COMMUNITY PRACTICE SKILLS

Dorothy N. Gamble
and Marie Weil

COMMUNITY PRACTICE SKILLS

LOCAL TO GLOBAL PERSPECTIVES

COLUMBIA UNIVERSITY PRESS ■ NEW YORK

COLUMBIA UNIVERSITY PRESS
Publishers Since 1893
New York   Chichester, West Sussex

Library of Congress Cataloging-in-Publication Data

Gamble, Dorothy N.
  Community practice skills : local to global perspectives / Dorothy N. Gamble and Marie Weil.
        p.   cm.
  Includes bibliographical references and index.
  ISBN 978-0-231-11002-0 (cloth : alk. paper) —ISBN 978-0-231-11003-7 (pbk. : alk. paper)
1. Community-based social services.   2. Community organization.   3. Community development.   I. Weil, Marie, 1941–   II. Title.
  HV40.G346 2009
  361—dc22   2009027820

Columbia University Press books are printed on permanent
    and durable acid-free paper.

This book is printed on paper with recycled content.

Printed in the United States of America
c 10   9   8   7   6   5   4   3   2   1

We dedicate this volume to those who keep us grounded and to our mentors.

Dee Gamble:

To George, who keeps me grounded but reminds me I am a citizen of the whole earth.

To Charles, who keeps me soaring but reminds me of the importance of a sense of place.

and

Mildred Ringwalt—Quaker meeting member in Chapel Hill who, while in her seventies, attended welfare mothers' meetings with me every Wednesday evening, sometimes in unheated buildings. *An organizer always needs a partner who can help you keep your balance.*

Charlotte Adams, Lucy Straley, Sadie Hughley, Tan Schwab, and other women who were leaders in the Women's International League for Peace and Freedom–Orange/Durham Chapter. *They showed me that you can keep a steady passion for peace and justice your whole life and do so with humor and humility.*

Hortense McClinton—First African American faculty member at the UNC–Chapel Hill School of Social Work. *All the reading and previous experience I had in civil rights did not touch my soul as deeply as her telling me the tragic story of Emmett Till.*

Marie Weil:

To Charlie, whose support and encouragement are invaluable.

To David and Kristen, who keep me focused on what matters—and on the promise of the future.

and

Anne E. Queen—Emeritus Director, YMCA, University of North Carolina, Chapel Hill; *Human rights champion, civil rights leader.*

Eleanor Ryder—Emeritus Faculty, School of Social Work, University of Pennsylvania; *Community practice teacher who guided with compassion and wisdom.*

Michael Blum—Director Emeritus, Nationality Services Center, Philadelphia; *Community practitioner and field instructor extraordinaire.*

Paul Schreiber—Dean Emeritus, Hunter College School of Social Work, CUNY; *Social justice visionary—scholar, mentor, and inspiration.*

Barbara B. Solomon—Provost Emeritus and Social Work Professor, University of Southern California; *Empowerment practice embodied— mentor for work and life.*

and

To our students, to community leaders, past and present, and to readers who will carry on the mission of community practice.

CONTENTS

ILLUSTRATIONS

FIGURES

TABLES

PREFACE AND ACKNOWLEDGMENTS

Our journey to completing this book is filled with both unique and familiar paths. Both of us came of age in professional social work in the 1960s. Dorothy "Dee" Gamble had just returned from two years in the Peace Corps, doing urban community development in Bucaramanga, Colombia, and enrolled in the Columbia University School of Social Work to focus on community organization. Marie Weil had worked with tribal members on the Tule River Indian Reservation in California, with the civil rights movement in North Carolina, done needs assessment work in very low-income communities in Philadelphia, and enrolled in the University of Pennsylvania School of Social Work with a major in community organization. We both had work experience in settlement houses during our graduate education, Gamble at Hartley House in New York City, Weil at University Settlement and Lutheran Settlement in Philadelphia.

As we engaged with our social work graduate studies and the communities surrounding Columbia and the University of Pennsylvania, we both became involved in civil, social, and economic rights movements. The continuing struggle for dignity among African Americans, Native Americans, Latinos/as, Asian Americans, women, the urban and rural poor, and those struggling with developmental delays had a profound effect on both of us as we saw people ignored, insulted, beaten, and even murdered for pursuing their human rights in one of the most respected democracies in the world.

These were the years before curb-cuts made it possible for people in wheelchairs to move about in cities and towns. These were also the years when many African Americans could not vote or apply to many universities; when mixed-race marriages were illegal in sixteen of the United States; when President John F. Kennedy, his brother Robert Kennedy, and the Rev. Martin Luther King Jr. were all assassinated. Informing and stimulating our passion for social work was the opportunity to participate in newly funded War on Poverty organizations such as Mobilization for Youth and citizens' groups focused on creating educational opportunity for African Americans. We were privileged to work beside courageous people struggling for human rights for their children and themselves, and to connect with historical as well as current theories, concepts, and models for community organization in the literature.

Gamble completed her master's degree at Columbia University and, after working with Head Start on Manhattan's Lower East Side, took a position in North Carolina to do rural community development and later worked with the Welfare Rights Organization. During the mid-1970s she spent two years in Venezuela working with International Social Service, after which she returned to the University of North Carolina at Chapel Hill to teach community organization at the School of Social Work and volunteer with the Women's International League for Peace and Freedom (WILPF), among other organizations.

Weil completed her master's degree in social work and worked first at University Settlement and then as deputy director of the Delaware Office of Economic Opportunity and the Wilmington Delaware Housing Authority, before studying for her doctorate at Hunter College/CUNY School of Social Work in New York City. After completing her degree, she joined the faculty at the School of Social Work of the University of Southern California where she engaged in consultation, research, and collaborative work with multiple Asian American communities, the Vietnamese refugee community, Latino groups, and pregnant and parenting adolescents. She also worked to develop services for women who were victims of domestic violence or rape/sexual assault.

During these years both of us worked in multicultural settings, sometimes finding ourselves the only Caucasian and the only woman in various programs and new projects. We both gained strong respect for grassroots community leaders and paraprofessionals and received profound lessons from the tenacity and courage of these wise street-level social advocates. We both married, raised our sons, and learned to juggle the double joys and demands of family and professional obligations.

In 1988 we met for the first time as faculty members at the University of North Carolina at Chapel Hill, School of Social Work, when Weil accepted the associate dean position. We connected on several levels. Both of us had grown up in humble surroundings, Weil in a working-class family in Raleigh, North Carolina, Gamble on a small farm in northeastern Colorado. We shared a passion for social justice and community work stimulated in part by past experiences. We also both understood that as women, taking a strong social justice approach in social work could be perceived as aggressive and would present some challenges. Our similar backgrounds naturally led to our discussion of current social problems and practice concepts. We both taught courses relating to community, planning, policy, and social administration in the School of Social Work and collaborated on many projects. Seven years later we proposed the first version of the eight models of community practice that is the focus of this book.

By the time we developed the conceptual framework of eight models for the Nineteenth Edition of the *Encyclopedia of Social Work 1995*, we each had more than a decade of practice experience and eighteen years of teaching experience. Weil's basic framework for teaching community practice, community development, and social planning was drawn from the work of Murray Ross, from sociological theory, earlier studies in philosophy, civil rights work, and practice experience. Gamble's model for teaching community organization, development, and practice came from Peace Corps training and experience as well as Jack Rothman's original elaboration of three approaches to community practice. Ross's and Rothman's approaches were taught in schools of social work across North America and in many countries across the world.

As we engaged with colleagues across the country, especially through the Association for Community Organization and Social Administration (ACOSA), and as we traveled abroad with summer study groups and to international meetings, we began to see a need for a more effective comparative way to help students understand the work we had both found so rewarding. Grassroots community groups and individuals had greatly enriched our understanding of community practice by sharing with us the realities, barriers, and resiliencies of their own lives. In addition, our students became our stimulus to dig more deeply as they asked questions and raised dilemmas, leading us to learn together. From these experiences as co-learners with colleagues, grassroots leaders, and students, we were persuaded to develop a set of models that could provide a more specific framework for practice. Hopefully, we could articulate a view that was more congruent with modern challenges to community practice and that was more easily understood by those who wanted to learn what community practice was all about, both here and abroad.

Our revised and updated framework places the models in a local to global context, recognizing that globalization with all its positive and negative effects will color the way we are able to practice in the twenty-first century. This revised framework also recognizes the issues facing internally displaced persons, immigrants, and refugees and affirms that community practitioners must increasingly engage in social justice work. We hope our models provide a clear and engaging perspective for those who wish to make community practice their life work. We especially hope that community practice workers across the globe will find the commonalities that draw us together as we work to build structures, relationships, and opportunities, especially for vulnerable populations, and for all people, everywhere, to develop to their highest potential in more socially just communities.

Many people provided helpful and encouraging comments as we engaged with this task. We have already mentioned our colleagues in ACOSA, too numerous to name, and our faculty colleagues and deans who sometimes raised their eyebrows at our "in-your-face" advocacy efforts, but gave us many nods of appreciation. Our students (now most of them colleagues) and grassroots leader/ partners have been exceedingly helpful in raising questions that made us both humble and persistent. From the past to the present, we think of people in the Bucaramanga, Colombia, barrio who did not have sufficient funds to feed their own families but were always available to help build a health center, guide young boys in a 4-H club, and sit on community councils. We think of Native American families and nations and African American communities where rights and opportunities have so often been denied by the majority society; yet members still rise and carry forward the vision for social justice—in building housing and economic opportunities, preventing hunger, supporting youth, and investing in the future. We think of urban residents in New York and Philadelphia who braved cold winters to help those less fortunate gain their civil right to an apartment with adequate heat, free of rats, and a working cook stove. We think of rural community leaders in North Carolina who built multicultural organizations to help identify and reach goals for all people who lived in low-wealth communities. Our experience with these communities, learning from the people we worked with, has shaped our practice and practice models. We honor and deeply appreciate their work.

Among those who have read and commented on our work and our ideas are Paul Castelloe and Craig White from the Center for Participatory Change, Sasha Vrtunski in the Ashville, North Carolina, Planning Department, John Hatch, founder of FINCA International, and Mat Despard from Durham CAN and the UNC–Chapel Hill social work faculty. For their encouragement and insight, we thank former students Karen Smith Rotabi, Emily MacGuire, Tezita Negussi, Claire Robbins, Denise Gammonly, Melissa Johnson, Josh Hinson, Andrea Bazan, Erik Simanis, Thomas Watson, and many others too numerous to name. Special thanks to Mary Rogge who would have been a fellow traveler with us on this journey but for unseen barriers. We thank all those who gave us encouragement and insight; the flaws in this book, of course, remain our own.

A special acknowledgment and appreciation goes to John Michel, our editor at Columbia University Press until his untimely death in early 2005. He had faith in our book concept, humor and patience in his response to our early efforts, and great courage in his fight for life. We also thank Lauren Dockett who paved the way for us to finish this project with Columbia University Press.

PART I

COMMUNITY PRACTICE: PURPOSE AND KNOWLEDGE BASE

Our goal in writing this book is to provide community practice workers with a comprehensive guide to skills for practice and with a knowledge base drawn from the values, purposes, and theories that form the foundation for work with communities. To help workers understand and differentiate among a range of intervention methods and skills for effective practice, we have developed a framework of eight different models illustrating approaches focused on specific goals. Our discussion for each model includes guidance for effective engagement and ethical practice, with examples drawn from both the United States and international contexts. This material will be useful not only to social workers but also to a wide range of community workers, including those involved with public health, city and regional planning, community sustainable development, and community capacity building.

We write from extensive experience in community practice with grassroots groups, community-based organizations, and the education of social workers in both the United States and international settings. Our primary interest is in expanding the work of anyone involved in building the capacities of community members and community institutions to improve the quality of life for people in community—whether that community is local or part of an extended regional, national, or global group.

We begin with a discussion of communities and community practice in the local to global continuum. In chapter 1, we discuss the meaning of community, processes associated with community practice, and social justice and human rights as the values that are the central focus of community practice.

Chapter 2 presents the table of eight models of community practice, the rationale for their development, a discussion of the "lenses" we believe will significantly influence the context of community practice in this century, and the roles associated with the different models of practice. Chapter 3 presents a broader discussion of guiding values and the evolution of the purposes and approaches to community practice. Building from that discussion, chapter 4 provides an overview of the concepts, theories, knowledge, and perspectives that guide community practice. Part II of the book, encompassing chapters 5–12, focuses on the scope of concern, basic processes, conceptual understandings, and roles and skills important for practice in each model. The companion volume, *Community Practice Skills Workbook* (Weil, Gamble, and MacGuire 2010; hereafter cited as the *CPS Workbook*), provides additional opportunities to engage in skill development with each model.

Issues of human rights and social justice are explored in each of the eight models of community practice analyzed in this volume. We are committed to building competencies and skills for social justice among future community social workers in all parts of the world. This commitment stems in part from the historical and heroic role of so many people who came before us and who showed the way to a more just society. We have learned lessons from Sojourner Truth, a courageous abolitionist born into slavery in New York in 1797, sold from her family at age 11, and yet spent the rest of her life working tirelessly for the freedom of slaves and the rights of women; from Jane Addams and her early work with families and organizations in Chicago's industrial slums; from Rosika Schwimmer, the Hungarian social worker and suffragist who worked with Jane Addams toward mediation to end the World War I hostilities and later fled to the United States when Jews were purged from Hungary, only to be denied U.S. citizenship because she was a pacifist; from Eleanor Roosevelt, who was instrumental in developing the Universal Declaration of Human Rights; from Mohandas Gandhi, who led the people of India in mass civil disobedience to a peaceful revolution, bringing them freedom and independence from Great Britain; from Cesar Chavez and Dolores Huerta, who built an organization to protect the rights of farm laborers throughout the United States; from the Rev. Dr. Martin Luther King Jr., whose message of freedom and peace still guides all people working against oppressive policies; from Nelson Mandela, who, even after spending twenty-eight years in prison, led his country on a path toward truth and reconciliation when South Africans at last overthrew apartheid and elected him to be their president; and from Wangari Maathai and Vandana Shiva, who connected our understanding of environmental restoration with women's rights and social justice in Kenya and India, respectively. There are so many more whose names may not be as well known, but whose deeds and words provide the guidance and wisdom to move human rights and social justice forward (Brueggemann 2006; Carlton-LaNey 2001; Maathai 2004; Mandela 1995; Shiva 2005).

These beacons of hope from both the past and today can be added to the list of people from your own life who have inspired you to work for social justice and human rights. Reflecting on such legends and inspirational models helps us get through the difficult times and keep our focus on the long term as we work to build democratic processes and empowered communities. Reflecting on the work of those who embody practice excellence can also help each of us develop our own essential skills that will be grounded in empowerment practice, human rights, and social justice.

1

COMMUNITIES AND COMMUNITY PRACTICE IN LOCAL TO GLOBAL CONTEXTS

Snowflakes, leaves, humans, plants, raindrops, stars, molecules, microscopic entities all come in communities. The singular cannot in reality exist.

PAULA GUNN ALLEN, AUTHOR OF *THE SACRED HOOP* AND *POCAHONTAS*

THE MEANING OF COMMUNITY IN THE LOCAL TO GLOBAL CONTINUUM

The meaning of community varies with each new generation, each distinct geographic location, and each community of interest. Scholars in the areas of sociology, psychology, anthropology, history, philosophy, and social work have all explored the meaning of community (Creed 2006; Martinez-Brawley 1995; Park 1952; Stein 1960; Warren 1963, 1966). Community can evoke the image of the traditional, bucolic village drawn from Ferdinand Tönnies's classic work that described small rural communities as characterized by *gemeinschaft*—that is, close-knit, face-to-face relationships imbued with a sense of mutual responsibility and obligation. Or community can call forth Tönnies's contrasting image, *gesellschaft*—that is, mechanistic relationships found in the growing industrial cities and characterized by larger, impersonal networks, broader working and exchange relationships, and weakened local ties (Tönnies, 1887/1957).

In small-scale geographic settings, bioregional location, socioeconomic assets, and cultural and political currents influence the human relationships and networks that give our lives meaning and purpose. These relationships and networks can be variably supportive or oppressive, depending on how inclusive and welcoming the accepted social, cultural, economic, and environmental norms are toward diverse individuals and family groups. Today, both the supportive and oppressive aspects of small-scale communities are inescapably affected by global political and commercial activity that may be initiated in faraway places.

In many parts of the world, elements of traditional, small-scale local communities remain very much alive, and supportive social and economic networks provide a basic community foundation. Today, however, we live in a world with unprecedented capacity for communication and travel that is expanding both our personal opportunities and our views of our local communities. Urban communities are exerting a strong pull as more people move to urban areas every year. By the year 2050, the United Nations predicts that 70 percent of the world's population will be living in urban areas (International Herald Tribune, February 26, 2008).

When the Apollo Mission astronauts sent the world the first photographs of Earth from space, most of us internalized the image of that beautiful blue marble as our home and "community." In that transformational moment, many began to think of community globally and to understand the larger sense of community as the interconnection of all living systems on Earth. From the perspectives of First Nation peoples and spiritual leaders, however, the interconnections go even deeper and wider across time and space (Berry 1990; LaDuke 2005). The rapid advances in technology and media have fostered this larger view of community by giving us instant access to events and images from around the world. This global access allows us to perceive that we are directly affected by each other's activity—whether that activity is downriver, downwind, across mountains, beyond borders, or across continents. Technology also helps us to create *communities of interest,* which connect people who wish to belong together because of loyalty and self-identification, and *functional communities,* which join people together in common causes for purposeful change in social, economic, and environmental arenas (Fellin 2001; Garvin and Tropman 1992; Park 1952).

William G. Brueggemann (2006) described community as

> natural human associations based on ties of intimate personal relationships and shared experiences in which each of us mutually provide meaning in our lives, meet our needs for affiliation, and accomplish interpersonal goals. . . . Our predisposition to community ensures that we become the persons we were meant to become, discover who we are as people, and construct a culture that would be impossible for single, isolated individuals to accomplish alone. (116)

In rural traditional communities, these relationships may encompass an entire village, whereas in townships, cities, and megacities, a sense of community is more likely to relate to a neighborhood, workplace, or other smaller geographic or functional grouping.

COMMUNITY COMPONENTS

Maureen Hart's practical picture of community incorporates social interaction and natural resources to describe the raw materials from which we create the

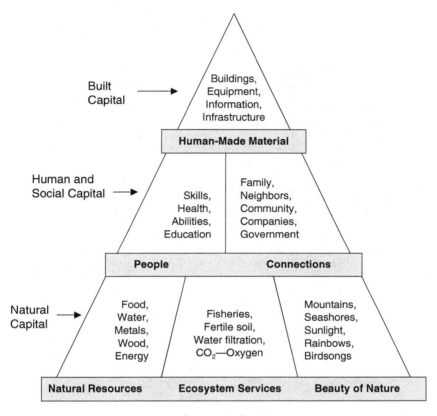

Community Capital

FIGURE 1.1 Hart's Community Capital Triangle

Source: Maureen Hart (1999), *Guide to Sustainable Community Indicators*, 2nd ed. (North Andover, MA: Hart Environmental Data), p 16. Available from Sustainable Measures. www.sustainablemeasures.com. Used with permission.

social and economic aspects of community (Hart 1999). Hart's Community Capital Triangle (see figure 1.1) describes community as a three-level pyramid that includes natural capital, human capital, and built capital. *Natural capital* forms the base of Hart's model and contains three systems: (1) natural resources, such as food, water, minerals, wood, and energy; (2) ecosystem services, including fisheries, fertile soil, water filtration, and carbon dioxide; and (3) the beauty of nature, such as mountains, seashores, sunlight, rainbows, and bird songs. In the pyramid's second level, *human and social capital*, Hart defined two categories: (1) people, which includes their skills, health, abilities, and education; and (2) connections, which includes relationships of family, neighbors, community, companies, and governments. At the top of the pyramid, supported by the other

KENYA

For the past thirty years, all over Kenya, Wangari Maathai, winner of the 2004 Nobel Peace Prize, has provided leadership to the Green Belt Movement with the aim "to mobilize communities for self-determination, justice, equity, poverty reduction, and environmental conservation, using trees as the entry point" (Green Belt Movement 2006). The Green Belt Movement has organized numerous community networks that are now caring for 6,000 tree nurseries across Kenya. These community networks have already planted more than 30 million trees throughout Kenya, transforming not only the environment but also attitudes about the future and thoughts of how to shape it. Currently, the Green Belt Movement has projects that move beyond Kenya's borders and that are continuing the mission of working with ordinary people to improve their lives and future, using tree planting as the motivational beginning point for community development and citizen involvement.

CHILE

For fifty years, and under widely divergent national governments, residents of La Victoria, a poor neighborhood on the edge of Santiago, Chile, have struggled to find meaning and justice in their lives. Even during the dark years of the Pinochet regime with its concentrated military effort to crush any popular movement, ordinary citizens continued to organize and to break down the fear created by the military. For example, during the Pinochet years, the people of La Victoria organized a huge outdoor tea on March 8 to mark International Women's Day. The women of La Victoria were seated at tables that stretched down the entire street, while the town's men and children served the tea and snacks that they had cooked in church kitchens. The people of La Victoria seized this and every other opportunity to have a public celebration, and in so doing, they "reclaimed symbolic power as they rejected the regime's imposed reality," thereby creating "spaces of possibility and resistance in the face of powerfully determining forces."

(Finn 2005:22)

five building blocks, is what Hart calls *built capital*, which is composed of all the things humans make and produce (e.g., buildings, equipment, information, infrastructure, art, music, clothing, roads). Hart's picture of community capital helps us understand the relationships between the resources available to community members and the way our communities can strengthen or preserve those resources.

COMMUNITY PRACTICE EXAMPLES

How do we engage with a community, in either a local or a global context, to work toward community improvement? Each of the boxed examples in this chapter provides a brief description of community from the perspective of

CHINA

In Guangzhou, a large city in the Guangdong Province of South China, more than 12 percent of the population is comprised of older adults, and 365 people are officially recorded as 100 years or older. To meet the needs of the growing population of older adults, especially older women, both the national and provincial governments are working with the families, who have traditionally been responsible for care of older relatives. Although much remains to be done to meet the needs of China's older adults, especially those living in rural areas, the provincial administration has shown a remarkable commitment to making adult services a priority. Already, adult services centers have been built in every neighborhood and district within Guangzhou city. The goal of these centers is to provide social, educational, recreational, health care, and respite care for the older adults and their families.

(Lee and Kwok 2006)

UNITED STATES

The nonprofit South Eastern Efforts Developing Sustainable Spaces (SEEDS) program in Durham, North Carolina, has been working to build community, neighborhood by neighborhood. SEEDS workers establish neighborhood programs that teach gardening, cooking, educational, and art skills to the children, youth, and adults of Durham. The overall goal of the SEEDS programs is to teach "respect for life, for earth, and for each other" (*City Farmer* 2006). The neighborhoods served by SEEDS are composed of a mix of African American, Latino, and Anglo families, reflecting the city's recent population changes. Children in the "Seedlings" program plant snow peas, and later carrots and onions, both to eat and to sell at the local farmers' market. Parents and other volunteers build raised gardening beds, teach classes, and help with the general focus of "gardening, nurturing, gathering, and education."

(City Farmer 2006)

people interested in community practice, whether in professional capacities or as neighborhood leaders. Although these examples focus primarily on local communities, they recognize connections to a larger environment, and some acknowledge both the past and present forces that are part of their experience.

These examples are representative of deep and enduring aspects of community. Equally important, they describe the varied roles of neighborhood leaders, organizations, and collaborative public and private efforts in strengthening and promoting community structures that are just and supportive. The community improvements and struggles described in these examples relate to *"meaning, context, power, history,* and *possibility,"* the five concepts Janet Finn and Maxine Jacobson (2008a) identified as defining a "just practice framework." According to these researchers, this framework emphasizes social work intervention guided by social justice, human rights, and progressive change (42–50). Throughout this volume we will discuss how the values of social justice, human rights, economic fairness and opportunity, and environmental protection and restoration are basic to all social work practice.

COMMUNITY PRACTICE PROCESSES

Community practice social workers generally engage with communities through a range of processes. Brueggemann (2006) has suggested that "of all the assets and tools that humans have for constructing their social environment, community is the most basic and the most important" (131). Thus, exploring the processes that underlie community practice is essential to the social work perspective.

Marie Weil (1993, 2005a) described the four major processes of community practice as *organizing, planning, development,* and *change.* These four processes are most easily observed in arenas where efforts are under way to improve community conditions and mitigate community problems. We have refined the terms, modifying *development* to *sustainable development* and expanding *change* to *progressive change.* These changes recognize that, to be successful, community development must incorporate the "triple bottom line" by working concurrently toward improvements in social, economic, and environmental conditions. Thus, we consider *sustainable development* a holistic term that encompasses those three arenas. Similarly, *progressive change* recognizes that the change we are working toward embodies positive movement toward social justice and human rights, which are basic values in social work.

Most efforts in community practice involve the four processes of *organizing, planning, sustainable development,* and *progressive change* in order to improve opportunities for all community members as well as to limit or eliminate factors that contribute to community degradation and disintegration. In addition, these four processes provide an overarching framework for the eight models of community practice that are the focus of our discussion in chapters 5 through 12.

ORGANIZING

Organizing includes efforts to engage citizens in developing their local leadership capacity and to equip them with the knowledge, skills, and organizational power to make positive decisions affecting their social, emotional, environmental, and economic conditions. Herbert Rubin and Irene Rubin (2007:5) describe organizing as "working with people to help them recognize that they face shared problems and to discover that by joining together they can fight to overcome these problems. [It] . . . builds upon and strengthens interpersonal, social, and community relationships while establishing ongoing organizations that enable people to sustain collective actions." The community considered in the organizing process may be defined by a geographic location or may apply to those with shared goals who are living and working in distant locations. Michael Reisch (2005b) described organizing that emphasizes achieving social justice as *radical community organizing* that is "focused on the attainment of social justice and fundamental structural and institutional changes in communities and society" (287). In his analysis of the root causes of social problems, Reisch bases his assumptions on the perspective that most existing social and economic structures have effectively prevented people of low wealth from reaching their optimum potential. He concludes that it is only with "the development of alternative economic, political, social, and ideological systems" that people of low wealth can hope to participate in community building (Reisch 2005b:278).

In his work in Brazil, Paulo Freire (1972) used adult education as a method for community organizing and development. His "problem-posing education" brought groups of people together to examine their current problems in light of their contextual past. Working and learning with the poorest people in Brazil, Freire learned that people, "for whom immobility represents a fatal threat, for whom looking at the past must only be a means of understanding more clearly what and who they are," can develop the capability to participate in and build their future (1972:57). Freire sought to foster this capability through a group discussion process that he called *conscientization*. This process involves bringing together a group to engage in reflection and analysis of their present situation, to plan for change based on understanding the past, to take action to change negative aspects of the present condition, and then reconvene to reassess and reflect. Freire's views on education and development are used in many parts of the world today (Castelloe and Gamble 2005; Chambers 1997; Hope, Timmel, and Hodzi 1995; Reisch, Wenocur, and Sherman 1981).

The principle that underlies organizing derives from the democratic value that emphasizes how important it is that people be involved in decisions affecting their lives (Austin and Betten 1990; Kahn 1991). However, not all organizing efforts will be equally effective. If the community members do not perceive the organizers as "legitimate," or if an institution outside the community imposes constraints on organizers' efforts, then organizing is unlikely to succeed (Schmid and Salman 2005). When organizing is successful, the process yields important effects on the psychosocial aspects of communities as well as benefits that improve the physical, social, and economic conditions of communities. These effects of the organizing process were noted by Mary Ohmer and Wynne Korr (2006), who found that organizing can influence citizen participation and its effects on participants [and] . . . can also facilitate personal and collective competencies among participants and increase their connections to their communities, including increasing self-esteem, personal empowerment, and community empowerment . . . leadership and political skills . . . and community pride and belonging. (142)

Another important aspect of organizing is bringing organizations together into networks or coalitions that can efficiently combine the separate efforts of many individuals or small groups to effect a specific policy or change (Brueggemann 2006; Homan 2008; Mizrahi and Rosenthal 2001).

PLANNING

Planning is a process widely used in community practice, and it will also be identified later in this book as one of the eight discrete models of community practice. Planning is recognized as having a fundamental role in working with community groups. Community planning involves identifying a shared vision for change and outlining the steps required to achieve the desired changes. The planning process seeks to engage citizens in identifying a condition for change, specifying the intended outcomes, and defining activities that will produce the desired outcomes. A number of researchers have examined the various aspects of planning. Murray Ross (1967), for example, advocated the use of both local and centralized social planning in social welfare and program development. Terry Mizrahi (2009), drawing on years of practical experience, identified planning as "a complex sociopolitical and technical process" (872). Marie Weil (2005b) reflected on the complex nature of planning and emphasized both the need for and importance of "participatory" planning methods. She defined planning with communities as "the process of social, economic, and physical planning engaged in by citizens and community practitioners to design services, community infrastructure, and neighborhood revitalization plans that are appropriate to given communities—urban and rural" (218).

In recent years, both the W. K. Kellogg Foundation and the United Way of America (UWA) have provided comprehensive planning manuals to community-based programs to help them practice step-by-step planning. The aim of promoting systematic planning is to help the community programs succeed and to better measure the results of their action strategies (Kellogg Foundation 2004; United Way of America 1996). In part, developing the planning manuals became necessary when both the community-based programs and their funding sources saw a need for concrete, specific information about the results of the program's actions. These planning manuals rely on the *logic model*, which takes participants through planning by requiring specific identification of program resources, inputs, outputs, activities, outcomes, and changes. Planning tools of this type can be useful with large groups because it allows each participant to better understand and envision the direction of the organization's efforts. Using a planning tool also provides an opportunity to gather comments and feedback from the entire group, which can increase engagement and the likelihood of reaching the group's intended goals.

In our recent work with grassroots organizations in North Carolina engaged in sustainable development projects, we co-created a workbook with members of community organizations, which they used as they planned, carried out, and evaluated hoped-for social, economic, and environmental changes. Our workbook expands the logic model process by incorporating the rationale behind the creation of the community-based organization. In addition, we integrated organizational and developmental theories with planned change theory to create a continuous planning model (see figure 1.2) for use by and with grassroots groups (Gamble, Weil, Kiefer et al. 2005). We describe the model's action plan in eight steps (represented by the eight boxes in the continuous circle), which were adapted from our experience and review of planning and evaluation literature. This body of literature is important because it aims not only to help community groups improve their collective effectiveness but also to improve the economic, social, environmental, and emotional aspects of community life (Arnold et al. 1991; Castelloe and Gamble 2005; Freire 1972; Kellogg Foundation 2004; Pretty et al. 1995; United Way of America 1996). The eight steps shown in figure 1.2 are intended to be iterative rather than sequential, which more accurately reflects the way groups function in the real world.

When elaborating the planning steps for any community project, whether local or global, it is important to ensure community participation at all points in the process (Fals-Borda 1998). Although organizers might assign specific responsibilities to task forces, action groups, or committees, guidance from the whole group is required throughout all stages—planning, implementation, evaluation, and reflection. This type of participatory planning takes time and requires the skills of a good facilitator, but it will yield big rewards in the number of people who actively support the plan and hope for its ultimate success. In addition, participatory processes embody widely valued democratic principles (Castelloe and Gamble 2005; Chambers 1997; Couto and Guthrie 1999; VeneKlasen and Miller 2002).

SUSTAINABLE DEVELOPMENT

Interest in sustainable development emerged in part from the dialogue among those working to alleviate social and economic disparities across the globe and those concerned with environmental degradation (World Commission on

The relationships among community/organizational issues, goals,
objectives, inputs, outcome evaluation/documentation, and reflection, with an emphasis
on the value framework of sustainable development.

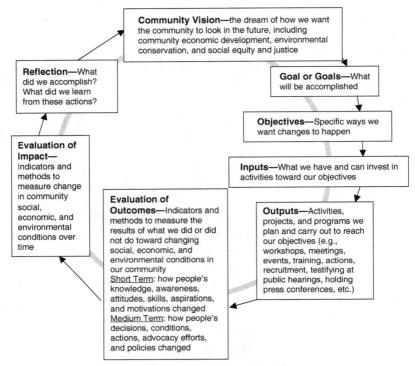

FIGURE 1.2 Continuous Sustainable Community Development
Model adapted from R. Arnold, R., Burke, B., James, C., Martin, D., and Thomas, B. (1991), *Educating for a Change* (Toronto, Ontario: Between the Lines/Doris Marshall Institute for Education and Action); Paul Castelloe and Dorothy N. Gamble (2005), "Participatory Methods in Community Practice: Popular Education and Participatory Rural Appraisal," in *The Handbook of Community Practice*, ed. Marie Weil (Thousand Oaks, CA: Sage Publications); Paolo Freire (1974), *Education for Critical Consciousness* (New York: Continuum).
Source: Dorothy N. Gamble, Marie Weil, N. Kiefer, and Resourceful Community Members (2005), *Measuring a Movement: Evaluating Outcomes in Community Sustainable Development* (Chapel Hill, NC: The Resourceful Communities Program of The Conservation Fund), p. 5. Used with permission from The Conservation Fund.

Environment and Development 1987). Although traditional wisdom suggested that market-based economic development was the single most important way to decrease poverty and increase opportunities, such narrowly focused efforts often came at the cost of the depletion of finite resources, lasting environmental damage, extreme gaps between wealthy and poor populations, and rapid extinction of plant and animal species (Daly and Cobb 1989; Escobar 1995; Korten 2001; Prigoff 2000). The movement promoting sustainable development emerged to foster human development in a more holistic way, protecting people, resources, and the environment. In describing the origins of sustainable development, Richard Estes (1993) focused on *global stewardship,* defined as human development that is just both socially and economically, while at the same time protective and respectful of the environment. Estes called for community workers to engage others (i.e., communities, nations, regions, and world organizations) in sustainable development. Practitioners in this movement now range from local entrepreneurs and farmers to multinational corporations (Hart 2007; Khor and Lin 2001; Soeteman and Harkink 2005; Wentzel 2003). In addition, many cities and countries have created task forces to focus on developing sustainable development goals, establishing benchmarks for protecting the environment, and promoting equal economic and social development opportunities. On a global level, the United Nations' Millennium Development Goals provide a broad, worldwide agenda aimed at achieving the first steps toward sustainable development by 2015. This program's special focus is on cutting extreme poverty in half, eliminating gender inequalities, preventing and treating HIV/AIDS and other deadly diseases, and ensuring environmental sustainability (United Nations Development Program 2003).

The United Nations evaluates a nation's efforts to achieve sustainable development in four areas: human development, environmental recovery, economic equality, and social justice. The principles and benchmarks used in these evaluations are included in the annual *Human Development Report* published by the United Nations Development Program (UNDP) since 1990. This publication includes the Human Development Index (HDI), which is a composite measure of a population's development progress combining health, education, and basic economic standards. The HDI incorporates a summary of three measures: (a) "a long and healthy life" (i.e., life expectancy at birth); (b) "knowledge" (defined by the adult literacy rate and the combined primary, secondary, and tertiary gross educational enrollment rate); and (c) "a decent standard of living," defined as gross domestic product per capita (UNDP 2005:341). For example, even though the United States had a relatively high per capita GDP in 2005, the nation ranked only tenth on the HDI because of its lower scores for education and life expectancy (UNDP 2005:219). In the 2007–2008 Report, the United States' ranking dropped to twelfth (UNDP:2007).

Gross domestic product (GDP) is the most frequently used measure of development, but it has significant shortcomings as a measure of the human population's true progress. Being strictly an economic measure (i.e., the total value of goods and services produced in a country), GDP excludes important development characteristics that cannot be measured in terms of money (e.g., voluntary care of children by grandparents, unpaid work in community-based service organizations). In addition, as a measure of a country's economic *output*, GDP incorporates as *positive* production such negative drags on the economy as the costs of illness resulting from toxic industrial and farming practices, the environmental toll of contaminated water and air, and the price of war and prison construction. In chapter 7, we present a further discussion of the sharp contrast between GDP and measures of human development by incorporating ideas from the Human Development Report and other progressive perspectives that set benchmarks for social, economic, and environmental well-being.

PROGRESSIVE CHANGE

The process of progressive change is often rooted in ameliorating negative conditions in local, regional, or global locations. In this book, we focus on purposive, planned change that seeks to produce better social, economic, and environmental outcomes for the most disadvantaged populations. Progressive change also gives particular attention to improving the lives of those who have been consistently excluded from community planning and decision making on the basis of race, ethnicity, gender, limited assets, ability, age, religion, or sexual preference. From our perspective, each community must individually define what kind of change would be "progressive" for them. When considering the meaning of progressive change for the local level, it may be useful to examine some international perspectives on change.

INTERNATIONAL EXAMPLES OF PROGRESSIVE CHANGE One example of an international perspective on progressive change is the Earth Charter, which outlines principles for "a time when humanity must choose its future" (Earth Charter 2008). Specifically, the Charter formulates principles that will guide a nation's transition from a system that exploits people and resources to a system that promotes sustainable development, and thus provides a global road map for change. The concept of the Earth Charter was born in 1987 within the UN World Commission on Environment and Development. Through the leadership of both Maurice Strong (former secretary general of the Rio Earth Summit) and Mikhail Gorbachev (president of Green Cross International), as well as the help of the government of the Netherlands, the idea of the Charter was rekindled in 1994 and launched as a civil society initiative. The Earth Charter, formally approved in 2000, outlines four main principles:

- Respect and care for the community of life
- Ecological integrity
- Social and economic justice
- Democracy, nonviolence, and peace (Earth Charter 2008:2–5)

The Earth Charter has been widely accepted by many international nongovernmental organizations (NGOs) as well as local, national, and international governing bodies. Overall, these groups recognize the Earth Charter as a consensus statement for the kind of change needed as countries move toward sustainable development. The Charter is also widely used as a resource for developing global standards and codes of conduct.

SOCIAL WORK AS PROGRESSIVE CHANGE AGENT The four principles of the Earth Charter resonate with the principles described in "Ethics in Social Work, Statement of Principles," which was adopted in 2004 by the International Federation of Social Workers and the International Association of Schools of Social Work. This Statement of Principles, including the definition of social work, is a central source for community practice social workers as they seek to ground their values and purpose and define progressive change.

Change in our physical, environmental, emotional, economic, and social condition is continuous. Community practice helps promote positive and progressive change, so that local conditions can help all people develop to their optimum potential—and without harming the environment that sustains them. In part II, we describe in depth the eight models of practice that work toward strengthening community leadership, social capital, planning skills, and action strategies, all of which can bring positive change to communities.

In the final analysis, community has meaning everywhere along the local to global continuum. We identify not only with our immediate neighbors as part of a community but also with others outside the community with whom we feel an affinity, incorporating them into our sense of global community. Communities can be geographic places, virtual groups linked by technology, functional groups with whom we work toward a specific purpose, interest groups with whom we play or pray, and ad hoc coalitions with whom we engage for short-term purposes. Each one of us is a member of multiple communities at any given time.

The social work profession promotes social change, problem solving in human relationships and empowerment and liberation of people to enhance well-being. Utilising theories of human behaviour and social systems, social work intervenes at the points where people interact with their environments. Principles of human rights and social justice are fundamental to social work.

International Federation of Social Workers and International Association
of Schools of Social Work, 2004 (IFSW/IASSW 2008)

JUSTICE, RIGHTS, AND EMPOWERMENT IN COMMUNITY PRACTICE

The eight models of community practice presented in chapter 2 and elaborated in part II of this volume are intended for use as practice reference points. The models illustrate how specific practice approaches might be considered as ideal types for comparative purposes (Weber, 1903–1917/1997). Each model presents different aspects of how community workers engage with communities in a variety of locations, cultures, and contexts to work toward specific purposes. The models have a twofold comparative purpose: (1) to serve as general guides to practice in organizing, planning, sustainable development, and progressive change; and (2) to raise questions about the "why" and "how" of different action approaches. All eight models are grounded in a set of principles based on promoting social justice and human rights. We provide an expanded discussion of values and approaches in chapter 3; here we introduce the value base related to social justice, human rights, and empowerment.

SOCIAL JUSTICE AND HUMAN RIGHTS

Social justice and human rights are critical values for social work and especially for community practice (Dominelli 2007; Finn and Jacobson 2008b; Ife 2006; Reichert 2007). Embedded in these two values are the right to a decent standard of living and the elimination of abject poverty, which we will discuss in relation to the UN Millennium Development Goals (MDGs), and the mission of empowerment in social work.

The profession has both recent and historical precedents on which to build a strong commitment to social justice and human rights. Social justice is one of the six core values identified in the U.S. National Association of Social Workers (NASW) Code of Ethics (NASW 2008). At the international level in 2004, both the International Federation of Social Workers (IFSW) and the International Association of Schools of Social Work (IASSW) adopted "Ethics in Social Work, Statement of Principles" (IFSW/IASSW 2008). In addition to the international definition of social work noted above, this document states that human rights and social justice are intrinsic, fundamental elements of social work. Furthermore, the document emphasizes human rights, human dignity, and social justice as the primary principles of social work practice (IFSW/IASSW 2008:1–2). Human rights and human dignity relate to "respecting the right to self-determination; promoting the right to participation; treating each person as a whole . . . within the family, community, societal and natural environments . . . ; [and] identifying and developing strengths . . . of individuals, groups, and communities and thus promote their empowerment" (IFSW/IASSW 2008:2)

These principles are intended for *all* social work interventions, whether used in direct practice or community practice. The understanding of social justice in "Ethics in Social Work" means "challenging negative discrimination; recognizing diversity; distributing resources equitably; challenging unjust policies and practices; [and] working in solidarity . . . towards an inclusive society" (IFSW/IASSW 2004:2–3). Such a universal statement will not have perfect agreement among all its stakeholders. However, the "Ethics in Social Work" marks an important first step in collaborative identification and definition of social justice and human rights for social workers around the world; it is a point of shared understanding from which we can move forward together.

The concern for the number of people in poverty, the number of children who die each day for simple lack of adequate nutrition, and the widening gap of access to wealth between the world's richest and poorest populations has been brought into clearer focus by a variety of United Nations organizations (notably, UNDP, UNICEF, and UNIFEM). Article 25 of the Universal Declaration of Human Rights states that

> everyone has the right to a standard of living adequate for the health and well-being of himself and of his family, including food, clothing, housing and medical care and necessary social services, and the right to security in the event of unemployment, sickness, disability, widowhood, old age or other lack of livelihood in circumstances beyond his control. Motherhood and childhood are entitled to special care and assistance. All children, whether born in or out of wedlock, shall enjoy the same social protection. (UDHR 1948)

In 2000, the world's political leaders adopted the Millennium Declaration and the eight Millennium Development Goals (table 1.1; see also boxed information, UNDP Human Development Report 2003); in accepting this declaration and set of goals, they made promises about how to respond to this disparity of income. The formal endorsement of the Millennium Declaration was a courageous step aimed at reducing poverty and advancing human development by the year 2015. According to the UNDP, many NGOs and national nonprofits have realigned their program goals in order to support the 2015 deadline and to work toward the Millennium Development Goals. However, more developed countries need to respond positively by providing the promised aid and debt relief; otherwise, the promises made in 2000 will be broken (UNDP 2003:1–14; InterAction, October 18, 2007). The current economic crisis should not be used as an excuse to abandon the MDG benchmarks. The devastating and destabilizing forces of global poverty require a broad and consistent response.

The Millennium goals give each of us an opportunity to work within our own countries to promote international collaboration and policies that will bring us

TABLE 1.1 Eight Millennium Development Goals with 2015 Targets

GOALS	TARGET FOR 2015
1. Eradicate extreme poverty and hunger.	Halve the proportion of people living on less than a $1 a day and those who suffer from hunger. More than a billion people still live on less than US$1 a day.
2. Achieve universal primary education.	Ensure that all boys and girls complete primary education. As many as 113 million children do not attend school.
3. Promote gender equality and empower women.	Eliminate gender disparities in primary and secondary education, preferably by 2005, and at all levels by 2015. Two-thirds of illiterates are women.
4. Reduce child mortality.	Reduce by two-thirds the mortality rate among children under five. Every year, nearly 11 million young children die before their fifth birthday.
5. Improve maternal health.	Reduce by three-quarters the ratio of women dying in childbirth. In the developing world, the risk of dying in childbirth is 1:48.
6. Combat HIV/AIDS, malaria and other diseases.	Halt and begin to reverse the spread of HIV/AIDS, the incidence of malaria, and other major diseases.
7. Ensure environmental sustainability.	Integrate the principles of sustainable development into country policies and programs and reverse the loss of environmental resources. Reduce by half the proportion of people without access to safe drinking water. More than one billion people lack access to safe drinking water, and more than two billion lack sanitation.
8. Develop a global partnership for development.	Develop an open trading and financial system that includes a commitment to good governance, development, and poverty reduction—nationally and internationally. Address the least developed countries' special needs and the special needs of landlocked and small island developing states. Deal comprehensively with developing countries' debt problems. Develop decent and productive work for youth. In cooperation with pharmaceutical companies, provide access to affordable essential drugs in developing countries. In cooperation with the private sector, make available the benefits of new technologies—especially information and communications technologies.

Source: Adapted from the UNDP *Human Development Report, 2006.*

closer to reducing poverty among world populations. Whether we are among nations with greater or lesser wealth, we all have policy-level and community-level work to do to increase opportunities for those living on less than $1 a day. We will return to the concern for poverty and the urgent need to engage in policy and community strategies in chapters 7, 12, and 13.

POWER AND THE MISSION OF EMPOWERMENT

The concepts of power and empowerment have a close association with social justice and human rights. *Power* is typically defined as the ability to exercise influence, control, or authority over decisions, resources, or outcomes. Power derives from a number of sources depending on the context and history of a situation. Power may come from historical events or conditions that influence a wide range of contexts such as the status of families, occupations, resources, policies, networks, religions, castes, gender groups, ethnic/tribal groups, age groups, or sexual preference groups. Negative uses of power often emerge as the result of a combination of discriminatory factors based on gender, race/ethnicity, religion, socioeconomic status, age, sexual orientation, geographic location, or disability (VeneKlasen and Miller 2002:337–39).

Feminist views of power include both power with and power to do, "an alternative to the patriarchal finite notion of power . . . power [is] a widely distributed energy of influence, strength, effectiveness and responsibility" (van den Berg and Cooper 1986:6). We discuss these kinds of power in greater detail in chapter 5. In her work *Black Empowerment: Social Work in Oppressed Communities*, Barbara Solomon (1986) presented the first social work text devoted to helping practitioners to assist people in freeing themselves from internally imposed restrictions and in developing empowerment strategies to overturn external challenges to their exercise of human, civil, social, and political rights.

According to Homan (2008), "Power is not dominance. Dominance is the way some people use power. . . . Power can be used in a spirit of cooperation as easily as it can occur in a climate of conflict" (131–32). It is important for community groups to study the history of power. Those seeking to change conditions need to understand the nature of power and influence and to be aware of differential access to resources and information. When exploring the meaning and use of power, it becomes clear that power can have both negative and positive results. The use of power can result in state-sponsored violence, or it can result in moral leadership, mediated equity, and peaceful revolutions.

The roots of this kind of empowerment in the Western historical development of social work were provided in Barbara Levy Simon's (1994) *The Empowerment Tradition in American Social Work*. Her analysis concluded that "full participation by citizens in the social contract hinges . . . upon the interrelated trinity of civil liberties, political rights, and socioeconomic entitlements" (1994:45). In that work, Simon points to the many influences in developing and broadening the social work knowledge base for empowerment, including Gandhi, African Independence Movements, Freire in South America, the civil rights and the black power movements in the United States, liberation theology in South America, feminism, gay and lesbian liberation, and the disability rights movement. Richard Estes (1993) and Paul Hawken (2007) added worldwide indigenous movements and the all important movements toward environmental protection and restoration.

People who have been working together toward empowerment often express their newly gained insight and collective efficacy in song, art, and drama. Si Kahn (1994), songwriter, singer, and community organizer, provided a manual, *How People Get Power*, to help organizers envision and carry out work that empowered people in local communities. Successful community workers from various corners of the globe have effectively facilitated the incorporation of local music, poetry, drama, and other cultural expressions into community awareness and empowerment activities (Boal 2000; Chambers 1997; Couto and Guthrie 1999; Kleymeyer 1994; Slocum et al. 1995).

VeneKlasen and Miller (2002) describe citizen empowerment as "a process of learning and action that strengthens people's self-esteem, analytical and organizing skills, and political consciousness so they can gain a sense of their rights and join together to develop more democratic societies" (59). As community groups become empowered, they are better able to engage in planning, action, and evaluation of programs and projects that will improve the quality of life for all community members. Measuring empowerment, evaluating how people become more engaged as social actors and how changes come about in the community, requires forethought and participation by community members to specify what the changes will look like.

Brueggemann (2006) suggests that when social workers engage with people to develop empowerment they should aim to "help people break the bonds of external and internal oppression, raise consciousness, challenge perceptions, and stimulate reflection" (488). Empowerment is an outcome we work toward and a process that we work through as we describe the eight models of community practice in part II.

CONCLUSIONS

In this introductory chapter we have set forth our perspectives on the meaning of community along a local to global continuum. We introduced a strong focus for incorporating social justice and human rights in the work of community practice, including a discussion of the importance of eradicating poverty and of developing community empowerment. Three additional chapters in part I establish the foundation for understanding and preparing for community practice. Chapter 2 presents the eight models of community practice, provides the rationale for selecting the eight models, explores the three lenses that we believe will color community practice in all parts of the world during the twenty-first century, and identifies the primary roles used by social workers in the eight models. Chapter 3 describes the evolution of values, the history of approaches to community practice, and the purposes of community practice work. Chapter 4 provides an overview of the theories, knowledge base, and perspectives that guide community practice.

In chapters 5 through 12, in which our community practice models and skills are presented in detail, we discuss specific philosophies, methods, and information technologies that facilitate the development of powerful and effective organizations. Helping people to engage in progressive community change, to develop an understanding of the change process, and to make use of participatory decision making, planning, strategy, development, and evaluation requires a skilled community practice facilitator. Through participation, people can be engaged in politics and policy development that can lead to progressive changes in social, economic, and environmental arenas from the ground up. Through engagement in the political process and the development of policy, people are more likely to take active roles and become participants in the efforts working for change. We understand that increased participation does not always lead in progressive directions, nor does political leadership necessarily help a population value diversity, collaborative engagement, responsibility for future generations, or environmental stewardship. However, the progressive changes we envision, and those that are convergent with the values of social work, include social justice, economic opportunity, and environmental restoration and protection.

Throughout this book we will frequently return to our perspectives on social, economic, political, and environmental well-being. *Social well-being* means that all people have access to the supports and opportunities offered by social institutions and relationships; *economic well-being* means that all people have opportunities to achieve a wide variety of livelihoods and that wages should pay enough to meet a family's needs for shelter, food, health care, and transportation; *political well-being* means that all people should have freedom to associate, speak, vote, and participate in the governments that make policy for them; *environmental well-being* means that present generations must not live beyond the resources in the biosphere and must repair, to the extent possible, damage to air, water, soil, fisheries, forests, and other species. In all the chapters that follow, we focus on the work of community practice social workers and the knowledge, roles and skills necessary for helping communities to identify goals and to work toward progressive outcomes for themselves, for their regions, and for the world.

2

CONCEPTUAL FRAMEWORKS AND MODELS FOR COMMUNITY PRACTICE

One is not born into the world to do everything but to do something.

HENRY DAVID THOREAU

How wonderful it is that nobody need wait a single moment before starting to improve the world.

ANNE FRANK, THE DIARY OF ANNE FRANK

INTRODUCTION

In this chapter we present an updated version of the eight models of community practice we first introduced in the nineteenth edition of the *Encyclopedia of Social Work* (Weil and Gamble 1995), along with the rationale for their organization. We also discuss three "lenses" that we believe will significantly influence the contexts of community practice in this century, and we examine the primary and related roles community practice social workers must adopt to engage in these eight models.

Many models and approaches are available for understanding community practice, historical and current, both from academic colleagues and from skilled practitioners. Currently, a number of authors present different frames for engaging with ideas related to macro practice, community practice, community organizing, community development, and social planning. William Brueggemann (2006) takes a wide view in describing how to work at social change with communities and with organizations at national and international levels. Michael Jacoby Brown (2006) and Mark Homan (2008) provide very practical guides to those wishing to engage in community, or even global change, by proposing frameworks for analyzing dimensions of power, guidelines for mounting a lobbying effort, ideas for how to mobilize resources, and a variety of nuts-and-bolts advice for grassroots community work. David Hardcastle, Patricia Powers, and Stanley Wenocur (2004) unravel the complexities of community-based social problems and pose a variety of strategic approaches using agencies, boards, committees, marketing, assertiveness, and advocacy as well as social casework to solve social problems. Dennis Long, Carolyn Tice, and John Morrison (2006) emphasize the strengths perspective of macro practice, with a focus on building strong community-based organizations prepared to engage in social planning and policy practice, all for the purpose of promoting social justice. Ellen Netting, Peter Kettner, and Steven McMurtry (2008) emphasize the change process and the way to engage with organizations and communities to plan for and monitor intended change for solving community and organizational problems. Herbert and Irene Rubin (2007) focus their work on organizing and development for progressive change, identifying twenty-two submodels of organizing and development that will defend the weak, diminish hardship, and work toward an equitable society. Jack Rothman (2007) has modified his three community intervention approaches—now called *planning and policy, community capacity development,* and *social advocacy*—showing that each of the three dominant modes is influenced by the other two, so that nine variations evolve that represent basic strategies for engaging with communities. Building on the work of these colleagues and our own experience, reading, and research on North American and international community practice, we have refined and updated our framework of eight dominant models currently applied in community practice.

EIGHT MODELS OF COMMUNITY PRACTICE, REVISED AND UPDATED

Since 1995 our table of community practice models has been presented in a variety of publications, the latest being in the twentieth edition of the *Encyclopedia of Social Work* (Gamble and Weil, 2008). Table 2.1 represents the most recent modification resulting from our effort to describe the major ways community work is now likely to be practiced in the United States and across the globe.

In addition to the five characteristics identified for each model, the table has two important side borders. The left border represents the values and purposes that we define as the application of social justice and human rights to the improvement of social, economic, and environmental well-being. The border on the right side represents the "lenses" we believe will significantly affect the contexts of community practice in this century: globalization, the increase in multicultural societies, and the expansion of human rights, especially rights for women and girls. Imagine that attached to these side borders are thin sheets of cellophane paper, each a different color, each an overlay influencing the work of community practice as it covers the whole table. The values and purposes "sheet" must cover all eight models all the time as a reminder of the fundamental

TABLE 2.1 Eight Models of Community Practice with Twenty-first-Century Contexts

COMPARATIVE CHARACTERISTICS	NEIGHBORHOOD AND COMMUNITY ORGANIZING	ORGANIZING FUNCTIONAL COMMUNITIES	SOCIAL, ECONOMIC, AND SUSTAINABLE DEVELOPMENT	INCLUSIVE PROGRAM DEVELOPMENT	SOCIAL PLANNING	COALITIONS	POLITICAL AND SOCIAL ACTION	MOVEMENTS FOR PROGRESSIVE CHANGE
Desired Outcome	Develop capacity of members to organize; direct and/or moderate the impact of regional planning and external development	Action for social justice focused on advocacy and on changing behaviors and attitudes; may also provide service	Promote grassroots plans; prepare citizens to use social and economic resources without harming environments; open livelihood opportunities	Expansion, redirection, and new development of programs to improve service effectiveness using participatory engagement methods	Neighborhood, citywide, or regional proposals for action by (a) neighborhood groups (b) elected body, and/or (c) planning councils	Build a multiorganizational power base to advocate for standards and programs, to influence program direction and draw down resources	Action for social justice focused on changing policies or policy makers	Action for social, economic, and environmental justice that provides new paradigms for the healthy development of people and the planet
Systems Targeted for Change	Municipal/regional government; external developers; local leadership	General public; government institutions	Banks; foundations; external developers; laws that govern wealth creation	Financial donors and volunteers to programs; beneficiaries of agency services	Perspectives of (a) neighborhood planning groups (b) elected leaders (c) human services leaders	Elected officials; foundations; government policy, and service organizations	Voting public; elected officials; inactive/potential participants in public debates and elections	General public; political, social, and economic systems that are oppressive and destructive

	Primary Constituency	Scope of Concern	Social Work/Community Practice Roles
	Residents of neighborhood, parish, rural community, village	Quality of life in geographic area; Increased ability of grassroots leaders and organizations to improve social, economic and environmental conditions	Organizer Facilitator Educator Coach Trainer Bridge Builder
	Like-minded people in a community, region, nation, or across the globe	Advocacy for particular issue or population (examples: environmental protection; women's participation in decision making)	Organizer Advocate Writer/Speaker Facilitator
	Low-wealth, marginalized, or oppressed population groups in a city or region	Improve social, economic, and environmental well-being; employ equality, opportunity and responsibility to guide human behavior	Negotiator Bridge Builder Promoter Planner Educator Manager Researcher Evaluator
	Agency board and administrators; community representatives	Service development for a specific population (examples: children's access to health care; security against domestic violence)	Spokesperson Planner/ Evaluator Manager/ Director Proposal Writer Trainer Bridge Builder Visionary
	(a) neighborhood groups (b) elected leaders (c) social agencies and interagency organizations	(a) neighborhood level planning (b) integration of social, economic, and environmental needs into public planning arena; (c) human services coordination	Researcher Proposal writer Communicator Planner Manager Evaluator
	Organizations and citizens that have a stake in the particular issue	Organizational partners joining in a collaborative relationship to improve social, economic, and environmental conditions and human rights	Mediator Negotiator Spokesperson Organizer Bridge Builder Leader
	Citizens in a particular political jurisdiction	Building the level of participation in political activity; ensuring that elections are fair and not controlled by wealth	Advocate Organizer Researcher Candidate Leader
	Leaders, citizens, and organizations able to create new visions and social structures	Social, economic, and environmental justice within society (examples: basic human needs; basic human rights)	Advocate Facilitator Leader

Source: Gamble and Weil (2008):355–68.

reasons we social workers engage in community practice. These values and purposes guide our choices of work and our practice behaviors. The "sheets" identifying the three contexts will shade the models as one or the other context becomes more or less influential with time and location. The context sheets remind us that global events and movements, larger than any community, will affect the work of community practice and the people with whom community practitioners engage. Each practice model interacts with the "lenses" in somewhat different ways. Although these contextual overlays have been important in the past, they will become even more significant in community practice in this century.

In order for you to incorporate the "lenses" and use knowledge about the models in practice, you need to understand the basic definition and essential purposes of models as ideal types.

As originally defined by Max Weber (1903–1917/1997), an *ideal type* (model) combines concepts (related to social actions and social structures) to form a "unified analytical construct," employed to study and understand social phenomena; it is an abstraction used to represent and explain reality. Although ideal types, or models, do not exist in their pure conceptual form in reality, they are intended to represent and explain the essential and most salient aspects of complex phenomena that combine behavior patterns, interactions, and social structures. The analytical constructs—ideal types/models—therefore enable us to compare complex and combined sets of actions and social structures, identify how they operate, and show how they are similar to and distinct from each other. Models provide condensed and simplified images and depictions of "types" of practice illustrating different emphases, purposes, scopes, and strategies for action. By gaining an image of a model's simplified form with related elements or characteristics, a community practice worker can differentiate among approaches and make sound decisions about which approach is most appropriate in specific contexts and situations. Understanding the differentiations among the models assists practitioners in comparing the possibilities for engaging in community work in actual practice.

We identified eight models in our first publication on this subject; in this volume we have retained the same models, updated them, and provided more current and specific names. We believe these eight types are the dominant, current models that encompass a wide variety of community work subtypes in many parts of the world. For example, *neighborhood and community organizing* can encompass grassroots organizing in diverse local settings (e.g., urban and rural). *Functional community organizing* can be related to various feminist, union, ethnic, spiritual, antipoverty, or antislavery causes or to any of the wide variety of organizing issues taken up by communities of interest. *Social, economic, and sustainable development* can be local or global but would tend to encompass any aspect of human development and community development, with the added concern to preserve and restore the environment. *Inclusive program development* relates to planning, implementation, and management of any type of program with a strong directive to engage with those who will benefit from the planned program. *Social planning* can have a focus, for example, on planning for public health outcomes, improved transportation, accident prevention, child protection, adult education or green building, and can encompass a neighborhood, region, or even a worldwide issue. *Coalitions* are groups of organizations that come together for short- or long-term goals around a range of social, economic, or environmental needs and can be local or global in their reach. *Political and social action* recognizes the need for policy change, or change in policy makers, in order to improve a whole range of social, economic, and environmental conditions. *Movements for progressive change* can also be local or global, working to engage with wide individual and institutional support throughout society. From our research, teaching, and experience in community work, we determined that employing this set of eight models was the most useful framework to introduce community practice students to the range of opportunities available in this rewarding work.

Our set of eight models differs from other established sets and recent presentations, while also drawing on earlier work. One of our sources is Canadian community practice pioneer Murray Ross, a scholar and researcher who played a major role in delineating community organization methods and workers' roles, as well as developing theory-based literature to guide curricula (Weil 1996). His first book, *Community Organization: Theory and Principles* (Ross 1955), centered on work processes and provided the first use of a range of social science concepts as central features tied into the achievement of practice goals. Ross held that practice methods were co-determined by useful theories from the social sciences and by social work values (Schwartz 1965). He specified three major approaches in community practice—reform orientation, planning orientation, and process orientation. Process remained central for Ross: he held that individuals and groups thrive through active participation. In *Case Histories in Community Organization*, Ross (1958) stressed workers' roles and activities in engagement with individuals and community groups using eleven well-developed case studies of work with different types of communities engaged with different types of problems, including a strong focus on international community development.

Our approach also bears similarities to and significant differences from Jack Rothman's earliest configuration of three community intervention approaches, for each of which he described twelve characteristics (Rothman 1968; 2001). Rothman's original approaches, which have had major influence on generations of U.S. social workers, were *locality development, social planning,* and *social action.* His locality development model comes closest to our model labeled *neighborhood and community organizing.* Our configuration and Rothman's each have a model or approach whose shared characteristics we have labeled social planning. In his latest iteration Rothman (2008) links planning with policy change, whereas we link policy change with social action. Our model of social planning in this volume is focused on planning at the community level. Rothman's third mode of intervention is labeled social action. Our combination of political action with social action is based on our experience and research, which indicates that one rarely engages in social action without also needing to change policies or try to change those who make policies (Jansson et al. 2005).

While some of our models are similar to Ross's three approaches and Rothman's original three modes, we also developed five additional models to encompass the breadth of community practice as we know it. Our model for *organizing functional communities* grew from our work and experience with feminist organizers, people organizing with families of the developmentally disabled, community leaders organizing for peace, groups organizing for Native American, African American, and Asian American rights, local farmers and consumers organizing for sustainable agriculture, and many other such efforts that grow from communities of interest. Although a number of our colleagues have provided excellent conceptual frameworks for social development (Midgley 1995), economic development (Johnson and Farrell 2000), and sustainable development (Estes 1993), we became interested in combining *social, economic, and sustainable development* in an effort to more vigorously link social, economic, and environmental well-being. The social work profession has tended to focus on social development, but we believe progress in human development requires the simultaneous incorporation of livelihoods and economic opportunities with the strengthening of social networks and institutions as well as the protection and restoration of the environment. Social workers may not have the requisite technical skills to accomplish all the work in such a complex model, but we do have excellent assessment, team-building, planning, and facilitation skills that are essential for this combination of human development activities.

Our *inclusive program development* model grew from combining two of the five original models presented in the work edited by Sam Taylor and Robert Roberts (1985)—"program development and service coordination" developed by Paul Kurzman (1985) and the "community liaison approach" written by Sam Taylor (1985). Inclusive program development emphasizes our belief that good community practice involves grassroots stakeholders who will benefit from engagement in all phases of the program from the beginning of plan-making to the evaluation stage. The *coalitions* model developed from our work with coalitions against domestic violence, for adolescent pregnancy prevention, campaign finance reform, changes in state policies, peaceful resolution of conflict and against war, and a clearer understanding of interorganizational dynamics that contribute to the success of coalitions (Mizrahi and Rosenthal 2001; Roberts-DeGennaro 1986). Whereas all models may incorporate aspects of *social planning* and *coalition building,* both of these models have generated significant bodies of literature, identifying sufficient characteristics to be labeled a discreet model in its own right. The *movements for progressive change* model came from our experience with the civil rights, women's, peace, and environmental movements as well as understanding of the history of social work and the need for fundamental changes in institutions and priorities to significantly reduce oppression, discrimination, and violence (Fisher and Karger 1997; Reisch and Andrews 2001; Rubin and Rubin 2007; Van Soest 1997). Although we recognize that social workers in these times are often not the leaders of social movements, we wonder why they could not more frequently take positions of leadership in promoting the values that are the foundation of our profession.

Our eight models comprise discrete types of community practice that can be examined through comparative analysis and that can help expand the understanding of intervention approaches. For additional comparison we identified five characteristics that apply to each model. Our interest was in providing sufficient descriptors to gain an adequate understanding of the model type, keeping it sharply focused, more easily understood, and therefore more easily compared. The five characteristics are: desired outcome, systems targeted for change, primary constituency, scope of concern, and social work/community practice roles. In part II, we describe and discuss these five characteristics for each model, with increased emphasis on the scope of concern and the primary roles engaged in by community practice workers for that model. We also explore the basic process, theoretical and conceptual understandings that inform the model, and significant skills and competencies we believe are important for community practice workers engaged in the particular model. Finally, we illustrate each model with several real-world examples, drawing on the work of colleagues and practitioners from across the globe. These real-world examples will demonstrate some mixing of models because, unlike ideal types, they represent the complexities of human engagement, community contexts, and change opportunities. A number of the real-world examples we introduce contain overlapping aspects of model types, which we will identify.

THE "LENSES" INFLUENCING COMMUNITY PRACTICE CONTEXTS IN THIS CENTURY

Earlier we identified the three lenses that will influence community practice in this century—globalization, the increase in multicultural societies, and the expansion of human rights, especially rights for women and girls. We describe each of these lenses in turn and discuss their influence on community practice models.

1. Globalization: The International Federation of Social Workers has defined globalization as

> the process by which all peoples and communities come to experience an increasingly common economic, social and cultural environment. By definition, the process affects everybody throughout the world. A more integrated world community brings both benefits and problems for all; it affects the balance of economic, political and cultural power between nations, communities and individuals and it can both enhance and limit freedoms and human rights. Social workers, by the nature of their work, tend to meet those who are more likely to have suffered the damaging consequences of some aspects of globalisation. (IFSW, International Policy Statement on Globalization and the Environment, 2008)

If globalization is understood as the exchange and integration of culture, technological innovation, travel, models of barter, and economic exchange, then it can be said to have ancient origins. Specifically, globalization might have been ongoing with the Mayan civilization stretching across Mesoamerica, with the Roman Empire, with the Han Dynasty and trade across Asia on the Silk Road, and with the intellectual and cultural centers of the Islamic Golden Age. In recent years, however, globalization has come to be identified with the Bretton Woods Conference, which created the World Bank and the International Monetary Fund (IMF) following World War II. These institutions were intended to promote growth and minimize disruptions and barriers to financial integration across national borders. In the years since, those who promote globalization, or more specifically those who support the parts of globalization identified with neoliberal free trade and free market policies, proclaimed major economic successes. Fewer people, they say, are now living in poverty in the world, except for sub-Saharan Africa, and the regions that have embraced global free trade such as East Asia and the Pacific have shown significant economic growth (Sachs 2005; World Bank 2006).

There is a negative view, however: some see the growth of enormous wealth for multinational corporations as paving a path of destruction for vulnerable populations. When farmers are left poorer in the developing world because they cannot compete with subsidized crops coming from agribusiness in rich nations, and when cheap labor and cheap natural resources in the developing world have been exploited, questions are raised about the so-called benefits of these policies and practices (Hurst 2006; Korten 2001; Stiglitz 2003). Furthermore, when the World Bank and the International Monetary Fund, following policies they labeled "structural adjustment," called for cutting poor countries' investments in education, health care, food, and fertilizer, global free trade and the international policies supporting its free rein looked more like a destructive force with no limitations (Cavanagh and Mander 2004: Klein 2007; Prigoff 2000).

While the economic implications of globalization are still being debated on both sides, the United Nations Development Program has been raising alarms about the growing gap between the rich and poor in the world. The *Human Development Report* for 2007/2008 indicated that the richest 20 percent of the world's population controlled 75 percent of the world's wealth, while the poorest 40 percent controlled only 5 percent of the world's wealth (UNDP 2007). Although newer methods are being developed to measure the disparity, more recent indicators seem to show an even greater gap between the world's richest and poorest populations. The effect of this diverging income gap focuses significant concern on how and to what degree globalization affects inequality in the world's populations and exactly what should and could be done to reverse the gap (Milanovic 2006).

In the end, the people who could benefit greatly from the work of community practitioners are those affected negatively by globalization factors such as multilateral and bilateral trade agreements, amassing and transfer of huge financial resources, or decisions by the World Trade Organization (WTO). These are the people who will need the involvement of a facilitator to help grow their capacity and empower their neighborhoods and community organizations to prevent additional negative effects on their local resources, livelihoods, social networks, and environmental quality. These are the people trying to save the special community services their disabled children need when those services are threatened by cutbacks because of the economic downturn. These are the people who, as their social and economic safety nets begin to crumble, will need assistance from an educator, promoter, and researcher to help them develop microcredit institutions and solidarity economics from the ground up. These are the people who will look for help from a social planner to measure the extent of local resources that can be applied to restore the social, economic, and environmental well-being of their communities and change policies to help them do it. These are the people who will need the help of a mediator or negotiator as they build coalitions across communities, regions, and continents to lobby and vote for positive local and global policies where global exchange and integration can be regulated to aid the most vulnerable populations rather than the richest ones. Finally, these are the people who will need advocates and leaders to move programs and policies toward progressive outcomes in social justice and human rights efforts. Understanding how international events can affect local conditions—whether wars, economic shocks, public health crises, political oppression, or natural disasters—is the first preparatory step for a community practice worker as he or she responds to the negative effects of globalization. In the chapters that follow, we describe how to build the skills to engage effectively with the available resources, often using the positive elements of globalization, and how to ameliorate or eliminate the negative effects of globalization. We use examples from Brooklyn to Bangladesh, from New Mexico and North Carolina to South Africa, and from Brazil to China, where we identify successful efforts that provide a window to community practice grounded in social justice and human rights (ASHOKA 2008; Cavanagh and Mander 2004; World Social Forum 2008).

2. **The increase in multicultural societies:** Nearly all of the world's societies are becoming more pluralistic in the sense that populations are becoming ethnically, racially, and culturally more mixed. The United States population, for example, was 83 percent white in the 1980 census but 75 percent white in the 2000 census. In New York City in 2004, 48 percent of the people said they spoke a language other than English at home (Hacker 2004). In the 2000 census of the United States, it was possible for the first time to identify oneself as a mixed-race person: 7 million people took advantage of the category to identify themselves as such (Orenstein 2008).

International migration accounts for nearly 3 million migrants moving from poor countries to wealthier ones each year. At the same time, migrations are increasing *between* developing countries such as from India, Egypt, and Yemen to the Persian Gulf States, from Bangladesh to India, and from Guatemala to Mexico (Population Reference Bureau, 2006). Although many cities, states, regions, and countries remain identified with a particular racial, ethnic, or cultural group, the populations in nearly all nations are more heterogeneous now than they were two decades ago. These changes are the result of both voluntary and forced migrations. Voluntary migration is often driven by economic factors. People immigrate to countries where there is a shortage of both skilled and unskilled workers. In addition, for those living in countries where wages are meager for both professional and unskilled positions, greater economic opportunity is a strong motivator to migrate.

Involuntary immigration, in contrast, is most often the product of war, genocide, famine, or natural disasters that force populations into refugee status. While recent and current refugees are primarily the result of wars, concern is growing for the number of refugees that may result from global climate change (UNDP 2007). During the Balkan wars in 1992, the Office of the United Nations High Commissioner for Refugees (UNHCR) provided assistance to 17.8 million refugees worldwide. Although that number steadily decreased to a low of 8.4 million in 2005, by 2007 it had increased to 11.4 million refugees outside their countries and 26 million displaced internally (UNHCR 2008). The

United Nations reported that the increase was largely due to the wars in Afghanistan and Iraq causing 3 million Afghans to seek refuge in Pakistan and Iran and 2 million Iraqis to flee to Syria and Jordan (Cumming-Bruce 2008). It should also be noted that there are ever-increasing numbers of people who cross borders for safety but are not considered official refugees. The UN estimates that beyond official refugees an additional 11 million people are *stateless*, meaning they have settled in a country where they are not recognized as citizens and have no legal rights (UNHCR 2007). Most of these refugees seek safety in a developing country near their country of origin, contradicting the misconception that Western countries provide most of the protection for refugees fleeing their own countries (Cumming-Bruce 2008).

The varied reasons driving the mobility and migration of people continue to bring people of different nationalities, races, cultures, and ethnic groups in closer contact with each other. To the extent that immigrants are welcomed, the opportunities for exchanging valuable cultural attributes over several generations are significant. When immigrant groups are large or easily identifiable because their dress or skin color is different from the dominant cultural or ethnic group, the blending of cultural aspects may be slower and fraught with discrimination. In addition to its damaging personal affects, discrimination militates against melding valuable cultural aspects from the two groups, and the dominant group has the power to exclude, diminish, and withhold resources and opportunities that would provide for continued human development for both groups. Each country and community struggles with the acceptance of cultural and ethnic diversity in different ways.

In the 1980s, Canada and some European countries adopted national policies supporting multiculturalism that legislated the acceptance of the cultures and subcultures that contribute to the whole society (About Canada 2008; Penninx, Berger, and Kraal 2006). These policies and legislative mandates promoted a kind of cultural pluralism allowing people to keep their cultural traditions while at the same time contributing to the whole country. As immigrant groups increased in size and visibility, however, the dominant population groups tended to exhibit less tolerance for the newer immigrants. In many cases, although the growth of immigrant groups was often fueled by the dominant group's demand for labor, the decreased tolerance led some European countries to retreat from their national multicultural policies, which drew criticism from both ideological extremes. Some making the case against multiculturalism are opposed to acceptance of cultural groups if it also means acceptance of all the cultural practices they bring with them, particularly those that restrict individual freedom and human rights, and that compromise the rule of law in their newly adopted country. This argument views the Western Enlightenment as the guide to values that support human rights and the rule of law (Cliteur 2007).

Feminists also criticize granting rights to cultural groups that would limit universal rights, especially if they restrict women from enjoying the full spectrum of human rights (Hirsi Ali 2007).

South Africa is a good example of a country struggling with the guarantee of human rights for its multiple cultural groups. Neither its African nor its white population is ethnically homogeneous, and the country recognizes eleven different official languages. The Constitution of the Republic of South Africa, adopted in 1996, is one of the world's most progressive and admired constitutions because of its broad human rights guarantees and its efforts to blend the strengths of its cultural mosaic. It is, for example, one of only six nations in the world that grants same-sex marriages. The Constitutional Court is gradually working through the application of this new Constitution and its Bill of Rights as the people explore its meaning for them as individuals and as groups (Constitutional Court of South Africa 2008).

The Center for the Study of Violence and Reconciliation (CSVR), based in Johannesburg, South Africa, has prepared excellent workbooks for use in youth discussion groups to explore the meaning of their diversity and rights (CSVR 2004). Working on training, consultation, research, and publications, CSVR provides opportunities for communities across the globe to make use of their experience in building a reconciliation and human rights culture wherever multicultural and multiclass issues threaten progress toward creating and maintaining democratic institutions.

Discussions of the kind promoted by CSVR (2008) are important in developing an appreciation of difference and diversity. Without question, because of our increasing migrations and mobility, most of the world's population will be living in communities where diversity of all kinds is common and continues to increase. We argue that community practice should encourage and facilitate discussions of the meaning of multiculturalism as well as the acceptance and appreciation of differences. Unfortunately, such reasoned discussion can always be thwarted and threatened by violence. Therefore, we must work to enhance the multicultural discussion and prevent violence through the promotion of normative behaviors based on the Universal Declaration of Human Rights and through legal prosecution of discrimination and hate crimes. The Southern Poverty Law Center in Montgomery, Alabama, provides educational material through its program "Teaching Tolerance" for schools to engage in multicultural discussion (Southern Poverty Law Center 2008). The center has also been involved in the tracking and successful prosecution of active hate groups (SPLC 2008).

In 2007 the National Association of Social Workers in the United States published *Institutional Racism and the Social Work Profession: A Call to Action*. The publication presents a clear definition of how structural situations trap all of us in racist behaviors, and it also provides multiple resources to guard against and change racist practices that are part of our everyday lives. The report's call to action states:

> The responsibility of individual social workers is to recognize that structural racism plays out in their personal and professional lives and to use that awareness to ameliorate its influence in all aspects of social work practice, inclusive of direct practice, community organizing, supervision, consultation, administration, advocacy, social and political action, policy development and implementation, education, and research and evaluation. (NASW 2007a:3)

Community practice workers should recognize their role in celebrating diversity and promoting collaborative efforts among different cultural groups and organizations in every one of the eight models of community practice we described earlier in the chapter.

3. The expansion of human rights, especially rights for women and girls: The discussion of diversity merges into the discussion of human rights, especially the rights of women and girls. As described in chapter 1, human rights is a major focus in the IFSW/IASSW "Ethics in Social Work, Statement of Principles" (2008), and it will continue to have prominence in this century. Social workers, as both scholars and practitioners, should embrace three particular human rights issues, as solutions are found for their application: (1) finding ways to ensure that cultural, social, and economic rights, especially the right not to starve or die from preventable diseases, have the same importance as civil and political rights; (2) helping neighborhoods, regions, and countries pull back from the extremes of cultural relativism and universal rights to a middle space where conflicting rights can be mediated; and (3) actively working for the rights of women and girls throughout society.

The history of the exclusion of women's voices is thousands of years long in both Western and non-Western societies. Women and girls who are excluded from participation in the issues that affect their lives are not only deprived of their human rights and the benefits of community resources, but they are also excluded from contributing in equal measure to the development of humanity (UNICEF 2006; Wetzel 2007). In its report, *The State of the World's Children 2007: Women and Children. The Double Dividend of Gender Equality* (2006), UNICEF calls for equality in the household, employment, politics, and government. When countries move to provide equality for women in these arenas, they reap a "double dividend" because of the significant effect these measures have on improving the lives of children. "For children to reach their fullest potential and to grow up in families and societies where they can thrive, gender discrimination must be banished once and for all" (UNICEF, *State of the*

World's Children 2006:69). Great gains have been made since 1945, with the election of increased numbers of women to political offices, more parity in girls' education, and even positive change in general attitudes toward women and girls. All the same, much more work is needed in this area. As of September 2006, the ratification of the Convention on the Elimination of All Forms of Discrimination against Women had been completed by 184 countries—not, however, by the United States. The promises of this Convention will require more work to ensure that girls are included in equal educational opportunities, to prevent violence and death from sexual abuse and from the lack of reproductive health provisions for pregnancy and childbirth, and to eliminate gender discrimination throughout the lives of women and girls (UNICEF, *State of the World's Children* 2006).

Women are working in all parts of the globe to identify strategic areas of action where social justice and human rights can have a gender focus. In the area of microfinance, for example, currently women make up approximately 85 percent of the poorest borrowers across the globe, in their effort to improve the economic prospects for their families (Daley-Harris 2007).

The Center for the Study of Violence and Reconciliation in South Africa, which publishes the *International Journal of Transitional Justice*, joined with the Human Rights Center at the University of California at Berkeley for their recent special issue, *Gender and Transitional Justice*, with a focus on the role of women as decision makers and strategists in the aftermath of sexual violence as a tool of war (Pillay 2007). These and many more lessons from the developing world are necessary for a full discussion of what women are thinking in a range of cultures and experiences outside of Western perspectives.

As with the two previous lenses, we know issues surrounding the rights of women and girls will be part of every one of the eight models described in our configuration. If they are not, the community worker should be prepared to integrate gender issues into the work so that they are not ignored or diminished. In an earlier work, we provided questions relevant to a feminist application for each model (Weil, Gamble, and Williams, 1998). These questions, as well as questions relevant to raising multicultural issues, are part of the companion *CPS Workbook*. They can be used with exercises in class or as relevant personal questions for assessing one's readiness for community practice.

PRIMARY AND RELATED ROLES ASSOCIATED WITH THE EIGHT MODEL STRUCTURES

One of the comparative characteristics we have developed to help shape the values, attitudes, behaviors, and engagement strategies of community practice social workers involves the identification and definition of roles. Table 2.2 describes the primary and related roles we have linked with the models.

The primary roles for these eight models are advocate, leader, organizer, planner, and researcher/assessor. These terms are relatively familiar, but we have given them more specific definitions as they are applied to the models. Sometimes the primary role will be found in several models. A related role with some variation in meaning will also be linked to several models. For example, being an *advocate* and thereby engaging in purposive change activities toward a more just social order is a role clearly linked to *organizing functional communities, political and social action,* and *movements for progressive change.* However, related roles such as *promoter, spokesperson,* or being a *writer or speaker for advocacy* definitely have a place in the models we identify as *inclusive program development* and *coalitions.* Consequently, advocacy and roles related to advocacy are related to at least five of the eight models we have identified.

Being a *leader,* or engaging in a role related to leadership such as a *visionary* or a *candidate* for public office, are roles related to the models we identify as *coalitions, political and social action, movements for progressive change,* and *inclusive program development.* Leadership—that is, serving as the initial director of a group that organizes to identify conditions of social injustice and human rights abuse, lack of opportunity, or unequal access to services or resources at a local, regional, national, or global level—has a primary place in at least four of the models we identify. Clearly, however, it is not a primary role in the model *neighborhood and community organizing* where the community social worker is trying to identify and build leaders among the grassroots participants who are seeking to improve their community or neighborhood. In the latter case, if the community social worker becomes the leader, he or she is likely to subvert the development of local community leadership. The role of visionary might be a common one in a number of models such as social planning and social, economic, and sustainable development; however, the role of candidate for public office would only be found in the political and social action model.

The role of *organizer* is perhaps the most common role for a person working in community social work practice. We define this role as systematically planning and working with individuals and small groups on community issues so that their efforts coalesce to form a whole organization to initiate change, improve the quality of life, and solve problems. In addition to the primary role of organizer, we identify seven related roles that are very closely associated to the work of an organizer. These roles are: *bridge-builder, coach, educator, facilitator, mediator, negotiator,* and *trainer.* Among these related roles, the work of a *facilitator* is perhaps the most skillful and useful in helping to ease the building of organizations by sharing techniques for communication, decision making, goal setting, strategy analysis, analysis of social, economic, and environmental conditions, and outcome

TABLE 2.2 Primary and Related Roles for Social Workers/Community Practice Workers in the Eight Models

PRIMARY ROLES AND DEFINITIONS	RELATED ROLES AND DEFINITIONS	MODELS RELATED TO ROLES
Advocate Researches and engages in purposive change activities toward a more just social order and/or supports and helps others to speak for and be able to take action and make changes on their own behalf that could result in more inclusive and equitable social and economic outcomes, with investments in improved human development, increased social capital, diverse economic opportunities, and recovered and protected environments.	**Promoter** Works actively in support of an idea and speaks about it positively and persuasively to multiple constituencies to gain resources and support from others. **Spokesperson** Literally, *spokesperson* means speaking *for* a project, program, or cause. It is a basic component of *advocacy.* Within community practice, *spokesperson* connotes the worker actively and directly speaking out for or representing a program or issue. **Writer/Speaker for Advocacy** Effectively makes the case in writing, speaking, and presentations for social, economic, or environmental justice and policy changes that could result in more inclusive communities and more equitable social and economic outcomes. Speaks and writes for development that emphasizes expanding livelihoods and restoring environments, especially for the most vulnerable populations and for species that cannot speak or write for themselves. Supports and coaches community members to expand their own writing and public speaking skills.	• Organizing Functional Communities • Political and Social Action • Movements for Progressive Change • Inclusive Program Development • Coalitions
Leader Guides or serves as the initial director of a group that organizes to identify conditions of social injustice and		• Coalitions • Political and Social Action

human rights abuse, lack of opportunity or unequal access to services or resources at local, regional, national, or global levels. Works to promote policies that increase social justice and human rights. While a community worker may take on a long-term formal leadership role, more likely at the policy level, a central goal for a community practitioner is to strengthen groups and engage in systematic leadership development so that members will learn to take on various leadership roles.

- Movements for Progressive Change
- Political and Social Action

Candidate

Chooses to stand for an elective office in order to speak, advocate, and legislate for community needs, sustainable development, supports and services for vulnerable populations and the poor, strengthening of human rights protections, and expansion of social justice.

Visionary

Being able to perceive solutions to problems and to conceive program goals and designs from a holistic standpoint. Having the foresight to identify potential barriers and identify solutions. Communicating and translating these perceptions into a clear vision with specific goals and measurable objectives

- Inclusive Program Development

Organizer

Brings people together by systematically planning and working with individuals and small groups on community issues so that their efforts coalesce to form a whole organization to initiate change, improve quality of life, and solve problems. Bringing people together also enables grassroots leaders and organizations to improve social, economic, and environmental conditions through collective action.

Bridge-Builder

Helps an organization to identify potential allies and resources outside their immediate geographic or network area so that they can collaborate, compare, convene, and connect with these allies. This process enables enlarging and tempering the group's analyses of social/economic/environmental conditions and refining their plans of action. This role is sometimes referred to as boundary spanning, and these skills are specifically intended to help grassroots groups engage in community collaborations, connect outside their area to other organizations from whom they can learn, locate organizations with whom they might negotiate a loan, find potential allies who can vouch for their approach, program model or evaluation plan; and identify and successfully connect with potential grant makers.

- Neighborhood and Community Organizing
- Organizing Functional Communities
- Social, Economic, and Sustainable Development;
- Inclusive Program Development
- Coalitions
- Political and Social Action
- Movements for Progressive Change

TABLE 2.2 (*Continued*)

PRIMARY ROLES AND DEFINITIONS	RELATED ROLES AND DEFINITIONS	MODELS RELATED TO ROLES
	Coach Identifies and calls attention to the strengths of individuals, groups, and organizations through supportive comments and communication. **Educator** Assists groups and individuals in locating information and resources regarding issues they want to learn about. In community practice, the educator role is always reciprocal with the worker learning from the community's history, vision, goals, strengths, and needs; and, in turn, sharing with community members the worker's knowledge and skills. The effective educator is always a co-learner with community members—each sharing his or her expertise and wisdom to co-produce new knowledge and understandings. **Facilitator** Makes the work of forming a purposeful organization easier and more systematic by sharing techniques for communication, decision making, goal setting, strategy analysis, social/economic/environmental analyses, and evaluation. In addition, the facilitator helps the group to think through and discuss their issues and analyses in greater depth, helping them to make shared decisions by raising critical questions (i.e., the *why, how, what if* questions). **Mediator** Works with members of an organization, or of multiple organizations, to resolve differences or conflicts by helping them hear each other and helping them move forward on an agreed plan. Mediators have an essential responsibility to hear the positions of each party, represent them accurately, and refrain from taking sides.	

Planner

Using a range of technical and process skills, works with problem definition, problem solving, program or plan implementation, monitoring and evaluation. In community practice, the planner's role is multifaceted and may be carried out at several levels from grassroots community groups to international development and service groups. In grassroots community practice, the planner works conjointly with community members, assisting them in meeting their goals for program and community development through a process of problem/need identification and documentation, problem solving, planning, program implementation, monitoring, and outcome evaluation.

Negotiator

Helps members of an organization or members of different organizations or groups come to an agreement satisfactory to both regarding a contested issue; works to identify a middle ground in the contested issue(s) that allows for win/win solutions; also coaches community members in learning negotiation skills.

Trainer

Provides information and demonstrations of skills and techniques, and tests the use of concepts and strategies useful to the group in forming their organization and carrying out action. The trainer also uses anticipatory guidance in the use of strategies and provides opportunities to practice the techniques so that individuals and groups develop comfort in using the techniques.

Manager

Works with the members of an organization to carry out policies and plans to successful operation. Major tasks to meet organization goals include planning innovative efforts, organizing people and resources to achieve goals, leading, guiding and coordinating implementation efforts, engaging in community liaison with external constituencies, monitoring implementation, and evaluating outcomes.

Proposal Writer

Works with others to develop an idea to respond to a community need, concern, or interest. The written proposal will document the *why, what, who, when, where,* and *how* the organization or community will implement and evaluate the process and outcomes of the proposed project.

- Social, Economic, and Sustainable Development
- Inclusive Program Development
- Social Planning

TABLE 2.2 (*Continued*)

PRIMARY ROLES AND DEFINITIONS	RELATED ROLES AND DEFINITIONS	MODELS RELATED TO ROLES
Researcher/Assessor Provides expertise for systematic inquiry in order to help organizations describe as fully and accurately as possible the extent of the impact of a social justice or human rights issue. The inquiry should include data collection as well as first-person accounts, in the words of those affected, showing the detail and nuances of social injustice, abridgment of human rights, and conditions of domination, exploitation, and discrimination. And when policies change, the inquiry should show if and how social justice and human rights have improved.	**Evaluator** Works with others to identify and solve problems in implementation (formative evaluation) and to assess the outcomes of a program, intervention, or plan in accordance with the goals and objectives of the organization.	• Social, Economic and Sustainable Development • Inclusive Program Development • Social Planning • Political and Social Action

Source: Dorothy N. Gamble and Marie Weil.

evaluation. The role of *organizer,* and the additional seven related roles, are associated with at least seven of the eight models we identify—all the models except social planning. Clearly, organizing activities is part of the social planning model; in our elaboration, however, it is not a primary role.

The role of *planner*—a role requiring a range of technical and process skills to engage groups in problem definition, problem solving, program or plan implementation, monitoring, and evaluation—figures prominently in three of the models. Obviously, planning as a skill is practiced in all eight models, but as a primary role it is linked to the *social planning, social economic and sustainable development,* and *inclusive program development* models. The role of planner can be found in these models at a very local grassroots level, as well as at a community, regional, national, or international level. Different skills will be required of planners working at different levels. In this volume we focus on the role of planner at the community level. Related to the principal role of planning are the roles of *manager* and *proposal writer.*

The role of *researcher, assessor,* and the related role of *evaluator* are found primarily in four of our eight models: *social, economic, and sustainable development, inclusive program development, social planning,* and *political and social action.* We would argue that research and evaluation skills are required in all eight models, though serving in the role of researcher, assessor, or evaluator could be a primary role in the four models we identify. Systematic inquiry carried out by a designated person or persons in an organization can help the organization describe as fully and accurately as possible the extent of the impact of a social injustice or human rights abuse. At the same time when policies, programs, and practices change, systematic research can show if and how social justice or human rights has improved or not. Equally important, an evaluator can work with members of an organization to identify and solve implementation problems and to assess program outcomes in accordance with the organization's goals and objectives. Special skills are required of persons in these research and evaluation roles.

In the eight chapters describing the models in greater detail, we will not reiterate the definitions we have presented in table 2.2. We will, however, describe how these roles are applied in the various models, and how community practice social workers can prepare themselves to be ready to engage in the roles demanded by the particular condition and context of their practice.

CONCLUSIONS

In this chapter we presented the most recently revised table representing our eight models of community practice. We also introduced the three lenses that we believe will significantly color the work of community practice in the twenty-first century. Further discussion of these lenses will be introduced as we cover each model in turn in part II of this book. Finally, we defined the principal roles related to the eight models to provide direction for social workers and community practice workers as they sharpen their values, attitudes, behaviors, and engagement strategies in preparation for this work. We hope this beginning framework will help the reader better understand our perspectives and at the same time encourage you to examine your own standpoint. We encourage you to apply critical thinking to all aspects of these models, lenses, and roles as you prepare for work in community practice.

3

EVOLUTION OF VALUES, CONCEPTS, AND COMMUNITY PRACTICE APPROACHES

The arc of the moral universe is long—but it tends toward justice.

MARTIN LUTHER KING JR., QUOTING ABOLITIONIST THEODORE PARKER

Without struggle, there is no progress.

FREDERICK DOUGLASS

VALUE BASE OF SOCIAL WORK AND COMMUNITY PRACTICE

This chapter examines the origins and evolution of values drawn from wisdom traditions, humanism, and democratic theory that have become the ethical value base of social work along with central ethical concepts and a brief history of approaches to community practice. The principles that support community practice represent the strongest human values promoting social justice and human rights, advocacy, and support for poor and marginalized populations, building connections among groups and communities, mutual assistance, and collaborative work for progressive change. Three ethical principles—altruism, enlightened self-interest, and interdependence—encourage enactment of these values. *Altruism* means "concern for the welfare of others" (*Merriam-Webster OnLine Dictionary* 2009) and is one of the most valued human qualities because it signifies a desire to protect, care for, and promote the welfare of others— and by extension, promote the welfare of society.

Altruism can be traced to human prehistory through early burial sites studied by archaeologists that document clothing bodies for burial and surrounding them with flowers, personal belongings, and symbolic objects in grave sites. These graves are indicative of actions and perhaps rituals that evidence concern, grief, and care for the body of a lost community member. Indeed, despite the capacity for human cruelty and the violence of war, altruism surfaces in even in the most horrific situations. For example, in *Man's Search for Meaning*, Viktor Frankl (2006), a psychiatrist and Holocaust survivor, describes the unspeakable conditions and horror of Nazi death camps, yet also depicts numerous acts of altruism and caring among prisoners. Altruism is not only valuable in times of major crisis; in truth, altruism is necessary for human survival because human infants are absolutely dependent on parents (or other adults) for nourishment, protection, and their very lives.

Because we all become human through interactions with others, and because we depend on each other at many levels across our life spans, interdependence is a cardinal human value (Dromi and Weil 1984). The ethics and values of caring for others have been essential parts of human cultures and have been enshrined in the world's major religious traditions. One does not need to be religious, however, to have a strong spirit of altruism. Humanist traditions vigorously support this value—and often without some of the exclusions exercised in religious contexts. The histories of the world's major religions reveal conquest and war in the name of religion, the establishment of patriarchal societies with the advent of the Bronze Age, and, frequently, oppression of women, slaves, and outsiders (Day 2009). Indeed, institutional religious practices in many traditions continue to support second-class status for women and hold other values that both negate equal opportunity and prevent human flourishing. Our focus here is not on institutionalized religion, or on the convoluted and disempowering aspects of democracies, but rather on the wisdom/spiritual traditions and humanistic and democratic theories that promote equality, social justice, and liberation.

The following discussion therefore focuses on the positive values inherent in traditions that have influenced social work and community practice. Throughout history, economic, political, and religious institutions have synergistically affected societies, and there are typically negative consequences for the poor and vulnerable resulting from these interactions when organized religion acts as a major institution rather than functioning as a spiritual tradition (Day 2009; Smith 1994). For example, religious intolerance has been responsible for many wars as well as pogroms and the atrocities of the Inquisition. In addition, institutional religious power and the economic and political forces that shape social welfare also often serve functions of social control (Day 2009).

Values for community practice, however, historically and currently focus on human rights, social justice, and liberating practices. Since community practice increasingly involves intergroup and cross-cultural work, it is important for practitioners to understand how wisdom traditions that arose in diverse areas of the world across many centuries share positive and liberating values that along with humanistic and democratic theories support community practice and may assist multicultural work.

EVOLUTION OF VALUES FROM SPIRITUAL TRADITIONS

HINDUISM

Hindu society and religion recognize and value interdependence. According to Vedic theology, society can meet everyone's legitimate needs if the various individuals perform their respective duties. These duties embody the ideal of extending God's shelter to others (Dipanwitha Bhattacharyya, personal communication 2008). For example, Hindu scripture obliges the householder to not turn away anyone who comes at mealtime and asks for food (Apastamba Dharma Sutra 1996:324). Similarly, the *Rig Veda* states, "Let the rich man satisfy one who needs help; and let him look upon the long view: For wealth revolves like the wheels of a chariot, coming now to one, now to another (*Rig Veda* 1982:10.117.1–6). The *Bhagavad Gita* (2000) expands these concepts in the following verse:

> Acts of sacrifice, charity, and austerity should not be abandoned, but should be performed, because sacrifice, charity, and austerity are the purifiers of the wise. Leading one's life according to the dharma [spiritual teachings] is essential for reaching moksha, or salvation. Fulfilling the dharma or one's religious duty requires that the wealthy give charitably to those in need. These charitable acts aid the person in the quest for nirvana.

The depth and richness of Hinduism are revealed in its multiple paths to spiritual unity—through love, work, knowledge, and the discipline of meditation. As the noted scholar of comparative philosophy of religion, Huston Smith, stated: "In supporting at once our own life and the lives of others, the community has importance no individual life can command" (Smith 1994:21). Hinduism holds that there is a deep divinity in human life and that the essential human task is to uncover and reveal that connection to the infinite. A major "path to God" is through *moksha*—liberation and unity with the infinite. One "way to God" is through work. This path can lead one to unselfishness and into commitment—to work for good unselfishly through love and as an "instrument of God." Smith noted that this "way" is suitable for people who strongly feel the emotion of love, while those who are more reflective work for good with the goal of enlightenment, which involves both a commitment to work and detachment from outcomes (Smith 1994). These are both forms of karma (work) yoga, and though distinct, they move toward the same goal (ibid.). The life of Mohandas Gandhi (1956, 1993), who led India's people in a nonviolent movement to free India from British rule, stands as an exemplar of the yoga of work and a life unselfishly devoted to the freedom and well-being of others.

BUDDHISM

Gautama Buddha began his examination of life during his early journey when he abandoned his father's palace and witnessed the realities of poverty, debilitating illness, other forms of suffering, and painful death in the world. His quest for enlightenment resulted in teachings focused on transforming suffering, and enacting charity and compassion for others. After years of practice in seeking to combine "rigorous thought and mystic concentration," the sutras recount that one night Gautama sat down under the bodhi tree and vowed that he would not arise until he had achieved his goal—enlightenment (Buddhist Scriptures 2004; Smith 1994). After experiencing numerous distractions and temptations, Gautama touched the earth signifying his concentration and connection, and the distractions melted away. Through the night he meditated and experienced what is termed the Great Awakening, in which he recognized the fullness of true being. This experience transformed Gautama into a *buddha*, an enlightened one, whose life combines wisdom and compassion.

The Buddha's teachings focus on living and are grounded in the belief that it is possible for any human to reach enlightenment. A particular teaching that is pertinent for social workers and community practitioners is his emphasis on compassion for all beings. Compassion is one of the "Four Immeasurable Minds," love, compassion, joy, and equanimity. *Love* in this sense is *maitri*, a concept that captures the capacity to offer to others both happiness and joy. To love in this way, one must have a deep understanding of what will make another person happy (not our own version of what we think should make him or her happy). In Buddhism, *compassion (karuna)* involves the "intention and capacity to relieve and transform suffering and lighten sorrows" (Hanh 1998:172). Contemporary teacher and scholar Thich Nhat Hanh has noted that, although compassion involves "deep concern," we do not have to suffer the same experience as another in order to feel *karuna*. Rather, we must listen carefully, look deeply, understand, and connect with the suffering of others but not lose the capacity to help (Hanh 1998:172). The fourteenth Dalai Lama's life and teachings serve as a contemporary model for attaining wisdom, living ethically, and acting with compassion toward all living beings (Dalai Lama 2001). Joy or *mudita* has to do with the concept of "dwelling in the present moment" and experiencing the simple lifting of mind and spirit that arises for example when looking at a beautiful flower or hearing children laugh. It has sometimes been called altruistic joy and is "filled with peace and contentment" (Hanh, 1998: 172).

The fourth concept of the four immeasurable is *upekash*, which signifies equanimity—expressed as "nonattachment, nondiscrimination, even-mindedness or letting go" (Hanh 1998:174). Upon first hearing, this concept is sometimes misunderstood to imply indifference. The true meaning, however, denotes "the wisdom of equality" which involves shedding all prejudice and discrimination—approaching everyone equally.

In Buddhism, the prayer of the *three refuges* is a central tenant, after "taking refuge in the Buddha and in the Dharma (the Buddha's teachings), the verse concludes with, 'I take refuge in the Sangha—the community that lives in harmony and awareness'" (Hanh 2000:69).

CONFUCIANISM AND TAOISM

Major wisdom traditions that have shaped moral philosophy and values in East Asia are Confucianism and Taoism. Both originated in China probably between 600 and 300 B.C.E.; and the influence of both traditions has shaped cultural values, belief systems, and social traditions throughout most of East Asia. Confucius was aware of the chaos experienced in Bronze Age China during the bloody period of the Warring States when invaders and internal wars had ripped asunder China's established cultural traditions and norms (circa 500–400 B.C.E.; Lau, Introduction to *The Analects* 1979).

After long study of the classics and with concern about cultural decline, Confucius took on the audacious task of reconstructing Chinese values and social norms, seeking to reestablish the social harmony valued during the Chou Dynasty.

Confucius's extraordinary accomplishment through his teachings and writing was to create a "deliberate tradition" drawing from earlier times, ancient texts, and his own thinking (Smith 1994). What he created was a social and moral philosophy and a system of ethics that spread after his death, becoming a new, conscious tradition—to be learned by all Chinese—inculcated in families and schools and intended to be expressed through benevolent governance of the state. For nearly two thousand years, Confucius's goal to create teachings for society that could rebuild the social fabric and recall people and society to the common good and social responsibility was achieved and spread throughout East Asia. His moral philosophy was grounded in two broad social norms—*cultural expectations of behavior* in four family relationships and in the relation of a benevolent ruler to the people and in a path (a "way," a *tao*) to be followed by those seeking to become a wise person (fully realized human being) living by the highest social ideals. To follow the *Tao*, one strives for "ideal moral character" and holds and enacts central virtues including *benevolence* (which combines two characters: *shu*—"the method of discovering what other people do or do not wish done to them"; and *chung*—doing one's best to act in accordance with what one has learned through *shu*) (Confucius 1979:14–16). The principle of benevolence and the other virtues were also expected of rulers. Scholar D. C. Lau (in *Confucius* 1979:32) states: "The ultimate purpose of government is the welfare of the common people (*min*). This is the most basic principle in Confucianism." The project Confucius expressed throughout *The Analects* was to promote essential virtues from the family to larger systems and from the ruler to all the people through benevolent governance. The social philosophy and ethics espoused by Confucius were explicitly taught for nearly two thousand years. Indeed, until the Communist revolution in 1949 led by Mao Zedong, which sought to replace Confucianism with Maoist principles, the first sentence every school child in China learned to write was the essential Confucian maxim: "Human beings are by nature good" (Confucius 1979). Perhaps illustrating the strength of culture, *harmony* is again the value promoted by the Chinese government and "Confucianism is back in China's public schools" (Smith 1994:121).

The wisdom tradition of Taoism as well as Confucianism and Buddhism has shaped culture and religion across East Asia. The founder of Taoism, Lao Tsu, wrote the *Tao Te Ching* (*The Way and Its Power* 1972, 1997), which remains the essential text for Taoist thought. Spiritually, the Tao is a transcendent "way of ultimate reality," more vast than humans can comprehend; it is also the "way of the universe," the driving power of nature, and Tao also "refers to the 'way of human life'" when it meshes with the Tao of the universe (Smith 1994:126). Taoism is expressed through three branches of practice: philosophical, religious, and "vitalizing Taoisms" (made up of the many physical and spiritual practices such as t'ai chi), all of which relate to gaining wisdom, which "empowers life." The power of the Tao is often described as similar to that of water; it adapts and accommodates—going around obstacles and seeking its own level. However, it is also infinitely strong, carving great canyons and wearing away rocks. The *Tao Te Ching* compares this strength to that of a good leader:

> A leader is best when people barely know that he exists.
> Of a good leader, when his work is done the people will say,
> "We did this ourselves." (Poem 17)

And again in Poem 10:

> Understanding and being open to all things. . . .
> Giving birth and nourishing,
>
> Bearing yet not possessing,
> Working yet not taking credit,
> Leading, yet not dominating,
> This is the Primal Virtue.

The *Tao Te Ching* promotes reflection on the self, society, nature, and the universe:

POEM 33:
Knowing others is wisdom: Knowing the self is enlightenment.

Of all the early sacred traditions, Taoism is perhaps the most connected to nature and to what we now would call environmentalism or deep ecology:

POEM 29:
The Universe is sacred.
You cannot improve it.
If you try to change it, you will ruin it.
If you try to hold it, you will lose it.

JUDAISM

Social justice is a value that characterizes Judaism and provides a particularly important legacy for Western social work (Day 2009; Schwarz 2008). For example, in the first book of the *TANAKH*— the Jewish Bible (TANAKH 1999; *Jewish Study Bible* [JSB] 2004), Abraham is instructed to "extend the boundaries of righteousness and justice in the world" (Genesis 18:19, JSB 2004; Schwarz 2008:5). An early teaching on charity and social welfare comes from the Book of Leviticus: "And when ye reap the harvest of your land, thou shall not wholly reap the corners of thy field, neither shalt thou gather the gleanings of thy harvest. . . . thou shalt leave them for the poor and stranger" (Leviticus 19:9, JSB 2004). The "stranger" is an oft-repeated ethical theme; for example: "You shall not wrong a stranger or oppress him, for you were strangers in the land of Egypt" (Exodus 22:20–21, JSB 2004). Judaic values of charity and justice are documented throughout the tripartite *TANAKH*: *Torah* (the Five Books of Moses); *Nevi'im* (Prophets); and *Ketuvim* (Writings). Together these three parts of the Jewish Bible recount two intertwined histories: the dialogic relationship between the Jewish people and their God; and the historical account of the people for about thirteen hundred years.

Jews have been called "The People of the Book." However, following from the *Jewish Bible*, other texts offer essential teachings and mark the Jews more accurately as the people of several connected books stemming from the *Torah*. These writings include the *Mishna*—which is a collection of laws and customs; the *Talmud*—which organizes laws and related teachings into several categories, and records diverse interpretations that draw the reader into deeper contemplation of meaning; and *Midrash*—which interprets biblical texts and is intended to reveal the "spirit" of the words by exploring meanings of stories, laws, and moral principles (Bank 2002). In Judaism, not only prayer is dialogic; the study of the scriptures involves readers in dialogue with the original text, with the various historical arguments and interpretations, and with each other.

From its beginnings, Judaism has focused on community, shared worship, and family observance in the home. The focus on family, community, and belief in a single omniscient, omnipotent God are all simply expressed in one of the most familiar Jewish prayers, the Shema:

> Hear, O Israel, the Lord is our God, the Lord is One. . . .
> And you shall love the Lord your God with all your heart, and with
> all your soul and with all your might.
> And these words that I command you this day shall be upon your heart . . .
>
> And you shall teach them diligently to your children,
> speaking of them when you sit in your house,
> when you walk by the way, when you lie down
> and when you rise up. . . .

Within Judaism there are also specific esoteric spiritual traditions such as that based on the Kabbalah; however, very frequently the expression of Jewish spirituality involves active engagement in work for social justice (Bank 2002).

The Prophet Micah proclaimed:

> He has told you, O man, what is good,
> And what the Lord requires of you:
> Only to do justice,
> And to love goodness,
> And to walk modestly with your God.
>
> MICAH 6:8, JSB, 2004

Study, service and worship, and acts of loving kindness were identified by Simeon the Righteous (2nd century C.E.) as the three pillars of Judaism (*Pirkei Avos: Ethics of the Fathers* 1:2).

Schwarz (2008:74) explores and abstracts the following core values inherent in Judaism:

SEVEN CORE VALUES OF THE RABBINIC TRADITION

1. Loving Kindness (Chesed)
2. Dignity of All Creatures (Kaved Habriot)
3. Seek Peace (Bakesh Shalom)

4. You Shall Not Stand Idly By (Lo Ta'amod [Leviticus 19:16])
5. The Ways of Peace (Darchei Shalom)
6. Loving the Stranger (Ahavat Ger)
7. Truth (Emet)

Rabbi Hillel (a spiritual leader who lived into the Common Era) selected a single principle as the essential guide for Judaism: "What is hateful to you, do not do to others. . . . The rest is commentary" (Schwarz 2008:4). And foreshadowing much more recent social thinking, the medieval Jewish philosopher, Maimonides, wrote of eight degrees of charity, citing the highest degree as working to prevent poverty (Twersky 1972).

CHRISTIANITY

The life of Jesus of Nazareth as told in the New Testament of the Christian Bible (*New Oxford Annotated Bible* 2007) recounts many of his sayings and parables that encourage community caring and responsibility to assist those in need. The "Golden Rule" (which also appears in slightly different forms in other religious traditions as early as Confucianism) enjoins individuals, "Do unto others as you would have them do unto you," while the Beatitudes lay out concerns for peace: "Blessed are the merciful for they shall obtain mercy. . . . Blessed are the peacemakers, for they shall be called the children of God" (Matthew 5:6–9). The parable of the Good Samaritan from the Gospel of St. Luke illustrates the injunction for compassion:

A certain man went down from Jerusalem to Jericho and fell among thieves, which stripped him of his raiment; and wounded him, and departed leaving him half dead.

. . . a certain Samaritan, as he journeyed, came where he was; and when he saw him he had compassion on him. And went to him and bound up his wounds, pouring in oil and wine, and set him on his own beast, and brought him to an inn, and took care of him. . . .

Which now of these three, thinkest thou, was neighbor unto him that fell among thieves? And he said, He that showed mercy upon him.

Then said Jesus unto him: Go and do thou likewise. (Luke 10:30–37)

The example from the Book of John of the woman taken in adultery who was about to be stoned illustrates the value and belief in extending compassion and empathy even to those viewed as transgressing community norms. When Jesus was invited to judge that the woman should be stoned, he did not respond but stooped down, "and with his finger wrote on the ground as though he heard them not." When they continued asking him, "he lifted up himself and said unto them, 'Let him who is without sin among you cast the first stone'" (John 8:3–11).

ISLAM

The Qur'an as recorded by the Prophet Muhammad commands all believers to enact charity as a central principle of Islamic practice; and one of the five pillars of Islam. Giving alms to the poor—performing *Zakat*—is a sacred duty of all Muslims, with particular emphasis on the importance of giving to orphans, the needy, and the stranded traveler (Qur'an 2008, 8:14). Islam, like Judaism and Christianity, is a monotheistic religion. Allah means *the* God—the One and Only God. The clarity of Islam's basic proclamation bears out this distinct commitment to monotheism: "La ilaha illa 'Ilah'"—"There is no god but God" (Lawrence 2006). In Islam, the created world is good, and "the world of matter is completely real." The remarkable accomplishments of Islamic science and medicine, "which flourished during Europe's Dark Ages," have been attributed to Islamic appreciation and investigation of the natural world (Smith 1994:157). Islam holds great respect for the prophets of Israel, especially Abraham, and also considers Jesus of Nazareth a great prophet (Lawrence 2006). The Qur'an is not only the spiritual guide of Islamic faith, it also provides a legal framework of laws and expectations of behavior for practicing Muslims. "It joins faith and politics, religion and society" (Smith 1994:164).

In Islam, believers are expected both to *do good* out of love of Allah and to shun evil. The Qur'an holds that believers should practice morality and kindness "in all places and toward all people and animals. The Ku'ran provides a stable, constant, and thorough moral system" (Anwar 2004:118–20). Faithful practitioners "understand from the Ku'ran that everything a person does in his or her life that is *good* is a form of worship" (ibid.).

Islam is not practiced just in the mosque; it is built into the actions of everyday life. When the Prophet Muhammad taught, "Worship Allah as though you see him," he was "indicating that worship should be pure, sincere, and overflowing with devotion" and that this devotion should show itself in virtues (Anwar 2004:120). Among the virtues of good character that Muslims should practice are the following: patience, kindness, truthfulness, and selflessness. Other virtues frequently mentioned in the Qur'an are humility, justice, generosity, sympathy, tolerance, and forgiveness. Selflessness is "the love of others more than the love of oneself," and a basic expectation is that Muslims will share money and food, and show generosity to those in need (Anwar 2004).

Those who spend their wealth in the cause of Allah, and afterwards make not reproach and injury to follow that which they have spent, their reward is with their

Lord; and there shall no fear come upon them; neither shall they grieve. (Qu'ran 2:262)

This is giving without expectation of reward and includes as sharing not just money, but "knowledge, shelter, food, and space. It is also extending a hand of assistance where it is needed" (Anwar 2004:124). Another aspect of Islam that others, especially community practitioners should know about, is this religion's emphasis on equality: "Islam stresses racial equality and has achieved a remarkable degree of interracial coexistence" (Smith 1994:168).

Whether one personally connects to one or more of these wisdom traditions, it is valuable for community practitioners to explore and seek to understand the meaning of cultural and religious practices in the communities we serve. Currently throughout the world our local communities are multicultural and increasingly connected to the global community and world events. Many tensions in the world still relate to cultural and religious differences as much as to political differences. Through intergroup and multicultural work, community practitioners can help to move communities and groups from intolerance to tolerance and beyond tolerance to active cross-cultural/interfaith engagement, mutual understanding, and recognition of shared values. Our study of these wisdom traditions reveals that the following values important to community practice are shared among them.

VALUES SHARED ACROSS MAJOR WISDOM TRADITIONS		
Social Justice	Loving Kindness/Compassion	Charity
Benevolence	Respect	Solidarity
Equality	Altruism	Enlightened Self-interest
Interdependence	Community	Liberation

Perhaps knowledge of the significant parallels in spiritual traditions, including essential values, can be used to help multicultural communities find common purpose to enact these shared values for the common good.

EVOLUTION OF HUMANISTIC VALUES

THE LEGACY OF GREECE

Western perspectives on both humanism and science are grounded in the Athens of the fifth century B.C.E. Multiple aspects of basic humanistic tradition and understandings about democracy are derived from the dialogues of

Socrates as recorded by Plato, while the empirical, scientific tradition evolved from the investigations and observations of Aristotle and other early philosophers.

Democracy, rule by citizens, was a central tenet of Athenian society. This first evolution of democracy worked well for freeborn male citizens, but all women and slaves were excluded from democratic participation. Slavery was common in the ancient world, as was marginalized social status for women. Although the Athenian development of democracy was a significant evolution in political structure, its denial of rights to those of lower status initiated a long lasting flaw in the evolution of Western democracies. For example, in the United States, the Emancipation Proclamation was signed by Lincoln in 1863; the Thirteenth Amendment to the Constitution in 1865 ratified the abolition of slavery. Black males received the right to vote through the Fourteenth Amendment in 1868, but women did not receive the right to vote until 1920 through the Nineteenth Amendment, and Native Americans not until 1924 (U.S. Constitution; Indian Citizenship Act). Societies across the world have differed widely in when and how they have granted basic rights of citizenship to women and marginalized groups.

Questioning accepted ideas and authority to arrive at truth were hallmarks of the Socratic Method. This form of inquiry remains a central practice in participatory methods of organizing, development, and planning. Freire's twentieth-century method of group discussion known as *conscientiatizion* (i.e., developing critical consciousness) builds on the Socratic tradition (Freire 2000, 2005). Currently, these methods of questioning, discussion, and participatory decision making remain essential aspects of community practice (Castelloe and Gamble 2005).

Early in the Common Era (396 C.E.) Augustine of Hippo, building on the work of Plato and Plotinus, wrote extensively about the concept of human *free will*, which became a central theme in medieval and twentieth-century philosophy. The question of free will has reasserted itself consistently in humanistic philosophical perspectives, including twentieth-century existentialism, which holds that *free will* and the human responsibility of *choice* (i.e., making the choices that shape our lives and that impact the lives of others) is the central project of human life (Sartre 2007). Concern for human free will is built into the values and ethical codes of social work.

WESTERN HUMANISM AND VALUE DEVELOPMENT DURING THE RENAISSANCE

The philosophy of humanism, which flowered during the final years of the fourteenth century, was an essential aspect of the Renaissance in Western Europe. This "rebirth" of civilization arose from the rediscovery and adulation of the humanist literature, art, political philosophy, and civilizations of ancient Greece and Rome and stimulated a renewed and vibrant interest in humanity as a species, in human capabilities, and in community. "From classical Greece and before, community was the center of society continuing into the 16th century" (Brueggemann 2006:123). The concepts of *community* and *democracy* reinforced each other throughout this era.

A *humanist* is one who is "concerned with the study and welfare of human beings" (*Merriam-Webster OnLine Dictionary* 2009)—a standpoint that is clearly consonant with social work and community practice. Petrarch, a prominent scholar in late fourteenth-century Florence, endorsed the writings of Plato (*The Republic*) and other philosophers such as Plotinus, who promoted human reason, ethical decision making, and the positive force of the human spirit (Hines 2004). Petrarch and his followers perceived themselves as reclaiming the "moral and imaginative fire" expressed in the classics (Tarnas 1993:209). One philosophical position taken by Plotinus and adopted by humanists in Florence held that since humans are part of nature, they possess a *divine spark*. This teaching became a pivotal point of humanism and interestingly is also a concept shared among numerous spiritual traditions from Hinduism through the Society of Friends (Quakers) (Hines 2004).

Civic or social humanism was a powerful philosophical and political tenet during the Renaissance. Ideas regarding democracy became a major focus during the early fifteenth century, and concerns about human welfare and community connections were evident in the arts, politics, and scientific pursuits of that period. This new republican ideology emphasized human capacity for autonomy (self-rule) as the means of creating the reality of *active citizens* and *citizenship*. Renaissance humanists encouraged participation in civic life as the essence of an effective polity and as a necessary aspect of being human. Free will, it was held, "should encourage humans to seek knowledge and truth" (Pico della Mirandola as cited by Tarnas 1993:215). This perspective, bearing seeds of both the social sciences and existentialism, places humans in charge of their own moral, ethical, and civic choices and can be viewed as a fountainhead of values espoused by social work and community practice.

AGE OF DISCOVERY

During the fifteenth through early seventeenth centuries, European explorers and their patron monarchs believed that they had "discovered" other continents and civilizations that had previously been "unknown" or little explored. In reality, of course, these civilizations had been experiencing their own social, economic, and political growth and development for centuries. Although there was knowledge of other civilizations from earlier Mediterranean, Middle Eastern, and Asian societies, the monarchs initially of Portugal and Spain and later of other European nations engaged in "discovery" and plunder of other civilizations with a vengeance—as one means to strengthen money economies and of establishing their national preeminence. The propensity of Westerners to assume that their appearance on the scene gives a greater reality to the cultures of others has long been, and continues to be, puzzling and offensive to peoples of the Global South.

One product of this global exploration was a new European perspective that grew out of interaction with other civilizations in Asia, Africa, and the Americas. Global exploration and exploitation heightened the focus on market economies, redefined commercialism in relation to international trade, and initiated a long period of European conquest and colonialism in many parts of the world. These changes propelled an early global market in commodities such as silver, gold, spices, and silk.

Global economic changes also resulted in a great expansion of slavery, primarily of Africans, for forced labor in the Americas, the Caribbean, the Middle East, and in Europe. Major crops (sugar cane, cotton, and rice) grown in the Americas depended on large labor forces of enslaved people to build local economies and to provide products and profits for Europeans. The slave trade and economic exploitation continued as hallmarks of colonialism. Today there are ongoing arguments about whether colonialism has indeed ended, despite the development of independent nation-states in formerly colonized regions.

SCIENCE, REASON, AND THE EUROPEAN ENLIGHTENMENT

During the European periods later named the Scientific Revolution in the sixteenth century, the Age of Reason in the seventeenth, and the Enlightenment of the eighteenth century, additional humanistic and democratic values gained prominence. Science gained ground throughout the sixteenth century, as did the Protestant Reformation. Protestantism, with its emphasis on individual salvation, and the Scientific Revolution were precursors to the rise of individualism as a central Western societal norm contrasting with the continuing communal norms of most contemporaneous civilizations (Day 2009).

Discoveries in the natural sciences changed worldviews, established new paradigms, reestablished and strengthened the position and methods of empirical research, and promoted efforts to identify and codify a system of "natural laws." Western understanding of the universe was forever changed by the work of Copernicus, who documented that the Earth revolves around the sun

(Tarbuck and Lutgens 2000). And throughout the sixteenth, seventeenth, and eighteenth centuries scientific study achieved major advances in many areas. The breadth of the early Scientific Revolution propelled philosophers and other scholars to reevaluate their knowledge of the nature of humanity, of society, and of politics in keeping with the new scientific discoveries. "Among these ideas was a new way of thinking based on mathematics and the laws of science: the view that the universe operated much as a mechanistic system and that humans also were subject to the laws of the physical universe" (Brueggemann 2006:124).

Building on this work, the English philosopher Thomas Hobbes (1651/1985), developed theories holding that human reason "was . . . a cost calculus in which individuals applied economic logic to maximize their own self-interests" (Brueggemann 2006:124). Hobbes's view, which attained considerable success over time, elevated individualism, the quest for wealth, and advancement of market societies, but diminished attention to communal life (ibid.). The triumph of individualism as first propounded by Hobbes and later by Locke, Hume, and Adam Smith is inextricably coupled with unfettered market economies.

> The stage was set for the gradual but inevitable transformation of the fundamental unit of society from family and community to individual, from intimate personal relationships to calculating, impersonal relationships, and from the economy as a restricted and minor element of civil society to a market society in which public and civic affairs became components of economic structures governed by the logic of the marketplace. (Brueggemann 2006:124)

Put most simply, communal man became economic man, and this largely mechanistic and reductionist model has had major negative effects on value perspectives as it denies the full scope of human potential and undermines the value of community. Social work values hold that we are not simply individualistic economic units. Currently, the continued dominance of the Western world's extreme individualism and overriding emphasis on market-based societies create challenges in different ways for community practice in both the Global North and South. However, community practice can also be seen as one force that can help to "re-humanize" societies.

The European Enlightenment (eighteenth century) was grounded in a more optimistic view holding the essential idea that reason itself (not monarchs, not religious institutions, not economic dictums) is the basis of true authority. Reason was to be applied to social and political issues through discussion, logical arguments, analysis, and structured approaches to problem solving.

THE EUROPEAN ENLIGHTENMENT AND THE FOUNDING FATHERS OF THE UNITED STATES OF AMERICA

Humanistic Enlightenment thought was a major influence on the Founding Fathers in designing the governance of the new nation. Most notably, the developers of the Bill of Rights and the Constitution were steeped in social thought related to human rights, democracy, and freedom. The Declaration of Independence states:

> We hold these truths to be self evident, that all Men are created equal, that they are endowed by their Creator with unalienable Rights, that among these are Life, Liberty, and the Pursuit of Happiness—That to secure these Rights, Governments are instituted among Men, deriving their just Powers from the Consent of the Governed.

And the Preamble to the Constitution of the United States of America begins:

> We the People of the United States, in Order to form a more perfect Union, establish Justice, insure domestic Tranquility, provide for the Common defence, promote the general Welfare, and secure the Blessings of Liberty to ourselves and our Posterity, do ordain and establish this Constitution for the United States of America.

Neither of these aspirational statements could have been written without knowledge of Greek philosophy, humanism, and Enlightenment social thought focused on reason and the innate equality of all men. Even so, it was radical, new, and revolutionary in 1776 to proclaim that governments derive their powers from the consent of the governed and that *freedom* and *liberty* would be the basic precepts of the new nation. Perhaps even more audacious was the concept of the *pursuit of happiness*. The major flaw in these radical documents was exclusion of women and people of color from basic rights and democratic participation.

Enlightened self-interest, the concept that our care for others is also a way to take care of ourselves, gained prominence at this time. Alexis de Tocqueville (1835/2000:500) reported that Americans seemed well able to employ enlightened self-interest: "Americans combat Individualism by the Doctrine of Self-Interest Well Understood" (i.e., enlightened). Much later, both altruism and enlightened self-interest would flourish during the American civil rights movement of the 1960s and 1970s, through massive social action, advocacy, and the essential principle "None of us are free, until all of us are free!"

Each of the traditions we have discussed—wisdom, humanist, and democratic—forms building blocks for concepts, values, and beliefs about human rights and social justice. The remainder of this chapter, and indeed much of this volume, deals with community practice as a field built on these values and concepts.

BUILDING A GLOBAL APPROACH TO THE STUDY OF HUMAN RIGHTS

Jim Ife, a noted Australian scholar of human rights, offers a thoughtful and challenging critique to the standard Western approaches that have been used to study, conduct research, and teach about values, ethics, and human rights. The established intellectual framework that treats three generations of rights—(1) *civil and political rights*, (2) *social rights*, and (3) *cultural rights*—he holds are insufficient and bound too closely to European history (Ife 2006). Equally problematic, Ife notes, is the fact that the three generation categories are not clear and distinct categories, which weakens their usefulness as an analytic tool.

Ife's categories form a more complete typology of human rights and he has developed a matrix framework to use in analysis. His distinct categories make it possible not only to trace the development of each type of rights for a nation or region, but also to conduct analyses to compare the development of one or more particular type of rights across nations over time. One of Ife's goals in carefully specifying and updating the earlier model for investigation of rights was to detach rights development from the particular evolution that occurred in Western Europe. Exploration of types of human rights using Ife's categories can be conducted free of specific timelines and free of assumptions about expected time sequences. In expanding and reframing this typology of categories, Ife (2008) effectively recognizes that different sets of rights can develop in different cultures in different time sequences. That is, his framework does not imply a specific evolutionary history. For example, some societies might develop environmental and spiritual rights before political rights, whereas another might build from economic to political to environmental rights. Ife's (2006) typology of rights is presented here along with the brief examples he provides to guide use of his "Human Rights Matrix":

IFE'S CATEGORIES OF RIGHTS

	SURVIVAL RIGHTS	SOCIAL RIGHTS	ECONOMIC RIGHTS	CIVIL/POLITICAL RIGHTS	CULTURAL RIGHTS	ENVIRONMENTAL RIGHTS	SPIRITUAL RIGHTS
List additional rights in each category	Life Food Water Shelter Clothing Health Safety	Family life Privacy Recreation/leisure Education Choice of: partner lifestyle sexuality housing	Basic living standard Earn a living Work Social security Savings Choice of spending	Free speech Free assembly Vote Fair trial Stand for office Join organizations Join union Strike	Cultural expression Cultural practices Clothing Religious expression Intellectual property Land rights	Pollution free Poison free Wilderness Beauty Sustainability Access to land	Choice Religious expression Rituals Experience nature Personal fulfillment Sacred land/ objects

Source: Ife (2006), "Human Rights beyond the 'Three Generations.'"

In the exercises included in the *CPS Workbook* you have an opportunity to chart the development of different rights for a particular nation or culture and to compare the development of specific types of rights across two or more cultures so that you can chart the differences in context and evolution. Rights can also be analyzed employing questions such as the following:

1. How is each category of human rights actively expressed in your area?
2. Are rights equal for everyone in your area?
3. Are any groups excluded? If so why?
4. Are there rights in your geographic area that need legislative protection?
5. What needs to be done to promote inclusion and to provide equal protection?

The value base that supports community practice is grounded in (a) respect for both the dignity of the individual and the interdependence of families and communities; (b) the development of legislative, political, and distributive justice; and (c) the expansion of human rights (Dromi and Weil 1984). The following discussion examines the translation of values and concepts into ethical codes to guide our practice.

PROFESSIONAL CODES OF ETHICS

Most of the values discussed above have been codified into professional ethics as represented by the Code of Ethics of the National Association of Social Workers (NASW USA), the codes of other nations, and the "Ethics in Social Work: Statement of Principles" of the International Federation of Social Workers and International Association of Schools of Social Work (IFSW/IASSW). We urge you to carefully study the NASW Code of Ethics (or your own national code) and the IFSW "Ethics in Social Work: Statement of Principles," and to engage reflectively in examining the major ethical issues we face in supporting the rights of clients, communities, and organizations. This reflection can help you in learning to apply critical thinking strategies to make ethical decisions. Critical analysis is especially needed in complex ethical situations and in situations where major conflicts of interest exist. You can access these codes through the following Web addresses: http://www.ifsw.org/en/p38000324 .html; and http://www.socialworkers.org/pubs/code/code.asp.

NASW USA CODE OF ETHICS The NASW Code of Ethics for social workers in the United States presents standards and principles to guide professional practice. The core values noted in NASW's mission reflect the profession's unique perspective and purpose: to provide service; promote social justice;

support the dignity and worth of the person; value the importance of human relationships, and to act with professional integrity, and competence (NASW, Web site). If you work under a different national code, make comparisons in order to determine similarities and differences between your national code and the international principles to assess how both support community practice.

IFSW/IASSW "ETHICS IN SOCIAL WORK: STATEMENT OF PRINCIPLES"
In 2004, two major international social work organizations, the International Federation of Social Workers (IFSW) and the International Association of Schools of Social Work (IASSW), adopted the IFSW/IASSW "Ethics in Social Work: Statement of Principles." Their definition of social work emphasizes basic values and states in part, "Principles of human rights and social justice are fundamental to social work." In reviewing the document online, you will see that the IFSW/IASSW principles emphasize human rights and dignity in one category and social justice in another. It cites the common standards incorporated into the Universal Declaration of Human Rights and six major United Nations conventions or covenants, and provides principles for professional conduct.

VALUES PARTICULARLY SUPPORTING COMMUNITY PRACTICE

In conjunction with the values and ethical principles specified in professional *Ethical Codes*, there are specific values that should guide community practice. Community practitioners, in contrast to many other professional groups, work to improve social and economic conditions within small and large communities; to empower poor communities and marginalized groups; to make service systems and bureaucracies more responsive to the needs of the disadvantaged; to change policies to be more just and equitable; and to make positive changes in the root causes of social problems such as poverty, discrimination, lack of care, or access to services. *In short, our work is to promote social justice, expand human rights, and engage in progressive social change.* To deal with the challenges that arise in community work and to carry forward our broad societal and international mission, we need to reflect on and continually seek to enact the community practice values illustrated in table 3.1.

These values are complex as they arise in daily practice, but their definitions help to guide action:

Interdependence: Being able to trust and rely on each other.
Empowerment Practice: Building partnerships with groups and communities; emphasizing strengths; development of human, social, and economic capital; recognizing groups and community members as active agents of

TABLE 3.1 Values and Ethical Principles for Community Practitioners

VALUES IN NASW CODE OF ETHICS OR SOCIAL WORK CODE OF YOUR NATION	PARTICULAR VALUES AND ETHICAL ISSUES CRITICAL FOR COMMUNITY PRACTITIONERS
Service	Interdependence
Social Justice	Empowerment Practice
Dignity and Worth of the Person	Reciprocity
Importance of Human Relationships	Partnerships and Mutuality in Work
Integrity	Citizen and Community Participation
Competence	Human Rights and Social Justice
	Structural Analyses and Approaches (work toward changing programs, policies, and root causes, not just manifestations of problems)

social change; and focusing on social justice for those who have experienced social exclusion and limitation of opportunities (Simon 1994; Solomon 1986; Weil and Gamble 2005).

Reciprocity: Creating mutual and cooperative interchanges and actions.

Partnerships and Mutuality in Work: Building equal and cooperative relationships especially through citizen and community participation.

Citizen and Community Participation: Promoting active, voluntary engagement of individuals and groups to change conditions and to influence policies and programs that affect the quality of their lives or the lives of others.

Human Rights: Advancing human rights which are "those rights, which are inherent in our nature and without which we cannot live as human beings. Human rights and fundamental freedoms allow us to fully develop and use our human qualities, our intelligence, our talents, and our conscience and to satisfy our spiritual and other needs" (UN 1987, *Human Rights: Questions and Answers*); having knowledge of human rights conventions and an understanding of basic social justice issues.

Social Justice: Opposing and challenging negative discrimination; recognizing and respecting diversity within societies; advocating for policies and practices to ensure that resources are distributed fairly according to need; challenging unjust policies and practice; and working towards an inclusive society. (IFSW/IASSW, 2001 Web site).

Structural Analyses and Approaches: Examining the root causes of social problems and documenting inequities in society; conducting research on unjust laws, systems, and discriminatory practices; presenting reports of findings and disseminating information broadly, particularly to those affected by inequities and those who can effect policy change.

ETHICAL DECISION MAKING WHEN VALUES ARE IN CONFLICT

In *Human Rights and Social Work*, Ife (2008) notes the controversies surrounding the "Western" cast of many of the values reflected in the Universal Declaration of Human Rights. Areas of disagreement connect to contrasting positions favoring either cultural relativism (local differences) versus essential (universal) rights that do or should apply to all people. Codes and principles of ethical practice are developed to help guide social workers in making decisions in complex situations and when different individuals, groups, and communities hold divergent views, and sometimes, incompatible interests. Such controversies often relate to arguments between a universalistic perspective versus a relativistic perspective on human rights and/or opposing views of what constitutes social justice. Social issues disputed from opposing ethical stances may relate to sharp differences in cultural beliefs and values and/or to very different political ideologies. In addition it is not unusual for there to be sharp divergence between a nation's stated principles and political/social reality. For example, while many nations have embraced the Universal Declaration of Human Rights and state that they oppose slavery, the practice still exists in numerous places in the world—through forced labor and in human trafficking (Nazer and Lewis 2002). What is the responsibility of community practitioners in the face of this critical issue? Although most UN member nations have signed the Convention on the Rights of the Child, children in many parts of the world are pressed into service in wars, subjected to abuse, indentured servitude, sexual slavery, beatings, and trafficking. What is the responsibility of community practitioners in the face of these unjust and inhumane practices? In some nations, social workers are expected to follow government dictates even if they conflict with professional responsibilities and client self-determination. How can a profession develop ethically under such circumstances?

Throughout the world, many controversial issues are related to gender—particularly to the rights of women and their status as independent or dependent beings. In a number of nations, for example, female genital mutilation (FGM) is practiced (Goodwin 2008; Hashi, Sharafi, and Ryan 2007), in others dowry killings or "honor killings" of women or girls occur, and perpetrators are frequently not held accountable. In some nations, babies are forcibly taken from very poor or indigenous women, and large profits are made by others through costly international adoption processes. What is the responsibility of community practitioners in the face of these practices? The *CPS Workbook* provides more detailed examples of ethical conflicts for analysis, discussion, and consideration of action.

Community practitioners can face ethical dilemmas of all kinds, including internal power struggles within the groups with which they are working, outside efforts to sidetrack community projects, and issues as serious as political oppression. Whatever the situation, when value conflicts arise, it is important to review and reflect on ethical codes and community practice values, to discuss these issues with the groups you are involved with, and to have trusted colleagues with whom you can discuss and analyze these conflict situations. It is consistently important to preserve your integrity and to maintain your stance as a professional by focusing on the needs of the people you serve rather than on your needs or the needs of the organization or agency in which you work. Useful guides are available for helping groups work through ethical dilemmas in community practice and broader social work and service areas when code directions seem ambiguous (Dolgoff, Loewenberg, and Harrington 2008; Markkula Center for Applied Ethics 2008).

ROOTS AND DEVELOPMENT OF COMMUNITY PRACTICE IN THE UNITED STATES

Every nation and region has its own history of communities coming together to accomplish common goals, improve quality of life for their members, seek social justice and solve community problems. Similarly, each nation has its own history of community support for vulnerable individuals, families, and groups. Because no single volume could cover the vast worldwide history of social responses, our strategy is to ask you to trace the history of community practice in your nation or region through several historical/economic eras. In the *CPS Workbook*, you will find an exercise that focuses on assisting you in documenting the history of community practice in your area. Following are highlights of this history in the United States.

RURAL COMMUNITY DEVELOPMENT AND PRACTICE

Rural community development efforts run deep in American history. In the second volume of *Democracy in America*, de Tocqueville recorded his astonishment at the differences in behaviors of American citizens in the 1830s as compared with the French and English. He observed Americans taking on responsibilities of mutual care (in what will later be termed the development of civil society):

Americans of all ages, all conditions, all minds constantly unite. Not only do they have industrial and commercial associations in which all take part, but they also have a thousand other kinds: religious, moral, grave, futile, very general and very particular, immense and very small; Americans use associations to give fetes, to found seminaries, to build inns, to raise churches, to distribute books, to send missionaries to the antipodes; in this manner they create hospitals, prisons, schools. Finally if it is a question of bringing to light a truth or developing a sentiment with the support of a great example, they associate. Everywhere that, at the head of a new undertaking, you see the government in France and a great lord in England, count on it that you will perceive an Association in the United States. (1835/2000:489)

De Tocqueville's observations portray the energy that Americans brought to the development of civil society in this early period and throughout the Industrial Revolution and following century. The United States still has the largest civil society sector in the world which still requires much work to increase inclusion and broad scale participation.

Later, rural survival was often the product of cooperation and reciprocal care related to systems to provide for electrification, access to clean water, marketing cooperatives, and the development of basic services from schools to volunteer fire brigades. In the 1930s a strong farming cooperative movement arose, and in some areas, Rural Community Councils were formed. Rural social development was also advanced by agricultural extension agents who used a low-key discussion approach in their leadership development and project planning to build citizen participation programs for rural development and technical assistance for crop development and home economics (Betten and Austin 1990; Carlton-LaNey, Murty, and Morris 2005).

Myles Horton and his staff at the Highlander Center in Tennessee began organizing the rural poor of the Appalachian region in the 1930s, and Highlander has remained a major training ground for both rural and urban citizen participation activists (Horton, Kohl, and Kohl 1990). They brought together blacks and whites in the South prior to the civil rights movement; Rosa Parks and other movement leaders participated in training at Highlander. Today, Highlander staff continue to train and organize citizens to take active roles in working for economic and environmental justice in rural America and across the globe.

The more recent rural population shifts to cities have prompted rapid increases in employment of migrant farm workers primarily from Mexico. The organization of grape pickers in California initiated by Cesar Chavez, Dolores Huerta, and Fred Harris in 1962 grew into a nationwide organization of crop harvesters called the United Farm Workers Union (UFWU), and its work continues nationwide. Still, migrant workers frequently continue to live in deplorable conditions and work for substandard wages. Undocumented migrant workers are even more vulnerable to exploitation. Organizations across the nation seek to support farm workers and ensure that those who tend and harvest the food the nation eats (as well as exports) receive fair compensation for their grueling work and have decent living conditions and access to health care and other services. Despite the need for their labor, political dissension centering on undocumented workers continues unabated.

THE INDUSTRIAL REVOLUTION, URBANIZATION, AND COMMUNITY PRACTICE

The Industrial Revolution in America propelled the rapid growth of cities based on migration from rural areas and arrival of immigrants who worked long hours in industrial plants, manufacturing, textile mills, and factory towns. This industrial growth and lack of policies to protect workers produced serious health problems and dangerous work conditions, while workers and their families lived in unsafe slum tenements.

Similar conditions exist today in newly industrializing nations. For example, China is dealing with the ever accelerating need for more urban labor while the massive population shift to cities leaves rural villages with a missing generation. This new industrial workforce presents familiar social problems relating to lack of adequate housing, frequent injuries to workers because of ill-regulated construction, manufacturing, or mining, and few, if any, health or disability benefits. In a number of nations, while the labor of such rural migrants is needed in growing industrial areas, they are not granted full citizen's rights and sometimes their children are excluded from schools. The fortunes of industrial and agricultural workers around the world are also increasingly subject to the vagaries of the global market. A number of Asian and African nations now face severe environmental problems and dislocated populations as a result of rapid industrial growth, construction, mining, and civil strife.

When the United States was industrializing, poverty and severe overcrowding in cities brought major public health problems, including lack of sanitation, lack of potable water, poor nutrition, and inadequate housing. The exploitation of the poor in sweatshops resulted in economic and social burdens, including 12-hour workdays for children, even longer workdays for adult laborers, and an underclass that was excluded from the political process. These problems spawned juvenile crime, prostitution, and other problems brought on by overcrowding, economic insecurity, exploitation, and lack of access to educational opportunities or political power.

Today displacements of people through shifts in industrial economies continue in many parts of the world—well-paying industrial jobs in America are "outsourced," and in developing nations, internal migrants leave rural areas for cities hoping for wage work and often find none. Large numbers of displaced and unemployed or marginally employed people crowd the streets of Mumbai and Deli in India, the Kibera slum in Nairobi, Kenya, the cities of Zimbabwe, and the favelas and barrios surrounding major cities in Latin America. The United Nations reports that throughout sub-Saharan Africa 72 percent of the population are urban slum dwellers (UN Habitat: UN News Center 2008). Although there are diverse reasons for massive population shifts, they all relate to global economic factors.

Across the world, in each region, social workers respond to changing conditions and shifting populations by developing new programs, organizing change efforts, planning local social and economic projects, joining social movements focused on increasing the well-being of marginalized groups, and promoting progressive development.

A very similar process occurred in the United States during the last quarter of the nineteenth century as a response to social problems created by rapid industrialization. Two major social organization movements were created to combat the multiple negative ills of early industrialization: the settlement movement and the charity organization movement. Indeed these two social movements form the taproots from which social work and community practice arose in the United States (Betten and Austin 1990).

Stephen Gurteen, an early leader in the charity organization movement, and Jane Addams, a leader in the settlement movement, both studied voluntary social organizations in Great Britain. At Toynbee Hall (the first settlement house), Addams learned about intensive community and group work with impoverished Britons and immigrant groups; and Gurteen studied operations of several Charity Organization Societies (COSs) in England. Back at home, each set to work developing American models and took steps to establish organizations intended to redress the wounds that the economic advancements of the Industrial Revolution inflicted on poor and immigrant populations. In 1877, Gurteen founded the first American COS in Buffalo, New York, and assisted in spreading the movement to other cities. Addams and Ellen Gates Starr founded Hull-House in inner-city Chicago in 1889.

The *settlement house movement* as exemplified by the work of Jane Addams and her colleagues at Hull-House initially focused on "getting to know the neighbors" as the largely immigrant participants in settlement work were called (Addams 1910/1960). "Settlers" sought to develop programs that truly reflected the interests, concerns, needs, and aspirations of their neighbors, including programs for nationality groups, citizenship groups, and neighborhood meetings for men and women that brought together people from many different backgrounds and worked with community groups on a full range of neighborhood problems.

Two special targets for Hull-House became social research and community change based on collecting information through tenement surveys (*Hull-House Maps and Papers* 1895). These detailed data collection efforts related to social and community health, recreation, and sanitation needs. The staff of Hull-House sought to build responsive programs for neighbors, provided leadership to develop public services such as juvenile court (Breckenridge 1934), and progressive social policies including labor (Sklar 1995) and child welfare policies at local, state, and national levels (Abbott 1938). Two Hull-House alumni would serve as director of the Federal Children's Bureau.

Major approaches to community work in organizing, planning, development, and community-based research all evolved from the settlement house movement. At their best, the settlements engaged, and continue to engage, neighborhood residents in educational reform, housing development, job skills training for youth and adults, children's programs, environmental actions, community action, program development, intergroup relations, and broad arenas of social and economic development. Such programs did and continue to embody the basic values of citizen participation and social justice.

The *charity organization societies* quickly spread to become a nationwide movement seeking to develop and rationalize a range of community services to alleviate the harsh conditions of the poor, assist them in acculturation, and consider ways to deal with major community social problems. The COSs worked on establishing the prototype of direct service practice through engaging middle-class women to serve as "friendly visitors" to the poor and provide them with models of behavior and adaptation. Mary Richmond (1907), for example, developed her model of casework through activities coordinated with COSs in which she studied their relationships with then nascent, small nonprofit organizations designed to assist the poor. Richmond envisioned social interventions as nested systems from small nonprofits to large public systems that should provide coordinated services to client families (Richmond 1907). She pioneered early work to document whether and how well specific services worked.

COSs helped coordinate the work of agencies to create rational service systems and sought to develop fair approaches to rationing services based on the assumption that needs would always be greater than available resources. The vision of the COSs was to ensure that charitable work was carried forward in an effective and efficient way through service development, community service planning, resource development, and coordination of human services.

Over time COSs morphed into Community Chests, which focused on federated fund-raising for charitable purposes and planning services for emerging needs. The next iteration was a broad national network of Health and Welfare Planning Councils that became essential components of social service planning and resource distribution in urban areas of the nation. With the increased need for resource development, Health and Welfare Councils evolved into the United Way movement, which initially had a dual focus on social planning and fund-raising. More recently, its focus has been limited to fund-raising and allocation. Currently, some United Ways have been taking steps to revive their role in social planning, but there is not yet sufficient research to report on the results of these efforts. This new process has brought to the surface longstanding tensions within United Ways between making a master plan to deal with one or two of the major serious social problems (such as homelessness) versus comprehensively serving the varied funding needs of the nonprofit sector.

In recent years, social planning councils have reemerged. The member organizations of the National Association of Planning Councils are one example. They receive local funding and seek external funding to plan and to conduct research examining social needs and program effectiveness. These councils collaborate with a range of nonprofits, public agencies, and local governments to plan and carry out programs and research needed to improve the lives and opportunities of groups with unmet needs (http://www.communityplanning .org/; see also chapter 9 in the present volume).

LATER INDUSTRIALISM—THE GREAT DEPRESSION AND ECONOMIC RECOVERY

During the Great Depression following the 1929 stock market crash, millions of Americans from every income bracket struggled for basic survival. Unemployment was at staggering levels, homelessness was rampant, food was inordinately expensive, and there was widespread fear of societal collapse. Franklin Delano Roosevelt (FDR), elected president in 1932, built his administration to allay fears, reestablish social and economic stability, and get people back to work. Social workers Harry Hopkins, a major planner and Roosevelt confidant, Frances Perkins, FDR's secretary of labor, and other committed reformers worked to establish multiple job creation programs building infrastructure and employing men and women on civic projects in both urban and rural areas. Eleanor Roosevelt pressed incessantly for rights and economic opportunities such as model farm communities for African Americans. She was a major force in the early work of the United Nations and development of the Universal Declaration of Human Rights.

Community practitioners responded to social needs, and the profession of social work was accorded considerable respect and appreciation. Practice leaders acted on commitments to community organization as an expansion of democracy, emphasizing that citizens should remain in control of decision making in their communities while professionals provided support, information, and specialized knowledge.

In this period, government supported community-focused work and research, and the Social Security Act of 1935 was likely the first federal statute to use the term *community organizing* and required "social and community planning in order for states to receive funds" (Betten and Austin 1990).

COMMUNITY PRACTICE IN THE 1940S AND 1950S.

Social workers were involved in operating services for war refugees abroad, including the Marshall Plan, and for those who immigrated to the United States following World War II. They assisted Jewish refugees and other survivors of the Nazi concentration camps, and had active roles in supportive work for community development in Asia and Europe. Social workers also assisted Japanese Americans as they were released from internment camps.

Murray Ross, the noted Canadian social work scholar, published seminal books on community organization practice during these years: his *Community Organization: Theory and Principles* (1955) focused on three primary approaches: reform orientation; planning orientation; and process orientation (which could be sequenced). *Case Histories in Community Organization* (1958) presented workers' roles and activities through eleven case studies in diverse communities including international development. At this time, the thirteen-volume *Social Work Curriculum Study* commissioned by the Council on Social Work Education and coordinated by Werner Boehm provided specialized volumes on macropractice methods in administration, community organization, research, and social welfare policy and services (Boehm 1959).

CONTEMPORARY APPROACHES TO COMMUNITY PRACTICE IN A CHANGING ECONOMY

EXPANSION OF COMMUNITY PRACTICE IN A PERIOD OF PROGRESSIVE CHANGE: 1960S-1970S

Major social shifts accompanied the widespread impact of the civil rights movement, and Michael Harrington's (1962) book *The Other America* brought increased attention to widespread and recalcitrant poverty. Social workers of all races worked to expand civil rights and alleviate poverty. The movement garnered support in many parts of the nation, and Martin Luther King's oratory and his "Letter from a Birmingham Jail" (1963) galvanized support from many sectors of society. King had become committed to nonviolence after studying the works of Gandhi (1956); and civil rights workers received careful training in nonviolence and nonviolent responses to the use of force. The televised demonstrations for civil rights made visible to the entire nation the violent tactics of those who opposed civil rights for African Americans. Racism was by no means limited to the South, but most Americans were shocked by the attack dogs and water cannons they witnessed on nightly television that were used against peaceful demonstrators. Waves of public concern and complaints were lodged with the federal government; President Kennedy finally sent federal officials to quell violence against civil rights demonstrators and from that point on, the movement began to make significant progress. The civil rights movement gave birth to a succession of related social movements, including the women's rights/feminist movement, the movement for the rights of people with disabilities, and the gay and lesbian rights movement

Throughout the 1960s and 1970s, the civil rights movement and War on Poverty programs encouraged a climate favorable to community organizing, social action, progressive politics, and growth in the nonprofit sector. The literature on community work continued to grow, and in 1968, Jack Rothman's article defining three models of community organization—locality development, social planning, and social action—was published (1968). Significant and highly influential works were also developed by George Brager and Harry Specht (1973), During this period, beginning in 1970, coauthors Jack Rothman, John Erlich, and John Tropman, originally with Fred Cox, developed two books, *Strategies of Community Intervention* (2008, sixth edition) *and Tactics and Techniques of Community Intervention* (2001, fourth edition) with continuing editions for decades, and Armand Lauffer, *Social Planning at the Community Level* (1978), among many others. Successive editions of the *Encyclopedia of Social Work* carried increasing numbers of entries on community organization, planning, and development.

RETRENCHMENT, NEOCONSERVATISM, AND COMMUNITY PRACTICE IN A RAPIDLY GLOBALIZING WORLD

The 1980s–1990s and the early years of the twenty-first century brought a return of socially conservative trends, although community practice and its literature continued to grow with work by Taylor and Roberts (1985); an expanded version of Rothman's work in 1995 (2008); and a framework of models by Weil and Gamble first published in the 1995 *Encyclopedia of Social Work*. Feminist treatments of macropractice in works by Cheryl A. Hyde (1986, 1989, 1995), Marie Weil (1986), and Ruth Brandwein (1981); along with approaches adapted by racial and ethnic groups, primarily Rivera and Erlich's *Community Orga-*

nizing in a Diverse Society (1998); and Gutierrez and Lewis (1994). Community development practice expanded to focus on residential development to improve housing stock and to encourage economic programs in inner-city neighborhoods.

The increasingly conservative environment of this period instituted by the presidency of Ronald Reagan continued through successive administrations: governmental retreat from the social safety net sparked the creation of new forms of community-based economic development (see chapters 7 and 9). More recently, social and economic development work in the United States and across the world has expanded to encompass concerns for sustainable development focused on social justice, human rights, and environmental protection (Estes 1993; Gamble and Hoff 2005; chapter 7 in this volume).

COMMUNITY PRACTICE VALUES IN A RAPIDLY GLOBALIZING WORLD

Community practice uses multiple methods of empowerment-based interventions to strengthen participation in democratic processes, to assist groups and communities in advocating for their needs and organizing for social justice, and to improve the effectiveness and responsiveness of human service systems. In our view, the purposes of contemporary community practice are as follows:

COMMUNITY PRACTICE PURPOSES

- *Improvement in quality of life:* Working to respond to basic human needs such as food and shelter, security, opportunities for education and basic health, freedom from violence, opportunities to organize in free spaces and participate in goals and decisions that will affect one's life, as well as the lives of one's family and community members.
- *Advocacy:* Doing research to determine what structures and behaviors limit people and their communities from reaching their full potential, then following up by working with people who wish to reduce the barriers or expand the opportunities for healthy development by planning purposive change activities.
- *Human social and economic development:* Assisting individuals and groups in learning new skills, gaining new knowledge, or other abilities that enrich their own capacities; working to improve life conditions in communities that can expand and improve people's livelihoods; and working with communities to enlarge their local economy through creation of cooperatives, establishment of microenterprise groups, and other asset-based

projects. Livelihoods are both the paid and unpaid work that people do either to gain income or to nurture families and communities.

- *Service and program planning:* Assessing needs whether for a whole community or a specific population, and developing plans, resources, and structures to meet those needs. For example, services may be modified, reorganized, or relocated to respond to a newly recognized need or an emerging population. New services can be developed to use a more effective intervention for a long-term problem. New intervention programs and services must be designed for new or emerging social problems.

- *Service integration:* Establishing a range of services and linking those services to create a continuum of care for the broad needs of particular populations. Examples include building services for the continuum of family support, preservation, and child welfare services; establishing a network of well-connected services for both healthy and frail senior citizens; or providing food, protection, relocation opportunities, and services for new starts for refugees and people who are internally displaced because of international or national conflicts.

- *Political and social action:* Engagement in the political process to change existing policies, establish new progressive legislation, or change policy makers. Activity in political and social action is direct, open, and nonviolent. Pursuing these actions requires free spaces in which people can gather, organize, and speak out, especially people who have been excluded from political involvement in the past. Political and social action seeks to foster institutional change for inclusion and equity, and increase participatory democracy and equality of opportunity in local, regional, and international institutions.

- *Social justice:* Building toward human equality and opportunity across race, ethnicity, gender, and nationality. Examples are working to ensure basic education for girls in all countries; full political participation for women; countries making reparations to those treated unfairly or exploited during war, invasion, and colonization. Building the fabric of civil and human rights laws both nationally and globally, and incorporating the articles of the Universal Declaration of Human Rights (United Nations 1948) as we develop social programs and interventions nationally and internationally. (Adapted from Weil and Gamble 2008)

Given these purposes, community practice faces significant challenges to upholding the values we have presented in this chapter. Community practice efforts that need to be expanded and strengthened include: (1) advancing the role of civil society in the world; (2) strengthening citizen participation and access to democratic institutions worldwide; (3) expanding human rights, social justice, and environmental protection; and (4) strengthening community practice efforts across the globe. The global challenges facing vulnerable people across the world make it critical that community practitioners advocate for national and international policies that can place people at the center of work for sustainable development. We also need to urge and pressure national and international leaders to meet commitments to the bottom billion, the poorest people in the world.

THE GLOBAL ROLE OF CIVIL SOCIETY AND NONGOVERNMENTAL ORGANIZATIONS

Globally, there are now more than 20,000 transnational nongovernmental organizations (NGOs) and registered networks (UNDP 2002). Civil society organizations are growing faster in low- and middle-income countries, and people in newly independent and postcolonial states in Africa, Latin America, Asia, and Eastern Europe are developing voluntary associations to respond to community needs, promote sustainable development, and engage in decision making with the public and private sectors. UN *Human Development Reports* document this growth and have increasingly emphasized promoting citizen participation through democratic governance (UNDP 2002).

> Participation promotes collective agency as well as individual agency—important because collective action through social and political movements has often been a motor of progress for issues central to human development: protecting the environment, promoting gender equality, fostering human rights. (UNDP 2002:53)

Inclusive citizen participation is a fundamental value of community practice. According to the United Nations Development Program (UNDP), seven basic universal freedoms ensure an individual's well-being, security, and human dignity:

- Freedom from discrimination—by gender, race, ethnicity, national origin or religion [and we add age, sexual orientation, and physical and mental ability]
- Freedom from want—to enjoy a decent standard of living
- Freedom to develop and fully realize the human potential
- Freedom from fear—freedom from threats to personal security, from torture, from arbitrary arrest, and from other acts of violence and intimidation
- Freedom from injustice and violations of the rule of law

- Freedom of thought and speech—freedom to participate in decision making and to form associations
- Freedom to engage in decent work without exploitation (UNDP 2000b:1)

These freedoms embody the values of social and economic justice, and basic human rights, and, if we add the freedom to have air, water and soil protected from pollution, we can incorporate freedom of environmental restoration and preservation. They parallel the "capabilities" described by Sen (1973) as the sufficient functioning required for people to exercise personal choice. Whether starting from the Universal Declaration of Human Rights or the seven freedoms outlined here, an audit of basic freedoms is a first step toward measuring inclusive citizen participation in any nation.

STRENGTHENING DEMOCRATIC INSTITUTIONS

Keeping in mind that not all democracies protect and promote human rights, a second step toward ensuring inclusive citizen participation is an audit of a nation's democratic institutions. Four challenges are often present in democracies that fail to ensure these basic freedoms and human rights:

1. The most persistent weakness of majoritarian democracies is discrimination against minorities and worsening of horizontal inequalities.
2. When elite groups act as if they are above the law or when elected representatives arbitrarily remove judges, civil servants, and others, faith in democratic institutions weakens.
3. Many democracies fail to address the economic and social rights of significant groups, typically because this neglect does not hurt the electoral outcomes of those in power.
4. Failing to deal adequately with the legacy of an authoritarian past can lead to the recurrence of violence and the reversal of democratic rule. (UNDP 2000b:59)

Strengthening democratic institutions and promoting an active civil society that demands institutional accountability can help to overcome these challenges. Many nations are called democracies, and it becomes increasingly important to be clear that holding a free election does not a democracy make. Democratic institutions must be strengthened at local and national levels through informed citizen participation and by the engagement of organizations and communities in work for more just societies. Well-established requisites for a stable and peaceful democracy include rule of law—even over officials— equitable systems of justice, a literate and informed people, free press, freedom of speech, checks and balances in governmental systems, checks and balances to protect minorities (Collier 2009), and the stability to support peaceful succession to leadership through free and fair elections.

CONCLUSIONS: HUMAN RIGHTS AND GLOBALIZING PRACTICE

Themes in this volume focus on working for social justice, expanding human rights worldwide, striving to help the disadvantaged reap benefits from the global economy, and finding ways to promote democratic and peaceful functioning in multicultural societies. Gender equality projects such as the work of the Central Asian Institute establishing schools for both girls and boys in Afghanistan and parallel efforts developing sustainable livelihoods for women carried out by Morning Star Development (http://msdev.homestead.com/) are prime examples of efforts needed in many parts of the world. Recent information about promoting human rights is available in Finn and Jacobson (2008a,b), Reichert (2007), and Stretch et al. (2003), which along with rights-oriented Web sites provide background and action guides.

Jim Ife (2007b) has emphasized areas of practice that are needed locally and globally to achieve goals of social justice and human rights; he maintains that all social workers should understand the scope and causes of poverty and inequality worldwide and develop the knowledge and skills to work toward drastically reducing the impact of these social ills. Unfortunately Ife notes, research on poverty and inequality has diminished within Western social work and has become a smaller part of social work curricula in Australia and the United States. Ife argues that this destructive trend must be reversed:

> It is the obscenity of global poverty, and the unequal distribution of global resources, that make international social work so necessary and so difficult, and that result in the massive lack of resources to provide adequate health care, housing, education and employment for the people of the Global South. But how can we do international social work if at home we define social work in such a way that poverty and inequality are no longer its core concerns? I would suggest that if social work education is to equip social workers to work internationally, a thorough study of poverty and inequality, nationally and globally, and a rediscovery of our profession's historical commitment, is fundamental. (Ife 2007b:12)

Ife recommends reclaiming this historical commitment by adopting a human rights framework for local and global work. Human rights and human responsibilities, he suggests, should be "embedded within our lived experience, and . . . enacted in our daily lives. Human rights as a participatory democratic project, where we share different understandings of 'the human' and what that means in terms of our rights and responsibilities, is a powerful basis for dialogue, and progressive social work practice" (Ife 2007b:6).

This global focus on human rights, social justice, and opportunity can help us all learn from the separateness of our earlier histories and cultures and prepare for more competent practice as we move inevitably into our shared, global human future.

4

THEORIES AND PERSPECTIVES FOR COMMUNITY PRACTICE

It is the theory that decides what can be observed.

ALBERT EINSTEIN

Whenever a theory appears to you as the only possible one, take this as a sign that you have neither understood the theory nor the problem it was intended to solve.

KARL POPPER, PHILOSOPHER OF SCIENCE

He who loves practice without theory is like a sailor who boards ship without a rudder and compass, and never knows where he may cast.

LEONARDO DA VINCI

No man can step in the same river twice.

THALES, 5TH CENTURY B.C.E.

INTRODUCTION

In chapters devoted to the eight community practice models presented in Part II of this volume we make use of theories to assist in explaining and developing understanding of each model and its specific focus. Some types of theories explain "big picture" issues, while others provide guidance for our practice. Theories help us understand *why* and *how* we practice as we do and enable us to test methods and approaches. Theories embody worldviews and perspectives on human and community behavior and, at least implicitly, include value bases that shape *how we think* and *what kinds of positive changes we believe are possible.*

Theoretical perspectives also help us to analyze relevant issues and concerns as well as social situations and options for action. Theories and perspectives guide our selection of strategies and shape our action plans. In addition, they serve as guides to assist us in reflecting on practice experiences and evaluating practice efforts and outcomes. We may find in practice that a theory is more useful than we had thought, or we might find that we have been using an inappropriate theory. For example, it is difficult to achieve empowerment outcomes if guiding theory supports the social/political/cultural status quo or if the theory propounds authoritarian strategies to promote grassroots progressive change. In this case the theory (authoritarianism) would be incongruent with the goal (empowerment). To be effective in working with communities and groups, a community practitioner needs to be a creative thinker and actor and also an observant and reflective evaluator. To become an effective practitioner—helping people to achieve their goals—we need to apply relevant theories, use them to analyze practice situations, and make use of the rapidly growing knowledge base to best serve dispossessed communities and vulnerable groups.

In this chapter we ask you to think about types of theory and the questions each type addresses. We present a framework for community practice theory grounded in five streams of theory that operate at different levels of change: community, interorganizational, organizational, group, and interpersonal. These theory streams originate separately but flow together in actual community practice to facilitate responses to diverse needs and varied scopes of concern. We emphasize *selecting, sequencing, or building the most relevant theory, or sets of theories, to guide your actions in particular practice situations.* That is, in most community practice efforts you will work with a range of individuals, with diverse types of groups, with multiple community organizations and social/human service organizations, with coalitions, and with communities and external power structures.

In the following case example you can see that Jane Addams and her colleagues at Hull-House had to learn how to work effectively, mutually, and collaboratively with quite diverse immigrant ethnic communities. In this brief example we can see how Addams and other Hull-House residents initially operated on an "expert theory" approach about nutrition—and from their mistakes gained valuable lessons related to cultural contexts and interests of the community. The example gives us a window through time to see an outstanding community practitioner learn the value of *participation*.

THEORIZING ABOUT THEORIES

As human beings, it is nearly impossible for us not to create theories that we can use in our lives and in our professional work. When we analyze practice situations or posit reasons to explain behavior, organize assumptions and structure them to interpret a situation, or seek to explain political, group, or individual behavior, we are engaged in a nascent process of theory construction—theorizing. We are trying to explain our world and to provide meaning that we

CASE EXAMPLE 4.1 JANE ADDAMS LEARNS THE IMPORTANCE OF PARTICIPATION

In *Twenty Years at Hull-House,* Jane Addams illustrates the importance of developing programs and facilities with the *participation* of people from the community rather than presuming to know what they need. She describes the experience of seeking to respond to community members' desires to have places where young people could dance and sports could be played and where all ages could have some refreshment—away from the saloon halls that "were the only places in the neighborhood where the immigrant could hold his social gatherings"(Addams 1910:102).

In an effort to respond to the need for a gathering place and to promote healthy nutrition, the Hull-House residents sent a member to cooking school and began serving "nutritious" meals to community residents at lunch. However, in this logical plan to improve health, they had overlooked the very diverse immigrant communities that they served and the reality that each community had its own culture of food—often more spicy than standard American fare of the time. Worrying about why the food program was failing, resident staff asked around, and one program participant stated firmly that she preferred "to eat what she'd ruther" than the tasteless foods that were called "nutritious."

Addams discusses what an important lesson this experience was in learning the central importance of community participation in planning and prioritizing the Settlement's work. As a result, their next decisions focused on developing facilities that neighborhood residents had actively sought.

Addams and her colleagues responded resiliently and she reported:

If the dietetics were appreciated but slowly, the social value of the coffee-house and the gymnasium [both requested by neighborhood participants], which were in the same building, were quickly demonstrated....

"From the beginning [of Hull-House], the <u>young people's clubs had asked for dancing,</u>" and nothing was more popular than the increased space for parties offered by the new gymnasium, with the chance to serve refreshments in the renovated room below. [Finding that "soft drinks" were not popular except with young children] and after "asking program participants questions, about their preferences—the staff decided to go with recommendations from a number of participants and <u>design the refreshment area like a coffee house.</u>

... The coffee house gradually performed a mission of its own and became something of a social center to the neighborhood as well as a real convenience. Business men from the adjacent factories and school teachers from the nearest public schools used it increasingly. The Hull-House students and club members supped together in little groups or held their reunions and social banquets, as, to a certain extent, did organizations from all parts of town. <u>The experience of the coffee-house taught us not to hold to preconceived ideas of what the neighborhood ought to have, but to keep ourselves in readiness to modify and adapt our undertakings as we discovered those things which the neighborhood was ready to accept.</u>

(Addams, Twenty Years at Hull-House 1910:102–3)

Underlining added for emphasis.

can understand. We construct theories to explain the actions of organizations, groups, and individuals, and we analyze social settings and community practice issues in light of implicit or explicit theories that we hold and act on. That is, as humans, we cannot *not* make theory.

In this chapter, we explore ways to theorize about community practice and to select appropriate theories for the problems and issues we are considering. We examine the intellectual tension between post-positivist approaches to theory and research and the approaches of social constructionists. We assess levels and types of theories available to help us understand, explain, or predict results: If we apply a particular theory to our practice issues, what will most likely happen—in comparison to what would more likely happen if we applied a different theory—and which theory is likely to be most helpful? The body of the chapter discusses streams of theory that contribute to community practice.

WHY IS THEORIZING IMPORTANT FOR COMMUNITY PRACTITIONERS?

Practice efforts have a greater chance of being effective—that is, we can help the people we work with achieve the goals they have set—when practice actions and strategies are guided by useful theory. Our efforts to achieve positive outcomes should be the result of applying theory in our practice. We should also assess the usefulness of theories in combination with reflective analysis of practice results. Groups need to consider their action choices in light of their values and the goals they wish to achieve. Congruency across goals, values, theory, and analysis facilitates evaluation of program effectiveness and outcome achievement. Knowing how to employ or construct theory is a critical component of community practice. Reflection and consensus building regarding choices and strategies help to build trust within groups. Freire's (2000, 2005) method, *praxis*, which involves continued, shared *analysis, reflection,* and *action*, is extremely helpful in group planning, decision-making, and evaluation processes and also helps to build group cohesion. As Reed (2005) notes, Freire's method assists us in three ways: in developing knowledge and applying it; in enacting knowledge through action; and in reflecting to test our knowledge and revise our theories to increase our chances of success. Furthermore, Reed specifies three reasons why theorizing in community practice is particularly important. Theorizing

- is an important tool for effective practice.
- helps practitioners to learn and improve their practice and knowledge about what is effective.
- is essential for community practice that has social justice goals. (2005:86–87)

Theory can be viewed as "systematically organized knowledge applicable in a relatively wide variety of circumstances; especially, a series of assumptions, accepted principles, and rules of procedure devised to analyze, predict, or otherwise explain the nature or behavior of a specified set of phenomena" (*American Heritage Dictionary of the English Language*, 4th ed., 2006). *Theorizing*, is an active process of formulating or analyzing theories (ibid.). More formally, this process is called theory construction. Using established theories and formulating theories for action (or practice) are both important activities for community practitioners. The most useful theories for community practice focus on change—promoting social justice at multiple levels and challenging injustices (Reed 2005). This focus is appropriate because the primary goal of community practice is to promote social justice through progressive change in communities, organizations, political/economic/social systems, and policies (Payne 2005). Reed also argues that community practice should promote participation and human well-being as well as work to prevent the development of problems. In order to effectively promote community capacity building and emphasize prevention strategies, she maintains that "one must also identify and intervene with those factors that either put communities at risk for developing problems or help protect them from problems. This usually includes developing leadership and capacity—among individuals, groups, communities, and institutions" (Reed 2005:86). Table 4.1 presents the utility of a range of explanatory theories for community practice.

Reed's table focuses on explanatory theories that predict or explain events and may indicate causality. Before applying other levels of theory, it is important to recognize that currently two distinct "ways of knowing" operate from divergent assumptions and indicate somewhat different methods of inquiry.

DIVERGENT VIEWS OF HOW WE KNOW WHAT WE KNOW

EPISTEMOLOGICAL DIFFERENCES—POST-POSITIVISM AND SOCIAL CONSTRUCTION IN SOCIAL WORK THEORY Selecting the most useful and relevant theories to guide specific work can be challenging. Some theories are not congruent with each other. Indeed, some theories complement each other, while others are contradictory. Two different theories used to analyze the same situation can produce quite different understandings. As Einstein said, "It is the theory that decides what can be observed." The theories we use can help us interpret behavior; at the same time, they also constrain the range of choices we are likely to have.

Incongruent theories can create problems if conflicting worldviews, ideologies, and values are used together. For example, strong degrees of difference are evident in the opposing positions of post-positivists and social constructionists. Post-positivism is the most recent incarnation of the long established empiricist

TABLE 4.1 Reed's Illustrative Types of Explanatory Theories about Society and Social Change

TYPES OF THEORIZING	BRIEF DESCRIPTION	RELEVANT QUESTIONS/ FUNCTIONS
Evolutionary—society and communities make progress over time	Assumes that change occurs in multilinear progressions, usually from more simple to more complex; some assume that changes improve society	What types of change are currently underway? What is the history of particular issues in a community and the society as a whole? What are the patterns and sources of change?
Political economy— concerned with polity (political processes) and economic systems	Assumes that economic and political bases of the global, national, and other external environments can create conditions for either change or stability	What are the consequences of the current political economic system and the political and economic circumstances that are impacting a particular situation and context?
Structural/functional— open systems, ecological (from theorizing about natural and social systems; could place role theory here)	Describes/analyzes structures and their functions, also processes within and between structures and boundaries. Tends to focus on what keeps things stable	What structures exist? What is the nature of their boundaries and relationships between and within them? What are the processes that occur within and among components of the system?
Conflict theories—strain, competing interests, scarce resources, power differences, competition among groups	Focuses on group differences, stresses and strains between societal and community components; assumes that conflict creates conditions that promote change	What groups in the community have conflicting interests and approaches? Who is competing for existing resources? What power differentials exist across group boundaries?
Construction of meaning— symbolic interactionism, some aspects of culture, theories about ideology, interpretive theories	Focuses on how ideologies (religious, political, cultural, and personal) are created and maintained, and internalized; includes how they explain and justify existing social and power arrangements	What rationales are given by whom about the existing state of affairs and the causes of perceived problems? What latent and manifest meanings can be discerned? What cultural and subcultural symbols and norms are operating?

(continued)

TABLE 4.1 (*Continued*)

TYPES OF THEORIZING	BRIEF DESCRIPTION	RELEVANT QUESTIONS/ FUNCTIONS
Social psychological— social learning, exchange, rational choice	Focuses at the personal and interpersonal levels, how individuals develop and learn, and influence each other	What community members are involved or could be? What characterizes them psychologically and relationally? What motivates their interests?
Co-construction—how everyday interactions shape behavior and institutions— each co-constructing and mediating the others	Examines how social structures and relationships co-construct each other; how everyday actions sustain social systems and vice versa; roles of human agency	How do social systems regulate and structure options for their members and vice versa? How do routines and transactions create/sustain the status quo? What sources of agency exist?
Critical feminist and critical race theories— emphasize power and oppression, with an advocacy stance	Have explicit goals for promoting improved situations for those most disadvantaged in society, seek to understand and challenge sources of oppression	How are existing power and inequality differences being created and sustained? What will disrupt, challenge, and change these? What would social justice look like?

Source: Adapted from Reed 2005:89.

tradition traced all the way back to Aristotle—observation and objective knowledge are central. Social constructionists argue that practice theory is constructed, that is, created and interpretive. Distinctions between these opposing positions are summarized next.

In general, *post-positivists* hold a set of principles that include the following:

- The world is orderly; there are natural rules; and we can come to understand them (Payne 2005).
- The world exists independently from human beings, and we can be removed and objective about it in observation (Brechin and Sidell 2000:6).
- Human beings behave according to their DNA and genetic code (ibid.:17).
- If we observe and analyze systematically, we can come to understand how the world works and the natural rules that affect its inhabitants (Kuhn 1970).

- From observation, analysis, and research we can develop knowledge and apply it to create desired changes (Payne 2005).
- We can be effective in interventions based on research knowledge because we can "explain how one action causes another" (Brechin and Sidell 2000:22).

On the other hand, the social constructionist position on the nature of the world and theories is interpretive.

Social constructionists hold the following beliefs:

- "Human beings are independent, free to follow their will as part of the world and in relationships, so cannot be objective" (Payne 2005:55).
- Society is separate from individuals so we can be most effective by understanding how other human beings understand the world (Payne 2005).
- "Participation in human relationships means that we influence the world we are studying; and our understandings about the world will influence how we behave—we are subjective" (Brechin and Sidell 2000:23).
- Human beings are subjects so our actions affect others, but also change ourselves—even though we may also be constrained by our environment (Payne 2005).
- Because of the complexity of the world, "it is not possible to collect all the necessary information to understand the rules of human life; so it is better to think about the world in a more flexible way" (Brechin and Sidell 2000:23).
- In our work, we enter into relationships, and "engage in mutual exploration of what is happening, for a full appreciation of what is happening. People's social objective and values in their relationships are always a factor" (Payne 2005:55).

IMPLICATIONS FOR PRACTICE Both the post-positivist and social constructionist approaches spring from the reasoning mind, and both are based on close observation—assessing situations and behavior and seeking to understand them. Yet they operate using separate streams of theory (and usually different research methods) because of differences in value perspectives, epistemology, ideology, and ideas about what constitutes proof and even "truth." Theory resulting from each of these perspectives can be used to guide practitioners in their work. However, the path to development of theories from each perspective is quite different; and what knowledge and what theories "count" vary considerably. To understand these differences, Payne (2005:54) notes that we have to understand their different views about epistemology—"that is how we understand and write about human knowledge." He argues that there are four viewpoints related to how "knowledge should be used in social work to provide the basis for theory" (Payne 2005:55–62):

EVIDENCE-BASED PRACTICE VIEWS

Evidence-based views argue that to be ethical, social workers should use knowledge that has been gathered and tested empirically in the most rigorous ways possible to provide evidence of the form of action that is most likely to achieve its objectives for the benefit of clients. (Representative authors: Gambrill; Macdonald; Sheldon; and Thyer 2001. *These ideas are associated particularly with cognitive behavioral theories.*)

SOCIAL CONSTRUCTION VIEWS

Social construction views argue that knowledge and understandings about the world come from social interactions among people. Knowledge is therefore constructed within cultural, historic, and local contexts through the language used to interpret social experiences. (Representative authors: Parton and O'Byrne 2005; Payne 2005; Slife and Williams 1995. *These ideas are associated particularly with social construction-oriented practice theories.*)

EMPOWERMENT VIEWS

Empowerment views argue that knowledge of situations comes primarily from clients and that social workers should use their own knowledge for further empowerment. The purposes of social work require workers to seek social justice. Community workers and members should be mutual partners in planning, development and organizing processes. (Representative authors: Gutierrez and Lewis 1999; Lee 2001; Simon 1994; Solomon 1986.)

REALIST VIEWS

Realist views are a fairly new perspective and hold that evidence of reality is not always available to empirical observation, so that knowledge *emerges* or is generated from human interpretations of successions of events that can be captured empirically. Often called "Critical Realism," these views seek to question assumptions about theory and research. Realist views argue that phenomena exist beyond social construction. (Representative authors: Beresford and Croft 1993, 2001. *These ideas are particularly associated with social and community development, ethnic sensitivity, empowerment and advocacy theories.*)

IMPLICATIONS OF PERSPECTIVES AND IDEOLOGY Each of these views represents a political standpoint within the profession, and it is important when you are engaged in practice that you understand the ideology, theory base, values, practice, and research methods most likely to be associated with the standpoint enacted by agency leaders, consultants, or teachers (even if they do not articulate a position). This analysis will help you understand why the agency's programs are designed as they are and the reasons certain types of interventions and research methods are selected. It is also instructive to discuss these ideas in classes and to reflect on the potential differences in impact on communities and clients depending on which types of theory and which types of research are employed.

Payne (2005), Robbins, Chatterjee, and Canda (2006), Slife and Williams (1995), and numerous other authors argue that since theory is constructed (and tested) by humans, it is inevitably shaped by values and perspectives. Max Weber, the father of sociology, famously noted that "there is no value-free social science" (Weber 1978). He argued that in addition to careful empirical observation of social phenomena, social scientists employ a method called *verstehen* (disciplined understanding—perhaps interpretation). Weber and many later social scientists recognized that theory is almost inevitably colored by ideologies. Ideologies may be socially progressive and focused on empowerment, they may implicitly support the status quo, or they may explicitly or implicitly support regressive forms of social control. Therefore, it is always valuable to assess the value base and assumptions of any theory. For example, the *structural-functionalism* of Talcott Parsons (1954), was based in part on his observations in India of people fulfilling their assigned roles in society; his justification of societal stability seemed to many to support the centuries of established structural inequities of the caste system. Other examples of repressive theoretical perspectives include the eugenics movement in America and its practices of involuntary sterilization of people believed to be "inferior" and the arguments more recently about which races "are more intelligent than others" espoused in *The Bell Curve* (Herrnstein and Murray 1994). Given the ethical questions that can be raised about many theories, the critical importance of assessing the purpose, ideology, and value base of theories is clearly an important step before applying them in community practice. You will need to understand what perspectives the people you work with are operating from and consider results that are feasible from each major theory or perspective.

TYPES OF THEORY

A continuum of theoretical approaches is used in social work practice and research moving from explanatory theory (the most abstract and broadly focused) through middle-range theory (less abstract, more specifically focused) to practice theory or theory of action (most concrete, most applicable to realities of practice). Explanatory theory seeks to explain phenomena, predict behavior, and, where possible, demonstrate causality. Since it operates at a fairly high level of abstraction, it is usually not applied in our day-to-day practice. Sociologist Robert K. Merton (1968) developed the idea of middle-range theory for theories that can be used to connect a more abstract theory to what we are observing empirically or experiencing in practice. Essentially, the purpose of middle-range theory is to give us the means, techniques, and tools to analyze reality and be able to discuss our theories and conclusions in an intelligible way. The ability to agree on the content of specific middle-range theories has enabled social scientists, social workers, and other professionals to discuss theory (reasons for behavior or phenomena) with others and know that we are meaning the same thing in using particular terms or descriptions.

As we understand and discuss our specific practice situations, we move closer to concrete reality employing specific practice theory or theory of action. Essentially, we take a practice theory and "lay it over" the interactions or experiences we are trying to figure out, and we examine, assess, and test to see whether the theory "fits." Does it fully account for what we are seeing? Does it make sense of a situation that has been confusing? Does it give us clues as to needed action? Practice or action theories offer us guidelines and, with testing, become a way of formalizing the theory and identifying best practices. Most often, we use practice theory or middle-range theory to analyze and make sense of our practice situations and determine strategies of action.

Theory for use in community practice can also be conceptualized as focusing on the scale of operation from large to small. Community practitioners are typically assumed to work "with communities." However, in reality we work with people in community organizations, in service and community-based organizations, and with many other types of groups as well as with individuals and very small groups. Focusing on theories of action or practice theories, table 4.2 provides a theoretical framework organized by scale of intervention from community to interpersonal that can be used to analyze and select theories appropriate for application at specific times in different community practice projects or programs. For example, to develop a community-based program to build social capital, you might employ interpersonal communication theory, intergroup theory, and collaboration theory with multiple, diverse community groups in order to study, document, and work to expand social capital in a particular

TABLE 4.2 Theoretical Framework for Community Practice—Macro to Micro Scale

THEORIES APPLIED IN COMMUNITY PRACTICE	SCALES OF INTERACTION			
	COMMUNITY SCALE	ORGANIZATIONAL SCALE	GROUP SCALE	PERSONAL AND INTERPERSONAL SCALE
Theory Streams	*Community and Community Practice Theories*	*Organizational and Interorganizational Theories*	*Group Theory and Empowerment Theories*	*Self, Self-Efficacy, and Interactive Theories*
Practice Theories and Theories of Action	• Community Building • Community Organizing • Organizing Organizations • Citizen Participation • Social, Economic, and Sustainable Development • Social Capital • Community Social, Economic, and Health Planning • Major Approaches —Development —Organizing —Planning —Social Change	• Meeting Management • Change from Below • Managing Up • Managing Out • Coalition Theory • Collaboration Theory • Exercising Influence • Leadership/ Management • Organizational Typologies • Organizational Theories • Organizational Development and Change • Organizational Action Theory • Interorganiza- tional Behavior • Interorganiza- tional Networks	• Group Process Theory • Group Facilitation Theory • Popular Education/ Conscientiza- tion • Decision- Making Theories • Task Group Theories (work group theories) • Intergroup Theories • Empowerment Theories • Empowerment Planning • Social Justice Theories • Ethical Theories • Participation Theory • Self- and Group Determination	• Use of Self in Organizing, Development Planning, and Change • Facilitation • Leadership and Leadership Development • Interpersonal/ Interactive Behavior Theory • Communica- tion Theory • Interactionist Theory • Exercising Influence • Coaching/ Training Theory • Positive Psychology Theory • Interpersonal Competence • People Skills

community. The *CPS Workbook* includes exercises you can use with case examples to determine what theories might be most useful for particular practice situations and levels of intervention.

The range of theories and scales of interaction that community practitioners undertake illustrate the importance of using theory, research, and the knowledge base appropriately to understand your roles and determine courses of action in all areas of community practice.

STREAMS OF THEORY FOR COMMUNITY PRACTICE

While systems theory is versatile in its applications, no single theory is adequate to explain the complex interactions of individuals, groups, communities, and service systems, and it is unlikely that such a theory could emerge. Social work draws from rich sociological, anthropological, psychological, political, economic, critical, and other bases of theory. Community practice particularly draws theories from across the social sciences and applies theories that function at different levels of human systems from individual to global interactions. We apply theories and concepts from multiple disciplines—for example, *collective efficacy* from psychology; *group, organizational, and interorganizational theory* from sociology; *ethnographic methods* from anthropology; *democratic theory* from political science; concepts about the *global economy* and about *poverty* from economics, sociology and political science; as well as concepts of critical theories on race or gender (for example) from multiple social science perspectives.

Social work has developed a broad base of practice theory. However, much of this theory base is focused narrowly on direct practice or too generally expressed to be useful in community practice. Expanded development of community practice theory relating to the central processes *development, organizing, planning, and progressive social change* is much needed. The following discussion focuses on theories for community practice, offers critique, and presents applications appropriate for one or more models of community practice. We discuss a range of theories proceeding from smaller to larger systems.

PERSONAL AND INTERPERSONAL THEORY: SELF-EFFICACY AND STRENGTHS PERSPECTIVES

SELF-EFFICACY THEORY Albert Bandura has conducted research on this theory for decades. Among personal and interpersonal theories, his perspective is particularly useful for community practice because it focuses on how people develop self-efficacy—a sense of mastery—to be able to face challenges, apply skills, and function with confidence in diverse situations. *Efficacy* indicates that we can accomplish something and achieve the desired result. According to Bandura, a sense of self-efficacy enables us to take greater control over the circumstances of our lives and to feel successful in working through challenges or solving problems. In *Self-Efficacy in Changing Societies*, Bandura (1995) asserts: "People make causal contributions to their own psychological functioning through mechanisms of personal agency. Among the mechanisms of agency, none is more central or pervasive than people's beliefs of personal efficacy. Perceived self-efficacy refers to the beliefs in one's capabilities to organize and execute the courses of action required to manage prospective situations" (2).

This theory can be used in work with individuals and in leadership development. In its individual and collective-efficacy forms, this theory deals with learning new skills, refining capabilities, and learning to identify and claim strengths. It is related to empowerment theory and to several roles that community practitioners take on with groups and members of communities, for example, coaching, training, and leadership development. Bandura discusses the ways that people come to believe in their own agency, and these learning experiences provide valuable lessons for community practitioners because we can provide support for these processes.

> People's beliefs concerning their efficacy can be developed by four main forms of influence. The most effective way of creating a strong sense of efficacy is through *mastery experiences*. They provide the most authentic evidence of whether one can muster whatever it takes to succeed. Successes build a robust belief in one's personal efficacy. . . . [efficacy requires cognitive, behavioral, and self regulatory skills].
>
> The second influential way of creating and strengthening efficacy is through the *vicarious experiences* provided by social models. . . . People seek proficient models who possess the competencies to which they aspire. . . .
>
> *Social persuasion* is a third way of strengthening people's belief that they have what it takes to succeed. . . .
>
> [Physiological and emotional states can also play a part in assessing one's efficacy.] The fourth way of altering efficacy beliefs is to enhance physical status [and] reduce stress. (Bandura 1995:3–5)

Just this brief sample of central ideas from self-efficacy theory indicates ways community practitioners can assist people in developing greater confidence, mastery, and belief in the new roles they take on in community development or other projects. Not incidentally, these same ideas can also assist students and experienced practitioners when confronting new experiences—if we can draw on previous mastery, we can better take on new challenges.

STRENGTHS PERSPECTIVE This perspective, developed by several scholars, including Saleebey (2005) and Weick et al. (1989), focuses primarily on work with individuals, families, and groups. Dennis Saleebey's *The Strengths Perspective in Social Work Practice* (2005), which provides a chapter applying this perspective to neighborhoods and communities, gave us a language consonant with community practice values. From the earliest community practice books by Murray Ross (1955, 1958), the perspective on the people whom we work with has been one of mutual relationships, transparent approaches, and shared planning for social change through organizing, development, and planning strategies. The relationship between community members and community practitioners is one of *partnership* rather than a relationship with the status difference of helper and client. The terms used in community work to describe these mutual relationships are *participants*, *partners*, *group members*, and *community members*. We work with people not in dependency relationships but in mutual relationships in their roles as *citizens, immigrants, refugees*—as *members of groups and communities*, and *member* carries a very different connotation than the dependency relationship implied with *client*; *member* connotes a person who belongs to a group or organization, while *client* implies dependency: "one for whom professional services are rendered" or "one dependent on the patronage of another" (*American Heritage Dictionary* 2006). Saleebey's description of the strengths perspective as presenting "a shift from an emphasis on problems and deficits defined by the worker to possibilities and strengths identified in egalitarian, collaborative relationships with clients" (2005:38) was indeed welcome—giving more elements of a common language to direct practice workers and community workers. However, community practitioners would more likely say "egalitarian, collaborative relationships with community members." The principles Saleebey (2005) developed for the strengths perspective in the last two decades have been cited by numerous authors and have been used by countless practitioners. Following is a version we have adapted specifically for community practice:

PRINCIPLES OF THE STRENGTHS PERSPECTIVE FOR COMMUNITY PRACTICE

People have many strengths (Saleebey 2005).
Motivation is based on fostering strengths (Saleebey 2005).
Community practitioners establish mutual working relationships and partnerships with community members, group members, and community-based organizations to nurture strengths and empower groups (Weil 2005a).

Strengths are present in all communities (Kretzmann and McKnight 1993).

Collective-efficacy empowers groups to take greater control over the circumstances of their lives and develop a sense of mastery by working through challenges or solving shared problems (Bandura 1995).

What we cannot do alone, we can do together (Legerton; see concluding case study in chapter 9 of this volume and in the *CPS Workbook*).

Community practitioners meet and work with people where they live, in their homes, in community centers, in schools, or in other community spaces. Each of these settings is unique, and the nuances of local realities, strengths, needs, and resources call on us to give careful consideration to our values, to community values, and to competing value stances as we work with people to develop projects and programs to improve the quality of life in their neighborhoods, towns, or villages.

TASK GROUP AND EMPOWERMENT THEORIES

TASK GROUPS Community practitioners perform the majority of their work with task groups. Although we work with individuals on preparing for meetings, practicing statements for council hearings, and making a presentation or other planning and development tasks, working with task groups is central to community work. Toseland and Rivas (2008) provide excellent, straightforward guidance in this area of practice. They describe group processes and worker responsibilities in a range of task groups and present relevant concepts and theory for work with committees, boards, social action groups, and coalitions. They distinguish between facilitation and direct leadership, and they depict workers' roles along a continuum of types of task groups.

EMPOWERMENT THEORY Community practitioners welcome the continuing development of empowerment theory. Barbara Levy Simon (1994) provides a detailed discussion of social work's empowerment tradition in her historical treatment, which traces "the century long evolution of social work practice that has been devoted to client empowerment" and explores "the social movements, ideas, and beliefs that have been most influential in the thinking of those who have forged the empowerment tradition" (xiv). Ideas related to empowerment have been evidenced in social work since the settlement movement, and contemporary presentations have established a strong practice theory perspective. In her groundbreaking book, *Black Empowerment: Social Work in Oppressed Communities* (1986), Barbara Solomon provided the following definition: "Empowerment refers to a process whereby persons who belong to a stigmatized so-cial category throughout their lives can be assisted to develop and increase skills in the exercise of interpersonal influence and the performance of valued social roles" (29).

Solomon identifies two types of barriers to empowerment: internal barriers, whereby members of oppressed communities may internalize stigma; and soci-etal barriers of exclusion, discrimination, oppression, and racism that prevent access to social and economic opportunities. She argues that social workers have responsibilities to work with people to overcome both the personal and societal barriers to active empowerment (Solomon 1986). Although many arti-cles have been written about empowerment in social work in recent years, the work of three authors in addition to Solomon is essential: Judith Lee's book, *The Empowerment Approach to Social Work Practice* (2001), offers in-depth treat-ment of empowerment theory and practice with individuals, groups, and com-munities. She provides valuable emphasis on group and community practice as major avenues for empowerment. Lorraine Gutierrez and Edith Lewis have developed major treatments of empowerment practice with women of color (Gutierrez 1992; Gutierrez and Lewis 1999; Lewis and Kissman 1989). Books examining social work theory now routinely include chapters on empowerment theory (Payne 2005; Robbins, Chatterjee, and Canda 2006). Robbins and col-leagues (2006:92) note that empowerment theories:

- Provide conceptualizations of social stratification and oppression.
- Identify the personal and political barriers and dynamics that maintain oppression.
- Offer value frameworks for promoting human empowerment and liberation.
- Identify practical strategies for overcoming oppression and achieving so-cial justice.
- Build on people's strengths, resiliency, and resources.

Simon (1994) cites the long tradition in social group work of assisting clients in developing social skills and group skills, particularly in consensus build-ing and democratic leadership (Coyle 1947; Lindeman 1949), and the long-established focus in community work of the practitioner working mutually with community groups and providing technical assistance (Simon 1994:159). In this regard, she describes the theoretical work of Harper and Dunham (1959), which assisted community organizations not only in conducting needs assessments and program evaluations, but also in teaching organization members compe-tencies such as proposal development, grant applications, and practice-based research (Simon 1994). These skills remain important for practitioners to learn and to be able to teach.

Numerous social workers who learned and taught these skills in the 1960s and 1970s expanded the role of technical assistants or advisers to work as advocates and mobilizers in teaching these skills in communities and working for social reform as "political tacticians," assisting community organizations in becoming forces to be reckoned with in their political milieu (Brager and Specht 1973). Hoffman (1989:81) argued that "the activist role was to mobilize communities to help themselves and to democratize the delivery of services."

Simon further cites the work of Weil and Kruzich (1990), building from feminist theory to connect skill development with power: "They credit feminist theory with reconceptualizing 'power as shared' and highlight the range of skills needed in effecting environmental transformations" (1–2). As noted, Gutierrez, Lewis, and colleagues have written extensively about empowerment practice and theory. Gutierrez and Lewis define *empowerment* as "a process of increasing personal, interpersonal, or political power so that individuals can take action to improve their life situations" (1999:10). Simon confirms the social reformer role of community practitioners and empowerment-oriented social work as follows: "The prevailing view of social workers dedicated to empowerment is that they will be directly responsible for participating in the reform of U.S. institutions, economic policies, and political processes as long as discrimination, poverty, violence, and sickness persist in affecting historically marginal groups disproportionately" (Simon 1994:167).

Empowerment theory has been useful in analyzing the growing strengths of specific populations. Weil (1986) presented an analysis of feminist theory and its empowerment orientation focused on perspectives from liberal, radical, and socialist political positions and from the perspective of women of color. Robbins and colleagues have provided useful discussions of the growing body of gay and lesbian empowerment theory (Robbins et al. 2006:106–110).

ORGANIZATIONAL AND INTERORGANIZATIONAL THEORIES

There is a vast body of organizational theory (Hasenfeld 1992; Hersey, Blanchard, and Johnson 2000; Schermerhorn, Hunt, and Osborne 2008), organizational development theory (Hatch 1997; Senge et al. 2006), and interorganizational theory (Bailey and Koney 2000; Cropper, Ebers, Huxham, and Ring 2008; Schopler 1987). All three of these arenas are major venues for community practice, and the theorists noted help us analyze complex organizational situations and develop strategies for dealing with internal organizational issues, while the following references assist in interacting effectively with external organizations and governmental bodies that may present barriers to community goals (Rothman 2008; Rubin and Rubin 2007). See chapter 10 of the present volume for discussion of coalitions and theories related to interorganizational collaboration.

COMMUNITY THEORY

Community work has a long history of utilizing the knowledge and expertise of a broad range of social sciences researchers; social workers; city and regional planners; public health workers; development workers; and grassroots community workers. This shared knowledge has helped those involved in community work gain greater understanding about community characteristics, needs, strengths, and arenas for collective action. Calvin Streeter provides an overview of contemporary community theory in the twentieth edition of the *Encyclopedia of Social Work* (2008).

HISTORICAL DEVELOPMENT Community theory has an interesting history built upon the work of early sociologists, particularly Robert E. Park (1952) and colleagues at the University of Chicago, Jane Addams and colleagues at Hull-House and later the Sociology Department and School of Social Welfare at the University of Chicago, and Howard Odum, who founded regional studies and established the School of Public Welfare at the University of North Carolina–Chapel Hill. Park spent his life exploring social, ecological, class, and racial conditions and meanings of *community*. At the University of Chicago, he directed his students to study cities and diverse neighborhoods to determine *how* to study communities from a sociological perspective and determine the best ways to describe and analyze them. He emphasized the systematic study of social systems and sought to ensure that his understandings and experience did not inhibit continued learning. Many sociologists who studied with Park continued community research; and human ecological theory emerged from the empirical research methods they learned under Park's mentorship.

It was also in neighborhoods surrounding the University of Chicago from 1889 through the next several decades that Jane Addams and the women and neighbors of Hull-House documented the living and environmental conditions of crowded immigrant communities. At the end of the first five years of their work, Addams and her colleagues provided an early model of neighborhood research and conditions in an industrial city through their publication of *Hull-House Maps and Papers* (*Hull-House Maps and Papers by Residents of Hull-House*, 1895). The intellectual discussions, research methods, and documents included in that publication provided direction for the planning and development efforts of the Hull-House neighbors and residents. This early work also helped to focus the Hull-House neighborhood-level activities on improving sanitation, creating parks and leisure activity sites, and ameliorating living and working conditions. In addition, the insight into community that Addams developed in those first years of study laid the foundation for the Hull-House efforts in community-level improvements, including labor organizing, intergroup relations, social and community development, children's programs, and social policy advocacy.

In contrast to Addams and her studies of urban communities, Howard W. Odum researched the livelihoods, cultures, and economic development of rural communities in the American South. His 1936 publication, *Southern Regions of the United States*, provided a broad view of rural life (Brazil, 1988). Odum was a founder of regional research and provided a wealth of data for state-level efforts in North Carolina to improve rural living conditions and family well-being. He was the founding director of the School of Public Welfare at the University of North Carolina at Chapel Hill, developed the university's Institute for Research in Social Science, and with his sons contributed to ecological theory (Rotabi 2004).

During the 1950s, the study of North American communities advanced through Roland Warren's research on selected community variables and his theoretical framework for analysis (1965). Warren's contributions to the field included his work as editor for *Perspectives on the American Community* (1966). Influential perspectives included in this work were Max Weber's views on community emergence as the result of economic and money-changing enterprises, Robert Park's theories of human ecology, and Violet Sieder's discussion of the "citizen volunteer." Warren (1963) also made earlier contributions to community research in his landmark book *The Community in America*, in which he discussed planned community change, vertical and horizontal relationship patterns in communities, rural and urban characteristics, and citizen participation.

Maurice Stein's (1960) analysis of sociological and anthropological studies of urban communities described the "polar processes of heightened functional dependence and diminished loyalties" (329). Stein noted that our loyalties, including national, regional, community, neighborhood, and family ties, decrease as we pursue individual interests in "commodities and careers" (329). According to Stein, cities are universally perceived as providing the densest concentration of opportunities to pursue material goods and the best careers. In contrast, he noted that cities increase the likelihood that the individual is "vulnerable to complete isolation" (333). In many settings, it is these dynamic, albeit polar, processes of community life that provide the impetus for the continuing deconstruction and re-creation of community.

Scholars and practitioners in many countries also explored communities, community change, and community conditions (Fals-Borda and Rahman 1991; Freire 2000, 2005; Simmel, 1964). In particular, anthropologists have contributed to the study of both rural and urban communities, and scholars from the range of social sciences and professional disciplines (e.g., public health, city and regional planning) have traced the direction of community change in shifting local, regional, and global contexts (Escobar 1995; Rahnema and Bawtree 1997). Collectively, these studies have contributed to our broader understanding of the settings where we develop our human roles, opportunities, and resources as well as the contexts in which we create the conditions that support or diminish human development.

CONTEMPORARY COMMUNITY CONCEPTS

More recently, social scientists have identified concepts that expand our understanding of the processes of change and conditions in communities. Currently, community perspectives encompass not only the structural, functional, geographic, economic, and political aspects of community, but also the cohesive connections commonly referred to as social capital (Portes 1998; Putnam 1993; Woolcock and Narayan 2000). In their study Woolcock and Narayan defined *social capital* as "the norms and networks that enable people to act collectively" (226). Furthermore, they differentiate between two types of social capital relevant for communities striving to improve their social and economic well-being: *bonding social capital,* which is the close local relationships that make it possible for poor communities to survive; and *bridging social capital,* which is the complex and wider set of external relationships that help a community to move out of poverty (227).

Both bridging and bonding processes focus on relationships and are important not only on a local level but also on a larger level of networks without boundaries, such as those created via Internet and satellite technology, which enable communication across borders, oceans, and continents (Lohmann and McNutt 2005). The connections within community were also the focus of work for Long and his colleagues as they examined community exchange beyond standard economic transactions and described community "by the amount of sharing that transpires in any given situation" (Long, Tice, and Morrison 2006:118). Emilia Martinez-Brawley (1995) described the importance of both structural and sociopsychological perspectives in defining community, but she gave *cohesion* particular value: "Although solidarity, that is cohesiveness or 'we-ness,' can be found in large and small units, in place and nonplace communities, the degree to which it can be observed justifies the extent to which the term 'community' can truly be applied" (540).

In his comparative analysis of regional governments in Italy, the political scientist Robert Putnam (1993) applied the term *social capital* at a broad level to the effectiveness of communities, and described this characteristic as "features of social organization, such as trust, norms, and networks, that can improve the efficiency of society by facilitating coordinated actions" (167).

Human capital refers to the qualities and capabilities of people in relation to the workforce and economic production. Putnam related his definition of social capital to people's capacity to increase economic success through their trust, norms, and networks. However, Couto and Guthrie (1999), who did their research in the Appalachian Mountains of North America, found Putnam's definition inadequate to describe the dense social networks of mountain communities because it failed to include the investment of public resources in community-based organizations. Therefore, Couto and Guthrie defined social capital as both "the moral resources *and public goods* that we invest to produce and reproduce ourselves in community" (xv). In this same work, Couto described how he came to understand "community-based organizations as agents of the democratic prospect of increased communal bonds and social and economic equality" (xv). He drew on the writings of Hirshman (1984) and agreed with his criticism of economic inquiry methods because noninstrumental outcomes were excluded. Outcomes such as striving to develop positive human qualities such as happiness, goodness, and community solidarity clearly differ from economic production and consumption.

Working toward justice and supportive, educational, celebratory, and recreational community institutions requires both an active citizenry and the support of public resources. These values and contributions of active citizens cannot be measured in monetary units, but communities and societies cannot thrive without them. Similarly, successful democratic institutions cannot be built without investment in public resources such as education, adequate infrastructure, access to health care, free spaces in which to associate, political institutions, and the protection and renewal of the environment.

COMMUNITY PRACTICE THEORIES

In one of the earliest texts on community work, Murray Ross (1955) gave careful consideration to issues of participation and argued for principles and methods of community practice that were grounded in adaptation to each local situation:

ABSTRACT OF ROSS'S PRINCIPLES FOR COMMUNITY ORGANIZATION PRACTICE

If means are to be consistent with ends, methods must arise from particularization of objectives in any setting. . . . a particular frame of reference must be developed for each setting. This frame of reference brings together certain assumptions that stem from one's general conceptions of values and one's analysis of the problem. In the community setting the principles which influence method may be stated as follows:

1. Communities of people can develop capacity to deal with their own problems.
2. People want change and can change. . . . [Resistance to change, Ross notes, is typically related to externally imposed change.] But our assumption here is that if blocks to free thinking and feeling are removed, all people everywhere will participate in change which promises to meet their communal needs more adequately.
3. People should participate in making, adjusting, or controlling the major changes taking place in their communities.
4. Changes in community living that are self-imposed or self-developed have a meaning and permanence that imposed changes do not have.
5. A "holistic approach" can deal successfully with problems with which a "fragmented approach" cannot cope.
6. Democracy requires cooperative participation and action in the affairs of the community. (Ross 1955:86–91)

CONCEPT AND PRACTICE OF PLANNED CHANGE

Community workers are used to the terminology of multiple systems as codified early on in the theory of planned change developed in the 1950s and 1960s by Lippit, Watson, and Westley (1958) and Bennis, Benne, Chin, and Corey (1976) and specified as practice theory by Pincus and Minahan (1973:63) among others. We may speak of ourselves and allies as *change agents* and discuss issues occurring in *community systems*. Community practitioners develop strategies to deal effectively with *target systems* to seek positive changes that will better serve vulnerable populations and/or provide support and resources to low-wealth communities. We are likely to work together with community allies and with *simpatico* organizations to educate or urge target systems to change problematic policies. With Pincus and Minahan we view *action systems* as being composed of all groups and organizations that will join in a community effort for planned change.

The current body of practice and action theories provides guidance in a range of practice arenas. Many sources are available. Some are noted here, and chapters 5 through 12 of this volume present theories to support particular models.

COMMUNITY DEVELOPMENT THEORY

Midgley (1995; Hall and Midgley 2004) and Midgley and Livermore (2005) provide solid grounding for the critical and expanding community development practice arena. Butterfield presents this growing body of theory in the new edition of the *Encyclopedia of Social Work* (2008), covering models, methods, trends, and opportunities in this major practice field. Friedmann (1992) originated alternative development theory to counteract the negative outcomes of earlier Western development practices.

Community economic development (CED) is presented in a sound framework by Rubin and Sherraden (2005). Rubin and Rubin (2007) focus on processes of social production. Sherraden (2008) holds that CED is a fully integrated approach to development intended to build capabilities, develop wealth, and promote empowerment in low-income communities. She describes the broad range of roles in CED that community practitioners take on to make lasting change.

Sustainable development theory provides community practitioners with guidance about protecting the natural environment in the course of human development. With increasing engagement in sustainable development work (Estes 1993; Gamble and Hoff 2005), they may also be using the concept of *deep ecology*, indicating an approach to work that emphasizes (Robbins et al. 2006:45) "the moral responsibility of human beings to engage in nonviolent, sustainable lifestyles and social behavior, based on a respect and spiritual awareness of the inherent worth of the entire planet, that supports the survival and growth of the entire life web."

From a framework of global practice, protection and rejuvenation of the natural environment becomes a worldwide cause so that Planet Earth can continue to support the development of human communities as well as the biosphere on which they depend. Gamble and Hoff have presented a wide-ranging treatment of sustainable development (2005).

COMMUNITY ORGANIZATION

Mondros and Staples (2008:387) present the history and theory of this essential form of community practice, analyze current issues promoting organizing, and discuss "trends in aging, immigration, diversity, and the labor force that suggest new opportunities for collective action." Rothman and colleagues (2008) present multiple examples of organizing strategies. Herbert and Irene Rubin's book, *Community Organizing and Development* (2007), is a classic text on this method and includes a strong focus on social production and building and sustaining organizations.

COMMUNITY BUILDING Milligan provides a useful summary of the growing body of literature on community capacity building (2008). She discusses current research on social cohesion in relation to participation and collective action and cites research on the effectiveness of community building strategies. Chaskin and colleagues' (2001) recent book provides an in-depth treatment of methods, theory, and current research.

SOCIAL MOVEMENTS In his article for the twentieth edition of the *Encyclopedia of Social Work*, Reisch (2008) presents an excellent discussion of the nature and history of social movements connecting the emergence of social work with several of the earliest social movements and chronicling the profession's strong connections to the progressive movement and subsequent movements for social justice. He provides an insightful analysis of new social movements and the challenges of globalization, noting: "As participants in the global social justice movements of the 21st century, social workers can help expose the consequences of globalization and develop viable alternatives to existing institutional arrangements" (2008:56). See also chapter 12 in this volume.

SOCIAL AND COMMUNITY PLANNING Jon Sager (2008) and Rothman (2008) examine types of social planning approaches, with emphasis on the classic rational problem-solving process and need for advanced technical skills. Sager (2008) raises realistic concerns about the small number of social workers now entering the field of planning and cites sound reasons why more social workers should take on these challenges. Recent advances in the technology of geographic information systems make this technology increasingly useful in planning from local to regional scope (Hillier and Culhane 2005). Rohe and Gates (1985) provide a review of the history and theory of neighborhood-based planning as well as analysis of their extensive study of effective planning strategies. Medoff and Sklar (1994) present a classic case study of citizen-led development in the Dudley Street neighborhood of Boston (see chapter 9 case example). Weil (2005b) has also contributed to the literature on community-based planning.

COMMUNITY INTERVENTIONS Rothman and colleagues have recently published the seventh edition of *Strategies of Community Intervention* with treatments of a broad range of practice approaches (2008). It redefines the parameters of community intervention and presents sets of articles focused on major approaches: planning/policy, capacity development, and social advocacy. Claudia Coulton (2005) has produced an extensive body of community and neighborhood-focused research with information on high-poverty urban neighborhoods and planning interventions. Chow and Crowe (2005) present sound methodologies for community-based research to ground interventions; and Brisson (2004) has presented sophisticated approaches to analyze social capital development in community-based interventions.

SYSTEMS AND ECOSYSTEMS THEORY

Systems theory—based on observing, studying, and understanding the inter- and intra-actions of components of diverse systems from small to large scale—is virtually built into macropractice. Macropractitioners working with communities and organizations consistently "check in" to see what parts of the systems they are connecting with are functioning collaboratively and which community and organization relationships "need work." A system represents a whole; and community practitioners engage with varied interacting systems including groups, intergroup, organizational, interorganizational, and community systems. This set of systems relates to each other and to larger state, national, and international systems and organizations. Similarly, community-based systems are grounded in smaller systems such as families, schools, and civic or religious groups. Frequently, community practitioners need to analyze and work to improve connections and communications, or deal with problems across systems of different scales.

In macropractice we seek to understand and work with community groups and subgroups (collaborating effectively or in conflict); we examine organizational and interorganizational behavior; in the case of a single organization we analyze what units are fulfilling the organization's mission and which need encouragement to get back on board; we also analyze how an organization relates (or does not relate) to the communities and populations it serves.

Community practice in all its forms is about creating more socially just organizations, communities, polities, and policies—it is about *change* through essential processes of organizing, development, planning, and social action (Weil 1993). Given the complexity of the service, systems at all levels are generally expected to experience some problems in functioning or responding to changing needs. They may benefit from consultation to move closer to the goals of a more socially just society or to create a learning organization (Senge et al. 2006). Community practitioners are not surprised when some human service organizations seek to maintain their stable status quo. With community-based organizations practitioners are quite likely to be among those who work to hold public and nonprofit agencies accountable to their missions and the people they serve (Medoff and Sklar 1994). Because of this focus on change, community practitioners are more likely to engage with concepts that relate to open systems and dynamic systems theories. As Robbins et al. state: "A distinctive feature of open dynamic systems is that they are both self-maintaining and self-transforming" (2006:40). They also discuss the basic reality that systems, between and among themselves, interact and interrelate in a nonlinear fashion and are inevitably engaged in or responding to change (41–43). Functioning as a self-maintaining and self-transforming system is a valuable and attainable goal for community organizations and community-based agencies.

One of the principles of system theory is its focus on adaptation, which is usually viewed as seeking a balance between systems with diverse goals. However, community practitioners seek not to help people adjust to unjust organizations or political systems, but to adapt organizations, institutions, and policies so that they can better and more justly serve communities. As social workers learn more about ecological theory in the natural/environmental sciences, it is likely that a more congruent ecological theory for social work will be developed (Rotabi 2004).

Essentially in community practice, the utility of dynamic systems theory is that it provides tools and language to analyze the connections, misconnections, and disconnections of communities, organizations, institutions, and societies in order to develop positive strategies for progressive social change. A principle of community practice is to understand and improve the well-being and life opportunities of groups and communities in their social and built environments. We can use systems analysis to assist in these complex tasks.

STRUCTURAL THEORY

This branch of theory is generally congruent with the values and practice strategies of community and development workers. As Finn and Jacobson (2008a) note, "Structuralists view the problems that confront social work as a fundamental, inherent part of the present social order wherein social institutions function in ways that systematically work to maintain social inequalities along lines of class, race, gender, sexual orientation, citizenship and so on" (182).

Finn and Jacobson cite Carniol (1990), and Mullaly (2007) as recent contributors to structuralist theory. This approach has connections both to classical Marxism and to other conflict theories. Structuralists use conflict theory and do not shrink from conflict, viewing it as necessary to redress social wrongs. Brager and Specht (1973) encourage use of the principle of least contest—seeking problem resolution at the least conflictual level feasible and escalating strategies as needed. Structuralists seek to develop and maintain power within grassroots and advocacy groups to build a critical mass of people and organizations to pursue needed social change—for example, the need for universal health insurance in the United States, or the need to increase opportunities for education and employment for the Muslim populations now in Europe—who chafe against their sense of exclusion and lack of opportunity.

A common criticism of structuralism holds that the theory casts clients as hapless victims. To us this seems to be a rather dated critique in that many community practitioners with structuralist views work consistently in mutual planning with members of low-wealth communities, knowing directly that community members are active agents engaged in efforts to improve their situations and communities. You do not have to see people as victims to recognize that poor and minority populations are often subjected to exploitation and conditions of inequality. Consider the women working in the maquiladoras on the U.S. border with Mexico; consider children in Southeast Asia locked in factories for 12-hour days or tied to looms to weave rugs for the upscale Western market; consider also the thousands of women in India who have joined the Self Employed Women's Association (SEWA) to develop their own businesses, learn trades, and become entrepreneurs. And consider the widows of rural Afghanistan, marginalized from society, and their new work with the NGO Morning Star Enterprises (2008), first making blankets to keep refugees warm—and parlaying that work into a major contract with the United Nations to make blankets for many worldwide relief efforts. The distinction between "victims" and successful microenterprise entrepreneurs is often that "victims" are isolated in their troubles, while "actors" have been able to join with a community group and/ or an NGO to work together for self-sufficiency, social support, and community development. Helping to make connections among people dealing with similar oppressive situations is a hallmark of community practice. Structural analyses, accompanied with Freierian analysis and reflection—conscientization— can move groups from acquiescing to oppression to working together to ensure their rights and well-being (Center for Participatory Change 2007). Although some of the structural theory literature may still focus on victims, workers on the ground with structuralist viewpoints see the oppression, and work with people to create new visions and new realities.

CRITICAL THEORIES

Critical theories in the social sciences related to social issues such as postcolonialism, feminism, and racism have developed rapidly in the last two decades in response to concerns about the limitations, ideologies, and biases recognized in the existing body of social science theory. Many established theoretical traditions had not taken into consideration the voices and perspectives of groups that have been marginalized in diverse ways. Often academic studies have made marginalized populations objects of study rather than active subjects and research participants who are able to articulate alternative explanations, explain their reality, and provide perspectives and grounding missing from earlier accounts. We do not have to go far into the past to recover perspectives that held, for example, that an adult female could not be both an "adult" and a "woman," as Braverman (1988) documented in her survey research on descriptors of adults compared with descriptors of women. Study results indicated that to be an adult one should be autonomous, able to make and act on decisions, and independent, whereas to fulfill the expected gender role of women at the time, a woman was expected to be dependent, appropriately feminine, and reliant on others to make major decisions. Less than twenty-five years ago, some schools of social work were still using human behavior texts that considered women as rather lesser creatures—less rational and less competent than their male counterparts, who embodied the "standard" human being. Women therefore could not represent norms for adult human behavior.

Theories and diagnostic categories that viewed homosexual men and women as deviant, sick, or psychologically maladjusted come from the even more recent past. The DSM finally removed the diagnosis of homosexuality as a disease in 1986. Somewhat further back in history, racist and pejorative notions permeated theories and studies of African Americans and many other people of color—anybody who did not fit the expected categories.

It is therefore not surprising that when African Americans, Asians, Africans, Latin Americans, and women from many parts of the world attained advanced "Western-style" educations and themselves became social scientists/researchers, they soon documented very different pictures of their cultures and the capacities of their people. From this work very different theories soon challenged the previous research of stalwart members of academic communities. Critical theorists raised uncomfortable questions about whose interests were being served in previous social "scientific" views of the world and its many peoples. They questioned the biases and the unacknowledged ideologies of many theorists and researchers and proposed new approaches to think about intercultural communication and interactions. Indeed, Agger (1998) among others has described the academic ferment as a "crises of theories" in the world of the social sciences.

The challenges to theories have also related to research approaches, identifying operating ideologies instead of objective scientific reasoning. The possibility of *objectivity* itself has been challenged. And beginning in Europe, new modes of considering the knowledge base of social science as well as how knowledge is ratified emerged to claim that knowledge and theories are socially constructed. Theories and the social phenomena that provoke them are not given in a single "objective" form, but will be seen and understood differently by different people from different social statuses and cultures, at different times. In critical theory terms, these differences represent different "standpoints" that will shape our views and color our interpretations of events or interactions. Critical theories challenge the certainties of positivism.

Critical theory, a multiplicity of theories united by several shared principles, generally includes postcolonial, postmodern, poststructural, feminist, and critical race theories. As noted, they all offer a critique of positivism, and all are particularly concerned about power and its uses, histories of domination, and patterns of devaluing differences by those in positions of high status. In contrast to these problematic issues, all critical theories also focus on the energy of human agency and the possibilities of social transformation through human agency and action. Knowledge is one of the areas questioned in critical theories because of its connections to power and risks of misuse (Foucault 1980).

The range of perspectives and ideas in the conglomerate of critical theories has engendered the authors' appreciation and respect for the direct discussion of complex concepts by Finn and Jacobson (2008a) and their careful work to realistically apply several important critical theory concepts to social work practice. They also explain how critical theories have helped to shape their own work on social justice and just practice (2008a). We trace their line of reasoning particularly in relation to carefully building social justice concerns into practice.

Finn and Jacobsen (2008a) demystify the essential concept of *discourse*, explaining that as used in critical theory it is not a means of discussion, but rather examining structures of knowledge and how they shape the ways we perceive certain realities. Finn and Jacobson state: "Thus, the concept of social work discourse brings critical attention to the mutual constitution of systems of knowledge—what counts as 'truth,' and systems of practice—what counts as problem and as intervention" (Finn and Jacobson 2008a:188).

For example, what do we discuss professionally—what can be talked about as compared to what is intentionally left unsaid? What were the multiple messages and judgments in a phrase that used to be heard frequently about lower income clients—that she or he "was not oriented to insight therapy?" How have words that express strong, positive societal values of compassion and connection such as "social welfare" and "liberal" come to be so devalued and discounted? Why is American culture so disdainful of "dependence" when all of us begin our lives totally dependent on others, and for most of us, the last stage of our lives will involve some level of dependence on the kindness of others? Finn and Jacobson ask: "What are the social and political consequences of omitting discussion of *interdependence* and *social* as well as *personal responsibility* from the welfare debates? These are questions of discourse" (2008a:189).

Domination in critical theory does not just connote power over someone; it also connects people and the "logic of capitalism." Several American scholars have sought to build on the work of Antonio Gramsci, who thought seriously about why so many people of moderate to lower income levels "buy-in" to the interests of powerful elites. Gramsci adopted the term *hegemony* to indicate this kind of nonviolent control. He discusses the ways that many people participate almost unthinkingly in the very systems that oppress them (Gramsci 1987). Finn and Jacobson conclude that they find Gramsci's work very useful in "helping us to think critically about questions of meaning, power, and history in the making of social problems" (2008a:190).

Oppression, Finn and Jacobson state, is a part of each of the major critical theory concepts and relates to the power and privilege of those in positions of relative status coupled with the exploitation and deprivation that can result for others. With Patricia Hill Collins, they hold that those in the dominant culture, not just those who are oppressed, should be studied and considered as we analyze social problems—particularly poverty (Hill Collins 2000).

Feminist theory recognizes that the lived reality of many women illustrates the concepts discussed above and also posits ways that women can seek and gain empowerment, that is, the ability to control their own lives and to influence community and political life. One of these means is through support and solidarity, recognizing common cause with other women; a related approach is through women engaging in community organizing and community development. The authors have written about both of these issues and see such involvement as a means of self-development through community development (Weil 1986; Weil, Gamble, and Williams 1998).

Critical race theory is the response to the long history of scientifically justified racism. These theories have examined the practice of racism as a part of everyday life as well as institutions and structures of society that perpetuate inequality and institutional racism. Women of color have done careful analyses of the intersection of the double oppressions of race and gender (Hill Collins 2000; hooks 1984). Recently, much more detailed work by African American and Latina theorists has enriched this area of study and should be part of any social work curriculum (Gutierrez and Lewis 1999; Moraga and Anzaldua 1984).

BUILDING A THEORETICAL PERSPECTIVE

Community practitioners in every part of the world will bring their own culture, their own languages (both of which frame the ways that we think), their own worldviews, their own values, knowledge, and perspectives to the challenges of community practice. Each of us in our own settings around the globe will therefore select differentially from the major streams of theory, knowledge, and relevant research. And from the communities that we work with we should add cultural content, specific theories, local knowledge, and approaches that can deal most relevantly with local, regional, national, and international issues and needs.

For example, the theoretical perspectives of many community practitioners in India will be shaped by the philosophy and theory of Mohandas Gandhi, grounded in human rights, equality, respect for diversity in culture and religion, and culturally sustained development (Gandhi 1956, 1995; Shiva 2005), as well as by the theories and methods that they study, which likely draw from both Eastern and Western sources. Similarly, practitioners throughout Latin America are often steeped in the theory and pedagogical approaches of Paulo Freire (2000, 2005), focused on *conscientization, reflection,* and *action* for social justice as described in *Pedagogy of the Oppressed.* Nelson Mandela, who following twenty-six years of imprisonment, led South Africans from the terrors of apartheid to a new democracy founded on human rights through a largely peaceful revolution (Mandela, *Long Walk to Freedom,* 1995), is a worldwide hero of liberation, human rights, and progressive social change. These three global icons of community work have left legacies in their writings as well as the extraordinary exemplars of their lives and commitments.

Other current leaders have had major impacts on worldwide problems. Wangari Maathi, who found creative ways to restore greenbelts in Africa and developed a major social movement promoting environmental restoration, has been recognized throughout Africa and the world. Aung San Suu Kyi, under house arrest for twelve of the last eighteen years in Burma for human rights work, is the symbolic leader of her people. She received the Nobel Peace Prize in 2007 and continues to work for human rights even from confinement. Another leader is Gro Harlem Brundtland, a former prime minister of Norway, who chaired the UN World Commission on Environment and Development, leading to the modern understanding of sustainable development, and who later headed the World Health Organization. These women leaders are exemplars of work for the kinds of change that community practice promotes. We often internalize much of our facilitative and leadership style from study, practice, and working with or reading the works of wise mentors. The six leaders just noted are internationally recognized and respected. There are also excellent mentors closer to home—we can learn the arts as well as the skills of facilitation from working with and or observing exemplary local leaders whether they are community members or other community practitioners. We combine the skills we practice and observe with knowledge to hone our own ways of sharing and nurturing leadership with groups. The types of facilitation and leadership development that we seek to impart will be shaped by the purposes of our engagement, the community's goals, and the model (or models) of practice employed.

CONCLUSION

As you work with diverse communities, groups, and organizations as well as their contexts, it is important for you to consider which theories in each framework category are most appropriate for the levels of engagement and kinds of work you are undertaking. For example in working with a community on multiple sustainable development projects, you might select self-efficacy theory and the strengths perspective for work with individuals; with community decision-making groups you might employ task group approaches; and you might use sustainable development theory to guide the overall project work. Our engagement with communities inevitably involves us with different scales of social organization. When current theories do not fit the work, you may theorize with community members and construct and test hypotheses, then construct theories of action and change, for the specific practice situations.

Although theories are formed from processes of rational analysis, they inescapably also emerge from the worldview (*weltanschauung*), culture, and experiences of those who perform the analyses whether in the natural or social sciences. Thomas Kuhn has contributed greatly to our understanding of the development of theory and processes of research through his work *The Structure of Scientific Revolutions* (1970), which examines the ways that scientific knowledge is developed and tested. Kuhn argues that the process of knowledge development and testing are almost always subject to the often unexamined operation of a *paradigm*—an accepted model or pattern of how things work (Kuhn 1970:23). Paradigms, whether acknowledged or unacknowledged, guide our observations and help to shape definitions and concepts; they also affect our notions of causality and change. The time-honored traditions of "normal science" are thus shaped not only from the basic principles of Western scientific tradition—systematic observations of nature and social systems—but from assumptions, beliefs, cultural biases, and ways of thinking that are embedded in the operating or mainstream paradigm in a particular disciplinary area. *Paradigms* are composed of basic axioms and beliefs that codify established methods and approaches for studying and understanding nature and human behavior.

Paradigms shape how we perceive the behavior or phenomena that we are observing; they form and constrain our development and application of theories; and they direct and organize theory construction. In short, paradigms are powerful influences on how we learn about ourselves and our world and how we develop our views of what is possible and impossible. Paradigms can be a great boon in that they encourage research and knowledge development and provide structures to work from, such as basic scientific methods.

However, paradigms can also blind us to changing needs and changing environments that would be obvious if we were not thinking and acting within a predetermined structure of thought and intervention. In both natural and social sciences, changes in reality that do not "fit" the current mainstream paradigms may be ignored or refuted. Kuhn (1970) provides numerous useful historical examples of mistaken paradigms beginning with the early Western theory that the sun rotated around the earth—replaced by Copernicus's theory holding that the planets rotate around the sun. His paradigm of heliocentric planetary motion still stands, long verified by scientific testing. A current paradigm accepted by the scientific community and supported by much scientific evidence enunciates the reality of global warming, which has been tested in many parts of the world by scientists in multiple disciplines. However, it has taken decades for mounting scientific evidence to be widely accepted, partly because of political positions in some nations that held it to be an "unproven theory." This opposition was tied to the risks and costs of alleviating the serious consequences of global warming for the people of the earth and the natural environment. Politically, if we recognize the problem, we are obligated to respond to its potentially devastating results. In the United States it took not only the work and advocacy of thousands of scientists, but the work of many activists— including Albert Gore Jr., whose book *An Inconvenient Truth* (2007) and documentary film of the same title—helped force acceptance of this scientific reality. In all parts of the world, investments to forestall negative consequences of global warming, changes in lifestyles, and adoption of new energy sources are required to respond to the realities of this now accepted paradigm that affects us all.

Although Kuhn wrote about the natural sciences, the same issues apply in the social sciences, where our worldview and often unacknowledged or unrecognized assumptions, values, beliefs, and particular research techniques shape our processes of research and thus color our findings (Mullaly 2007). Reed describes this process as follows:

> The concept of paradigm allows us to analyze the relationship between scientific thought in a discipline and the social context in which it arises. Paradigms help those who hold them to locate and organize information, select methods for their work, and shape meaning for the results. Paradigms are grounded in ideology— they represent certain idea sets and values about the way things are and ought to be. They organize and order our perceptions of nature according to their rules. Theories are developed by following the paradigm's rules and when viewed through

the ideological lens of the paradigm, these theories appear reasonable to scientists, scholars, and others who share the paradigm. Practices that arise from a particular paradigm may not appear to be valid or reasonable to observers who do not follow the paradigm's rules or ideology. (Reed 2005:85)

Given the power that paradigms have over individual and public thought, we not only have to carefully examine the paradigms we ourselves have accepted, community practitioners around the world continually have to actively oppose negative paradigms that demean the people we work with—particularly the most vulnerable and impoverished. Most nations have their own versions of the pejorative views of the poor that still have major effects in Anglo-American social welfare policies evidenced in carryovers from Social Darwinism and the Elizabethan Poor Laws and embodied in terms such as "unworthy poor" or "deadbeat dads," and assumptions that individuals could—if they were not "lazy," "indolent," or "inferior"—easily work their way out of poverty. These negative views deny the reality of market economies that depend on surplus labor, and they deny the essential humanity of the dispossessed. Critically, these views also deny the reality of structural causes of social problems. Paradigms and political/economic beliefs are major aspects of shared "worldviews" on which policies and allocation are based. Locally and globally, community practitioners are among those working for the broad acceptance of new paradigms—promoting human flourishing and environmental protection that are grounded in principles of social, economic, and sustainable development

Given that macro-focused community practitioners from a variety of disciplines and professions engage in community practice throughout the world, an initial, critical analytic step in community work is to determine whether a particular theory or paradigm has relevance to a particular village, neighborhood, or city—examining the ideologies (political, social, scientific, and religious), philosophical underpinnings, cultural settings, and values of the community. A later step, if the theory proves useful, may be to test what aspects of the initial project or program (and what theoretical precepts) could be generalizable to other communities and what aspects need to be tailored anew to different settings.

As you move through reflection and discussions of the community practice models in the second part of this volume, give consideration not just to strategy, but to the knowledge and theory bases that should assist you in determining which approaches to action will work best in which practice situations and how you can theorize and use theories and positive paradigms to promote empowerment among the people you serve.

PART II

EIGHT MODELS OF COMMUNITY PRACTICE FOR THE TWENTY-FIRST CENTURY

In part II we analyze each model in turn to present the scope of concern, the basic process, and the theoretical underpinnings and conceptual understandings that are important to the model. In addition, we identify the primary roles, skills and competencies, used by practitioners for each model. Our end goal is to help successful community practitioners develop the knowledge and skills needed to engage in this important work.

The eight models represent types of work that we have actually engaged in or closely observed in the United States and other parts of the world. They are intended to provide a comparative framework for critiquing community practice approaches and to determine which approach seems most appropriate for the presenting context and needs of the community group. In chapters 5 through 12, as we describe each of the models in turn, we incorporate examples from a wide range of practitioners in different parts of the world. The case material, sometimes found in smaller segments throughout the chapter, with longer case examples at the end of chapters, helps us connect with hundreds of community practice partners who are engaged in efforts to increase social justice and human rights all across the globe. Accompanying this text is a companion volume, *Community Practice Skills Workbook*, that presents additional case studies, experiential exercises, and issues for discussion. We hope the *CPS Workbook* will assist you in strengthening skills and deepening your thoughts about the people we serve.

The models as presented in the table and in our chapter discussions are discrete approaches to community practice and will help practitioners determine why a particular approach is more effective for certain outcomes than others. Paying close attention to desired outcomes, systems targeted for change, primary constituencies, and the scope of concern will help the practitioner determine which model, roles, and skills will be most successful in the community practice efforts they undertake. At the same time the practitioner needs to remain flexible and attentive to the nuances of changing contexts, power relationships, cultural and ethnic perspectives, historical overlays, ethical challenges, and opportunities for change. In the real world of practice, some mixing and sequencing of models may be the most effective choice. Because case examples are drawn from the real world, they often present lessons for more than one model.

Chapter 5, with its focus on neighborhood and community organizing, is a lengthy chapter because we provide a detailed discussion of how the worker can gain knowledge and practice skills necessary for community work. In the remaining chapters, we will not discuss skills development in as much detail, but will provide initial assessment and assignment suggestions, discuss groups of skills called for in each model, and direct the reader to additional exercises in the CPS Workbook. Most of the participatory group-assessment and self-assessment tools we will provide will be found in the CPS Workbook; however, some tools, tables, and figures that are designed to help clarify the model have been included in this volume.

Engaging with the exercises will help you to determine which approaches and skills best suit your own abilities, and to decide for which approaches you may wish to find partners and allies in order to bring a broader array of knowledge and skills to the tasks required to more effectively engage with communities.

5

NEIGHBORHOOD AND COMMUNITY ORGANIZING

In democratic countries the science of associations is the mother science; the progress of all the rest depends upon the progress it has made.

ALEXIS DE TOCQUEVILLE, 1835

We come and go, but the land is always here. And people who love it and understand it are the people who own it—for a little while.

WILLA CATHER, *O PIONEERS!*

INTRODUCTION

Pass Christian, a Mississippi coastal town, is located halfway between New Orleans and Mobile, Alabama. It has been hit twice by major hurricanes in recent years. On July 17, 1969, it was hit by Hurricane Camille, and then at 4:30 a.m. on August 29, 2005, it was hit by Hurricane Katrina. Winds of up to 130 miles per hour pummeled Pass Christian, and the storm surge that followed leveled the town for more than a half mile inland. The storm destroyed or damaged all but 500 or so homes; twenty-five residents of Pass Christian died as a result of the hurricane. Before Hurricane Katrina, the town had about 6,500 residents; more than two years after the devastation, only an estimated 4,000 have returned.

When City Attorney Malcolm Jones became the acting mayor of Pass Christian after the storm, he began to take stock of what and who was left. Jones soon realized the city had only three out of nineteen police cars left, no fire trucks, a failed sewer system, and only one public building was left standing. They had no cell phones, no telephones, and no electricity. Eighty percent of the residential buildings in the town and 98 percent of the commercial buildings had been "washed away as though nothing had ever been there" (Jones 2008:40).

Jones began to pull together the community's remaining leadership for the immediate tasks of rescue, recovering bodies, providing water and food for survivors, protecting the remaining town from looters and "disaster sightseers," and responding to an entire community that was basically homeless. The scale of the emergency could have overwhelmed Jones and his fellow community leaders who were working 18- to 20-hour shifts.

A week after the storm, the director of AmeriCorps in St. Louis came to Pass Christian with a team of AmeriCorps volunteers. Jones was skeptical. He needed people with skills. What he soon learned was that the residents in Pass Christian and the AmeriCorps volunteers could establish a good partnership. Together, the community members and the volunteers surveyed the primary needs of the community and sites from which to coordinate services. They worked together to distribute food and water, to manage tents and communication centers, to begin repairs to homes and replanting gardens, as well as to manage the emergency shelters. The AmeriCorps volunteers stayed for more than two years and were especially helpful in providing the "hands and boots" to move and distribute the volume of material and supplies that soon arrived in the town. Their efforts included helping to coordinate and direct the work of short-term volunteers who came from distant cities and towns. In return, the town folk cooked special meals for the AmeriCorps volunteers and made craft articles for them as they completed their tours of duty and were replaced by new team members. Jones wrote that upon facing the task of rebuilding the town that was physically devastated, "Our hearts were broken. These young people helped get us grounded again emotionally" (Jones 2008:41).

Neighborhood and community organizing takes place when people have face-to-face contact with each other, allowing them to feel connected to a place. Even though our ability to engage with people has been greatly facilitated with the use of electronic communication technology, we still feel the need to belong to a place. Exploring a "sense of place" has always been the special province of poets, novelists, city planners, ecologists, and bioregionalists (Berry 1992; Kriesberg 1999; Lynch 1960, Stegner 1993; Xu 1995). A local place where one can experience face-to-face communication is a space of collective identity and sociocultural heritage. It is a physical place for developing cultural awareness and providing the soil where your roots can take hold. It is a landscape that provides opportunity for a variety of human purposes and the place where childhood memories and morals germinate. The social planning and social service organizations in which most human services professionals work are rooted in a local place (Hardcastle, Powers, and Wenocur 2004). Community as a geographic place has a number of useful definitions in social work literature (Chaskin 1997; Cottrell 1976; Marley and Rogge 2008; Martinez-Brawley 1990; Rogge 1995).

Generally, we think of a neighborhood, parish, village, township, or even a large municipality as the geographic locations where neighborhood and community organizing can occur (Gamble and Weil 1995; Hallman 1984; Homan 2008; Lee 1997; Mizrahi 2009; Weil, 1996). Although it is possible to have statewide and regional organizations where face-to-face communication occurs on an irregular basis, building consensus for neighborhood and community organizing requires the trust that grows from personal contacts. This neighborhood and community organizing model does not exclude developing links and learning opportunities with people and organizations outside the community. Rather, it means that the direction of collective action will be decided by people who reside in and are connected to a geographic place. The focus of work happens in a close geographic setting where people interact on a regular basis to plan, to learn, and to take action.

SCOPE OF CONCERN

Neighborhood and community organizing has two main goals: building the organization and taking action for progressive change. Although these goals can develop in tandem, the initial focus must always be on building a strong and effective organization. When community members develop their capacity to study critical issues that relate to the quality of their lives they are also developing the leadership qualities and skills to make an organization strong and effective.

Rubin and Rubin used the term *social production* to describe the complex process that includes the development of the organization, its ability to provide local services, and the emergence of community empowerment and capacity building. When community members engage with external social, economic, and political systems through a formal mechanism (e.g., electoral politics, litigation) or through direct-action campaigns (e.g., media events, and demonstrations), they describe this process as *social mobilization* (2007:17).

Developing leadership capacity and organizational maintenance capacity are important skills for people who want to build an organization. Simple tasks such as developing agendas, maintaining records of discussions and decisions, keeping account of dues and other resources, forming formal organizational structures, establishing decision-making procedures, and coming to consensus on democratic and respectful rules of organizational conduct are not innate. All of these organizational building skills must be learned, and they are best learned within the context of the social, cultural, economic, and environmental conditions of the geographic location. As people learn these skills, they increase their capacity to build a strong organization and to contribute to the general social capital of their community (Aspen Institute 1996; Castelloe 1999; Krishna and Bunch 1997). Ohmer and Korr (2006) reviewed recent literature on community practice interventions and, drawing from the work of a number of other scholars (Itzhaky and York 2002; Knight 1997; Vidal 1992; York and Havassy 1997; Zachery 1998), concluded that organizing community members can "facilitate personal and collective competencies among participants and in-crease their connections to their communities, including increasing self-esteem, personal empowerment, community empowerment, leadership and political skills, and community pride and belonging" (142).

The second goal of neighborhood and community organizing, as already noted, is to take action for progressive change. This means that the community members must find ways to build an organization that will have the capacity to reduce an identified negative community condition or install a positive condition. It is the organization's ability to make progressive changes that will improve the quality of life for a large number of residents.

Frequently, new neighborhood groups are organized to prevent something bad from happening (e.g., to stop the toxic waste dump, to stop the school from closing, to stop the drug dealers from coming into the neighborhood). Some-times, too, neighborhood groups organize around efforts to help something good to happen (e.g., to get a preschool or teen recreational program started, to orga-nize a cooperative grocery store, to establish a cultural center). Whatever the objective, organizations can consider a number of approaches when they are planning for action. Engagement with social, economic, and political systems can be *collaborative* in nature, such as problem solving and persuasion; or it can be more of a *campaign*, such as political maneuvering, bargaining, and negotia-tion; or it can involve *adversarial conflict*, such as direct action, disruption, boy-cotts, civil disobedience, and noncooperation (Brager et al. 1987). Successful community organizing actions can have positive outcomes for local and regional residents (Ewalt, Freeman, and Poole 1998; Uphoff, Esman, and Krishna 1998).

Changing ourselves to become active community members and making our organizations more effective is easier than changing the well-established and powerful forces that sustain social injustice, unfair economic policies, and envi-ronmental degradation. In their review of recent literature on community prac-tice interventions, Ohmer and Korr (2006) noted that "it may be easier for com-munity practice interventions to positively affect citizen participation and its effects on participants (i.e., collective action, personal and political skills of participants, etc.) than it is to influence and improve complex physical, social, and economic problems in poor communities" (142). For this reason, it is im-portant for community organizers to effectively engage the community partici-pants in an analysis of power, an exploration of local economics and livelihood opportunities, and an investigation into social policies that support basic needs and open opportunities for education and asset development. Although using collaborative or campaign strategies would be the propitious way to improve conditions affecting quality of life, often external targets remain intransigent. The kinds of changes that must take place to ensure basic human rights for all community members and to provide significant economic opportunities for the poor require "an analysis of the root causes of inequality, injustice, and oppression, with a particular emphasis on examining the fundamental distribution of resources and power . . . the reformulation of social goals, and the reordering of policy priorities" (Reisch 2005b:290–91). Indeed, changing policy priorities often requires confrontation and direct-action strategies. Social researchers have established that the increase in community capacity has great potential to change local economic and agricultural production methods as well as health, nutrition, and water supply practices (Krishna, Uphoff, and Esman 1997). However, additional research is needed to understand the effects that community-level organizing can have on larger social, environmental, and economic changes that often are controlled by external institutions.

Throughout this chapter we refer to two case examples. One is included at the end of this chapter—"South African Community Work in Practice: Langa KwaNobuhle Self Help and Resource Exchange"—and the other is in the *Community Practice Skills Workbook*—"Farmer-to-Farmer Integrated Rural Development for Smallholders in Guatemala: Organization in the Face of Natural Disaster and Civil Conflict." It may be helpful to read through the two case studies now so that you can envision how neighborhood and community organizing might work. Discussion questions for each case example are available in the *CPS Workbook*.

The Guatemala example describes work with the Cakchiquel Indians to improve their crop production for increased nutrition and better health outcomes in the region. The organizing and technical assistance was done by World Neighbors with funding from Oxfam America. The example at the end of this chapter is from a local organizing effort in the Eastern Cape of South Africa. The organizer of the Langa KwaNobuhle Self Help and Resource Exchange (SHARE) program, a social worker, describes the difficulties of organizing a community that had been oppressed by years of apartheid policies. In both cases, local organizing was able to produce successes even though the people faced formidable barriers to making progress. Comparing these cases with neighborhood and community work in your own local setting can provide special insight as you try to understand issues of context, history, and possibility. Perhaps someone working in a local community organization would make a presentation to your class or write a three- or four-page example for use in your class for comparison purposes.

BASIC PROCESS: TEN GUIDING STEPS

Many authors provide guidance for engaging in effective community organizing as it relates to neighborhoods and communities (Bobo, Kendall, and Max

1991; Bradshaw, Soifer, and Gutierrez 1994; Brager, Specht, and Torczyner 1987; Brown 2006; Brueggemann 2006; Eichler 2007; Fisher 1994; Homan 2008; Minkler 2004; Netting, Kettner, and McMurtry 2008; Rubin and Rubin 2005, 2007). There are many sources of wisdom to help make this work understandable and available to the community practice worker.

Drawing from community practice literature and from our own knowledge and experience, we have developed guidance for each model that provides an approach for engagement with groups and organizations for that model. Some of the guiding steps we present are used in multiple models. Each model represents a distinct approach for practice based primarily on the desired outcome, systems targeted for change, and scope of concern.

What follows are ten guiding steps for this model to help neighborhoods and communities come together to improve their quality of life (see figure 5.1). Rarely does organizing of any kind take place in a step-by-step linear fashion. Steps may be repeated or evolve in a different sequence depending on the context and timing of organizational development. In addition to the process outlined here, a community practice worker must be grounded in the values of social justice and human rights, and have a deep understanding of local and global contexts described in chapter 2.

1. Identify and establish a *working relationship* with a neighborhood or community. This relationship includes clarifying with yourself and community leaders why you are doing this work and under whose auspices you are engaged with the community. In this initial phase, you must take care to be a co-learner with members of the community, becoming a student of their experiences and perspectives. The organizer who shows respect for the local knowledge and appreciation for the historical context of the community's conditions will have a greater chance of becoming a community partner (Castelloe and Watson 2000). Appreciation for the community's history helps the organizer prepare for a joint analysis of the problems and collaborative development of an action plan.

People are motivated to form groups for change—whether social, economic, or environmental—because they have the freedom to organize, they realize that acting alone has less effect on the condition, they have ideas of how to improve conditions for their community, and they believe they can succeed in making a change (Zander 1990). Imminent threats can also spur people into community action. For example, people can be motivated to try to change outcomes when a corporate decision is made to relocate a community's largest employer to another state or country, uprooting economic opportunity; or with the forced removal of a population, as occurred with Native Americans in the United States, squatter settlements around Latin American cities, and communities-of-color in South Africa. In addition, pressures from long-term oppression, neglect, and violence

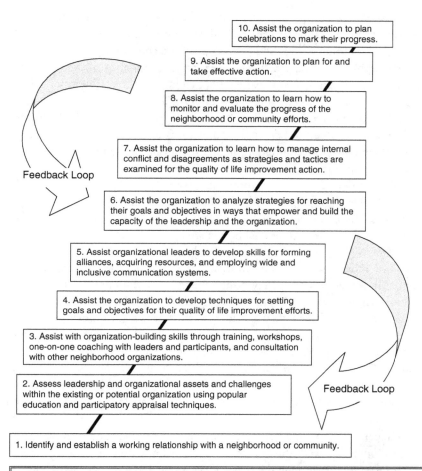

10. Assist the organization to plan celebrations to mark their progress.

9. Assist the organization to plan for and take effective action.

8. Assist the organization to learn how to monitor and evaluate the progress of the neighborhood or community efforts.

7. Assist the organization to learn how to manage internal conflict and disagreements as strategies and tactics are examined for the quality of life improvement action.

Feedback Loop

6. Assist the organization to analyze strategies for reaching their goals and objectives in ways that empower and build the capacity of the leadership and the organization.

5. Assist organizational leaders to develop skills for forming alliances, acquiring resources, and employing wide and inclusive communication systems.

4. Assist the organization to develop techniques for setting goals and objectives for their quality of life improvement efforts.

3. Assist with organization-building skills through training, workshops, one-on-one coaching with leaders and participants, and consultation with other neighborhood organizations.

2. Assess leadership and organizational assets and challenges within the existing or potential organization using popular education and participatory appraisal techniques.

Feedback Loop

1. Identify and establish a working relationship with a neighborhood or community.

Guiding steps for facilitators/organizers working with neighborhood and community groups. Feedback loops represent returning to previous steps for rethinking when new information is acquired or alternative perspectives need to be incorporated.

FIGURE 5.1 **Guiding Steps and Feedback Loops for Community Organizers**

can motivate people when a catalytic event occurs to bring them together. Sometimes a neighborhood response to a local issue can lead to a regional or national movement. Examples are the Montgomery, Alabama, bus boycott in 1955–1956 that touched off the activist phase of the American civil rights movement, and the campaign against violence in Northern Ireland that evolved from actions taken by Betty Williams and Mairead Corrigan in 1976. A few brave people's work to transform a neighborhood may eventually lead to the transformation of a whole nation.

2. **Assess leadership and organizational** *assets and challenges* **within the existing or potential organization.** This process requires engaging with individuals, small groups, and different sectors of the community to identify existing strengths and resources (Kretzmann and McKnight 1993); to specify the barriers to positive organizational development; to recognize the historical perspectives regarding social, cultural, economic, and environmental justice; to identify embedded resiliencies; and to determine people's visions for the future. This engagement can be accomplished by using a range of participatory techniques. We make the assumption that most communities today are composed of diverse populations that are the result of forced and voluntary regional and global migration. The various groups comprising today's multicultural populations will likely have different norms and expectations for creating community. Because such differences loom large in their day-to-day existence, often groups cannot see the more distant benefit and strength that can come from joining together.

When groups initially focus on their differences, *facilitated intergroup dialogue* can sometimes effectively bring individuals and groups together to promote learning about each other's strengths (Dessel, Rogge, and Garlington 2006). This type of dialogue works to open the lines of communication among people with polarized perspectives and enables them to discover shared values and common goals. In addition, techniques developed in South America, Asia, and Africa known as *popular education* and *participatory appraisal* can also be successful in eliciting the real and varied voices of neighborhood and community members (Castelloe and Gamble 2005; Chambers 1997, 2002; VeneKlasen and Miller 2002).

In recent years, oil and gas companies have aggressively sought and received permission to drill wells throughout the Rocky Mountain federal lands (stretching from Montana through the states of Wyoming and Colorado, all the way to New Mexico) and, in the process destroyed the mountains and contaminated the water and grazing lands. Formerly, these federal landholdings were leased primarily to ranchers for cattle grazing and were used by hunters, fishermen, and outdoor enthusiasts for recreational and spiritual renewal purposes. In Montana people were able to prevent wholesale drilling of oil and gas wells because environmentalists, ranchers, and hunters were able to overcome their differences and entered into dialogue to learn why each group so valued the beauty and natural resource of this unspoiled land (Herring 2008). When people understand and appreciate each other's perspectives, powerful associations can be created.

In the process of assessing leadership and organizational assets and challenges in a community, the worker can explore the kinds of changes the community has in mind, how they see their future and that of their children, what the community values about their particular location, and how they view the forces that keep negative conditions in place. This step also helps the facilitator develop respectful engagement behaviors and identify the organization's strengths.

3. **Assist with *organization building skills* through training, workshops, one-on-one coaching with leaders and participants, and consultation with neighboring organizations.** This process might involve participatory assessment of community assets and deficits through the use of community mapping; well-being ranking; or difference analysis based on characteristics such as gender, age, social groups, or occupations (Chambers 1997, 2002). In addition, this step might provide an opportunity to facilitate workshops on understanding the various forms of power such as *power over* (including *visible* and *hidden power*), *power with,* and *power to,* which are more collaborative uses of power (Vene-Klasen and Miller, 2002). This step might also involve visits to nearby communities that have struggled with social, economic, or environmental change and were successful in taking action to improve negative conditions. Building such regional connections with communities working on similar issues has a powerful ability to diminish the isolation often felt by communities struggling with a strong adversary.

4. **Assist the organization to develop techniques for *setting goals and objectives* for their quality of life improvement efforts.** Facilitating discussions of social, economic, and environmental justice issues of concern to this particular neighborhood or community is a precursor to discussions of goal setting. Workshops help the community members learn about alternative decision-making techniques and encourage practice in stating specific goals and indicators that will help the community document progress essential to this process. Questions for starting dialogue should relate to what is best about the community and its people. For example, typical questions might include, "What would you like to preserve in the community?" or "Identify things that tell you this is a good place to work, play, raise a family, stay healthy, or grow old." Generally, this discussion includes ideas of changes that should occur within the community itself as well as needed changes that are external to the neighborhood or community. Follow-up questions might relate to future visions and how the community will look with improvements in twenty years. Along with changes that need to occur within the community, members of the community will need to identify internal assets and strengths as well as barriers to progress. It is of particular importance to include a discussion of the fundamental structural and institutional forces that perpetuate conditions of poverty, exclusion from resources and opportunities, barriers to economic and livelihood development, and environmental pollution.

To facilitate a full, open exchange of ideas, these discussions must take place in settings that allow all the people who represent the diversity of the community to have a say. Sometimes cultural norms or embedded traditions require that the first level of discussions take place in segregated spaces (e.g., for women or for people of different cultural traditions, sexual orientations, ages, or religious beliefs) to feel safe in discussion. Training for the whole group can emphasize the importance of cultural, economic, social, and religious diversity for building strong organizations and communities. Training can also include decision-making techniques, planning for cycles of goal setting, action, evaluation, and reflection, and learning methods to evaluate outcomes that result from their efforts (see figure 1.2, Continuous Sustainable Community Development, in chapter 1, and the "Cardstorming" technique in the *CPS Workbook*).

5. Assist organizational leaders to develop *skills for forming alliances, acquiring resources, and employing wide and inclusive communication systems.* Helping community leaders to develop effective communication methods that reach out to all members of the community can assist the organization to grow in a transparent and open way. Sometimes organizations become secretive in an attempt to hide their mistakes in development. Even though the development of an organization may have many bumps and stumbles, a secretive organization where only the "in crowd" is welcome or "in the loop" of what is happening will never become successful in building strength or accomplishing its progressive objectives. Therefore, it is essential that communication remain open and that any new participants should always feel welcome.

In addition, helping community members take account of their own economic and social power to build their organization is a way to identify and vitalize the community's assets, including leadership, knowledge, materials, and connections. An assessment of the extent and strength of networks community members already have *outside* their community will be valuable information. This process relates to the concept of "bridging social capital," which we will discuss more fully later in this chapter. In any community action effort, internal strength is as important as external allies. This step also involves building bridges among members of the community with various groups outside the neighborhood or community that might be supportive of their efforts, such as the initial process of identifying and making contact with external funding sources and other like-minded organizations.

6. Assist the organization to analyze *strategies for reaching their goals and objectives in ways that empower and build the capacity* of the leadership and the organization. This process requires consideration of both ethical and effective actions. Minkler and Pies (2004) suggest that community organizing and community practice can be ethically problematic for social workers, health educators, and community facilitators because of conflicting loyalties. For example, a social worker may be challenged by the conflict that arises between his or her internalized professional commitment to work for social justice and the

very real need to start from the point where the local group is in regard to its needs and goals. It is easy to impose one's own agenda when first introduced to blatant social injustice. Minkler and Pies suggest facilitators take time to analyze problems related to the following issues: "(1) conflicting loyalties, (2) dealing with funding sources, (3) eliciting real rather than symbolic participation, (4) addressing cross-cultural miscommunication and real or perceived racism, (5) the unanticipated consequences of organizing, and (6) the matter of whose 'common good' is being addressed through the organizing effort" (2004:117).

In addition to the International Code of Ethics (IFSW/IASSW, 2004), each country has a code for professional conduct and ethics that should be the guide for professional behavior. Dolgoff, Loewenberg, and Harrington (2008) provide an "ethical principles screen" as a guide when professional codes fail to provide specific guidance.

Although the social work organizer has an ethical responsibility to work for social justice and human rights, progress toward such goals, and the strategies to reach them must be identified and affirmed by the members of the community. The organizer/facilitator may have differences of opinion with community members about how particular problems are best tackled. However, the organizer's primary role is to help the community members determine their own strategies and to explore the outcomes and risks of particular strategies.

The organizer/facilitator in the example from South Africa at the end of this chapter demonstrates how she had to maneuver between polarizing and dangerous political factions as she organized in the waning years of apartheid. The Langa KwaNobuhle SHARE community group had to carefully evaluate each source of potential funds to help the organization because some funds were offered by apartheid institutions to "buy off" the organization. Other funds were offered by groups outside South Africa but could be accessed only with the approval of South African groups for whom conflict strategies were seen as necessary to bring about change. The organizer/facilitator struggled with both ethical and practical dilemmas. As funding opportunities were evaluated, many local and international financial resources were rejected to preserve the organization's neutrality.

Discussion of strategies requires that the community group have a full dialogue about the interim goal they will reach as the result of an action. In the Center for Victims of Torture's "New Tactics in Human Rights" resource, strategies and tactics are differentiated as follows: "Strategy defines what is important to do, tactics embody how to do it. The relationship between 'the what' and 'the how' is an important one in understanding—and demystifying—the concepts of strategy and tactics. Tactics—which may be activities, systems, techniques or even institutions—are one of the key building blocks of strategy" (Johnson 2004:19). Starting the analysis of how to make change by considering tactics has the potential to get a group's discussion closer to the conditions they hope to change and often makes it easier to see how the effort will affect the condition.

In the Guatemalan farmer-to-farmer example in the *CPS Workbook,* trained farmer "extensionists" created experimental plots on their own small acreage to show their neighbors and those from neighboring villages how to construct drainage ditches and build terraces. This example shows the very successful tactic of utilizing trusted and respected neighbors to be the teachers, and having those farmers/teachers turn their hillside farms into the school (Krishna and Bunch 1997).

As described in step 1, the strategies and tactics used to reach goals can be of a collaborative nature in which the community and the policy-making institutions share a common interest concerning needed changes. A second level of strategies can take the form of a campaign in which political maneuvering, bargaining, and negotiating are the primary methods used to reach the desired goals. When social change cannot occur because existing institutions and social structures rigidly resist the control of resources and opportunities, a more profound effort to bring about change may be needed. The third strategy level is contest or conflict that includes tactics such as direct action, disruption, and violation of normal behavior or legal norms through civil disobedience or noncooperation. Sometimes these three types of tactics are used in combination by different groups working for similar changes. In the Gandhian view, they would be used sequentially, with civil disobedience being the final stage that is taken only after less confrontational efforts to change the positions of those who keep discriminatory and oppressive policies in place have proven unsuccessful.

A strategy that has the capacity to move beyond conflict is intergroup dialogue work, also known as dialogue and deliberation. This strategy seeks to help groups with conflicting or opposing views explore each other's perspectives in a nonthreatening, facilitated dialogue (Dessel et al. 2006). Dialogue can lead from communication for understanding to forms of collaborative action described as *appreciative inquiry, future search,* and *study circles* (National Coalition for Dialogue and Deliberation 2007). Opportunities for dialogue work are expanding as people across the globe acquire experience with facilitated deliberation.

In many parts of the world where people feel they have few options for making their case against injustice and inhumanity, they may feel compelled to use civil disobedience. One of the objectives of nonviolent civil disobedience is to create awareness in the larger society that an oppressed group has been denied their human rights. Mohandas Gandhi and Martin Luther King Jr. both effectively used nonviolent civil disobedience in their efforts to obtain independence for India and civil rights for African Americans in the United States, respectively. In these circumstances resistance to negative structures, power building, and mobilization of allies can bring about social movements for change. However, nonviolence cannot succeed if those who hold complete power do not see the oppressed group as human, as was the case for Native Americans who sought redress against white colonialists, slaves in the United States in the 1860s, and the Jews in Nazi Germany in the 1940s (Brager, Specht, and Torczyner 1987).

Although the goals of community work are serious, strategies and tactics seem to be more effective when they possess an element of humor or fun. For example, in 1991, as part of their effort to gain public funding to fight HIV/AIDS, the Treatment Action Group of the AIDS Coalition to Unleash Power (ACT UP) wrapped a giant "condom" over the suburban Washington, D.C., home of former North Carolina Senator Jesse Helms. The Helmses' home was targeted because of the senator's particularly vitriolic antihomosexual position and comments to the media. The condom was taken down as soon as police asked for it to be removed, but it stayed in place long enough to make the national news (Allen 2006). The tactic was considered both dramatic and humorous. In his later years Senator Helms was persuaded to fund some HIV/AIDS services designated for Africa. There are many humorous examples such as this that are used to draw public attention to the serious needs of a particular population group, but the context and ethical issues should always be evaluated beforehand. Community groups should thoroughly discuss the potential implications and consequences for all strategies and tactics so that the group can judge the potential effectiveness of the action for reaching their goals as well as the ethical implications of their actions.

7. **Assist the organization to learn how to *manage internal conflict and disagreements* as strategies and tactics are examined for the quality of life improvement action.** All organizations experience internal conflict. Disagreements can help clarify and broaden the understanding of the issues, but useful disagreement can only occur in open, safe, and structured settings that allow any member of the community to raise their concerns. The facilitator can introduce the opportunity to establish respectful rules of engagement and discussion in early meetings. The facilitator might propose a structured dialogue through which group members would take time out from their process toward goal setting to look at issues in a safe, unhurried way for the simple purpose of hearing each other's perspectives. Group members can be trained as group mediators so that they can take turns facilitating the discussion of two people with widely divergent opinions. Such mediated discussion whereby the mediator simply helps the two people hear each other's perspectives can promote an understanding of how oppressive forces affect different people and their families.

Priority-setting techniques such as the Nominal Group Technique have proven to be more satisfactory ways to make decisions than simple majority voting (Delbecq, Van de Ven, and Gustafson 1975). Fair representation in leadership and committees should reflect the population characteristics of the community or neighborhood in terms of diversity. Taking care to form committees, task groups, and action plans that are representative of a broad spectrum of the community can diminish intergroup conflict.

8. **Assist the organization to learn how to** *monitor* **and** *evaluate* **the progress of its neighborhood or community efforts.** Monitoring keeps track of program implementation and provides information about progress toward goals. Evaluation involves careful assessment following the implementation to determine its effectiveness and efficiency (Netting, Kettner, and McMurtry 2008). This step involves helping the neighborhood or community group identify in words and pictures exactly how things will progress, and to describe specific ways people and conditions will be different at interim points. Evaluation documents how well the action has achieved social, economic, and environmental justice.

Preserving a record of the planning process and the early action taken provides the needed information for making decisions about adapting or changing tactics if the group finds itself moving in a direction it had not intended. The community's discussion of an action's usefulness or effectiveness toward long-range goals is similar to the Freirean concept of "action-reflection" (Hope, Timmel, and Hodzi 1995). Taking time for the community to think through the total result of their action and its positive and negative consequences, in the context of their local place and vision, provides ways to identify what worked and what did not.

Stoecker (2005) provides a research methods guide for communities that frame their action as projects. Among the methods that should be of special interest to community organizers are *participatory research* and methods that ensure the voices of all stakeholders are recorded and reported in the evaluation documents. Methods such as oral histories, photographs, dramatic presentations, mural paintings, quilts and other textiles, sculptures, and songs are legitimate ways to represent community concerns and change efforts (Kleymeyer 1994; Stoecker 2005). Evaluation that incorporates empowerment research methods helps the community group assess its needs, identify strategies for change, and document processes and results of planned action (Eng and Parker 1994; Pennell, Noponen, and Weil 2005). Through her work in India, Helzi Noponen has been particularly successful in helping organizations develop evaluation tools composed entirely of community-produced graphic representations of household and community progress (Noponen 2002). These tools work especially well in communities where not all members are literate. In her *Guide to Sustainable Community Indicators,* Maureen Hart (1999) provides creative ways to think through and identify the complex changes that can occur in communities when social, economic, and environmental improvements (e.g., "the triple bottom line") are combined. In the Guatemalan case example, farmers were able to see within one season how the changes they had made, such as terracing and soil enrichment, were helping to rebuild the fertility of their soil and increase crop yield. Because they were willing to experiment on their own fields, these farmers saw that "forage crop as perennial cover plus contouring increased yields six fold within seven years . . . [and they] doubled yields again on their own after the project ended" (Uphoff, Esman, and Krishna 1998:115).

9. **Assist the organization to** *plan for and take effective action.* All the work that has gone on in the organization to get to this point is the foundation for effective action. In addition to having a detailed plan of the logistics for the action, perhaps the most important way the facilitator can assist the organization in taking effective action is to help the participants think through the range of tactics and the likely consequences of the action. A useful discussion includes all the "what if" questions that will help people think through both the worst and the best possible outcomes, and how they will respond to the whole continuum of possibilities. Being unprepared to win can be as dangerous and unproductive as being unprepared to lose. In the case example from South Africa, the SHARE director was prepared for the white apartheid government representatives to thank her for her ideas, then effectively table the issue by asking her to return when she had a fully developed proposal. In anticipation of the bureau's tactics, she always went to government meetings with a fully developed proposal ready to hand to the committee chair.

In taking action, it is also important to think through the range of diversity represented among those who will be the "public face" of the organization during the action. This should not be a contrived arrangement but rather the result of work from the beginning to be an inclusive organization. The leaders of the group should not select a "token" or "poster child" to constantly represent a certain sector of the community. Effectively including all members of a neighborhood or community demonstrates the diversity of the community. When the time comes for public action, the organization will be modeling the affirmation of diversity for the community at large. Preparing for a press conference or public encounter requires role playing with community members and rehearsing communication strategies since typically there will be a brief chance to communicate the group's central message.

10. **Assist the organization to** *plan celebrations that mark the progress* **of leadership, organizational development, and action victories.** We have learned that celebrations of leadership growth, organizational milestones, affirmations of diversity, and successful actions are all reasons for public congratulations.

Celebrations can connect a wide range of community members in a social setting, and they present an opportunity to alert the wider community to the organization's vitality and success. Celebrations can be a venue to raise much needed funds for the organization. There are many reasons to celebrate active citizen involvement, and the facilitator should encourage and support such events.

The Concerned Citizens of Tillery, in Halifax County, North Carolina, for example, understand the true meaning of using celebrations in their organizing work. Established in the 1930s as an African American "New Deal Resettlement Community," the Tillery community began to organize in the last twenty-five years to protest several problematic conditions. Among Tillery's concerns were the loss of land by Black farmers, the closing of schools that served broad needs in their community, the need for health services, and the loss of environmental quality from the pollution of large corporate hog factories. To celebrate their successful organization, Tillery holds an annual Miss Black Earth pageant honoring the community's youth and their connection to the land. There is an annual "Senior Prom" celebrating the elders in their community that is organized by the Open Minded Seniors, who have also sponsored "Joyful Sounds" gospel concerts. The Nubian Youth group celebrates achievements at summer camp, college graduation, beach trips, basketball, and Kwanzaa, among many other events. The Grown Folks group, which was organized to improve the quality of life of families in Tillery, holds an annual Red and Black Ball on Valentine's Day. The Halifax Environmental Loss Prevention (HELP) group and the Economic Development Committee organize other community celebrations. For the Tillery Community history project, a community member wrote a play, *Predny and Yestidy*, depicting the social, economic, and political struggles of families in the community. These are examples of the way one community celebrates its history, achievements, and potential. These celebrations reach out to all ages and all people in the community. News coverage helps to broadcast the vitality and enduring contribution this community provides to the whole county and beyond (Concerned Citizens of Tillery 2003).

These ten steps are intended to serve as a guide for people undertaking the roles of organizer, facilitator, educator, coach, trainer, and bridge-builder in working with neighborhoods and communities. In this model, as in later models, it should be understood that in practice organizers might employ these steps as a systematic guide; however, to be successful organizers must remain flexible. There will be many times in the organizing activity when the organizer and community members will feel the need to take a few steps back to reflect on new information or differences in perspectives. The steps, therefore, should be thought of as incorporating a system of feedback loops as indicated in figure 5.1. The feedback loops are internal monitoring activities for the organization to gauge the progress and direction of their effort, and indicate when the group needs to take necessary corrective action that might require returning to an earlier step. Feedback loops answer questions such as, "Do we have sufficient information and resources to make a decision?" "Now that we know one of our key opponents is supporting us, should we change our strategy?" and, "What if the outcome appears to benefit only a small number of our leaders rather than the whole community?" Feedback loops also help the facilitator and neighborhood leaders identify the specific strengths and challenges faced by the organization as it moves through a community building effort. In practice, organization and leadership building require considerable flexibility and the recognition that working with neighborhoods and communities is multifaceted and never a simple linear path. There are common processes, but every neighborhood and community is a unique place.

We have not included a step that calls for the organizer to end his or her relationship with the neighborhood or community. In some cases, as in the Guatemalan farmer-to-farmer case, the organizers informed the community at the outset that they were working toward a specific end date, by which time the community was expected to be running the program. In the South African Langa KwaNobuhle case, the organizer eventually resigned from her position at the social service agency and from board membership to become the first director of the new community organization. Neighborhood and community organizations go through many changes as they evolve, and the organizer has to adjust to these changes. An essential aspect of the organizer's relationship with the community members is the need for direct and open communication to clarify the shared understandings of their agreement.

THEORIES AND CONCEPTS THAT GROUND THE MODEL

Central theories and concepts that ground neighborhood and community organizing are drawn from five major streams of theory discussed in depth in chapter 4: *personal and interpersonal theories; group and empowerment theories; organizational and interorganizational theories; community theory; and theories of globalization and social change.* Here, we focus on concepts from those theory streams, drawn primarily from theories for action, that we hold are most useful to the work of organizing neighborhoods and communities. Those concepts include

- group process and facilitation
- principles of democratic participation
- power and empowerment

- social capital
- collective efficacy

These concepts can be relevant for anyone working with community-based social services, but they are particularly relevant for those working to organize neighborhoods and communities because they inform the processes people go through as they come together to build organizations and make progressive changes for their quality of life.

GROUP PROCESS AND FACILITATION

According to Toseland and Rivas (2008), "A group's entire social structure, its communication and interaction patterns, cohesion, social controls, and culture evolve as it develops" (85). How can a community organizer assist a group or organization to make relatively smooth transitions as it evolves from its embryonic to more mature stages? How do small groups of people come together, share common interests, establish common goals, engage in strategies to build skills, improve the quality of their neighborhood, and build lasting community organizations? Perhaps the most useful theoretical understandings for those who will work in community practice relate to group process and the facilitation of group development. Understanding the patterns and challenges of human interaction is basic knowledge for community practice. Facilitation relates to the coaching and teaching activities that make it easier for a group or an organization to move through the developmental stages. A facilitator, as an outside observer with knowledge about group development, can help an organization when it faces a crisis or an obstacle. A facilitator does not solve the crisis, but rather helps the group to see possible options for moving forward.

Some groups may not need a full-time facilitator. Others have difficulty sorting through issues that concern them in order to engage in citizen action. It is not uncommon for groups to become bogged down when they confront really challenging issues. Kaner et al. (1996) have suggested that

> most groups do not know how to solve tough problems on their own. They do not know how to build a shared framework of understanding—they seldom even recognize the significance. They dread conflict and discomfort and they try hard to avoid it. Yet, by avoiding the struggle to integrate one another's perspectives, the members of such a group greatly diminish their own potential to be effective. (32)

In the early 1970s, considerable work focused on understanding the difference between unstructured interactive meetings and structured meetings. Andre Delbecq and his colleagues (1975) summarized these differences based on their work to help modern organizations benefit from the breadth of creative potential available in groups. Typically, unstructured meetings generate a small number of ideas because particular members of the group tend to dominate the discussion and there is pressure to conform to the established norms and hierarchy. These kinds of meetings can leave many participants feeling excluded and uninterested in taking part because the ideas seem old and hierarchies are very rigid. In developing new techniques for participatory decision making, Delbecq et al. (1975) focused on ways to help groups maximize the participation of *all* members toward more productive and creative outcomes. Use of the Nominal Group Technique (NGT) ensures a high quality and specificity of creative ideas, member equality, and a high feeling of accomplishment by participants (Delbecq et al. 1975:32). The ideas behind NGT are the basis for many other techniques that continue to ensure the inclusion of people of color, women, youth, the elderly, and other groups in community planning activities.

NGT can be used with any size group. For example, the technique could be used in a large gymnasium or auditorium with hundreds of participants working in small groups of five to nine persons, with two trained facilitators assigned to each group. This method allows every participant to be involved and also completes a significant amount of work in several hours time. The basic rules for conducting NGT sessions are available at a number of Web sites noted in the *CPS Workbook*.

Cardstorming, a method of facilitating brainstorming and conceptual clarification in groups as large as forty people, is based on the NGT theory of structured group process. We have used Cardstorming with international women's groups, student governing groups, grassroots community groups, and community planning groups. The rules for facilitating this method are also described in the *CPS Workbook*. Both NGT and Cardstorming are face-to-face activities, which are especially useful for neighborhood and community organizing. The Delphi Technique is a form of NGT that involves mail or e-mail ballots rather than face-to-face discussion and voting. One of the important lessons of using structured techniques that involve visual representation (e.g., pictures or short phrases) is that the different perceptions of people are quickly revealed and more readily absorbed by the larger group members as each one sees the representations appear in front of the room.

Another structured method for engaging community members in defining the perception of community concerns is a six-step computer-assisted process called *concept mapping* (Kane and Trochim 2007). The *concept-mapping* process involves community stakeholders in a number of the steps, especially brainstorming, sorting and rating, data interpretation and analysis, and building consensus for data utilization (Ridings et al. 2008). Over the several months of the process, community members build their understanding of how the variable perceptions of participants can be incorporated into the effort to set community goals for action programs.

Kaner and colleagues (1996) provide a guide to help community practitioners see the differences between "conventional groups" and groups that are facilitated to be participatory. Understanding the differences between unstructured and structured groups is of particular importance in working through controversial issues where competing interests are likely to be part of the process. Structured facilitation can help group members confront and solve highly charged issues with satisfying results. A key to being successful is to engage a capable facilitator who can help the group choose appropriate structures for the task as well as help the group move through the process to achieve satisfying agreements.

In recent years, additional forms of facilitated dialogue and deliberation have come into practice (Dessel et al. 2006). The National Coalition for Dialogue and Deliberation (NCDD) described some dialogue techniques as "establishing ground rules, emphasizing the importance of listening, utilizing trained facilitators, encouraging storytelling and reflection on personal experiences and perspectives" to "help ensure that everyone at the table has a real voice" (Heierbacher 2006:9). According to Heierbacher, "Deliberation promotes the use of critical reasoning and logical argument in decision making. Instead of decision making by power, coercion or hierarchy, deliberative decision making emphasizes the examination of facts and arguments and the weighing of pros and cons of various options" (2006:9). In any of these techniques, either the structure or the facilitator must ensure that hierarchical power structures have been diminished and member equality is protected.

PRINCIPLES OF DEMOCRATIC PARTICIPATION

In the 1980s and 1990s, the world watched the self-generated emergence of democracies across the globe. The walls of many authoritarian nation-states came tumbling down as Latin American and African military dictatorships were replaced with elected leaders, and newly independent states in Central and Eastern Europe struggled to build democratic institutions (Barker 1999; McCoy 1999). However, the loosening of authoritarian social and economic structures did not always provide the opportunity to move directly to democratic practices. In some countries, centuries-old ethnic hatred, sometimes exacerbated by colonial oppression and intolerance, positioned itself against the development of civic infrastructure (Kumar 1998). "During the 1990s the number of refugees and internally displaced persons grew by 50%," largely as a result of intrastate conflicts (UNDP 2002:11). Civil society and democratic institutions to protect freedoms cannot grow in an environment of violence. Violence includes not only the grotesque statistics of civilian and combatant deaths in wars, but also deaths from preventable childhood diseases and extreme poverty, deaths at the domestic or community level from oppression and abuse, and slow deaths from treatable chronic diseases and polluted water and air. Perhaps Shirin Ebadi, the 2003 Nobel Peace prize winner from Iran, said it best in her Nobel Lecture: "A human being divested of all dignity, a human being deprived of human rights, a human being gripped by starvation, a human being beaten by famine, war and illness, a humiliated human being and a plundered human being is not in any position or state to recover the rights he or she has lost" (Ebadi 2003:3).

In a speech at McGill University in 2004, Ebadi reiterated her basic perspectives on building democratic institutions: "Democracy is a historical process. It's not an event that happens overnight. It's not a gift. . . . Human rights are not established by throwing cluster bombs on people. You cannot introduce democracy to a country by using tanks" (Westlake 2004:1).

In the tenth anniversary of the *Human Development Report,* the United Nations Development Program outlined seven basic freedoms that form the basis for human rights and human development: freedom from discrimination; from want; from fear of threats to personal security or torture; from injustice; to develop and realize one's human potential; to have decent work; and the freedom to think and speak, to form associations, and to participate in decisions (UNDP 2000b:1). We would add freedom to live in a community where the air, water, and soil are protected from pollution.

Without some measure of these basic freedoms, it is very difficult, if not impossible, to organize a community or neighborhood. On a local level, problems with the denial of these freedoms may be the very issues that stimulate people to organize. These freedoms must ultimately be linked to vertical institutions that are regional, national, and even international in scope to gain permanent support. Part of democratic participation is having the opportunity to identify how such freedoms affect human development, identify ways a local community can work to make positive changes in such issues, and organize to take action toward changes.

There are many models of democratic institutions, and they must be developed in the context of the particular society that is reaching for the freedoms and human rights that such institutions can bring. Building democratic institutions for civic participation requires an environment that is not only free of violence, but also full of opportunities for education and learning for all people, both girls and boys, women and men. Every person who wishes to work in neighborhood and community organizing must have a basic understanding of the Universal Declaration of Human Rights. As discussed in chapter 1, the "Ethics in Social Work, Statement of Principles" (IFSW/IASSW, 2004) holds that social workers should know not only the Universal Declaration of Human Rights but also the contents of the six additional covenants and conventions they have identified. These additional criteria form the "common standards of achievement, and recognize rights that are accepted by the global community" (IFSW/ IASSW 2004:2).

Vandana Shiva describes democratic participation in her discussion of *Earth Democracy* as "based on diversity . . . on multidimensional and multifunctional expressions of creativity and productivity in humans and nature" (2005:83). Shiva, a physicist by training, has spent the past three decades deeply involved in environmental and livelihood issues in her native India and in global issues concerning natural resource privatization, cultural theft, consolidation of food production by agribusiness, and violence against women. Her concept of Earth Democracy is based on a set of ten principles, one of which is the need for people to be engaged in *living economies* and *economic democracy*. Economic democracy is an essential principle of Shiva's Earth Democracy because the process of producing and purchasing local food and materials "internalizes social and ecological costs in our production and consumption systems. . . . Localization constantly responds to ecological feedback from nature and political and cultural feedback from people. . . . Localization creates honest economies based on real costs" (2005:82–83).

The international organization, CIVICUS, the World Alliance for Citizen Participation, is bringing more attention to the value of *civic engagement*: the voluntary local activity of people in both formal and informal settings for contributing to the community. The organization holds that "the health of societies exists in direct proportion to the degree of balance between the state, the private sector and civil society" (CIVICUS 2009:home page).

Citizen participation has been a strong thread found throughout the larger history of democratic development as described in chapter 3. We sometimes assume that citizen participation is a given in Western democracies. In fact, most democracies have a long way to go in the struggle to create inclusive and participatory organizational structures in neighborhoods and communities.

In all societies, even those that encourage and sometimes require participation, some groups are systematically excluded from participation because of the combined effect of various barriers. People are typically excluded from participation because of their limited formal education, lack of access to information, and differential treatment by more powerful groups. People may not press to participate when powerful groups deny their participation based on gender, racial/ethnic minority status, or lower socioeconomic status. In addition, marginalized groups often experience the negative effect of barriers, whether perceived or real, such as being made to feel unwelcome or humiliated, not being understood, and being discounted, ignored, or even endangered simply because they are present. Sometimes those in power choose to carry out the discussion using esoteric and technical language in an effort to confuse others. The social justice work of organizers and facilitators working in neighborhood and community organizations involves work with citizens and participants to break down these external and internal barriers to democratic participation and build up the capacities of those who are excluded from participation.

Expanding the legal guarantees and regular involvement of all groups in the community decision-making process is not an easy effort. Commitment to basic freedoms that sometimes takes years to put into law can be easily diminished or eliminated in crisis situations. As neighborhood and community organizers work toward the ethical and professional commitment to build democratic processes, they need both a tougher and a more sophisticated worldview.

POWER AND EMPOWERMENT

All relationships embody some aspects of power. Power can be used to discriminate against and oppress people, thereby preventing them from reaching their optimum potential. Or worse, power used to discriminate can lead to abuse or even genocide. In contrast, neighborhood and community groups can also use power to change negative conditions and improve their quality of life. Organizers and facilitators of community organization who are committed to social justice and human rights need a full understanding of power as it relates to the neighborhoods and communities with which they work. It is of particular importance to understand power and power relationships specific to a place because the horizontal and vertical networks, social and economic institutions, and historical sources of power differ in each locality.

Power used to discriminate begins with differentiation and grouping of people often based on race, ethnicity, gender, age, religion, socioeconomic status, sexual orientation, geographic location, disability, dress, or a combination of these identifiers (Lee 1997; VeneKlasen and Miller 2002). Srilatha Batliwala described basic concepts of power as follows:

> Power can be defined as the degree of control over material, human, intellectual and financial resources exercised by different sections of society. The control of these resources becomes a source of individual and social power. Power is dynamic and relational, rather than absolute—it is exercised in the social, economic and political relations between individuals and groups. It is also unequally distributed—some individuals and groups having greater control over the sources of power and others having little or no control. The extent of power of an individual or group is correlated to how many different kinds of resources they can access or control. . . . Our understanding of power would be incomplete, unless we recognize its partner, ideology. Ideology is a complex structure of beliefs, values, attitudes,

and ways of perceiving and analyzing social reality. Ideologies are widely disseminated and enforced through social, economic, political and religious institutions and structures such as the family, education system, religion, the media, the economy and the state, with its administrative, legislative and military wings. The economic, political, legal and judicial institutions and structures set up and mediated by the state tend to reinforce the dominant ideology and the power of the dominant groups within it, even though their stated objectives and policies may be superficially egalitarian. While ideology does a far more effective job of sustaining an unequal power structure than crude, overt coercion and domination, we should not forget that it is always being reinforced by the threat of force, should anyone seek to rebel against the dominant system. But neither power, ideology, nor the state is static or monolithic. There is a continuous process of resistance and challenge by the less powerful and marginalized sections of society, resulting in various degrees of change in the structure or power. When these challenges become strong and extensive enough, they can result in the total transformation of a power structure. (1993, *Women's Empowerment in South Asia—Concepts and Practices* from the Asia Pacific Bureau of Adult Education, as quoted in VeneKlasen and Miller 2002:41)

Most people who have worked for social change understand that altering the way power is established and allocated often involves conflict because there will be resistance to changing the power structure (Alinsky 1971; Brager et al. 1987; Freire 1972; Horton, Kohl, and Kohl 1990; Kahn 1994; Lee 1997; Mondros and Wilson 1994; Reisch 2005b; Rubin and Rubin 2007; Shiva 2005). In their effort to initiate social change, neighborhood and community members often overlook the complexity of power, including their own power sources.

VeneKlasen and Miller described both positive and negative sources of power as a way to more fully understand expressions of power. *Power over* is described in all of its negative connotations, including "repression, force, coercion, discrimination, corruption and abuse." When people are asked to describe power, often they will only describe these negative views of power. If this negative connotation is the only meaning of power understood by people, it unfortunately also becomes the way people may behave when they suddenly acquire power. VeneKlasen and Miller suggested that when people with this singular view gain new leadership positions, "they sometimes 'imitate the oppressor,' [becoming themselves oppressive and abusive]. For this reason, advocates cannot expect that the experience of being excluded prepares people to become democratic leaders" (2002:45). The analytical understanding of the structural aspects of power—for example, how those in positions of authority, such as the police, the military, or judges are simply applying the rules in a larger oppressive structure that is kept in place by unjust economic and social forces—is valuable learning.

The concept of *power over* is challenging to analyze given that such power is often embedded in the institutions as described earlier by Batliwala: family, religion, education, media, the law, and ideology. Exploring the sources of *power over* requires tenacious and clever research because some power is visible, some is hidden (i.e., it is hard to discover but does have a paper trail), and some is invisible (i.e., it is not available in recorded documents but is evident in behaviors and practices). VeneKlasen and Miller described three ways that neighborhood and community groups might try to analyze *power over* (2002:47–49). One approach is to look for the *visible or observable sources of power* by examining laws, political parties, elections, corporate policies, and budgets. Once identified, these sources can be analyzed for ideological bias. Grassroots teams can divide the work of collecting data on different power sources and plot their findings on charts and diagrams for discussion. This dissection of power helps develop an understanding of the social, economic, and environmental factors that can be either a help or a hindrance to progressive change.

A second approach is to dig deeply for the *hidden sources of power* that are buried in privately established committees, private reports on issues such as toxic pollution, corruption, domestic violence, corporate privilege, child labor, and land and water rights. Sometimes reports on conditions that affect people negatively, especially people who are less powerful, are labeled "private" or "sensitive" or "high security" as a way of limiting access and keeping the issue out of the media, away from the public, and off the political agenda. Having a free and an effective press is an important asset to discover hidden power. Another asset is training people at the grassroots level to do the research of digging into public records so that they can develop a detailed picture of the issues that affect their community. An example of this approach was the training of citizens in Appalachia to go to public records offices in eighty counties across six states to copy thousands of pages of information about who owned the land, who owned the mineral rights, and who paid taxes, including how much. The analysis provided significant information about concentrations of corporate and absentee land ownership, inequities in property taxes, the exploitation of land and minerals for external gain, and the way the extraction of coal fouled the land and left behind impoverished economies, schools, health centers, and community services (Gaventa 1981). Although these records were public, they effectively remained hidden until people were willing to be trained to collect and analyze the data so that it could become useful to their organizational effort.

Finally, *invisible power* is the most insidious form of *power over* because it shapes people's beliefs and interprets meaning so that people who perceive themselves to be superior believe it is a natural relationship, and those who feel inferior believe it is their natural role. As VeneKlasen and Miller stated, "Processes of socialization, culture, and ideology perpetuate exclusion and inequality by defining what is normal, acceptable and safe" (2002:48–49). The concept of *mobilization of bias,* as described by Schattschneider (1975), operates in this kind of *power over.* Mobilization of bias is not necessarily a negative concept. If something is stated over and over again, especially if it is stated by people who have socioeconomic power, people come to believe it is true. Schattschneider's perspective holds that in most societies the freedom to organize around issues, and thereby define what is good and acceptable, tends to establish a bias in favor of social and economic elites. It is people who have social status and economic resources who will have the most control of media (e.g., newspapers, TV, radio), and the media are sometimes combined with coercive power to direct bias. This kind of *power over* can make it very difficult for people to even question injustice and violations of human rights.

In working against these three sources of *power over,* VeneKlasen and Miller described three collaborative methods they have used to help people explore the meaning of power: *power with, power to,* and *power within.* The social change and development literature frequently refers to *power with* and *power to* by the term *agency. Power with* is the power acquired when groups of people begin to build common interests and collective efforts to work toward improving community conditions together. *Power to* is the power felt by individuals when they have experienced new learning and expanded options and are enabled to take charge of conditions that affect them personally. *Power within* describes the new conceptions people have about themselves, their self-worth and dignity, their roles in family and community, and their confidence in their abilities. This power allows people to appreciate their individuality and personal perspectives while also respecting the differences of others (2002:45). The work of VeneKlasen and Miller has been employed and evaluated primarily in Asia, Africa, and Latin America, but it has also been effectively applied in the industrial West. The authors have framed their descriptions of power and their methods for analyzing power with neighborhood and community groups in ways that can be used universally.

Helping people to discover the power they have must be done in a very sensitive way because it can lead to direct action that can have dangerous outcomes for those working toward social justice, economic opportunities, and environmental protection and restoration. Mondros and Wilson (1994) described three methods that can be used to work toward empowerment: grassroots organizing, lobbying by building large organizations through public interest research, and mobilizing through mass education. There are many ways to help people discover their *power with, power to,* and *power within.* Once people have discovered these powers, their group empowerment can be used to make changes in social and economic opportunities and environmental protection. As Gandhi stated: "I have learnt through bitter experience the one supreme lesson: to conserve my anger, and as heat conserved is transmitted into energy, even so our anger controlled can be transmitted into a power which can move the world" (Mohandas Gandhi as quoted in Lee 1997:iii).

SOCIAL CAPITAL

When people are voluntarily engaged in their communities, through either formal or informal activity, they contribute to the dense network of relationships and trust that form social capital. Grassroots citizen organization was highlighted by Robert Putnam (1993) in his work on social capital, which extended the earlier work of James S. Coleman (1990). Putnam described social capital as "trust, norms, and networks, that can improve the efficiency of society by facilitating coordinated actions" (1993:167). Voluntary grassroots citizen organizations can flourish only where democratic institutions allow people to freely associate. As people develop the capacity to become group leaders or members in a neighborhood or community organization, they build trust and networks that can enlarge both their personal and organizational ability. Putnam concluded that "networks of civic engagement foster sturdy norms of generalized reciprocity and encourage the emergence of social trust" (1995:67). Understanding the development and utility of social capital is important for social workers who wish to work in neighborhood and community organization.

Michael Woolcock and Deepa Narayan (2000), who define social capital as "the norms and networks that enable people to act collectively" (226), keep their definition narrow for research purposes but do recognize the connections among horizontal, vertical, and institutional networks. They proposed that the value of this definition is its focus on the sources of trust and reciprocity rather than the consequences and that it allows for the exploration of different dimensions of social capital such as "close-knit 'bonding' social capital" and "more diffuse and extensive 'bridging' social capital" (2000:226). Finally, this definition "presents the community (rather than individuals, households, or the state) as the primary unit of analysis" (2000:227).

Richard Couto, whose research has focused on small communities in the Appalachian Mountains in the United States, described social capital as "the moral resources *and public goods* that we invest to produce and reproduce ourselves in community" (Couto and Guthrie 1999:xv; emphasis added). Couto suggests that a focus solely on *local moral resources* (i.e., trust, norms, and networks) is insufficient in that it does not take into consideration the important role of *mediating structures* as a necessary part of a community's ability to build social capital. Couto defines mediating structures as "the social and political provision of material goods and services such as health care, education, housing, employment, environmental quality, and the other factors" that are provided in communities primarily through the policies of local, regional, state, and national governments (1999:68). The networks and trust people develop among themselves must be combined with public funding that contributes to individual, family, and community well-being in order for communities to develop democratic institutions. Couto holds that "mediating structures exercise their democratic potential by extending trust, cooperation, and other moral resources from local organizations and institutions into broader, horizontal and vertical, organizational and institutional networks" (1999:69). These mediating organizations and institutions include nonprofit and public service organizations that contribute to the basic needs of families and communities.

Measuring social capital is difficult because of the complexity of its dimensions and the fact that we have no long-term measures of social capital in different countries. Anirudh Krishna (2002), who wrote from his experience in Africa, Central America, and especially in India, warned against using membership in formal organizations as the only measure of the density of social capital: "In developing countries, particularly in rural areas, it is informal rather than formal associations that have most value for citizens" (5). Thomas H. Sander and Robert Putnam, working through the Saguaro Seminar at Harvard University, are doing extensive research to expand knowledge about levels of trust and community engagement with surveys in U.S. communities (Putnam and Feldstein 2003; Saguaro Seminar 2006). Canada's Policy Research Initiative prepared an assessment of the effect of social capital on reducing poverty, improving wellness among the elderly, settlement of new immigrants, aboriginal educational advancement, youth engagement, and crime prevention in their report "Social Capital in Action" (Policy Research Initiative 2005).

Community practice organizers need a good understanding of the role of social capital and its potential application in responding to the needs of disenfranchised and excluded people in all nations. Woolcock and Narayan recognized that "social networks of the poor are one of the primary resources they have for managing risk and vulnerability," and suggested several cautionary notes in the application of social capital to development interventions (2000:243). "It is critical," they suggest, "to invest in the organizational capacity of the poor, and support the building of 'bridges' across communities and social groups" (Woolcock and Narayan 2000:242–43).

COLLECTIVE EFFICACY

Self efficacy and collective efficacy theories have been described in some detail in chapter 4. Castelloe (1999) drew on Albert Bandura's (1985, 1986) social-cognitive and collective efficacy theories, and Paulo Freire's (1972) popular education theory to deepen the concept of collective efficacy. From his observations and work with grassroots groups, Castelloe posited that from social capital we understand the trust and networks that can emerge from participation in civic engagement, and from social-cognitive theory and popular education we understand the next step of learning that can make a positive difference for the community. Finally, community members consciously take action on behalf of the community or neighborhood to improve life for the residents when they can see the incentives for doing so. Building on these theoretical perspectives, Castelloe described *collective efficacy* as "the realization among community members that they can participate in the building of a new future for their community, and the hope that springs from this realization" (1999:7). This understanding of collective efficacy is fundamental to any work we do to organize neighborhoods and communities.

Witnessing collective efficacy happening in a community is so emotionally stimulating it can take your breath away, especially if you are helping to make it happen. When people in neighborhoods learn how to analyze their conditions; develop the capacity to structure themselves in a democratic, participatory organization; develop the social capital to trust each other, their organization, allied institutions, and neighborhoods; and mutually plan and take action for the improvement of their community, they have engaged with all the theoretical concepts we have described in this chapter.

SOCIAL WORK/COMMUNITY PRACTICE ROLES

The roles of a community practice worker are, to say the least, multifaceted and require a wide range of skills and knowledge. Chapter 2 provides a definition and discussion of roles in community practice; the roles we have identified as most salient for this model are as follows:

- Organizer
- Facilitator
- Educator
- Coach
- Trainer
- Bridge builder

WHAT THE COMMUNITY ORGANIZER IS NOT When you are involved in neighborhood and community organizing, it is important to remember you are *not* the leader. You are not the leader because you are organizing people to develop their own leadership skills and democratic organizations. You are not the leader because you are teaching people how they can become effective leaders and members. You are not the leader because you are the coach who supports the new leaders when they are sagging and celebrates the new leaders when they have done well. You are not the leader because you are facilitating the growth of participatory democracy as you help the neighborhood group engage in decision making, problem solving, and action planning.

WHAT THE COMMUNITY ORGANIZER IS   In the farmer-to-farmer case example from Guatemala, the organizers from World Neighbors were clearly outsiders. To be effective organizers, they needed to be open co-learners to gather knowledge from local people about soils, traditional crop production practices, roles of men and women in household economies and community maintenance, ethnic tensions, social stratification, and health and welfare concerns. Although the organizers arrived with considerable knowledge about soil erosion and sustainable agricultural practices, it was a technical knowledge that had no value to the local people until it was combined with their own local knowledge. All of the roles—organizing, facilitating, educating, coaching, training, and bridge building—were played by the World Neighbors staff as they went about engaging with the local people. The staff practiced empowerment strategies by turning local farmers into the educators, facilitators, coaches, and trainers, so that by the end of the first year the local farmers had test plots where they demonstrated to themselves, neighbors, and other villagers the improved conditions of their soils. In the second year, the farmer-educators helped neighbors and farmers in nearby villages learn the techniques of terracing, placement of drainage ditches, and appropriate fertilizer application. In this case example, both the transformation of leaders to teachers and the acquisition of knowledge were so successful that the community continued to make gains in crop yields after an earthquake, after horrible civil conflict, and long after the outside organizer/facilitator team left the community.

In the SHARE case example from South Africa, the organizer/facilitator was not the leader while she was beginning to gauge how the community might come together to form a self-help organization "to break the bonds of dependency." She first approached leaders in the community to see if they might be interested in working toward creating such an organization. Although employed by a national welfare organization, she was also a resident of the same neighborhood, and therefore the township leaders encouraged *her* to chair the committee exploring the idea of a self-help organization. This case presents a slightly different path to leadership because the facilitator/organizer was an "insider," a resident of the township being organized as well as an external professional. As a professional social worker, she was building bridges between the members of the township and potential allies in institutions that were connected to resources (e.g., her employers, town council members, and other professionals who were aware of the limited services available to people in the Black townships). When the organizing committee finally had funds to hire a director, they asked the organizer/facilitator to lead the organization. She resigned her position with the national welfare organization as well as her position as chair of the township organizing committee. As the director of SHARE she was then responsible to the organization's newly formed board. She was very clear about her need to formally resign her earlier positions when the time came to step up to lead the newly formed organization. In her case, the organizer continued to play the roles of educator (e.g., attending workshops, facilitating other staff to attend trainings, and mentoring other newly organized community-based organizations); coach (e.g., learning with and from the newly established board, negotiating the political land mines); trainer (e.g., helping the board and staff learn how to manage an organization); and bridge-builder (e.g., connecting with the institutions and organizations that could help the newly established organization gain resources).

Building bridges with external organizations, resource institutions, and neighborhoods is an important part of exploring action options. Although the organizer can easily make these connections on his or her own because of previous connections and knowledge about what resources are available beyond the neighborhood, the external contact should be done *with* one or more representatives from the neighborhood. The connections should be cemented between the representative of the external organization and the members of the community being organized, often increased by multiple meetings. If the organizer makes all the external contacts, no bridges are built, and the contacts evaporate when the organizer leaves.

There may be many occasions when the organizer will be called on to mediate and facilitate solutions to internal conflicts in the organization. Early in the work, the organizer should teach decision-making techniques to limit the need for conflict resolution, as well as group-mediating practices and group-imposed discussion rules that will help the organization solve internal conflicts. Another role played by the organizer is providing coaching to members with specific roles to help them master the skills the organization needs. One area that requires careful coaching is any position that is entrusted with access to the organization's funds, such as the treasurer, or those positions with spending power. Keeping account of the organization's funds should be a transparent activity. It often works best when at least two people share the responsibility providing for dual oversight. Many organizations have failed, leaving their noble goals incomplete because funds were misused or the accusations of misuse could not be adequately disproved. As the organization develops structures and processes to solve internal conflicts, and as individuals develop skills to build the organization effectively, members will know the empowerment process is evolving.

There will be occasions when the strategies and tactics decided upon by the organization will bring members into conflict with external institutions and groups. Part of the organizer's role is to prepare the organization for possible conflict. In preparation for exploring goals and strategies and taking action, the organizer should help the members think through the outcomes of each step. In such discussions, the organization should analyze reasons for conflict with external groups and institutions, and the organization's members should carefully decide on their engagement strategy. The organizer should never suggest or condone planned violence as part of the strategy. As Brager and colleagues state, "If revolution is the goal and violence is the means, then community work is the wrong field" (1987:339). However, even an organization's planned nonviolent tactics can elicit a violent backlash from external forces. The focus of the organizer would then be to protect, support, and advocate for the organization and its members.

Empowerment strategies hold significant meaning and guide the engagement between organizers and the people they wish to help (Gutierrez et al. 1998). Respect for human dignity means that people, individually and as groups, should have the opportunity to make their own decisions. When such decisions are made in the interest of redressing social injustice, they can elicit negative responses from powerful institutions. These are critical times when the organizer must stand with the person or group to support their action.

A most useful guide for acting in accordance with the empowerment tradition as a social worker doing neighborhood and community organizing comes from Barbara Levy Simon (1994:xiv). We have adapted her five points in the following list. A community practice organizer acts in the empowering tradition by engaging in the following activities:

1. Constructing collaborative partnerships with community leaders and organizations through a process of co-learning and respect.
2. Emphasizing the capacities of community members and their organizations rather than their incapacities.
3. Sustaining a dual working focus to strengthen community leaders and build the capacity of their organizations as they work to improve the social, physical, political, economic, and environmental conditions of the community.
4. Recognizing community members and their organizations as active participants with interrelated rights, responsibilities, needs, and claims.
5. Choosing consciously to work with historically disempowered groups and their members.

A social worker or other professional working as an organizer/facilitator is a partner with neighborhood members and leaders, and must recognize that both parties have something to contribute. The engagement with community groups is always done as a co-learner. Emphasizing the capacities of neighborhood residents moves the professional into a role of coach and facilitator to help expand neighborhood strengths. Recognizing residents as active, dynamic participants moves the facilitator/organizer into the roles of educator and trainer to help residents learn new skills that will make their organization building work easier. Choosing to work with neighborhoods and communities that have been consistently disempowered embraces the value position of social work community practice.

CORE SKILLS AND COMPETENCIES FOR NEIGHBORHOOD AND COMMUNITY ORGANIZING

In this section, we discuss five competencies and skills important to effectively organize neighborhoods and communities. A skilled and competent organizer will have sufficient knowledge, judgment, and skills to engage with neighborhoods and communities to improve problematic social, economic, and environmental conditions identified by the community group. We define skills as not only the knowledge of methods to accomplish tasks, but also application of knowledge through the ability to carry out tasks. Competency involves adequate judgment as well as knowledge and the ability to apply methods.

The five core competencies and skills we identify and discuss are

- Culturally sensitive engagement
- Facilitation/dialogue
- Teaching decision-making techniques
- Mediation
- Planning for action

Skills that are discussed in later models might also be applied to neighborhood and community organizing, just as skills discussed here can also be applied in the other models. Learning skills for practice must ultimately be part of an experiential learning activity. In this chapter we discuss in some detail ways to assess one's current skills and suggestions for developing skills through experiential learning. The accompanying *CPS Workbook* also contains exercises that can contribute to building skills and competencies for community and neighborhood organizing. In this chapter, we engage the reader in much more detail about processes, methods, and skills for practice than we do in the following chapters focusing on different models. Our hope is that the framework presented here will be useful to you in developing your own plan for ongoing skill development.

In most schools of social work, learning practice skills is done in supervised fieldwork settings where the student is given many opportunities to test skills in the real world. In addition, this supervised learning allows opportunities to review your work with a skilled community practitioner who can help guide you to work ethically, effectively, and in a culturally respectful way.

CULTURALLY SENSITIVE ENGAGEMENT

In the ten guiding steps for organizing neighborhood or community groups that we described at the beginning of this chapter, we began with engagement, that is, the establishment of a positive working relationship with the community group. Some communities may seem more homogeneous than others, but even in seemingly homogeneous groups individuals have different perspectives and needs. The social work principle to value "the worth and dignity of each individual" requires that we prepare ourselves to be sensitive to, and respectful of, difference.

ASSESSMENT AND PREPARATION A number of authors provide guidance for acquiring multicultural sensitivity (Anderson and Carter 2003; Bankhead and Erlich 2005; Guadalupe and Lum 2004; Gutierrez and Alvarez 2000; Gutierrez and Lewis 1994; Hyde 2005; Lum 2006; Rivera and Erlich 1998). Knowledge from these authors should form the basis for understanding multicultural issues. Prior to engaging in practice, we suggest the organizer do a personal assessment of his or her qualities, skills, and experiences that can be applied to organizing. An organizer could ask, "What knowledge, judgments, and skills do I have and feel confident being able to offer to this community group?" A checklist of questions, adapted from Christine Robinson (1996), could be helpful with such a self-assessment.

- Who am I? How do I describe myself physically, and in terms of my personal philosophy, motivations, expectations, fears, cultural values, religious beliefs and tolerance, and gender expectations?
- Who are the people in this community? What is my knowledge of their beliefs, motivations, expectations, fears, and cultural values? Are there people in the community I might find harder to reach? Do I have a strategy for getting to know the range of diverse people who live in the community?
- How will the community view me? What previous experience does this community have with organizers? How will the community members regard my age, sex, sexual orientation, language, education, dress, and spiritual beliefs?

- What are my best competencies (knowledge, judgment, skills) for joining in a partnership with members of this community to promote improved social, economic, and environmental conditions?

Following a self-assessment of qualities and skills, an organizer should do additional reading and research in preparation for engaging with the specific neighborhood or community, including the ethnocultural perspectives of different groups within the community and social, economic, and environmental concerns affecting the community. The following list of questions can help the organizer to think through the preparation that may be necessary.

- Where can I access existing economic reports, historical documents, and social and environmental data about this community to gain a basic understanding of the conditions? Who in the community might be helpful to this learning?
- What are the areas of exploration I will need to undertake to be a co-learner with community members regarding their life experiences?
- What are the informal activities I can be part of (easily and appropriately) that will help me understand the livelihoods, hopes, fears, and traditions of this community? What are the best ways for me to be a co-learner to enlarge my understanding of gender and ethnocultural perspectives in this community?
- Do I have a grounded sense of my framework for social, economic, and environmental analysis as it relates to this community? Am I prepared to be open to learning what their framework is for analyzing their social, economic, and environmental conditions?

PRACTICE (SIMULATION AND GUIDED EXPERIENCE) The next step is to gain some experience in engaging with communities. If you are in a student setting, the classroom may be a good opportunity to discuss your responses to the self-assessment questions. Classrooms can also offer opportunities for role plays. Alternatively, you might use your home community as a place to do additional research and consider how you would respond to the preparation questions if you were to work in the community where you live. If you are lucky and can have a guided experience as part of your field assignment, that will be the best place to practice engaging with a real community. If you are extremely lucky, you will have the opportunity to work with a partner so that you can observe and critique each other's efforts.

Participatory Rural Appraisal (PRA) is a collection of participatory methods designed to guide those who engage with local communities to assess needs and assets, plan for change, and take action and evaluate outcomes (Chambers

1997, 2002). The PRA method is more than simply engagement with the community. Chambers suggests a series of questions that helps the organizer/facilitator realize that community members are the experts on their own community because they have deep knowledge based on lived experience and shared history. Only community members are likely to be able to answer questions such as the following: Who knows most about water resources? How do children and parents regard schools? Who settles disputes? Who knows most about home gardens? Who knows most about the elderly? What happens when someone's house burns down? (Chambers 1997:117). This emphasis on the community's expertise cannot be overstated, especially during the engagement phase.

EVALUATION AND REFLECTION Once an organizer actually engages with a community group, it is wise to establish an ongoing series of questions to help assess how well practice efforts are going. The questions might be posed monthly for the first three months, then every quarter after that. This allows for the development of personal benchmarks to measure growth of skills and competencies. Such questions might include the following:

- How do I know that I am acting in a culturally respectful way?
- How will I know that community members have begun to trust me?
- How have I demonstrated that I am a co-learner in the organizing process?
- What are the new understandings I have about this community that I have learned from community members and could not have learned without them?
- What groups in the community (e.g., youth, elderly, men, women, ethnic groups, religious conservatives, outcasts) do I still have too little knowledge about or have no meaningful connections with?

These are clearly generic questions and should be designed more specifically as the organizer develops a clearer sense of self and a better understanding of the community. Making time for such reflection is a valuable way to examine and strengthen practice.

FACILITATION AND DIALOGUE

Facilitation, as we have noted earlier, is the introduction of techniques to make the work of the group easier, along with raising critical questions to help the group consider issues in greater depth. Dialogue brings together people with differing perspectives for "shared exploration towards greater understanding, connection, or possibility" (Atlee 2009: dialogue page). Look for opportunities to help task groups think more deeply in analyzing community issues, (e.g., assessing and documenting types of power, power networks, internal and external resources, and processing outcomes through reflection). The organizer must be clear about the goal to help community members clarify their own issues and reach for a common understanding on issues they wish to change. The organizer should be an expert facilitator, but not *the* expert in framing the issues or determining which strategies are best to respond to identified problems. The organizer helps group members clarify their thinking by asking critical questions. The patient and trustworthy organizer will eventually be a co-creator of knowledge and perspectives about social, economic, and environmental conditions.

ASSESSMENT AND PREPARATION The practice assessment phase of learning to be an expert facilitator can include observing good facilitators in the organizer's life experience such as in school, work, community, sports, or music. A set of questions can also help the organizer assess his or her knowledge and skills:

- What has been my experience as a participant in structured groups and formal dialogue settings?
- What experiences have I had in facilitating discussion with groups?
- What was effective in my facilitation? Why?
- What areas of facilitation worry me the most? Why?
- How well can I handle disagreement during group discussions? How well can I handle divisive comments such as those that are racist, sexist, homophobic, or ageist? Am I patient enough to allow for silence in discussion?
- How deep is my repertoire of techniques such as those for facilitating community assessment, power analysis, decision making, community mapping, tactical mapping, and community dialogue?

Numerous sources are available that offer approaches and facilitated exercises that lead toward participatory involvement. Some are available in print, and others can be found on the Internet (Arnold et al. 1991; Atlee 2009; Castelloe and Gamble 2005; Chambers 1997, 2002; Delbecq et al. 1975; Freire 1970; Hope, Timmel, and Hodzi 1995; Kaner et al. 1996; Lee and Balkwill 1996; National Coalition for Dialogue and Deliberation 2007; VeneKlasen and Miller 2002).

It is not sufficient to have a large repertoire of facilitative techniques; it is also critical to have good judgment about how those techniques can be helpful or how they can be adapted to be more culturally respectful given the context of the community. Perhaps the most important understanding an organizer can have is knowing how to ask questions that encourage in-depth thinking without being directive. Many community groups have experienced so much adversity and oppression that they are weary and are looking for a savior to come in and change their desperate situation. As was true in the South African case example that is described at the end of this chapter, the community wanted the organizer to *fix* the problems. However, no empowerment accrues to the community if someone from the outside comes in to solve their problems, and there are no more solutions to be found once such an organizer leaves. When people go through a participatory way of identifying issues, setting goals, deciding how to make changes, initiating action themselves, celebrating the change, and evaluating the new reality, they then own the experience. That ownership builds capacity, empowers the community collectively and individually, and establishes the building blocks to change other negative conditions in their lives. Excellent facilitation is what makes it possible for a community to move to that place of ownership and empowerment.

The organizer will do well to find out if community members have had any experience with a facilitator, structured participatory experiences, or dialogue. Their experiences may have been negative, and they might be suspicious of outside facilitators. In addition, communities sometimes have strong gatekeepers who feel the need to protect or direct the neighborhood's response to outside involvement and, therefore, do not want participatory activity to take place in their neighborhood. It is not uncommon for communities that have been severely oppressed to build a strong protective wall against outsiders because they have been taken advantage of so frequently. In this case, an organizer's engagement phase of work needs to focus on building trust in the community. Sometimes whether the organizer is an insider or an outsider to the community, engagement is not possible and respectful consultation is a sufficient outcome.

PRACTICE (SIMULATION AND GUIDED EXPERIENCE) Many opportunities arise to practice facilitation. If you are in a classroom, you can select hypothetical or real problems in your setting and facilitate discussion about the problems. You can practice many of the techniques such as Cardstorming (see the instructions in the *CPS Workbook*) for focusing the language of the issue, or tactical mapping, which allows groups to explore tactical solutions for the issues they wish to change (Johnson 2004). In addition, you can practice facilitation in everyday settings with groups (e.g., hobby, sports, spiritual or work groups) or wherever you engage with a group that is trying to solve a problem. If you are lucky enough to have a guided field experience, opportunities may be available in the community for facilitated discussion Many communities are now using dialogue techniques to engage community members from different backgrounds and value perspectives in structured discussion through *study circles, conversation cafés,* or *issue forums.* The National Coalition for Dialogue and Deliberation (2007) has guidelines and resources for four streams of dialogue practice:

exploration, conflict transformation, decision making, and collaborative action. Dialogue as a technique is becoming more common in many communities across the United States (Dessel et al. 2006; Gutierrez et al. 2005) as well as in international settings (Comprehensive Dialogue among Civilizations 2007). With either facilitation or dialogue, practice is the only way you will develop confidence in using these techniques.

EVALUATION AND REFLECTION Again, we suggest that the potential organizer perform a self-assessment of his or her practice experience and develop benchmarks of his or her skill level. Some helpful questions to include in the assessment might include the following:

- How well did I handle the facilitation? What worked? What needs improvement?
- Am I listening well enough to the perspectives that are being presented, or am I pushing my own agenda in the discussion (i.e., my view of social justice, economic opportunity, and environmental security)?
- What additional personal behaviors will help me listen "fully, deeply, and actively"?
- Is the group moving to a better understanding of the conditions they wish to change? Can the group infer the relationship between personal problems and structural conditions that keep the status quo in place? What questions could I pose to help them explore those issues in greater depth?
- Is the group sensitive to being inclusive in their discussions? Do they notice certain voices missing from the discussions (e.g., women, youth, outcasts, religious conservatives, elders)? How can I move the group to become more inclusive without insisting?
- Is the group beginning to identify allies (e.g., other neighborhoods, university advocates, elected officials, news media) who are external to their community and might be helpful to their effort?

Again, these questions are only suggestions for self-evaluation after practice experiences. The organizer must outline questions that make sense for her or his development as well as those that relate to the specific characteristics of the community and the tasks at hand.

TEACHING DECISION MAKING

Decision-making techniques can make the work of an organization easier and more satisfying. They can also go a long way to minimize lingering disagreements within a group. First, a group has to understand a range of methods for making decisions (e.g., consensus, majority vote, Nominal Group Technique, leaders decide). Once a group has an understanding of different techniques, they should then agree which methods work better for them under what circumstances. If a decision is needed on a particular subject, unstructured discussion with a majority vote at the end of the discussion can have many shortcomings. Hierarchies exist in every community, and the person who speaks the loudest or is the most eloquent may not represent the general feeling of the larger community. If unstructured discussions are to be held, the group should at least agree on general rules of engagement (e.g., one person speaks at a time, no one speaks twice until everyone has had a chance to give their opinion, specific time limits will be imposed only if needed to ensure everyone has an opportunity to speak, we will agree to try to stay on the topic).

ASSESSMENT AND PREPARATION In the assessment questions, the organizer again will want to review how life experience has prepared him or her to understand and facilitate decision-making techniques. Some assessment questions might include the following:

- Do I understand the meaning and different uses of Robert's Rules of Order (parliamentary procedure), majority rule, consensus, Nominal Group Technique, and Cardstorming?
- Do I know what patterns of decision making people from this particular community are most familiar with or use most frequently?
- Can I be effective in helping the group discuss common, respectful rules for general discussions?

As we have mentioned earlier, when a community group has a good understanding of different ways to make decisions that they consider fair, many conflicts among group members can be eliminated.

Basic information about decision-making techniques such as consensus and the Nominal Group Technique (Delbecq et al. 1975) should be studied along with basic rules for parliamentary procedure (Robert et al. 2004). Powerful institutions have sometimes used parliamentary procedure to exclude people with less formal education. Anytime a structured method for conducting discourse is used to exclude citizen participation it should be discarded and replaced with a more inclusive method, or the excluded group should learn the method well.

Sometimes organizations develop their own decision-making techniques by combining several methods. Development of the Nominal Group Technique (NGT) by Delbecq and his colleagues (1975) is based on research conducted during the U.S. War on Poverty to get people from all sectors of society—the poorest people as well as bankers and corporate officers—to work together to develop plans for fighting poverty in U.S. urban and rural communities.

It will be important for the organizer to explore what kinds of decision-making models have been used previously in the neighborhood or community and if they worked well or instead created dissension. It is particularly important for groups to learn that no single method for conducting meetings and discussions, and making decisions is necessarily the best. The decision-making method should suit the group and their purpose and may therefore vary according to their situation and needs.

PRACTICE (SIMULATION AND GUIDED EXPERIENCE) There are many opportunities to observe and practice different decision-making techniques in everyday life. Again, we suggest that the potential organizer might use a classroom for a simulated experience or look to their sporting, social, artistic, and religious clubs as venues to practice decision-making techniques. Many of our former students have used NGT and Cardstorming with student organizations, both in learning new techniques and in reaching satisfying decisions. In addition, students make use of these brainstorming and priority-setting techniques in community field settings.

EVALUATION AND REFLECTION After facilitating the development of either consensus or one of the brainstorming or priority-setting techniques, the organizer can again develop a set of questions that will provide benchmarks for personal development in the area of decision making. Such questions might include the following:

- What were the most effective decision-making experiences I have facilitated in the last month? What made them effective (e.g., satisfying to participants, effective, inclusive)?
- Have I been able to train members of the community to be facilitators of these methods?
- What new methods should I introduce to this community to help them expand the choices of decision-making methods available to them?

These questions should be expanded to best reflect the experience of the organizer and the specific nature of the neighborhood and the conditions the community wishes to change.

MEDIATION

There are three generally considered formal methods for settling disputes within an organization or a community:

- Mediation—"any process for resolving disputes in which another person helps the parties negotiate a settlement" (Beer and Stief 1997:3).
- Negotiation—"back-and-forth communication designed to reach an agreement when you and the other side have some interests that are shared and others that are opposed" (Fisher, Ury, and Patton 1991:xvii).
- Arbitration—another person is chosen to settle the issues between parties in a dispute.

In this section we will focus primarily on mediation as a generic process for work with communities, which may from time to time include aspects of negotiation and arbitration.

Whether working with small task groups or large communities, opposing views should be expected as part of human social interaction. Opposing views are useful in exploring wider perspectives about an issue and as such should not be seen as negative or unhelpful. Conflicting or opposing views become problematic only if the two views prevent a community from moving forward toward building common ground for changing the negative conditions that are the larger target of the community. Sometimes key people in the community will have opposing views about how to interpret a condition or how to challenge a situation. If the organizer has some knowledge and experience in mediation, he or she may well be able to help the people with opposing perspectives to reach a more common viewpoint by helping them to clarify, explore, and hear each other's perspectives. This process can be carried out if the two parties agree to mediation. The mediator helps the two people to express their views, to hear each other's views, to express their concerns about the other's views, and to describe their hoped for outcome. By this measured method with its focus on outcome or the future, it is possible for two people to understand each other better and reach an amicable agreement.

Mediation is useful in small groups and communities because it is often seen as more effective than litigation, which usually means the outcome will produce one winner and one loser. Or in the case of building a community organization, litigation usually divides the group into two or more factions. In many communities, dispute resolution centers exist to help community groups resolve disputes, and such centers are often a free resource to those who are willing to give mediation a chance before taking their case to a court of law. Mediation settles many disagreements between people in neighborhoods and communities, culminating in more satisfying and less expensive outcomes.

For some, mediation has more potential for international disputes in a globalized world where legal jurisdictions are less clear and litigation is seen as long and costly. For mediation to be successful, both parties must agree to the mediation process and a knowledgeable and trained mediator must be available as a neutral third party. Mediation may not be appropriate in some cases, especially when one of the two parties has much more power than the other.

ASSESSMENT AND PREPARATION The first step is an assessment of the mediating knowledge and skill possessed by the organizer. Some questions that might be helpful in such an assessment are:

- Do I understand the differences among mediation, negotiation, and arbitration?
- Have I had training in mediation? Can I get training in mediation locally?
- Have I ever mediated a disagreement?

Dispute resolution centers are now common in most countries. These centers often offer training in mediation techniques. *The Mediators Handbook* by Beer and Stief (1997) is also a useful resource for the community organizer. Assessing the extent of mediation training available in the larger community and determining whether any community members have had mediation training is an important step that the community organizer should take early on. Parents of children in public schools are often aware of such training because it is used widely in schools to help with conflict resolution among students.

PRACTICE (SIMULATION AND GUIDED EXPERIENCE) The organizer might begin by observing mediation if it is formally available in the larger community. If not, students in a class could read Beer and Stief's (1997) handbook and practice mediation through role playing in the classroom. The classroom is also a good place to practice negotiation, which is one-on-one problem solving without the use of a third-party mediator as described in *Getting to Yes* by Fisher et al. (1991). By practicing both mediation and negotiation in the classroom, students can begin to see the different uses of both methods for solving disputes. If the student has a guided field experience, she or he might well be able to practice mediation either in the community or in a human service agency connected with the community.

EVALUATION AND REFLECTION As with other skills described earlier, the organizer should develop a set of self-assessment questions that can help measure development. Such questions might include the following:

- How well have I been able to mediate disputes between two parties in the developing organization? What made the mediation work? What made it fail?
- What are the things that seem to cause most disagreements among members of the neighborhood or community organization (e.g., personalities, miscommunication, perceptions of difference and discrimination, different worldviews)?
- Can I train others in the organization to take responsibility for mediation?
- Does the group have ideas to minimize internal disagreements that could be used rather than mediation?

These questions should reflect the needs for growth in the organizer as well as the specific needs and characteristics of the community organization.

PLANNING FOR ACTION

A group ready to take action has spent considerable time to plan and prepare for it. This work includes facilitating community assessments; discussing power relationships and networks; examining the social, economic, and environmental conditions the community wishes to change; setting goals; exploring strategies and tactics that will accomplish the goals; and determining what resources the community has available to take the action. All of that work will have to be accomplished through facilitation of the organizer, hard work of community members, the collaborative co-learning of both the facilitator and community members throughout the process, and the emotional, physical, and cognitive readiness of community members to take action.

In their work with communities all over the world, VeneKlasen and Miller often used the SWOT (i.e., strengths, weaknesses, opportunities, and threats) analysis to gauge a community's internal strengths and weaknesses and to measure opportunities and threats posed by the external forces (2002:211–22).

Internal → Strengths and Weaknesses
External → Opportunities and Threats

In the internal assessment, the community organization assesses the strengths and weaknesses of its leadership, technical skills, funds and material resources, clarity of purpose, commitment and participation, organizational planning, responsibility, skills, and relationships with external allies.

The external assessment examines threats and opportunities such as the available resources beyond the community, relationships with individuals and organizations outside the community who are supportive of the community's plans, and the "political and policy space" available to make changes in the conditions targeted by the community. In addition, the community conducts a power analysis of the opposition forces by creating a "power map" that identifies all the threats and the potential strength level of each of the identified threats (VeneKlasen and Miller 2002:221–22).

The SWOT assessment puts the community members in a good position to identify all of the activities that need to go into the plan for action, including methods for evaluation and opportunities for reflection based on the evaluation tools and data. The action plan should identify each person who will be responsible for carrying out different parts of the plan and include the time when each part or task will be accomplished. The plan for action is very similar to event planning in its detail.

ASSESSMENT AND PREPARATION The set of questions a potential organizer may use to assess her or his readiness to assist in planning for action might include the following:

- What is my experience in planning events and actions? Do I have wisdom, insight, or experience to offer the community in this area?
- How much do I know about other communities' experience in developing successful strategies and tactics for change? Are there nearby communities with leaders and members who could be helpful teachers and allies?
- Do I have enough knowledge about the internal and external forces at work in this setting?
- Are there ways in which the group can incorporate humor in their action?
- How will I determine whether the planned action will include and represent the diversity of people in the community? How can I help the community assess their diversity representation?
- Am I and the community group prepared if the response to the action should become violent?

A well-prepared organizer will have read many examples of strategies and tactics used by different communities to accomplish their goals (Bradford and Gwynne 1995; Fauri et al. 2008; Krishna et al. 1997; Nyden et al. 1997; Weil 2005c). The most significant assessment the organizer can complete with members of the community is thinking through and talking through all the possible actions that might be successful in changing the conditions in the community, in addition to all the possible reactions to those actions.

Along with clarifying strategies and tactics, the organization should revisit the goals and objectives of their effort. By clarifying *what* should be changed and *how* it should be changed, the organization members are poised to be able to evaluate their outcomes.

PRACTICE (SIMULATION AND GUIDED EXPERIENCE) Simulating plans of action may be useful, but the best practice is to perform the complex and detailed planning for real action to see what the outcomes will be.

EVALUATION AND REFLECTION As in earlier parts of this section, we pose questions for the organizer to use as a way of developing benchmarks for the skills they will have mastered and will continue to master. Such questions might include the following:

- How thorough were the plans for action? Did we cover all the parts of the action that were expected to be successful?
- How effective were the members of the community in carrying out their respective responsibilities?
- How well did the whole community participate in the action? Were those who participated in the action representative of the community's diversity?
- Was any follow-up promised, and if so, was it delivered?
- Has the evaluation of the action been completed?
- Has reflective discussion of the outcomes been conducted by the community leaders?
- Have new relationships with external organizations been established as the result of the action?
- What was the most positive outcome resulting from this action?
- What was the most negative outcome resulting from this action?

As noted earlier, other skills and competencies are described in later chapters, and some of these might also be applied to neighborhood and community organizing. We consider the five skills listed here as basic skills for community organizing with neighborhoods or communities. The process of gaining skills and the ability to apply knowledge and skills with sound judgment requires practice and is enhanced through the benefit of peer consultation.

CONCLUSIONS

In this chapter, we have defined neighborhood and community organization, offered ten guiding steps for engaging in neighborhood and community organization, described theories and concepts that ground this model, provided some examples from the United States and abroad, and described the basic roles, core competencies, and skills needed by an organizer working in this model. We have also outlined methods for learning these needed competencies and skills.

The work of organizing is complex and circumscribed by the context and history of the place in which the organizer is working. Finn and Jacobson (2008a:42–50) helped to raise our consciousness about context and history in their thoughtful questions: "How does context inhibit or facilitate possibilities for mutual learning? What is context specific about the process? How do past histories and experiences of participants shape the encounter and process of relationship building? How does historical consciousness inform future action?" Being able to respond to these kinds of questions builds and deepens our understanding that organizing is not just a set of steps and techniques, but also judgments informed by values and principles relating to social justice and human rights.

The two case examples associated with this chapter, Integrated Rural Development for Smallholders in Guatemala, which can be found in the *CPS Workbook*, and South African Community Work in Practice, at the end of this chapter, are examples of place-based, geographically local community practice. Although they are both success stories, the organizers and community members encountered barriers and challenges along the way. Because they come directly from the real world of practice, the description of their evolution is more complex than our discreet models developed for comparison. Consequently, you will see that the Guatemalan case organizes farmers to take risks on experimenting with new agricultural techniques but also involves education and leadership development and employs methods for social, economic and sustainable development. In the South African case, the practitioner is sequentially involved in inclusive program development, in social planning, and in direct community organizing. While practice models may be mixed or sequenced, it is critically important for the community practitioner to know at which times and in what ways methods of specific models are being employed in order to increase one's effectiveness.

As we suggested earlier, direct learning about neighborhood and community-based organizing can be significantly enhanced by finding a local organization that represents characteristics of this model, interviewing members, observing meetings, and writing up your own case example. Having the opportunity to discuss the group's development with the organizer provides even more learning. In addition, we hope it stimulates excitement for work in neighborhood and community organizing.

SOUTH AFRICAN COMMUNITY WORK IN PRACTICE: LANGA KWANOBUHLE SELF HELP AND RESOURCE EXCHANGE (SHARE)

NOMINISE JOYCE GOGO, MSW, DIRECTOR, SHARE

Langa KwaNobuhle SHARE (Self Help and Resource Exchange) is a social development NGO located in the Eastern Cape Province of South Africa, north of Port Elizabeth and 4 kilometers from the city of Uitenhage. Although SHARE serves all people in the Eastern Cape Province, it was created to focus on the residents of KwaNobuhle and Langa Townships. Langa Township is the oldest African township in Uitenhage. In 1967 the apartheid government forcibly removed the majority of African households from Langa Township to the more distant KwaNobuhle. This forced removal of people typically occurred whenever African communities were considered to be living "uncomfortably close" to the white population. Today KwaNobuhle has a population of 150,000.

Socioeconomic Conditions of the Area

Population data for the people in the Eastern Cape Province as reported in the *State of South Africa's Population Report for 2000* indicates that among the 6.5 million people who live in the province 68 percent had no access to electricity, 45 percent had no access to telephones, and at least 50 percent had no access to safe drinking water. Nearly 60 percent are below the age of 24. People in the province struggle with basic human needs as well as with the current scourge of HIV/AIDS.

Uitenhage's economy is dependent on the motor industry. Volkswagen has approximately 5,000 employees, and the Goodyear Tyre Company is the next largest company with approximately 2,000 employees. Various other small motor component factories also provide employment to substantial numbers of people. Despite these facts, unemployment remains very high, with estimates of up to 55 percent of the potential workforce unemployed. There is a high rate of alcohol abuse and violence against women and children, including abuse of the elderly. These problems are compounded by the lack of community facilities to house even rudimentary community service efforts by community groups.

The Developmental Milestones of Langa KwaNobuhle SHARE

Upon receiving an MSW at Clark Atlanta University in the United States, Nominise J. Gogo went back home to Langa Township in 1988. She later relocated to KwaNobuhle Township where she was able to buy a house for her family. The country was still under the rule of apartheid, creating political tensions and violence that filled people with suspicion and intimidation. Having grown up in this area, she was very familiar with all the social problems and political dynamics in the Eastern Cape Province. She wanted to organize the community members to take charge of their lives and social conditions and to help them break the bonds of apathy and low self-confidence. Putting community work theory into practice was, however, much more difficult than textbook directives, especially in the face of the South African racial context where black people were required to wait for the white government to do things for them. African community members complained endlessly

CONTINUED

about the failure of the white government to respond to their needs and remained despondent living in a context in which they felt helpless to do anything about it.

Ms. Gogo began by contacting several prominent people in the KwaNobuhle community, who suggested convening a community meeting to hear her ideas. From the community meeting a committee was established to work on the idea of building an organization that would help people break the bonds of dependency and begin, through self-help actions, to "ensure provision of accessible and viable social developmental welfare programs at community level throughout the Eastern Cape Province," and to "start where the people are, and with what they have, and build from there." In KwaNobuhle, there was a dilapidated and unused single man's hostel (migrant housing for workers from ethnic homelands) with twenty residential units. The community organization negotiated with the KwaNobuhle Township authority to receive it as a donation for use in the development of social welfare and development programs. After collaborative community renovation, it provided housing for the new community organization: the SHARE Community Development Complex.

Ms. Gogo became chair of the fledgling community organization while still working as a professional consultant for one of the national welfare organizations in South Africa. "It was at that organization where I learned the practical aspects of how to run and manage an organization," she notes, "something I did not learn at the university!" When in 1990 SHARE was able to hire its first two employees, it selected Ms. Gogo as the best person to lead the newly established organization. It was the same year Nelson Mandela was released from prison.

Ms. Gogo resigned her position as both chair of the organizing committee and employee of the national welfare organization to accept the new responsibilities as director of SHARE. SHARE's purpose is to serve as "an empowering social agent that works with individuals, groups, and communities to ensure provision of accessible and viable social developmental welfare programs at the community level throughout the Eastern Cape Province," and its mission is to "restore human dignity and self-respect . . . while releasing people from dependency and moving them to enhanced self-reliance."

Building an organization that could be an advocate as well as help people to organize services in the midst of a very unstable political environment required a variety of skills. Skills related to strengthening the community and building an organization included negotiating internal disagreements, giving leadership training, providing participatory decision making, and creating alternative opportunities. Skills related to advocacy and targeting systems for change involved education and community awareness, advocacy, lobbying, boycotting, and engaging collaboratively with specific local political organizations as network partners.

During the height of the rioting in South Africa, some political groups were so suspicious they presumed that Ms. Gogo, having recently returned from the United States, was a CIA spy. Some of the political groups wanted to control SHARE, so that it would be *their* social welfare arm. Even the South African police wanted to give SHARE a donation. Ms Gogo continues:

> Though SHARE was desperate for financial resources, they declined such donations because acceptance would have killed the initiative, or even threatened the lives of committee members who would have been labeled "sellouts" by other

CONTINUED

members of the community. You can imagine my horror when during the *Truth and Reconciliation* hearings, I learned that the Police Public Relations Officer, who was so desperate to give SHARE a donation, was actually the notorious police interrogator who tortured the detainees mercilessly!

The four years between Mandela's release from prison and his election as president were very dangerous times to be sorting out alliances in South Africa. During some periods of high unrest, elected committee members would not turn up for meetings. There were times when only three members were active in the organizations. To have waited until there was a quorum as was required in the organizational constitution would have meant a collapse of the organization before it got off the ground.

Ms. Gogo worked through a community needs assessment and facilitated a power analysis of social welfare resources with community members. "I focused on Paulo Freire's *Pedagogy of the Oppressed*, principles of popular education, and the need for connecting with perspectives of people who would gain from SHARE's efforts, for my primary theoretical guidance," she notes.

On the one hand, South Africa was made ungovernable by political riots, but local political activists, though suspicious, also realized that the idea of starting a social developmental community-based NGO would bring needed (and then nonexistent) services to the township. White-run organizations like Child Welfare and the Mental Health Society had been established in the center of Uitenhage but provided no outreach to the African townships. Consequently, community-based organizations, the local government authority, and health service personnel supported the ideas behind SHARE.

Even the apartheid government wanted to subdue the political opponents by seemingly supporting the "non-threatening welfare organization." Overseas donors were flooding South Africa with resources prior to 1994 to support the struggle. The efforts of Rev. Leon Sullivan in the United States to promote the Sullivan Code among international corporations brought the possibility of receiving corporate funds because corporations wanted to be seen to be supporting an NGO rather than the apartheid government. But SHARE refused to be a wing of any political organization, even though NGOs without the endorsement of the underground political parties did not have access to the large external donors. Staying neutral and focused on the mission had a negative impact on funding during the political upheaval but paid off in terms of building "dignity, humanity, and self-respect."

Being a woman leader of an NGO had some positive spin-offs. "As a woman and a professional, I delivered on what was agreed upon: I did the spade work and all necessary follow up needed to get the job done, and consequently men in powerful positions would support me," Gogo notes. The board chair, having earlier experience in dealing with white government officials, provided advice for strategies to expedite results when making appointments with them.

Ms. Gogo recounts: "I would make an appointment for a board committee and myself to see the relevant official. After I verbally presented our proposal, the official would say 'This is good, Ms. Gogo. You must just write your proposal down and send it to me.' Then I would respond, 'In fact Sir, here is a written proposal' and I would hand it to him. Now the official was not prepared for that and so I managed to cut out any delaying tactics on his part.'"

CONTINUED

At the same time some political activists struggling for South Africa's freedom were harassing Ms. Gogo for refusing to comply with their wishes to have SHARE come under *their* wing. She recounts:

> The chairman and treasurer of SHARE, both men, would accompany me as I would be summoned to answer allegations or demands. I would just be there and the men would answer and defend my actions based on positions taken by them as board members of SHARE! I had a significant role in fundraising and in proposing strategies for our goals, but always with the approval of the board. At that time, most people, both women and men, dared not defy the freedom fighters. So, the male board members respected this "brave woman who would tell them that her Social Work profession gave her the mandate to assist with the social wellbeing of her people and improve the quality of their lives," and as she is not interested in politics, that is her own contribution to the "struggle for liberation"!

SHARE Matures and Diversifies into Community Development Activities

Through boycotts, community education, and publicity, the *right* to social welfare service delivery was forcibly brought to the attention of the government and the community as a whole. Today, in addition to its advocacy role, SHARE supports the Ithembalethu Youth Support Center, which provides fifty out-of-school youth infected and affected by HIV/AIDS with immune boosting food parcels, skills training, and, for those who can work, job placement. Ithembalethu further provides a protective workshop for mentally disabled youth, where they learn to care for themselves, form relationships in a nonthreatening and supportive environment, and learn survival and hand work skills. SHARE also supports the Lukhanyiso Home for more than forty children, from babies to 22-year-olds, who were abandoned, orphaned, or suffer from abject poverty.

When requested, SHARE provides mentoring services to newly established community-based organizations. These organizations are fiercely independent and are vigilant against being exploited by established organizations as they often were in the past. Formerly, some well-established organizations would approach these emerging organizations to find out what they were doing and how. They would promise to help them seek funds and provide them professional guidance to improve their services. Unfortunately, when funds were secured, they would be used mostly to sustain the administration of these established organizations and the people in the emerging organizations would often be ignored and marginalized.

Depending on available funding, SHARE provides skills training projects for women and has a fully equipped catering kitchen and bakery. They hold workshops on HIV/AIDS, children's rights, child trafficking, child pornography, as well as public education workshops on selected government legislation, so that people know about and can begin to access their rights and services. House-to-house campaigns promote awareness about birth registrations, child sexual abuse, and violence against women. SHARE also provides an after-school program for both the Lukhanyiso Home children and children from the surrounding neighborhood.

Through Community Outreach, a soup kitchen feeds sixty to ninety-five children per day at least three times per week. A new Self Help Group Approach spreads SHARE

CONTINUED

services through the outskirts of the Nelson Mandela Bay metropolitan municipality reaching out to displaced farm workers living in informal settlements in the outskirts of the metropolitan area. The Self Help Group Approach focuses on establishing Savings Clubs as a vehicle for creating sustainable self reliance. With ten established groups, the target goal is to organize 150 such groups, which would then later create a federation of self-help groups in the metropolitan area.

The community members of KwaNobuhle are politically alert and now know and demand their rights. There are a lot of talented and motivated youth who unfortunately, due to lack of avenues to express their talents and skills, end up destroying themselves through alcohol abuse. SHARE would like to "unearth this youth talent and channel it into community building and thus mak[e] a contribution to strengthening their hard earned liberation." SHARE rents office space and workshop space to other community-based organizations, emerging nongovernmental organizations, and budding entrepreneurs. Operating from a fixed address facility that is traceable and easily accessible assists emerging NGOs registered as Not For Profit Organisations (NPOs) and youth groups to increase their chances of accessing all the government initiatives to improve their quality of life.

SHARE was finally recognized as a viable social developmental welfare organization when the Eastern Cape Department of Social Development approved its funding application and subsidized social work, social auxiliary work, and administrative posts for the organization. SHARE is recognized by many in the province as one of the best run community based NGOs.

SHARE Community Developmental Complex
Jabavu Street, KwaNobuhle, Uitenhage
Eastern Cape Province, 6230, South Africa
e-mail: SHARE@MAIL.NGO.ZA

6

ORGANIZING FUNCTIONAL COMMUNITIES

A Cherokee grandfather spoke of two wolves engaged in a terrible fight inside of him. One wolf represented fear, arrogance, lies. The other represented joy, faith, and generosity. "Which wolf will win?" a grandchild asked. "Why, the one I feed," the elder answered.

FRIENDS COMMITTEE ON NATIONAL LEGISLATION, MARCH 2008

We will surely get to our destination if we join hands.

AUNG SAN SUU KYI, BURMESE POLITICAL LEADER

INTRODUCTION

Karen Tse grew up in Los Angeles, California, the daughter of Chinese immigrants. After completing law school in the United States and working in the San Francisco public defender's office, she took a position working on legal reform in postwar Cambodia in 1994. In Cambodia she founded the Cambodian Defenders Project and Legal Aid of Cambodia, and trained prison guards, police, and judges through the United Nations Center for Human Rights. She returned to the United States in 1997 to enter Harvard Divinity School. By the time she finished, she had founded International Bridges to Justice, a voluntary organization that connects legal aid and human rights volunteers, usually lawyers and citizen groups, who form "Communities of Conscience" with public defender's offices in other countries, including China and Vietnam. International Bridges to Justice, a citizen organization, has a formal agreement with the Chinese government to work with legal aid bureaus and the criminal justice system in thirty-one provinces. Under Karen's leadership, people who have a primary commitment to human rights and fairness in judiciary systems have collaborated across oceans to build infrastructure and train practicing attorneys in legal aid and criminal law (ASHOKA 2009).

In Uganda, Africa, Mary Kafuko completed her social work education when she was 34 years old, after five of her children were born. She lost her husband in the factional violence that has claimed the lives of too many in Uganda and its neighboring countries, and she now works in Jinja, Uganda, on the shores of

Lake Victoria. Jinja is a city of more than 100,000 people where the average annual household income is estimated to be US$100. Still, many young people are drawn to the city to escape ethnic and political conflicts and to access economic opportunities lacking in the rural countryside. Mary Kafuko and her colleagues have formed the Adolescent Development Network, an organization that works with young people, children and adolescents, who live on the streets (Kafuko 2007).

With her colleagues Kafuko started a vocational school for girls who have worked primarily as prostitutes. Little by little, the girls are learning to make things they can sell such as clothes and crafts. Kafuko says, "The girls I have helped mostly go out to help other girls themselves. My goal in life is to help other people. Sometimes you are very tired, but it gives new energy whenever you see a girl who used to earn her money with prostitution now working as a hairdresser assistant" (Kafuko 2007). Kafuko also works in villages outside the city where, in collaboration with the village chiefs and community members, they have built water systems, improved roads, and begun cultivating abandoned land for vegetable crops that can be sold at the village market. With this new income, it is hoped young people will not experience so much pressure to migrate to the city where many, unable to find job opportunities, turn toward dangerous livelihoods.

Mary Kafuko and Karen Tse are what we call functional community organizers. Both of them are working with their colleagues, sharing common interests, even though one works in a city and surrounding region and the other works across continents. In the Adolescent Development Network, the common interest is in changing the negative outcomes for young people, especially girls, who come to the city for work, and in helping them to find other economic opportunities in the villages from which they come. International Bridges to Justice works to support human rights along with contributing to social development and justice systems with integrity. They have created communities of interest that function together to make specific changes, one group focusing on human rights and criminal justice, the other on opportunities for street youth and young prostitutes.

Functional communities are composed of people who have a common interest about something they would like to change but may not live in close proximity to one another. The functional communities we describe are interested in taking actions toward social justice goals and in expanding education and information about their issues to the wider public. The people in these functional communities organize to respond to the needs of children with developmental disabilities, to support people with HIV/AIDS, to prevent trafficking of women and children for slavery and sexual exploitation, to establish services for the frail elderly, to eliminate landmines, and similar social justice interests. Because they are not necessarily located in close proximity to one another, they make extensive use of newsletters, conferences, telephones, teleconferences, and Internet sources as their primary means of communication.

Organizing functional communities is the practice of bringing people together who are like-minded to work for specific social justice outcomes. The work involves not only changing behaviors and attitudes of the general public and government institutions, but also providing services for the organization's target population. Making services available is sometimes the catalyst for organizing wider social justice efforts because engagement with people who are oppressed—such as young girls who become prostitutes because they cannot find other work in the city, or people who are arrested for crimes but are never charged and sometimes languish in subhuman prison conditions—provides the content and context for organizing social change. As already noted, the people who become part of such an organization may or may not live in close proximity, so communication becomes particularly important to the organizing process.

SCOPE OF CONCERN

Functional community organizing may be seen as having three main goals: identifying and clarifying the particular conditions that contribute to a specific social injustice; providing services to individuals and families affected by the conditions; and developing strategies to stop or mitigate the negative conditions and promote supportive and positive outcomes. In the examples we have described, Mary Kafuko's interest started in providing services for desperate youth who found themselves living in the streets of Jinga, Uganda, when they could not find work. This interest led her to probe the larger concern of how and why they were coming to the city in such large numbers. With the creation of her organization she identified more people with similar concerns. These were people who could engage with the youth in providing services and in turn could learn the stories told by the youth that would expand understanding of the context and content of their conditions. Once their stories were better understood, the organization could begin working with the chiefs and refugee leaders in the villages surrounding Jinga, where they could be supported in developing preventive measures. Now Mary Kafuko has a Web site that not only describes the work of the Adolescent Development Network, but also shares pictures and stories of the youth with whom the functional organization works (Kafuko 2007).

Karen Tse learned about the plight of the low-wealth detainees in working with Vietnamese refugees in Thailand and Hong Kong, as well as with human rights advocates in Cambodia. She not only clearly learned the culture of the criminal justice systems in these locations, she also learned about the unavailability of training for legal defenders. In many cases, volunteers are unwilling to assist with criminal defense of the indigent because it is unpopular and may even be dangerous. Karen built her International Bridges to Justice organization with a focus on three goals: securing the agreement of governments by working toward the mutual interest of developing good international reputations; developing partnerships within the countries of people who could provide practical services; and bridging those groups of practical local people with groups of citizens from the international community who could provide supportive, technical assistance (ASHOKA 2007).

BASIC PROCESS: TEN GUIDING STEPS

Many of the ten guiding steps described in chapter 5 are similar to those for functional community organizing, with variations focused on the desired outcomes for this model. Again, the guiding steps are not intended to be followed in lockstep sequence. Sometimes a step forward requires two steps back to reevaluate the issues, incorporate new information, and rethink goal specification and strategies. The list is a guideline for the community worker, helping the worker to think systematically about potential opportunities for effective engagement with functional communities.

1. **Identify and establish a working relationship with a functional community organization or help to create an organization if needed.** In this step the community worker helps an organization that is already forming around a particular interest, or helps a group of people with a common interest to form an organization to be able to prevent or diminish negative outcomes for a common concern. The community worker needs to be grounded in the values of social justice and human rights prior to beginning work. These are the values underpinning the community worker's desire to become involved with people around a common interest. In addition, the community worker would want to have some special knowledge about the common concern. For example, if the group had concerns about how the community could adequately respond to the needs of children and young adults with developmental disabilities, the community practice workers would need deeper knowledge about developmental disabilities, their origins, legal and service support systems, family support systems, and best practice intervention methods. Another example could be work with an organization focused on regional food security. Such work would require deeper knowledge of the context and history of food deficits and resources, food surplus

opportunities, nutrition and health concerns, and development of community gardens. Building a relationship with the group requires developing a deep knowledge about the issues from research and historical sources, while at the same time keeping open to the group members' knowledge and perceptions so that a process of co-learning and mutual trust building can occur.

2. Assess the leadership and organizational assets and challenges within the existing or potential organization using popular education and participatory appraisal techniques. This step requires a collaborative assessment in order to help the community worker understand how the organization hopes to develop and what she/he could be doing with the organization to help them reach their desired goals. People may be motivated to form or join an organization based on their affinity with the common concern, but each person may bring a different agenda to the organization. In addition, the organization may be at a very beginning stage of coming together to identify concerns about a similar issue (e.g., developmental disabilities, food security, discrimination against immigrants, land mine injuries, care for the frail elderly, health needs of children). They may also be at a stage of trying to establish services to respond to the common concern (e.g., services for battered partners or homeless teens). The organization may be primarily concerned about the contributing factors of the common interest and may wish to work on preventive measures (e.g., stopping the trafficking in people, drugs, or munitions). They could be organizing regionally, nationally or internationally to develop a greater interest in their common concern. Their organizing members may be primarily people who are the victims of the concern or advocates against its negative outcomes, or both. Engaging with the people who are forming, or have already established, the organization is a collaborative process designed to continue building respect, knowledge, and trust between the community practice worker and the organizational members.

3. Assist the organization to learn about the range of interventions—service, advocacy, prevention—in order to help them identify where to apply strengths and resources. In this process, the community worker will want to consult with wide networks of service and advocacy organizations in order to collect wisdom from successful functional community organizations. The community worker may have been chosen by the organization because of her or his previous work with service or advocacy efforts. In 1992, for example, six nongovernmental organizations came together around their common concern for the proliferation of landmines. Landmines and cluster bombs keep exploding long after the wars are ended, and their victims are usually children and farmers. The destructive nature of these antipersonnel munitions brought victims and advocates together to form the International Campaign to Ban Landmines (ICBL 2009).

In this effort, the ICBL sought the help of Jody Williams, who had worked with programs providing medical aid to El Salvador and had coordinated educational programs in Central America following the Contra Wars. Williams's organizational skills and postwar knowledge would help facilitate the group's broad flexible network as they worked toward their goals of an "international ban on the use, production, stockpiling, and transfer of antipersonnel landmines, and for increased international resources for humanitarian mine clearance and mine victim assistance programs" (ICBL 2009:1). Williams combined her own understanding of international conflict in Central America with the specific information about landmine devastation provided by such groups as Handicap International, Human Rights Watch, and the Vietnam Veterans of America Foundation. Within five years this group of people with a common interest developed the strategies needed to sufficiently awaken the world about the need to stop this destructive human activity by collaborating with citizen organizations, one country at a time. For each country the goal was to establish legislation for an antipersonnel landmine weapons ban. In September 1997, 130 nations signed on to the International Ban on Landmines in Oslo, Norway (ICBL 2009:1). The mutual learning between Jody Williams and the human rights, humanitarian, children's, veterans', arms control, religious, environmental, medical, development, de-mining, and women's groups from sixty different countries led to the synergy of knowledge and political will necessary to move the campaign forward, country by country. In 2008, a total of 156 countries had signed on to the convention; regrettably the United States has still not become a member of that group, although President Barack Obama did sign a law within two months of taking office in 2009 to restrict the export of nearly all cluster munitions.

4. **Assist organizations to develop techniques for setting goals, objectives, outcome measures, strategies, and tactics for reaching their goals.** Organizations have many different ways of reaching decisions and coming to terms with how to establish priorities for action. In the International Campaign to Ban Landmines, the original coalition of six organizations welcomed any organization to join them as long as they signed a commitment to the three goals of the campaign: a ban on the use, production, stockpiling, and transfer of antipersonnel landmines; increased resources for humanitarian mine clearance; and mine victim assistance. No dues were collected, and no specific directions were given for how each collaborating NGO worked in their own country to persuade their governments to sign on to the international ban. However, open communication was critical to keeping each group connected to the wave of efforts that eventually brought the 156 countries to sign the ban, 130 in Oslo and 26 countries since 1997 (ICBL 2009; Peace Talks Radio 2007).

Technologies for reaching consensus, setting priorities, deciding on goals, and developing strategies and techniques range from very basic paper voting to weighted ranking as in Nominal Group Technique (NGT) or facilitated inter-group dialogue. The modification of NGT particularly designed for distant participants is the Delphi Technique (Delbecq, Van de Ven, and Gustafson 1975). Because collaborating members of functional organizations are often not located in the same region or country, Internet discussion and ranking can be employed. Whatever methods are used, the community practitioner should take care to incorporate all the voices from among the common interest group members.

5. Assist the organization leaders to develop skills for forming alliances, acquiring resources, and employing wide and inclusive communication systems. Effective communication is part of the key to forming alliances. If people can easily understand what an organization is doing, they might more readily join in the effort. Thus, it is probably inconceivable that a functional community would not have a Web page and an electronic newsletter. For functional communities whose members may not easily meet face to face, the full range of telephone, Internet, text messaging, video, and teleconferencing, discussion forums and blogs may be part of the communication repertoire (Homan 2008). Functional communities may also want to make use of radio and television public service announcements, newspapers, and even billboards.

Following the success of the International Coalition to Ban Landmines, a related organization initiated a campaign to ban cluster munitions—bomblets usually dropped from the air in a big bomb and scattered across the countryside. Many of these munitions, sometimes as many as 30 percent, do not explode upon impact. Unbelievably, some of the cluster bombs dropped in Afghanistan were the same color as small food parcels dropped to villagers high in the mountain valleys (Mortenson and Relin 2006). The cluster munitions ban campaign again has brought together a wide group of concerned organizations to persuade individual countries to sign on to the convention. The American Friends Legislative Committee organized a tour across middle America to support the campaign. They toured states with influential senators, bringing with them international advocates: the father of a small child who had died in Lebanon while celebrating his birthday in a park, a 17-year-old who lost both legs in Afghanistan, and the mother of a soldier who had died while engaged in a bomb-clearing effort in Afghanistan, a duty for which he had volunteered. Communication within the group of concerned beneficiaries and advocates is of primary importance, but communication with the external public, with people who may have the power to influence progressive change, and with people who will support service and policy efforts, is equally critical.

6. Assist the organization to develop strategies that incorporate both the voices of those who will benefit from the intervention as well as the advocates for change. In some functional community organizing efforts, all the strategies are developed by those who will benefit from change or their immediate guardians. In many programs for children with developmental disabilities, it is the parents of these children who become the leaders, trainers, community spokespersons, lobbyists, and educators. In programs working to diminish the spread of HIV/AIDS, it is often those who are living with the disease who have become the most effective and persuasive advocates for needed prevention and service programs all across the globe. Campaigns to reduce homelessness are frequently composed of advocates for affordable housing as well as people recently or still homeless in a community. The important concept here is that people who are the most oppressed by a condition should be included in discussions about how it should be changed. They should also be encouraged to participate in carrying the message about the change needed to the public and to policy makers.

7. Assist the organization to learn how to manage internal conflict and disagreement as the organization grows and as a range of strategies are implemented. All organizations will have internal disagreements because of the variety of perspectives people bring to issues. As ideas are promulgated to confront and contravene the negative conditions that sustain the concern, and as plans for services unfold, differences of opinion will be discussed. It should be assumed that disagreements are part of the ongoing dialogue to find solutions for problems. Methods and practices to encourage the openness of communication, to facilitate sufficient airing of perspectives, and to build consensus should be part of the workings of the organization from an early point. It is preferable to have some agreed upon rules of discussion that can norm civil discussion without shutting off important counterpoints. Often it is the community practice worker who provides the options for this kind of discussion and who can keep a neutral position on opposing views and help the group explore the potential outcomes of the views and strategies. It is also sometimes necessary for growing organizations to consider a complete reorganization of their structure as they consider the future and their evolving goals. The existing structure may not be sufficiently robust, inclusive, and flexible.

8. Assist the organization to monitor and evaluate their progress toward goals. Even before strategies are implemented, the organization should spend time discussing how success will be evaluated, as well as the usefulness and effectiveness of the outcomes. These evaluation and monitoring processes could be quite simple, or they could be complex, but thinking about them before action is taken ensures a better measurement effort. Outcome information can be used to solicit additional funding or to call for more heroic efforts, or it can be

used to celebrate the organization's periodic successes. In the Campaign to Ban Land Mines, the 130 individual governments that met in Oslo, Norway, in 1997 to sign on to the ban was a simple but powerful measure of the flexible but fierce five-year organizing effort of more than 1,000 nongovernmental groups in more than sixty countries.

9. **Assist the organization to plan for and take effective action.** Action taken by communities of interest or functional communities might include mounting a successful campaign for policy change or developing an effective program of service. Although planning for a policy change and planning for a program are very different activities, both require significant attention to detail. All of the who, how, when, what, why, why not, and what if questions should be considered before the action is taken. A broad range of actors should be involved in the effort, both to be inclusive and to exert strength. An action taken by only a few leaders, or a program planned by an elite few, will not have the depth of support needed to be successful. In the model for social planning discussed in chapter 9, we provide a more comprehensive framework for making plans for action.

10. **Assist the organization to plan celebrations that mark the progress of leadership, organizational development, and action victories.** The work that functional communities do to diminish and eliminate social injustice is serious work, whether undertaken to ban landmines, to provide services for children with disabilities and their families, to connect with frail elders living alone, to stop the spread of HIV/AIDS, or to stop hunger in the world. That is all the more reason that celebrations—art, music, poetry, drama, festivals—all these things should be incorporated into the work of a social justice organization.

All human development, in the words of the Chilean economist Manfred Max-Neef, requires subsistence, protection, affection, understanding, participation, leisure, creation, identity, and freedom (Max-Neef 1992). According to Max-Neef, these needs are "the same in all cultures and all historical periods" (1992:203). Many of these needs can be partially satisfied when an individual can engage in an organization with which they feel some passion and common concern. Opportunities for participation and creation can be available in an organization that lights the fire within its members, and celebration of the victories and milestones in functional organizing can satisfy the needs of affection, understanding, participation, leisure, creation, identity (i.e., personal meaning), and freedom.

THEORIES AND CONCEPTS THAT GROUND THE MODEL

The theories and concepts that ground functional community organizing can be drawn from four major streams of theory discussed in depth in chapter 4:

social change theories, group and empowerment theories, organizational and interorganizational theories, and *communication theories.* Here we focus on some concepts from these theory streams that we believe are most useful to the work of organizing functional or communities of interest drawn from a wide range of research and practice (Finn and Jacobson 2008a; Gutierrez and Lewis 1999; Hawken 2007; Homan 2008; Rivera and Erlich 1998; Rubin and Rubin 2007; Staples 2004; VeneKlasen and Miller 2002; Weil 2005c). The concepts most relevant to this model are as follows:

- Deep understanding of the issues: specifically issues related to power, empowerment, and identity of interest group participants (e.g., ethnic, social, sexual orientation, spirituality, acculturation, and human rights).
- Strategies for advocacy (e.g., education, campaign, collaboration, contest, direct action).
- Communication methods for inclusive networking: accessibility and appropriateness.

DEEP UNDERSTANDING OF THE ISSUES

A "deep" understanding of the issues requires efforts on the part of the community practice worker to read and engage beyond the obvious and superficial. Deep means far down and way back from the front. We are not using the term *comprehensive* because we don't want to imply all inclusive or exhaustive knowledge—sitting on the sofa and reading for five years, or engaging in endless research before being able to act. There is a middle place where one reads thoroughly, engages with the actors who are bearing the injustice, and engages with research that discovers the nuances of best approaches or interventions in preparation for action. Using the term *deep* also positions the community practice workers to use critical thinking as they stay current with new knowledge, new developments, and new opportunities to diminish social injustice. "Deep" requires engagement and action as part of the learning process, and staying alert and open to new learning. Of specific importance is gaining knowledge and experience with issues related to power, empowerment, and identity (e.g., ethnic, social, sexual orientation, spirituality, acculturation, and human rights) as these are interpreted by interest group participants.

As with neighborhood and community organizing, the organizer working with functional communities cannot neglect understanding group process and facilitation, principles of democratic participation, social capital, and collective efficacy. Power and empowerment analyses are needed to understand how the people concerned identify themselves in relation to the issue (e.g., citizens, advocates, service beneficiary, victims, etc.). Similarly, one must understand how the different constituencies describe and define the usefulness or availability of service resources. The constituents of interest groups will have cultural perspectives and beliefs that shape the ways they define the problem. Particularly, how do the constituent groups and individuals relate themselves to such identities as ethnicity, social class, sexual orientation, gender, spirituality, religion, family groups, community groups, and advocate groups, given the multiple identities we all carry with us? Examples could be how a whole family is affected by the disability of one member or how HIV/AIDS threatens whole ethnic populations.

We have stressed the importance of human rights, but especially the rights of women and girls as key factors for community practice in the twenty-first century. It is very likely that functional community organizers will at some point be working with women's and girl's groups around issues that relate to equity and human rights. It is not, however, so simple to identify a list of women's issues or women's rights without taking into consideration the social, cultural, class, and environmental contexts of issues. A helpful way to begin a deep understanding of women's issues could be to use Finn and Jacobson's "just practice matrix" (see table 6.1) as a framework for analyzing the particular issues of a women's group with whom the community practice worker intends to engage (2008a). Supposing a community practice worker wanted to help a group of people work to diminish trafficking of women and girls. The "just practice matrix" provides focus for questions to help the worker engage with the group in a respectful and deep way.

At first glance antitrafficking work might seem a fairly easy topic around which to build consensus. In fact, when a deeper understanding of cultural, gender, historical, and social factors are examined, it soon becomes more complex (Stop the Traffik 2008). In a recent critical analysis of the discourses surrounding trafficking in women and female migration, Deliana Popova looks at different perspectives as communities of interest try to frame a response to trafficking (2006). The Protocol to Prevent, Suppress, and Punish Trafficking in Persons, adopted by the United Nations in 2000 and entered into force in 2003, has heightened our awareness of this terrible problem, which has devastating effects, especially for vulnerable women and children from economically depressed countries (United Nations Office on Drugs and Crime 2007). But as Popova states, the two primary antitrafficking groups are not in agreement about how to enforce the protocol because of their differing views about prostitution. One group, led by the Global Alliances against Trafficking in Women, believes a distinction must be made between sex work, which can be a "free choice," and "forced" prostitution, which should be considered trafficking. The perspective of the other group, led by the Coalition Against Trafficking in

TABLE 6.1 Using Finn and Jacobson's "Just Practice" Concepts for Deep Analysis

KEY SOCIAL JUSTICE CONCEPTS AS IDENTIFIED BY FINN AND JACOBSON	QUESTIONS FOR AN ORGANIZER ENGAGING WITH A GROUP OF PEOPLE WORKING AGAINST TRAFFICKING OF WOMEN AND GIRLS
Meaning	What is the significance of the encounter and relationship between the organizer and the group working against trafficking? How do the different parties involved interpret the concern/issue? How do the group members interpret their relationship with the organizer?
Context	How do interpersonal, organizational, and social contexts shape relations and trust building? For example, are the people involved most interested in prevention of crimes and prostitution, in human rights protections, or other approaches? How can the context be examined in order to facilitate common interests, engagement, and collaboration?
Power	How do differing positions of participants shape their engagement with the organizer? Are women involved in the discourse and interpretation of the issues? How does gender play into the interpretation of problems, resources, goals, and desired outcomes? What forms of power need to be addressed in the engagement process? How can available power be exercised to promote justice in relationships and in the change efforts?
History	How do past histories and experiences of participants shape the encounter, the process of relationship building with each other and relationship with the organizer? What prior knowledge and assumptions might promote or inhibit the engagement and change processes?
Possibility	What are the possible relationships that can be formed and strengthened in this change effort? What new perspectives and understandings should be incorporated in the analysis? What spaces for hope and trust can be opened that might facilitate a change process?

Source: Adapted from Finn and Jacobson 2008a:202.

Persons, is that prostitution is a "moral evil" and no women would voluntarily enter into its practice (Popova 2006:73–74). Apparently, neither of these groups has incorporated into their analysis an even deeper concern for the role of "racism, xenophobia, and social prejudice against migrants and prostitutes" and against the poor, which are significant factors in why trafficking is able to flourish (Popova 2006:74).

No matter what the issue, an organizer working with a functional community needs to explore in some detail forces that keep problems in place and examine barriers that prevent movement toward solutions. This analysis should be done from the perspective of both the organizer and the people involved with the issues. The organizer may not agree with the analysis of the people wanting to change the conditions, but some compatibility in understanding the causes, context, history, influence of race, gender, culture, social construction, and possibilities for change would be important in establishing a working partnership.

STRATEGIES FOR ADVOCACY

Participants in functional or interest communities will be advocates for changing the conditions, attitudes, and actions that keep oppressive, regressive, harmful, exclusionary, and neglectful situations in place. These are the conditions, attitudes, and actions that prevent people from developing to their fullest potential and that destroy natural resources and human capital. They are conditions that resist change for a variety of reasons: society's lack of awareness, competing values, unfair power balances, or even coercive enforcement. These are the conditions that require a wide range of intellectual tools and critical analyses to help community workers become partners in seeking anti-oppressive solutions to problems (Fook 2002; Mullaly 2007).

The strategies and tactics for advocacy will be guided by an organization's mission and goals, resources, organizational strength, and leadership, as well as the context and opportunities for change. Brager, Specht, and Torczyner have described three types of tactics as collaboration, campaign, and contest (1987: 340–404). In their view, *collaboration* involves problem solving, education, joint action, and persuasion; *campaign* involves political maneuvering, bargaining, negotiation, and mild coercion; and *contest* involves direct action and disruption. An example of a problem that requires the whole continuum of tactics— education, collaboration, campaign, contest, and direct action—is the problem many communities face with drug and substance addiction. We can demonstrate this continuum of tactics from the experience of a small community in New Mexico.

The state of New Mexico leads the United States in the number of deaths from drug overdoses, reporting deaths from unintentional/undetermined drug overdoses at a rate of 17.5 deaths per 100,000 persons in 2003, more than twice the national average (Drug Policy Alliance 2007). The village of Chimayó, New Mexico, is known by tourists and pilgrims as the beautiful, bucolic community that is home to the healing chapel called the Santuario de Chimayó. The dark side of Chimayó and its surrounding county of Rio Arriba is that in the mid-1990s and continuing into the new century, it is the place in the United States with the highest rate of deaths from drug-related overdoses (Centers for Disease Control 2005; New Mexico Department of Health 1996).

The residents of Rio Arriba County have deep roots in the land, with nearly three quarters of the population being of Hispanic or Latino heritage, 14 percent Native American, and the remainder European American (Rio Arriba County Data 2000). No one in this community wanted to speak openly of the drug scourge even as the signs and death rates increased. Nor could anyone in the community ignore the senseless killings, roads littered with drug paraphernalia, and wasted and damaged youth that the surge of heroin use had contributed. In her personal and political story about the struggle to rid the community of drug abuse, Chellis Glendinning describes how the deep scars of colonial oppression became the receptors for the global drug trade (2005). In time, the community used all the tactics available—education, collaboration, campaign, contest, and direct action—to decrease the rate of drug addiction and drug overdoses in their county.

It took a while for people from different parts of the county to discuss who and how to bring the issue of drug abuse into focus when addictions touched nearly everyone in some way. An elderly woman in a wheelchair persuaded Los Hermanos Penitentes to lead the community in an Interfaith Procession to End Violence from Drugs and Alcohol (Glendinning 2005). The Procession, held in May of 1999, brought together nearly 500 people, marching through the villages and past the drug dealers' houses to the Santuario, calling forth their historical roots together with their various religious traditions in an effort to send up a cry to the heavens and a plea deep into the earth to help end the scourge of drugs. This was the education and collaboration phase. To acknowledge they were members of a community in which more of them died from drug overdoses than anywhere else in the United States was a first step. This effort was inclusive, pulling together all the area's faith traditions as well as activists, county government representatives, and family members of the murdered, the addicted and the vulnerable youth.

In the next phase, existing organizations as well as new efforts began to focus on how to respond to reestablishing family health, with a specific concern for drug addiction prevention, treatment, and harm reduction. Glendinning describes how representatives from the Eight Northern Indian Pueblo Council came together with county health department representatives, police, and treatment and counseling professionals to share ideas and approaches for intervention. In addition, "a Pentecostal minister, two Roman Catholic priests, a Presbyterian minister and several Hermanos traveled together to a week-long training given by the Pacific Institute for Community Organizing (PICO) in California" (Glendinning 2005:131).

Contest and direct action came into play as representatives from the local community carried jars of used needles they had gathered from the roads and streambeds in the villages into offices of state officials to make their case for additional funding for treatment and prevention. The combined federal, state, and local police officials participated in their own direct action by arresting thirty-one people, including members from five of the main drug dealer houses, in September 1999 (Glendinning 2005).

The battle to take back "sovereignty" continues in a community that lost its way as the history of colonization and forces of modernization resulted in psychological trauma and internalized racism, pushing people from a land-based to a wage-based, dependent, consumerist existence. Today, however, people in Chimayó have a better understanding of how they must acknowledge the problems of drug addiction, face the demons of history, cultural destruction and personal apathy, and take the action necessary to rebuild a community that values its combined cultural traditions and the health of its families. The work is collective, collaborative, and constant. The effort involves building a Health Commons that will co-locate numerous health services so that referrals for drug treatment can be made by walking a patient across the hall rather than providing the patient with referral information for a later time and place that may never be acted upon (Rio Arriba County Comprehensive Plan Draft, January 24, 2008). The work against drug addiction will continue to require community leaders to use all the tactics of advocacy—education, collaboration, campaign, contest, and direct action—to reconnect families to their cultural strengths and land-based roots, even as economies and resources change around them and their youth struggle to find an identity that will carry them into the future (Hands Across Cultures 2007; Hoy Recovery Program 2007).

COMMUNICATION METHODS FOR INCLUSIVE NETWORKING

Today organizers and organizations have at their disposal many different methods of communication. This opportunity for wide-ranging communication methods is particularly helpful to functional community organizers. In order to be inclusive, however, methods of communication must be accessible to all potential stakeholders in the functional community. Using the Internet for communication can facilitate quick communication within a geographically dispersed group, even globally, at very little expense. The rapid advance of information storage and processing and the equally rapid development of communication through improved technological transmission of information make the Internet an easy choice in communities and countries where it is accessible.

In late 1995 there were fewer than 20 million Internet users, but by 2000 there were more than 400 million users, with the expectation of reaching 1 billion by 2005 (UNDP 2001:32). As of 2008, about 1.5 billion people, or 22 percent of the world's population, had access to the Internet (International Publishers 2008).

Still, a large portion of the earth's population does not have accessibility to the Internet or even to telephones. According to the United Nations Development Report, "Thailand has more cellular phones than the whole of Africa. There are more Internet hosts in Bulgaria than in all of Sub-Saharan Africa (excluding South Africa)" (UNDP 1999:62). Communication in developing countries, and sometimes in industrialized countries, is often complicated by high costs and limited services in rural areas. Even in the United States, in rural Rio Arriba County, New Mexico, described above, nearly 12 percent of the population does not have home telephone service (*Rio Arriba County Comprehensive Plan* 2008). On the positive side, some rural areas are benefiting from the opportunity to purchase telephones in small rural villages through microcredit programs. Grameen Bank reported that they have provided microcredit to 74,422 women to buy mobile phones in Bangladesh. These "Telephone-ladies" now are able to offer phone services to "nearly half of the villages of Bangladesh" (Yunus 2004:16).

Communication in this model is less face to face and more person to person, whether it is by telephone or e-mail, in conference calls, by personal letter, in newsletters, or in conferences (Homan 2008). People who want to work against a particular social injustice, or for improved quality-of-life measures, will want to build their power base by finding other people who have similar concerns and understandings. These people may live across the street or on the other side of the planet. Understanding the use and appropriateness of the variety of methods of communication in order to help functional communities build organizations and networks will be important to community workers in this model.

The Blue Ridge Women in Agriculture (BRWIA), located in Watauga County, North Carolina, provides an example of how a variety of communication techniques can work effectively to build an organization and help its like-minded members reach their goals. The people of the western Appalachian region of North Carolina historically built their economy on the land, similar to the people of Chimayó, New Mexico. Most of the small farms, with an average of 70 acres, previously grew burley tobacco. As industrialization and the service economy grew across the country, and as farm economies diminished, most farm families had to have at least one, and sometimes two, wage earners working in service or manufacturing jobs. More recently, as tobacco became less productive and less popular because of its threat to health, farm families had to make a transition in order to keep their land and continue the viability of a land-based community (conversation with board members of the Blue Ridge Women in Agriculture, December 2004).

Sue Counts, the Watauga County Extension director, realized that for farm women in particular, some of whom farmed independently, new opportunities needed to be explored to help families keep their farms economically viable and their communities strong. She stimulated the idea among several farm women, who soon came together to form Blue Ridge Women in Agriculture (BRWIA). Initially, their communication was fairly local, with small meetings held at the Cooperative Extension offices in Boone, North Carolina, or at local restaurants. Soon, however, their network and resources expanded as they connected with other women in neighboring high mountain counties and specialists in sustainable agriculture at universities across the state: Appalachian State University, NC Agricultural and Technical State University, and NC State University.

The next level of communication required e-mail and many small and regular meetings to bring their ideas into focus and build a stronger organization. In 2004, when they planned their second annual conference, their sophistication in communication techniques was obvious, and they were able to demonstrate their focus on sustainable agriculture.

The food for the conference—chicken, eggs, cabbage, potatoes, rolls, raspberries, and peaches—all came from local growers, many of them women. Their conference sessions covered topics related to growing and marketing crops and developing business plans for the production of mushrooms, flowers, exotic fruits, organic and heirloom vegetables, pastured chickens, Christmas trees, roadside markets, and agritourism (e.g., bringing urban school kids and adults to the farm for activities such as tours, labyrinth walks through corn fields, and gourmet dinners using farm produce).

This conference provided farm women with contact information to connect with specialists from universities outside the state such as Clemson and Cornell universities. By e-mail, phone, or mail, they knew how to contact people who would help them learn how to produce goat cheese or medicinal herbs. The list of Web sites they shared ranged from general information at Appropriate Technology Transfer for Rural Areas (ATTRA), a project of the National Center for Appropriate Technology, to very specific sources for growing a particular medicinal herb or finding seeds native to their geographic region (BRWIA, August 2004).

Their organization developed a Web site for posting upcoming events, advertising classes, and recounting discussions from their regular board meetings (BRWIA 2007). Their communication methods are sophisticated, yet organic, realizing that some farm women are not yet comfortable with the world of cyber communication. Meeting at each other's farms to see directly how certain problems were solved and to spark creative thinking about how to link their efforts with local restaurants and public schools continues to provide the one-on-one communication that will build their organization. At the same time, they share ideas with a ramp producer in Tennessee, or a goat farmer in upper New York State, or even the International Slow Food Movement organization headquartered in Italy (http://www.slowfood.com/). They participate in regional Appalachian high country meetings as well as statewide sustainable agricultural conferences to deepen their understanding and commitment to the role of women in agricultural production.

Organizers of functional communities who understand the variable uses of communication methods and have skills or access to training that can help connect the organizations to appropriate communication techniques will contribute to the success of such organizations.

SOCIAL WORK/COMMUNITY PRACTICE ROLES

The work for this model again requires a multiskilled person with broad knowledge. Roles for working in functional community organizing as defined in chapter 2 are:

- Organizer
- Facilitator
- Advocate
- Writer/Speaker

In addition to these four roles, a functional community organizer will on occasion also assume roles we will discuss later (in chapter 10) related to building and sustaining coalitions. Those roles relate to *mediation, negotiation,* and *bridge building,* skills that become necessary when functional communities move in the direction of establishing alliances with groups that have the same or similar missions.

As was true of neighborhood and community organizers, the functional community organizer is usually not in a leadership role because she or he is working to build leadership in the functional organization. There are times when the organizer will speak on behalf of the organization, but their best work will be in helping leaders and members of the functional organization advocate on their own behalf. We will not reiterate our discussion of the roles of *organizer* and *facilitator* already discussed in the previous chapter, but will focus here on the role of *advocate,* including writing and speaking related to advocacy.

ROLE OF ADVOCATE

The role of advocate is critical in social work and community practice. The U.S. Council on Social Work Education (CSWE) has affirmed the importance of advocacy in social work education through its policy statement that graduates of social work would "understand the forms and mechanisms of oppression and discrimination and apply strategies of advocacy and social change that advance social and economic justice" (CSWE, EPAS 2001, Revised October 2004:7, 3.0 #4). Numerous scholars have reviewed the history and practice of advocacy in social work and its role in successful community change (Ezell 2001; Hardcastle, Powers, and Wenocur 2004; Hick and McNutt 2002; Jansson 2007; Schneider and Lester 2001). In "Ethics in Social Work, Statement of Principles," the international social work organizations state that "social workers have a duty to bring to the attention of employers, policy makers, politicians, and the general public situations where resources are inadequate or where distribution of resources, policies and practices are oppressive, unfair or harmful" and "have an obligation to challenge social conditions that contribute to social exclusion, stigmatization or subjugation, and to work towards an inclusive society" (IFSW and IASSW 2004:3).

Being an advocate is an important role in organizing functional communities and will also be identified in chapters 11 and 12 as significant in two additional models: Political and Social Action, and Movements for Progressive Change. Hardcastle, Powers, and Wenocur describe advocacy as "championing or speaking for the interest of clients or citizens" (2004:356). They identify three different kinds of advocacy: *ensuring individual rights*— rights assumed to belong to everyone; *public interest advocacy*—participating in public priority setting and redistribution of benefits; and *transformation*–engaging in bringing about profound institutional changes (2004:357–58). Each of these kinds of advocacy requires different kinds of research and action plans for different arenas.

Ensuring individual rights assumes that specific national and universal rights are agreed upon, and the work of advocacy tries to make certain that everyone can enjoy those rights. Although the rights enumerated in the thirty articles of the Universal Declaration of Human Rights are a standard from which to measure human rights, they are not yet codified or accepted in all countries and all cultures. In the new constitution of South Africa, for example, many rights such as food, housing, health care, education, and even the right of gay and lesbian persons to marry, are all guaranteed to individual citizens. A guarantee of rights can be denied if structures are not in place or if resources are not available to insure them. The South African government, under pressure from citizen advocacy groups, continues working to come to terms with economic and social resources that could make such rights accessible for all the citizens.

Public interest advocacy relates to efforts to incorporate nonexisting rights into public policy so that certain rights or conditions can be officially guaranteed and funded for all citizens. Health care, for example, is not a guaranteed right in the United States, as it is in most other industrialized countries. Many organizations in the United States are working to make health care universal so that citizens will have similar health benefits as do citizens of Spain, Canada, Japan, or Costa Rica, for example. A number of states in the United States have established policies, or are working toward policies, that will provide wider, if not universal, health care coverage for their citizens, and national advocacy groups continue to raise issues for the nation as a whole (Citizen Health Care Working Group 2007; Health Care Now 2007; WHO 2000). The new administration of President Barack Obama has called for a universal health insurance program. In the meantime 47 million people in the United States do not have health insurance.

Transformation is the most profound kind of advocacy because it draws on one's understanding of how structural circumstances keep oppressive conditions in place and of the complex social, economic, cultural, religious, political, and environmental changes necessary to eliminate or mitigate the conditions (Fook 2002; Mullaly 2007). In the case of the campaign against the high rate of drug overdoses in Chimayó, New Mexico, community leaders understand that change has to occur at the personal, family, community, state, national, and international levels. Although some changes in policies are necessary at all levels, changes in attitudes, lifestyles, opportunities, understandings, and perspectives are also necessary. In transformational advocacy, profound changes are required in the way that society perceives, defines, interprets, and engages with social, economic, and environmental conditions. When the Rev. Martin Luther King Jr. wrote his letter from the Birmingham jail in 1963 defending the use of direct action and civil disobedience to overturn 350 years of African American oppression in the United States, the society at large did not expect that profound changes would take place in a matter of years (King 1963). Of course, the transformation required to eliminate racism and xenophobia, which are structurally embedded in social, cultural, economic, and environmental arenas, is a continuing struggle.

In our definition of advocacy, we also embrace the notion of championing the interests of vulnerable and oppressed populations, emphasizing that all advocacy activity should be directed toward the transformative outcome of a more just social order. Furthermore, we identify the importance of helping people become their own advocates for more inclusive and equitable social and economic outcomes as well as recovered and protected environments (see table 2.2). Helping people and organizations engage in advocacy for themselves contributes to the building of a sense of capacity and empowerment in the work they may do in the future.

A technique for helping groups advocate for their own issues is available in the *CPS Workbook* in the form of "A People's Hearing." Women on public assistance and their allies used the format in the 1970s to help the broader local community understand the specifics of pending legislation to change welfare programs. Most of the population did not understand the complex legislation, nor did they have much interest in welfare reform. With the "People's Hearing" the people most affected by the legislative changes were able to draw in the larger community and frame the issues in terms of personal repercussions for low-income families. People's Hearings were held all over the United States, contributing to the defeat of the legislation. Equally important, welfare mothers' organizations gained significant experience and a sense of empowerment from learning how to use this form of advocacy.

ADVOCACY IN WRITING AND SPEAKING

Members of a functional community organization are often the best speakers and writers about the particular oppressive conditions that need to be changed. A woman who has been the victim of trafficking, a former child soldier, a family without health insurance or access to health care—these will be the legitimate voices of those who have been oppressed. But there are times when organizational members are not available, or cannot frame in writing the deeper story that needs to be told to a particular policy or funding organization. The most helpful role often played by functional community organizers is to do the necessary research to accurately frame the breadth and depth of the conditions that should be changed. We emphasize here *accurately* framing the issue.

In their *Action Guide for Advocacy and Citizen Participation,* VeneKlasen and Miller describe an action flow for advocacy that begins with "information and analysis," moves to "position," then "argument," and finally "message" (2002:233). The information and analysis relate to the deep understanding of the issues we have described above. Framing the issues in a focused message is the final step when the functional organization has determined who will be the particular audience. However, the message must have its origins in the group's deeper, social justice analysis.

CORE SKILLS AND COMPETENCIES FOR FUNCTIONAL COMMUNITY ORGANIZING

In this section, we discuss four competency/skill areas that are important to effectively organizing a functional community. In our use of competencies, we intend to incorporate the meaning of having sufficient *knowledge, judgment,* and *skill* to engage in the work, not simply adequate skill. Skill is the practiced ability to carry out a set of tasks. Combined with competencies, the skills used by a community practice worker will be based on good judgment about when and why to use certain skills, application of ethical wisdom as well as knowledge about the issues, effectiveness of intervention strategies, and sensitivity to cultural and gender issues that apply to the functional organizing tasks. As in the previous chapter, we define skills as not just having knowledge of the skills, but as actually being able to apply the skills and carrying out the tasks toward human rights and social justice goals.

The competencies/skill areas we identify and discuss here are:

- Analyzing human rights and social justice issues
- Advocacy
- Speaking and writing with respect to advocacy
- Building leadership and networking skills

It is our expectation that these skills can only be honed with experiential learning opportunities and with practice. Obviously, the experiential learning is best done with a mentor, guide, or even a partner who can provide feedback and appropriate questions to help the organizer become more ethical, effective, and culturally respectful.

ANALYZING HUMAN RIGHTS AND SOCIAL JUSTICE ISSUES

Earlier, we described the importance of having a good understanding of the Universal Declaration of Human Rights. We believe that establishing and safeguarding human rights, especially the rights of women and girls, will be an enduring priority throughout the next fifty years. Six additional covenants and conventions are identified in "Ethics in Social Work, Statement of Principles" as documents important for social workers:

- The International Covenant on Civil and Political Rights
- The International Covenant on Economic and Social and Cultural Rights
- The Convention on the Elimination of All Forms of Racial Discrimination
- The Convention on the Elimination of All Forms of Discrimination against Women
- The Convention on the Rights of the Child
- Indigenous and Tribal Peoples Convention (IFSW/IASSW 2004)

The Protocol to Prevent, Suppress, and Punish Trafficking in Persons, which entered into force in 2003, is yet another important document for social work familiarity (UN Office on Drugs and Crime 2007). In countries that have ratified these covenants and conventions, the citizens and their advocates can reference the rights outlined as they take action against the oppressive forces that sustain these conditions. Advocates in countries that have not yet ratified these basic human rights documents may want to start or join a campaign in favor of their ratification. The contents of these documents provide some basic knowledge to begin analysis of specific conditions.

The organizer should identify a social justice analysis framework before engagement with a functional community organization has begun. We have used Finn and Jacobson's framework—meaning, context, power, history, and possibility—as an example earlier in this chapter (2008a). Cohen, de la Vega, and Watson, having worked for many years in a variety of cultures, are clear that a value-based analysis is necessary for social justice advocacy (2001:9–10). We draw from these authors, as well as from VeneKlasen and Miller (2002), to suggest a beginning guide for social justice analysis. A social justice analysis would be

- People- and community-centered, drawing on the experiences of people who have experienced social, economic, and environmental injustices.
- Amplified by drawing on basic rights and justice documents that are recognized by global institutions.
- Representative of the knowledge and expertise of scholars and activists who have collected data about the issues.
- Cognizant of where and how to raise critical questions normally avoided by those in power.
- Able to explore, discover, and create public spaces in which debates and dialogues can be safely undertaken to examine options for change. (Adapted from Cohen, de la Vega, and Watson 2001, and VeneKlasen and Miller 2002)

ASSESSMENT AND PREPARATION As the organizer of a functional community prepares to engage with a group of people who have made a commitment to work for change in a particular social, economic, or environmental arena, a number of questions about readiness could be helpful.

- Am I sufficiently familiar with the Universal Declaration of Human Rights and the six additional conventions and covenants described in the IFSW/IASSW "Ethics in Social Work, Statement of Principles"?
- Do I understand how these documents provide basic standards for the issues at hand, are silent on some aspect of the issue, or contradictory on some aspect of the issue?

- What is the human rights/social justice framework that is most helpful to me in doing an analysis about this issue? Does this analysis framework include historic, cultural, and structural factors that keep oppression and injustice in place? Is this framework compatible with the values and understandings of the group with whom I will engage?
- Do I know where to access first-person experiences about this issue?
- Do I know where to access scholars' and other practitioners' knowledge about this issue? How will I evaluate these sources?

The analysis of issues related to functional community organizing will relate to the organization's mission, goals, and resources. As noted earlier, generally functional communities have three related goals: to identify and clarify the particular conditions that contribute to specific social, economic, or environmental problems or injustices; to provide services to individuals and families affected by the injustice; and to develop strategies to stop or mitigate the negative conditions and promote supportive and positive conditions.

Many specific issues relate to social injustice. Some people, however, believe that a focus on basic needs such as food, water, shelter, health care, or income security misses the point of a larger issue looming over all of human kind (Gore 2007). Gerald O. Barney was the director and primary author of a report published in 1980 called the *Global 2000 Report to the President* (Barney 1980). It was undertaken at the request of President Jimmy Carter to integrate "the long-term (25-year) global thinking and analysis from fourteen government agencies," from a human rather than an American citizen's perspective (Barney 2007:5). Barney discovered that most federal agencies projected biased optimistic future scenarios, perhaps wanting to make the future look good to their leader, when in fact global models actually indicated a world that was more polluted, crowded, and vulnerable in ecological and social spheres than they normally reported (1980). Since that time, Barney's analysis has continued to deepen, so that today his view is that "our largest institutions implicitly or explicitly endorse our ruthless exploitation of Earth. We are suffering from a cultural disorder—a cultural pathology—that has roots very deep in our history, religion, and sense of identity" (Barney 2007:3). It is useful to determine the depth and focus of your own values and your sense of the application of social justice and human rights values. The exercises in the *CPS Workbook* for this chapter will help you to focus and anchor your perspectives.

PRACTICE (SIMULATION AND GUIDED EXPERIENCE) Gaining experience in social justice analysis can and should first be practiced in the classroom. Together a class or agency group can study a variety of social justice analysis frameworks and examine their potential appropriateness or usefulness for understanding social, economic, and environmental injustice. All of the following authors provide some guidance for developing human rights and social justice analysis frameworks: Cohen, de la Vega, and Watson (2001), Finn and Jacobson (2008a), Ife (2006, 2007a), Reichert (2006, 2007), and VeneKlasen and Miller (2002).

Firsthand experiences can also be gained by working in nearby communities that are organizing to change policies or programs related to such issues as HIV/ AIDS, developmental disabilities, drug addiction, homeless teens, and women's concerns. Going to conferences can expose the organizer to firsthand experiences from people who are organizing on a national or global scale—for example, conferences about preventing domestic violence, banning landmines and cluster bombs, training people in nonviolent conflict resolution, and preventing trafficking in women and children. At such conferences, attendees may have the opportunity to hear from people from different cultures and perspectives, views of the world that are different from the normative views acquired in the organizer's experience. Hearing the points of view from different cultures and different experiences is helpful in evaluating one's social justice analytical framework.

Volunteering to work abroad with an organization that is linked with functional organizations, such as Earthwatch Institute, Habitat for Humanity International, Volunteers for Peace, or WorldTeach, can also provide direct experience for social justice analysis. Many schools of social work also have study abroad programs that can provide a supervised arena from which to do social justice analysis. Georgetown University has a summer abroad program specifically designed for social justice analysis (Georgetown University Summer Abroad 2007).

REFLECTION AND EVALUATION Once the organizer actually engages with a functional community organization, it will be important to establish a systematic way to regularly evaluate one's skill and ability to do the necessary analysis that is essential for organizing. A set of questions might be addressed on a three- or five-month basis to provide a time for reflection and evaluation. Some questions might be as follows:

- Am I sufficiently knowledgeable about the Universal Declaration of Human Rights and other widely accepted rights conventions and covenants that I can make reference to them as I analyze the issues of the group with which I am engaged?
- What are the primary and secondary structural barriers that keep the problem in place (e.g., social, political, economic, or environmental barriers)?
- How do people who are affected directly interpret the causes of the problem? How well can they see the structural forces such as history, social

construction, power, economic conditions, and gender roles as part of the analysis of the problem?

- Is my interpretation of causal factors or conditions similar to the interpretations of functional community members? Why or why not? Is my interpretation of causal factors or conditions similar to that of scholars in the field? Why or why not?

Reflection on these or similar questions helps functional community organizers assess their competencies to do social justice analysis and to feel confident in the positions they have taken.

ADVOCACY

Earlier, we discussed advocacy strategies including education, collaboration, campaign, contest, and direct action with regard to the efforts by the people of Rio Arriba County, New Mexico, to reduce their area's high rate of deaths from drug overdoses. We talked about advocacy again with reference to social work roles used in organizing functional communities. Here we will discuss the kinds of skills necessary to do advocacy work with functional communities.

A priority for the functional community organizer will be to help leaders and others in the community of interest to be able to advocate on their own behalf, perhaps through coaching, role plays, and simple practice sessions. There will be times when the organizer also has to serve as an advocate for the desired outcome and therefore must be prepared in terms of understanding the issues, barriers to solutions, and options for positive results.

Like other efforts at community change, functional community organizations should have an agreed-upon mission, long- and short-term goals, and measurable objectives associated with the goals. VeneKlasen and Miller describe "SMART" objectives: Specific, Measurable, Achievable, Realistic, and Timebound (2002:176–77). Spending time on developing a specific set of timebound objectives will make evaluation of the outcomes much easier.

Working toward change as an advocate may require the organizer and the community of interest to work in a number of arenas. Earlier, we talked about advocacy for individual rights, for public interest, and for transformation (Hardcastle, Powers, and Wenocur 2004). Any one of these advocacy strategies may involve intervention in at least five different dimensions. In fact, VeneKlasen and Miller report that social justice advocates around the world indicate that transformative success can only result if change occurs in all five dimensions:

- The government arena (e.g., laws, policies, programs, elections, budgets)
- The private sector (e.g., business policies, corporations)

- Civil society (e.g., civic and neighborhood organizations, nonprofit organizations, agenda setting, community planning)
- Political space and culture (e.g., making it safe and useful for individuals and groups, especially women, to participate in the political process)
- Individual level (e.g., changing the skill and attitudes of individuals so that they are engaged with decisions that affect their lives and feel positive about the opportunities and abilities open to them for progressive change) (Adapted from VeneKlasen and Miller 2002:178–79)

Making changes in all five dimensions requires the complex effort of setting goals and objectives for each arena, even though the interventions may occur sequentially. When change occurs in all five arenas, we can say that transformation is occurring.

ASSESSMENT AND PREPARATION How does the organizer develop the knowledge, skills, and judgments to become an effective advocate? We again suggest a set of prepractice assessment questions.

- Have I had any previous experience in doing advocacy? What was the experience? Was it a successful experience? Why or Why not?
- Have I had any previous experience in helping someone become an advocate on his or her own behalf? Was it successful? Why or why not?
- What are the ethical concerns that should guide my judgment in determining when a person with experience in the issue should be the advocate and when I should be the advocate?
- Of the five dimensions of advocacy work (government, private, civil society, political, and individual), in which arenas am I most knowledgeable and comfortable? Which arenas will require considerable learning and increased skill for engagement?

Examining your knowledge and skills prior to practice will keep you alert to learning and skill-building opportunities as you enter practice. In addition, you will want to make use of some of the advocacy skill-building exercises for this chapter in the *CPS Workbook*.

PRACTICE (SIMULATION AND GUIDED EXPERIENCE) Practicing advocacy could first begin in your university or in your agency. A class at your university could take on issues such as access to child care opportunities for students or concern for distant peer groups of students who suffered from a natural disaster such as a hurricane or tsunami. Or a group of people in your agency could decide to advocate for adjudicated youth who must be sent to a treatment facility 150 miles away because there is no facility nearby, for example. In each case the issues first require research. Research must be collected from the first-person voices of the people for whom the problem is a direct concern as well as from wider sources, data, and knowledge of scholars, to measure the depth and extent of the problem. The group should decide upon goals and "SMART" objectives. An ambitious effort might include goals and objectives for each of the five arenas: government, private sector, civil society, political space and culture, and, individual. The group should determine who might be most effective in the group to contact each of the different arenas and how those arenas should be contacted. In evaluating strategies, the group should analyze the effectiveness of education, collaboration, campaign, and the use of contest and direct action if necessary.

A local or regional organization might have an excellent learning opportunity if it is working on an advocacy issue, such as seeking change in state or national policy regarding those in need of adequate mental health services, or for children who need dental care, or laid-off workers who need a longer period of benefits so they can take advantage of additional education or opportunities for self-employment. The organizers' initial engagement with such regional, statewide, or national groups should be done with a qualified supervisor or mentor.

REFLECTION AND EVALUATION Following engagement in advocacy, the organizer should plan a regular assessment to reflect on her or his growth and personal development. The following questions might facilitate this assessment:

- What range of resources did I use to build my knowledge about this issue? Were they sufficient? What additional sources of knowledge could have helped me improve my social justice analysis?
- Am I effective in developing and helping others develop goals and objectives for change? Are the objectives generally specific, measurable, achievable, realistic, and timebound? Was I able to help the community of interest evaluate and reflect on the outcomes?
- Among the range of advocacy strategies—education, campaign, collaboration, contest, and direct action—which were the most effective for the different arenas or dimensions of change? Why?
- Was I able to coach functional community organization members in how to use advocacy strategies?

SPEAKING AND WRITING WITH RESPECT TO ADVOCACY

As we described earlier, speaking and writing as an advocate for a particular issue first requires extensive research. Collecting information about the factual, emotional, and collateral oppression that is at the heart of the issue around which the functional group has organized provides the basis for the public message and argument for change. In providing guidance for developing the message for change in written or spoken form, VeneKlasen and Miller suggest the following ten-point checklist:

a. Know your audience.
b. Know your political environment and moment (e.g., controversies, big issues, fears, and what is considered left, right, and center).
c. Keep your message simple and brief.
d. Use real-life stories and quotes.
e. Use precise, powerful language and active verbs.
f. Use clear facts and numbers creatively.
g. Adapt the message to the medium.
h. Allow your audience to reach their own conclusion.
i. Encourage audiences to take action.
j. Present a possible solution.
(VeneKlasen and Miller 2002:232)

The messages can be packaged in a number of different ways from formal news releases to street theater. Again, from VeneKlasen and Miller's experiences working with groups in Africa, they learned from the local community that some messages worked better than others because they were humorous, used popular expressions, were adaptations from popular songs, metaphors, stories, and poetry, were brief, rhythmic, and witty, were linked to a respected person or institution, and were appealing to children who helped inform parents and adults (VeneKlasen and Miller 2002:234).

ASSESSMENT AND PREPARATION Doing an assessment of an organizer's competence for writing and speaking as an advocate might begin with the following questions:

• What experience do I have with writing statements that advocate for a particular change as it related to social, economic or environmental oppression? How successful do I think the written document was? Why?
• What experience do I have with speaking as an advocate for a particular change as it related to social, economic, or environmental oppression? How successful do I think the speaking experience was? Why?
• How well did I use first-person experiences and expert data and knowledge in my previous advocacy efforts?

- What experience have I had in helping others advocate on their own behalf by helping them think through the message, medium, and potential outcome?

PRACTICE (SIMULATION AND GUIDED EXPERIENCE) Practice simulations can easily be organized in a class or in an agency task group. Some exercises are suggested in the *CPS Workbook*. For twenty-five years one of the authors regularly assigned her students to write a "letter to the editor" about a current issue related to poverty or racism. The students could choose the issue and the medium, even going on TV if they wanted, and they were required to shed "light" rather than "heat" on the issue. Students responded to this assignment in a variety of ways. Most wrote a letter to the editor of the campus or local newspaper, responding to an issue of racism or poverty that had recently appeared in that paper. A few testified at public budget hearings on behalf of a particular service slated for a budget cut, indicating the effect such a cut would have on the fight against poverty and/or racism. One student drove to Washington, D.C., on a long weekend to testify at a public hearing against a proposal to eliminate a subway stop in Anacostia, one of the poorest neighborhoods in the city. Happily, the subway stop was built in Anacostia.

Additional learning for the students was a requirement to examine how effective they presumed their statement would be and how the experience of making a public statement felt to them. This was important because the instructor's expectation was that the students would be helping many people in the future to advocate for themselves, and it is ethically problematic to ask people to take a risk that you would not be willing to take yourself.

REFLECTION AND EVALUATION After an organizer has had the opportunity to engage with a functional organization and participate in writing an advocacy statement used by the organization, it is a good time to reflect on the outcomes. Some questions that could help with such a reflection might be:

- How effective was I in researching and writing an advocacy statement used by the organization? What were the strengths and weaknesses of the statement? Why?
- How effective have I been in helping the organization frame its message?
- How effective have I been in helping the organization identify with the range of outlets available for getting their message out?
- How has the organization evaluated its ability to educate and persuade community members and policy makers about the needed changes in policy, program, or perception of the issue?

- Did the organization's message have the intended result? How should the message or the medium be altered to extend and deepen its persuasive effect?

This section implies that the organizer must develop all the skills necessary for communicating the message. Nowadays, with the explosion of technology for communicating messages, it is probably not possible for the organizer to be skilled and competent in all the methods of communication. The organizer should be able to identify key media people, write a press release, and organize a press conference. It will be the organizer's responsibility, along with members of the organization, to keep the message accurate and as closely tied to the experiences of the people who suffer the oppression as possible. This is part of the organizer's ethical responsibility

BUILDING LEADERSHIP AND NETWORKING SKILLS

Communities of interest generally seek to expand their connections, either in building coalitions or loose affiliations with groups that have similar interests. In numbers there is strength. In chapters 10, 11, and 12 we will speak more about the building and sustaining of coalitions, political and social action, and movements for progressive change. In this chapter we focus on building leadership that seeks to broaden the mission of the functional organization.

Leaders of functional community organizations will generally be good advocates and have good communication skills focused on the oppressive issues they hope to change. However, communication and networking responsibilities can become complex for functional organizations because they have multiple goals—educating the public about the issues, providing services for those who suffer the social, economic, or environmental injustice, and initiating specific policy and/or transformational changes that will diminish the causes of injustice and oppression. With these multiple goals it is good for such communities of interest to groom multiple leaders that can help the organization develop action in a variety of spheres. It is also very helpful to link with like-minded organizations regionally, nationally, and globally in order to learn about other strategies and tactics employed that result in improved knowledge about the issues in the broader community and improved services and resources made available to mitigate the negative conditions and promote the positive conditions influencing the issue.

Leadership that grows other leaders will decrease burnout and increase people power by keeping many different members of the functional community organization involved in the wide range of duties required to keep an organization moving and growing. Leadership that is open to dialogue and that is comfortable engaging with new ideas and new arenas will be the most helpful to functional organizations. VeneKlasen and Miller talk about leadership roles that are both formal and informal, shared and transformative (2002:299–301). Marleen Nolten of the Netherlands Organization for International Development Cooperation describes feminist leadership as "*transformative* in the sense that it questions and challenges existing power structures; *inclusive* in the sense that it takes into account the views and fosters empowerment of the most marginalized and poorest groups of society; and *holistic* in the sense that it addresses all forms of social injustice" (VeneKlasen and Miller 2002:301). Although these characteristics of leadership are described as those of feminist leadership, both women and men in many parts of the world practice these characteristics.

In April 2007, the Leadership for a Changing World Partners (i.e., the Institute for Sustainable Communities, Research Center for Leadership in Action at New York University, and the Ford Foundation) released a report from their research over several years entitled *Quantum Leadership: The Power of Community in Motion* (Milewski 2007). The report documents the strategies and methods leaders use to build their community efforts and identifies seven critical steps for success. The seven drivers of quantum leadership are the activities related to building anchors and networks to strengthen community practice efforts. For *transforming the community* the research group identifies three elements:

- Build strong community relationships.
- Open the space for community initiative.
- Find the deep sources of strength.

For *transforming the community's environment* the research group identifies the following four elements:

- Face the wind and bend without breaking.
- Stretch and build the relationships outward.
- Encourage purposeful learning.
- Bring the future into the present. (Milewski 2007:44)

For each of these drivers, the report is filled with examples from neighborhood and functional communities that bring to life the essential inward and outward networking that contributes to the organization's success. The report also speaks of leadership teams that are open and outward looking in their work. These drivers for transforming the community and transforming the community's environment might also be compared with the bonding and bridging social capital discussed earlier.

PERSONAL ASSESSMENT AND PREPARATION Functional community organizers will want to understand their personal strengths with regard to building leadership and developing networks within an organization. Identifying and supporting the development of good leadership is an important skill. Each of us can think of occasions when as part of a group or an organization we could identify leaders who seemed well grounded in their beliefs and values, which helped them remain open to understanding new perspectives. Leaders who are able to connect fresh ideas to larger and more complex ways of framing issues provide opportunities for organizational growth and networking. At the same time, leaders who are insecure and doubt their ability to manage the group's growth and development are sometimes controlling and unsettled by new perspectives.

Some questions to help an organizer establish an understanding of his or her current skills regarding building leadership and networks might be the following:

- Have I had experience in developing leadership for a group in the past? What kind of partnership/relationship is required to assist in the development of leadership without taking over as the leader?
- Am I comfortable being a passionate advocate for a particular issue without having to be in the front of the issue at all times?
- Do I understand issues related to building networks without giving up organizational "sovereignty"? Do I understand the structural aspects of organizations that build internal strength while at the same time stay open to the wider community?
- What experience do I have in organizing networking events such as conferences or summits, or producing networking communication mediums such as newsletters, Web pages, blogs, or teleconferences?

PRACTICE (SIMULATION AND GUIDED EXPERIENCE) Opportunities for guided/supervised field experiences in helping organizations build networks will strengthen the organizers' confidence and competence. Organizers can be assigned to particular functional organizations for the purpose of helping the organization expand its leadership team and its networking relationships. For example, an organizer might work with a regional group whose goal is to diminish the rate of adolescent pregnancies. In addition to working with the organizational members, the organizer might engage with youth who understand the pressures for adolescent sexual encounters. The result of these broad contacts can provide a greater understanding of the organization's goals and mission as well as the needs of youth who can benefit from the organization's services.

Searching widely for innovative strategies and tactics builds bridges to knowledge and effective experience. Being able to connect members of the Adolescent Pregnancy Prevention Program in North Carolina, for example, with the work of the Center for the Study of Violence and Reconciliation (CSVR) in Braamfontein, South Africa, may seem like a stretch (CSVR 2004). However, the CSVR has developed an adolescent curriculum for young people to help them understand their rights regarding unwanted sexual advancement that may be helpful to the group in North Carolina working to prevent adolescent pregnancy. By making such connections, the community practice worker can suggest exercises or examples that will fortify the organization's leadership team-building and network-building capacities (Milewski 2007; VeneKlasen and Miller 2002).

Practice can involve organizing conferences and developing communication tools such as newsletters or Web pages with a local or regional functional community. Regular feedback from the mentor/supervisor/partner in the guided learning experience will be important to the organizer's growth and skill development. Feedback from members of the functional community organization with whom the organizer is working will also be very helpful.

REFLECTION AND EVALUATION Following the actual work with a functional organization, the organizer will want to do regular assessments to measure his or her effectiveness in developing transformative leadership and building community networks. Some questions that might be included on such an assessment are:

- What particular actions of the organizational leaders demonstrate their transformative, inclusive, and holistic qualities (e.g., leaders analyze and challenge existing structural barriers to change; take into account the views and foster empowerment of the most marginalized and poorest groups of society; address all forms of social injustice)? What role have I played in helping to strengthen those qualities in leaders with whom I have worked?
- What can I do as an organizer to help the leadership team become more transformative, inclusive, and holistic?
- What particular indicators demonstrate that the organization has increased its networks? How effective are its communication methods within its region? How effective are its connections with similar groups across borders?

- What can I do as an organizer to help the leadership team increase its networks?

Formal reflection sessions with organizational members that will explore the questions "How am I doing as an organizer for your group?" and "Am I helping you to reach the specific goals and outcomes you have identified for your organization?" can be helpful to the growth and development of the organizer.

CONCLUSIONS

In this chapter we described the work that a community practice organizer can accomplish working with functional communities or communities of interest. Sometimes the work will involve helping the organization identify and clarify particular conditions that contribute to a specific social injustice. It may also involve helping the organization provide services to individuals and families affected by the condition or issue. And it can also involve developing strategies to stop or mitigate negative factors and promote attitudes and actions that will result in positive outcomes.

The important roles the community practitioner can play in this model are as organizer, facilitator, advocate, and writer/speaker in effectively making the case for social, economic, or environmental policies that could result in more inclusive and equitable outcomes for the targeted population. Community practice social workers can evaluate their effectiveness by assessing specific outcomes of the organization, or networks of organizations, with whom they work to:

a. improve the optimum functioning of people affected by a negative condition through the establishment or expansion of services, rights, and resources;
b. increase the social capital and successful change efforts of communities struggling with a negative condition by building the leadership and networking capacity of the organization; and/or
c. recover and protect the environments that provide basic resources for people and their future generations in terms of good health, productive livelihoods, beauty, and serenity.

The measurability and specificity of these outcomes will be established by the organizations themselves.

Developing one's skills for this work requires the willingness to practice under the direction of a field instructor or mentor, and requires personal assessment of one's abilities as well as feedback from the people with whom one works in the functional community organization. There are hundreds of opportunities to work toward social justice and human rights with communities organized around special interests. Skilled community practice workers in this model are highly valued.

7

SOCIAL, ECONOMIC, AND SUSTAINABLE DEVELOPMENT

In these opening years of the twenty-first century, as the human community experiences a rather difficult situation in its relation with the natural world, we might reflect that a fourfold wisdom is available to guide us into the future: the wisdom of indigenous peoples, the wisdom of women, the wisdom of the classical traditions, and the wisdom of science.

THOMAS BERRY, *THE ECOZOIC READER*

When we tug at a single thing in nature, we find it attached to the rest of the world.

JOHN MUIR, NATURALIST, FOUNDER OF THE SIERRA CLUB

Recall the face of the poorest and most helpless person you have ever seen and ask yourself if the step you contemplate is going to be of any use to them. Will they be able to gain anything by it? Will it restore them to a control over their life and destiny?

MOHANDAS GANDHI, 1948

INTRODUCTION

In 1972 two dedicated social entrepreneurs returned to Bangladesh from studies abroad to begin the task of developing programs and services for the poor in their newly independent country. Both had received formal educations in Britain and the United States, one in finances and the other in economics. They worked independently, but their common interest was in making changes for the destitute. Soon both discarded the Western theories about development and economics they had learned abroad for a more grounded understanding of what was really happening to the poor in Bangladesh and what they needed. People's lives had been disrupted by the war for liberation and by devastating cyclones. The two social entrepreneurs drew their knowledge for action from understanding people's dignity and livelihoods. They set aside the idea of top-down grand plans for homegrown solutions that would respect the social and cultural heritage of the people.

One of those entrepreneurs, Fazle Hasan Abed, founded BRAC (formerly Bangladesh Rural Advancement Committee, now Building Resources Across Communities) as a small rehabilitation and relief project to assist refugees returning to Bangladesh. Today BRAC, one of the largest nongovernmental organizations in the world, has a staff of about 30,000 and works to expand services for microfinance, skills training for income generation, women's legal rights education, a women's health and family-planning program, and a nonformal education program for children of BRAC microfinance borrowers, while still responding to the devastation of cyclones that plague the low-lying delta provinces (Rao, Stuart, and Kelleher 1999). BRAC's microcredit program serves about 7 million borrowers (100,000 of them are the extremely poor, including beggars) and reaches 11 percent of the nation's school children who would not be in school except for the BRAC informal schools (ASHOKA, Conversations Network 2007; RESULTS 2008a).

The second person to return to Bangladesh in 1972 was Muhammad Yunus, who took the post as head of the Economics Department at Chittagong University. He and his students explored the poverty in the villages around the University. They learned that forty-two local craftspeople together needed a loan of only US$30 to be able to avoid the high interest rates charged by the traders who purchased their crafts. At first Yunus used his own money to lend to small vendors and craftspeople, but after some years of working with people who could not get loans from banks because they had no collateral and could not complete the complicated forms demanded of banks, he founded the Grameen Bank, a people's bank, in 1983. "Credit" says Yunus, "is a kind of key, a passport to explore the potential of a person" (Yunus 1997:10).

Thus began the grand experiment in micro lending that earned Yunus the Nobel Peace Prize in 2006. Grameen microcredit and the BRAC microfinance programs served as models for thousands of programs worldwide that today allow an estimated 134 million clients, and more than 400 million family members, to benefit from very small loans that can make significant differences to their well-being (Daley-Harris 2007). More than 85 percent of the borrowers are women. Often a first loan is used to buy back a child who might have been sold into slavery because their mother couldn't feed the others, or to pay for both girls *and* boys to attend school since the family could only afford to pay for the boys' schooling before receiving the small loan.

On the other side of the world, and in a project that spans an ocean, the Tuscany, Italy, Slow Food Foundation for Biodiversity is funding a project in the American Southwest where Diné (Navajo) people are using traditional sheep-herding methods to restore the rare Churro sheep breed, originally introduced by Spanish explorers 400 years ago. Navajo Churro sheep provide high-quality wool, large quantities of milk, and lean, sweet meat. The breed had declined significantly in part because of a federally imposed interbreeding initiative as well as the loss of Diné cultural sheepherding traditions (Nabhan and Chanler, 2008). Now the Navajo and their supporters are working to establish economic viability as well as restore a culture and way of life for future generations (Quivira Coalition 2008).

In the examples above we are describing the interconnections between social, economic, and sustainable development. BRAC and Grameen Microcredit respond to the basic needs of people by providing them a hand up instead of a handout and by allowing people to work within their social and cultural networks to develop their own economic viability. In addition, providing education to women and girls, the vast majority of microcredit borrowers and nonformal school beneficiaries, increases the health of families and decreases the birth rate. This in turn decreases the demands on Bangladesh's natural resources. The collaboration between the Slow Food Foundation and the Diné Lifeways Program works to preserve a heritage breed of sheep, one that is desert-hardy and requires less water and food than other breeds, which increases the diversity and resiliency of livestock. At the same time, the Navajo Churro sheep provide meat, milk, and wool for market and home use in the Diné communities of New Mexico and Arizona, in ways that are congruent with the social and cultural traditions of the people.

It has taken social workers, social scientists, political scientists, ecologists, biologists, economists, environmentalists, spiritual advisers, health providers, and others a long time to realize that atomized disciplines often provide atomized knowledge. In recent years people have begun to realize that human societies need more integration of the fragments of knowledge generated by these different disciplines. Perhaps what is needed even more is a new set of principles that can guide how we humans integrate the knowledge produced by disparate disciplines.

This model—social, economic, and sustainable development—is defined by the complex synergies that take place when people can move toward sustainability by integrating social well-being, economic well-being, and environmental well-being (Hall and Midgley 2004). In social work we have long held the perspective that people in their environments are the focus of our work. Consequently, social workers engage with people to improve the conditions that affect them by accepting them as individuals but recognizing the influences of family, neighbors, community, work, health, education, gender, sexual orientation, and physical and mental ability, for example. Too often social work has neglected the effect of the natural environment (i.e., resources of the earth's biosphere) on human conditions (Hoff 1994; Rogge 1998).

What effects do the quality of air, water, food, and the opportunity to experience the beauty of nature have on the lives of people with whom we work?

Equally important, what effects do the economic and exchange systems in a particular location have on both the development and functioning of individuals and groups of people and their institutions? On the one hand, community practice workers in the United States seem to recognize a variety of social and political systems that can enhance human development, but we social workers seem to be fixed on capitalism as the single, perhaps the only, viable, economic system that can serve as the structure for progress in development. The bias toward unregulated capitalism (Gibson-Graham 1996; Klein 2007), as compared with a more humane capitalism described by Rubin and Sherraden (2005), is widespread in Western society. Exploring alternative economic systems will be germane to this chapter.

Some would say social work has broken with its earlier orientation toward progressive ideals of social justice and concern for the poor. By accepting the oppressive outcomes of current economic and power systems, we are unable to help our traditional clients find any opportunity to move out of conditions of poverty, discrimination, injustice, and abuse of human rights (Dominelli 2007; Mullaly 2007; Reisch, 2005b). In this chapter we provide a range of ways to think about social, economic, and sustainable development as it applies to community practice. We also provide some principles that could be used as guides to help direct work in this model.

SCOPE OF CONCERN

In chapter 1 (figure 1.1) we presented a perspective of community described by Maureen Hart that stacks the elements of community capital in a pyramid, with the building blocks of natural capital (e.g., water, air, minerals, fertile soil, and the beauty of nature) forming the base of the pyramid; human and social capital (e.g., health, education, families, companies, governments) forming the middle layer; and built capital (e.g., buildings, information, infrastructure) making up the peak at the top (Hart 1999:16). We borrow from Hart to create a related perspective. Our diagram reconfigures the three levels as three integrated spheres of resources, redefining built capital as the economic sphere, and adding perceptions about the quality of human interactions between the spheres to move societies toward sustainability (figure 7.1).

SOCIAL, ECONOMIC, AND ENVIRONMENTAL WELL-BEING Human communities make progress toward sustainability when they can improve social well-being, economic well-being, and environmental well-being. We define *social well-being* as the ability of all people to have access to the supports and opportunities provided by social institutions and relationships. In other words,

Human societies have three spheres of resources—social or human capital, economic or built capital, and the environment or natural capital. The social sphere includes such things as families, neighbors, community, the arts, and governments, as well as the individual and cumulative education, skills, abilities, and health status of people. The economic sphere contains buildings, information systems, infrastructure, livelihood opportunities and the barter and exchange systems different societies have created. The environment, or natural capital, includes all the life-sustaining elements of the biosphere: water, food, metals, wood, minerals, fisheries, fertile soil, oxygen, and the whole realm of beauty in nature from mountains to rainbows to bird songs (Hart 1999).

These are our building blocks, and we must determine how best to use them to provide for current populations without harming the resources for future generations. To do so requires human behavior that integrates **equality, opportunity, and responsibility**. In human actions *equality* or justice is necessary in the shared use of social, environmental, and economic resources. This requires judgments about fairness as well as a respect and an acceptance of diverse contributions and needs of people everywhere. In addition, to reach their full potential people must have *opportunities* or the right and ability to access social, economic, and environmental resources (Sen 1998). Finally, the sustainability of human development requires *responsibility*. Responsibility can be thought of as the requirement in the social work codes to be an advocate for social justice and human rights and for the needs of the most vulnerable populations. In addition we add humility as a species in the recognition of connections with all other creatures in the biosphere, and to take account of the result of overconsumption on the part of the most advantaged populations, locally and globally.

Because of the diversity and ingenuity of human cultures, there are infinite ways to create social and economic systems that embody equality and opportunity. On the other hand, the biosphere of our planet is unique among the three resource spheres in that it is fragile and finite, requiring our collective responsibility. (Estes 1993; Falk 1971; Gamble and Hoff 2005; Rogge 1995).

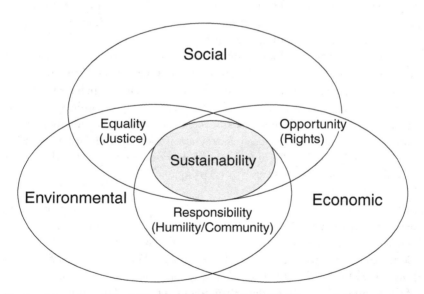

Moving toward sustainability: Human interaction with life-sustaining spheres of social, economic, and environmental resources

FIGURE 7.1 **Human Interaction toward Sustainability**

Source: Dorothy N. Gamble.

everyone should have access to supportive families, neighborhoods, and communities. Everyone should have the opportunity to engage in education, recreation, cultural organizations, spiritual institutions, and political organizations. Families, neighborhoods, and communities must have supportive health, welfare, educational, security, and political organizations so that they can continue to reinvest in future generations (Couto and Guthrie 1999).

Economic well-being means that all people have opportunities to achieve a wide variety of livelihoods and that wages should pay enough to meet a family's needs for shelter, food, health care, and transportation. Livelihoods are ways of life as opposed to jobs. Livelihoods encompass all the striving people do for themselves, their families, and their communities. Economic well-being requires economic and exchange systems as well as information, infrastructure, and building systems. Economics relates to the production, distribution, and consumption of commodities and services, including opportunities for paid and unpaid work, wealth, assets, and income. The exchange systems relate to how we place value on particular commodities and services, and the reciprocal patterns of activities we develop to trade services and commodities. For example, how do we value parents and extended family members in helping to care for and rear children, the work performed by formal and informal teachers, a local farmer's organic produce, a work of art, the volunteers who deliver meals to people who are not ambulatory or are frail elderly, or planting trees in a public park? Civilizations value all of these strivings, yet economic formulas often undervalue or exclude entirely the value of some of them.

The elements of social and economic well-being are obviously creations of human societies and will be as diverse as human ingenuity and human cultures make them. *Environmental well-being,* on the other hand, depends on finite resources. These resources include all the elements of the biosphere we use or affect in the creation of our social and economic worlds. The environment, or natural capital, includes water, food, metals, wood, minerals, fisheries, fertile soil, oxygen, and the realm of natural beauty we might think of as the sunset, a rainbow, a mountain, or birdsongs (Hart 1999).

THE CONCEPT OF SUSTAINABLE DEVELOPMENT Although people have been concerned about sustainable development for many decades, the label and its meaning are primarily connected with the 1987 report by the World Commission on Environment and Development (WCED), *Our Common Future: From One Earth to One World.* The report, often identified with the chair of the Commission, Gro Harlem Brundtland, who was then prime minister of Norway, defined sustainable development as "paths of human progress which meet the needs and aspirations of the present generation without compromising the ability of future generations to meet their needs" (WCED 1987:2). The Commission recognized that as human populations increased and satisfied their insatiable appetites for more than basic needs, our environmental resources were rapidly disappearing. The Commission's work helped people recognize that poor people with limited choices will burn precious rain forests for fuel, and rich people with unrestrained choices will allow precious rain forest to be turned into cattle pasture for more hamburgers. What remained of the biosphere was becoming extinct or fouled to an extent that it threatened the very existence of future human societies. The report raised the moral question of what responsibility everyone might have to preserve resources for future generations.

Although many continued to doubt the relationship between how we humans actually affected the earth's biosphere, environmentalists turned out reams of studies detailing the planet's degradation (e.g., Carson 1962; Odum 1997; Odum and Odum 2001). At the same time, questions were being raised about the implications of global industrialization and unregulated economic systems on the environment and on people, particularly the effects on the most vulnerable populations (e.g., Hawken, Lovins, and Lovins 1999; Henderson 1996; Korten 2001). Finally, questions about our social systems the world over began to focus on excluded populations, discrimination because of race, ethnicity, gender, class, ability, and religion, and the significant disruptions to development caused by wars and violence at all levels (e.g., Dominelli 2002; Hoff 1998; Van Soest 1997). The more these studies and perspectives were circulated, the more understanding grew about their interconnections. New material emerged demonstrating the connections between the social, economic, and environmental spheres and conceptualizing principles that might guide the integration of the spheres. The wisdom of ancient cultures and indigenous peoples that spoke of the need to live in harmony with one's surroundings and to respect the earth provided guidance. The principles focused on how human societies could make progress without further contributing to negative outcomes for people and the planet in general (e.g., Thomas Berry 1990; Wendell Berry 1992; Chief Seattle Speech 2008; Estes 1993; Falk 1971; Shiva 2005; Swimme and Berry 1994).

In figure 7.1 we have identified three spheres of resources that human societies can draw from to enhance and improve their well-being—limitless kinds of social and economic resources and a finite quantity of environmental resources. Recognizing the interconnections among these resource spheres, we understand that activity in one will inevitably affect the other two. Consequently, as we take actions in a social sphere we must be cognizant of the effects on the other two. And if we take action in the environmental realm, we must be aware of the effects on the other two. What then can we use as principles to guide our actions as we strive to make progress? How can our actions reflect improvements in social conditions, economic opportunities, and environmental restoration and preservation at the same time?

GUIDANCE FOR SUSTAINABLE COMMUNITY DEVELOPMENT A number of authors and institutions have provided direction for how to think about human action as we go forward. In chapter 1 we described the Universal Declaration of Human Rights (1948) and the Earth Charter (2000), which provide principles for the integration of social, economic, and sustainable development. Richard Falk, writing in 1971, identified seven values as guides to reorienting our integrated actions:

- Unity of humankind and unity of life on earth.
- The minimization of violence
- The maintenance of environmental quality
- The satisfaction of minimum world welfare standards
- The primacy of human dignity
- The retention of diversity and pluralism
- The need for universal participation (Falk 1971:293–312)

Richard Estes (1993) provides a detailed set of fourteen principles to guide social work toward sustainable development, indicating that "the most fundamental problems confronting humanity are essentially political, social and moral in nature" (1993:15). Other principles have emerged from a variety of organizations in the Global South. Vandana Shiva, physicist and activist who has worked in her native India and across the globe in support of women's rights and protection of native seeds and agricultural methods presents the Declaration of Interdependence in her book, *Earth Democracy*. Its six principles recognize "responsibilities to the common goods and liberties of humankind as a whole" (Shiva 2005:143).

In our model we describe human interaction with the three life-sustaining spheres as guided by three major values: *equality*, which we relate to social justice; *opportunity*, which we relate to human rights; and *responsibility*, which we relate to both humility and community. Equality reminds us to use judgment about fairness as well as to have respect and acceptance of diversity in all three resource spheres. To reach their full potential people, must have opportunities that include the right and ability to access social, economic, and environmental resources. Responsibility can be thought of as the requirement in the social work codes to be an advocate for social justice and human rights. It can also reflect the ideas of Estes (1993) and Hoff (1994) to be humble as a species in recognition of our connections with all other creatures in the biosphere, to respond to the needs of the most vulnerable populations in the world community, and to reduce overconsumption.

Earlier we described how the principles of social justice and human rights are emphasized in both the national and international value systems described in the NASW Code of Ethics and the IFSW/IASSW "Ethics in Social Work:

Statement of Principles" (2004). The very basis of ethical statements is to help professionals take responsibility for their actions and conduct. Responsibility, in our view, with its related aspects of humility and community, recognizes the "unity of life on earth": we are one with all other species on earth, and we have common interests with all other human communities on earth. As the most powerful species, we have an obligation to be humble in our behaviors toward other species and in our use of resources in the biosphere. Overconsumption has a direct negative effect on current populations and a particularly onerous effect on future generations. Responsibility can therefore be thought of as stewardship for the resources of the biosphere, so that by restoring and protecting natural resources we have provided for the opportunities of future generations. Finally, as intelligent, professionally committed community practice workers, we have the responsibility to recognize and take particular care of the most vulnerable human populations.

In this model the scope of concern is necessarily complex and wide ranging. Connecting three significant spheres of resources in a way that can help people and communities develop without having negative outcomes, either for people or any of the resource spheres, is a very big task. In the following sections we will break down the issues so that they might be more easily understood. We also recognize that this model especially lends itself to teamwork. No one has all the knowledge or skills necessary to work in such complex efforts. This work requires the wisdom of community members as well as many other skilled experts. In this model the most important role of the community practice worker, in addition to explicating the meaning of sustainable development by keeping a simultaneous focus on all three resource spheres, may be to integrate and coordinate the various threads of wisdom.

BASIC PROCESS: TEN GUIDING STEPS

We begin our guidelines of this model with the familiar caveat that no community work will ever take place in such a linear, direct way as outlined here. Keep in mind the feedback loops in figure 5.1 to remain flexible and open to new information, changing contexts, and organizational/community changing needs.

1. Identify and establish a working relationship with a neighborhood or community group that has concerns for social, economic, and/or environmental issues. You may live in a city that is plagued with pollution, as was Chattanooga, Tennessee, in 1969 (Rogge 1998). Or you may be part of a rural community that has lost most of its small manufacturing and mining jobs like Ivanhoe, Virginia (Hinsdale, Lewis, and Waller 1995). Or, you may work in a city filled with congestion, inequity, unemployment, squalor, and disease, as was Curitiba, Brazil, prior to 1972 (Hawken, Lovins, and Lovins 1999). There is no shortage of social, economic, or environmental problems that communities are trying to work on across our country and across the planet. The difficulty for both the community worker and the neighborhood or community organization itself is how to work with the connecting aspects of social problems, economic problems, and environmental problems all at once. The most reasonable way to engage with a community is to start with the most pressing issues and work through the analysis so that the connections can be understood and the problem solving can gradually become more holistic.

We make the assumption that working on one or two of these problems at the same time is more likely to happen than engaging with what is often called the triple bottom line—social, economic, and environmental issues—all at once. To demonstrate how these guidelines might be applied, we use the unusual story of Curitiba, a city of 2 million people located in the south of Brazil. Curitiba's story provides parallels for the way a community practice worker might begin work with a community. This real case has been described by Bill McKibben (1995, 2007), as well as Paul Hawken and his collaborators (1999) and others. Unless otherwise noted, the material describing Curitiba is drawn from Hawken, Lovins, and Lovins (1999:288–308). Characterizing Curitiba, Hawken and colleagues write: "Though starting with the dismal economic profile typical of its region, in nearly three decades the city has achieved measurably better levels of education, health, human welfare, public safety, democratic participation, political integrity, environmental protection, and community spirit than its neighbors, and some would say than most cities in the United States (Hawken, Lovins, and Lovins,1999:288).

The initial changes in Curitiba were directed by an architect and planner, Jaime Lerner. After working with his students on hypothetical plans to turn the squalid city into a livable urban center, he became the mayor and promptly put the plans to use. The city was about to demolish its old center to widen the central main street and construct an overpass. Lerner, the new energetic mayor, whom Hawken describes as "intensely practical, with the brain of a technocrat and the soul of a poet," had other plans (Hawken et al. 1999:289). He sided with the people who wanted to preserve the old city, but knew that transporting people around the city and dealing with flooding problems had to be solved as well.

2. *Assess the leadership and organizational assets and challenges within the neighborhood or community using popular education and participatory appraisal techniques.* The mayor of Curitiba had earlier used the "charette," a collaborative workshop planning technique, to bring people together to collect their perspectives and ideas about how the city might be developed. He knew

that there would be opposition to some of the ideas to try to make the city center a more livable space, not the least of which was that the new ideas seemed counterintuitive to what was then defined as progress or modernization. So he moved quickly.

Lerner started by transforming the central boulevard into a pedestrian mall within 48 hours. The work began on a late Friday afternoon in 1972. By the following Monday morning the pavement had been replaced by cobblestones and tens of thousands of flowering shrubs, and plants were located around newly installed kiosks and street lights. When the mall started filling with people on Monday morning, the skeptical shopkeepers soon took a positive attitude about the radical change. Car owners organized to take back the pedestrian mall as a street the following weekend. However, city workers laid out rolls of newsprint and pots of paint to invite children to use the mall as the space for their Saturday art class. At first people stole the flowering plants, but they were quickly replaced by city workers and the stealing soon stopped, especially after employing some gang members as gardeners. People began to think of their city center as a beautiful, clean, and friendly place.

3. *Help the neighborhood or community to deepen their understanding of sustainable development by exploring with them how their work toward improved social and/or economic outcomes is necessarily linked to environmental conditions, or how their work to improve environmental conditions is necessarily linked to social and economic outcomes.* Health issues in Curitiba are one way the city leaders helped the citizens connect the dots between economic, social, and environmental indicators. From 1972 to 1996, a total of eighty-eight health stations were installed throughout the city; each has a drugstore connected to it that distributes eighty-one free commercial and traditional medicines. A number of the health stations are open 24 hours a day. Family-planning information and prenatal and postnatal care are provided. Poor children are required to take advantage of free regular health assessments. A focus on children and the importance of preventive care is evidenced in health programs in day care centers, schools, and teen centers. Through a campaign called Garbage That Isn't Garbage, more than 70 percent of the population participates by sorting recyclables for curbside pickup. According to Hawken "Sorting stations, built from secondhand parts, hire the homeless, the disabled, and recovering alcoholics [to prepare recyclables for sale and reuse]. Landfill use has been reduced by one-sixth in weight, and even more in volume. Groundwater is protected from contamination by leaching garbage. . . . Paper recycling alone saves 1,200 trees a day" (Hawken et al. 1999:301). In addition, the city operates a program called the Green Exchange that trades sacks of food for sacks of garbage. People in the poorer neighborhoods collect trash along streambeds and along streets too narrow for garbage trucks and in return get surplus produce purchased from local farmers. This solution is a triple win: it helps the neighborhood stay free of garbage, it helps the people get nutritious local produce, and it helps the farmers stay on the land.

4. *Assist the neighborhood or community to develop techniques for setting goals and objectives for improving their community that integrates improved social, economic, and environmental outcomes.* As noted earlier, the leadership in the city frequently used participatory "charette" workshops to focus on their problems and solutions. This included the involvement of neighborhood associations, representatives from municipal agencies, private firms, utility companies, nongovernmental organizations, individuals, and community groups for effective integrated problem solving. Two big problems the city faced almost immediately were the transportation problem and the flooding caused when two major rivers and five smaller ones overflowed after rains. The presumed "modern" solution for moving people and cars was to demolish the old city, widen the street, and build an overpass. The presumed "modern" solution for controlling flooding was to line stream channels with cement and direct the water through the city. Both presumed plans were rejected by the citizens and leaders.

Mayor Lerner and his advisers tried to focus on alternatives that would be "simple, fast, fun, and cheap" (Hawken et al. 1999:298), but to do so by constantly connecting the solution to a holistic plan, and meeting human needs, "especially the requirements of the poorest" (1999:293). In considering transportation, they made three primary changes. First, they limited a main two-lane city street for use by buses and local traffic. Two parallel streets were made one way, in opposite directions, and designed for more efficient auto and taxi traffic. Second, they designed a bus system with many facets to carry people to every section of the city. The largest double articulated buses can carry up to 270 passengers with five extra-wide doors for easy entry and exit. Finally, they designed slightly elevated glass cylinder "tube stations," level with the bus doors, that would accommodate handicapped individuals and could fill and disembark the buses through automatic controls in about 30 seconds. The express buses carry 20,000 passengers per hour and work a lot like a subway except they are much cheaper. The flat-rate fare, which allows for an unlimited number of transfers, is divided among the ten bus companies that run the system based on the number of miles their route covers. The city contributes the streets and stations, but otherwise the bus system finances itself and provides a profit for the ten companies. The citizens of Curitiba still have cars, but three-quarters of all the commuters use the bus, cutting the use of fuel and the pollution of the city significantly.

Instead of lining the rivers and streams with cement, the city bought the land bordering the waterways, protected riparian zones, and turned the banks and floodplains into lake-studded parks for leisure and sports activities. Instead of fighting the floods, the city exploited the resource, and nearby citizen groups take responsibility for keeping the parks clean and unpolluted. Many of the parks have an ethnic focus, reflecting the many different ethnic groups that inhabit the city. The grass in the parks is trimmed by municipal shepherds and their flocks of sheep.

5. Assist the neighborhood or community organization leaders to develop skills for forming alliances, acquiring resources, and employing wide and inclusive communication systems. While children's needs are a high priority in Curitiba, services and programs for adults are equally evident. Both children and adults benefit from what are called "Lighthouses of Knowledge." These 52-foot-high libraries, shaped like a lighthouse, each hold about 7,000 volumes and provide free Internet connections. Each Lighthouse of Knowledge has a light and a police officer on its very top floor in order to provide safety for children as they come and go. The aim is to have a lighthouse library within walking distance of every home.

Children from boarding schools, many of whom work part-time, get city-organized support for sports and computer courses. Apprenticeships are available to many older children who can develop environmental skills in water pollution control, public health, forestry, and ecological restoration. Sixty-four centers respond to the needs of school dropouts with a variety of programs to help them earn self-respect as well as some income while they are gaining skills in jobs.

As is true in a number of Latin American cities, more than a thousand peasants arrive in Curitiba monthly from the rural countryside. The city works to organize and license small vendors, rather than harass or ignore them. Recyclable collectors, handcart vendors, and shoe-shiners are organized to help them earn some money. Some of the larger bus terminals house what are called "Citizenship Streets," where efforts are made to decentralize city services so that people can access training opportunities, business loans, and a myriad of municipal services. From children to adults, the tone the city has set is to build respect and responsibility for oneself and one's community. People are proud of this place, and all of these efforts have an effect on strengthening civil society in Curitiba.

6. Assist the neighborhood or community organization to think through strategies for reaching their goals and objectives in ways that empower and build the capacity of both primary and secondary leadership. Earlier, we described the participatory methods frequently used by the leadership and municipal employees of the city to draw in the ideas, energy, and responsibility of the city's citizens. Constantly bringing together private, public, nonprofit, and interest-affiliated groups and individuals is the key to problem solving. In the early years, when land was still reasonably priced, the city purchased 16 square miles of land outside the city for an "Industrial City," providing space for clean economic development. Since the land was 7 miles from the city center, a bus station was immediately installed, connecting to feeder bus systems, and provisions were made for affordable housing, schools, cultural facilities, and open space. The nonpolluting industries that were recruited had to dispose of their own solid waste on their own land.

Although Curitiba has tried to house the newly arriving migrants from the rural areas in its low-income dwellings scattered throughout the city and near the Industrial City, it is now moving toward an owner-built project to house poor families. The city set aside 170 lots for a pilot project with a goal of eventually being able to house up to 50,000 migrant families. City leaders recognize that many rural migrants come to the city with building skills. Upon qualifying, they are provided with a plot of land, a title, two trees, and a one-hour consultation with an architect. The architect helps them design a unit they can afford that might be added to as they increase their income and family. A line of houses already constructed helps them determine the style and building materials they might use, after which they are given some building supplies and can begin constructing their own house. Such a project results in a variety of styles and appearance, as well as pride in the construction and in the neighborhood. As the houses are built, solidarity develops when offers of help are made between neighbors for particular construction tasks. The new homeowners take pride in themselves, in their neighborhood, and in the city that helped them with a hand up.

7. Assist the neighborhood or community to learn how to manage internal conflict and disagreement as their organization grows and confronts new challenges. Curitiba has not yet solved all of its problems. At first glance, it may look like any other city except for what is believed to be the finest bus system in the world and the large number of parks, gardens, and greenspaces in the city. Upon closer examination, one has to ask how the city has been able to develop in such a people-centered way. Those who have seen the city and talked at length with Jaime Lerner and his equally capable consultant, Jonas Rabinovitch (who is now a senior urban development adviser and manager with the United Nations Development Program), say that the success of Curitiba was the result of

hundreds of multipurpose, cheap, fast, simple, homegrown, people-centered initiatives harnessing market mechanisms, common sense, and local skills. It flourished by treating all its citizens—most of all its children—not as its burden but as its most precious resource, creators of its future. It has succeeded not by central planning but by combining farsighted and pragmatic leadership with an integrated design process, strong public and business participation, and a widely shared public vision that transcends partisanship. (Hawken et al. 1999:288)

The city democratized its amenities by scattering cultural facilities, schools, affordable housing, work, clinics, day care centers, sports facilities, and food distribution centers throughout the city. Land speculation was discouraged through the use of open land-use plans and rules, and a public Geographic Information System (GIS) that makes information about land available to everyone. The city makes available a number of telephone and Web-based hotlines and resources. People vote for improvements they would like to see in their neighborhood when they pay their property taxes. Transparent, honest, and accountable government is what people have come to expect in Curitiba. The sense of ownership of the city is so strong that rather than seeing graffiti on walls you might see a poem taped to a utility pole. To highlight the importance of the citizens as owners of all public assets, Hawken quotes Lerner, "If people feel respected, they will assume responsibility to help solve other problems" (1999:308).

8. *Assist the neighborhood or community organization in learning how to monitor and evaluate the progress of their effort and to share those outcomes inside and outside the community.* In Curitiba, where inflation of the national currency can sometimes make it difficult to evaluate the cost of a particular project or service, some have begun to use the comparison of the cost of putting asphalt on 1 kilometer of city street. A "Lighthouse of Knowledge" costs the equivalent of 0.2 kilometer of asphalt, for example, or, a new tube bus station costs the equivalent of 0.5 kilometer of asphalt. But in Curitiba there are also annual benchmarks for collecting the data to describe the details of the city's livability. The measures are very similar to those created by Maureen Hart (1999), which we will describe later in this chapter in more detail. The benchmarks help the city move forward by measuring such things as literacy, high school education, basic vaccinations, owner-occupied households, households with drinking water and electricity, trash collection, poverty rate, life expectancy, newspaper circulation, public libraries, radio stations, orchestras (they have three, including their famous harmonica orchestra), cultural buildings, and greenspace, including private and public parks. All these basic changes were being made while the annual per capita income for Curitiba was less than US$8,000. The news of their accomplishments has spread throughout their country and the world. Lerner has consulted with more than eighty cities around the world who want to learn from the successes and mistakes of Curitiba.

9. *Assist the neighborhood or community organization to plan for and take effective action.* Probably the most significant indicator of how the citizens of

Curitiba have taken effective action to focus on quality of life over the traditional definition of progress is to note the progressive local legislation they have passed in the last thirty years. Examples include 5-yard setback requirements for any new building outside the center to allow for gardens; tax relief for planting woods and gardens; requirements to plant two trees if you get a permit to cut down one of your own trees; recycling everything, including the city's excellent busses that get retrofitted and turned into neighborhood job-training centers; the "green exchange" program that pays citizens in poorer neighborhoods where garbage trucks can't go, exchanging bags of garbage for tickets to buy bus tokens, food, or school notebooks; schools that serve children by day and adult learners at night; more than 200 day care centers that stay open 11 hours to accommodate working families and serve four meals a day; tax waivers for companies that provide day care positions; and neighborhood health clinics. In addition, among the new mayors elected since Jaime Lerner, though politically diverse, none has retreated from the direction created to build a livable city. The citizens seem to have taken the idea to heart that they own the assets of the city, even the municipal government.

10. *Assist the organization to plan celebrations that mark the progress of leadership, organizational development, milestone outcomes, and action victories.* Every Saturday morning, since the transformational pedestrian mall was built in 48 hours in 1972, the rolls of newsprint and paint pots are laid out on the cobblestone for children to create their own visions of wonder and beauty. No cars even consider spoiling their fun. Festivals and ceremonies fill the linear environmental parks, the woods, and gardens. The open-air opera house can seat 10,000 people. The city of Curitiba itself has become a celebration.

As noted earlier, Curitiba has not solved all its problems, but the pattern for solving them is now deeply etched into the minds and hearts of the citizens, some of whom were the first children to paint on newsprint laid out on the new pedestrian mall back in 1972.

THEORIES AND CONCEPTS THAT GROUND THE MODEL

The theory streams discussed in chapter 3 that inform this model include theories from *development, economics, politics and governance, poverty and asset development, construction of social realities, ecology and environment, and population and migration.* In this chapter we focus on conceptual understandings that are derived from these theory streams that are most useful to community practice in social, economic, and sustainable development. The conceptual understandings are:

- Human development
- Livelihoods
- The measurement of social, economic, and environmental well-being

As with previous models, we have chosen several central concepts for discussion in this chapter in the interest of directing the community practice worker to particular areas of knowledge. Building one's knowledge for work in community practice is an ongoing task. Focusing on the three areas will open up new avenues for exploration and the opportunity to increase your basic knowledge of issues to be encountered in working in this model.

HUMAN DEVELOPMENT

In our work we relate the concept of human development primarily to the Human Development Index (HDI) developed by the United Nations Development Program (UNDP). The HDI was first conceived by Mahbub ul Haq as a response to the need to measure people's progress in a particular country by something other than a country's gross national product (GNP) or the more commonly used gross domestic product (GDP), both of which are considered "blind to the social aspects of people's lives" (UNDP 1999:23). In 1990 ul Haq and his colleagues developed a composite index that was a better measure of people's capabilities and their ability to make choices and enlarge their opportunities. He considered it an incomplete but better measure of what people did and could actually do with their lives. The index was a composite measure of people's ability to *lead long and healthy lives* (measured by life expectancy at birth), their *knowledge* (measured by adult literacy and the combined primary, secondary, and tertiary gross school enrollment), and their ability to have *a decent standard of living* (measured by per capita income). Every year since 1990 the Human Development Report has listed countries of the world and their rank based on these measures. In the 2007–2008 Report, the UNDP analyzed 177 countries for which they had sufficient data. Although human development is considered more complex than any simple measure might capture, the HDI has become a standard for beginning to explore the actual capabilities of people in a country, proving much more useful in terms of social progress than the GDP.

In recent years, the Human Development Report has included different measures of people's lives, so that today each report also has rankings for the Human Poverty Index (HPI), the Gender-related Development Index (GDI), and the Gender Empowerment Measure (GEM). The Gender-related Development Index (GED) measures the same three capabilities as the HDI, but it reflects the inequalities between men and women (UNDP 2002:255). The Gender

Empowerment Measure (GEM) is a composite of three indicators: (1) political participation and decision making comparing men's and women's percentage of parliamentary seats; (2) women's and men's percentage shares of positions as legislators, senior officials and managers, and professional and technical positions; and (3) economic power as measured by a comparison of men's and women's earned income (UNDP 2002:257).

The rich content in each Human Development Report provides information on the status of major international human rights instruments, the health and technology diffusion indicators, and since 2000, the progress of countries on the Millennium Development Goals. The Report is now fully available on the Internet, and interactive tools are available for additional calculations. Many cities throughout the world base local planning documents on the Human Development Index, using the UNDP's calculations as benchmarks for their own social, economic, and environmental planning.

From a global perspective we now shift to a more local, even personal, perspective on human development. Given the urgent focus on global climate change, it would be unusual for a community practice social worker not to be aware of how individual and community conduct affects the environment. One way to engage with that kind of learning is to do the Internet calculation for your "Ecological Footprint."

In 1996 Mathis Wackernagel and William Reese developed a conceptual framework and calculations to help people understand the relationship between their individual social and economic behavior and the ability of the planet to provide for their needs. Their idea was to help individuals, companies, communities, cities, states/provinces, and countries determine how much of the earth's resources were necessary to sustain their living habits. Wackernagel and Reese drew from the wisdom of economists, sociologists, biologists, ecologists, philosophers, and others to help frame a simple picture of biosphere resource needs based on the behaviors of individuals. The result of those calculations would determine how many earths were needed to sustain all the people on earth at that level of use. Their model for calculating the number of acres or hectares to maintain one's own lifestyle was quickly adopted by a number of organizations for educational use. One organization that incorporated the Ecological Footprint in their Web material is Redefining Progress, founded by Ted Halstead in 1994 (Redefining Progress 2008b).

Redefining Progress (RP) created its own composite index for measuring human progress identified as the Genuine Progress Indicator (GPI). The GPI is more complex than the Human Development Index but was also a response to the frustration felt by many that GDP was an inaccurate measure of progress. The GDP is based on *all* spending and therefore does not take account of the negative aspects of spending (e.g., pollution-related health care costs; costs related to crime and drug addiction) or the effects of present spending on future generations (e.g., borrowing to pay for wars; overuse of finite resources). Redefining Progress used ten indicators to create its own measuring stick for progress in 1995. You will find it at their Web site and can compare it with the UN Human Development Index and the GDP (Redefining Progress 2008a).

Although the Human Development Index, the Human Poverty Index, and the Genuine Progress Indicator have significant value for people working in community practice, none takes sufficient account of the effects of state-sponsored or civil wars. Wars present enormous costs against human development. They deprive resources that could be used for health, education, and other social well-being measures, and they prevent the development of public and private infrastructure such as public transportation, clean water sources, and alternative energy sources.

The horrific cost of wars continues long after the violence has ended. The costs of war in loss of life, mostly the lives of children and young people, deprives societies of the creative and productive human capital these people might have contributed to community well-being. Although there are estimates of the cost to heal the mental and physical trauma of war, such trauma is endless for the victims of war. The wars in Iraq and Afghanistan have been financed on borrowed money, meaning those who have to pay will be the next several generations (Stiglitz and Bilmes 2008). By 2008 the cost to wage the combined Iraq and Afghanistan wars was US$16 billion a *month*. "Sixteen billion dollars is equal to the *annual* budget of the United Nations. . . . Even so it does not include the $500 billion we already spend per year on the regular expenses of the Defense Department" (Stiglitz and Bilmes 2008). The 2009 budget presented by President Bush requested over US$1 trillion for the military, a 70 percent increase over military spending at the beginning of his term (Center on Budget and Policy Priorities 2008). One trillion is hard to comprehend because it has twelve zeros, but a number of organizations help us get a clearer picture (Friends Committee on National Legislation 2009).

To help U.S. citizens connect with the meaning of the expenditure of war, the National Priorities Project provides a budget trade-off calculator to compare the tax dollars spent on the Iraq War in your state, city, or congressional district, for example, with the cost of public safety officers, or homes with renewable energy, or Head Start spots for children, or university scholarships (National Priorities Project 2008). As indicated in earlier chapters, the work to diminish violence at all levels, including internationally, is a responsibility of everyone in social work, especially those working in community practice.

LIVELIHOODS

In this section we focus on the meaning of livelihoods rather than simply using the word jobs to describe the range of work performed by community members. Livelihoods more broadly includes such activities as caring labor, work and living wages, microcredit, asset development, and solidarity economics.

CARING LABOR The paid and unpaid work people do in a holistic way for family, neighborhood, and community can be thought of as caring labor. Social care, for example, described as the personal care for infants and young children, moral and supportive guidance for children, personal care and stimulation for people who are temporarily or permanently infirm, or care of the frail elderly is often done voluntarily and is seldom counted in economic production formulas, even though no society could prosper without it (UNDP 1999). Much of this work is done by women, and the market penalizes rather than rewards social care. The UNDP suggests three reasons for social care receiving a financial penalty: "Gender bias is one factor. A second is the intrinsic reward people get from helping others, allowing employers to fill jobs at lower pay. A third is that people feel queasy about putting a price on something as sacred as care" (UNDP 1999:80).

WORK AND WAGES Work for wages, with a particular focus on *adequate* wages, has been a stimulus for research and grassroots organizing during the last several decades in the United States. Jared Bernstein, director of the Living Standards Program at the Economic Policy Institute, calls the policy approach to work and wages during recent years in the United States "YOYO Economics"—*you're on your own*—as far as retirement accounts, health insurance, and unemployment insurance is concerned (Bernstein 2007). Although means-tested programs are intended to cover the gap between low wages and needs, according to Nancy Cauthen with the National Center for Children and Poverty at Columbia University, studies show that only about 5 percent of low-income families actually get these benefits. Cauthen recommends a list of principles that should guide the development of programs designed to support working families (i.e., work supports):

- Full-time work and family benefits should be sufficient to support a family.
- Earning more should not be a disincentive and should always improve a family's bottom line (currently, a family is disqualified for whole programs if their income reaches a certain level).

- Funding for work supports needs to expand during economic downturns and therefore needs to be countercyclical.
- Work supports should be efficiently administered and easily accessible.
- Work supports should provide a bridge to the middle class. There should be a continuum of services, "progressive universalism," so that we are not separating low-income families from everyone else.
- All this should supplement jobs that pay higher wages, jobs that provide family leave, paid sick leave and better retirement benefits. (Cauthen, October 2, 2007)

These kinds of principles, Cauthen believes, should also be applied to work-support programs for adults who work but don't have children, and for noncustodial parents, if we expect to develop respect rather than resentment for children.

Although the United States has had a minimum-wage standard since 1938, that standard has never been considered sufficient to provide for the needs of a family with one member working full time. In 1959 the United States established a basic-needs poverty level to be used in considering applicants for certain federal programs. Unfortunately, this threshold is so insufficient a marker of basic need that programs providing child health benefits routinely certify applications by doubling the poverty level in their calculations (Cauthen 2007). In its history the minimum wage has never reached as high as the poverty level. Measuring its value in constant 2007 dollars, the minimum wage in 2007 was as low as it has ever been in fifty years (Smith 2007). After years of neglect, the federal minimum wage was finally increased to US$5.85, with intended increments to $6.55 in 2008 and to $7.25 in 2009. With the value of wages not keeping pace with the cost of living, American workers have had to work longer hours and use an ever greater proportion of their income for housing, food, and transportation (Roberts and Povich 2008). This punishing wage policy, together with the inability of the national government to make necessary changes, has been the impetus for the grassroots Living Wage movement. Coalitions of workers, labor organizations, religious groups, and other community groups have successfully lobbied for municipalities and states to increase the minimum wage to an adequate standard.

A living wage, based on the basic needs for housing, food, child care, transportation, and health care in a specific locale, is a beginning step toward establishing social, economic, and environmental well-being. Fred Brooks's excellent review of the Living Wage movement indicates that more than 140 coalitions have been successful in changing the wage laws of states and municipalities in the United States and that the movement has spread to Canada, New Zealand,

Australia, and the United Kingdom (Brooks 2007). The case example incorporated at the end of this chapter provides the story of one such campaign in Santa Fe, New Mexico, that was successful in increasing the wages for everyone who works within the city to $9.50 beginning January 1, 2008, with future increments tied to the cost of living index. In the neighboring state of Nevada, social work faculty and students joined with the Nevada Chapter of the National Association of Social Workers and numerous other progressive organizations in a multiple-year campaign to support a statewide minimum wage, also tied to the cost of living (Chandler and Jones 2003).

MICROCREDIT AND ASSET DEVELOPMENT Eliminating poverty, at least eliminating the need for people to live on only US$1 a day, should be central to any sustainable development effort. In addition to increasing wages to meet the basic needs of people, two additional strategies for alleviating poverty have been *microcredit,* described at the beginning of this chapter in the examples of BRAC and the Grameen Bank in Bangladesh, and *asset development,* used primarily as a strategy in developed countries. Microcredit consists of providing very small loans without the need for collateral to help a poor person buy a cow, or supplies for selling sweets on the street, or to pay necessary fees so the girl child can go to school. This poverty-fighting strategy now serves more than 400 million family members around the world, often with loans as small as US$5–20. RESULTS, a citizen lobbying group, in their work to increase the resources invested in microcredit programs, focuses on Millennium Development Goal #1: "To cut in half the number of people living on less than US$1 a day, from 1.2 billion to .6 billion, by 2015" (RESULTS 2008a). RESULTS aims to increase the United States' contributions for microcredit to a level of $250 million, with at least half of that devoted to the very poor and to increase the amount the World Bank devotes to microcredit, which, shamelessly, is less than 1 percent of its total budget.

Asset development has received significant attention as a strategy to reduce poverty in developed countries, especially in the United States (Mckernan and Sherraden 2008; Sherraden 2001, 2008). Asset development is accomplished primarily through Individual Development Accounts (IDAs). These formal programs assist the poor to develop savings accounts by matching their savings with public and private funds to maximize growth. Families in these programs also generally receive some financial education. Withdrawal of the funds is "only allowed for specific, asset building purposes, such as purchase of a home, starting a small business and post-secondary education" (Birkenmaier and Tyuse 2005:70–71). The Jacobs Center for Neighborhood Innovation in San Diego, California, has taken the asset development idea one step further in its construction of a 10-acre shopping mall, Market Creek Plaza. The residents in a low-income neighborhood known as the Diamond were involved in the planning and design of Market Creek Plaza and are now part owners of the mall. The neighborhood stakeholders can become stockholders with an investment as small as $200 (Jacobs Center for Neighborhood Innovation 2008).

SOLIDARITY ECONOMICS Finally, we discuss the idea of solidarity economics, which brings us back to the more holistic idea of livelihoods. Quietly emerging on the edges of traditional economies is what is known as *economia solidaria*, or solidarity economics. The impetus originated in the developing world where it doesn't seem so radical to become an entrepreneur outside a strictly capitalistic model. The idea, formally discussed at the 1998 World Social Forum held in Porto Alegre, Brazil, focuses on the small entrepreneurs who find success for their production in the horizontal networking and cooperative exchange patterns they use in their communities. According to Ethan Miller, many of these experiences grew from the "structural adjustment programs imposed by the International Monetary Fund, [that] forced many communities to develop and strengthen creative, autonomous and locally-rooted ways of meeting basic needs" (2006:1). These initiatives, often known in Latin America, Asia, and Africa as the informal sector of the economy, may include "worker and producer cooperatives, neighborhood and community associations, savings and credit associations, collective kitchens, and unemployed or landless worker mutual-aid organizations" (Miller 2006:1). These developing world networks are beginning to connect with cooperative organizations in developed countries created by people frustrated with the "dominant market economy" and responding to basic needs of housing, child care, food, and health. These efforts seem to acknowledge the feminist understandings of economics described by Gibson-Graham (1996) and the rejection of the one-dimensional human being designed simply for maximizing profit. Muhammad Yunus suggests that we have followed a very narrow interpretation of capitalism for too long and that the result is a failure of "conceptualization": "Everyday human beings are not one-dimensional entities, they are excitingly multi-dimensional and indeed very colourful" (Yunus 2008:1). Taking the needs of the whole human being into account in our work recognizes the need for jobs, helping children learn values, enjoying arts and leisure, cooking supper, investing in neighborhood parks by volunteering to plant a tree or clean a streambed, being a companion for an adult with developmental disabilities—indeed, all the aspects of living that people do in all parts of the world. Obviously, having the resources to engage in life fully requires work that pays a living wage.

KEEPING A FOCUS ON THE TRIPLE BOTTOM LINE A focus on reducing poverty and supporting a living wage is basic to our efforts toward sustainable development. However, sometimes the work toward economic and social well-being leaves out important aspects of environment. Majora Carter founded Sustainable South Bronx in New York in 2001. Together with her colleagues and neighbors she has transformed parts of a blighted neighborhood into tree-lined streets, riverfront parks, and a new "green-collar" job training center (Sustainable South Bronx 2008). The initial impetus was to keep out yet another waste dump designated for a minority, poor neighborhood. Across the American continent in Oakland, California, Van Jones co-founded the Ella Baker Center for Human Rights in 1996. When Oakland was designated as the site for a giant youth prison in 2003, the Center started the "Books Not Bars" campaign to successfully stop its construction and at the same time reduce the youth prison population in California by more than 30 percent. Jones has been effective in steering the job-creating activities of the Center toward the environmental needs of the city and the state through creation of the Green Collar Jobs Campaign and the Green Job Corps (Ella Baker Center for Human Rights 2008).

Another example of livelihood extension with environmental protection comes from Vandana Shiva, who works on protecting plant seeds, food, water, and the people who grow and depend on traditional seed crops. Although her work is global, she maintains a particular focus on the needs of people from her home country, India. In response to the U.S. Department of Agriculture and the W. R. Grace Company's application for a patent in the European Patent Office on the Indian neem tree in the mid-1990s, Shiva writes:

> Neem, or azad darakht to use its Persian name, which translates as free tree, has been used as a natural pesticide and medicine in India for over 2,000 years. As a response to the 1984 disaster at the Union Carbide's pesticide plant in Bhopal, I started a campaign with the slogan: "no more Bhopals, plant a neem." A decade later we found that because W. R. Grace was claiming to have invented the use of neem, the free tree was no longer going to be freely accessible to us. We launched a challenge to the neem biopiracy and more than 100,000 people joined the campaign. Another decade later, success—the European Patent Office revoked the patent. (Shiva 2005:146)

These kinds of efforts help people understand the global connections of social, economic, and environmental well-being.

THE MEASUREMENT OF SOCIAL, ECONOMIC, AND ENVIRONMENTAL WELL-BEING

In figure 7.1 at the beginning of this chapter, we provided a conceptual perspective to show how social, economic, and environmental resources are linked to provide for human and biosphere well-being. We focused on the importance of equality, opportunity, and responsibility as the guides for human interaction in drawing from the three life-sustaining resources. Measuring progress toward sustainability is not always easy. Parris and Kates indicate that, while nearly every country, and the United Nations itself, is working on measures of sustainability, there still seems to be too little specificity and too much ambiguity in the efforts. They therefore recommend an analytic framework with clear goals, indicators, targets, and trends (Parris and Kates 2003).

The latest guidelines for measuring sustainable development, published by the UN in October 2007, linked progress to the Millennium Development Goals (MDGs) with indicators focused on poverty, governance, health, education, demographics, natural hazards, atmosphere, land, oceans/seas/coasts, freshwater, biodiversity, economic development, global economic partnerships, and consumption and production patterns (UN Department of Economic and Social Affairs 2007).

In our view, Maureen Hart and the Hart Environmental Data Web site provide the best resource to help communities establish indicators (Hart 1999). Hart provides another graphic perspective of the social, economic, and environmental link using three different-sized spheres, one inside the other. The largest sphere is the environment; the second, located inside the environment, is society; and the smallest, located inside society, is the economy. According to Hart:

> The economy exists entirely within society, because all parts of the economy require interaction among people. However, society is much more than just the economy. Friends and families, music and art, religion and ethics are important elements of society but are not primarily based on exchanging goods and services . . . Finally, the environment surrounds society. . . . The parts of the environment unaffected by human activity are getting smaller all the time. However, because people need food, water and air to survive, society can never be larger than the environment. (Hart 1999:4)

Hart's manual, *Guide to Sustainable Indicators*, second edition, takes communities through the steps of thinking and action to establish specific indicators for their needs. The manual is very clear and helps community members understand the value of an indicator, learn how to organize indicators for particular categories of interest in the community, and look for measurability in all three spheres. A particularly instructive part of the manual helps communities see the difference between traditional measures of progress and measures that reflect the integration of social, economic, and environmental progress. Table 7.1 shows the difference between some traditional indicators and Hart's suggested sustainability indicators.

TABLE 7.1 Hart's Comparison of Traditional and Sustainable Community Indicators

TRADITIONAL INDICATORS	HART'S SUSTAINABILITY INDICATORS	ADVANTAGE OF SUSTAINABILITY INDICATOR
Median income per capita	Hours of work at the average wage required to support basic needs	Links economy to other aspects of community, including housing, health, education, and society
Number of housing starts	Number of housing units built at different income levels compared to the number of people at those levels	Measures how the economic activity meets the social needs of the community, also a measure of income diversity
Cost of electricity, gasoline, natural gas, or oil	Percent reduction in energy use from nonrenewable sources	Highlights major sustainability concern: dependence on nonrenewable energy
School dropout rates compared to state average dropout rate	Participation in continuing and adult education classes	Measures investment in social capital; individuals' commitment to improving their skills and abilities
Number of hospital beds	Births to women with inadequate prenatal care	Highlights connection between health of mother and child's future well-being
Number of child care slots available	Number of parents with satisfactory day care arrangements	Measure of social capital— reflects an economic structure that allows parents to provide the level and type of care they prefer

Source: Adapted from Hart 1999:52–90. Used with permission.

This small sample provides some comparison between traditional indicators linked only to a one-dimensional understanding of an issue and a more complex measure that can help community members link social, economic, and environmental resources. Categories can be created for land use, ecosystems, population, participation, diversity in government, and any other category the community feels is important to their measure of sustainability. It would not be expected that every indicator could make the triple link, but with practice community members can incorporate a more complex understanding of how their community is actually making progress in all three areas—social, economic, and environmental well-being.

The need for conceptual understanding is much deeper than the points we have highlighted in this section. With experience, the community practice worker will be directed to knowledge and understanding in many related topics.

SOCIAL WORK/COMMUNITY PRACTICE ROLES

The roles we have identified as most important for social, economic, and sustainable development, already defined in chapter 2, are the following:

- Negotiator
- Bridge builder
- Promoter
- Planner
- Educator
- Manager
- Researcher
- Evaluator

There is no doubt that Jaime Lerner did a lot of *negotiating* to create the radical transformation of Curitiba in his intermittent terms as mayor (he served three different terms because of term limits in the city). Our sense is that Lerner negotiated from a position of strength. The strength of his plans grew from the participatory involvement of citizens of the city from a wide range of organizations and neighborhoods and from the principle to plan with respect for people and for the environment. Still, the plans that eventually created an efficient bus system, vast greenspaces all across the city, and child- and family-centered educational, health, and cultural resources, went against most traditional planning wisdom at the time. Going against "traditional" economic wisdom, for example, whether in supporting solidarity economics or working for a living wage, pits progressive community groups against the powerful voices that tell us we will all be doomed unless we pursue unlimited growth through the maximization of profits in the market (Miller 2006; Yunus 2008). Negotiating from strength will help communities reach more successful outcomes for social, economic, and environmental well-being.

In chapter 5 we described the role of *bridge-builder* in relation to helping the Guatemalan farmers connect with helpful knowledge and resources outside of their immediate community. We also described the importance of making external resource contacts *always accompanied by* a member of the community with whom you are working. Two important benefits derive from doing bridge building with a community member. First, the community member needs to make a judgment about the external resource contact to assess the value and usefulness for the community. As a person with many external resource contacts, the community practice worker is more likely to be ready to accept an association with a new potential resource. The worker's uncritical acceptance of the contact can unknowingly lead to "recolonizing" the worker's relationship with the community. The community member, on the other hand, has a set of judgments to make based on an assessment of need grounded in her or his own community context and history. The second reason to contact outside resources with a community member is for the experience. If the community member makes a judgment that the external resource is useful, the community now has acquired a new direct contact and adds experience on which they can build networks for their own community.

The role of *promoter* is important to building interest, enthusiasm, and excitement for a potential progressive change action. The promoter role is similar to the role of *promotora* described by Arizmendi and Ortiz (2004) in their work in the Mexican *Colonias*, or *animador(a)* used in other parts of Latin America and described by Finn and Jacobson (2008a:325) and by Reisch, Wenocur, and Sherman (1981:115). Building interest and enthusiasm for a particular change effort, especially one that speaks to social/cultural, economic, and environmental well-being can be done by the community practice worker as well as by community leaders and members. If you ever have the opportunity to hear Jaime Lerner in person, or to see him in video, you will see directly how much energy goes into being a good promoter.

The role of *planner*, as noted in the definition, is "multifaceted and may be carried out at several levels." The most important aspect of a planner's activity is to make certain that community voices are part of the planning process. The only way to break the cycle of the most powerful voices always making the plans, always deciding how a problem should be defined, always coming up with the perfect solution, is to make certain that less powerful voices are at the table for every decision and that the least powerful have a significant role in the plan making. It is the responsibility of the community practice planner to know where the most excluded segments of the community are and how to access their voices for the planning process. This requires creativity, persistence, and a commitment to social justice and human rights.

The role of *educator* in this model will be broad because of the many concepts involved in becoming knowledgeable and grounded in understanding social, economic, and environmental well-being. The importance of this role is to combine one's expert knowledge with the indigenous knowledge learned from people in their context and from their perceptions. Collaborating to build an analysis of the problems and a vision of how the future could look is the process of co-learning. The very vulnerability of accepting the fact that expert knowledge is only partial knowledge, and may not provide the answer to the problem engenders an openness to accept new information. Combining expert knowledge with indigenous knowledge provides new perspectives and understanding for everyone involved.

It took the catastrophic accident in the Bhopal, India, pesticide plant to generate the idea that the natural pesticide produced by the Neem tree was a freely available pesticide, and the tree was eventually kept free through the efforts of Vandana Shiva and others who fought the attempt to patent its use (Shiva 2005). It took the threat of locating a new waste dump in the Bronx, New York, to stimulate Majora Carter and her colleagues to move her community from the bottom rung of environmental degradation to leadership in developing "green-collar" jobs and community riverside parks (Sustainable South Bronx 2008). Sometimes a challenge can be the spark that builds new knowledge and new solutions, but it generally comes from a collaboration between grassroots ways of knowing and expert wisdom.

When a program to improve the social, economic, and environmental well-being of a community, city, state or nation is adopted, it will then fall to the *manager* to carry out the policies and plans of the program to successful completion. The Continuous Community Sustainable Development Model (figure 1.2 in chapter 1) describes the activities a manager will direct. A good manager works with the organization to establish and reassess goals, define specific objectives, organize the inputs and outputs, evaluate the outcomes as well as the long-term impact, and help the organization reflect on accomplishments, new understandings, and challenges. The manager is required to perform many different tasks, not the least of which is organizing people and resources to achieve goals. The manager must successfully direct the internal tasks of the organization as well as stay engaged with the external constituencies of the organization to be effective. Valuable guidance for the internal tasks required in management is provided by Robert Weinbach (2003) and the late Ralph Brody (2004). Management guidance for the internal tasks, as well as the external tasks—specifically the challenge of engaging with the external constituencies including consumers, boards, foundations, and competing values in the community—is provided by David Austin (2002) and Yankey and Edwards (2006).

This model requires both the roles of *researcher* and *evaluator*. All the models need to demonstrate how change will be directed and systematically measured, especially the quality and quantity of change that takes place once a program or action plan is initiated. Our focus on the roles of researcher and evaluator in this model recognizes the complexity of work to direct and measure as best we can the integrated outcomes of social, economic, and environmental well-being. Some research may explore the quality of community interactions to measure the degree to which equality or social justice, opportunity or human rights, and responsibility for the broader community and the biosphere serve as the principles or guides for community action. Other research may look more specifically at the outcomes or long-term impact on improved social, economic, and environmental indicators. Defining indicators that measure the quality of interactions, or the impact on social, economic, and environmental well-being, will be the task of the community members, working with a skilled community practice researcher and with helpful resources such as *Guide to Sustainable Community Indicators* (Hart 1999). The research and evaluation efforts in community practice must reflect the perspectives and voices of the people who will benefit from the findings (Chambers 1997; Jacobson and Rugeley 2007; Pennell, Noponen, and Weil 2005). Equally important is the way community members can best make use of and disseminate research findings, remembering that drama, art, and music can be effective media for this task.

These roles are considered critical for the community practice social worker. They are also roles that one should make use of as an aware and responsive human being. They are roles that can be used as a neighbor, community resident, or a person who wants to bring sustainability concepts to any group. As we have suggested earlier, no community practice worker will be skilled in all these roles. Looking for collaboration across disciplines and across organizations can be very helpful. The wise community practice worker will look for skills both within and outside the community that can be applied to the tasks at hand.

CORE SKILLS AND COMPETENCIES FOR SOCIAL, ECONOMIC, AND SUSTAINABLE DEVELOPMENT

In this section, we discuss three skill/competency areas that we believe are essential areas for working in this model. Sufficient knowledge, judgment, and skill are needed to engage in the complex effort to help people improve their social, economic, and environmental well-being. A community practice worker, or any social worker for that matter, may work in only one of the three areas of well-being, but the connections among the three and the principles that guide the work toward the more holistic outcome of sustainable development should be understood.

The three skill areas we will discuss are as follows:

- The application of human rights and social justice principles to identify basic human needs
- Combining social, economic, and environmental analysis and practice
- Sustainability outcome measures

We have suggested that these kinds of skills can only be acquired through study, practice, and reflection; then study, practice, and reflection again. We remind you that it is especially helpful to have a guide, field instructor, mentor, team leader, or partner as you do this work, so that you will have the opportunity to reflect on your skill development and the challenges you encounter.

Since you now know the pattern of how we suggest you might prepare yourself for practice, engage in practice, and then evaluate your efforts, we will simply pose the questions related to the three skill areas and follow up with some suggested practice opportunities.

APPLICATION OF HUMAN RIGHTS AND SOCIAL JUSTICE PRINCIPLES TO IDENTIFY HUMAN NEEDS

- What articles in the Universal Declaration of Human Rights relate to social well-being? economic well-being? environmental well-being?
- In the area I work, which population groups have the least opportunity and the least equality, and show the least responsibility with regard to the three resource spheres—social, economic, and environmental? What prevents opportunity, equality, and responsibility for these groups? What supports opportunity, equality, and responsibility for these groups?
- How do I know this information? Do I know what to do to get better information if I can't answer the questions above?
- What are the Millennium Development Goals, and how are they related to my own well-being, my region's well-being, and my country's well-being?
- With my knowledge of basic needs identified by the Human Development Index and others (e.g., Falk, Estes, Max-Kneef, Shiva), what are the principles that can guide my work toward meeting the basic needs of people anywhere?

COMBINING SOCIAL, ECONOMIC, AND ENVIRONMENTAL PRACTICE

- How knowledgeable am I about the basic meaning of sustainable development?
- What use can I make of the Ecological Footprint Quiz to increase my own understanding of sustainable development?
- What use can the community members with whom I am working make of the Ecological Footprint Quiz in understanding personal and regional consumption patterns?
- What is the difference between the gross domestic product, the gross domestic (or per capita) income, and the Genuine Progress Indicator?

- What aspects of a community's needs are not accounted for in gross domestic product? in the Human Development Index? in the Genuine Progress Indicator?
- How can I help community organizations use the UN's Human Poverty Index, Gender-related Development Index, and the Gender Empowerment Measure in an analysis of social, economic, and environmental well-being?

SUSTAINABILITY OUTCOME MEASURES

- What are the basic categories that could reflect the integration of social, economic, and environmental well-being in any community?
- How can I help community members relate to the integration of the three resource spheres—social, economic, and environmental?
- Does the community have locally focused information on the Human Development Index, on the Genuine Progress Indicator, or on Sustainable Development?
- Using Hart's Guide to Sustainable Community Indicators, how can I help community members identify specific indicators?
- What additional resources are available to help the community specify local indicators to measure sustainability?
- Where will the community members find the information (data) they will need to measure the indicators?

Perhaps the biggest question a community practice worker might have about building skills in this area is where to find a practice opportunity. We suggest a number of opportunities such as the Peace Corps, AmeriCorps, African Impact, American Jewish World Service, Catholic Relief Services, Earthwatch Institute, Foundation for Sustainable Development, Habitat for Humanity, Partners of the Americas, or Volunteers for Peace. Although these are primarily volunteer experiences in developing countries, there are also many opportunities for work in communities in the developed world where we have too often excluded or ignored the social, economic, and environmental well-being of people who are from low-wealth neighborhoods and mostly communities of color. As we described earlier, there are people such as Majora Carter in the South Bronx and Van Jones in Oakland, California, who are stopping negative and oppressive development and opening their communities to green-collar jobs and community-centered livelihoods. We suspect there are projects of this sort going on in your own towns and cities. Find the integrated projects and try to get a position with them.

Social workers are working in Canada, the Philippines, Hawaii, Australia, and Brazil to help communities reject the widening gap between the rich and poor in their countries and are helping to build communities that can engage in solidarity economics (Hoff 1998; Miller 2006). Mary Rogge formed a coalition of social workers, biologists, and environmentalists to explore the level of toxic risk experienced by children in schools and adults in polluted sectors of urban Appalachia (Rogge 1998). From the Carolina Farm Stewardship Association in North Carolina to the Quivira Institute in New Mexico, and from the work being done by Sustainable Seattle to the more than twenty communities throughout the United States who have developed an effort to rid their community of commodities purchased in sweatshops, there is no shortage of opportunities to practice social, economic, and sustainable development. In addition, there are many guides to help community workers gain understanding for approaching this work; among them are those by David Cox and Manohar Pawar (2006), Lynne Healy (2001), Susan Mapp (2008), Terry Hokenstad and James Midgley (1997), Chathapuram Ramanathan and Rosemary Link (1999), and Karen Sowers and William Rowe (2006).

These roles and skills can apply to any field of social work, but especially to community practice. Once you find an opportunity to practice, how will you know you are making progress developing the roles and skills necessary for this work? How can you make sure you are not simply marking time but are constantly giving yourself goals and challenges to hone your roles and skills? We suggest partnering with someone to help identify each other's strengths, joys, and challenges in this work. Knowing what you can do well, and where you need more awareness and practice to do better, is always valuable. Understanding what gives you the most joy, as well as the most frustration, about this work is also important. With a supportive partner, or a supportive group where you assess each other's progress in positive ways, personal growth can be identified and celebrated as you become a more effective community practice worker in this model. From experience we also know the sagest advice about community practice effectiveness often comes from the grassroots leaders who are our partners and key community informants in this important work.

CONCLUSIONS

The goal of this chapter is to bring the student of community social work closer to an understanding of sustainable development and the potential for integrating work toward social, economic, and environmental well-being. Although social work is committed to equality through social justice, to opportunity through human rights, and to responsible use and stewardship of the earth's resources, we have too often neglected the content that will help us engage in this work in our curricula. Being able to critique the various indicators of human progress, understanding personal and community overconsumption through use of the

Ecological Footprint Quiz, and learning how to develop a community sustainability indicator help us to increase our knowledge and to develop skills for this work.

In the decades ahead we have parallel paths to traverse. One path calls upon us to work toward improved social, economic, and environmental well-being for all people on the planet. The other path calls upon us to struggle against the negative aspects of globalization, work toward the expansion of human rights, especially rights for women and girls, and facilitate positive dialogue among the diverse cultures and populations in our communities. Jim Ife cautions that the inevitability of global warming requires us to act now to lessen the potential devastation of the earth's resources, and to be prepared to respond to the most vulnerable populations as climate change occurs (2007b). At times it seems undoable, but with appropriate knowledge, skills, and commitment to the values of social justice and human rights, community practice social workers are up to the task.

HISTORY OF THE LIVING WAGE CAMPAIGN IN SANTA FE, NM, USA
CAROL OPPENHEIMER, CO-CHAIR, SANTA FE LIVING NETWORK

The First Ordinance

In the fall of 2001, Jimmie Martinez learned that his employer, Furr's Super Market, was going out of business. Soon after, he learned that his particular store, in Santa Fe, had been purchased by Lowe's, an anti-union firm from Texas. When Lowe's reopened the store, it refused to hire back most union people, and salaries were reduced from a $10 to $16 an hour range with benefits to $6 per hour without benefits.

Jimmie was angry. He had been a member of the United Food and Commercial Workers, Local 1564, in Albuquerque but was never active. Coincidentally, Jimmie was a city councilor in Santa Fe. Therefore, he, along with Councilor Frank Montano, in the fall of 2001 introduced a proposed living wage ordinance that applied to city employees, city contractors, and the private sector generally.

With the help of a long-time community activist, a hastily put together campaign, with limited union and community support, did produce results. A few weeks before the March 2002 election, the City Council unanimously adopted a traditional living wage ordinance (adopted by over 100 localities around the country). It applied to City of Santa Fe employees and contractors. The Ordinance would raise the minimum wage to $8.50 beginning July 1, 2003; $9.50 beginning July 1, 2004; and $10.50 beginning July 1, 2005. City of Santa Fe unions—the American Federation of State County and Municipal Employees, the International Association of Fire Fighters, and the Fraternal Order of Police—in the months after the ordinance was announced, negotiated agreements that brought all their members above the $8.50 level.

CONTINUED

The City Council also established a Living Wage Roundtable to be made up of four "labor representatives," four "business representatives," and one neutral. The groups' purpose was to explore ways of extending the living wage to the private sector. In the 2002 election, Jimmie Martinez lost his Council seat to a candidate opposed to the living wage.

The Living Wage Roundtable

The Roundtable business and labor representatives were quickly at loggerheads. It became clear early on that the business representatives would never agree to any increase in the wages of their employees. They were trying to bog down the process and exploit any mistakes the labor representatives might make.

The Living Wage Network

After the initial Roundtable meetings, it became obvious that there was a need to start putting together a broader community/labor alliance to build real support for a living wage. The Roundtable asked for an extension of time, until the end of 2002, in which to report back to the City Council. This gave more time to organize support for a strong pro-worker ordinance.

The first organizational meeting of what was soon to be termed the Santa Fe Living Wage Network took place in August 2002. Some of the key people and groups in the Network included a representative from the National Education Association; a Democratic Party activist; a Green Party activist who knew a lot about campaign organizing; a labor pension specialist who was also a good writer; two labor attorneys; an operating room nurse who was active in a union produced Living Wage buttons for everyone to wear; and a dozen other people from housing groups, environmental organizations, unions, gay and lesbian organizations, and an immigrant rights group. Many became more active as the campaign gained strength. A local artist, who designed the logo, and her partner, a local general contractor, were fervent supporters and brought to the table a progressive small-business perspective. The labor representatives on the Roundtable were essential to building the campaign.

The Campaign

The campaign started with two large meetings, one a general organizational meeting and one specifically to discuss what the proposal of the labor representatives on the Roundtable should be. About fifty people came to each meeting. Several labor representatives on the Roundtable attended the meeting to learn about people's concerns. This started the buzz and gave the labor proposal some legitimacy.

A living wage "speakers' bureau" was started, sending speakers to church, community, and school groups. We spoke to almost fifty different organizations over the course of the campaign and got additional names on "interest cards." Using those interest cards, we enlisted the help of numerous volunteers to contact or call hundreds of people to ask them to sign on to an ad that would be run in the Santa Fe *New Mexican,* just before the councilors voted. The Network worked on this for at least three months. Our goal was to have 1,000 names by the time the city considered the proposal. We also started a Web

CONTINUED

site and developed a strategy for op-ed pieces and appearances on radio talk shows. The Network collected over 1,500 names of individuals, unions, and community organizations. Fifty businesses and most of the union locals in the state also signed on.

In the final stages of the campaign, volunteers phoned every one of the people on the list of supporters. Our core of activists phoned everyone they knew to urge them to come out the night of the vote. A union group personally called 800 union members in Santa Fe a few days before the Council meeting. Six hundred people came out the night of the vote, the biggest crowd ever at a City Council meeting. Two-thirds wore an "I support a Living Wage" sticker with logo. With only one minute per person, a wide range of living wage supporters spoke for over 2½ hours including labor and community activists, low-wage workers, struggling single mothers, business owners, lawyers, college students, high school students, teachers, politicians, and many, many others. It was an impressive display of democracy in action.

The Final Vote

The final ordinance passed the City Council 7 to 1. Like the original proposal, the ordinance passed that night phases in from $8.50 to $10.50 per hour, but it does so over four years rather than two and covers only 60 percent of Santa Fe employees rather than the 75 percent originally proposed. That was accomplished by raising the threshold for applicability to businesses with twenty-five or more employees (9 percent of Santa Fe employers), rather than the original ten or more employees (20 percent of Santa Fe employers). The Council also added a provision that a research firm hired by the city would establish an economic "baseline" before the ordinance went into effect, so that it could be compared to data to be collected right before the first step up to $9.50 per hour.

Potential Delays

Immediately after the ordinance was enacted, in early March of 2003, the Chamber of Commerce and several local businesses filed a state lawsuit challenging the legality of the living wage. Amicus briefs were filed to help the city defend the lawsuit—one to explain the social justice and economic principles involved and the other on the issue of home rule. A District Court judge ruled that the living wage ordinance was legal and ordered that it take effect immediately.

Several attempts were also made to have a preemption bill introduced into the New Mexico State Legislature that would have taken away Santa Fe's right to pass a living wage law. All these attempts were defeated.

The Raise to $9.50

In the summer of 2005, months before January 1, 2006, when the living wage was to rise to $9.50 per hour, a town councilor who had voted against the living wage in 2003, introduced an amendment to delay the increase until completion of the study of the effects of the living wage being done by the Bureau of Business and Economic Research (BBER) of the University of New Mexico. The BBER was to give a preliminary report on the living wage prior to January, but the final report was not to be completed until June 2006.

CONTINUED

The BBER report showed that the living wage did not seem to have caused any damage. In fact, 1,700 new jobs were created in Santa Fe after the law came into effect, and the number of recipients of Temporary Aid to Needy Families fell 10 percent in Santa Fe while remaining the same in the rest of the state. The unemployment rate was much lower in Santa Fe than in other major New Mexico cities and the state as a whole. Although there were some reports of increases in prices, curtailing of overtime, and some hardship for some nonprofits (e.g., job placement for people with developmental disabilities), in general the report was positive. The Network did not want a delay.

The evening of the City Council meeting, hundreds of supporters of the living wage attended; 75 spoke in favor; and only 4 people spoke against the $9.50. In fact, many more businesses testified in favor of the $9.50 than against it. At the end of the evening, the Council voted 7–1 to proceed to $9.50. However, they also amended the ordinance so that any future increases would need to be approved before going into effect.

A Living Wage for Everyone—No Exceptions

On July 12, 2007, Santa Fe's mayor announced a compromise agreement on the future of Santa Fe's Living Wage Ordinance. First, the living wage would be extended to cover *all* employees in Santa Fe, not just those in businesses with twenty-five or more, starting on January 1, 2008. Second, the requirement that the City Council approve all wage increases was removed and replaced with a cost-of-living increase. Finally, the living wage would not go to $10.50 per hour on January 1, 2008, as had been set out in the original ordinance, but would *stay at $9.50 until the cost-of-living increase on January 1, 2009.*

The Living Wage Network ran a campaign over the next few months entitled "A Living Wage for Everyone—No Exceptions" supporting the compromises. The Network also circulated a petition that received almost 4,000 signatures and phoned living wage supporters to call their councilors. In the final week before the vote, a newsletter was mailed to 4,000 supporters urging them to come to the Council meeting, and "pro-living wage" yard signs were distributed around the city. In addition, we were able to get many students and young people involved through an event with Barbara Ehrenreich. Especially helpful was the mayor's announcement of the first "community read" which featured Ehrenreich's book *Nickel and Dimed.*

The City Council considered the proposed changes on November 28, 2007. Over 250 people overflowed the Council chambers. After hearing from seventy-five supporters of the changes and one opponent, the Council approved the changes unanimously. On January 1, 2008, a minimum wage of $9.50 an hour went into effect for everyone working inside the city limits of Santa Fe.

The full history can be found at http://www.santafelivingwage.org/history.html.

8

INCLUSIVE PROGRAM DEVELOPMENT

There are those who look at things the way they are and ask why . . . I dream of things that never were and ask why not.

ROBERT F. KENNEDY, QUOTING GEORGE BERNARD SHAW

In spite of poignant experiences, or perhaps, because of them, the memory of the first years at Hull-House is more or less blurred with fatigue, for we could of course become accustomed only gradually to the unending activity and to the confusion of a house constantly filling and refilling with groups of people. The little children who came to the kindergarten in the morning were followed by the afternoon clubs of older children, and those in turn made way for the educational and social organizations of adults, occupying every room in the house every evening.

JANE ADDAMS, *TWENTY YEARS AT HULL-HOUSE*, 1911:147

INTRODUCTION

This chapter presents three approaches (submodels) of program planning and development: the basic rational planning model, inclusive program development, and the interpretive planning-emergent approach. We illustrate two approaches with case examples, discuss the distinguishing features of each approach, and suggest some guides for choosing the optimal program planning and development approach in differing circumstances.

In the twenty-first century, a major change in principles underlying program development is under way. Experiences in many parts of the world have brought recognition that it is poor practice and ethically problematic to design and implement new local service programs or community development efforts without the involvement and active participation of community members and members of the population to be served or engaged in change. The shift is from traditional expert-based program design to inclusive program development, which involves active and continuous participation of community or service population members. Both the inclusive approach and the emergent/interpretive approach embody this level of engagement. For decades the predominant approach to program development in the literature was based on the skills of planners well trained in the rational planning model where participation of clients in planning and evaluation was given little emphasis. Indeed, historically it was not unusual for clients to be viewed strictly as people to be helped rather than as people who could also participate productively in needs assessments, program development, and evaluation. Recently, instead of this unequal relationship of "expert to client," it has been found that neighborhood-based programs can foster empowerment and become continuous processes of positive organizational and community change (Aspen Institute 1996; Butterfield 2008; Castelloe and Gamble 2005; Chambers 1997, 2002; Chaskin 1997; Couto and Guthrie 1999; Eng and Parker 1994; Fals-Borda 1998; Fetterman and Wandersman 2004; Gaventa 1982; Hinsdale, Lewis and Waller 1995; McBride and Sherraden 2004; Medoff and Sklar 1994; Minkler 2004; Mortenson and Relin 2006; Noponen, 2001, 2002; Rohe and Gates 1985). This shift in relationships and processes in program development is driven by increased confidence in participation and participatory planning. The ascendance of empowerment theory and the strengths perspective, as well as the growing movement in community development for strong participation, support this movement toward participatory planning. Participation in program design and development processes by community or service population members can take place in all three of the approaches we present. The task for community practitioners is to understand the power of participation and to promote and facilitate empowerment-oriented processes. While community participation can be emphasized in all three approaches, the level of participation generally accelerates from the expert/rational model to the inclusive model to the emergent/interpretive model, which is fully participatory in all processes.

Currently, participation by the people we serve and engage with is becoming an expected aspect even of organizational governance and evaluation. Participation can occur in a variety of ways and with different levels of intensity. This chapter and the exercises in the *CPS Workbook* present a range of case studies that illustrate the principles of participation and inclusive program development. While discussing all three approaches, this chapter focuses primarily on how to carry inclusive program development forward. The case example "Participatory HIV/AIDS Education in Ethiopia" illustrates a strong participatory and inclusion focus.

Prevention education programs are a critical component in the global fight against HIV/AIDS; and this program offers several positive examples of good program design. First, the youth brought to Addis Ababa for the prevention training were within the age group generally most at-risk of contracting HIV. They were already skilled in general health education techniques and knew that they needed to learn about HIV/AIDS to help stop its advance. Perhaps

PARTICIPATORY HIV/AIDS EDUCATION IN ETHIOPIA

The Global Health Report from Ethiopia in 2003 provided heartening news that the rate of HIV prevalence was dropping among pregnant teenagers. This positive change followed the implementation of an educational intervention program designed and carried out by fifty-one youth who work as health educators. The program, Ethiopian Youth: Planning for HIV/AIDS Prevention Education, was sponsored by the National Ministry of Health, which adopted participatory learning and action (PLA) methods to train the health educators.

The program engaged participants in a learning, planning, and coaching process to assist them in helping others in rural and urban communities improve their health and avoid HIV/AIDS infection. Following their training, the young people participated in planning an assessment of HIV/AIDS prevention educational needs. In practice, these health educators then have an opportunity to expand program participants' knowledge about basic health and HIV/AIDS prevention strategies for themselves and their communities. The training made it possible for young women and men to talk more freely about sexuality and HIV/AIDS.

Following their own training, the youth leaders designed and then conducted participatory workshops among youth and adult stakeholders in rural and urban settings to heighten awareness and assess learning needs of local HIV prevention program staff.

After conducting assessments, the youth leaders learned to analyze their data and to validate the earlier findings through regional consultations with a broader representation of youth from across the country. "They brought their results to the first National Youth Consultation on Sexual and Reproductive Health and HIV/AIDS in Addis Ababa, Ethiopia . . . and developed their national youth charter and action plan at the Consultation, outlining specific recommendations conducive to sexual and reproductive health."

Global Health Council 2008
Case developed by Tessita Negussie and Emily MacGuire

most importantly, their training was conducted using *participatory learning and action* methods, which engage groups in identifying what they already know, determining their learning needs, and building knowledge and skill for action in local communities (Chambers 2002; Pretty et al. 1995). Participatory learning and action is an effective empowerment practice strategy, and the Ethiopian program enabled health educators to carry their participatory learning and action training forward in each community engagement. They provided local training, assessed needs, and trained local health workers in the content and exercises. Local health educators carried the intervention forward encouraging sound prevention strategies and modeling ways of increasing participation in social and health learning. Across the world, a range of diverse HIV/AIDS prevention, support, treatment, and long-term services are needed. In the *CPS Workbook*, another case example describes the highly participatory development of a program to serve HIV/AIDS survivors in a small town in western North Carolina. Following the epidemic-level progression of HIV/AIDS throughout the United States, a considerable number of young gay men who had earlier moved to urban areas and contracted the virus had "come home to die;" and the local Hospice program began to provide services. However, the introduction of more effective drug treatments meant that many who had expected to die young were now surviving. The case study describes how the Hospice director, Kevin Branch, recognized that young men now living with, rather than dying from, AIDS needed quite different supports and services. Branch organized AIDS survivors, family members, and other service providers into a coalition, and together they designed a participatory, community-based *AIDS support and service program*. Several things are important about this new response to a new need. In a very low-wealth rural area, concerned service providers and people living with AIDS were able to design, secure county funding for, and implement a low-cost and mutual aid-focused program for a population that had been stigmatized and even feared. With the global epidemic of HIV/AIDS, this program provides hope that with increasing access to effective antiretroviral drug treatments, people in every populated continent can survive this scourge and live productive lives. It also illustrates collaborative and low-cost ways to initiate support services for survivors and their families that can help them reintegrate into their communities.

PROGRAM DEVELOPMENT: SCOPE OF CONCERN

DEFINING PROGRAM DEVELOPMENT The Ethiopian prevention education effort and the western North Carolina program are examples of *programs and program development*. This essential aspect of working with people and communities to improve their lives and shared quality of life has been described in a range of ways. Royse, Thyer, Padgett, and Logan (2006) define *program* as "an organized collection of activities designed to reach certain objectives . . . a series of planned actions that are designed to solve some problem" (5). Yuen and Terao (2004) see a program as "a coordinated change effort that is theory-based, goal oriented, often time limited, target population specific, and activity driven" (1). It is also, they note, "an evolving process" (1).

Overlapping points in these definitions identify central components and prompt the authors to the following definition: *programs* are *dynamic*—they are composed of a set of *coordinated activities* intended to *promote positive change* for individuals, groups and communities and to *meet desired goals*. An assessment of needs, interests, and desires for a particular program should be undertaken with members of the local community and service providers to see whether the program is warranted and whether the design ideas fit local concerns (Mulroy 2008). To plan programs with community members, practitioners need to be grounded in or actively learning about the culture, goals, and aspirations of community members or population to be served.

New programs (a) may be initiated by an organization or government body outside the community seeking to respond to a social or health need; (b) may be developed within a community by people living with the problem (or concern) and allies—both service professionals and volunteers; and (c) in addition, can be an expansion or a redirection of efforts to improve service effectiveness (Brueggemann 2006).

INCLUSIVENESS AND COMMUNITY LIAISON A program might be initiated "solo" by a local human service agency—but at its peril if it has not built collaborative processes with community members to ensure the fit of the program with local interests, goals, and aspirations. In this usage, *inclusiveness* connotes "involving as part of a whole," that is, ensuring that all who need to be engaged in planning a program are engaged and that their perspectives are taken into account. It is a principle that should operate in all stages of program design and operation. Inclusiveness from the get-go and community liaison through consistent, interactive communication should be critical parts of this practice model from early planning through ongoing evaluations. Inclusion signifies that community members sit on committees, participate in focus groups, and review reports, and are sought out by staff for advice and consultation. Programs or services are more likely to meet needs identified by the community and attain desired outcomes if they have been jointly planned.

SCOPE The central goal and desired outcome of this model is to co-design and implement new programs, services, or community change processes that have been identified as needed by participating community or population members. The interaction of the community with service programs is strengthened through the involvement of potential consumers and citizens in the needs assessment process and development of boards and advisory bodies. Mechanisms that encourage consistent feedback to and from the community are valuable in keeping new programs on target. The scope of concern for inclusive program development is designing and developing programs or change efforts *with* community or population members, and tailoring activities to their needs and hopes with a sufficiently flexible design that workers can adapt projects or programs to respond to environmental, political, or economic changes.

Inclusive program design involves a process that continually engages community members as well as workers in identifying unmet needs, community concerns, or opportunities, then assessing that need or concern, and designing and structuring a program, or set of programs, to respond to the concerns or needs. A useful amplification is provided by Netting, O'Connor, and Fauri (2008), who note:

> Like ideas, programs come in all sizes and forms. Some have large sets of interconnected services with complicated regulations and guidelines attached. Others are quite simple and straightforward. The term *program* is so much a part of common parlance that it is often taken for granted. Yet program roles are complicated and powerful. They are the critical units or components within human service organizations. They translate organizational mission into action. They are the pivot points of evaluation and outcome measurement. Program success or failure affects organization survival and individual, community, and even social change. (33)

CULTURAL COMPETENCE, PROGRAM DEVELOPMENT, AND CONGRUENT ORGANIZATIONAL CULTURE

In community practice, multiple levels of cultural competence are needed: individual, programmatic, and organizational. Initially, the worker needs to be knowledgeable about the culture, context, interests, and needs of the community or population to be served. This learning need is heightened if the community practitioner is from a different cultural/ethnic/racial/nationality and/or social class background from community members. How you relate face to face with community members or the service population will have a significant effect on the culture of the program and participants' sense of belonging. There are numerous good books about cultural competency with client groups that can be helpful to you in this first level of cultural competence (Harper-Dorton 2007; Lum 2007; Peterson 2004; Sue and McGoldrick 2005). With regard to community or population, you also need to understand their history, cultural traditions, potential issues of exclusion or oppression, and their sense of "place" in the larger society in which they live. In addition, you will be working with groups and organizations to plan and implement your program; it is critical that you learn about organizational culture—how to build on strengths and how to solve communication issues, turf battles, internal conflict, or other problematic issues.

It is particularly important to structure your organization so that the guiding internal, organizational culture supports broad inclusion, encourages active learning about community culture and diversity, and makes organization culture an issue to be discussed openly. In short, organizational cultural competency should remain an agency priority (Iglehart and Becerra 2000; St. Onge 2009). Organizational culture is not "just" the sum of the individuals in the organization; it becomes its own entity—"the way *we* do things"—norms about staff or member relations in agency or organizational work. Leadership is often signaled as the "creator and sustainer" of organizational culture—and leaders do have a great deal to do with "setting the tone" for collaborative work; still all members of a group affect its culture. Typically, leaders determine aspects of how formally—or informally—communication occurs, how bureaucratic or democratic the process of meeting management is, and how genuinely the organization "walks the talk" of organizational and programmatic cultural competency. Essential skills for working effectively with issues of cultural competency within and outside the agency are facilitation, active listening, reframing issues to promote learning and problem solving, and learning from the people with whom you engage. If we are comfortable with the skills of facilitating discussions democratically, planning sessions so that all perspectives will be heard, attending to different cultural styles and using participatory decision-making processes with groups, we are likely well on the way to being able to assist groups in their chosen activities as well as blending cultural responsiveness and competency into this work (Hogan-Garcia 2003)

Although there are times and places when community practitioners take on the mantle of expert, planner, leader, or evaluator, most often we are working with and coaching community members in building skills in these roles themselves. We need always to bear in mind with groups and staff that everyone is simultaneously representing two or three "cultures" at one time. An outreach worker may be a member of the community, belong to an ethnic group that is different from most of the staff, and perhaps be the only male staff member in a program. Another staff member—perhaps an associate director of programs and resource development—may be a member of the same ethnic/racial/cultural group as community members. However, she or he may have a bachelor's or master's degree, may come from an upper-middle-class socioeconomic status, and not "be from here." As a facilitator, you need to recognize that in any meeting many diverse "cultures/selves/roles/and statuses" are represented, and sensitivity to this complexity is helpful to nurture positive interpersonal and professional behavior. It is important within the agency and in the community to negotiate with respect when there are disagreements about such issues as "Who really understands the community?" "How should we determine priorities?" or "Who has the right (or power) to make this decision?" Cheryl Hyde provides useful guidance about building and sustaining multicultural staffs in order to serve multicultural communities well (Hyde 2003, 2004; Hyde and Hopkins 2004).

INTERACTION AND ADAPTATION

Programs often need to be redesigned, expanded, or redirected to be more effective, respond to changing conditions or new populations, or complement other services. These adaptations are important for organizational survival. Interaction among citizens, potential clients, and agency staff is critical in the conception of this model. The interaction between the community and service programs can be strengthened in a variety of ways. Aside from intentional work to promote broad inclusion, you may find it valuable to utilize focus groups of potential consumers or related staff, as well as working on problem areas with advisory- and policy-making boards. Providing the same messages to each of these constituencies, and being sure that concerns from each are transmitted to the others is a central practice for achieving organizational congruence. As the program is designed and implemented, mechanisms for feedback to and from the community are valuable in keeping new programs on target The *desired outcomes* for a specific program are achieved (or not) though carrying forward practice activities intended to lead to the changes or development that community members and staff think will best respond to the identified needs or concerns.

TARGETS FOR CHANGE AND RESOURCES

All programs have specific targets for change—typically, multiple systems are targeted. Depending on the resources in the community and whether a new program is nested in an existing organization or is a new venture, planners will need access to resources to carry out program goals and activities. For a new venture, resources may come from the community, or preparation of a grant proposal may be required to seek external funding from financial grantors. If the new program will be lodged within an existing nonprofit or governmental organization, planners will need "buy in" and support for the program from staff, volunteers, board, and community members in order to carry the program forward as intended, or to modify it if environmental or population changes warrant. Because there are many organizational activities that consume staff time, it is useful to hold periodic meetings to review program visions and discuss mission and goals. The reward for staying on mission is the increased probability that participants in the program or change process learn new skills, find more effective ways to deal with problems, and achieve goals for personal (human capital) and community (social, economic, and sustainable) development.

Social legitimacy and accountability are important for any program. If a proposed program takes a new direction, staff, supervisors, and managers need to work closely with the agency board or local leaders who give community legitimacy to the program. If a program is new to an area, community representatives can provide local legitimation and feedback to improve the program. Participants in services or programs are the "end-user" constituency, and accountability to them should be a high priority. In the last two decades, expectations for program accountability to multiple constituencies have greatly increased. Too often the literature has framed accountability only in terms of meeting responsibilities to program funders; this can result in goal displacement, with a focus only on efficient use of resources. In community practice, the pivotal foci for account-ability are program participants and the community, with efficiency incorpo-rated into good management practices. The agency's staff and staff of other service agencies are also part of the accountability chain, but if a program is not meeting its service and change goals, it needs to be redesigned so that vulnera-ble people or low-wealth communities are not harmed. Frequently, lack of com-munity response or outright failure of a program results from insufficient in-volvement of community members in the planning (Greg Mortenson, personal communication, April 2009); and the cure for failure is often going "back to the drawing-board" with all who should have been involved in the first place.

COMPARATIVE APPROACHES TO PROGRAM DEVELOPMENT

Whether a program is totally "homegrown" within the community, is spon-sored by an organization, or has to seek external funding, the planning work places community practitioners near the center of a complex process that de-pends on: (1) facilitating the steps of the process, (2) relating consistently and transparently with community members and participants, and (3) simultane-ously designing and carrying forward steps of a participatory evaluation process. The community practitioner will need to assist with several additional processes and tasks to effect useful planning. These include (1) processes of engagement— with organizational staff, with community members, and with other stakehold-ers; (2) hearing local perspectives on needs, hopes, and aspirations and collect-ing and organizing information; (3) preparation of a participatory strengths and needs assessment; (4) shared decision making with community and staff mem-bers about essential program purpose and features; (5) development of a partici-patory evaluation plan that can demonstrate if and how desired outcomes will be achieved; (6) completion of the program design—goals, objectives, delinea-tion of activities, and delegation of tasks; (7) implementation of the program concurrent with monitoring by staff and community members; and (8) an ongo-ing process of evaluation to see what may need to be changed to increase the success of the program (Kettner et al. 2008; Netting, Kettner, and McMurtry 2008; Yuen and Terao 2004).

RATIONAL PLANNING AND PROGRAM DESIGN

Most of the U.S. literature on program planning practice is guided by a specific, well-established approach derived primarily from rational planning theory. Ra-tional planning for program development has considerable utility, as it lays out tasks in logical steps and assists in structuring both implementation and evaluation (Kettner et al. 2008; Mayer 1972). In their book, *Comparative Approaches to Program Planning*, Netting, O'Connor, and Fauri (2008) explain that to be "rational in this sense means to move forward with purpose toward a pre-identified goal" with assumptions that one can know the problem if one analyzes it well enough; that one can solve a problem if a clear direction of how to proceed can be identified; and that there are logical ways in which to move through this *problem solving process* (69–70).

Essentially, this approach to rational planning is both strictly linear and prescriptive. Netting and colleagues (2008) trace the history of this prescriptive approach to Chester Bernard and Herbert A. Simon, who held that information about centrally made decisions would trickle down through the organization. Substantial criticisms of this approach have been made even by proponents. For example, as Friedmann and Hudson argue (1974), it is generally accepted that this model does not give sufficient weight to the reality of uncertainty and the high likelihood that changed circumstances can derail a well-planned program. In addition, earlier assumptions were made by decision theorists that when an organizational decision was made, "it would be implemented with minimum friction" (164). Over time the rigidity of some positions within the rationalist school sparked the most frequently voiced criticism that the model can be so rarefied as to "neglect the human side of planning" (ibid.).

Despite these and other problems with this planning submodel, the increased demand for accountability from funders, both government and private, has rendered it the standard and accepted model for proposals, program designs, and evaluations. Pressures from several federal agencies, the total quality management approach, and mandated performance measures for federally funded, state, and local governmental programs have driven the adoption of performance measures and use of prescriptive planning models (Kettner, Maroney, and Martin 2008). These pressures also explain the increasingly frequent requirement of logic models in proposals for funding as one means to explain the rational process of a specific intervention or program (McLaughlin and Jordan 1999).

These political and accountability pressures have increased the prescriptiveness of rational planning approaches, with one benefit being the increased sophistication of a variety of useful planning procedures and sophisticated technical tools (Kettner et al. 2008; Pawlek and Vinter 2004; Royse, Thyer, Padgett, and Logan 2006). This "rational" model is useful for its clarity, its step-by-step process—the linearity that can cut both ways—and its logical process of development and implementation.

The basic components of the rational model and the order in which tasks are carried out in community practice–focused work are delineated in table 8.1.

TABLE 8.1 Components of Rational Planning Process for Program Design Adapted for Community Practice

COMPONENTS	PURPOSE AND FUNCTION	PARTICIPATION STRATEGIES
Select Community Issue or Concern to Be Addressed	Determine issue or concern most likely to have useful positive impact on the community and that is feasible to undertake	Seek information from community members about areas of interest and concern. Use this issue to assist in constructing the needs assessment.
Problem Analysis: Specifically Define and Conduct Analysis of Community Concern or Problem	• From assessment analyses and other data, identify problem causes and community concerns. • Identify desired conditions, strategies and actions that should remedy problem that are feasible for the organization or community to take on. • Clearly define and specify problem areas. • Frame the issue for intervention focusing on changes that can be promoted at the program level. Consider root causes and determine whether they can be addressed programmatically.	
Conduct Needs Assessment: Information Gathering and Synthesis	• Collect data and use multi-method analyses of community issues to determine broad-scale needs or needs/service gaps in the particular area of program concern (services for children). • Gather data in geographic area of concern with information from potential clients, community leaders, organizations and institutions and service providers as well as essential demographic data for area and issue of concern (original data + census, etc.). • Use the needs assessment analyses as the basis for designing a program to respond	• Survey potential participants and community members in needs assessment.

TABLE 8.1 *(Continued)*

COMPONENTS	PURPOSE AND FUNCTION	PARTICIPATION STRATEGIES
	to the identified needs and to produce positive change with individuals, families, groups, or the neighborhood/community as a whole.	
Construct Hypotheses	• Develop hypotheses: working intervention hypotheses and program hypotheses	
Selection of Community Intervention Strategies	• Select best strategies to guide interventions with individuals, families, groups, or community at large. • Design the program's interventions based on testing or replication of an evidence-based practice model where possible, or best practice models adapted to local conditions, or best knowledge base available that accurately fits the problems/concerns identified.	
Develop Program Goals and Objectives Process Objectives Outcome Objectives	• State the broad vision for the program—what will be different for participants and the community if the program succeeds? • Set goals that can reasonably be met by the intervention. • Design objectives that are clear, specific, and measurable (accomplishing the objectives should add up to meeting the program's goals). • Develop outcome objectives that can reasonably measure improvements in quality of life for program participants or the community at large. • Build formative evaluation design on process objectives.	

(continued)

TABLE 8.1 (*Continued*)

COMPONENTS	PURPOSE AND FUNCTION	PARTICIPATION STRATEGIES
	• Build outcome (summative) evaluation on the achievement of outcome objectives.	
Design Program and Program Activities	• Describe/illustrate program components in logical format identifying steps and activities participants will be involved in to promote positive change. • Specify program activities.	• Discuss potential program components with potential participants.
Program Design Decision Making	• Focus services/interventions on activities directly affecting the desired changes for participants and community. • No single program or community intervention can deal effectively with all issues related to the problem of concern; • Be prepared to adapt and refine the program design based on formative evaluation and new information.	
Design Intervention Research Early Development and Pilot Testing	• Specify elements of intervention. • Specify procedures for data collection. • Specify measures and methods of analysis. • Conduct pilot test.	
Implement and Monitor Program	• Conduct program activities. • Monitor program activities.	• Observe program activities. • Conduct satisfaction surveys with participants.
Conduct Intervention Research and Program Evaluation	• Collect and analyze data. • Refine the intervention.	• Involve program participants in assessment of program. • Collect qualitative data from participants related to program outcomes.

The table is also designed to present the purpose and function of major steps and to illustrate potential participation strategies which make the model more adaptable to the participatory nature of community practice.

The rational planning approach is most likely to be required in applications for federal- and state-funded grants. Some foundations will request use of several typical features of this submodel such as a logic model or Gannt chart time and task implementation schedule. In contrast, the closer to grassroots planning and development a program will be, the greater the expectation and local pressure will be for more inclusive processes (Medoff and Sklar 1994). While there is much utility in this approach, in community-based planning it is increasingly important to employ participatory methods and inclusive processes.

INCLUSIVE PARTICIPATORY PROGRAM DEVELOPMENT

The inclusive planning model depicted illustrates a less formal approach to planning that is grounded in the context and realities of a particular community and is consistently engaged in communication and feedback processes with community members and participants—an approach that can also make use of the planning tools and product production associated with the rational planning model. This inclusive approach should be useful: (1) to ensure ongoing and productive communication, feedback, and guidance for needed change from community members or sponsoring groups; (2) if your community has local, governmental, or other support for a new program; (3) if you will need to submit a proposal to external funders; and (4) if you work with an interested sponsor who focuses on site visits to monitor or evaluate programs.

Table 8.2 illustrates a model of inclusive participatory planning that seeks to effectively use and combine major aspects of both participatory and rational planning models (Linnell et al. 2002; Netting, O'Connor, and Fauri 2008; Weil 2005b). To remain grounded in the community and its needs and directions, this approach explicitly includes frequent reflection, discussion, interaction with and guidance from community members. This approach allows for the production of frequently needed technical documents, and can be adapted flexibly as specific program development needs dictate.

The table, along with discussion and case examples, illustrates a program design process proceeding from vision to evaluation. This process draws from several sources, including Linnell et al. (2002:3–14); Netting, O'Connor, and Fauri (2008); Fetterman and Wandersman (2004); Suarez-Balcazar and Harper 2003; Hogan-Garcia (2003); Chambers (2002); Estrella et al. (2002); and Pawlek and Vinter (2004), to form a strongly participatory community-based planning process. Inclusive participatory program design, illustrated in table 8.2, provides a workable combination of intensive community involvement and participatory processes

TABLE 8.2 Inclusive Program Design: From Vision to Valuation

PLANNING AND DEVELOPMENT TASKS	PROCESSES OF ENGAGEMENT AND PARTICIPATION
Engage with and respond to community members and/or population to be served.	Formally and informally meet with community members. Focus on listening. Learn their concerns and solicit their ideas and worker concerns and ideas. Be attentive to expressions of community concerns, needs, and ideas for development. Engage with community members; engage with staff if an organization is initiating the process; engage with other service providers for collaboration and support. Involve these primary stakeholders in discussion of needs and strengths in the community and encourage new ideas for how to improve quality of life, increase social capital, and promote new skills or endeavors. Provide time to reflect on ideas and directions.
Assess community strengths and needs and examine local context.	Explore community context and work with community members to formulate and conduct a strengths/needs assessment related to the program idea, its general purpose, and the strengths the community and service programs can bring to bear. In communities with multiple services, assess whether other auspices provide the kind of program being considered; consider how the idea will fit within the current and emerging environment; adapt ideas based on knowledge, resources, and opportunities; and consider strategies to deal with barriers to development of the idea into a program. Discuss and reflect on what information you need and how the group wants to use it.
Work with community members to build a vision, purpose, and goals for programs or projects they wish to develop.	Engage with community members to hear their dreams and facilitate their work to build a vision, purpose/mission, and goals for changes they want to work for. Create a dialogue with community and agency constituencies and others such as board or village elders, as appropriate to context. Test ideas in group discussions, focus groups, and community meetings as well as with other potential stakeholders. "Use community feedback to begin to focus a 'good idea' into program purpose and concrete goals. Use feedback to define what the outcomes of a particular program initiative should be" (Linnell et al. 2002:13). The community's desired outcomes may be quite different from those organization staff may have considered. Therefore, it is very important to facilitate open discussion, be sure all perspectives are heard and assist the group in moving toward a consensus on the viability of vision, purpose, and goals with the understanding that they can be revised as needed.

TABLE 8.2 *(Continued)*

PLANNING AND DEVELOPMENT TASKS	PROCESSES OF ENGAGEMENT AND PARTICIPATION
Gather available data and conduct research as needed about issues, concerns, options and goals.	Involve community or service population in research about their issues of concern, about different strategic approaches to meet their goals, about the population or community to be served and about comparable programs. Identify and review any existing research on comparable programs or issues and meet with community groups to assess applicability to local context. Work with small groups to develop drafts of vision, purpose and goal statements. Check out stakeholder responses to the drafts. As information and data are analyzed, convene small groups to review and reflect on what is being learned and consider alternate causes.
Facilitate planning group discussions to determine program objectives linked to each goal.	Use small group meetings and exercises to document how they will know whether the program's purposes have been achieved. This process will answer the question: "What difference does the program/project make in people's lives (in the life of the community) (the environment)?" Check out objectives with stakeholders to see if they make sense.
Work with small groups to specify desired outcomes and indicators for each goal and objective.	Coach planning groups in techniques of writing outcomes and determining indicators that will show whether goals have been met.
Hold group discussions and employ experiential exercises to determine needed program components. Then have the groups design specific activities or actions that will fulfill the purpose of the program or project.	Work with groups to design program components and activities/actions "that will flow from each goal and lead to hoped for outcomes," (Linnell et al. 2006:13) and assure through continued dialogue that the activities fit with community interests and with previous information and research. Present the program design to small groups and ask them to mentally or physically "walk through" program activities, reflecting on what it feels like to be involved in the program.
Develop a logic model for the proposed program or project. Have planning group present the program design and logic model to community/neighborhood meetings.	Given the context and requests of potential funders, you may need to work with a smaller group to develop a Logic Model for the program/project that illustrates the *Resources* brought to the program (Inputs); *Program Outputs*, that is, Program Activities and Participants; *Outcomes*: Short-Term and Medium-Term Program Results (or Program Effects); and *Program Impact*: Long-Term Outcomes/Community Impact/ Program Effectiveness.

(continued)

TABLE 8.2 *(Continued)*

PLANNING AND DEVELOPMENT TASKS	PROCESSES OF ENGAGEMENT AND PARTICIPATION
Determine with planning group if the community or organization needs to seek external funding.	Coach planning group members to practice presenting their case to potential funders, NGOs or government agencies.
Develop a program model diagram that illustrates the activities and progression of program/project activities.	In the program model diagram illustrate the components and pathway for project/program development. Show what actions or activities participants will complete. Also illustrate the staffing pattern, volunteer roles, resources, and community outreach needed to carry out the planned activities of the program. Illustrate who will do what and how the components will fit and work together.
Work with committees to develop the plan and methods to evaluate the program or project.	Design the program evaluation using both qualitative and quantitative methods if possible (this step may be very simple or complex, depending on the program), and develop and pilot-test evaluation instruments. Funders expect to see an evaluation plan as evidence of accountability. Train committee members in evaluation processes, techniques, and data analysis procedures.
Prepare leadership group to assist in resource development and fundraising.	Hold community or neighborhood meeting to share and review the plan with residents. Invite potential funders; prepare group members to speak for the proposal, to facilitate the meeting and solicit feedback and additional ideas from those attending.
Develop the budget with finance committee.	Whether you will need external funding or not, construct a budget for the program/project that covers funding and resources needed to carry out the program, including staff, space, equipment, supplies, and any indirect costs.
Develop program timeline.	Construct the timeline for implementing the program, including the steps for start-up and timing for participant and community feedback and for evaluation.
Complete proposal for funding if needed.	If needed work with planning committee to complete proposal and seek external resources as needed.
Build support for the program.	Promote program with community members and local agencies, local government. Make careful searches for external funding to match your program's purpose to funding sources priorities. If external funding sources are needed develop good contacts with foundation officers or government liaisons. Promote program at local celebrations and keep community leaders aware of progress.

TABLE 8.2 (*Continued*)

PLANNING AND DEVELOPMENT TASKS	PROCESSES OF ENGAGEMENT AND PARTICIPATION
Implement the program.	Engage community members or other program participants in program activities. Be sure that staff and/or volunteers are well trained and competent in their responsibilities. Be sure that some project participants serve on the board and advisory board of the organization. Seek frequent feedback from participants, community members, and staff. Adapt program as needed related to changing needs, new information, or changes in environment. Seek participant feedback on a regular basis.
Monitor project implementation, troubleshoot for problems, maintain good communication and seek participant feedback and feedback from relevant constituencies. Set up a monitoring committee.	Monitor the program's progress and take corrective action as needed. Develop instruments for monitoring and program review and initiate use of formative (process) evaluation procedures and instruments.
Evaluate implementation process and conduct a participatory/empowerment-oriented evaluation of program outcomes (and impact).	Continue to refine program as needed to achieve desired goals and examine goals to see if additions or changes are needed.
Develop a program implementation and evaluation report.	Use the report as needed to secure additional funding, to build other support for the program, and to educate others about the program, outlining both its effects and its effectiveness.
Work with community members on other issues and opportunities.	Build ongoing planning and evaluation into community work.

with use of specific analytic approaches and planning tools. It draws strength from both of these sources, honoring inclusive participatory processes and providing documents and materials that will be required by many funding agencies.

The inclusive planning approach can respond to the demands and ethical stance supporting community and service population involvement in program development. It is also amenable to use of several of planning tools that help to make the plan and implementation design visually understandable to a wide range of people because of immediately apprehendable pictorial presentation.

INCLUSIVE PROGRAM DEVELOPMENT

Increasingly, program development and implementation guides are emphasizing the ongoing responsibility to be "learning organizations" and to "learn for sustainability," so that programs can adapt and grow with changing environmental demands or population preferences (Senge et al. 2006). These learning approaches fit well with the inclusive and interpretive models for program planning as they focus on changes in context, seek new information, and indicate clearly that we continue learning as we proceed with a process. The following case example began as an emergent process that demanded change in "business as usual" practice methods in child welfare. Following considerable interpretive planning between Maori leaders and New Zealand child welfare staff, planning switched to a strongly participatory approach and also employed several components of the "rational" model to produce a design for practice that in combination with positive research reports encouraged the adoption of the new Family Group Conferencing (FGC) model throughout New Zealand.

When a child is at risk of being removed from her or his family of origin and the FGC program model is in place, this step is not taken without pulling together all available members of the child's extended family. After hearing from all involved social agencies, it is the extended family's responsibility to use the opportunity of a Family Group Conference to develop a working plan that provides for (1) safety of the child; (2) the child's care and nurture within the extended family; and (3) congruence with child welfare mandates to protect children from abuse and neglect.

ELEMENTS OF PROGRAMS   The Maori example of inclusive planning, as well as the Ethiopian HIV/AIDS prevention education program and the program in western North Carolina developed for people living with AIDS, illustrates several aspects of participatory program development. All three programs are based in *empowerment and participatory practice strategies.* The participatory learning and action methods employed in the Ethiopian prevention program engage community members in shared learning, discussion, and action for use in prevention and health education programs. It was reported that some participants had little knowledge of their body and that making the body maps in the sand was in itself empowering; not only did the participants gain knowledge about their own body and its functions but they later were able to take part in broader health education for their own communities. The New Zealand FGC program

---

THE MAORI AND FAMILY GROUP CONFERENCING
JOAN PENNELL AND MARIE WEIL

The development of Family Group Conferencing (FGC) as a required aspect of the child welfare process provides a clear example of strong partnership in program design. FGC was first legislated in New Zealand and is now practiced in many nations (Burford and Hudson 2000; Nixon, Burford, and Quinn 2005). The formal system of child welfare that originated and operated from a Eurocentric perspective often failed to understand the power of the extended family in Maori culture and its traditional means of group-based problem solving (Rangihau 1986).

The Maori are the indigenous people of New Zealand, outnumbered by immigrants from Europe. The dynamics of urbanization and the encroachment of a new dominant culture have upset the cultural norms and social supports within the Maori population. Recognizing these conflictual issues, Maori leaders along with child welfare workers and administrators worked to resolve problems associated with the child welfare process and to plan and implement services that would build on traditional Maori problem-solving methods.

The new approach was called Family Group Conferencing. Through this program, in cases of alleged child abuse or neglect within the Maori community, after information has been gathered, child welfare workers communicate with all the members of the extended Maori family and bring them together for a conference. Typically, a respected Maori elder opens the conference with a brief ceremony and prayer, and the key worker explains the process for the day. Staff from all of the agencies that are working with the family then share the facts of what has happened with the assembled family group, after which all agency workers leave the meeting. The extended family works together to develop a plan for the child that will assure safety and lodge the child with a family member, while the agencies continue to work with the parent(s) on issues that initiated a child welfare report. One family member is appointed as facilitator and the group discusses the matter until they reach consensus on a plan. The key child welfare worker is then told about the plan and is asked to review it. If it meets child welfare standards, the agency adopts the family's plan, and the worker remains in contact with the child, the caregivers, and the parent(s), working toward reunification.

Families and workers who take part in FGC like the process because it helps them build effective partnerships within and around the family. Notably, FGC is a way of countering institutional racism by bringing together the family and their informal supports, to plan safe ways to keep children and young people connected to kin without further endangering child and adult family members.

(Pennell 2007; Pennell and Anderson 2005)

was also empowering to family members and caregivers because it brought home the realities of living with AIDS and helped to diminish the fear and stigma that had previously isolated families. The entire FGC process is designed to empower extended families and to establish child welfare as a shared community issue.

All three programs were community-based, and all were adapted to the particular population to be served. Through these processes and staffing decisions, all the programs became culturally competent. Although much of the literature about program development focuses on the importance of technical processes such as needs assessment, monitoring, and evaluation, the value to the population and the contribution to program success should not be underestimated (Lum 2007; Pennell et al. 2005; Weil 2005b).

To act in accord with the values of community practice, planners need to listen and work closely with the community to be served. Within that process, programs may be designed by nongovernmental organizations or public agencies with strong community involvement, or the planning process may be community led.

RESOURCES If the community and existing agencies can provide the majority of needed resources, the project may well be interpretive and emergent, growing from the community's exploration of issues and options (Netting, O'Connor, and Fauri 2008). If the program design is developed collaboratively by social agencies and community members, and if it requires external resources from a larger NGO or from government or international sources, it is more likely that the process will need to produce a number of the formal products required in a funding request proposal.

STAGES OF DEVELOPMENT IN THE INCLUSIVE PARTICIPATORY PROGRAM APPROACH

Inclusive Program Development incorporates three broad stages that will demand different roles and skills from the community practitioner. In this section, we discuss the tasks of each of these implementation stages—early, middle, and concluding stages—along with the skills needed to ensure the development of a participatory and broadly inclusive program.

EARLY STAGES The early stages in program development involve the community practitioner in paying close attention to the desires of community members. The New Zealand child welfare system had worked with Maori families for many decades before community-based child welfare workers and Maori spiritual and political leaders came together for the sake of the children's future. It was necessary for workers knowledgeable about Maori culture and customs and Maori representatives to commit to training and support of child welfare staff and staff of related agencies to help them transition from an agency-led to a community-led process. In this example, ongoing engagement and response provided the base for long-term commitment to system change and new ways of engendering community responsibility for children.

Several types of instruments can be used to assess the needs, resources, and context for program planning. Community members or planning committee members can be trained to conduct door-to-door surveys to seek information about residents' perceptions of needs and priorities for action. In addition, members might conduct interviews with subsamples of residents, or focus groups could be conducted using just a few structured questions to promote discussion about needs, priorities, and program or project preferences.

As collected data is analyzed, the group will set action priorities. The community may, for example, wish to press forward with reclaiming a park and will accordingly secure safe outdoor play equipment for younger children and a soccer and baseball field for older children. After these infrastructure development goals are met, a neighborhood committee that includes youth should be responsible for weekly programming in the park, plans for special community-wide events, and upkeep of the area. Another program priority might be construction of affordable housing and financial counseling for local families who wish to relocate into planned developments that include safe play areas, community gardens, a community kitchen, and multipurpose meeting rooms. Subgroups will need to work on building the vision, mission, and purpose of the proposed program and gain agreement from community associations. Only then can they proceed to the more detailed tasks of gathering additional data and information, drafting the proposed program activities or tasks, building program objectives from goals, and connecting objectives to desired outcomes. During this early stage, response and reflection times for block groups or subcommittees and the planning committee can be built in, and larger meetings can be held for feedback when new information, documents, or designs become available.

MIDDLE STAGES During this phase, your group may need to conduct a strengths/needs assessment using participatory methods to document resources, interests, concerns, and community needs that residents report (Kretzmann and McKnight 1993; Mulroy 2008).

> **Strengths and Needs Assessment**—An evaluation that is designed to identify community resources and strengths of residents, community groups, and institutions. It is also used to determine what goods and services are lacking in a community, as well as identify existing services and resources. Such assessments ask: What resources and strengths already exist that can be built upon? What is needed? By whom? This type of evaluation is especially useful before starting a new program to determine whether there is sufficient need to justify it. (Adapted from United Way of America)

This information can help you to determine whether ideas that have been voiced fit the concerns expressed by the broader community (Kretzmann and

McKnight 1993). You may test ideas in group discussions, focus groups, community meetings, and with other potential stakeholders, and assess if these ideas are congruent with earlier discussions. *CPS Workbook* provides opportunities to review and critique an inclusive needs assessment process.

It may be useful for your planning group to develop a logic model for the planned program that provides a picture of the resources to be provided to the program, the program activities, and short and long-term outcomes. The *CPS Workbook* also includes templates and exercises to develop a logic model and other types of program documentation useful in program implementation and resource development.

Building the vision, describing the purpose, and setting the program's goals are essential elements in program development. A well-developed vision and purpose statement comes from Professional Assistance for Development Action (PRADAN) in northern India—a group of committed development professionals who work to help lift rural communities out of severe poverty. The organizational overview at their Web site states:

> Established in Delhi in 1983, PRADAN was pioneered by a group of young professionals, all of whom were inspired by the conviction that individuals with knowledge resources and empathy for the marginalized must work with communities at the grassroots level in order to help them overcome poverty.
>
> PRADAN believes that the path towards conquering economic poverty is through enhancing the livelihood capabilities of the poor and giving them access to sustainable income earning opportunities. In the process, the poor must be enabled to break free of the past, develop an alternate vision of their future and set achievable goals. They must be equipped with the technical, organisational, negotiating, and networking skills that will facilitate the fulfillment of their goals. (Professional Assistance for Development Action 2009)

Following the purpose statement and program goals, program or project activities are designed to fulfill each goal and achieve desired outcomes. Program/project activities can be as various as cooperative development of a community garden, prenatal care and well-baby checkups in isolated areas, learning skills to develop microenterprises, mentoring and job skills training for youth, installation of pumps or plumbing for domestic water coupled with maintenance skills training, or Motheread activities in which women who have not had the opportunity to read learn with their young children. The progression of program activities and components is often depicted in a "program model"—a graphic representation that makes it easy to grasp the operation of the entire program.

CONCLUDING STAGES Participatory and empowerment evaluations are the most appropriate assessment approaches for highly participatory, community-based programs. Most critically, in collecting evaluation data, it is important that your work group use methods that seek out the diverse voices of the community. People in community work practice evaluation all across the globe and use multiple methods to collect the perspectives of people in the community—even people who may not be literate. In some very low-income communities in India, people have developed a logic model for their community program plans and have used assessment workbooks developed by Helzi Noponen for PRADAN, which are designed in symbols and pictures (Noponen 2001; 2002; Pennell, Noponen, and Weil 2005). Noponen designed a pictorial Likert-type scale with assessment points ranging from a very unhappy to a very happy face of an Indian woman. PRADAN women's groups could then use this scale to assess each resource and need in their villages. The pictorial assessment books illustrated many community features with each feature connected to their "Happy to Sad Face" rating scale and included, for example, drawings of well pumps to relate to their supply of water; drawings of cattle or goats to indicate assets; and large grain jars to illustrate reserve food supply. The most important aspect of using assessment and planning aids is that everyone in the community is encouraged to have their say in how the future should be envisioned.

To help ensure desired outcomes, program implementation should be accompanied by a carefully crafted evaluation plan designed in concert with early program planning (Unrau, Gabor, and Grinnell 2007). Evaluations need to include two parts: an evaluation of program development and implementation processes; and an evaluation of program outcomes, ideally focused on immediate, intermediate, and long-term outcomes (or program impact). In this chapter we focus primarily on evaluations characterized by citizen participation and an orientation to empowerment of participants and community members. Evaluations of community programs should focus on assessment of effectiveness measured through use of both qualitative and quantitative methods and are intended to uncover "what works and why" to help participants achieve desired goals.

INCORPORATION OF PARTICIPATORY EVALUATION INTO INCLUSIVE PROGRAM DEVELOPMENT

Program evaluation originally developed as a research process carried out by external evaluators—presumed to be objective because they had no vested interest in program outcomes. Expectations of methodological sophistication tended to drive evaluation processes. As the early "rational planning models" depended on professional expertise, so did evaluations. However, this objective distance sometimes meant that evaluations "missed the mark" through misunderstandings and limited firsthand knowledge about programs. While very formal external evaluations are required in some situations, it is much more common now for program or project evaluation processes to employ participatory methods (Israel, Eng, Schulz, and Parker 2005) or to be guided by an empowerment evaluation focus (Fetterman and Wandersman 2004). In these evaluation approaches, the evaluation process itself becomes an intervention because program staff and/or program participants learn new skills and engage with each other actively to assist in assessing program effects and effectiveness. As noted earlier, community programs are more successful when they utilize local knowledge of residents, and listen to their perspectives and ideas about needs, strengths, and directions. Similarly, many people may be unwilling to participate in an evaluation constructed by and implemented by "outsiders."

Currently, the social sciences and helping professions are taking in and acting on a newer paradigm of participatory and empowerment-oriented research (Fetterman et al. 1996; Israel et. al. 2005; Kindon 2008; McIntyre 2007; Suarez-Balcazar and Harper 2003). This is not an "alternate" paradigm, but an additional one; and we should choose our frameworks, methodologies, and research procedures in light of the issues we are studying and the questions for which we want answers (Kuhn 1970). As participatory and empowerment evaluations have gained stature it is no longer considered strange to involve those who know the most about the context, strengths, and needs of their communities (Chambers 1995; Gaventa 1982). Their experiences and perceptions, as well as their abilities to communicate effectively, enrich the research work, help to gain accurate responses, and offer grounded perspectives on results.

PARTICIPATORY EVALUATION   Practice wisdom has long honored the maxims to "start where the people are" and to "trust the process." Starting "where people are" is still critical, and community practitioners need to construct program planning processes that are transparent and trustworthy. Transparent (understandable) methods and evaluators' efforts to build and maintain trust with program staff, participants and representatives of the community are critical both to ethical practice and to assure that the information gathered is accurate and useful.

Recently refined methodologies for evaluation such as participatory evaluation, self-evaluation, and empowerment evaluation now provide frameworks for evaluation and research that are congruent with the values, theory, knowledge, and practice methodologies of community practice. *Participatory evaluation* involves community members in the research process to greater or lesser degrees. Through this methodology, sometimes community members are trained to conduct house-to-house surveys or co-facilitate focus groups. In more intensive participatory processes, community members are involved in all stages of the evaluation process—from designing the evaluation in conjunction with program design throughout all steps of evaluation, including data analysis and reporting on results (Chambers 1995, 1997; Estrella et al. 2002; Minkler 2004).

Empowerment evaluation methods have recently been built and expanded from principles of participatory evaluation. A number of useful books present the methodology and good examples of evaluation strategies that are intended to empower the people and communities involved as well as to evaluate community programs and change efforts (Fetterman, Kaftarian, and Wandersman 1996; Fetterman and Wandersman 2004; Suarez-Balcazar and Harper 2003).

All of these emergent research methodologies take time, commitment, and the capacity to work in a "learning environment," along with the frustrations and lengthy discussions that are likely to be part of the process. When carefully conducted, these participatory methods can effectively ground evaluation of a program in its local context and become an in-depth participatory learning project in itself—thus building community capacity and shared social capital to assess current programs and design new ones.

The *CPS Workbook* includes tools and techniques for drafting goal statements, preparing program budgets, and developing timelines. In practice, when your proposal is completed, you and members of your planning committee will seek external resources as needed. Several useful books provide detailed information about proposal and resource development (Brueggemann 2006; Linnell, Radosevich, and Spack 2002).

During the final stages of program development, you will need to work in the community to build support for the program. When you submit your proposal to potential funding sources, you will also hold meetings with the larger community to review the program. Hopefully, you will receive requested funding and proceed to implement the program, seeking frequent feedback from participants, community members, and staff, in order to adapt the program to changing needs, contexts, or new information. Research responsibilities at this stage of implementation include monitoring the program's progress and taking corrective action as needed. Final steps in the implementation process will involve you and your planning committee in two phases of research: to complete the evaluations of the program's implementation process, and its outcomes. When the evaluations are completed, a final task is to develop a program implementation and evaluation report. You may use the report as needed to secure additional funding, to build other support for the program, and to educate others about the program.

The case study in this chapter on the Women's Wellness Network from the "Bootheel" area of Missouri presents a clear example of a need, an idea, and a program conceived and pursued by a group of women concerned about lack of access to mental health services.

WOMEN'S WELLNESS NETWORK: MENTAL HEALTH IS PART OF EVERY WOMAN'S WELLNESS
SARA K. PRICE, 2005

In the spring of 2001, problem recognition and a desire for change brought together a dozen women from entirely different walks of life, and they all wanted to talk about one thing: why were so many women in their community depressed, and what could they do about it? One of these women recently had a neighbor who experienced the death of a baby. She contacted a bereavement support organization in St. Louis, which was about 2 hours north of her community for assistance. To her surprise, a social worker drove out from that organization to visit with her neighbor, bring her information, and offer to help her create a social support network for herself and others with similar issues. Somewhere, a spark had been ignited, and I, that social worker from St. Louis, was about to get caught up in a fire of inspiration.

Over the next several months, a collaboration began to emerge among several agencies formed to address the growing disparity in fetal and infant mortality in this rural community, along with service providers concerned about access and services for women's mental health. An opportunity for funding had been presented through Healthy Start for communities desiring to enhance screening, recognition, and treatment for maternal depression. As the Women's Wellness Network began to work together, the fundamental challenge of the proposed project emerged: no one wanted to talk about "depression." Yet, the group was committed to changing core community beliefs about mental health because we believed that we could enable and empower women to seek the support they needed if women were able to name their own concerns and define their own level of treatment and support. So, we decided on a name, the "Women's Wellness Initiative," and a tag-line, "Mental Health Is Part of Every Woman's Wellness."

The Women's Wellness Initiative targeted all women in the rural community equally with the assumption that everyone was in this project together: providers, consumers, those with and those without resources, those impacted by mental health directly and those whose lives were impacted by the mental health of others. First, educational materials were produced and widely distributed to differentiate the facts and myths of depression. Second, community service agencies sent staff members for training to integrate screening and education regarding depression into their ongoing general community services. Third, social workers with bachelor's degrees from within the community were hired to work with women who were experiencing or were at risk for depression. Finally, the Women's Wellness Network reached out into the community and offered seed money to grassroots causes and groups who wanted to add services in their neighborhoods, churches, and communities that could enhance women's mental health and self-esteem.

The role of community practice in the Women's Wellness Initiative was never an easy or a straightforward one. As the primary community organizer and project director of the grant submission, I was involved in a number of challenging situations. For example, there was the general disagreement over whether "non-mental-health" providers were adequately trained to deliver mental health education and support ser-

CONTINUED

vices. In hiring staff members for the project's direct work, I relied heavily on the ability to distinguish individuals who would resonate with the needs of the community and adopt a "learn as we go" approach surrounding concrete knowledge of depression and mental health. Prospective applicants were reviewed by a community panel of consumers and providers who rated their ability to connect with and understand the needs of the community.

Once these initial tasks were completed, the larger challenge of community practice became stepping back and allowing the community members to develop their own expertise and leadership in changing core attitudes, beliefs, and behaviors within their community. Through an empowerment evaluation approach (Fetterman, Kaftarian, and Wandersman 1996), the Women's Wellness Network began to take charge of their own measurements for process and outcome evaluation.

These participatory approaches to community practice are essential for trust and autonomy to develop, but that trust building was a gradual evolution from providing extensive start-up support and resources to a slow process of stepping away while the community's leaders stepped in to positions of increasing leadership.

The tools of empowerment evaluation also brought a new recognition to the community leaders that helped them understand the processes of measuring "success" and eventually provided the infrastructure needed to secure additional funding.

The biggest challenge for the Women's Wellness Initiative was the rapidly escalating level of need within the community at a time of diminishing resources. Severe cuts in Medicaid spending at the state level, combined with a massive economic impact of lost jobs within the community and a dramatic increase in drug use, were all problems that we had to deal with. This continues to be a severe challenge for the community as time goes on and little changes in the economic and social infrastructure of the area.

The outcomes for the Women's Wellness Initiative were extremely positive. For instance, during our four years of funding, over 3,000 women were screened for depression and received psychoeducation. Over 200 women received professional case management and support services, and of those women, 87 percent actively engaged with other mental health services in the self-help, primary care, and/or specialty mental health sector.

The Women's Wellness Initiative provided major life lessons for me (Price 2005), but also significant learning opportunities for social work and community practice in the area of maternal depression and service utilization for women of reproductive age.

This case combines work with a small functional community—women concerned about mental health issues (initially postpartum depression)—that employed organizing and planning processes to achieve their goals through service and network development and community education. The steps involved combine serious attention to context and use of interpretive planning and an emergent process for development, along with later use of rational planning tools and methods of empowerment research. The results for the Wellness Initiative indicate an effective sequencing of approaches and consistent use of methods with a strong community focus.

INCLUSIVE PROGRAM DEVELOPMENT ROLES AND SKILLS

Roles and skills in program development typically focus either on facilitating processes or on assisting groups in task accomplishment. Some of the task areas involve coaching in technical planning skills or use of particular planning tools. We will first review process-oriented roles, then those that typically have a fairly equal balance of task and process, and finally those roles that are primarily focused on specific planning or grant preparation tasks. More information and sets of exercises are included in the *CPS Workbook* to assist in learning these skills.

ESSENTIAL PROCESS ROLES AND SKILLS FOR INCLUSIVE PROGRAM PLANNING

Netting, O'Connor, and Fauri (2008) describe four critical process skills that have similar roles in both interpretive and rational planning models: *gaining entry; becoming oriented; engaging in critical thinking;* and *making ethical decisions.* These skills require the community worker to become a learner and explorer.

SKILLS IN GAINING ENTRY TO THE COMMUNITY These skills involve sharpening your interpersonal skills, working hard to build trust and credibility, and especially identifying those who can help you build relationships. The community-based planner cannot work effectively without gaining legitimated access to the community and attending to local realities of power and protocol, without building relationships with a range of people by establishing commonalities, and without establishing mutuality and rapport by listening, responding, and observing carefully to understand local customs, communication patterns, and the concerns and motivations of the people you are connecting with (Mondros and Wilson 1994; Netting, O'Connor, and Fauri 2008; Weil 2005c).

BECOMING ORIENTED THROUGH EXPLORATION In order to work effectively with any group or community, you must observe and analyze their context—physical, social, and economic—as well as carefully observe the operation of power dynamics and also identify current formal and informal leaders. You need to understand each of these elements in relation to the planning process that is part of your purpose in their midst. This is when all "closet anthropologists" have the opportunity to focus on learning about the community you are entering and its people. Active ethnographic skills are important for figuring out salient aspects of the culture and coming to understand people's roles (Hammersley and Atkinson 1983). You are initiating a process of discovery that is especially intensive initially. In some ways, this discovery process involves refreshing the skills you had as a child—looking intently, observing everything, taking in what is going on, and also learning to ask questions that are respectful in the local context. Your gender, race, age, or culture may impact local expectations of your behavior (and that is well worth knowing), though it has been our experience that if some members of a community have decided that you are authentic in your self presentation and worthy of trust, they and often other community members can be very forgiving and willing to educate well-intentioned strangers. It can be very helpful early on to have someone give you a community tour and introduce you to a range of people, especially those who might be stakeholders in the program planning process. There are typically going to be neighborhood gathering places whether you are entering an urban neighborhood, a smaller town, a rural community or village, ranging from the general store to the local coffee spot or teahouse. Take time to talk to people about general topics, and as you get to know people, ask them about community issues and potential program or project interests. If you are working in a local organization or agency, use these same skills to get to know the people, the culture, and the context of the organization and explore the organization's relationship to its community and to other organizations.

ENGAGING IN CRITICAL THINKING Critical thinking is a term that is often heard and not always understood. It involves a combination of reasoning skills, and you will need to practice them individually and sequentially (though not in a fixed pattern) to learn all you need to know to engage citizens and staff in program planning. Aside from specific analytic and reasoning skills, critical thinking involves honing your skills in listening and observing, body language, and visual and cultural cues to make sense out of the information. Kroeger and Thuesen (1988) have carefully examined critical thinking skills, and we have developed critical thinking exercises for the *CPS Workbook*. The essential critical thinking skills move up a ladder of complexity beginning with copying; then comparing; computing; analyzing; coordinating; and finally synthesizing information so that it is understandable (Kroeger and Thuesen 1988). According to Netting, O'Connor, and Fauri (2008):

> Critical thinking, as deep thorough thinking results in examination of assumptions, goals, questions and the various elements of evidence. It involves the use of reflection focused on what to believe or what not to believe. Critical thinking is part of problem-solving, not just an effort in appraisals or claims or arguments. Critical thinking critiques mistakes in one's thinking and strives for a deeper understanding of issues. No matter the planning approach, the planner thinks critically. What differs may be the focus of the critical thinking. (13)

SKILLS IN ETHICAL DECISION MAKING

We all have our own personal ethical standards that give our lives guidance in decision making. In addition, as community practitioners, there are professional values that we have agreed to uphold. Reconsider the discussions in chapter 3 and the values and codes of ethics that call us to work toward empowerment of disadvantaged groups, to seek more just policies and practices, and to weigh the potential power issues inherent in all professional decision making. In planning there are complex decisions about who will be included in programs, what community goals will be advanced, whose interests are being served, and, in very difficult decisions, how we can choose so that the interests and concerns of those most disadvantaged are given priority. As John Rawls has argued, when inequitable distribution is made, it is just to assure that those with the least are not further disadvantaged (Rawls 2001). In our field, we are challenged to a higher standard than utilitarianism dictates (working to produce the greatest good for the greatest number). We are challenged to work toward a redistribution of society's goods so that policy and program decisions are made to advantage the least advantaged. Meeting this challenge requires moral courage, willingness to speak truth to power, steadfastness not to yield to powerful counterforces, and stamina to consistently subject community planning and policy issues to ethical assessment (Kim Strom-Gottfried, personal communication, August 22, 2008).

Skills that are associated with the roles of visionary, planner/designer, communicator/engager, bridge-builder, proposal writer, spokesperson/advocate, and evaluator/researcher/assessor are also critical for this model (see *CPS Workbook*).

VISIONING SKILLS Visionaries tend to "see things whole," recognizing and understanding a social problem or concern—and often after reflection—almost literally seeing (envisioning) both the end goals (how things will be with the problem resolved) and the programmatic strategies to make what needs to happen, happen. The Grassroots Support Project of Southern Rural Development Initiative (SRDI) provides an example of a vision statement:

VISION STATEMENT

SRDI's Grassroots Support Project works to strengthen the effectiveness and sustainability of grassroots support organizing efforts that respect, honor, and preserve local culture, heritage, and the natural environment while simultaneously working to resolve the crippling legacy of racism and other oppressions in the rural South. Specifically, we are working to deepen the impact of rural grassroots support organizing efforts that increase income, assets, and racial equality for marginalized populations. (Thomas Watson, director of Grassroots Support Project, SRDI 2008)

Internally, Thomas Watson's vision for work with grassroots organizations is to help them increase their effectiveness and strengthen their leadership capacities. Externally, his vision is to assist grassroots organizations in connecting with each other, with nongrassroots partners, and with larger systems to help them develop resources, build community assets, and establish sustainable projects and organizations. Having clarity about the long-term vision, program purposes, and components of grassroots support that he takes on, Watson and the groups he works with receive the necessary guidance.

The role of *visionary* is crucial in program development. The community worker/planner may or may not be the initial visionary in program development. For example, Muhammad Yunus was the visionary for development of the Grameen Bank, which has had worldwide impact on asset development for very low-income people. It could just as easily be a community member, or members, who from deep knowledge of local conditions recognize a transformative way of reshaping services or beginning a program of support. In the Missouri Women's Wellness Network case example, the vision of the Network was born from the work of a small group of women who had concerns about the lack of mental health services in their rural region. Through their group discussions with the regional health worker, these women envisioned future programs. Together they identified who the programs would serve; how they would respond to local conditions; what benefits they would have for participants; and what they could accomplish in the larger community. Vision, however, does not arise unattended, as Einstein said of genius; it is the result of 10 percent inspiration and 90 percent perspiration. Vision, that is, arises from our experience and knowledge, our connections with people, and our openness to possibilities.

ROLES AND SKILLS THAT BALANCE PROCESS AND TASKS

Central skills for a program planner/designer are to be able to work through group processes in order to determine the purpose and desired outcomes for a new program. In fact, process and facilitation skills are needed from the initial idea until implementation and evaluation. Equally important for program designers are technical skills used to assess needs, present materials, and conduct evaluation research. Building your skills in both of these major areas is essential, especially if you need to prepare a proposal for funding a program or community project.

COMMUNICATION SKILLS These skills are needed in all phases of program planning. In particular, the planner needs to use good communication skills in facilitating work within small groups such as the planning group and staff groups, and with larger groups of community partners and representatives who will need to know a lot about the program and how it will work. Relevant external organizations and funders will be interested in meetings that provide briefings about the program and reports that provide up-to-date information on program accomplishments, expenditures, and program and budget management. The CPS Workbook provides communication exercises and recommendations.

The SRDI vision/purpose statement example is a standard in a proposal and is of great value to clarify a program's purpose. Equally important is learning to write goal statements that indicate what will be different for program participants or the community when the program is concluded. For example, all too often a program for early childhood education may select a goal such as "To end poverty in our county." This aspiration is laudable but hardly a workable goal statement. Much more realistic examples of goals for this program would be to:

1. Ensure that all children participating in the program will enter first grade prepared and ready to learn.
2. Provide parents with training in job readiness skills and computer literacy to assist them in seeking employment in the county's job market.

GOAL STATEMENTS Goal statements define what the program will do and what it seeks to achieve. With sound goal statements, participants, staff, sponsors, and community members should be able to read your proposal and know what this program will do and how the lives of participants, or the community itself, will be different as a result of participating in it.

A program planner typically needs to design, in graphic form, a model of how the program will work and what its components will be. In the CPS Workbook, you will have the opportunity to conceive of a program and develop the "working model." A program model illustrates several things: (1) The components of the program—what participants will do in what sequence. For example, how will the parents in the support program noted above learn job readiness skills? What skills will be fairly easy to master and therefore build motivation and commitment? (2) What staff will be working with participants? What instructional methods are likely to be most effective with parents who have not previously achieved major success in school or the job market? and (3) How will program staff and the participants know when they have achieved specific goals? mastered specific skills? When are they ready to compete in the local job market?

Being able to answer these questions will help you draw the design of your program and identify what participants and staff will do, as well as how the evaluation will capture and demonstrate the skills they have mastered. Participants' development of skills is a major immediate outcome of the program. For the longer-term successful outcomes, participants will not just have developed skills, but they will have found a job that uses those skills and have successfully maintained the job for six months or a year. In the *CPS Workbook*, more content and program planning tools will be presented to assist you in learning how to lay out a logic model, program timelines, the budget, the evaluation plan, and other more technical tasks.

SPOKESPERSON/ADVOCACY SKILLS   Direct advocacy skills are discussed in other chapters. It is important to note here that spokesperson skills are needed for you to be prepared to speak to a variety of kinds of groups—funders, community members, other social agencies or NGOs, governmental agencies, and civic organizations. Your purpose will be to build support for your program, engage others in networking and collaborating with your program, and possibly assist your participants in finding jobs or accomplishing other program goals.

Think through whether you will use technical equipment, videos, DVDs, slide shows of program activities, or photograph posters, and handouts. Analyze what each group's desired relationship with the program is, and then tailor your talk and your visual aids to emphasize the most relevant points for these various constituencies. Each of the constituency groups mentioned may want some different information from you. You may well have brochures or flyers and certain basic general information that will be distributed to any groups you speak with or with any media outlets—newspaper, radio, television. Be sure, however, insofar as possible, that you select the most relevant material for each audience. You might ask those who attend to write questions down on note cards, or you might mention a couple of areas that may be controversial for questions, or use other strategies to encourage discussion and questions. If you are going to be speaking to groups or organizations with the intention of resource development, you may want to meet with groups, more than one time, and be sure that you have provided the stories they need to hear and the results that will matter to them.

EVALUATOR/RESEARCHER/ASSESSOR SKILLS   A broad range of skills are needed in this complex role set that involves technical strengths in research methods and project management. In community practice, most program research employs empowerment and participatory approaches; therefore, it is important that researchers also have very strong "people skills" such as relationship building or coaching. In this way they can effectively lead staff and community representatives through the process and engage with community constituencies to discuss the purpose, methods, and use of the research. Maintaining good communications is an essential skill.

Researchers take on major roles when they develop instruments for Strengths/ Needs Assessments, for focus groups or other group related processes, and for Qualitative and Quantitative measures for program evaluation. A major task in participatory research is training staff and community members in collecting needed data. An important skill is designing needed instruments for both a process and an outcome evaluation of the program, supervising data collection, compiling and analyzing data, briefing groups and community members about findings, and writing the program evaluation report. The CPS Workbook provides more information on participatory and empowerment methods (see also Fetterman and Wandersman 2004; Israel et al. 2005).

INTERPRETIVE PLANNING AND EMERGENT APPROACHES

According to Netting, O'Conner, and Fauri (2008), the emergent approach to program planning grows out of a community-centered value perspective focused on mutual respect and relationship building. A particular concern is to see that all voices and perspectives are heard in planning processes, that leadership is relational not directive, that preconditions are not set, and that the program design will grow out of the process of interaction. Indeed, Netting et al. liken rational planning approaches to straight lines with clear initiation and ending points and a sequential logic; whereas they see emergent planning approaches as more closely resembling an upward spiral of cooperative, iterative processes. The emergent approach demonstrates sensitivity to context, history, cultural norms, and ethical decision making. Although the process is not linear, and the "plan" may not be clearly identifiable until after the fact, the program when launched will benefit from strong engagement and commitment to truly shared goals. In support of emergent and participatory planning processes, Mortenson (personal communication, March 31, 2009) sees these approaches as much more congruent (than expert planning efforts) for international development work with small, rural communities. Indeed these approaches build on local (or indigenous) knowledge and require the "external" planner to be more connected to her/his own intuitive sense and intelligence (Mortenson, personal communication, March 31, 2009).

Netting, O'Connor, and Fauri (2008) provide useful analysis and illustrations of Interpretive Planning and Emergent Approaches drawn largely from their own experience in community development in several nations and building on feminist theory, participatory theory, social learning, social constructivist theory, and participatory research. This approach has elements that are similar to the change theory developed earlier by John Dewey (1967); Lippitt, Watson, and Westley (1958); and Bennis, Benne, Chin, and Corey (1967/1976). Although some might view this model of program design as resembling the time-honored British process of "muddling through" (Lindbloom 1959), our own experiences in similar complex community processes bring the current authors to a strong appreciation of this model. It is often very applicable in community development program planning in small communities. It is especially valuable in its recognition that program development "in situ" is often nonlinear and that circumstances can alter well-laid plans at any moment. The "interpretive/emergent" model provides a means of meeting communities and potential participants "where they are," and promotes flexibly adapting as needed when new knowledge and experiences gained through consistent engagement of community members warrant. The following assumptions (Netting, O'Connor, and Fauri 2008:118) guide this approach:

ASSUMPTIONS FOR INTERPRETIVE PLANNING AND EMERGENT APPROACHES

- Interpretive planning and the emergent approaches create a viable framework for competent program planning, even though planning will be different from rational, prescriptive approaches.
- Interpretive planning focuses on understanding stakeholders' perspectives as a means of continual information gathering and analysis.
- Interpretive planning is nonlinear in that engagement, sense-making, and discovery interact continually as a program design unfolds.
- Data collection in this type of planning tends to be both formal and informal with whatever structure that is applied being tentative and open to reformulation depending on what is being learned.
- The planning process is continually emergent by being attentive to time and context.

This approach provides guidance for situations that are not appropriate for the standard rational model. In addition, it focuses closely on inclusion of diverse groups, and it specifically incorporates relationship building into the planning process.

Interpretive planning occurs in many situations when professionals recognize that they will "lose the community" if they continue with pre-set plans. The varied impacts of economic globalization, especially in the Global South, make it even more important for community-based planners to ground planning and development programs in local realities, and to work within the local culture. An excellent case example that embodies this point and illustrates the

AIDS ORPHANS AND THE PIG INTERVENTION

Staff in a faith-based nongovernmental organization (NGO) were witnessing a rise in child-headed households (CHHs) in an African country where many adults were being felled by AIDS. Because there were so few facilities to care for these "AIDS orphans," many of the children were remaining in their family homes rather than becoming street children. A European farming concern offered to donate 2,500 baby pigs to the agency over a three-year period, assuming that the CHHs, helped by the agency, would raise the pigs, butcher them, and then use the butchered hogs for their own consumption. The thinking was that the pigs would be a good source of food and would provide manure to enrich depleted agricultural land. The first round of CHHs was selected and trained in the care and feeding of pigs and seemed ready to raise the pigs. However, shortly after the first 500 pigs arrived, it became clear that most of the CHHs had other ideas. They wanted to take the pigs to market quickly in order to obtain capital as quickly as possible. With the direct financial help of the European pig concern, the program was modified by having the NGO purchase the pigs, putting funds in the hands of the participants while also extending the program by distributing the purchased pigs to the new CHH participants (O'Connor and Netting 2007).

In this example, well-intentioned planners responded to an opportunity that had unexpected results. The projected outcome for this program was a child-headed household having adequate food. However, the children wanted to participate in the local economy, not simply be passive recipients of food supplies. This CHH decision had implications for the larger community and its economy. In the process of discovering what the children wanted and the fears of existing pig farmers related to what might happen, rational planning rightly switched to an emergent approach in which persons in authority began to realize the implications of the program design and the need to change the plan (O'Connor and Netting 2007).

A combination of rational and interpretive planning was needed in this example and was eventually utilized. One cannot mobilize the distribution of a large number of pigs without a rational approach to detail. On the other hand, the children saw pigs as a source of income, and this perspective conflicted with the planners' assumptions. So for this context, a far better approach required rethinking and adjusting the program as information was gathered through experience. That redesign resulted in a self-sustaining effort with positive outcomes for all stakeholders.

(Abstracted and adapted by the authors from Netting, O'Connor, and Fauri 2008:173–76.)

value of employing the "interpretive/emergent" approach focuses on efforts to create sources of food (Netting, O'Connor, and Fauri 2008).

"AIDS Orphans and the Pig Intervention" clearly illustrates the need for flexibility, for "going back to the drawing board," and for being responsive to local needs and knowledge. By moving from the original plan to an interpretive response and an emergent approach to what was actually happening "on the ground" to better meet local needs, the planners were able to "save" an intervention that would have been assessed a failure under the original rubric.

SOCIAL LEARNING, CONSTRUCTIVIST, AND SENSE-MAKING THEORIES

Employing *social learning, social constructivist,* and *sense-making theories,* Netting, O'Connor, and Fauri note that approaches grounded in these theories are likely to be "more collaborative and less reductionistic" than the traditional model in planning and decision-making processes (2008:12–14). They draw from older sources on collaborative planning, from Lindbloom's (1959) early incremental planning work, and from newer organizational theories including Miller, Hickson, and Wilson (1996); Hudson (1979); Weick (1995); Westley, Zimmerman, and Patton (2006); and Senge et al.'s (2006) approaches to building "learning organizations."

Netting, O'Connor, and Fauri (2008) describe emergent processes as having "directionality" and being similar to the famous toy, Slinky, through its circles of coiled energy (16–17). Emergent logic for planning is "developed from attention to context, and since no two contexts are exactly alike, each planning process will unfold differently" (Netting, O'Connor, and Fauri 2008:134). In line with networking theory and information exchange, emergent processes are expected to promote creativity and innovation. Table 8.3 presents the dimensions that are inherent in emergent approaches to interpretive planning and illus-

TABLE 8.3 Dimensions of an Interpretive Planning Process

DIMENSION	FUNCTION
Engagement	Assures that multiple perspectives are heard and reinforces their validity Provides a mutual respect and relational focus Assures understanding of and attention to context Assures a complexity focus
Discovery	Draws from multiple data sources Assures validity and complexity of information
Sense-making	Uses compromise and consensus-based decision making Assures complexity, sophistication, and validity in decision making Respects context by assuring that decisions fit and work for particulars of the situation
Unfolding	Assures options and possibilities for the particulars of the situation Builds on what was learned and attends to continued learning Privileges complexity rather than reductionism Assumes continual revisioning

Source: Netting, O'Connor, and Fauri 2008.

trates its distinctions from traditional planning models (Netting, O'Connor, and Fauri 2008:136).

CONCLUSIONS

This chapter has presented three approaches to program planning: a rational planning model; an interpretive/emergent approach; and an inclusive participatory model—"from values to valuation." We have used a variety of case examples to illustrate program development and several vignettes to explain processes and skills.

The central component in program design is to develop a new idea for how to solve a long-term problem, or to develop a novel approach to deal with an emerging problem, always with the involvement of community partners. David Bornstein's 2007 book, *How to Change the World: Social Entrepreneurs and the Power of New Ideas,* provides inspiration for this work. He begins:

> Is it possible to eradicate poverty? Extend health care to every corner of the world? Ensure that every child in every country receives a good education? These visions may seem beyond reach today, but the stories in this book reveal that we can, in fact, change the world in ways that seem unimaginable. There is a hidden history unfolding today: an emerging landscape of innovators advancing solutions that have the potential to transform life around the globe. (ix)

Bornstein chronicles the stories of ordinary people from many nations who have had ideas and carried them to fruition. Although he focuses on the single entrepreneur, the ideas carried out often depend on numerous people and can come from a group, such as the women in Missouri, or from members of a community. Bornstein prefers the term *social entrepreneur* to *nonprofit leader* or *community organizer,* and emphasizes the ingenuity of the individual, noting two recent winners of the Nobel Prize for Peace: Wangari Maathai, who founded the Greenbelt Movement in Africa (awarded in 2004), and Muhammad Yunus and the Grameen Bank (awarded in 2006). While we honor the stories of such humanitarian heroes, no movement occurs in a vacuum, no project is the product of a single person, and one of the responsibilities of community practitioners is to engage with others to develop ideas, to share the work and share the credit. Looking at the rapid growth in the nonprofit/NGO sector, Bornstein discusses its growing importance in many parts of the world.

This work involves innovation and creativity. Innovative organizations, Bornstein (2007) holds, have at least four common practices:

They institutionalize listening.
They pay attention to the exceptional.
They design real solutions for real people.
They focus on the human qualities.

These ideas are very powerful and are very likely to emerge in inclusive, participatory programs. Corollaries to these practices have long been found in community practice through principles such as those we have summarized here:

- Listening is a critical component of engagement and relationship building.
- Be observant and mindful of what promotes success, what ideas resonate with people, what new ideas can solve old problems, and what creative approaches can deal with emerging concerns and issues.
- Learn from the people you work with and be grounded in their realities. Connect their local wisdom and experience to new knowledge.
- Maintain focus on individual strengths, needs, aspirations, and hope, and the shared strengths, needs, aspirations, and hopes of communities.
- Consistently value human dignity, independence, and interdependence; and through empowerment practice, work for social justice and expansion of human rights.

Throughout the world there are myriad social issues waiting for solutions. Some will require very high-tech, highly specialized knowledge. Many problems, however, can be dealt with first by simply seeing them for what they are—perhaps seeing them anew and working with others to plan participatory programs—and then taking action to carry out your innovative ideas and build programs that make real differences in people's lives.

9

COMMUNITIES AND SOCIAL PLANNING

The good we secure for ourselves is precarious and uncertain until it is secured for all of us and incorporated into our common life.

JANE ADDAMS, FOUNDER OF HULL-HOUSE

If you don't know where you are going, any road will get you there.

ANONYMOUS

INTRODUCTION

Since 1989 the people of Porto Alegre, Brazil, have engaged in an innovative community planning process called *participatory budgeting*. It is a form of participatory planning and direct democracy that can engage a broad and diverse group of people in setting priorities for some portion of their municipality's budget. Historically, the budgeting process in most towns and cities throughout the world has been a power lodged with political, socioeconomic elites—and more recently also technical/professional elites. Participatory budgeting opens doors to larger scale participatory planning and community empowerment over its resources and direction. The initial Porto Alegre experiment in participatory budgeting was the culmination of a long process of social mobilization that produced a new democratic constitution for Brazil and opened "the possibility of direct participation of civil society in public issues" (Lorenz and Menino 2005:1).

In 1989 about 40,000 people in Porto Alegre participated in the year-long process of participatory planning and budgeting, which involves neighborhood assemblies, "thematic" assemblies, and meetings of representative delegates for citywide coordinating sessions to plan for the use of resources to improve the well-being of residents (Goldsmith 2006). The participatory budgeting process in Porto Alegre has increased civic activity, built social capital and planning skills, and increased the availability of local resources:

- Instead of two public day care facilities, there are now 120.
- Twice as many children now attend school than before, and fifty-seven new schools have opened.

- The percentage of homes with running water and sewer service has increased from 46 to 85 percent.
- The transit system is modern, affordable, efficient, and widely used. (Pibel 2006:45)

These changes in Porto Alegre's social and economic infrastructure have taken place because the priorities and concerns of the wider community were imposed on a process that formerly was the exclusive domain of a smaller group of less diverse representatives. It presents a prime example of changes that can take place in communities when a broad spectrum of residents from diverse neighborhoods have the opportunity to document local social and economic needs and engage in face-to face discussions and deliberations with each other and with city staff and officials.

Having been established in Brazil, participatory budgeting is now practiced in about 250 municipalities in Latin America and Europe and is being tested in China (Chen 2006). China has become very interested in local participatory planning, which is being sponsored by the government, with over twenty-two projects in urban areas and rural towns. Participatory budgeting in pilot towns has been quite successful, prompting expansion and more community-based planning projects. A case example from Xinhe, Zhejiang, China, written by Chen Jiagang, is included in the *CPS Workbook*.

BASIC PROCESSES AND SCOPE OF CONCERN: SOCIAL PLANNING

DEFINITIONS OF SOCIAL PLANNING Definitions of social planning share major content, yet differ with respect to scope, focus, and functions. We provide several definitions here that move up the scale of complexity and scope of operations. Weil defined planning *with* communities as

> the processes of social, physical, economic, and environmental planning engaged in by citizens, community organizations, representatives of social agencies and local governments, and community planners/practitioners to promote social and economic development, build community infrastructure, design and coordinate services, develop environmental protections, and neighborhood revitalization plans that are appropriate to given communities—urban, rural, or international. (Weil 2005b:218)

In his classic book, *Social Planning at the Community Level*, Armand Lauffer provides a definition focused on social services: "*Social planning* refers to the

development, expansion, and coordination of social services and social policies" and is a method of practice and application of rational problem-solving
that occurs organizationally on a continuum from local to societal (Lauffer
1978:583).

The definitions offered by two other scholars, Jack Rothman (2008) and Jon
Sager (2008), address a broader scope and a more specifically technical oriented
focus. Rothman points out that, with changes in technology and communication, social planning now constitutes *organized social change* and each of the
strategies is driven by a particular "strategic engine." He describes his Planning
and Policy model as being data driven, and he notes that persuasion is the major communication method to "convey the truth as revealed in empirical facts"
(Rothman 2008:142). Findings of the data should then lead "toward proposing
and enacting particular solutions" (142). Sager's definition is similar to Rothman's; it treats the public and voluntary sectors, and it presents a broad range of
settings in which social planning takes place:

> Prototypical social planning is the application of rational problem-solving tech-
> niques and data driven methodologies to conceiving, developing, coordinating,
> and delivering human services. Social planning occurs in federal, state, county
> and city bureaus, and in the voluntary sector, including community councils, United
> Ways, Area Agencies on Aging, voluntary associations and faith-based organiza-
> tions. Planning can be carried out locally, regionally, nationally, or internationally,
> and addresses such problems as poverty, child and family welfare, aging, housing,
> crime, delinquency, mental health, and so forth. Social planners function in a va-
> riety of disciplines, including social work, urban planning, public administration,
> health care, and public policy. (Sager 2008:57)

Each of these definitions is a good "fit" with at least one of the five submodels of social planning presented in this chapter. There are three major categories of skills in social planning, and the amount of time spent with each category helps distinguish the subtypes. We discuss scope and processes of social
planning in relation to the submodels and will discuss theories, roles, and
skills generically.

SCOPE OF SOCIAL PLANNING Social planning focuses on community renewal combining social and economic development, building housing and
community infrastructure, and/or coordinating social services and community
programs. The geographical scope may be neighborhoods, entire cities, larger
rural areas, or multistate regions. Traditionally, planning is known for using rational problem-solving approaches and now increasingly incorporates grassroots

groups, citizens' groups, and a broader range of community voices in participatory planning (Weil 2005b).

SUBMODELS OF SOCIAL PLANNING PRACTICE

Throughout the literature on community practice, *planning* is described as a method in itself and also as a generic process that is integral to most community practice activities—in organizing, community development, social change, and policy activities, and as a component of program design. Currently, there are five arenas differentiated by geography, participants, staff, focus of work, and skill emphasis where social planning is the major practice responsibility. For purposes of this discussion, we will refer to these distinct approaches as "submodels" of planning as illustrated in table 9.1.

The table illustrates that as the planning models move up in scale, their focus on advanced technical skills and scope of tasks intensifies. International programs may be very locally focused on basic needs of refugees, poverty alleviation programs focused on microenterprise, or these same foci may be carried out at global levels through international NGOs or even the United Nations.

Although there are multiple ways of categorizing strategies, models, or approaches to planning practice, several comparable areas of responsibilities are found across the models presented below. Rothman's (2008) set of strategies provides a "pure rationalistic planning model" that can blend either with local capacity building or a strategy that blends with advocacy. Brueggemann (2006) describes three approaches that have time-honored places in social work's history of planning: social welfare planning; social agency planning; and neighborhood planning. Social welfare planning corresponds directly with the authors' model of sectorial service planning. The approaches to neighborhood planning by Brueggemann (2006) and Weil (2005b) are well matched. Brueggemann's social agency planning approach corresponds in several ways to our discussion of program development in chapter 8. In addition, however, he describes a broader scope of planning work lodged in large public agencies such as Departments of Child Welfare and work within specific organizations entirely focused on social welfare planning.

Community practice planning often involves a greater concern for the needs and life opportunities of the poor and oppressed than is found in larger-scale city planning. Planners at all levels always need to ask, "Who plans for whom?" and "Who benefits and who suffers from public policies and decisions?" (Drake 2001). These questions ground the rationale for planning *with* communities. When decisions are made centrally, low-income communities

TABLE 9.1 Five Submodels of Planning

DIFFERENTIATING FACTORS	1 PLANNING WITH NEIGHBORHOODS AND SMALL COMMUNITIES	2 SECTORIAL PLANNING BY TYPES OF SERVICE	3 COMMUNITY-WIDE PLANNING—NONPROFIT SECTOR	4 CITY AND REGIONAL PLANNING; USUALLY PUBLICLY FUNDED	5 INTERNATIONAL, MULTINATIONAL, AND GLOBAL PLANNING
PLANNING BODY	Community Organization or Group A local agency	Coordinating Body such as: Area Agencies on Aging; State Planners for Child Welfare; Interagency Coordinating body to prevent, and treat AIDS/HIV	Community Planning Council United Ways Jewish Federations Other nonprofit Planning Groups	Staff of a City's Planning Department Staff of a Regional Planning Department	Local and External and International NGOs Community National Planning Agency Global Org. such as the United Nations Red Cross UNICEF
STAFF	Community Practitioner	Community Practitioner/ Planner	Community Planner/ Practitioner	City and Regional Planners	Community Practitioners; Governmental and NGO Staff
PARTICIPANTS	Residents of Neighborhoods/ Communities; Members of Community	Staff of Social Agencies in that Sector of Practice; Representatives of community;	Staff of Planning Organization; Members of Planning Council; Governmental Reps.	Staff of CRP Department; and Other Governmental Agencies;	Residents of Villages, Communities; Members of Community Organizations;

	Organizations	Representatives of Client Populations	Neighborhoods/ Populations to Be Served	Advisory Board; Nonprofit Staff and Citizens	NGO Partners Representatives of Local, State, Federal Governments and International Bodies
FOCUS	Social, Economic, and Sustainable Development in Communities; Program Development in Communities or Neighborhoods; Comprehensive Community Initiatives	Development of Quality Services for an Underserved Population; Or a New or Emerging Population Collaboration to Develop a Continuum of Services for a Population	Developing the Range of Programs Needed to Serve Diverse Members of Communities, Vulnerable Populations; Promoting Collaboration among Members to Broaden or Re-envision Services; Evaluating Services; Conducting Assessments	Planning for City or Regional Infrastructure, Transportation, Water and Sewer; Leading Planning Groups for Special Projects, e.g.: Re-planning for a Devastated Neighborhood. Working to Develop Mixed-use Neighborhoods; Assisting Community Groups in Planning Neighborhood Recreation Areas, etc.	Social, Economic, and Sustainable Development in Communities; Responding to Natural or Manmade Disasters Development of Quality Services for a New or Emerging Population Developing Long-range Plans for Major Projects: such as Ending Poverty; Accomplishing Millennium Goals. Resettling and Developing Services for Refugees or Internally Displaced Persons

(continued)

TABLE 9.1 (*Continued*)

DIFFERENTIATING FACTORS	1 PLANNING *WITH* NEIGHBORHOODS AND SMALL COMMUNITIES	2 SECTORIAL PLANNING BY TYPES OF SERVICE	3 COMMUNITY-WIDE PLANNING—NONPROFIT SECTOR	4 CITY AND REGIONAL PLANNING; USUALLY PUBLICLY FUNDED	5 INTERNATIONAL, MULTINATIONAL, AND GLOBAL PLANNING
GEOGRAPHY	Local Rural Area; Village; Community; Urban Neighborhood	Rural or Urban Region; County; City; State; National	Urban Communities; City + Suburbs; Counties; Multiple Counties	City; City and Counties; Region; State	Anywhere Humans Inhabit the Earth
EMPHASIS PRIORITY PROCESS TASK OR TECHNICAL SKILLS	1. Process 2. Task 3. Technical	1. Task 2. Technical and Process Balanced	1. Task 2. Process and Technical Balanced	1. Technical 2. Task 3. Process	Priorities May Be Different Due to Setting and Context

typically lose, suffering the negative consequences of freeway placement, loss of economic base, burdens of toxic waste, and other major physical and environmental problems that more powerful communities are able to prevent (Hall 1988).

Community-led planning can help to reverse these negative impacts and over time with organizing and social action build both social and political power within communities. Participatory community planning is one measure of the engagement of citizens in a democratic society; it can also move groups toward democratization.

PLANNING WITH NEIGHBORHOODS AND COMMUNITIES

All participatory planning efforts hold values of furthering social justice by building and nurturing citizen participation in community planning and decision making. To illustrate the adaptability of this submodel of planning, consider the differences in scope and location between (1) the detailed guidance provided for urban citizens in *The Community Planning Handbook* (Wates 2002), prepared in England for broad use in "official" neighborhood and town planning; (2) case studies in the *CPS Workbook*; and (3) "AIDS Orphans and the Pig Intervention" in chapter 8 of this volume. Despite the great differences in the contexts of the case studies, they share a number of similarities in the processes of engaging people in planning and taking action for their own communities.

Lauffer (1978), Medoff and Sklar (1994), Netting, O'Connor, and Fauri (2008), and Temkin and Rohe (1996, 1998) all have written about neighborhood-based planning with a strong participatory focus. This approach is well illustrated in the following case example examining the Dudley Street Neighborhood Initiative, which continues to be a strong citizen-led effort in the Boston area. You can also view their video and read about current projects on their Web site (http://www.dsni.org/). In other efforts, intensive long-term development may be taken on primarily by residents with some city funding, or they may be partially funded by a major foundation, or through partnerships with local foundations or governmental units. Neighborhood-based planning and development is usually very participatory by nature. Still, caution is needed to see that initiatives do not become sidetracked by vested interests and that planning projects operate transparently with members and supporters.

THE DUDLEY STREET NEIGHBORHOOD INITIATIVE CASE STUDY In their major quantitative study of neighborhoods in Pittsburgh, Temkin and Rohe (1998) found that "neighborhoods with relatively large amounts of social capital are less likely to decline when other factors are held constant" (1998:26). These neighborhoods had strong community-based organizations able to carry forward two important functions: they had the strength and support to act on behalf of residents, and they had earned respect from institutional actors within and external to their communities (Temkin and Rohe 1998:21–26). The revitalization of the Dudley Street area illustrates these strengths and provides an example of positive change through participatory planning in a low-income inner-city area (Medoff and Sklar 1994).

DUDLEY STREET NEIGHBORHOOD INITIATIVE CASE STUDY, BOSTON

Dudley Street is a multicultural neighborhood in Boston with a history of high levels of poverty and neighborhood deterioration. The story of the Dudley Street Neighborhood Initiative (DSNI) is recounted in *Streets of Hope: The Fall and Rise of an Urban Neighborhood* (Medoff and Sklar 1994). The neighborhood was plagued with illegal waste dumping, arson perpetrated by slumlords in both empty and occupied housing, drug traffic/substance abuse, and hundreds of abandoned cars. While a number of service agencies worked well with the neighborhood and several religious congregations were concerned about neighborhood issues, for years the area had lacked the social cohesion and neighborhood mobilization needed to counter these serious problems. The Riley Foundation, seeking to promote better conditions, held meetings with representatives of about thirty community agencies to discuss possibilities for neighborhood revitalization in 1984. The agencies and Riley representatives developed such a plan and then called a community meeting. The meeting was large, and residents understandably did not appreciate having outsiders presume to plan for them; the plan was rejected in part because neighbors had not been part of the process.

With careful facilitation and willingness to work together on both sides, a collaborative was formed that included residents, businesspeople, agency staff, and staff from religious organizations. A new effort was set in motion that involved residents in the planning process, and the Dudley Street neighborhood Initiative was born. Their governing board included representatives from two Community Development Corporations, representatives of the diverse ethnic groups in the neighborhood—African American, Hispanic, Cape Verdean, and white—service agency staff, and religious and business organizations. With Riley funding, they were able to hire staff. Many residents were involved in a survey of neighborhood issues. After considerable work themselves and pressure on the city, DSNI was able to get the abandoned cars towed, close illegal dumps and illegal trash transfer sites, obtain new street lights, and eventually get a rail stop to downtown Boston. Success in these engagements brought more and more residents into the revitalization work, building both bonding and bridging social capital.

In 1987 DSNI completed its plan for the area: *The Dudley Street Neighborhood Initiative Revitalization Plan: A Comprehensive Community Controlled Strategy,* with the intention of creating an urban village with good housing, shops, recreation, and improved quality of life for residents. Thirteen major strategies were included in the plan.

CONTINUED

Summary of DSNI Master Plan

Development. Creation of an entity "to plan, finance, market and manage development projects."

Financing. Pursuit of both public and private financing. Establishment of a land trust. Development of alternative ownership through cooperatives and sweat equity.

Antidisplacement measures. Information and assistance to residents to stay in neighborhood. Qualification for financing and subsidized rental. Community action to curtail speculation.

Marketing research approach. Use of focus groups to determine community priorities.

Community review. "Increased local control of human service program priorities and resource allocations" and promotion of collaboration.

"The Force." Promotion of "pride, dignity, energy, and self help." Mobilization of volunteers, communicators, and role models in efforts to fight crime and drugs and to encourage job development and other projects.

Strengthening racial, ethnic, and cultural identity and diversity. Assistance to Cape Verdean community for human services and encouragement of interagency collaboration regarding diversity.

Child care. Establishment of a neighborhood registry for providers and consumers. Advocacy for additional child care services and youth programs.

Recreation and athletics. Establishment of a resident planning committee for R&A. Development of a master plan for R&A to present to city Department of Parks and Recreation.

Orchard Park planning process. Assistance to Tenants Association "to fund and develop a comprehensive plan."

Employment and training advocacy. Inventory residents' employment needs, aspirations and skills. Identify support services and tap existing programs.

Earning/learning project. "Work with public and private agencies to develop a comprehensive program of individual training—providing child care and other appropriate support services."

Neighborhood-based business development and training. Work with government, agencies, and business schools to "provide entrepreneurial training and support" to residents.

DSNI continues its work with considerable evidence of neighborhood improvement in regard to housing and neighborhood amenities. The central aspects of the master plan have not been changed; however, as is expected in any community development project, it has often taken longer to complete projects than was initially thought. DSNI's first executive director, Peter Medoff, has said, "Deep, grounded community development takes time. . . . You have to have patience and you have to have faith in the people who live in the neighborhood" (Boston Foundation 1992:3).

(Adapted from Medoff and Sklar 1994.)

Planning *with* communities is an approach that can increase the chances of reviving a shared sense of neighborhood as well as promoting community building, physical improvements, and economic development (Wates 2002). This approach to community revitalization focuses on work with members of communities, and while planning is an initial and central focus, methods of both community organizing and development are also employed. Planning provides the guidance for all three methods; successful organizing can bring people together and build political influence. Community development methods are used throughout the implementation of a neighborhood plan, and its results can in part be measured by the quality of the plan and the planning process. The organizing activities and processes focus on increasing participation. This perspective seeks to create ongoing processes of positive community change that can build infrastructure and support opportunities for children, youth, and adults.

SERVICE SECTOR SOCIAL PLANNING Major sectorial planning is carried out by planners and midlevel administrators in agencies such as departments of child welfare, area agencies on aging, and regional public health programs. In this submodel, the planning focus is likely to be on a specific population— elders with dementia; children with developmental disabilities, or other groups needing specialized services. The following example presents intensive planning with organizations in thirty counties for the implementation of programs specifically designed for family support, family preservation, or family resource centers. One of the authors was the principal investigator based in a university who consulted with state staff, local citizens and agency representatives to plan, develop, and evaluate the programs planned by each of the family support and preservation project's thirty pilot counties.

Sectorial planning can also be done through coalitions focusing on particularly vulnerable populations such as people who are homeless (Roberts-DeGennaro and Mizrahi 2005). *Together We Can* provides useful information about coalitions and collaborative planning focused on the educational sector (Melaville, Blank, and Asayesh 1993; http://www.togetherwecan.org/). Collaboration and collaborative planning processes, as will be discussed in chapter 10, often address the multiple needs of a particular population and use methods of coordination and collaboration to shape the ways that agencies communicate and work with each other (Morrison 2005). Research increasingly documents best practices and factors that can promote successful collaboration (Mattesich, Murray-Close, and Monsey 2004).

MULTISECTOR OR COMMUNITY-WIDE SOCIAL PLANNING Several types of organizations engage in multisector and community-wide social planning. One of the most interesting trends in the last two decades has been the revitalization

NC FAMILY SUPPORT AND FAMILY PRESERVATION INITIATIVE
JOAN PENNELL AND MARIE WEIL

During the 1990s, social work faculty and graduate students from UNC-CH engaged in a process of participatory planning and evaluation to jump-start the state's Family Support and Family Preservation Initiative. Through a social indicator analysis undertaken by the School of Social Work team focused on countywide indicators that were relevant for child and family poverty, thirty counties with the most problematic indicators were selected as the potential cohort for the initial planning year. A joint team from the State Office and the university visited all thirty counties where multiple organizations—social agencies and community organizations—had been approached and asked to bring together a diverse group of citizens and agency representatives who might be interested in sponsoring and working on planning the new programs to support and preserve families in their communities. All thirty counties convened such groups, and the planning began. Participants had some concerns about engaging in a state-sponsored and university-related project because they had had negative experience or knew about previous examples of communities being let down, or "used" by the state or a university when they became the objects of research rather than participants in a mutual process. In the FS/FP initiative, the community groups did design their programs with support from consultants and technical assistance from the university team. The groups also participated in planning for the statewide evaluation, and with consultation from the UNC-CH team, each group also developed its local plan for ongoing local evaluations—which they knew they would need to seek additional funding.

Marie Weil and Judith Dunlop developed *Family Centered Services Community Planning Manual* (2008), which provides guidance for every stage of program implementation and evaluation planning; and consultants representing the local state university branches (primarily Historically Black Colleges and Universities) were hired to work with the county groups and facilitate their work in planning the programs that they wanted to initiate. The consultants brought program and planning experience, community connections, and cultural competency to the counties they worked with; and each county completed its plan and received implementation funding. Each county developed a one-year and a five-year implementation plan for Family Support and/or Family Preservation services.

The university teams and state staff visited programs to respond to questions and facilitate planning. In addition, two statewide conferences were held each year so that counties had rich opportunities for peer learning. These larger meetings provided participants with confirmation about their direction and the opportunity to learn from each other, and also created a strong sense of connection in carrying the program across the state.

The central goal of the planning year was for each county planning group to complete their own program design and plan for implementation. In addition, they participated in planning for the statewide evaluation and with technical assistance and consultation designed their own longer term plan for self-evaluation which could assist in continuation when state dollars were expended. All thirty counties completed their plans and went on to develop a network of services across the state.

of local Planning Councils. After two decades of decline, these organizations are again alive and well. Planning Councils focus on social issues and carry out essential planning tasks: they implement needs assessments, identify emerging needs, conduct research, and develop programs needed in their locale. Councils provide a base of planning talent and are able to respond to conduct research or work with agencies to design pilot programs. Planning Councils have proven their mettle in staying with the planning, research, and program piloting format and are nimble in their abilities to combine planning and research and juggle multiple projects. The National Association of Planning Councils Web site (http://www.communityplanning.org/) provides information and examples of programs. Because they are usually well respected in their communities, Councils can serve as trusted advocates for service programs and at the same time are viewed as objective colleagues who can bring together representative groups to begin planning processes for particular communities or needs. Councils are expected to have a broad perspective on their communities and to track shifting needs and emerging issues. As demonstrated in the following case example, Councils have high research standards and present valuable research findings in comprehensible reports.

The Jacksonville, Florida, Community Council has been engaged in numerous broad-scale and population-focused planning and research efforts over the years. It collaborates effectively with other organizations seeking to improve the quality of life for residents of the area. The following case study presents a particular program effort evaluated by the Council that has proven to be very effective.

JACKSONVILLE, FLORIDA, COMMUNITY COUNCIL—TEEN PREGNANCY PROGRAM
BEN WARNER, DIRECTOR, JACKSONVILLE COMMUNITY COUNCIL

The Jacksonville Community Council Inc. (JCCI) was founded in 1975 as part of a sustained governmental and civic reform movement that reshaped Jacksonville, Florida's public governance in significant ways. The reforms emerged from multiple crises of pervasive political corruption in both city and county governments, deaccreditation of all the high schools in the county's public-school system, and an ineffective civic process to successfully tackle and resolve these crises.

Major institutional reforms, in addition to achieving reaccreditation of all the public schools, included:

- Consolidation of former city and county governments into a **new joint city/county government** with professionalized bureaucracy and non-corrupt elected officials—1968.

CONTINUED

- Establishment of private nonprofit entities to foster:
  - community volunteerism (**Volunteer Jacksonville**—1973),
  - civic leadership (**Leadership Jacksonville**—1975), and
  - citizen involvement (the **Jacksonville Community Council Inc.**—1975).

JCCI's purpose was—and remains—to *improve the community's quality of life by engaging citizens, stakeholders, and community institutions in consideration of significant community issues, using a consensus-building/problem-solving approach that combines mutual learning and effective advocacy.* Success of the "JCCI process" relies on two major commitments, to which JCCI has firmly adhered since its inception:

- Excellence in the professional performance of community-based research
- Inclusiveness in the involvement of the full spectrum of diverse people and interests in the community

JCCI annually produces the *Quality of Life Progress Report, A Guide for Building a Better Community.* The report is a collection of indicators that quantitatively measure the quality of life in Northeast Florida and identifies trends in education, economy, natural environment, social well-being, arts and culture, community health, local government, transportation, and safety. In a unique process, JCCI responds to these community indicators through in-depth, citizen-based study of problem areas. Each study combines research with citizen participation and creates a set of recommendations for positive change. An advocacy process follows the study and empowers volunteers to promote community action. Ultimately, trends are impacted in a positive way through this process. Concerned about the medical, social, and economic consequences of teen pregnancy, JCCI convened the community to address the issue of teen pregnancy in 1982. The effort resulted in the formation of a highly regarded multiservice teen center, successful in addressing the issue among the youth it served but insufficient to significantly impact the community trend in teen pregnancy. Recognizing ongoing and disheartening indicator trends, a second study was launched in 1995. The study led to the formation of the Jacksonville Alliance for the Prevention of Adolescent Pregnancy. The Alliance linked citizens, service providers, and teens to address teen pregnancy prevention from family planning and youth development perspectives. In addition to the creation of the Jacksonville Alliance for Prevention of Adolescent Pregnancy, the JCCI Study Committee made a number of other recommendations focused on welfare-reform legislation, family life education, media efforts, and the assistance of social service providers. Following the release of JCCI's study, many of these changes did in fact take place.

As a result of broad-based community efforts, the birth rate for girls under 14 years of age in Jacksonville dropped by more than half from 1995 to 2006—from 2.0 to 0.8 per 1,000 girls. The birth rate for teens ages 15 to 17 was cut by nearly 60 percent from 1990 to 2006 in Jacksonville, including a 52 percent drop from 1995 to 2006, and the teen birth rate for all ages (10 to 17) dropped 58 percent from 1990 to 2006 (48 percent since 1995)—faster than the national rate during the same period, even before the national rate started inching upward in 2006 while Jacksonville's rate continued to decline. The National Association of Planning Councils highlighted Jacksonville as a national model for "bending the trends" in teen pregnancy.

CONTINUED

Nature of the Indicator Project

JCCI's quality of life indicators serve as internal benchmarks for local government and many other institutions, including media, health and human service providers and funders, private foundations and businesses. The report enables them to:

- Make fact-based decisions
- Promote evidence-based public policy
- Establish priorities, and
- Strategically plan

JCCI's *Quality of Life Progress Report* reaches far into the community and is by design brought to the attention of key decision-makers who use the document in a variety of ways. For example, the United Way of Northeast Florida incorporates the Report in its fund allocation process. In fact, the *Quality of Life Progress Report* is a key resource for their 2006 Community Impact Initiative which will determine areas for targeted support. Newly elected government officials use the report as an orientation to the needs of their constituents; the Jacksonville Regional Chamber of Commerce discusses the indicators at their annual Board of Governors meeting; Leadership Jacksonville presents the Report to each new leadership class and to participants in its annual New Leadership Summit; and the Human Services Council recommends the document as a resource for the social service agencies they fund in Northeast Florida.

The indicators in the *Quality of Life Progress Report* become powerful agents for change as JCCI pairs them with a unique citizen study process. Problem areas targeted by negative trends often become the focus of an in-depth process that yields a set of recommendations. Advocacy follows to promote community action and ultimately, trend lines are moved in a positive direction.

JCCI's *Quality of Life* process begins with the collection of quantitative data from more than 60 established sources by JCCI's professional staff. Data is also collected from the surveying firm, American Public Dialogue, to track perceptions in the community related to the nine areas in the Report. Professional staff prepare trend lines and summarize what each indicator measures. Next, 15-20 volunteers, recruited for relevant expertise and experience, review the indicator set for clarity and completeness and make suggestions for improvement, revision or replacement of indicators or their presentation. The review committee then assesses progress toward community goals and identifies problem areas requiring additional community attention. The incoming president of the Jacksonville Regional Chamber of Commerce traditionally leads the review. Following the review, a professional document is published, publicly released and distributed throughout the community to key decision-makers such as City Council members, the Mayor and his administrative staff, the Duval County School Superintendent, Duval County School Board, the Sheriff, all major media, and is posted on the JCCI website which receives more than 100,000 hits per month.

JCCI's *Quality of Life Progress Report* currently presents 119 indicators with data spanning a 20-year period. An explanation of what each indicator measures and a summary of how we are doing as a community are offered. Expanded data in a spreadsheet and web links to additional data sites are also provided for manipulation by individuals and

CONTINUED

organizations for their own planning purposes. In 2003, a compact disk was produced to accompany the print version of the *Quality of Life Progress Report* containing the full print version of the report with all accompanying data.

Following the release of the *Quality of Life Progress Report*, JCCI conducts an in-depth citizen study of an issue that impacts a large segment of Jacksonville's population. Problem areas identified by negative trends in the *Quality of Life Progress Report* are considered for study, as well as issues solicited from the community at large.

Community Change

Teen pregnancy in Northeast Florida has been significantly impacted by JCCI's work with indicators and its model for community improvement. Indicators identified a negative trend in teen pregnancy which was worse than the national average. In-depth study followed and led to community planning and action. *As a result, the birth rate for teen girls ages from 15 to 17 from 1991 to 2006 in Jacksonville dropped 56 percent—faster than the national rate (43 percent decline) during the same period. The National Association of Planning Councils highlighted Jacksonville's work as a national model for addressing teen pregnancy.*

Mechanisms for Change

The JCCI model begins with the identification of a community issue through review of quantitative data. Research, careful study, citizen involvement, plans for action, advocacy and community action follow. Community change can be assessed by positive movement in trends for key indicators.

Concerned about the medical, social, and economic consequences of teen pregnancy, JCCI first convened the community to address teen pregnancy in 1982. A committee of 35 concerned citizens determined that data on teen pregnancy in Jacksonville was incomplete. The group made a number of recommendations. One addressed the availability of data through the office of Vital Statistics. Another addressed the need for a multi-service center for teens. In large measure because of this study, The Bridge of Northeast Florida, was created. The Center has since been identified by the Pew Partnership for Civic change as one of 19 *Solutions for America*. While this first study had a positive impact on young women, especially in one low-income neighborhood of Jacksonville, it did not turn around the community-wide trends. By 1994, in fact, the teen birth rate had dropped only 4 points in Jacksonville.

Three years after the first study of teen pregnancy, JCCI pioneered work with community indicators with its *Quality of Life Progress Report*. The purpose of the Report was to provide an accurate, quantitative measure of where we were as a community and where we needed to be.

In 1995, JCCI launched a second study of teen pregnancy. At that time, the rate of teenage births per 1,000 young females in Duval County was higher than it was for Florida and the nation. A study committee of 48 concerned citizens embraced the vision to break the cycle of children having children in Jacksonville, a problem that is closely linked to social conditions such as poverty, [low] high school graduation rates, child abuse and neglect. The Committee realized that to make a difference, pregnancy prevention services must be well coordinated and the community collaborations must be formed.

CONTINUED

At the conclusion of the study, the Duval County Health Department, a respected public entity, got behind the study and was able to parlay public money to address the issue of teen pregnancy with services in neighborhoods with high rates of teen pregnancy. In addition, the Duval County Health Department was awarded a 2-year planning grant and subsequently a 5-year implementation grant from the Center for Disease Control (CDC) for an Adolescent Pregnancy Prevention Program to mobilize the community, form broad based partnerships, determine the needs of youth in the community and prepare a community action plan. The Jacksonville Alliance for Prevention of Adolescent Pregnancy, an important piece of the Program, linked citizens, service providers, teens and concerned others to address teen pregnancy prevention from family planning and youth development perspectives and secured more than $4,000,000 in grant dollars for services to the Jacksonville Community.

The Adolescent Pregnancy Prevention Program continues to provide staff expertise to the Jacksonville community in program planning and development around teen pregnancy prevention initiatives, to identify best practices and to work with the Healthy People 2010 Healthy Jacksonville Coalition.

In addition to recommending the creation of a major community-wide initiative to encourage the coordination of teen parent services, the JCCI Study Committee made a number of other recommendations focused on welfare-reform legislation, family life education in public schools, media efforts, a free health hotline and the assistance of teen parent social service providers. Many changes took place in the Jacksonville community following the release of JCCI's Teenage Single Parents and Their Families:

- The Jacksonville Children's Commission was awarded a grant by the WAGES Coalition to lead teenage pregnancy prevention efforts for the children of WAGES participants. Case workers were placed in 5 area high schools to assure that adolescent children received sex education and were enrolled in positive youth development programs.
- The Jacksonville Children's Commission required all of its funded organizations to include teen pregnancy prevention as one of its stated goals.
- The Duval County School Board adopted a new health curriculum.
- The Jacksonville Jaguars Foundation sponsored an annual televised Teen Forum around this issue.
- Planned Parenthood established a Facts of Life hotline that delivered information about health-related issues and provided referrals.

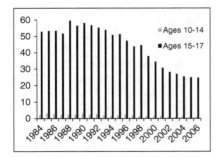
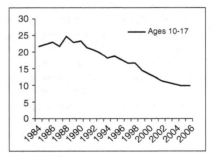

CONTINUED

Because of research, informed citizens, advocacy, increased public awareness, and community mobilization, trends in teen pregnancy have been positively impacted in Jacksonville. In recognition of the importance of this accomplishment, in August 2005, at JCCI's 30th anniversary celebration and on the 20th anniversary of the Jacksonville *Quality of Life Progress Report,* the Jacksonville Community Council presented JCCI Milestones Awards to the chair of the Teen Single Parents Study and the chair of the study's Implementation Advocacy Task Force. The National Association of Planning Councils has recognized Jacksonville as a national model for addressing teen pregnancy.

COMMUNITY DEVELOPMENT CORPORATIONS Many community development corporations (CDCs) engage in physical and social planning in communities, which is typically focused on housing and the creation of new community services and infrastructure ranging from day care services for children and seniors to planning for housing and physical environment improvement, to job training or business incubators, and to development of cultural institutions. Similar functions are evident in CDCs such as Bethel New Life Community Corporation (BNLCC) in Chicago, which sponsors multiple programs and services to fulfill its mission by empowering individuals, strengthening families, and building neighborhoods through community-driven, solution-oriented, and value-centered approaches. Bethel New Life, a neighborhood church, began community planning with the single goal of providing some good-quality affordable housing. Staff went through an extended housing planning process, and as they began construction and then completion of houses, they discovered that housing alone was not sufficient to meet community needs. They went back to the drawing board and planned a successive range of programs and services, implementing components over time, so that they were involved in a continuing cycle of planning, development, and evaluation. You can learn more about Bethel New Life Community Corporation at their Web site, http://www.bethelnewlife.org/. In terms of accountability, Bethel New Life has developed indicators to measure success for each program area. They use the indicators to determine what needs to be done to strengthen programs. *The Bethel New Life Key Indicators Report* provides a good guide to developing outcome/success indicators and can be downloaded from their Web site.

Chicanos Por La Causa, Inc. (CPLC) is a statewide community development corporation in Arizona committed to building stronger, healthier communities as a lead advocate, coalition builder, and direct service provider. CPLC promotes positive change and self-sufficiency in its efforts to enhance quality of life. Its Web site states:

Today, Chicanos Por La Causa is one of the largest CDCs in the nation. It has grown from a small group of student activists to a huge corporation with over 350 full-time staff and several offices throughout Arizona. Among its recent successful projects is the Museo Chicano Cultural Center in downtown Phoenix and a self-help housing program in Somerton that enables families to use low-cost mortgages and their "sweat equity" to construct their own single-family homes. CPLC's current president and CEO, Pete Garcia, does not measure his organization's success by its phenomenal growth, however, but by its tremendous impact on the Mexican-American community. It has opened numerous doors, built leadership and instilled pride among Chicanos. What is more, it has built respect for Arizona's Latino community within mainstream corporate and government circles. (http://www.cplc.org/)

From CPLC's earliest program development, the organization has had a strong planning focus documenting needs, concerns, and aspirations in the Latino community and responding with plans and implementation of a multitude of programs with a strong focus on youth development, employment/job training, and economic development.

CPLC began its major planning efforts in 1975 after being awarded a Special Impact Program (SIP) grant from the federal Community Services Administration. This was a complex planning process with emphasis on Latino community participation as well as working in collaboration with local government officials in Phoenix. Through this process, CPLC needed to maintain its grassroots connections as well as build credibility with governmental agencies and increase its business expertise.

CPLC had to develop a long-range plan for instituting economic development programs and expanding other services. With the award of the SIP implementation program, CPLC started small business development—a food plant. However, they were perceived as ignoring existing small businesses when ten Mexican American food manufacturers brought legal action related to unfair competition. The court ruled in CPLC's favor; however the growing organization learned a hard lesson "about the need to establish clear communications with the community. Upon reflection, Espinoza [then CEO] concluded that CPLC should have reached out to local manufacturers to explain the organization's mission, the purpose of the project, and how it would have ultimately benefited the whole community. "It is important to recognize that money and power are not your strengths," he stated. "Your strength is your community. If you don't have that, then you don't have a CDC. That is a point that people sometimes lose track of." (http://www.cplc.org/)

This "lesson learned" has meant that CPLC is consistent in engaging community members in planning processes for new programs or redirecting existing programs. What happened to CPLC is a frequent problem with CDCs—when the business model takes precedence over community connections (Twelvetrees 1989). As community-based programs and CDCs grow larger, it becomes even more crucial for the organization to maintain contact with its community and to have representatives on planning committees and the board.

Comprehensive community initiatives (CCIs) are broader-based planning and implementation efforts combining social, organizational, institutional, and physical development while improving services, housing, parks, recreation facilities, community centers, public safety initiatives, and promoting economic development and community governance (Brisson 2004; Halpern 1995; Medoff and Sklar 1994; see also Mulroy et al. 2005).

CITY AND REGIONAL PLANNING A number of social work scholars writing about planning in the 1970s—including Brager and Specht (1973), Gurin (1970), Kahn (1969), and Rothman (1968)—described planning as a more elitist process than any other form of community practice. They viewed social planning as relying primarily on the technical expertise and judgment of the planner and formal community leaders. These writers viewed planning as operating within a strictly "rational" process. Indeed, rationality is viewed as the central criterion for work. Brager and Specht (1973) held that within planning projects, major value tensions can arise between those holding to the "expert planning" approach and those supporting community participation. If expertise "resides" only with the planner, the risk of elitism and removal from community concerns is high. However, Ecklein and Lauffer (1972), after intensive case studies of work with community-based planners, reclaimed the importance of planning work with community residents. Use of logical processes is, of course, a major component of planning. In contrast to more elitist approaches, Ecklein and Lauffer and later community-based planner-advocates also focused on participatory planning and the use of newly developed group decision-making facilitative techniques (such as the Delphi method) and other participatory strategies that can be used to maintain a level playing field, ensure that all voices are heard, and build consensus for planning and neighborhood improvement.

There is a clear and present need to reinvest in inner-city neighborhood social, housing, and economic renewal through community building, economic development, microfinance programs, and community development corporations. Larger scale efforts possible in comprehensive community initiatives cannot only make physical and housing improvements, but also consider environmental and economic sustainability for communities within the current context of globalization.

A risk that city and regional planning offices face is that it is easy to become so involved in data analysis and task force work that connections to grassroots groups are weakened or lost. As Sager (2008) indicates, social workers should be employed in city and regional planning both because of their value perspective and because social workers have a great deal to offer planning programs in terms of technical as well as "soft skills." In both urban and rural areas there is a continuing need for social work–trained, community-based advocate planners and for social work–trained planners in the public sector who have the requisite technical skills and who are committed to "speaking truth to power" in order to represent the concerns of low-wealth communities.

INTERNATIONAL, MULTINATIONAL, AND GLOBAL SOCIAL PLANNING

Nongovernmental programs (NGOs) such as Oxfam, World Vision, ACCION, and the Soros Foundation are examples of organizations that take on international and multinational planning and development projects in areas such as community development, microenterprise projects, educational projects, and the welfare and health of children. Other internationally focused programs organized by the United Nations and the Red Cross/Red Crescent national programs work continually to have in place plans to provide for timely intervention to relieve victims of large-scale disasters throughout the world (Simmons 2008).

Given the press for increased democratic participation in many parts of the world and the challenges many communities face as negative effects of the global economy increase, participatory planning can serve as an antidote. That is, elected leaders, community leaders, staff of NGOs, and community members can act together to preserve human and social capital in low-wealth communities and promote a sustainable economic base on which to build civil society and create a "new localism" better prepared to be proactive in rapidly changing times (Figuera-McDonough 2001; Korten 2009; Shiva 2005).

The planning and development of a village in Kenya governed by women offers a particularly interesting example of local planning and development:

KENYA: UMOJA AND MADRE
KAREN SMITH ROTABI

Kenya is a well-known travel destination, celebrated for its beautiful savannahs through which large game migrate annually. The villages bordering game parks in Kenya often have vendors that sell a variety of folk art, including the colorful beaded jewelry which is the craft of indigenous Kenyan women.

An observant visitor to one such village, Umoja (which means unity), may notice that the community is no ordinary place. Most obviously, the village is governed by women, and it has been declared a "no violence against women zone."

CONTINUED

The planning and development of this village that embraces peace and the empowerment of women is historically rooted in violence. The Samburu women who founded the village are survivors of rape carried out by members of the British army. As is typical in traditional communities, survivors of rape are often stigmatized and even subjected to further violence as their husbands blame the victims and may respond with domestic violence. The Samburu women who experienced this double injustice found their post-rape, violent environment to be personally unbearable and unacceptable for the socialization of their children.

As a result, they planned and built their own village governed under the founding principle of nonviolence. They chose a geographic location where they could sell their crafts to tourists and financially support themselves and their children with microenterprises. The women planned the village layout, coordinated the building of homes, and worked to create a good environment for their children. Building from principles of nonviolence, the women developed guidelines for how the village would function and planned construction of their school and community spaces. Through discussion processes facilitated by Rebecca, the woman the community chose to be their leader, the women of Umoja planned their consensus model for self-governance and have successfully negotiated relationships with local communities, NGOs, and governmental bodies.

Today, Umoja village is a home and shelter for women who have rejected and escaped from rape and violence. It is a village where artists who work with beaded jewelry are able to sell their crafts, exercise their self-determination, and manage their own household and expenses. As mothers raising children in Umoja, they are able to socialize their children in their feminist, nonviolent value system and empower their children with information about human rights.

As a village, Umoja provides a school for the village children, and the women consider it to be an important agent for change. Along with the ordinary curriculum, the school also teaches the children about the *United Nations Declaration of Human Rights,* the *Convention for the Rights of the Child,* and other relevant conventions. Both boys and girls learn about their rights in the context of practical issues, including information about how to prevent HIV/AIDS. Even more difficult, but highly relevant, issues like female genital mutilation are also addressed openly with *both* boys and girls. The quality of education at the Umoja school is so well respected by the local peoples that boys and girls from surrounding communities attend, including the villages in which the Samburu women previously resided.

The independence of the Umoja women has come at a cost. They turned their backs on their husbands and built a feminist village. And although some men have come and resided in the village, they often do not stay long. The men complain that the women are unreasonable and too demanding because they express their expectations for equality.

Umoja has a village governance system in which the women engage in a democratic process, making decisions for the good of the group. In addition to selling beaded jewelry, they also manage animal husbandry projects as both sources of food and as microenterprises. These activities, in addition to their well-organized school, have been financially supported, in part, by the international development organization, MADRE.

Another organization, called MADRE, founded on the principles of human rights and equality, works to support projects around the world that embrace women's rights and feminist values. Originating in Central America while that region experienced intense

CONTINUED

civil wars, MADRE began work with an initiative in Nicaragua. Today, MADRE supports numerous development initiatives that focus on creating opportunities for women. MADRE has not only supported the school in Umoja by providing assistance in the development of human rights education, but also has funded smaller village projects and microenterprises, including goat herding. MADRE sponsors projects and programs for women's social and economic development in many parts of the world. Their projects now include work in the ongoing fight for basic human and civil rights for gays and lesbians around the world, bringing attention to the oppression and violence this group has often experienced. For more information about Umoja, the indigenous Samburu people, and MADRE's human rights initiatives, go to www.madre.org. For more information about the rape of Kenyan women by soldiers of the British army, go to www .globalwomenstrike.net.

Midgley and Sherraden (2000), Noponen (2001, 2002), and others have discussed aspects of this type of international program focus as operating from a developmentalist perspective to improve human well-being and support sustainable social and economic projects. Particularly for social workers, it is important not to focus only on the creation and operation of services but on opportunities for skills and empowerment-focused economic development. In this example, bonding and bridging capital are developed as results of Umoja's engagement in community building and asset development.

FOUNDATIONS OF SOCIAL PLANNING

Brueggemann's (2006:151) "foundations" for community planning stress the following principles: "The entire process should be empowerment oriented, future directed, democratically aimed, advocacy based, and practically engaged. Through involvement in community planning, participants broaden their perspectives, come to understand different agendas, limitations, and varied commitments, while agreeing on rules and boundaries, avoiding jargon, and maintaining honesty" (151).

At its simplest, planning can be interpreted as the ability to envision a future that is better than the present. Visions for plans and projects, however, are largely shaped within a framework of competing values, different interests, political and social ideologies, and conceptions of "the good" (Edwards et al. 1998; Friedmann 1979; Quinn 1988). In community practice, one major goal is to promote and facilitate citizen participation—especially that of low-income or marginalized groups—so that their own views of what is good for their communities is articulated and carried out. "Citizen initiated groups that work voluntarily on complex social problems are the heart of a democratic, pluralistic society. They are also the means through which oppressed groups, which are often marginalized by government structures, can affect positive change in their communities" (Gamble and Weil 1995:483).

More recent studies of low-wealth neighborhoods have documented the disinvestment of government, and authors have written more frequently about a "permanent" underclass (Halpern 1995; Wilson 1987). The problems that Brager and Specht (1973) documented have not disappeared, and indeed, some seem even more entrenched. Currently, the poverty rate in the United States is higher than it has been in over twenty years, and the income gap between the lowest 20 percent of families and the highest 20 percent is greater. Newer approaches to social planning *with* communities offer promise for longer-term improvement in quality of life and community infrastructure in low-wealth urban areas, towns, and rural communities.

Municipal governments that often initiate local planning may still create tensions between official expertise and broad-based grassroots participation. However, approaches to planning now operate on the basis of investment in human capital, social capital, and development of community capacity (Chaskin et al. 2001). These terms may be primarily more capitalist-friendly versions of older concepts, but they resonate and receive increasing attention in a range of disciplines and professions—city and regional planning, economic development, urban studies, public policy, and public affairs as well as in community practice (Brisson 2004). Initiatives sponsored by community development corporations and comprehensive community initiatives often employ strategies to increase *human and social capital* and build *community capacity* at least in part because these terms make sense to governmental bodies, progressive business leaders, and other policy and community decision makers.

Approaches based on assessments and utilization of community assets (Kretzmann and McKnight 1993) and social investment based on asset-building approaches (Midgley and Sherraden 2000) can also garner larger professional, governmental, and public appeal. While some have criticized assets development programs as being too focused on individuals as compared with neighborhoods, asset development approaches do not exclude more community- and cooperative-based approaches operating conjointly (ACOSA Symposium 1998). As Friedmann (1992) states, the means of moving households out of absolute poverty requires connections to bases of social power within and external to their communities. Kretzmann and McKnight (1993), Portes (1998), and others emphasize the assets of communities and individuals and how they can be marshaled to create bonds and build opportunities. Gun and Gun (1991) hold that true development occurs only in combination with efforts to broaden the practices of democracy, and like Friedmann (1992), they see a necessary role for the state in this development process. Although CDCs offer considerable opportunity for economic development, they can become problematic and separated from the community if they do not attend to social development, continued community interaction, community norms and level of cohesion (Matsuoka 1997; Twelvetrees 1989).

Strategies for planning with communities can be drawn from the analyses by Brager and Specht (1973), Figuera-McDonough (2001), Friedmann (1992), and Kramer and Specht (1975) and can be adapted to fit local contexts and needs. In addition, strategies can be built on guidance from Ross (1955, 1958) who strongly emphasized planning *with* rather than *for* communities. Castelloe's (1999) proposal to combine efforts to develop social capital and community competence to construct and enlarge collective efficacy for community revitalization can also be combined with Lauffer's earlier recommendations for community planning (1978). Lauffer supports the position of the community social work planner as an advocate for the community and stresses the importance of citizen participation in planning processes. Although almost all texts on planning emphasize a rational process with specific and logical steps from problem identification through evaluation of efforts, planning processes are equally, if not more, dependent on development and maintenance of relationships and good communication—with community groups, with agencies, and with governmental bodies.

Technical expertise (Kahn 1969) is typically seen as a central characteristic of the planner's role. However, in planning with communities, the need and expectation are for the community practitioner to have not only a wide range of technical skills but, equally, to bear responsibility to teach and coach community residents in the understanding and use of assessment, planning, and evaluation tools; community research methods; and negotiating skills for use with a range of organizations, including funders, governmental bodies, human service organizations, and other community groups. Process and task skills and relationship as well as technical skills are needed if community-based planners are to take up the important challenges to (1) work *with* communities to plan for strengthening social and physical infrastructure, (2) engage in mutual work and learning with community members, (3) develop supportive services, (4) establish sustainable social and economic development programs, and (5) promote strong and broad participation to improve quality of life.

Figuera-McDonough (2001) argues for the possibility of local regulations from stronger communities to be able to limit corporate exploitation. She also states that "as the nation state declines, the local community becomes the focus of hope for collective power to maintain everyday life. The potential strengths of communities as important units in the democratization of economic strategy derive from the evidence that the economic and political development of communities is closely interwoven" (2001:166).

Figuera-McDonough maintains that community activism did not die with the demise of the War on Poverty. Rather, agreeing with Flacks (1995) and Anner (1996), she states that this pessimistic view is more the result of poor reporting than of actual decline in communities' efforts to win a larger voice in policies and decisions affecting their future (Figuera-McDonough 2001). Community organizing initiatives, she notes, "reinforce the importance of democratic involvement for economically vulnerable communities and the potential of this involvement for generating political energy" (Figuera-McDonough 2001:166). The key to such combined planning and development lies in finding and maintaining the ability to obtain "external resources while maintaining local control over their use" (166). Along with presenting sophisticated models for assessing communities to ascertain appropriate approaches for local development, Figuera-McDonough argues for and presents examples of synergy in the creation and cooperation of private, local, and governmental partnerships for planning and development. The new localism that Figuera-McDonough espouses does not assume self-sufficiency in communities; rather, it recognizes the importance of interdependence and cooperation within and between communities.

THEORIES AND CONCEPTS THAT GROUND THE MODEL

John Friedmann's (1992) book, *Empowerment: The Politics of Alternative Development*, describes the serious results of absolute poverty in the Global South. Friedmann is among the international development scholars who early on identified the failures of market-based development techniques in the Global South. As a champion of empowerment of local people, he constructed a model of "alternative" development that focused on livelihoods and the networks and bridges needed to help the poorest of the poor move out of "absolute poverty." He was among the first to carefully examine the foundational importance of livelihoods in assessing a nation's true economy and to discuss the realties of the informal sector to which so many women and considerable numbers of men are consigned. Following a carefully worked out critique of Western policies that often did as much harm as good in developing nations, he examines the concept of the whole economy (formal and informal with household livelihoods at its base).

Friedmann integrates theoretical perspectives on civil society and poverty and constructs empowerment approaches to community development that include gender equity and the ability to develop both bonding and bridging social capital. Figure 9.1 illustrates Friedmann's depiction of the overlapping government, religious, civil, and corporate sectors of society; and he argues that a stronger civil society can help check the unfettered power of the corporate world.

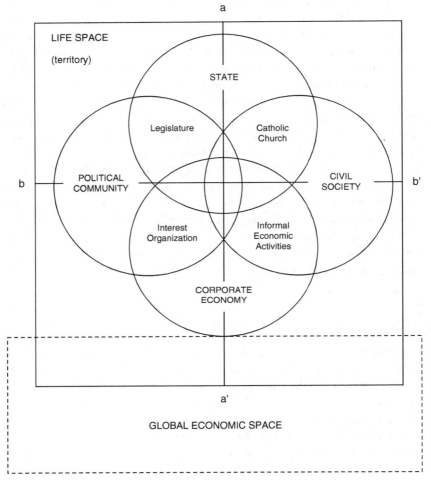

FIGURE 9.1 Friedmann's Four Domains of Social Practice

Source: Adapted from John Friedmann (1992), *Empowerment: The Politics of Alternative Development* (Cambridge, MA: Blackwell Publishers/Ingraham).

Worldwide, the central social problem of the early twenty-first century is the stark reality of poverty and extreme poverty across the globe in developing, industrial, and postindustrial societies (Sachs 2005). For example, the United States is a postindustrial nation and is considered to be one of the wealthiest countries in the world; yet the U.S. Census in 2005 reported that 13.3 percent of Americans (38,231,000) lived below the poverty line, as did 10.2 percent of families (7,605,000) (U.S. Census 2008). Currently, these percentages are even higher. *Extreme poverty* has been defined by Jeffrey Sachs and in UN documents as living on less than one U.S. dollar per day (Sachs 2005).

Planning and development projects growing out of postcolonial efforts to improve agricultural technology and other economic efforts in the Global South were built from analyses of how economic advancement had occurred in the Western democracies of the global North. Therefore, development projects frequently employed inappropriate and unsustainable techniques and technologies. Friedmann charts a different course—one that builds on both locally controlled development and support from the state. However, the state needs to be made more "accountable to poor people and more responsive to their claims. But without the state's collaboration, the lot of the poor cannot be significantly improved. Local empowering action requires a strong state" (Friedmann 1992:7).

Friedmann does not romanticize villages and rural communities; he contends that there are serious "fault lines" in small communities emerging from differences based on race/ethnicity, class, caste, religion, language, and the "universally subordinate role of women" (1992). These and other issues prompt territoriality and escalate competition for resources. Local life *is* political: it is based in competing claims and challenges about resources that can become regional and national issues. In many societies, local power has been lodged in some elite families with continued exclusion of the poor seen perhaps as unfortunate but as a basic reality nonetheless. Friedmann asserts that his conception of an alternative development is based on a "politics of claiming" and on "removal of those structural constraints that help to keep the poor poor" (Friedmann 1992:7).

Alternative planning and development is grounded in advocacy for social and political empowerment, for building on local knowledge, and for stressing civic engagement as well as for using planning expertise. Friedmann provides an additional diagram which places the household economy as the central concept surrounded by a set of external resources in an outer ring. These resources can serve as portals out of absolute poverty. He discusses the resources that the extremely poor must have access to, and he indicates that connections for a number of these resources need to be made outside the neighborhood. The poor need peer (or horizontal) bonding with members of their neighborhood. Just as critically, if not more so, they need access to external resources in the form of people, materials, and finances that can assist them in gaining skills and knowledge, accumulating tools for work, and making external connections in order to take the first steps toward moving out of absolute poverty. Figure 9.2 illustrates the connections needed by the poor to begin to move up the basic economic ladder. This diagram serves as an excellent guide for students and other groups as they analyze local situations and determine steps for planning and action. Indeed, the resources illustrated can become bases for empower-

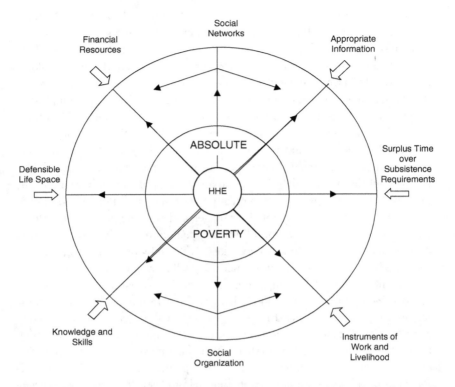

FIGURE 9.2 Friedmann's Conception of Poverty as Lack of Access to Bases of Social Support

Source: Adapted from John Friedmann (1992), *Empowerment: The Politics of Alternative Development* (Cambridge, MA: Blackwell Publishers/Ingraham).

ment to help those who have been impoverished build human and social capital and begin to develop assets.

To engage in development-focused community planning, it is ethically imperative that we work toward the creation of opportunity and economic advancement for those who have not yet experienced it. Sachs describes the situation of one-sixth of the world population as follows:

The greatest tragedy of our time is that one-sixth of humanity is not even on the development ladder. A large number of the extreme poor are caught in a poverty trap, unable on their own to escape from extreme material deprivation. They are trapped by disease, physical isolation, climate stress, environmental degradation, and by extreme poverty itself. Even though life saving solutions exist to increase their chances for survival—whether in the form of new farming techniques, or essential medicines, or bed nets that can limit the transmission of malaria—these families and their governments simply lack the financial means to make these crucial investments. (Sachs 2005)

In addition to extreme material deprivation and the social forces identified by Sachs as creating the "poverty trap"—disease, physical isolation, climate stress, and environmental degradation—a number of other forces can effect severely negative changes in a community.

PROCESS OF COMMUNITY PLANNING

Castelloe (1999) identifies six factors that form the basis of a community's infrastructure: physical, economic, educational, social, civic, and organizational. The specific combinations of positive and negative internal and external forces within a community affect both social ties and infrastructure and form the context in which a community's capacity (Chaskin et al. 2001; Fellin 2001; Ross 1958) and social capital are located—whether those "stores" of such capital are low, moderate, or high. The strength or weakness of social capital and community competence will significantly shape a community's responses to internal and external threats.

Three potential outcomes can be predicted given the status of infrastructure and threats to any given community (Castelloe 1999):

1. If a community has high social capital and community capacity, it is likely to be able to meet external challenges and exercise collective efficacy for positive community change.
2. If a community has moderate social capital and community competence, it has the potential to respond to internal and external threats.
3. If a community has low competency and low social capital, community deterioration is likely to result from external and internal threats.

In the first condition, the community is likely to have collective efficacy and be able to mobilize and plan for community action, act to strengthen horizontal and vertical linkages to aid in improving community infrastructure, and preserve social and cultural heritage that over time can lead to strengthening ties. In the third instance, low community competency and low social capital leave a community much more vulnerable to internal and external threats. Social capital and community competency are components of collective efficacy (Bandura 1997). Without this sense of shared efficacy, community deterioration over time is the most likely, but not an inevitable, outcome if effective community building occurs that can support planning and action.

In the second or intermediate situation, popular education (Castelloe and Gamble 2005), empowerment research (Pennell et al. 2005), and strategies for planning with communities and initiating community development (Rubin and Sherraden 2005) can be employed to build collective efficacy and develop skills, organization, and action to greatly increase the likelihood that positive social and economic community development that also preserves culture and heritage can prevail. Even from the low social capital and competency example, positive outcomes are possible if precursors to effective community planning and action are enacted. An adapted and abbreviated version of Castelloe's (1999) model illustrates this process (see figure 9.3).

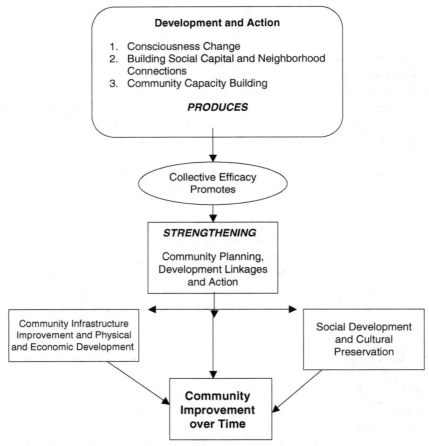

FIGURE 9.3 Castelloe's Community Capacity Frame Adapted

Sources: Adapted from Paul Castelloe (1999), "Community Change: An Integrated Model," in "Community Change and Community Practice: An Organic Model of Community Practice." Ph.D. diss., Chapel Hill, NC: University of North Carolina at Chapel Hill, School of Social Work; and Marie Weil, ed. (2005a), *The Handbook of Community Practice* (Thousand Oaks, CA: Sage Publications).

The precursors to community action ground planning with communities in popular education tactics to assist community members in analyzing their community—scrutinizing the factors affecting it physically, socially, and economically. To move into the practices recommended in this section, the community practitioner needs to take on a wide range of roles.

COMMUNITY PRACTICE ROLES IN SOCIAL PLANNING

These roles have been defined in chapter 2:

- Researcher
- Proposal writer
- Communicator
- Planner
- Manager
- Evaluator

A more detailed way to think about these and additional roles is provided by the National Association of Planning Councils' list of roles and functions for planning, which can be found on page 319.

CORE SKILLS AND COMPETENCIES FOR SOCIAL PLANNING

ENGAGEMENT IN COMMUNITY-BASED PLANNING

Although planners focused on community-level work may come from a variety of professional disciplines or may rise through the ranks in grassroots projects, the distinctions for social work community practice arise from social work's values, ethical principles, and strong commitment to plan *with* rather than *for* people in communities.

In this context, community practitioners engaged in planning will first be involved in establishing a relationship of trust with members of a community and with exploration of roles in the planning process as well as goals. Ross (1958) articulated several principles for this form of community work. In contrast with those who see planning primarily as research, setting priorities, and the production of a planning document, Ross holds that planning "represents the whole act from the stirring of consciousness about a problem to the action taken to resolve that problem" (1958:136). Planning processes and methods of work with community members must fit the specific context and work toward resolution of a particular problem or set of issues in a specific milieu and also initiate action to implement the proposed solutions. Within this perspective, planning that is community-led is also described as *participatory* or *action planning.*

Planners need interpersonal and facilitation skills along with technical and analytic skills to work with community members on establishing the planning process and carrying out specific efforts (Brager and Specht 1973; Ecklein and Lauffer 1972). While a city planner's role may most often be that of the technical expert, a community practitioner working with members of a community to plan for neighborhood or service improvement must first of all have excellent skills in facilitation—in bringing people together and developing a process through which they can lay out their ideas and transform them into a working plan (Gamble and Weil 1995). In this situation then, skills in relationship building, interpreting and reframing ideas, facilitating discussions and meetings, and coordinating tasks are primary requisites. Facilitation is indeed the central role in participatory planning.

Planners also need good skills in writing, strong skills in methods for conducting both needs/strengths assessments (Mulroy 2008) and research on community infrastructure and social conditions such as poverty (Blank 1998; Coulton 2005; Pádilla and Sherraden 2005). It is increasingly important to use mapping not only through residents' engagement in mapping, photographs, and renderings but also employing census data and GIS methods to map infrastructure, services, transportation, and other community variables. Planners also need skills in budgeting, proposal writing, and increasingly fundraising and marketing skills—all of which the planner committed to work *with* communities will teach and coach residents to use as needed. Political skills are also requisite to work not only with community groups but also with the range of nonprofit and governmental organizations with which they and neighborhood committees will need to engage and negotiate agreements. Indeed, because of the complexity of tasks called for in planning *with* communities, planners need competence in most of the major skills for community practice.

The desire to plan within a community typically arises from dissatisfaction or concern about neighborhood conditions or problems, or lack of needed services, opportunities, or facilities. For community members to invest time and energy to develop a plan and find means to carry it forward, there must be sufficient concern for change to maintain momentum in action. Planning takes time, as does implementation, and a community-based planner will need to invest in leadership training to build community capacity and carry interest forward so that community members can direct different aspects of the process.

Since planning and implementation involve an extended time frame, small gains—such as the clearing of a vacant lot—should be celebrated (Medoff and Sklar 1994; Melaville and Blank 1993).

Competencies combine knowledge and skills. The National Association of Planning Councils lists the following core competencies for social planning on its Web site:

**NATIONAL ASSOCIATION OF PLANNING COUNCILS'
CORE COMPETENCIES**

- Building community infrastructure
- Developing, nurturing, and sustaining organizations and communities by enhancing their abilities to achieve the common good through convening groups to address issues, training and technical assistance, and leadership development.
- Mobilizing resources
- Identifying and filling gaps in community services by redirection of existing or development of new resources.
- Research and evaluation
- Producing and sharing credible and meaningful community-based research and program evaluation that informs and influences health and social policy and practice.
- Public policy analysis
- Producing timely, valuable, and accurate information on policy choices for use by citizens and policy makers in developing solutions for community problems.
- Community organizing
- Helping people and organizations most affected by public policies, services, or community conditions develop and carry out activities that build community and neighborhood capacity and enhance health, economic conditions, and social well-being.
- Advocacy
- Engaging people in use of effective approaches to influence policy makers, opinion leaders, and general public in decisions benefiting the overall community's quality of life.
- Information services
- Producing and disseminating timely, accurate information for health and human services planning, fund distribution, policy development, and services referral.
- Facilitation
- Creating a safe, unaligned environment for the resolution of community problems and engaging multiple community sectors in addressing identified community issues.

VALUES AND ETHICS

Underlying these skills and competencies are values and ethics of practice. The values that members of the National Association of Planning Councils subscribe to are presented on their Web site. The complexity and variety of planning responsibilities and roles a well as the politicized nature of social planning indicate that social planners need to carefully assess potential conflicts in values and consistently be aware of ethical choices. Significant efforts to open up planning processes, including strong consumer and community participation, are becoming the norm.

MULTICULTURAL PLANNING IN ACTION

Putting planning and intervention skills into practice is well illustrated in a case example from Robeson County, North Carolina. This ethnically diverse county, through its Center for Community Action, works on eight levels of social transformation: individual, family, community, institutional, systematic, cultural, environmental, and moral/spiritual. It does so through five strategies of intervention: social relief, social support, social development, social reconstruction, and social witness. The full case example, exploring all the challenges of planning over time, is available with study questions in the *CPS Workbook*. We close this chapter with the "lessons learned" from this decades-long rural planning and transformation work.

WHAT WE CAN'T DO ALONE, WE CAN DO TOGETHER—SOCIAL PLANNING AND SOCIAL CHANGE IN ROBESON COUNTY, NORTH CAROLINA
MAC LEGERTON, EXECUTIVE DIRECTOR, THE CENTER FOR COMMUNITY ACTION

Many of us understood the truth of this message when we came together to form a multiracial, grassroots organization in rural Robeson County, North Carolina, in 1980, the Center for Community Action (CCA). What we didn't understand is what and how much it would take, and the sacrifices that we would be required to make in order to manifest this truth. Robeson County, a large rural county, three-quarters the size of the State of Rhode Island, is the home of the Lumbee, the largest tribe of indigenous people in the U.S. that live East of the Mississippi River. Its multiracial population of 123,000 is 38% Native American, 32% European American, 25% African American, and 5% Latino/Hispanic. The Asian population is less than 1% (U.S. Census Bureau).

"Lessons Learned: Comprehensive Social Planning Is So Much More Than Starting from Where the People Are"

The basic maxim of "starting where people are" (re the concerns and goals of members of a community) is generally understood to be an essential principle in planning with communities. It is also true that the process of comprehensive social planning involves much deeper and broader based processes. The following principles and examples barely scratch the surface of lessons gained through CCA's work to establish comprehensive social planning in our rural area. The principles we have learned and adopted include:

1. **Organize and cultivate grassroots and professional participation** in planning, but consider separate processes first in people's natural settings. When you bring them together, facilitate and structure the meeting along grassroots cultural values and indicators more than those of professional culture. Our professional culture is more hegemonic and exclusionary.

2. **Utilize traditional, cultural practices and values in your planning processes** that build relationships and community among participants. This includes an openness to everyone and an honoring of diverse perspectives, holding hands, sharing insights and wisdom, listening to stories, and singing. Modern, or conventional, cultural frameworks focus on the tasks at hand more than the relational and spiritual dimensions of planning. A balance of perspective and practices enhances creativity and spontaneity.

3. **Planning can either be reactive or proactive,** focusing on the prevention of further harm, or on the introduction of new practices and policies that are more caring, creative, and just. We need significantly more proactive planning. With only reactive planning, our communities will experience a zero sum gain or net decline.

4. **Identify and review creative strategies and models**, learning of effective and successful practices of similar work to what you are imagining and considering. Find out about them, and if you can, learn "through" them. "Take the best and leave the rest!"

5. **Planning can be comprehensive or focused in its scope,** focusing on a holistic view of what is needed and the resources and assets on which to build or on only what one's organization or program will and can do. Both forms are needed and the comprehensive planning enables organizations to see where their work fits and supports a broader, more systems approach to social transformation. We need transformation at all levels with all types of interventions. We need to get far beyond our own biases and defenses toward what needs to be done, engaging in our work while partnering with others engaged in other types of interventions that address other levels of transformation.

6. **Planning is more than just performance-based, organizational, and program planning.** There is a deeper, more reflective level of planning that includes identifying the explicit assumptions, values, principles, and indicators within our programs (see the writings of Dr. Jack Mezirow on critical reflection and transformative learning).

7. **Continue planning but don't settle on a plan.** Planning is something we do: it's a verb. A plan is something we have: it's a noun. Be cautious of "having" a plan to

CONTINUED

the point that the plan blinds you to its own shortcomings and lack of insight. Even a plan developed yesterday or even this morning cannot be followed to the "letter." Life, and each day, is filled with unanticipated events. Plans are for people who demand a plan. Prepare for your day and prepare your programs through constant planning. But always be flexible and learn from what your experience and new knowledge is teaching. Remember, time and truth are both our friends. They are not our adversaries. Stay flexible and adapt.

8. **Planning is both short-term and long-term.** Our organizations, projects, and programs need both processes. We need to decide what it is we want to do over 1 year, 3 years, 5 years, 10 years, and 50 years. We need to imagine the steps and phases in reaching our vision and goals, being constantly aware of the unanticipated events on every level of our work and lives that can hasten or extend the time it takes to reach our destinations, both near and far. Again, recognize and trust the relativity of time, advantaging new opportunities and meeting new challenges with proactive and creative strategies, particularly in the face of new and sometimes tragic obstacles.

9. **Discern and assess your organization's capacity to carry out your goals and objectives.** Do this with foresight as a part of your planning process. Also, trust the spiritual and business dimensions of your life and work that support risk-taking. Being proactive involves taking risks, joining in new partnerships, being an advocate with others, and often spending money and acquiring it later.

10. **Our needs for improved practice, research, and policy development and leverage are inextricably linked.** Comprehensive planning designs strategies, activities, and supports on all three levels of our work. Research and policy change are often left out of many planning processes, and those who do research and policy work are often not rooted in community and community partnerships. It's a wonder that our social conditions aren't even worse than they are when we reflect on our own practice. The organized power of practitioners, researchers, and policy developers goes largely untapped. What we can't do alone, we can do together. The Center on Integrating Research and Action (CIRA) at UNC-Chapel Hill is one of the best, new models of multisector collaboration.

11. **A lot is made of the differences between need-based and asset-based planning, but both are needed.** Alone, both can blind us to different dimensions of our social responsibility that are a part of a comprehensive planning process. An extreme focus on needs overlooks the resources available and how to utilize and build on them. An extreme focus on assets overlooks the barriers and inequities that exist in the practice, policies, and cultures of our institutions and systems. A comprehensive planning approach will address all levels of transformation, utilizing all available and new resources.

12. **Horizontal Social Change:** I have learned that social change is more horizontal than vertical. While successful social justice work is based in organization on the grassroots level, it is never limited to it. Successful social change operates and performs on multiple levels and combines units of organized influence on many different levels in order to achieve its goals. This understanding has been key to our success for we realize that there is a role for everyone in social justice work. Every perceived adversary is a potential ally. Our planning needs to be inclusive and utilize the power that all people have to partner and participate in transformative programs, honoring their own interests while inviting them to broader ones.

13. **Push and Pull of Social Change:** I have learned that social change has two major dimensions—(1) organized influence that pushes for change, [and] (2) visions and efforts that pull and draw change forward. This is why planning is so important. There is power and unity in a common and concrete vision, and in goals, objectives, and strategies that demonstrate evidence of success and hope. A clear vision combined with successful action raises our people's anticipation and hope for change, motivating and supporting them to take risks and learn from action at the boundaries of their own experience. The literature emphasizes the forceful and often coercive nature of "power politics" and social conflict. As a contemplative, I am much more aware of the more subtle but powerful and proactive influence of love, patience, and forgiveness in the midst of human struggles. Dr. D. D. Williams writes in *The Spirit and Forms of Love* that "love is a whisper . . . in the clamor of history." We need to make space in our planning to be pulled forward by the very visions that we find and create, deepening our hope and understanding of the possibilities for effective and successful action.

"We Have Achieved Major Successes . . ."

We have achieved major successes in Robeson County, N.C. on all 8 levels of transformation identified in this study. In our ethnically diverse and economically challenged rural community, we have made major changes that are a model for other rural communities across our nation.

We utilize our intellectual capacity, heart, and will to make major improvements in both our quality and equality of life. With effective and successful organizational and program planning and implementation, we access both the private and public resources necessary to support our extensive work and sustain it over the last 28 years. At the same time, we reach across our state and nation and join with others to improve our public policies to promote and protect the lives and livelihoods of our people. Then, we also reach across the globe, embrace other cultural and faith traditions, and join to shape a new vision and practice towards genuine and lasting social justice throughout the world.

Mac Legerton's journey in social planning, program development, and action provides an exemplary illustration of the kind of transformational practice needed in many rural and urban areas in both the Global North and South. Although specific situations will be different, many principles for practice are similar and the roles and skills presented here, when adapted for cultural differences, should prove to be core competencies for effective planning practice that connects to development and social production. We hope that the examples presented in this chapter and in others inspires you with Legerton's conviction that "What We Can't Do Alone, We Can Do Together."

10

BUILDING EFFECTIVE COALITIONS

Faced with what seems like an impossible task, a group of folks will do well to remember the African proverb: When spider webs unite they can tie up a lion.

JOHNNETTA B. COLE, FOUNDER, J. B. COLE GLOBAL DIVERSITY AND INCLUSION INSTITUTE

Coalitions are like orchestras composed of autonomous and talented people linked together by a conductor and by a score.

DIAL NEUGARTEN, EXECUTIVE DIRECTOR,
NATIONAL LEADERSHIP INSTITUTE ON AGING, DENVER, COLORADO

INTRODUCTION

What could such a seemingly benign product as infant formula have to do with organizing coalitions? IBFAN, the International Baby Food Action Network, emerged from a shared concern about unfair marketing practices used by corporations to promote their infant formula products as superior to breastfeeding (IBFAN 2008; Baby Milk Action 2008). These aggressive marketing campaigns often have devastating effects on infant health and mortality rates, especially in low-wealth neighborhoods and less developed countries. The producers of infant formula heavily promote their products, especially in less developed countries, without regard for the mothers' access to resources to buy formula or the availability of a safe water supply for preparing the formula. After the initial free supply of formula is used—and the mother's body has ceased producing breast milk—many low-wealth mothers overdilute the powdered formula to stretch their supply, which results in malnutrition for their infants. Mothers are sometimes given inadequate instruction in safely preparing the formula, and many mix formula with contaminated water—often their only source of water—that frequently results in severe infection, dehydration, and death from diarrhea. In addition, the companies promote their products as nutritionally superior to breast milk despite the well-established evidence that mother's milk contains antibodies that protect babies from certain illnesses. Current estimates hold that millions of babies die each year because mothers use infant formula rather than breast milk (Kean and Allain 2004a).

In response to this problem, the U.S.-based Infant Formula Action Coalition (INFACT) was formed in 1977 to boycott Nestlè, a Swiss manufacturer of chocolate and the largest supplier of infant formula to the world market. Two years later, INFACT became one of the founding members of the international coalition IBFAN, and the organization quickly grew to 200 autonomous citizen groups in ninety-five countries. IBFAN's mission is to monitor the actions of all producers and distributors of infant food and related products for inappropriate and aggressive marketing.

The IBFAN coalition was instrumental in getting the World Health Assembly to adopt the International Code of Marketing Breast Milk Substitutes in 1981, which prohibited corporations from certain kinds of advertising and aggressive marketing. The boycott of Nestlè products was temporarily suspended in 1984 to give the company, and other infant formula companies, a chance to comply with the International Code standards. However, the boycott was resumed in 1988 when IBFAN's monitors found that Nestlè, which controls 40 percent of the infant formula market, and other companies were violating the international code and again flooding health clinics and hospital maternity wards with free and reduced price supplies of infant formula. Currently, Baby Milk Action in England serves as the coordinator of the global boycott, which continues to alert many countries to the hazards for babies of using alternatives to breast milk. Many countries have adopted the International Code established by the World Health Assembly, which has allowed IBFAN to sue the corporations in those countries to halt their marketing practices. Although IBFAN's efforts have ended the most blatant, inappropriate formula marketing, their recent monitoring reports indicated code violations by many of the world's largest formula producers including Nestlè; Dutch-based corporations Nutricia (NUMICO), and Dumex; U.S.-based corporations including Mead Johnson, Abbott Ross, and Wyeth; Germany's Hipp and Humana; Japan-based Morinaga and Meiji; and the French-based Danone Corporation (Kean and Allain 2004b). In addition, the Sanlu Corporation in China was recently forced to recall its product because the milk formula it produces was tainted, sickening 50,000 children.

This global example provides a window to why a coalition might become organized and how it could gather the power to influence policies and monitor commitments to those policies. In this example the concern started small, probably among nurses and public health providers. While understanding the great value of infant formula for new mothers who could not produce breast milk, they also noted the negative outcomes of aggressive marketing approaches for a significant number of infants whose mothers were able to breast-feed. Formula is often marketed as "superior" to breast milk, and many mothers are duped by the message to buy the formula. This is a stunning example of how marketing methods can change behaviors, in this case negatively. To be successful, the campaign against such marketing had to involve lay health workers in villages and neighborhood clinics, and eventually new mothers themselves. In a sense this coalition, organized locally to decrease high infant mortality rates, evolved into a global movement for progressive change: many people agreed to join the international boycott of any products made by infant formula companies, including chocolate.

There are all kinds of coalitions on a local to global continuum. Generally, there are five recognized types of coalitions that use collaboration or alliance formation to come together for different purposes: information and resource sharing; technical assistance; self-regulating purposes such as setting minimum standards; planning and coordination of services; and advocacy or social, economic, and environmental change (Roberts-DeGennaro 1997). These coalition types overlap, as we see, for example, coalitions for the developmentally disabled or for women's issues combining information and resource exchange with technical assistance and advocacy. In addition, we see coalitions to prevent child abuse or domestic violence combining information sharing, planning and coordination of services, and advocacy. In this chapter we will focus on coalitions that are more local or community based and that focus on advocacy and community change. We will use examples from the United States and abroad as we define the scope of concern of community-based coalitions, the basic process of organizing successful coalitions, the theories and concepts that provide the foundation for this work, and the roles and skills required to do successful organizing.

SCOPE OF CONCERN

Coalitions are often defined simply as "organizations of organizations" (Homan 2008:315), as "interorganizational, cooperative, and synergetic working alliances" (Wandersman, Goodman, and Butterfoss 2004:293), and more specifically, as "an organization of organizations whose members commit to an agreed-on purpose and shared decision making to influence an external institution or target" while maintaining their autonomy (Mizrahi and Rosenthal 2001:63).

Another useful definition of coalitions is the one offered by Tom Wolff (2008a), whose work with hundreds of Area Health Education Centers in the United States as well as other national and international coalitions, has shaped his understanding of their potential: "Coalitions are partnerships of the many sectors of a community [that] gather together collaboratively to solve the community's problems and guide the community's future." (2008a:2). With our focus on community practice, we will assume that the problem-solving focus and community direction will be toward improved social, economic, and environmental conditions.

Researchers and organizers who contribute to building coalitions make a distinction among three organizational processes commonly practiced in coalitions. These processes, *coordination, cooperation*, and *collaboration*, often used interchangeably, have specific meaning when applied to the relationships of alliances and coalitions. Karen Ray from the Wilder Foundation sees these relationship terms on a continuum, with collaboration representing the most intense degree of relations: "It is not better or worse than cooperating or coordinating; it is simply the most intense commitment" (2002:17). She describes organizations that make a commitment to collaboration as agreeing to be influenced by each other for changes needed in a community, while still maintaining separate identities (2002:17).

Darlyne Bailey and Kelly McNally Koney (2000) see the continuum beginning with cooperation and ending with *coadunation*, a new term and a fourth process. They describe *cooperation* as involving shared information and mutual support, *coordination* as having compatible goals and common tasks, *collaboration* as having a collective purpose and integrated strategies, and *coadunation* as involving a unified structure and combined cultures—the point at which organizations merge or consolidate (Bailey and Koney 2000:7–10). From our perspective, and for clarity, collaboration seems to be the best way to describe the processes and nature of alliances in most coalitions.

THE BASIC PROCESS: TEN GUIDING STEPS

Wolff (2008b) describes two approaches among people trying to build coalitions. One group believes that the basic method for creating a coalition is to do so through *community organizing*, which implies using power-based strategies for social change. The other group believes that the basic method should be *community building*, which implies building relationships among all the diverse sectors of the community. Power-based organizing sometimes leads to conflict when the key organizational members are loath to collaborate with traditional service providers and existing political groups they believe are part of the problem, or at least represent the forces that keep the problems in place. On the other hand, relationship-focused community builders have high hopes that their good relations with these same entities will influence effective changes within entrenched service programs and political groups, but may have their hopes dashed when the changes never materialize. Wolff believes that only a balance or a mix of these two approaches can accomplish the social change intended by the community coalition.

In their work analyzing the definitions of success among leaders of forty co-alitions in the New York metropolitan area, Mizrahi and Rosenthal (2001) iden-tified internal and external elements of successful coalitions. Similarly, Mattes-sich, Murray-Close, and Monsey (2001) reviewed forty relevant research studies from a two-year period and interviewed university and foundation researchers to identify factors reported as important to the success of collaborations. Table 10.1 provides a comparison of the results of these two approaches to identify suc-cessful elements/factors in coalitions and collaborative efforts.

In the following guiding steps for building coalitions, we draw on these au-thors to blend the organizing and relationship approaches as well as the elements that make coalitions successful.

1. Identify and establish a working relationship with a community coali-tion. When an organizer engages with a coalition, or a collection of represen-tatives from organizations who hope to start a coalition, four general aspects of the coalition, as identified by Mizrahi and Rosenthal, should be clarified: *con-ditions, commitment, contributions,* and *competence.* The timing and the op-portunity to form a coalition are often based on favorable social and political community *conditions.* For example, new awareness concerning an issue such as homelessness may be sparked by the onset of cold temperatures, or the dis-covery of a family sleeping under a bridge. To stimulate interest in the concern a recently elected member of the local governing board may become an advo-cate. These two factors could provide the opportunity to develop favorable so-cial and political conditions for renewed action to decrease homelessness.

The next two aspects, *commitment and contributions,* related to exchange theory, question what individual organizations gain from entering into coali-tions and what an organization must give to the coalition in return. Representa-tives from organizations, and deeply involved individuals who may join the ef-fort, must be sufficiently committed to the issue to be willing to give time to the creation and maintenance of a coalition. This commitment may come from the recognition that, in numbers, the group has more power. For example, youth advocates, community police, drug prevention advocates, youth groups, and parent groups may have a strong commitment to a coalition for creating alterna-tives for youth activities because they believe that together they will have power to be successful. In addition, together they can have a broader reach to potential youth participants than they could through their individual efforts. The third aspect, contributions, relates to what each organization is willing to give or to do in order to build a coalition that is viable, legitimate, and successful. Habitat for Humanity, for example, gives some of its power and legitimacy to an afford-able housing coalition when it becomes a member, and the coalition in turn

TABLE 10.1 Comparative Elements for Success in Coalitions

ELEMENTS/FACTORS FOR SUCCESS IN COALITIONS AND COLLABORATIONS	MATTESSICH, MURRAY-CLOSE, AND MONSEY (2001)	MIZRAHI AND ROSENTHAL (2001)
Membership	Mutual respect, understanding and trust; appropriate cross section; see self-interest in collaboration; ability to compromise	Mutual trust, respect, and tolerance; broad-based constituency of members; continued contributing of resources; providing benefits to coalition members
Purpose	Concrete, attainable goals and objectives; shared vision; unique purpose	Commitment to goal/cause/issue; commitment to coalition unity work; achieving interim victories
Process and Structure	Members share stake in both process and outcome; multiple layers of participation; flexibility; development of clear roles and policy guidelines; adaptability; appropriate pace of development	Equitable decision-making structure and process; shared responsibility/ownership; adequate time to address issues; appropriate division of labor; good operating structure
Communication	Open and frequent communication; established informal relationships and communication links	Right connections and contacts
Resources	Sufficient funds, staff, materials, and time; skilled leadership	Competent leadership; adequate staffing; adequate funding
Environmental Factors	History of collaboration or cooperation in the community; collaborative group seen as a legitimate leader in the community; favorable political and social climate.	Previous history of working relationships; the right timing; critical issue; appropriate target; community climate of openness and flexibility; responsive target; and no opposing coalition or organization

may give Habitat some additional clout when Habitat goes to the community council to get approval for a new housing development.

Finally, there is the aspect of *competency*. Who among the leaders likely to step forward to provide guidance for the coalition has recognition in the community as a clear-thinking social justice advocate? Who has the reputation for effective communication and framing of issues to be able to negotiate consensus on goals and strategies? And who is known as a trustworthy, follow-through person who can be depended upon to do the necessary head and leg work to make sure things get done? In the analysis of leadership competence, the organizer will want to weigh the balance between leadership that can carry the advocacy challenge with leadership that can carry the relationship development necessary for the coalition to be successful. Because coalitions are generally impermanent and leadership is shared, there may be elements of all these types of leadership among the organizations coming together to develop the coalition. That could be a very good outcome if coalition members see the usefulness of shared leadership.

In addition to these four aspects, the organizer should also acquire some understanding about the time frame envisioned by the organizational representatives. Some coalitions are very ad hoc and are intended to last only until the primary purpose is achieved. Other coalitions, those that are established to standardize services, monitor policy shifts, or coordinate technical assistance, information, and resources, may have multiple goals and a longer term perspective.

2. Assist the coalition to develop a broad-based membership with representation from as many stakeholder organizations as possible. Tom Wolff describes a number of coalitions that have passed into oblivion because their primary membership was composed of the same leadership that tried to solve a community problem before without success (2003). In the last several decades, foundations and other funding sources have often required recipients to have broad community coalitions to be engaged in planning for the resource expenditure. Building a diverse coalition is comparable to building a diverse organization of any kind. Wolff proposes that

> membership in coalitions needs to be inclusive, allowing all members of a community who endorse the coalition's mission to join in the coalitions' efforts. Inclusive membership will occur only through active recruiting of the two power extremes in the community—the most powerful (business, clergy, city hall, etc.) and the least powerful (neighborhood groups, youth, people of color, the poor, etc.). The coalitions' basic principles must celebrate diversity and must value the multicultural characteristics of their communities. Institutional racism needs to be identified and addressed. (2008c:1)

Sometimes such coalitions are formed with token representation from parts of the community that are commonly not at the table. When the token representative drops out, the coalition resembles the "usual suspects" who have always been in charge of solving the community's problems—problems that are still unsolved. In such a scenario the community's attitude may be reduced to "Ho hum, business as usual."

Rosenthal (2004) provides an "Inclusivity Checklist" for coalitions to use in their periodic self-evaluations. Among the questions she includes are those asking how sensitive the coalition is regarding religious and cultural holidays, customs, recreational and food preferences, and how thoroughly representatives from different sectors of the community are incorporated into speaking, presentations, and decision making at the coalition meetings.

Mulroy (2001) and Mulroy and colleagues (2005) suggest starting small and taking a slow approach to building the membership of a coalition. Developing community partnerships will require time for the coalescing of multiple perspectives: problem definition, strategic response, and desired outcomes. Although the coalition may be responding to a community crisis, taking time for a broad range of partners to build trust will, in the end, make the response more effective and empowering.

3. Assist the coalition to build trust, understanding, and respect for differences with the involvement of different kinds of organizations and different cultural perspectives about the vision and goals. In addition to seeking diversity in the membership of the coalition, diversity should also be part of the way the organization makes decisions, conducts meetings, holds celebrations, takes action, and shares leadership. In other words, it is important that membership diversity not simply be used for "show," but be an integral part of the coalition's functioning.

Building a coalition that is inclusive and connects across different cultural, gender, age, or racial groups requires special attention to trust-building activities. Trust must include the ability for the coalition to form effective structures for efficiently conducting business. Traditional theater-style meeting rooms and formal Robert's Rules-style meeting formats may have to be set aside. Some meetings might begin or end with everyone in the room taking two minutes to tell what one thing made them most proud to be part of the coalition during the last month. Other meetings might begin with elementary school students sharing team-created posters depicting their vision of the community of the future, with a focus on the coalition's primary issue. In at least one celebration for the year, the coalition might have every member bring a guest who will be at least twenty years older or twenty years younger than themselves, and have the visitors describe the most important legacy the coalition could provide for future residents.

As noted earlier, trust and respect are critical aspects of success identified by most researchers examining relationships in coalitions. Trust develops over time as the coalition meets in formal and informal settings and as they carry out planned actions. Coalitions to prevent oil and gas drilling on western lands have been organized with cattle ranchers, environmentalists, hunters, and forest advocates as members. Trust could only happen with such a diverse group when they could hear each other's concerns and identify their common interest. Building trust among members of international coalitions such as the International Baby Food Action Network (IBFAN) or the Campaign to Ban Land Mines (CBLM), described in earlier chapters, must rely heavily on telephone and Internet communication to develop the trust needed to carry out their significant efforts.

4. Assist the coalition to use participatory techniques to come to a consensus on mission, vision, goals, and outcome objectives. A coalition's mission and goals have to incorporate the self-interest of the different member organizations. Negotiating the specifics of a mission statement, goals, and objectives "requires both a willingness to set aside personal agendas for a common good, and a realistic understanding that addressing the self interests of participants is crucial" (Wolff 2008c:1). Visioning techniques such as "Cardstorming," introduced earlier, and use of "house meetings" described in the case example "Durham CAN" at the end of chapter 11, are potential methods for refining the interests and commitments of coalition members. Whatever method is used, it must allow for the voices of each organizational representative or member to be heard and understood.

Sometimes coalitions get stuck on who should be the designated representative of a certain group or organization. Some considerations might include representation from the breadth of the geographic area as well as a range of relevant organizations, taking into account the need to hear the voices of different community representatives. Usually, the basic criterion for membership in a coalition would be that the person be a resident of the area for which the organization hopes to change conditions. Does that mean that an agency representative who lives outside the geographic area cannot be part of the planning? Does it mean someone's pastor who has parishioners in the geographic area but who does not live there can participate? Should membership be exclusive to those who have been selected as the official representative by their organization's board? These are questions that should be decided in advance, and one should remember that the membership of a coalition tends to be very fluid, with members coming in and out. Karen Ray provides a number of options for avoiding conflict in collaborations by urging groups to decide, before a problem arises, the procedure for settling conflicts (2002). Whatever the decision, keep in mind the importance of being as inclusive and as welcoming as possible, and if need be, flexible enough to change a decision that earlier seemed right but now seems too rigid.

5. **Assist the coalition to adopt and implement open and frequent communication links with its membership, both formal and informal.** The combination of a good Web site, regular newsletters, and regular social events is probably the minimum kind of communication necessary to keep a coalition functioning well. A coalition cannot function without reasonable and regular communication; however, long or frequent meetings can very quickly kill enthusiasm for the issue that initiated its formation. Internal communication, or sufficient communication among the members so that they can come prepared to meetings and events ready to act, can be accomplished in a regular and efficient way by mail or e-mail, depending on the members' accessibility to the Internet. Once mission, goals, and outcome objectives have been clarified, every effort should be made to move toward the action goals in the most efficient way. Coalitions that work to be inclusive will also make the information available in any language that is needed and will make certain that reading- and hearing-impaired members will be able to easily participate.

Social events, whether to celebrate successes or to advertise the efforts of the coalition to the whole community, should be part of the coalition's plan and budget. Social activity, whether internal for coalition members or external to be shared with the community at large, often provides informal opportunities to cement trust and respect. Community celebrations to emphasize cultural diversity organized by a coalition working for immigrants' rights, a youth arts expo organized by a coalition for youth services and programs, and a community tree planting at a river park organized by an environmental coalition have all been successful ways to spread information about these coalitions throughout the community. In addition, they have provided opportunities for coalition members and other community members to share work and fun together. Working side by side with anyone for a noble cause can provide a transformational experience for both partners.

6. **Assist the coalition to think through strategies for reaching their goals and objectives in ways that empower and build the leadership's capacity and increase the legitimacy of the organization to accomplish positive change.** Empowerment comes from building a strong and wide base of leadership. One author worked with a group of women who were receiving public assistance (e.g., food stamps, public housing, Aid to Dependent Children). Although these women were living at the edges of life—selling hot dogs out of the back door of their apartments and "doing hair" for extra cash when food stamps did not last the whole month—most were in classes to get a high school equivalency, nurse's aide, or secretarial certificate. Suddenly, new national welfare reform legislation was announced, legislation that would seemingly make life even more

difficult for these women. They formed a coalition with faculty members from the school of social work, leaders from the League of Women Voters, clergy who were sympathetic to the indignity suffered by the poor, and students from the university who understood the structural causes of poverty. The coalition planned "A People's Hearing on Welfare Reform," the advocacy technique described in the *CPS Workbook*.

With help from analyses done by national legislative watchdog organizations, these women sorted through the items in the bill that could potentially diminish their ability to provide for their families. They divided up the points in the legislation, assigning two issues to faculty members, one to a respected community leader, and taking five items for themselves. Each person assigned an item prepared a four-minute speech to present that issue in the legislation. The women rehearsed their presentations in front of their own organization several times. On the evening of the People's Hearing, with the "Listening Panel" in place (e.g., elected officials, editors, and local business owners), the details of the pending welfare reform legislation were presented. The women on welfare performed as planned, except for one who became very emotional over the fact that a community audience would witness how diminished she and her children felt about accepting government help. She tossed her speech aside and spoke from the heart, sharing her understanding of how the new rules would make the taking of help even more demeaning than it already was while not providing the hand-up she needed. She spoke for more than the four minutes allowed, but no one wanted to stop her. The audience roared its approval when she finished. After that evening, members of the women's welfare organization were invited to speak throughout the university in departments of sociology, medicine, and social work. The idea that a wider community audience had heard, and presumably understood, their perspectives was both astounding and empowering to them. Several went from welfare to jobs with the university, with the hospital, and with the city transit system.

The forum gave these women the opportunity to affirm their knowledge and emotional understanding of how our systems to aid the poor really demeaned them. It provided assurance that they were quite capable of interpreting how their lives intersected with policy. It empowered them as a group and contributed to the self-efficacy they experienced as some moved from public assistance to work and others continued to fight for assistance programs that would actually help their families. For a time, this experience reminded some university faculty that shared learning, from books *and* from real people, is more profound and transformative than simple learning inside the classroom. Nowadays some social work programs still work with families on the economic edges of life. Two such programs are the Kensington Welfare Rights Organization in Philadelphia and the Poor People's Economic Human Rights Campaign, which references the Universal Declaration of Human Rights as one justification for their actions (Bricker-Jenkins, Young, and Honkala 2007; Kensington Welfare Rights Organization 2008; Poor People's Economic Human Rights Campaign 2008).

7. Assist the coalition leadership at all levels to engage with internal disagreements and conflicts in ways that encourage openness, growth, and transformation of coalition members. In her discussion of how to make a collaboration nimble, Karen Ray (2002) describes ten "principles of resilience" for groups involved in coalitions. One of these states that "conflict is expected and is managed effectively" (Ray 2002:56). Because conflict is part of any organization and inevitably will be part of "an organization of organizations," plans and specific ways to resolve conflict should be outlined in the beginning.

Ray and others provide examples of structures and rules used by coalitions across the United States to help move the coalition's mission forward while recognizing the autonomy of the various organizational members (Ray 2002; Wolff and Kaye 1995). Additional structures and rules are available from international organizations such as the Campaign to Ban Land Mines and the International Baby Food Action Network.

8. Assist the coalition to learn how to monitor and evaluate the progress of change as outlined in their goals and objectives, and to use these data to evaluate the flexibility and adaptability of the coalition's structure. Evaluating the results of the work of a coalition is not an easy task. Wolff and Kaye (1995/2008 e-version) suggest, for example, that "if all a coalition can claim as its success are programs designed and implemented by professionals, then its commitment to empowerment must be questioned" (4).

Among the excellent online consultation services to help coalitions develop evaluation tools is the University of Kansas Work Group (The Community Tool Box, KU Community Health Work Group 2008a). The University of Kansas can provide grassroots coalitions with low-cost and no-cost systems that can track the activities, number of people involved, products, and resources. In addition, the Cooperative State Research, Education, and Extension Service of the United States Department of Agriculture has mounted a community collaboration campaign to improve the well-being of children, youth, and families, which inevitably seeks changes in communities. They provide an online checklist for self-evaluation of community coalitions based on the following criteria:

- **Communication**—The collaboration has open and clear communication. There is an established process for communication between meetings.
- **Sustainability**—The collaboration has a plan for sustaining membership and resources. This involves membership guidelines relating to terms of office and replacement of members.

- **Research and Evaluation**—The collaboration has conducted a needs assessment or has obtained information to establish its goals, and the collaboration continues to collect data to measure goal achievement.
- **Political Climate**—The history and environment surrounding power and decision making is positive. Political climate may be within the community as a whole, systems within the community, or networks of people.
- **Resources**—The collaboration has access to needed resources. Resources refer to four types of capital: environmental, in-kind, financial, and human.
- **Catalysts**—The collaboration was started because of existing problem(s) or the reason(s) for collaboration to exist required a comprehensive approach.
- **Policies/Laws/Regulations**—The collaboration has changed policies, laws, and/or regulations that allow the collaboration to function effectively.
- **History**—The community has a history of working cooperatively and solving problems.
- **Connectedness**—Members of this collaboration are connected and have established informal and formal communication networks at all levels.
- **Leadership**—The leadership facilitates and supports team building, and capitalizes on diversity and individual, group, and organizational strengths.
- **Community Development**—This community was mobilized to address important issues. A communication system and formal information channels permit the exploration of issues, goals and objectives.
- **Understanding Community**—The collaboration understands the community, including its people, cultures, values, and habits. (Borden and Perkins 1999)

Tracking the "output" and the participation of community members in events and other coalition activities is only part of an evaluation. Gathering sufficient data to describe outcomes for reflection on what really happened as a result of the coalition's efforts provides a more thorough evaluation. One important aspect of this reflection might be to examine how each individual organization has become more responsive to community needs, more sensitive to social justice and economic opportunity, and more responsive to environmental protection. Although the coalition's intended mission may not have been to change the organizational members, if the systems of operating within the individual organizations were to be transformed so that the whole community would be better served, these would be welcome institutional changes.

Reflection is also a time to examine the coalition's basic purpose and structure. It may be a time for changes that will make the coalition more robust, or it may be a time to turn the coalition into "compost" (i.e., send it to rest for a few years to see what better response could come from the next generation of community leaders). The National Community Building Network, founded in 1996 to connect leaders of community building organizations from across the United States and Puerto Rico, evaluated its purpose and decided to end the organization in January 2008. While still believing that neighborhood residents are the best builders of improved community conditions and institutions, the Network determined they were no longer the best vehicle to serve new community leaders.

9. **Assist the organization to plan for effective action.** Assuming you will be working with a robust coalition, it is important to plan for effective action. As noted earlier, if a coalition is marked by endless meetings with endless reports, it will quickly lose steam and members. Plans for action should examine how much power and wisdom the coalition has gained from its multiple partners. The Santa Fe Living Wage Case described at the end of chapter 7 started its action before the coalition was firmly in place. The organizers and leaders had to pull back from an ordinance for a living wage introduced too early in the city council until they had a sufficiently robust and broad-based coalition in the community ready to back the ordinance.

No plan can possibly consider every contingency that results from an action or an event. However, poorly thought out action plans, or too thin a coalition, can significantly damage efforts to move the issue forward. On one hand, it takes people a long time to forget an ill-planned affordable housing initiative, or a poorly planned youth center, or an unplanned free medical clinic. On the other hand, people have welcomed the creation of well-planned community drug courts introduced by coalitions of mental health providers, police, probation officers, and families and friends of those in need of mental health services. People have also welcomed community mediation centers introduced by coalitions of women's organizations, lawyers, and peace activists. The creation of space for new ways of interpreting and responding to old problems is one of the important contributions coalitions can make to any community.

10. **Assist the organization to plan celebratory events to mark its successes and disseminate information about real change accomplished in the community.** We have already described how celebrations should be part of the coalition's ongoing activities. Celebrations have several purposes, one of which is to provide happy relief for an action well done. Another is to provide an informal trust-building event among the coalition partners and between coalition members and the community. A third purpose is to expand the coalition's message about its mission to the community.

Celebrations should be planned in the same spirit as the regular work of the coalition; that is, they should be totally inclusive. Take stock of the coalition partners' perspectives, and listen well to how they celebrate, what they would like to communicate to the rest of the community, and carefully examine who in the community might not feel welcome at a particular planned event or celebration. Be clever about how to organize celebrations, using unexpected venues, for example. At a recent Santa Fe, New Mexico, citywide campaign to encourage families to read more instead of watching television, permission was granted for volunteers to read short stories aloud on a Saturday morning all over the city—in grocery stores, nursing homes, hardware stores, restaurants, dry-cleaning establishments, art galleries, and exercise gyms, as well as in libraries and bookstores.

Celebrations are an important part of life, and we sometimes learn that better when we travel to other countries. On a recent student study tour to Mexico, we became aware of the number of public celebrations that were part of the regular rhythm of every community and neighborhood. In one interactive session with a group of people, all of whom had worked in the United States illegally during their recent past, we asked if they would like to move to the United States permanently. Their reply was an emphatic "No way! You folks never see each other, you are always inside, you never seem to have celebrations, it can be very lonely to live there."

THEORIES AND CONCEPTS THAT GROUND THE MODEL

The theory streams that inform this model are organizational and interorganizational theory, collective efficacy, power and empowerment, group theory, communication theory, leadership theory, and exchange theory. These concepts have been explored in more detail in chapter 4. The conceptual understandings from these theory streams important for this model are:

- Building and maintaining coalitions
- Cooperation, coordination, and collaboration
- Group dynamics and teamwork
- Tension between self-interest and altruism

These conceptual understandings, some of which we have mentioned earlier in this chapter, will help an organizer think through the task ahead in organizing coalitions.

BUILDING AND MAINTAINING COALITIONS

Certainly coalitions are not a new form of organization. Throughout history an affiliation of people who did not ordinarily work together, or who had different experiences, came together to pool their wisdom, wealth, and energy to create cities, build hospitals and universities, and tackle major health epidemics. In human services we know coalitions were responsible for establishing the first child welfare agencies, a more humane response to people suffering from mental illness, and policies to respond to the needs of the elderly.

In recent years, development of new coalitions has been stimulated by a number of national and international forces. Research among public health providers globally stimulated the World Health Organization's call for "Healthy Cities" and "Healthy Communities." In 1986 the World Health Organization meeting in Europe identified eleven key components of a healthy city, most of which speak to basic human needs, healthy connections with culture and community, safety, and a diverse economy (Encyclopedia of Public Health 2008).

The Ottawa Charter for Health Promotion, also promulgated in 1986, indicated that health for community residents could be achieved only through a collaborative process with a focus on "peace, shelter, education, food, income, a stable ecosystem, sustainable resources, social justice and equity" (Ottawa Charter for Health Promotion 2008). The Healthy Communities Movement was the response to the World Health Organization and the Ottawa Charter's call for a process that would involve people's participation in changing the determinants of health, which were identified with social, economic, and environmental conditions rather than illness. In the United States the Area Health Education Centers (AHEC) provided the staff and became the catalyst for developing participatory activities in communities across the country, large and small, in an effort to change health indicators.

The AHEC Healthy Communities Movement was, in effect, a top-down stimulus to go into communities, especially low-wealth communities, for the purpose of forming coalitions focused on changing the social, economic, and environmental conditions negatively affecting health. From these efforts a significant body of research and practice wisdom has developed about organizing and building communities and developing community coalitions (Minkler 2004).

At about the same time as the Healthy Communities Movement was emerging, national policy changes in the United States were pushing the responsibility for human services decision making and funding to state and local levels. A new local perspective developed for approaching social and economic problems that stimulated grassroots groups to look locally for solutions to such issues as increasing affordable housing, minimum wages, and services for the developmentally disabled. Foundations also began requiring that proposals they received involve a broad cross section of providers and community residents, especially residents from low-wealth communities, in the planning in order to receive funds.

Looking for solutions from inside communities was an important step, and many communities turned to the work of Kretzmann and McKnight (1993) for guidance in exploring community assets. Identifying and strengthening community assets is an important aspect of coalition building because it recognizes the importance of often undervalued and ignored wisdom and strength from low-wealth communities joining the coalition's change mission. Expecting solutions to come solely from communities long denied investments by both private and public institutions, however, cannot happen unless new investments are made in education for children and adults, libraries, job training institutions, economic opportunities, housing rehabilitation, and health centers in those communities.

Tom Wolff, who has worked with AHEC in Massachusetts and across the country, recently summarized the research evaluating the process and outcomes of community-based coalitions. One observation was that many civic organizations seem to be moving toward similar goals (e.g., health, safety, smart growth, good schools, etc.), but they are parallel organizations that do not often see the value of joining forces in a larger comprehensive coalition (Wolff 2003:25). Active coalitions in communities often focus on a single issue (e.g., living wage, health access, violence, etc.), and only recently have they begun to make the connection between their increased empowerment and environmental aspects of their communities (Brooks 2007; Wolff 2003).

One common barrier to more effective collaboration seems to be the strong cultural value U.S. society places on individual rather than community well-being. Too often grassroots representatives are still not included in the planning for change, and instead programs are controlled by professional service providers whose norm is to focus services on individuals, one by one. In addition, the meager government funding available is rarely directed to community organizations. Wolff writes:

> Supporting healthy communities requires that government 1) understand and endorse the concept of the social determinants of health, 2) support working in a comprehensive and integrated manner across all government departments, and 3) cede power to communities for them to identify issues and implement solutions. This is a tall order in an American society that focuses more on the individual than on the community; and a society that has a service delivery system heavily slanted to individual remedial care rather than to community-based prevention. A healthy communities approach seems more compatible with the politics and economics of other governments; thus we see healthy community programs flourishing in Europe and Canada. (Wolff 2003:23)

Wolff warns those working hard to develop coalitions that sometimes they may be expecting coalitions to behave in ways that they cannot. He reminds us of a number of caveats emanating from his own experience and from the work of the MacArthur Foundation's Collaboration Project.

- Coalitions are not externally run or driven.
- They are not human service organizations.
- They are not an automatic link to the grassroots communities.
- They are not cure-alls.
- They are not necessarily efficient because trust building and reaching consensus takes time.
- They are not a money-saving solution.
- They are not the only way to solve problems. (Wolff 2008a:1–2)

Another challenge that community coalitions often face is that neither foundations nor government funding sources seem willing to fund community organizers, a position essential for community coalitions to be developed and thrive. Indeed, Alter (2000) suggests that, as a minimum, coalitions require skills in management, program planning, direct practice, and community organizing. In addition, coalition participants must agree with the vision and working styles that embrace teamwork and cooperation and have a "commitment to social justice as a core principle; [and a] culturally sensitive concept of community" (Mulroy et al. 2005:466).

Even with these reservations, the power of coalitions to transform communities when they work is heartening. Successful coalitions, whose partners include organizations that traditionally count their success by providing individual services as defined by their expertise, are now helping one another to see the whole person. More importantly, coalition partners are connecting the dots between the whole person's well-being and the health of community supports that affect the resilience of families. The efforts to build community coalitions continue, and numerous research materials, training guides, and consultants are available for moving toward their success (Bailey and Koney 2000; Mattessich et al. 2001; Minkler 2004; Mizrahi and Rosenthal 2001; Mulroy and Matsuoka 2008; Ray 2002; Roberts-DeGennaro and Mizrahi 2005; Weil 2000; Winer and Ray 1994; Wolf and Kaye 1995).

COOPERATION, COORDINATION, AND COLLABORATION

The dictionary definitions of the relationship terms *cooperation, coordination,* and *collaboration* have some overlapping meaning. *Merriam-Webster's OnLine Dictionary* (2009), for example, defines *collaboration* as simply "to work jointly with others"; *coordination* as "the harmonious functioning of parts for effective result"; and *cooperation,* seemingly closer to the work of coalitions, as "association of persons for common benefit." Research, of course, depends on concise and clear meaning, and the researchers and trainers have for the most part chosen "collaboration" as the word that defines the processes and relationships of coali- tions (Ray 2002). Mizrahi and Rosenthal (2001) identify "collaboration" as the operative process for coalitions, and they emphasize a focus on social change partnerships that are voluntary and have an external focus.

Bailey and Koney (2000) have identified "coordination" as the operative word to describe the processes and relationships of coalitions, associations, and federations. In addition, Teresa Hogue (1994), from the Oregon Center for Com- munity Leadership, embraces the continuum of terms from less to more formal commitments and relationships with coalitions identified as a less formal rela- tionship than collaborations, as follows: networking; cooperation or alliance; coordination or partnership; coalition; and collaboration. Although all of these definitions are useful to our understanding, sometimes one or the other is more appropriate to the particular research or training approach at hand. For our general purposes we will focus on collaboration as the term that describes rela- tionships in coalitions.

As noted earlier, Karen Ray describes collaboration as the most intense rela- tionship on the continuum, requiring a formal agreement among the partners, a common new mission statement, clearly defined and interrelated roles, dis- persed leadership, shared risk, and pooled resources. In all three relationship terms—cooperating, coordinating, or collaborating—the partner organizations retain their autonomy. Cooperation is described as an informal relationship; coordination is more formal, involving planning and role specification; and col- laboration requires significant planning and communication with potential risks for partners' resources and reputations (Mattessich et al. 2001:60). In the end, the details are in the formal agreements that partners elaborate and sign as their model for initial operation. A number of different models and rules can guide the relationships among the partners in the coalition. It will be helpful for any newly forming coalition to explore the range of models to determine which one best fits the context of the community and interests of the partners.

GROUP DYNAMICS AND TEAMWORK

Building and maintaining coalitions involves complex dynamics and provides opportunities for imaginative kinds of teamwork. As we have discussed, avoid- ing conflicts in group dynamics can often be managed with effective structures and rules of decision making. Do the partners all have the same idea of what the organizational and the decision-making charts look like? Are financial rec- ords transparent and clearly understood? Ray (2002) suggests that rules be short and act as guidance for the mission and goals of the collaboration rather than too prescriptive. The following is an example of a coalition that has only four rules:

- Don't do anything illegal.
- Don't spend more money than is allocated to the task or the result we want.
- Use consensus-driven decision-making processes.
- Excellent customer service—as perceived by the customer—is preeminent. (Ray 2002:63)

At the same time, conflict should be expected because organizational partners come and go as changes in life and jobs create transitions, some partners have a history of mutual ill will and find it hard to trust each other, or some partners believe they should have more influence in decisions and others should have less. These are the normal dynamics of any partnership and should be anticipated, openly approached, and resolved. Conflicts that are not solved and remain simmering under the surface can gradually destroy any norms of trust and respect that have earlier been created.

A coalition that has solved most of its basic collaboration issues should begin to develop structures and processes that help it work more efficiently. Coalition models that spread out the work, the leadership, and the decision making using different task groups will be useful. Organizers should always be mindful of the need to be inclusive rather than exclusive as task groups and task activities are assigned.

THE TENSION BETWEEN SELF-INTEREST AND ALTRUISM

Generally, organizations choose to join coalitions for both utilitarian and ideological reasons (Mizrahi and Rosenthal 2001). Some coalition partners may be motivated by the potential increase in power created by the collective and by possible resources that accrue to them as partners. Other partners may have an ideological or altruistic motivation if they believe that working for the coalition's goal will be "good" for the community. These alternative motivations can sometimes cause tension in the relationships when they are not openly discussed and understood. If it appears that one partner must contribute more time and information than was at first anticipated, will the altruistic motivation be strong enough to retain that partner's commitment? If the mission or goal seems less focused on real change than one partner anticipated, will the power and legitimacy gained from being part of the group be enough to allow the acceptance of the lesser "good," keeping that partner involved until a deeper change opportunity presents itself at a later time? In coalition partnerships there will always be tensions because people are participating in a give-and-take relationship and the value of their needs and gifts will be variable. Acquiring some understanding of the motivational interests of the coalition partners will be critical as a community practice worker engages with coalitions.

SOCIAL WORK/COMMUNITY PRACTICE ROLES

The practice roles for this model identified in table 2.1 and defined in table 2.2 are the following:

- Mediator
- Negotiator
- Spokesperson
- Organizer
- Bridge-builder
- Leader

You will recognize that four of these roles have already been discussed in previous chapters: negotiator, spokesperson, organizer, and bridge-builder. Here we will only discuss the roles of *mediator* and *leader*.

A mediator is an important role for a community practice worker in this model because of the built-in opportunities for conflict when bringing together autonomous organizations that have their own philosophy, goals, approaches, and ideas about what constitutes success. Building a coalition requires lots of listening so that groups can hear each other's needs and concerns. In the mediator role, one is very careful to help the groups listen and hear each other, to help groups affirm their understanding of each other's interests, and to help groups clarify their interests when unintended words, behaviors, and actions interrupt the trust necessary to continue. Mediation requires practice because from the time we are young we are taught to show our reactions to events and conditions. Keeping our own opinions to ourselves, including not showing feelings in facial expressions while helping groups hear each other, is not just a role, but an extremely valuable skill community practice workers will use in this model and in others as well.

This is the first model in which we identify the role of *leadership*. For the most part we stress the roles of organizer, facilitator, coach, and advocate when working with grassroots groups because the effort should be to build the leadership capacities of people, strengthen the effectiveness of the organizations, and empower groups and organizations to take action on their own behalf. When a community practice worker takes the role of leader, it generally indicates that a community leader is not yet available to step into a critical position needed to champion social justice, human rights, and environmental protection. When a coalition is forming, at times a community practice worker is the natural leader to bring organizational partners together to move a critical issue to the forefront of a community. Someone working with a homeless population, for example, may be the right person to lead a coalition for affordable housing or a coalition to establish day treatment facilities or a community court. Someone working with homebound elderly might be the right person to take a leadership position in forming a coalition to advocate for the frail elderly or for elderly co-housing facilities. Many leadership opportunities are likely to present themselves as community practice workers take on the social justice, human rights, and environmental protection needs of any community. In thinking about leadership roles, the community practice worker would do well to consider the range of qualities suggested earlier as needed to bring the issue to a successful completion. Alter (2008), in describing the qualities of leaders for a range of interorganizational practice interventions, suggests that the best leaders are risk takers. In addition:

> They must be future-oriented and believe that the future can be better than the present. They must have a positive attitude toward change. They must be inventive and view innovation as a key to organizational survival and even as a way to strengthen their organization and make it grow. . . . The capacity to tolerate a degree of uncertainty during the development process is another important personal asset. (Alter 2008:5)

These qualities relate to being a strong and effective advocate for social justice, having effective relationship building skills, including the ability to communicate easily with all sectors of the community, and having the steady energy to keep an organization moving, with both the head and leg work required to juggle many concerns at once. Only the rare individual has all these qualities, but because all these characteristics are needed, it is important to consider a leader's strengths and how those strengths can be matched by spreading the leadership throughout the coalition with others.

CORE SKILLS AND COMPETENCIES FOR EFFECTIVE COALITIONS

The core skills and competencies for this model involve a range of proficiencies needed to build and maintain effectively functioning coalitions. We agree with Alter (2000) that, at a minimum, planning, managing, direct practice, and community organizing are necessary, if not always sufficient. In addition, we endorse the perspectives of Mulroy and colleagues (2005) that skills alone, without a commitment to social justice, cultural sensitivity, and participatory methods, are insufficient. The skills identified for building and maintaining coalitions would not likely be found in a single individual, just as the range of leadership characteristics (e.g., champion of social justice, excellent relationship builder, dependable follow-through) would rarely be found in a single person. It would be wise to seek out among the leaders and organizers of a coalition a core group of people whose skills will be complementary. Putting these ideas together, the leadership and organizing skills needed to build effective coalitions are the following:

1. Planning, especially employing the use of participatory methods
2. Managing, especially being dependable with follow-through
3. Direct practice, especially the ability to build relationships
4. Cultural sensitivity, demonstrating inclusiveness
5. Organizing and leading as a champion of social justice

Earlier, we described the basic workings of a coalition as well as the thrust of community coalition activity introduced by the Healthy Communities Movement and the leadership provided for this movement by Area Health Education Centers. Currently, there is a groundswell of coalitions forming in the United States to work toward gaining a living wage for all workers, health care access for all citizens, alternative economic opportunities such as organic farms, cohousing, cooperative preschools, and new practices to ensure food security (Brooks 2007; Miller 2006; Pollan 2008). With these opportunities available in communities, and a significant body of research that provides a knowledge base for the worker, there is opportunity for learning and practical experience. As in previous models, we ask community practice workers to prepare a personal assessment of their readiness for this work:

- What is my previous association with a coalition? as a partner? as an organizer? as a casual observer?
- What are my understandings and perspectives of the values and limitations of coalitions?
- What characteristics seem to identify coalitions with success in this community?
- What characteristics seem to deprive coalitions of power and legitimacy in this community?
- Among the roles identified as important for working with coalitions (mediator, negotiator, spokesperson, organizer, bridge-builder, and leader),

and skills (management, planning, direct practice, and community organizing), in which have I had experience? In which would I have strengths? In which do I feel competent?

• What strategies and plans can I make to strengthen my skills?

Following this assessment, the community practice worker should seek out practice opportunities with an eye toward gaining new experiences and honing skills that may already have been acquired. As we suggest in all the models, practice should be done with a guide, field instructor, partner, or someone who can both observe your work and help you dig more deeply as you describe the challenges as well as the excitement of this practice. We have suggested a number of community-based practice opportunities. In addition, regional and state-/ provincewide or countrywide coalitions may offer opportunities to practice.

Following is a recent letter sent to the Association of Community Organization and Social Administration (ACOSA), which describes a ready-made opportunity to jump into the tasks of building a coalition for action.

Dear ACOSA members,

I thought you might be able to provide some direction on a major community organizing project ADA Watch and the National Coalition for Disability Rights (NCDR) is about to launch. Our hope is that we could tie our organizing efforts to social work programs around the country to provide learning opportunities and to assist in organizing.

I am very grateful for my social work professors who insisted I take community organizing classes back when I was so certain I was going to only be doing clinical social work! I just returned, with my wife and two young boys, from a yearlong, cross-country bus journey and traveling exhibit promoting disability rights and organizing around legislation to restore the Americans with Disabilities Act (ADA) after years of being weakened in the courts. (www.roadtofreedom.org)

As we approach the 20th anniversary of the ADA in 2010, we are planning to launch a series of regional, state and local organizing events that will focus on public education as well as organizing and mobilizing the grassroots disability rights community. Focus areas will include civil rights and discrimination, economic and social justice, youth, and disability rights history. Our journey around the country reinforced our view that the community is significantly fragmented and, especially in light of the tough economic times ahead, we need to build a "bottom up" strategy and infrastructure for social change.

We have the backing of most major disability, civil rights, and social justice organizing at the national and state level, but I am unclear about how best to reach out

*to social work educators to engage social work community organization programs in
our efforts.*

I appreciate any direction you could provide in this regard.

Best,

James P. Ward, MSW
Founder and President
National Coalition for Disability Rights (NCDR)
601 Pennsylvania Avenue, NW, Suite 900S
Washington, DC 20004
Direct Voice: 202-415-4753
Email: jimward@ncdr.org

Our Programs:

ADA Watch: www.adawatch.org <http://www.adawatch.org>
Road To Freedom bus tour and traveling exhibit: www.roadtofreedom.org
Wired On Wheels: www.wiredonwheels.org <http://www.wiredonwheels.org>
The Disability Rights Concert
Campaign for Fair Judges

After a period of practice, and throughout your professional career, you
should reflect on your progress, your increased and effective skill and competence, and the satisfaction you acquire from this work. Some questions to guide
such reflection might be the following:

- How would I describe the success of the coalition with which I worked in
  its ability to accomplish its mission?
- Was the coalition able to be inclusive in its membership development?
- How successful was the coalition in its ability to foster empowerment
  among groups that have been excluded from participating in community
  improvement?
- How successful was the coalition in its ability to actually change a condition to improve social justice, human rights, and/or environmental protection and restoration.
- What could I have done to make the coalition more successful, more inclusive, more committed to social justice and economic justice, human
  rights, and environmental restoration?

Shepherding the growth and success of coalitions requires a steady and skilled
community practice worker.

CONCLUSIONS

In this chapter we described organizing coalitions as a practice model. We provided the insights of those who work in building community coalitions from social work, from community health, and from the cooperative extension programs. Examples of coalitions were also identified, some connecting organizations to global issues and others to very local issues.

This work requires excellent community organizing knowledge and skills to develop the multiple complex interrelationships that make coalitions work effectively. In the end, building community coalitions increases the social capital of any community. Networks are increased as people who may not have known each other before begin to trust each other. A sense of empowerment emerges as people see they can be successful in bringing real change to situations that earlier engendered helplessness and hopelessness. It would be well, however, to remember that working collectively without the support of governmental institutions is only half the battle. As Couto and Guthrie noted, the networks of social capital, the deep trust and collective work required to improve community conditions, can work well only if public goods and resources are also invested in the effort (Couto and Guthrie 1999). It requires both the energy, wisdom and commitment of grassroots organizations *and* the resource support and recognition of local, regional, and national governments to bring about sustainable community transformations. Coalitions can provide the structure, process, and action needed to bring local, state, and national resources together for progressive change (Roberts-DeGennaro and Mizrahi 2005).

11

POLITICAL AND SOCIAL ACTION

When will our consciences grow so tender that we will act to prevent human misery rather than avenge it?

ELEANOR ROOSEVELT, 1884–1962

Framing is about characterizing values, concepts, and issues. Frames define the underlying problems, and by reframing one can point out when the real problems lie elsewhere.

GEORGE LAKOFF AND SAM FERGUSON, 2006

INTRODUCTION

We begin this chapter by referencing the last section of the NASW Code of Ethics as it sets the tone for our focus on the political and social section model. This section of the Code is often overlooked in the education of social workers and community practice workers—perhaps because it comes last and a crowded curriculum squeezes it out. Or the reason may be that we social work educators are simply too unfamiliar with these policy and participation directives, making us reluctant to integrate them into the whole of social work practice. Section 6.02 of the Code simply states, "Social workers should facilitate informed participation by the public in shaping social policies and institutions" (NASW 2008). Section 6.04 of the Code, enlarging on the ideas of social and political action, states:

> (a) Social workers should engage in social and political action that seeks to ensure that all people have equal access to the resources, employment, services, and opportunities they require to meet their basic human needs and to develop fully. Social workers should be aware of the impact of the political arena on practice and should advocate for changes in policy and legislation to improve social conditions in order to meet basic human needs and promote social justice.
>
> (b) Social workers should act to expand choice and opportunity for all people, with special regard for vulnerable, disadvantaged, oppressed, and exploited people and groups.

(c) Social workers should promote conditions that encourage respect for cultural and social diversity within the United States and globally. Social workers should promote policies and practices that demonstrate respect for difference, support the expansion of cultural knowledge and resources, advocate for programs and institutions that demonstrate cultural competence, and promote policies that safeguard the rights of and confirm equity and social justice for all people.

(d) Social workers should act to prevent and eliminate domination of, exploitation of, and discrimination against any person, group, or class on the basis of race, ethnicity, national origin, color, sex, sexual orientation, age, marital status, political belief, religion, or mental or physical disability.

(NASW 2008)

In addition to the NASW Code of Ethics, articles 19–21 of the Universal Declaration of Human Rights (which celebrated its sixtieth birthday in 2008) give us additional direction for the model we have identified as political and social action:

Article 19: Everyone has the right to freedom of opinion and expression; this right includes freedom to hold opinions without interference and to seek, receive and impart information and ideas through any media and regardless of frontiers.

Article 20: (1) Everyone has the right to freedom of peaceful assembly and association.

(2) No one may be compelled to belong to an association.

Article 21: (1) Everyone has the right to take part in the government of his country, directly or through freely chosen representatives.

(2) Everyone has the right of equal access to public service in his country.

(3) The will of the people shall be the basis of the authority of government; this will shall be expressed in periodic and genuine elections which shall be by universal and equal suffrage and shall be held by secret vote or by equivalent free voting procedures.

(UDHR, 1948; Eleanor Roosevelt argued for use of nonsexist language in the declaration, but she was overruled.)

How does this model manifest itself in the directives in Section 6 of the Code of Ethics, and how are these directives applied in everyday practice? What role should social work and community practice workers play in helping citizens understand Articles 19–21 in the Universal Declaration of Human Rights? We believe the following examples demonstrate the action that grows from this model.

BOLIVIA CHIQUITANO PEOPLE In the 1700s, the Spanish relocated indigenous Chiquitano people from the eastern forests of Bolivia to haciendas where they were forced to work tapping rubber trees. In the past decade, Oxfam America has begun working with these indigenous people to help them to reclaim and return to their original community territories. Restoring these homelands to the Chiquitano has involved legal and technical work, mapping territorial boundaries using satellite positioning data, and making use of a 1996 agrarian reform law that will allow them to control and plan for how the trees, minerals, and water will be utilized. The restoration work went against the logging and ranching interests whose hired thugs burned down some of the Chiquitano community buildings and equipment and physically beat and intimidated some of the organizers. In June of 2007, the president of Bolivia announced that the legal work was completed and that the Chiquitano were now the legal owners of the forest area called Monte Verde (Hufstader 2007).

U.S. CIVIL RIGHTS MOVEMENT OF THE 1950s AND 1960s During the most recent U.S. civil rights movement, African Americans took the lead in researching and responding to the oppressive and inhumane laws and practices that discriminated against them. Americans across the nation, some of whom were social workers, joined the effort to eliminate these laws and practices by using direct action, nonviolent confrontations, legal challenges, boycotts, and street demonstrations. The era began with the 1954 public school desegregation decision by the U.S. Supreme Court. Significant actions included student "sit-ins" at the Greensboro, North Carolina, lunch counter where African Americans had customarily been denied service; the bus boycott in Montgomery, Alabama, where African Americans refused to ride the city busses until they could sit where they chose without having to give up their seat to a white person, and the organization of the Mississippi Freedom Democratic Party that tried to be seated at the 1964 Democratic National Convention, erupting in a major national controversy. The reaction to these efforts was harsh and violent, resulting in many deaths. Examples include 14-year-old Emmett Till who was killed in 1955 for allegedly whistling at a white woman in Mississippi, and the Rev. Martin Luther King Jr. who was killed while mediating a sanitation workers strike in Memphis, Tennessee, in 1968. Although much remains to be done to eliminate racism and discrimination against people of color, these efforts resulted in the passage of the Twenty-fourth Amendment, the 1964 Civil Rights Act, the 1965 Voting Rights Act, and the 1968 Housing Rights Act prohibiting discrimination in the sale, rental or financing of housing (Bullard 1994; Dierenfield 2004).

THE DINÉ (NAVAJO) IN ARIZONA The Navajo Nation in northern Arizona has been struggling against mining interests for many years. Peabody Energy, the transnational parent company of Peabody Western Coal, is interested in extending its mining interests into Black Mesa, an area that has endured the removal of 14,000 Diné (Navajo) families since 1974. The Navajo contend that families and livestock were removed through a fabricated land dispute with the Hopi tribe in order to access the coal beneath the mesa. Environmental groups and community members used regulatory mandates to influence the closing of the Mojave Generating Station in 2006. This Mojave Generating Station, located in Nevada, provided electricity to Nevada, Arizona, and California, even though the Hopi and Navajo living on Black Mesa have no electricity or running water. The collaborating advocates exposed the fact that the Peabody mine, 270 miles from the Mojave Station, was pumping crushed coal in a "slurry line" using water from the Navajo and Coconino Aquifers. These fragile western aquifers provide high-quality water to Hopi and Navajo families on their ancestral lands, lands that could be even more prone to drought conditions in the near future. The Elders among the Native Americans describe coal as Mother Earth's liver. The work continues to protect Black Mesa, bringing together coalitions of environmental groups, youth, and Elders in work to protect the sacred and natural land (Black Mesa Indigenous Support 2008; Black Mesa Water Coalition 2008).

Using examples from real-world situations helps to bridge understanding between the comparative ideal model types presented in chapter 2 (see table 2.1) and the real world where instructive lessons can be identified. In all three examples described above the advocacy groups were able to expand interest and action for their goals. Eventually policies, and in some cases policy makers, were changed, allowing the Chiquitano people in Bolivia, African Americans in the United States, and Diné people in Arizona to achieve some measure of redress for past injustice. As in previous chapters, we draw from these and other case examples throughout this chapter to expand the knowledge and understanding of skills related to this model.

SCOPE OF CONCERN

Political and social action is primarily action for social justice that seeks to change oppressive policies and, when necessary, change the policy makers who have a stake in keeping oppressive policies in place. These actions often require years of effort and can be more permanent and less divisive if they are waged in a nonpartisan way. The case described at the end of this chapter, Durham CAN, is a good example of nonpartisan approaches in action where all political parties are subject to questioning by the empowered coalition members. Durham

CAN has created a multiracial, multifaith, multineighborhood coalition with deep grassroots support. As you will see from reading the case, this kind of organization does not spring up overnight.

Rothman (2007), in his latest conceptualization of approaches to community intervention, describes one of his three dominant intervention modes as social advocacy. Social advocacy in its predominant mode "relies on pressure as the core instrument of change with the aim of benefiting the poor, the disadvantaged, the disenfranchised, and the oppressed" (Rothman 2007:28). In our eight-model configurations, we specifically join *political action* with *social action*; changing institutional or structural conditions almost always involves engaging with political processes. In addition, we want social workers and community practice workers to embrace political activity—voting, proposing, and supporting progressive policy options, engaging in lobbying, and even becoming a political candidate—as expected behavior for themselves and for their clients in work toward social justice and human rights. The only one of these activities that may need to be partisan is becoming a political candidate. All the other actions can and should be carried out in vigorous nonpartisan efforts and should be seen by social workers as part of their skills repertoire (Rocha 2007). The struggle against oppressive and tyrannical policies is not just a struggle to eliminate policies, institutions, and practices that oppress; it is also the struggle to promote fairness and equity as the normative approach to establishing policies, institutions, and practices in any society.

BASIC PROCESS: TEN GUIDING STEPS

As in previous models, we enumerate a systematic pattern to help identify what one actually does in this model. In actual practice, you will not find an organizer who follows these steps in a linear fashion; life is too filled with unknowns and opportunities. The guiding steps can help an organizer or community practice worker remember what must be completed while also remembering the feedback loops from the diagram in chapter 5 (figure 5.1) that signal the need for opportunities to take steps back in order to reevaluate understandings and actions before moving forward.

In work directed toward political and social change, the resulting outcomes generally require some power shifts or power sharing, both of which may present challenges for the organization and its leaders. People the world over are challenging the status quo and working in a variety of ways to secure social justice, human rights, and environmental restoration for their communities (Hawken 2007). Most do so in a climate of civility, but as we see from the examples at the beginning of this chapter dangers can be present and sometimes unexpected.

1. **Identify and establish a working relationship with a politically or socially active organization, or help create one where needed.** This step, similar to that in the other models, relates to engagement. The community worker should be alert to organizations in the broader community that are working to change conditions they believe are unjust, conditions that may require changing policies or policy makers.

In some communities in the United States, social workers have engaged with, or helped to start, organizations that promote a more humane and compassionate response to immigrant workers and refugees, who are often without rights and excluded from services for very basic needs (e.g., National Network for Immigrant and Refugee Rights; Immigrant Solidarity Network). In communities in many parts of the world social workers, mental health community workers, and mental health patients have helped to change policies that neglect and denigrate people who are in need of mental health services (World Health Organization 2008). Women's organizations throughout the world have also worked tirelessly to gain passage of the Convention on the Elimination of All Forms of Discrimination against Women (CEDAW 2008; The People's Decade of Human Rights Education 2008). These are examples of areas where local communities have significant interest in the problem and existing organizations are providing leadership to mitigate policies that prevent immigrant workers, people with mental illness, and women from gaining their full human rights.

2. **Assess the leadership and organizational assets and challenges within the existing organization using popular education and participatory appraisal techniques.** This step should be regarded as a mutual interview. The community practice worker wants to understand what the strengths and challenges are within the organization to determine whether he or she has the skills and knowledge necessary to help the organization develop and succeed. The organization needs to understand what it actually needs from a social worker or community practice worker in order to maximize its efforts toward policy change.

This mutual interviewing stage encourages the community worker to engage with as many key actors in the group as possible in some participatory discussions or activities. The community practice worker should be taking account of who the "key actors" are that have come forward to participate, and who the "missing actors" might be if one were to think of the whole range of people who could be involved in the policy issues identified by the organization. By the same token, the organization leaders will want to see how the potential organizer responds to a range of people, fellow collaborators, as well as challengers, not just the leadership.

There will be occasions when the social worker finds herself in a situation where policy changes are desirable but an organization has not yet emerged to take on this action. Assuming the community practice worker decides to take some leadership in forming a new organization, the worker will find that the assessment tasks are similar. The worker looks for the range of people who may be concerned about specific policy change, assesses the strengths and challenges that will present themselves as the policy issues are exposed to the wider public, and makes some judgment about the likelihood of developing a strong organization to move the policies in a more progressive direction.

3. Assist the organization to deeply analyze the social, economic, environmental, and political aspects of the issues they are confronting. Earlier, we made "deep understanding of the issues" an essential skill for community social workers in a number of the models. In the political and social action model, we again see the importance of Finn and Jacobson's (2008a) analytical framework for social justice—understanding the history, context, meaning, power, and possibility for decreasing social injustice and promoting progressive, humane policies.

A focus on immigration issues helps to illustrate this guideline. Migration of populations, whether voluntarily because of economic and social forces or because of war and violence, will continue to be an issue for many countries in the years ahead. The United States has struggled with reaching a consensus for immigration policy in recent years partly because the complexity of immigration issues has been framed very differently by different groups, sometimes resulting in policy extremes. One very important way to gain a deeper understanding of migration and immigration issues is to examine how the issues are framed historically and in the current context (Public Agenda 2008).

Although the United States is historically a country of immigrants and its Statue of Liberty proclaims a welcoming message to immigrants, after 9/11/2001, national voices warning of terrorism framed concerns about immigrants in national security language. The presence of immigrants in some communities has changed the look of "Main Street," which now caters to food, clothing, and recreational interests of the new immigrants. These cultural and language changes have created unease in many communities, and policies have been proposed to respond to the changes.

People who fear the dilution of perceived national cultural attributes or have deep fears about national security tend to use terms such as *illegal, alien,* and *undocumented* to describe immigration issues. When these concepts are used to frame the problem, the focus on solutions is also seen in narrower and more direct terms, calling for building fences at the borders and increased policing to ferret out criminal behavior. People who view the issues from a deeper, more historical perspective, however, might examine international economic and trade agreements, depression of wages, and availability of cheap labor. They are more likely to use terms such as *economic refugees, forced migration,* and *humanitarian crisis* to describe what is happening to migrants entering the United

States (Lakoff and Ferguson 2006). Their focus on solutions would require more involvement of foreign policy. From this wider, deeper perspective of immigration, we would be asking questions such as the following:

> How has U.S. foreign policy placed, or kept, in power oppressive governments which people are forced to flee?
>
> What role have international trade agreements had in creating or exacerbating people's urge to flee their homelands? If capital is going to freely cross borders, should people and labor be able to do so as well, going where globalization takes the jobs?
>
> Why has nearly ten percent of Mexico's population been willing to face death to move north?
>
> Such a framing of the problem would lead to a solution involving the Secretary of State, conversations with Mexico and other Central American countries, and a close examination of the promises of NAFTA, CAFTA, the WTO, the IMF and the World Bank to raise standards of living around the globe. It would inject into the globalization debate a concern for the migration and displacement of people, not simply globalization's promise for profits. . . . The immigration problem, in this light, is actually a globalization problem. (Lakoff and Ferguson 2006)

In 2007 some policy makers in North Carolina were interested in making it possible for successful high school graduates of undocumented immigrants to apply for admission to the state's community college system as long as they paid out-of-state tuition. This policy already exists in some states. The arguments of advocates for such an admissions policy were framed to emphasize workforce development, the advantage of graduating bilingual/bicultural workers for the state, issues of fairness since these students had successfully completed high school in North Carolina having come to the United States as children, and the fact that out-of-state tuition exceeds the actual cost of community college education (El Pueblo 2008). The reaction to this proposed policy was violently negative, involving personal threats to the families of policy makers and advocates. These reactions were a response to the fears and antagonisms shaped by those who took a more shallow, immediate perspective, framing immigrant children as criminals and their options for more education as unfair advantage. The harsh negative sentiment caused all the gubernatorial candidates, Republican as well as Democratic, to question or condemn the policy. In the end, the courageous director of the community college system kept the policy in place as long as possible, serving about 350 such students.

Deeper analysis of history and context is especially important work in this model because it brings out aspects of the problem many people have not considered. In our discussion of conceptual understandings later in this chapter, we will explore deeper analysis of policies that affect people who suffer mental ill-ness as well as policies relating to human rights concerns for women and girls.

4. Assist the organization to develop techniques for setting goals, objec-tives, and outcome measures for reaching their policy changing goals. The United States has had a minimum wage law since 1938. Over the years Congress has been slow to increase the minimum wage, resulting in a wage standard that has ranged between 53 and 62 percent of the U.S. poverty level in the period between 1985 and 2007 (Department of Labor 2008). This abysmal policy to fa-cilitate the availability of cheap labor has forced many heads of households to work two full-time jobs just to meet some of their basic housing, food and trans-portation needs. The smallest jolt to this squirrel cage existence, such as a health emergency or an auto accident, frequently spells catastrophe for such families (Roberts and Povich 2008).

More than a decade ago advocates for the poor throughout the United States began to recognize the greater potential of getting municipalities and states to adopt a "living wage" rather than to depend on a shift in national policy. Na-tional and local advocacy groups have also done analyses of wage structures and family budgets showing how families barely survive on the current federal mini-mum wage. For instance, the Economic Policy Institute has calculated family budgets for six different family sizes in 400 different locations of the United States, providing an effective cost of living analysis for determining what it costs a family to pay for food, clothing, housing, health care, child care, and transpor-tation for nearly any locale (Economic Policy Institute 2008; Living Wage Re-source Center 2008).

Baltimore, Maryland, passed the first municipal living wage ordinance in the United States in 1994, requiring a wage of $6.10 an hour, $2 more than the federal minimum at that time, which applied to any one doing significant business with the city (Brooks 2007). Fast forward to January of 2008, after many years of effort by a coalition of labor, church, immigrants rights, and other groups, Santa Fe, New Mexico's municipal wage was established at $9.50 an hour for any one do-ing business inside the city limits (Living Wage Network 2008). The case exam-ple of Santa Fe's Living Wage Campaign at the end of chapter 7 provides insight into the long-haul effort that pays off when a broad coalition is motivated and some external expert assistance can rally when needed.

Organizations that can help to determine how and where to engage with an issue to make policy changes are those that have some experience in that arena. For policy changes such as those in living wage campaigns, David Reynolds, who teaches at the Labor Studies Center at Wayne State University in Detroit, and Jen Kern, who presides over ACORN's Living Wage Resource Center in Washington, D.C., published a manual drawing from the campaigns of a num-ber of cities to help other groups think through goals, objectives, and outcome measures before engaging in strategies (Reynolds and Kern 2003). Data on the number and percentage of people in each of the states below the poverty guidelines and the family budget standard for that state are invaluable for use by economic change activists (Economic Policy Institute 2008).

5. Assist the organization leaders and members to develop skills for forming alliances, acquiring resources, and employing wide and inclusive communication systems. People with mental health conditions require a very broad continuum of community services. With an effective network of different levels of service, most people with mental health needs can continue to be productive members of any community. An effective network requires forming alliances with persons in need of mental health care, their families, inpatient and outpatient facilities, police, the courts, employers, housing providers and educators. In recent years mental health community workers have felt a great deal of frustration as their clients were released from inpatient treatment facilities and weeks later were incarcerated for a petty crime that could have been avoided with a closer monitoring of medication and talk therapy. Without some kind of coordination and adequate funding, people in need of mental health services and their families have often been shunted from one service to another, resulting in failed treatment and diminished human beings who often end up on city streets. This is a problem all over the world. The call for more comprehensive services and adequate funding is especially strong as soldiers, both adult and child soldiers, return from civil and state-sponsored wars, many of whose lives have been torn asunder by physical and emotional wounds.

People in need of mental health services, especially those with dual diagnoses of drug addictions and mental illnesses, depend on very empathetic family and friends, but may also come in contact with many different therapeutic service and public control providers, including therapists, hospital workers, police, judges, prosecutors, defense attorneys, housing providers, educators, and parole authorities. Recently, a number of communities in the United States have organized groups that advocate for an alternative approach to meeting the needs of these people by forming what are called Mental Health Drug Treatment Courts, Community Resource Courts, or, simply, Drug Courts. These courts identify certain people who have substance abuse and mental health issues and provide community-based treatment and supervision to help the person avoid circumstances that would send them to jail or to an inpatient facility. Once a patient is selected for the program, he or she is required to engage in a variety of treatment interventions with frequent supervision as well as regular drug testing. Establishing these courts required securing collaboration from families, patients, and providers; establishing new policies for how to effectively engage with these patients; and obtaining new and steady funding. In New Mexico, where problems with DWI are among the highest in the nation, a research study indicated that only 36 of the 341 people who had graduated from the Drug Court Program had been rearrested for DWI since the program began, a recidivism rate of only 10.6 percent. Now the state is working to establish drug courts in every one of its thirty-three counties (New Mexico Drug Court 2008).

Fortunately, these voices of concern for adequate mental health services have now been joined by the World Health Organization, which has established a World Mental Health Day and provides a Web site where people can record their stories—indicating both useful and unhelpful experiences in their search for healing strategies for emotional and behavioral traumas (World Health Organization, Regional Office Europe, "Vahid's Story," 2008).

6. Assist the organization to think through strategies for reaching their goals and objectives in ways that empower and build the capacity of the leadership and the organization. The living wage campaigns described earlier have been particularly effective in engaging a wide coalition of ordinary working folks in the more than 200 cities in which they are active. This beginning effort to bring low wages out of the cellar and into the twenty-first century has ignited the energy of many people. According to Fred Brooks (2007), coalitions for economic justice around the country have taken on "numerous other issues such as health insurance, immigrants' rights, expanding of state earned income tax credits, monitoring of living wage ordinances, and statewide increases in the minimum wage" (437). Santa Fe, New Mexico's Living Wage Campaign, as well as Nevada's Living Wage Campaign, are instructive cases for how a broad-based coalition effectively comes together to change policy, even in the face of national inertia and local legal challenges against their goal. These broad-based efforts will build the leadership, strengthen social capital, and empower the people who work hard for economic justice.

Another example of social and political action that has empowered and built the leadership capacity of people has been the "Coke-Pepsi Free Zone Campaign" in India. A Coca-Cola plant began producing 1,224,000 bottles of Coke a day in Plachimada, in the state of Kerala, India, in 2000. Unfortunately, they began to illegally pump millions of liters of water from underground wells for use in the production, causing wells used by families for drinking and farming to either dry up because the water table dropped or become contaminated by waste products pumped out of the production plant. Women from Plachimada began sitting at the gates of Coca-Cola in 2002. They also filed a public interest lawsuit against the Coca-Cola Company in the Kerala High Court, and in 2003 the court ordered the plant to stop pirating water. The cola giant was finally ordered completely closed in 2004, stimulating the efforts of thousands more people across India to challenge other Coke and Pepsi plants that were robbing or contaminating local water. Vandana Shiva (2005) writes that "the victory of the movement in Plachimada was the result of creating broad alliances and using multiple strategies. . . . [it] triggered recognition of people's community rights to water in law, while also triggering movements against the 87 other Coca-Cola and Pepsi plants where water is being depleted and polluted" (168–72). In addition, young people were brought into the campaign as hundreds of schools and colleges across the country declared themselves "Coke-Pepsi Free Zones."

7. **Assist the organization to learn how to manage internal conflict and disagreement as the organization grows, and the range of strategies are explored, remembering that changing institutions can generate hostile external reactions to the goals and strategies.** We have explored this step in some detail in other models. Suffice it to say that participatory methods are essential technologies to draw out the variety of the organizational members' points of view. The community worker should expect these views to be divergent at times, and their open discussion is exactly what helps the membership learn about the nuances of issues, how perspectives differ and their potential to uncover creative solutions. A wide range of participatory methods, including popular theater, can contribute to the deep analysis and building of conceptual frames about issues that are grounded in the experiences of people in the organization (Finn, Jacobson, and Campana 2004). Discussions of social and political issues generated from participatory methods generally promote greater clarity about the problem. This increased clarity doesn't always bring greater consensus, but it does help to focus strategies that emerge to reach the identified goals. Mediation methods and participatory organizational methods, such as Appreciative Inquiry, may still be in order to help the organization deal with internal divergent perspectives. Certainly, the more people can clarify the issues for themselves in their own words, the more likely they are to be committed to the group effort.

The Durham CAN example at the end of this chapter demonstrates how this multiracial, multireligious, grassroots organization was able to build a broad coalition that could influence social and economic policies in their city. Building their agenda from the ground up allowed its diverse membership to manage potential differences in intimate discussions.

8. **Assist the organization to learn how to monitor and evaluate their progress toward goals.** Plans for evaluation should be made long before the strategy and action phases are initiated. The most readily available evaluation tool for organizations seeking to influence social justice through policy change is to determine whether the targeted policies, practices, and institutions have actually changed as identified by organizational goals. If the goal has been to establish a "living wage," or put in place a new program that replaces disconnected revolving door services for people needing mental health services, or to stop the stealing of minerals and water by transnational corporations, the first level of

evaluation is to measure the outcome. Hopefully, the outcome will be positive. But that is never the end of the work. Part of outcome measurement requires reflection to see what was learned in the process of struggling toward the goal (see the continuous sustainable development diagram in figure 1.2). In reflection, the organization also explores any untoward results that have occurred in reaching the goal and examines how the process could have been altered to be more inclusive, empowering, and efficient. Monitoring the outcome to make sure that the new policy is enforced and adequately funded is another step. Policy change without monitoring and enforcement would be a hollow victory.

As we suggested earlier, the outcomes can be measured by an outside group, or they can be measured internally. Outside evaluators generally are considered to be more "objective" and therefore more legitimate in arriving at results. They may, however, also be costly and may not necessarily be more objective because it is very difficult to eliminate all value judgments from evaluation questions and protocols. The concerns for reliability and validity should be discussed in preparation for participatory evaluation (Finn and Jacobson 2008a). Internal evaluation should take place whether or not the organization hires an external evaluator because it necessarily involves reflection contributing to the continued growth and skill development of organizational members.

9. Assist the organization to plan for and take effective action and to protect its members from hostile external reaction. The strategies for action should include all of the legal means available to change policies or policy makers in order to eliminate or diminish policies that are oppressive and unjust. Throughout history those measures have been rebuffed and people may decide to take direct action. Peter Suber's (1999) philosophical discussion of the pros and cons of civil disobedience provides a broad perspective for thinking about the range of actions relating to peaceful protest. Direct action is sometimes confronted by rigid and angry reactions from the forces that wish to keep the status quo. Resistance to change, especially institutional or policy change, can be direct and even violent or can be subtle and insidious. Examples from recent years include the U.S. civil rights movement, the South African fight against apartheid, the multifaceted coalition demonstrating against the World Trade Organization and the World Bank because of concerns about the negative aspects of globalization, Indian people's protest against Coca-Cola and Pepsi for stealing and contaminating water, and the Burmese monks' demonstration against national policies that diminish democracy (Mandela 1995; Prigoff 2000; Shiva 2005; Yunus 2007). In each instance when direct action was planned, a great deal of training was necessary to help people involved in direct action resist taunting and to prevent their harm. Examples of guides to peaceful protests are available

from the American Friends Service Committee (2008), Wilderness Society in Australia (2008), Act Up (2008), and the Liberty Guide to Human Rights (2008).

People who plan to take a peaceful stand against injustice are unknowingly connected with thousands of other people throughout the world who are doing similar work. They must, however, plan for the contingency that they may be arrested. Planning should include arrangements to have available legal representatives, news media, medical personnel and clinical social workers to assist on such occasions. Even in the face of violent response, peaceful demonstrators often recommit themselves to go forward in a cause they believe should be solved in civil discourse.

10. Assist the organization to plan celebrations that mark the progress of leadership, organizational development, and action victories. Just because this step is last, the community practice worker should not mistakenly think it should be tended to after all the other work is finished. Organizing for social and political change must involve some fun along the way because it is usually serious work. Keeping a balance between the steady work toward organizational goals and a lightness of heart to provide relief and reality to the effort is always important. Organizers should never take themselves too seriously. Celebrations, street fairs, block or village events, drama, singing or art competitions honoring elders and youth, or organizing a water or forest walk will be essential to keeping the work and the people involved vibrant. These kinds of celebrations also attract the talents of a wider group of people from the community. Where would the United States' civil rights movement have been without Pete Seeger's widespread sharing of "We Shall Overcome" or Bernice Johnson Reagan and her group, Sweet Honey in the Rock (*Pete Seeger: The Power of Song* 2007; Reagan 1993)?

THEORIES AND CONCEPTS THAT GROUND THE MODEL

The theory streams that ground political and social action, previously discussed in chapter 4, are *power and empowerment, leadership theories,* and *perspectives relating to human rights and social justice.* Related to these theories and perspectives are conceptual understandings that we believe are most critical for social workers and community practice workers engaging in political and social action.

The essential conceptual understandings are

- Social justice applied in community settings
- Basic human rights instruments with a focus on the rights of women and girls

- Universal and equal suffrage and the right to take part in government, directly or through freely chosen representatives (Article 21 of the UDHR)
- Professional ethics

SOCIAL JUSTICE APPLIED IN COMMUNITY SETTINGS

Social justice has been an abiding theme throughout this book, and its application has been discussed in other chapters. At the beginning of this chapter, we indicated its importance as described by the NASW Code of Ethics and in the IFSW/IASSW "Ethics in Social Work, Statement of Principles." The social work dictionary defines social justice as "an ideal condition in which all members of a society have the same rights, protections, opportunities, obligations and social benefits. Implicit in this concept is the notion that historical inequalities should be acknowledged and remedied through specific measures. A key social work value, social justice entails advocacy to confront discrimination, oppression, and institutional inequities" (Barker 2003:405).

How does the community practice worker connect with this ideal while reckoning with the weight of historical inequities that manifest themselves in institutional discrimination and oppression in innumerable facets of community life? Although many aspects of social injustice are intertwined, it is always useful to focus on specific areas of concern, or even just *one* specific area. Familiarizing oneself with the history, context, and insidious nature of social injustice requires developing personal relationships with people in a community who are concerned about or have experienced injustice. It requires engagement with people who have felt the sting and hurt of a personal injustice. It requires hearing the story from that person's perspective. Learning about fair wages directly from a grocery clerk or casino cleaning woman, learning about child care options from a mother with two toddlers, and learning about health insurance options from newly independent young workers are places to begin one's education.

Community social workers who wish to work for social justice in their communities must engage with homeless teens or adults, with single parents who are working two jobs and don't have adequate child care, with the poor in many countries who must sell one child in order to have money to feed the others, with women who move into prostitution in order to feed their children, with men who make the dangerous, often deadly crossing into the next country where even meager wages can earn the possibility of paying for a new roof or medical care for a sick child back home, with the destitute elderly left behind when the young were swept into wars, or with communities left with no jobs after global economic shifts took industry to places where wages are cheaper.

Unfortunately, there is no shortage of social justice arenas in which a community social worker could engage.

BASIC HUMAN RIGHTS INSTRUMENTS WITH A FOCUS ON THE RIGHTS OF WOMEN AND GIRLS

In the aftermath of World War II, the world's leaders began the process of establishing normative rights that could become standards guaranteed to every citizen in his or her country. The Universal Declaration of Human Rights (UDHR) was adopted by the United Nations General Assembly on December 10, 1948. The UDHR is still regarded as the basic standard from which to measure and promote human social, economic, and cultural rights, even though it is sometimes considered too strongly influenced by Western Enlightenment (Ife 2006). One of the shortcomings of the UDHR is that the nation-state is responsible for enforcing the human rights outlined in the UDHR, as well as judging and punishing violations (Dominelli 2007). We are sometimes in the situation where the state is the violator and therefore not likely to enforce the basic right. Another problem is that the rights are guaranteed to individuals because they are citizens of a particular place, leaving refugees, asylum seekers, and other noncitizens without similar rights. Finally, poverty, "which significantly undermines all other rights" and is, according to Dominelli, largely due to structural conditions such as trade agreements and control of capital financing established by rich corporations and countries, cannot be overcome through the guarantee of individual rights (Dominelli 2007:40). Even so, the Kensington Welfare Rights Union in Philadelphia, Pennsylvania, has joined with the Poor People's Economic Human Rights Campaign in using Articles 23, 25, and 26 of the UDHR as their national and international rallying points to organize poor people across the United States (Bricker-Jenkins, Young, and Honkala 2007). In planning public events they have juxtaposed their stark poverty and the deplorable conditions of their neighborhoods with the noble words found in the UDHR about one's right to work and to have an adequate standard of living.

To establish the universal acceptance of rights and the ability to make use of such rights as legally binding laws, UN member states have passed additional rights instruments relating to specific human needs. The "Ethics in Social Work, Statement of Principles" identifies six rights as essential for social work knowledge. (The dates in the following list indicate when the convention entered into force.)

- The International Covenant on Civil and Political Rights (1996)
- The International Covenant on Economic Social and Cultural Rights (1996)

- The Convention on the Elimination of All Forms of Racial Discrimination (1965)
- The Convention on the Elimination of All Forms of Discrimination against Women (CEDAW, 1979)
- The Convention on the Rights of the Child (1989)
- Indigenous and Tribal People's Convention (1991) (IFSW/IASSW 2008)

Additional rights instruments that should be of concern to social work are the UN Declaration on the Right to Development, 1986; the Convention against Torture and Other Cruel, Inhuman and Degrading Punishment, 1984; and the Protocol to Prevent, Suppress, and Punish Trafficking in Persons, Especially Women and Children, 2000 (UNODC 2008). The Convention on the Elimination of All Forms of Discrimination against Women (CEDAW) was ratified by 180 UN member states but not by the United States. Only two countries have not ratified the Convention on the Rights of the Child: Somalia and the United States.

Some people believe the push for economic, social, and cultural rights has been less energetic than that for civil and political rights. The Vienna Declaration of 1993, however, confirmed that civil, political, economic, social, and cultural rights were "universal, indivisible, interdependent and interrelated" (World Conference on Human Rights 1993:para 5). Even so, some scholars believe the fact that civil and political rights seem to have more enforcement power than economic, social, and cultural rights may be due to a "hidden gender bias" (Staub-Bernasconi 2007). If the right to education, equal pay for work, or to marry whom you choose were enforced, rights for women and girls would increase. Staub-Bernasconi (2007) argues that the hostility toward economic, social, and cultural rights by some governments is misguided because it is "precisely these rights— education, food, employment, decent housing, and medical care—[that] would make at least the same contribution as political and civil rights to a safer and more secure world" (149).

In no country do women have rights equal to those of men. Girls are particularly handicapped when they are denied education, not provided health care and excluded from opportunities to become entrepreneurs. Janice Wood Wetzel, who is the IASSW NGO representative to the United Nations and chair of the UN Committee on Mental Health, argues forcefully that

it is wrong to physically or psychologically restrain and control women, regardless of religious insistence on their subservience. It is not all right to demand dowries when women marry, regardless of ritual beliefs. Nor is it acceptable to genitally mutilate girls and women, regardless of ancient mores. To pay women at lesser rates than men for the same work is not all right, regardless of common practices. To expect women to work all day outside the home for inequitable wages, in addition to having responsibility for unpaid home maintenance and child care, is wrong, even if "everyone does it." And to blame women for being poor or not having a home when their wages are less than life-sustaining, and when affordable housing is unavailable, is not all right. Women's human rights are being violated. (Wetzel 2007:166)

UNIFEM, the United Nations Development Program for women, has been working to improve women's rights country by country (UNDP-UNIFEM 2008). The Gender Empowerment Measure (GEM), found in the annual *Human Development Reports*, is also an excellent data source for evaluating the status of women's participation in political and economic arenas in any country of the world.

Women and children, who make up 80 percent of the world's refugees, are particularly vulnerable to social injustice and human rights abuse. Rapes are endemic in refugee situations, scarring women and girls for life. To protect human rights during and following civil wars and catastrophic natural disasters, where people are displaced internally, the UN in 1998 passed the Guiding Principles on Internal Displacement, with a particular focus on preventing displacement and helping people return safely to their homes when displacement occurs. The Institute for Southern Studies recently used these guidelines to determine how the United States was applying the principles to the million people displaced from their homes in the wake of Hurricane Katrina in 2005. Their report indicates that the U.S. government failed to meet the standards outlined in the guidelines (Kromm and Sturgis 2008). In their press release Chris Kromm stated, "Based on interviews with hundreds of Gulf Coast leaders and residents and an analysis of reams of data and research reports, the Institute concludes that the U.S. government failed to live up to the U.N. standards during all stages of the disaster—with many Katrina victims still suffering the consequences" (Kromm and Sturgis 2008).

The hurricane disaster affected both men and women, but because they were viewed as primarily poor and Black the news media often referred to them as "refugees." As Cornel West said:

What we saw unfold in the days after the hurricane was the most naked manifestation of conservative social policy towards the poor, where the message for decades has been: "You are on your own." . . . Well, New Orleans was Third World long before the hurricane. It's not just Katrina, it's "povertina." People were quick to call them refugees because they looked as if they were from another country.

They were. Exiles in America. Their humanity had been rendered invisible. (West 2005)

The broad spectrum of human rights—civil, political, social, economic, and cultural—should be seen as "universal, indivisible, interdependent and interrelated," just as the Vienna Declaration confirmed in 1993. This is the message community social workers should take with them in their daily work against social injustice.

UNIVERSAL AND EQUAL SUFFRAGE AND THE RIGHT TO TAKE PART IN GOVERNMENT

In Article 21 of the Universal Declaration of Human Rights we are reminded that "everyone has the right to take part in the government of his country, directly or through freely chosen representatives," and that "the will of the people shall be the basis of the authority of government" (Article 21 of the UDHR). A Gallup International Survey in 1999 asked more than 50,000 people in sixty different countries "if their country was governed by the will of the people. Less than a third of the respondents said yes. And only 1 in 10 said that their government responded to the people's will" (UNDP 2002:1).

In the 2004 U.S. presidential election, the combined cost for the presidential candidates, the convention, and the general election was conservatively estimated to be $1.2 billion (Center for Responsive Politics 2009). The presidential election of 2008 is estimated to have cost $2.4 billion (Center for Responsive Politics 2009). The total seems shocking, but the real story lies in the details of where these large amounts of money are coming from and in the implications for the privileged access it allows.

Although campaign finance laws have imposed limits on certain contributions and required the reporting of contributors over certain sizes, the work to make elections more reflective of "one person, one vote" has been assumed by a variety of state and national nonprofit organizations such as the Center for Responsive Politics, Clean Election Institute, Common Cause, Democracy North Carolina, and the League of Women Voters. These organizations track campaign finance issues and work on state and national policy changes that will increase the diversity of candidates running for office, decrease the amount of money coming from corporate political committees, lobbyists, and wealthy individuals whose political action committees can generate significant campaign funds, and increase the number of people who actually vote.

Controlling the vast amounts of money spent on political campaigns has been complicated because of First Amendment challenges establishing the right to give unlimited campaign funds as a free speech issue. In the United

States a public financing system was established for presidential candidates following the Watergate scandals in the early 1970s. According to the League of Women Voters, "almost all of the Democratic and Republican presidential candidates between 1976 and 2000 used the system to finance their presidential races in the primary and general elections," but now the legislation needs to be adjusted to keep pace with the cost of running presidential campaigns (League of Women Voters, December 6, 2007). Fourteen states currently have legislation that provides some form of public financing for state-elected officials (Common Cause 2007). Generally, a candidate wishing to accept public funds must first establish himself or herself as a serious candidate by securing a minimum number of signatures and contributions (as low as $5.00 per contributor). Then, to qualify for public funding they must voluntarily refuse to accept additional private funds for the primary or general election. State laws vary as to which state offices can qualify for public funding and how a candidate qualifies. Arizona has had "clean election" legislation since 1998, and its governor until 2009, Janet Napolitano, was elected to two terms as a "clean election" or publicly funded candidate (Clean Election Institute 2008).

Voting rights are particularly important to social workers and community workers because of the NASW Code of Ethics focus on ensuring "access to needed information, services and resources: equality of opportunity: and meaningful participation in decision making for all people" (NASW 2008).

Following blatant, long-entrenched voter discrimination prior to the civil rights movement, Congress passed the Voting Rights Act in 1965. In 1993 the National Voter Registration Act was also passed to increase voter registration by expanding registration opportunities at motor vehicle departments and at service agencies such as those certifying people for food stamps and Medicaid. Because lower-income Americans were the most likely people to visit these certifying centers, it was expected that more of these citizens would be brought into the voting process. Even though the effort to increase political participation among the poor has not been very successful, for social workers and community workers committed to "equality of opportunity: and meaningful participation in decision making for all people" (NASW 2008), the work to help secure suffrage for all people, young and old, wealthy and poor, should be in their consciousness and part of their effort (Kavanagh et al. 2005).

Many countries have their own watchdog groups that assist in monitoring political freedoms and political participation. Both the United Nations Development Program and Freedom House (2008), a nongovernmental organization founded in 1941 to monitor global progress toward freedom of participation in the electoral process and freedom of the press, are good places to begin exploration.

PROFESSIONAL ETHICS

In all community practice work, professional ethics is very important. In this model where the worker and the community are collaborating on specific policy changes, a reminder about ethical practice may be helpful.

For American community practice social workers, there is no more clear directive about *when* to act than can be found in NASW's six Ethical Principles and Section 6 of the Ethical Standards (NASW 2008). The directive in "Ethical Principles" should compel the community worker to "pursue social change," to focus on "issues of poverty, unemployment, discrimination and other forms of social injustice," and to "ensure access to needed information, services, and resources; equality of opportunity and meaningful participation in decision making for all people." Added to these principles are directives in "Ethical Standards" that call on social workers to "promote conditions that encourage respect for cultural and social diversity within the United States and globally," and to "advocate for programs and institutions that demonstrate cultural competence and promote policies that safeguard the rights of and confirm equity and social justice for all people." Finally, they should "act to prevent and eliminate domination of, exploitation of, and discrimination against any person, group, or class on the basis of race, ethnicity, national origin, color, sex, sexual orientation, age, marital status, political belief, religion, or mental or physical disability" (NASW 2008). The question of "when to act" seems to be very clear. The problem often is "where to focus" since no person can act on all the social injustices in any community at once.

The National Association of Black Social Workers Code of Ethics directs its membership to "be guided by our Black consciousness, our determination to protect the security of the Black community and to serve as advocates to relieve suffering of Black people by any means necessary" (NABSW 2008). This code recognizes the multiple identities of people as they focus on their professional role and their relationship with the people whom they will serve.

The IFSW/IASSW "Ethics in Social Work, Statement of Principles" has an equally strong focus on social justice, but it adds concern for human rights and dignity, drawing on the Universal Declaration of Human Rights and the six additional rights instruments already identified. Although there will be concern in any particular locale about *when to act* if action is risky or dangerous, each community practice worker will have to make that decision in consultation with colleagues and advisers. In the end, *when to act* seems relatively clear given the language in the Codes.

"How to act"—that is, how to define the specifics of the injustice, how to focus the change effort toward social justice, how to engage with groups that wish to make change, and which direction to take change—also has ethical implications.

Again, the NASW Code seems to provide some general direction for the "Ethical Principles." We are directed "to help people in need," to "respect the inherent dignity and worth of the person," to "recognize the central importance of human relationships," to "behave in a trustworthy manner," and "to practice within our areas of competence" (NASW 2008). As far as professional conduct is concerned, the IFSW/IASSW "Ethics in Social Work, Statement of Principles" directs each national organization to develop and update their own codes while at the same time providing some general guidelines (IFSW/IASSW 2008).

Community practice experience tells us that competing interests, even competing ethical directives, will sometimes force us to weigh decisions carefully. This should always be done in an open discussion with the people and organizations with whom you are working. Guidance for ethical decision making, especially ethical rules and screens, can be found in Dolgoff, Loewenberg, and Harrington (2008).

SOCIAL WORK/COMMUNITY PRACTICE ROLES

The roles we have identified as most critical for political and social action are the following:

- Advocate
- Organizer
- Researcher
- Candidate
- Leader

Earlier, in chapters 6 and 10, we described the roles of *advocate* and *organizer*. Although the roles are similar for this model, the constituency and scope of concern are different. In this model the community practice social worker will definitely go beyond establishing new programs and services or changing behaviors. The organizing and advocacy work in this model seeks to make specific policy changes that will promote targeted social justice and human rights improvements.

The role of *researcher*, described in chapters 7 and 9, is also similar. In this model the research seeks to initiate systematic inquiry into the particular social justice and human rights policy that is the focus of the organization. In the Durham CAN example later in this chapter, research must explore a variety of indicators that measure the well-being of families in different neighborhoods, and must demonstrate how policy changes would improve the conditions of families. Data sources such as the Economic Policy Institute, which can provide data for specific areas, though valuable resources, will not be able to collect the first-person accounts, in the words of those affected, showing the detail and nuances of social injustice, abridgment of human rights, and conditions of domination, exploitation, and discrimination. These first-hand accounts may be collected through focus groups, surveys, drama, photo workshops, participatory video, time and trend analysis, mapping, past and future graphing, and a variety of ways people might use to express how they understand and describe problems from their experience and in their words (Chambers 1997; Chaskin and Rosenfeld 2008; Finn, Jacobson, and Campana 2004). Empowerment research methods "realign power so that people can direct their individual and collective destinies" and contribute to "a theory of indigenous knowledge to guide social inquiry" (Pennell, Noponen, and Weil 2005:620). In both the description and detail of how the problem is presented, as well as in the evaluation of change following political and social action, the inquiry should be participatory and the reports should be usable by the organization and the community.

At times the community practice social worker will decide to become a *candidate* for elective office; this would not be unusual. When one is working side by side with people who are experiencing social injustice and human rights abuse, it is a short walk from proposing policy options that could improve human rights and social justice to becoming a candidate for the opportunity to actually make the changes. In 2007 ten members of the National Association of Social Workers served in the U.S. Congress. Jane Addams herself, a leader in the late 1890s settlement house movement, campaigned to be appointed garbage inspector in her Chicago slum neighborhood after she and her neighbors had no success in improving the existing garbage removal system. In a nonelective leadership role, Addams also took a strong stand against World War I as the leader of the Women's Peace Party and later as the head of the Women's International League for Peace and Freedom (Addams 1922/1983).

Jeannette Rankin, a graduate of the New York School of Philanthropy, was active in gaining women's right to vote in 1916, and she was the first woman elected to Congress. In her campaign, she described herself as a peace candidate, and after voting against U.S. entry into World War I she was defeated. Later she was reelected to Congress from Montana, and she again voted against the U.S. entry into war, this time World War II in 1941 (Lopach and Luckowski 2005; Smith 2002).

A recent significant example of a community worker who sought elective office is Barack Obama. Though trained as a lawyer, Obama worked as a community organizer in Chicago, gaining early experience with people who suffered social injustice and human rights abuse. He became a civil rights attorney, a member of the Illinois State Senate, and then a member of the U.S. Senate before being elected president of the United States in 2008 (Obama 1995/2004).

In describing *leadership,* earlier we made a distinction between the role of *facilitator,* which we describe as developing, supporting, and growing leaders; the role of *manager/director,* which we describe as leading service organizations to effective performance; and *leader,* which we describe as providing direction and cohesion for organized efforts to diminish social injustice and human rights abuse. Understanding these differences helps the worker and the organization with whom the worker is engaged to be clear about which role he or she is assuming so that the actions of the worker are understood.

Brueggemann (2006) describes macro social work as embodying two kinds of leadership: social leadership and task group leadership (78). Social leadership is the kind performed, for example, by Jane Addams, Mohandas Gandhi, Cesar Chavez, the Rev. Martin Luther King Jr., Nelson Mandela, and Marion Wright Edelman. They conceptualized social problems from their experience and study and were able to make the issues understandable to larger groups through their speeches and writings. They were able to frame the impact of social injustice and human rights abuse in ways that helped ordinary people see the issues more clearly. This kind of leadership comes closest to the leadership role we refer to in this model. In the case of Durham CAN, both facilitation and leadership seem to be relevant roles for people working in the organization. Different group members may serve in facilitative and leadership roles as the organization evolves. The community practice workers role will be based on worker strengths and group needs.

The task group methods and skills, described by Toseland and Rivas, and the task group leaders described by Brueggmann are useful for "integrated work teams, project management teams, conflict management groups, quality circles, and problem-solving task forces" and are more relevant to the work of managers and directors which we identified in chapters 7, 8, and 9 (Brueggemann 2006:84, Toseland and Rivas 2005).

CORE SKILLS AND COMPETENCIES FOR POLITICAL AND SOCIAL ACTION

As in previous chapters, we link competencies and skills to form a more complete description of action that demonstrates sufficient knowledge, judgment, and skills. The action taken by the community practice social worker in this model would involve engaging with people in political and social action for the purpose of changing policies, or, if need be, changing the policy makers through democratic efforts, in order to promote social justice and human rights. The knowledge acquired should be gained from wide sources, including direct experience with people who suffer the consequences of injustice and human rights abuse. Judgments should be made after carefully reviewing the knowledge acquired, codes of ethics, human rights instruments identified as essential by IFSW/IASSW, and the needs of the people with whom you are working. Skills should be honed in the area you intend to work to promote social justice and human rights.

The skill/competency areas we identify and discuss here are as follows:

- Organizing and coordinating action groups
- Analyzing policies for economic, social, and environmental outcomes,
- Measuring economic, social, and environmental outcomes for all sectors in the community
- Advocating to promote social justice and human rights.

As in previous chapters, we believe these skills can only be acquired through study and practice, reflection, and then study and practice again. A helpful mentor, guide, field instructor, or partner can provide feedback through appropriate questions that will help you dig more deeply into your beliefs, reasons for involvement, effectiveness, strengths, and challenges.

ORGANIZING AND COORDINATING ACTION GROUPS

We have defined an organizer as someone who brings people together by systematically planning and working with individuals and small groups so that their efforts eventually form a whole organization or affiliation. The organizer in political and social action will have identified an issue, or engaged with an organization that has identified an issue, where the only effective change effort would be changing policies. In order to help organize and coordinate the action needed to effect the policy change, the community practice social worker may become the leader/organizer of the group or may become a candidate for public office.

The Durham CAN case example at the end of this chapter clearly describes how the organization was built and how organizational development can involve many detailed tasks. In the Durham CAN organization, the group organized from the principles of the Industrial Areas Foundation (IAF), which has a long history and methodology of how to build strong, grassroots organizations. The group operates on a strictly nonpartisan basis (i.e., it is not affiliated with any political party); builds an agenda for action through small "house meetings" held in homes, coffee shops, or laundromats where the agenda grows from people's lived experience stories; and evolves into "action teams" that do further research into issues such as health care, jobs, education, and housing. Big efforts go into building relationships across racial, income, religious, and interest differences; therefore, action outcomes are built on holding policy makers accountable without being intentionally confrontational. The organization's motto is that "the work of leaders is to cultivate more leaders," so that the leadership bench for public and organizational events is very deep. Thinking about the work that must go into keeping this organization going is a good way to examine your readiness to work in political and social action.

ASSESSMENT AND PREPARATION Prior to accepting the role of an organizer for an organization doing political and social action, you might ask yourself the following questions to gauge your readiness.

- Have I studied the issues relating to the particular social injustice or human rights abuse that is the focus of the organization with which I will work?
- Do I, or does the organization, have a commitment to a particular kind of organizational method or model? What are the strengths and challenges of that method?
- Do I have sufficient knowledge about organizational development and maintenance to be an effective adviser and partner in this effort? What are my strengths? In what areas will I be challenged?

PRACTICE (SIMULATION AND GUIDED EXPERIENCE) Organizing and coordinating action organizations for political and social action is very difficult to do inside a classroom. Some schools do have regular legislative days where students can go as individuals or as a member of a professional association to the state legislature to lobby for social issues or human rights concerns of their choice (e.g., increasing funds for child health, setting a moratorium on death penalty executions, increasing the standards for nursing homes, etc.). These are good exercises that will help people get acquainted with policy-making arenas and policy-making rules. If a policy is targeted for change, the organizer should have as much familiarity with the policy-making body, their rules, their formal and informal practices, and the individual members as possible. Real learning comes from the actual practice of helping to build an organization and working to actually engage in a policy-level change.

EVALUATION AND REFLECTION After actually organizing a group for action, the community practice social worker might engage in reflection questions with the organization, as well as with a trusted mentor.

- How effective was our organization in reaching its goals?
- How effective was I in my leader/organizer position to help the organization reach its goals? In what areas do I feel most challenged?

- How effective was I in helping the organization grow its leadership and its membership?
- What are the things I might have done to help the organization become more cohesive, larger, effective, flexible, resilient, and diverse?

As is often the case, these guiding questions are only the opening to additional questions you and the organization will want to explore in order to build your skills as an organizer.

ANALYZING POLICIES FOR ECONOMIC, SOCIAL, AND ENVIRONMENTAL OUTCOMES

Although our focus here is on social justice and human rights, it is important to examine the extent to which the issues that concern us have local, regional, national, and international connections, and it is useful to have some understanding of their relationship to economic, social, and environmental factors. Katherine van Wormer provides an excellent background for approaching this kind of analysis (2004). An analysis framework for the specific problem of homeless youth, for example, might take the following form:

Social Justice and Human Rights Analysis Issue
Homelessness among Youth

ECONOMIC, SOCIAL, AND ENVIRONMENTAL FACTORS THAT OPERATE TO PREVENT SOLUTIONS	ECONOMIC FACTORS	SOCIAL FACTORS	ENVIRONMENTAL FACTORS
Local			
Regional			
National			
International			

Using the same format, a second part of the analysis would be to explore "economic, social, and environmental factors that might *support* solutions." Without a deeper analysis of the problem, a solution might be too narrowly framed. Obviously, in this specific problem the interest is in getting housing for the homeless youth as soon as possible. As the wider factors and levels of influence are explored, however, the organization can begin to see that the problem is embedded in historical, contextual, political, and power frames.

ASSESSMENT AND PREPARATION Depending on the social justice and human rights issue, the community practice social worker will want to do as much reading and engaging with people who would benefit from a policy change as possible. Some questions to help the worker determine their readiness to engage with an organization might be:

- How does this particular issue relate to the Universal Declaration of Human Rights? to directives from my own country's code (e.g., NASW Code) or the IFSW/IASSW Code?
- How well do I understand the linkages of this issue to economic, social, and environmental factors at different levels?
- How well do I understand the positions of people who wish to solve this problem in a humane, progressive way?
- How well do I understand the positions of people who wish to keep the focus of the problem on individual behavior rather than structural or policy changes?

PRACTICE (SIMULATION AND GUIDED EXPERIENCE) Practicing analysis can be done in the classroom, with an action organization, and with a group of colleagues. An issue can probably be analyzed in limitless ways. The sample chart suggested in the preceding section gives some depth in examining an issue. Others have used a social justice framework that explores the influence of history, meaning, context, power, and possibility on the problem and its potential solutions (Finn and Jacobson 2008a), and a framework that analyzes changes needed in five arenas—the government, the private sector, civil society, political space/culture, and the individual level when seeking transformative change (VeneKlasen and Miller 2002). Participatory methods for examining the depth of social injustice and human rights abuse are always best because the more data-based wisdom and lived-experience wisdom that can be brought together to gain a more complete picture of the condition, the more likely the worker and the organization will learn how to make effective changes.

EVALUATION AND REFLECTION After you have had experience, hopefully with a number of different ways to engage in analysis, you will want to spend some time in reflection to examine how effective you were. Some questions to help you think through your completed work might be the following:

- What aspects of the Universal Declaration of Human Rights helped me understand this issue? Are there other international conventions or protocols that could be relevant to the analysis of this issue?

- Was I able to relate this issue to directives in the NASW Code (or my own country's professional code) that relate to social justice and human rights? to the IFSW/IASSW Code?
- Can I present the issues that need to be changed in this example of social injustice or human rights abuse in a coherent, logical way so that other people can easily understand what sustains the problem and what needs to be changed?
- Am I knowledgeable enough about the perspective of people who do not want change to occur that I can provide them with new data, help them engage with other views, and bring a clearer focus to the social justice and human rights perspective?

MEASURING ECONOMIC, SOCIAL, AND ENVIRONMENTAL OUTCOMES

When and if a policy is changed, how will we know whether the change has happened and in what direction it has gone? As we have suggested earlier, the best time to establish specific goal outcomes is when one is planning strategies for change. As described in chapter 6, VeneKlassen and Miller (2002) suggest stating change outcomes in terms of SMART objectives: Specific (narrowly focused), Measurable (exact in terms of who, what, where. and when), Achievable (within the power and resources of the organization), Realistic (a balance between idealism and realism to avoid failure), and Timebound (time specific) (176–77). The important aspect of this skill is to remember to measure the outcomes for all sectors of the community—across specific groupings such as gender, class, age, race/ethnicity, sexual orientation, marital status, religion, and mental/physical ability—to make sure the intended outcome has not bypassed a particular group for unexpected reasons.

In the case of the Santa Fe Living Wage Campaign, the city hired an outside evaluator in order to engage a firm with expert knowledge and to evaluate a number of different aspects of change. The evaluators were able to determine that jobs in the city increased after the living wage was begun, the unemployment rate was lower in Santa Fe as compared with the rest of the state, the number of people receiving public assistance had decreased 10 percent as compared with the rest of the state, and overtime work had decreased. The evaluators did learn that nonprofit organizations were having the hardest time meeting the increased payroll and placing people with developmental disabilities in work situations.

Although the organizer/leader should not be expected to have all the skills to do this kind of evaluation, he or she should know what kind of evaluation is needed and how to procure it. The following questions will guide community practice workers in assessment of their readiness and in assessment following a practice experience.

ASSESSMENT AND PREPARATION

- What particular measures will be important in determining success for a specific social justice/human rights effort?
- What skill do I have for these tasks?
- Where can we secure pro-bono skills in the community to apply to these tasks?
- What groups should be included in discussions of how to measure success and effectiveness?

PRACTICE (SIMULATION AND GUIDED EXPERIENCE) Practice experience can be gained through an internship working alongside people who do this kind of evaluation, especially if it is an evaluation with a focus on social justice and human rights efforts. Faculty from social work, public health, psychology, geriatrics, anthropology, political science, city and regional planning, African Studies, Women Studies, and a range of other departments may be involved in a study that requires fieldwork assistance for evaluation. Gaining direct experience in such an evaluation study could be helpful.

Following practice or action, the community practice worker will want to reflect on the activity to determine growth and need for additional experience. The following questions may be helpful in that reflection.

EVALUATION AND REFLECTION

- What kinds of new skills have I gained in working with measures of success/effectiveness related to social justice/human rights efforts?
- What groups have I identified in the community that have skills and interest in measuring outcome efforts for social justice/human rights, either at no cost or low cost to political and social action organizations?
- How helpful was I to the political/social action organization in providing for or locating expertise for measuring outcomes?

ADVOCATING TO PROMOTE SOCIAL JUSTICE AND HUMAN RIGHTS

We discussed advocacy earlier in chapter 6 as both a potential role for organizing functional communities and a skill to be acquired by the community practice worker in that model. Advocacy is equally important in this model as both a role and a skill. We have defined the role in table 2.2 as researching and engaging in purposive change activities toward a more just social order, or supporting and helping others to be able to make changes on their own behalf that could result in more inclusive and equitable social and economic outcomes, with investments in improved human potential, increased social capital, and recovered and protected environments.

A community organizer working in political and social action will serve as an advocate for the desired outcome and therefore must be prepared to understand the issues, the barriers to solutions, and options for positive results. Like other efforts at community change, organizations working in political and social action should have an agreed upon mission, long- and short-term goals, and measurable objectives associated with these goals. Working toward change as an advocate may require the organizer and the political and social action organization to work in a number of arenas. We have talked earlier about advocacy for individual rights, for public interest, and for transformation (Hardcastle, Powers, and Wenocur 2004). Any one of these strategies of advocacy can involve the organization in at least five different dimensions. As noted earlier, VeneKlasen and Miller report that according to social justice advocates around the world success can only result if change occurs in all five dimensions:

- The government arena (e.g., laws, policies, programs, elections, budgets)
- The private sector (e.g., business policies, corporations)
- Civil society (e.g., civic and neighborhood organizations, nonprofit organizations, agenda setting, community planning)
- Political space and culture (e.g., making it safe and useful for individuals and groups, especially women, to participate in the political process)
- Individual level (e.g., changing the skill and attitudes of individuals so that they are engaged with decisions that affect their lives and feel positive about the opportunities and abilities open to them for progressive change) (Adapted from VeneKlasen and Miller 2002:178–79)

Making changes in all five dimensions requires setting goals and objectives for each arena, even though action may not happen in all of them at once. Prioritizing the action will be an important process.

ASSESSMENT AND PREPARATION How does the organizer develop the knowledge, skills, and judgments to become an effective advocate? Some of these questions will be similar to those provided in chapter 6.

- Have I had any previous experience in doing advocacy? What was the experience? Was it a successful experience? Why or why not?

- Have I had any previous experience in helping someone become an advocate on his or her own behalf? Was it successful? Why or why not?
- What ethical concerns should guide my judgment in becoming an advocate for this particular social injustice or human rights abuse?
- Is my level of understanding sufficient (data and direct experience wisdom) to be able to adequately defend a particular change of policy for this issue?
- Of the five dimensions of advocacy work (government, private, civil society, political, and individual), in which arenas am I most knowledgeable and comfortable? Which arenas will require considerable learning and increased skill for engagement?

Examining your knowledge and skills prior to practice will keep you alert to learning and skill-building opportunities as you enter practice.

PRACTICE (SIMULATION AND GUIDED EXPERIENCE) Practicing advocacy could first begin in your university class or in your agency. A class at your university could discuss issues such as homelessness, the deportation of undocumented workers who were forced to leave their children behind with relatives, or the lack of a living wage for employees at the university. Or a group of people in your agency could decide, for example, to advocate for people in need of mental health services who are caught in a revolving door of inpatient treatment and incarceration, or for domestic partner rights to gain the same economic and social protections held by people who are married. In each case, research must be collected from the first-person voices of the people for whom the problem is a direct concern. Research must also be collected from wider sources of data and expert knowledge in order to measure the depth and extent of the problem. Leadership can be dispersed so that different people with different skills might lead teams to work in specific arenas, such as in the Durham CAN example. The group can assess strategies for each arena to determine the most effective use of the range of change strategies—education, collaboration, contest, or direct action.

A local or regional organization offers an excellent learning opportunity if it is already working on an advocacy issue, such as seeking change in state or national policy regarding those in need of adequate mental health services, or for children who need dental care, or laid-off workers who need a longer period of benefits so they can take advantage of additional education or opportunities for self-employment. The organizer's initial engagement with such regional, statewide, or national groups should be done with a qualified supervisor or mentor.

EVALUATION AND REFLECTION Following engagement in advocacy for political or social action, the organizer should plan a regular assessment to reflect on her or his growth and personal development. The following questions might facilitate this assessment:

- What range of resources did I use to build my knowledge about this issue? Were the sources sufficient? What additional sources of knowledge could have helped me gain a deeper social justice and human rights analysis?
- Am I effective in helping others develop goals and objectives for change? Are the objectives generally specific, measurable, achievable, realistic, and timebound? Was I able to help the political/social action organization determine how best to evaluate outcomes?
- Among the range of advocacy strategies—education, campaign, collaboration, contest, and direct action—which were the most effective for the different arenas or dimensions of change? Why? Which proved to be most effective in change effort for social justice and human rights? Why?

CONCLUSIONS

Work in political and social action will require the roles of advocate, organizer, researcher leader, and perhaps candidate. A thorough knowledge of internationally accepted rights instruments is an essential part of the preparation of a community practice social worker who wishes to work in this model. Familiarity with a variety of policy practice guides will also be important (Jansson 2007; Rocha 2007; Schneider and Lester 2001). People working in this model will find they have many colleagues across the globe working at many different levels of change to make the world more humane and just (Hawken 2007; UNDP 2007/2008; WEDO 2008; WHRnet 2008). While social justice, and human rights and dignity are the primary goals of this model, we urge a special focus on the rights of women and girls. The efforts to deprive women and girls of an equal share of rights and resources are embedded in a thousand years of cultural traditions. For women of color the struggle for rights is always greater. When rights are unequal, we must always ask "why." Such a focus increases the rights of all humanity and brings all human actors into the work of building a more humane world.

DURHAM CAN: MULTIRACIAL, MULTIFAITH GRASSROOTS POLITICAL AND SOCIAL ACTION, DURHAM, NC, USA

Durham Congregations, Associations, and Neighborhoods (Durham CAN) is an affiliate of the Industrial Areas Foundation (IAF), the oldest and largest national, congregation-based, community organizing network in the United States, founded in 1940 by the legendary Saul D. Alinsky. Durham CAN was formed in 1997 when members of four founding organizations recognized the need for an inclusive broad-based citizens' organization in a community divided by race, economic class, and disconnected institutions. Durham CAN is comprised of thirty member organizations, including Muslim, Jewish, and Christian faith communities, representing over 5,000 residents in Durham, North Carolina, a racially and ethnically diverse community of a quarter of a million residents.

An initial round of house meetings in 2000 involving 1,600 participants produced the first organizing agenda. Since then, Durham CAN has compiled a list of many accomplishments in the areas of living wage policies, job training, health care access, rental housing quality, and public safety.

Durham CAN's approach to political and social action is intentionally (1) local and (2) nonpartisan. Durham CAN believes that residents' quality of life can be impacted by affecting local institutions, even concerning issues of state and national importance, such as the lack of health insurance. While understanding that long-term solutions to the problem of uninsurance are best addressed at the state or national level, Durham CAN nonetheless sees opportunities for the uninsured to gain greater access to health care *now*, not later. It ignores the concerns of some advocates who worry that such an approach nullifies the need for fundamental social change in favor of securing concrete quality of life improvements. Durham CAN has no political affiliations, does not issue political endorsements, nor does it engage in political lobbying at the state or federal level. It does, however, deal directly with locally elected officials and holds them accountable for institutional changes desired by its members.

As an example of its nonpartisanship, a recent mayoral candidate launched a series of "robocalls" to the homes of registered voters that many members regarded as offensive to Latino immigrants (i.e., voters were asked leading questions concerning whether Durham should continue to act as a "sanctuary city" for undocumented immigrants). Durham CAN took no position on the candidacy of this politician, yet invited him to a meeting to explain his position on a number of community issues, including immigration. He was the only candidate not to respond to the invitation. As one organizer stated, "his empty chair at the event will speak for itself." Meanwhile, a different city council candidate appeared at a planning meeting during the election season hoping just to "listen in." Despite impressive credentials as a neighborhood organizer, he was politely asked to leave the meeting. In essence, Durham CAN's nonpartisanship could be viewed as a means of exercising good boundaries with politicians.

Like other IAF affiliates, Durham CAN's commitment to political and social action is predicated on Alinsky's Iron Rule, "Never, never do for others what they can do for themselves." As part of its political and social action approach, CAN employs community organizing strategies that include four key components:

CONTINUED

- Relationship building
- Leadership training
- House meetings
- Action research and issue campaigns

1. **Relationship Building.** This component is based on what Edward Chambers, executive director of IAF and author of *Roots for Radicals,* discusses as relational meetings. Durham CAN asks its members to hold one-on-one meetings with friends, neighbors, and colleagues to identify personal interests and concerns. A typical question might be, "What do you like about Durham?" or "What would you like to be different about your community?" Relational meetings are intended to help people make connections with one another and to see the possibility of collective action through Durham CAN as a means of addressing their concerns. The emphasis on relationship building can be likened to what Robert Putnam and other scholars call *bonding* capital. Durham CAN also seeks to facilitate relationship building among its member organizations, many of which are faith communities. A recent general assembly of Durham CAN was held on a Sunday at a local synagogue, causing a speaker to quip, "Who but Durham CAN holds a meeting on the Christian Sabbath at a synagogue with Muslims in attendance?" The speaker was in part referring to Ar-Razzaq Islamic Center, which had recently joined Durham CAN as its inaugural Muslim faith community. Ar-Razzaq happens to be located just down the street from Immaculate Conception Catholic Church in the West End neighborhood of Durham. Immaculate Conception was one of the founding organizations of Durham CAN and has a significant Latino in addition to Anglo membership. In addition to its multi*faith* identity, Durham CAN also claims a strong multi*racial* one, priding itself on being a "brown-black-white" coalition. This racial and ethnic consciousness is seen through actions such as ensuring a racially balanced slate of speakers at meetings and actions and making sure that "not all the white people are sitting in front," as an organizer recently said in a planning session. Durham CAN also believes in cultivating relationships with local institutions, which are often the targets of issue campaigns. Like relational meetings, effort is made to get to know individuals who represent institutions to understand *their* self-interest and concerns so that "win-wins" can more easily be identified and to demonstrate that Durham CAN can be trusted as an organization that does not believe that confrontation is inevitable. That Durham CAN will exert pressure through actions such as accountability sessions is well known and unnecessary to state. Thus, by attending to relationships between individuals, among its organizational members and with institutions, Durham CAN seeks to cultivate both bonding *and* bridging capital. Durham CAN's efforts to grow its social capital embody Alinsky's principle of "power precedes program."

2. **Leadership Training.** Durham CAN embraces the fundamental axiom in organizing work that the job of leaders is to cultivate more leaders, not followers. Simply put, Durham CAN understands that it loses credibility if the same small group of advocates appears in every meeting acting as the organization's elite group of brokers, negotiators, and agitators. Thus, time and effort is made to train emerging leaders in IAF's methods using popular education approaches. Although

CONTINUED

leadership training comprises its own set of activities in addition to time and energy expended on issue campaigns, the *process* of participating on action teams and on issue campaigns is intended to offer "on the job" training as well. For example, individuals who will speak at general assemblies representing various action teams are coached and offered peer feedback during rehearsals. The commitment to leadership training serves very practical purposes, such as ensuring that there is a constantly changing group of actors that comprise the public face of Durham CAN, lending an impression that it is a very large organization.

3. **House Meetings.** House meetings are the way Durham CAN builds its action agendas in a very intentional grassroots manner. Organization leaders don't sit in a room and come up with action agendas; individuals develop the agendas through a series of informal, small-group discussions in people's homes, coffee shops, and other settings that center around people's lived experience and stories. Participants are asked to share a story about how they are affected by different community issues and events. Meeting facilitators start by sharing their own story to create safety in the group. After someone shares a story, the facilitator asks for reactions with questions such as "Can anyone relate to Mary's story? Have you experienced something similar?" in an attempt to identify shared experiences and interests. Qualitative data from the house meetings is summarized and analyzed to produce an action agenda that represents the top priorities of members. This means that not everyone's concerns can be addressed. Durham CAN understands that it cannot spread itself too thinly across too many action teams and issue campaigns.

4. **Action Research and Issue Campaigns.** The agenda produced by the house meetings creates action teams that conduct research, develop strategy, and hold meetings with institutional representatives. Action teams currently include Health Care, Jobs, Education, and Housing. With the assistance of local university faculty and students, the Jobs Action Team has been studying local economic incentives policies with the guiding question, "To what degree are tax incentives offered for new businesses based on the number of people from Durham who offered living wage jobs?" The Health Care Action Team has been guided by the question, "What can local health care providers, businesses, and government do to ensure that lower-income uninsured persons get the medical care that they need?" Action teams report at general assemblies on the progress of their research, strategy development, and negotiations with institutions. The culmination of this work comes when such institutional representatives are invited to attend a general assembly to state their commitments to change concerning an agenda item before what is typically a crowd of 300 to 400 Durham CAN members. Institutional representatives are never "ambushed" in these assemblies, knowing well ahead of time what will be asked of them publicly. In fact, it is not uncommon for the statement of commitments to be almost ceremonial, since so much work through a series of "win-win" negotiations and planning meetings takes place prior to the assemblies. Nonetheless, the public statement of commitment helps ensure follow-through; few public officials and other institutional representatives can muster the courage to face the same 300 to 400 residents to explain why they did *not* make good on their promise.

CONTINUED

This case example likely echoes the story of many other, similar grassroots organizations across the United States engaged in political and social action at the local level. It serves as a pleasant reminder that, despite the growing influence of money in politics, lack of voter turnout, and other indicators of civic disaffection, the democratic promise of forbearers such as Alinsky is alive and well.

Contributors
Mat Despard, Clinical Assistant Professor
School of Social Work at UNC-Chapel Hill.
Ivan Parra, Lead Organizer with Durham CAN and,
Organizer with the North Carolina Latino Coalition.

12

MOVEMENTS FOR PROGRESSIVE CHANGE

I have walked that long road to freedom. I have tried not to falter; I have made missteps along the way. But I have discovered the secret that after climbing a great hill, one only finds that there are many more hills to climb. I have taken a moment here to rest, to steal a view of the glorious vista that surrounds me, to look back on the distance I have come. But I can rest only for a moment, for with freedom come responsibilities, and I dare not linger, for my long walk is not yet ended.

NELSON MANDELA, *LONG WALK TO FREEDOM*, 1995:625

Only the construction of another society based on total human development can politically and humanly emancipate men and women . . . and eradicate poverty and inequality. It will only be possible if social movements have the force to resist the barbarism already installed, and modify the relations of current forces, promoting construction of another world; . . . From my point of view, social workers from all over the world should position themselves in service to this proposal.

ANA ELIZABETE MOTA, JULY 25, 2005, INTERNATIONAL CONSORTIUM FOR
SOCIAL DEVELOPMENT KEYNOTE ADDRESS, RECIFE, BRAZIL

INTRODUCTION

There are many metaphors in nature to describe social movements: a little spark starting on dry prairie grasses that begins as a small fire and soon spreads across the whole landscape; a small dust devil you see in the distance, raising a little sand but soon turning into a full-blown tornado, changing everything in its path; a spring rain that seems innocuous enough until it continues for days, soaking the ground, forming springs that cut gulches into the soil as it runs down to the river, filling its banks as it rages down to the sea.

The spark is like the person chopping up chicken parts on her "mac-nugget" factory shift who decides one day that the company has sped up the assembly line yet again and her aching arms just won't take it any more. The little dust devil is like the woman who is raped because the rapist is physically stronger and can usually count on her humiliation to allow him to go free, except this time when the dust devil turns into a full-blown tornado representing every woman and man who believes rape is a human rights violation. The spring rain is like a community of people waking up to the realization that the violence of war and the threat of war do not have to be the standard answer to ethnic, gender, resource, ideological, or even international disagreements, and that "constant mediation," if supported by enough local to global institutions, can become the healing water that prevents the cruel destruction of war.

In this model we speak of "movements for progressive change" recognizing that social movements can be destructive and regressive as well as positive and progressive. Progress means "gradual betterment" (*Merriam-Webster Online Dictionary* 2009). Although the United Nations Development Program has developed a system for measuring progress in human development since 1990, recently the Organization for Economic Co-operation and Development (OECD) has embarked on a new effort to define the complex aspects of progress (OECD 2009; Stiglitz 2009). *Progressive*, for our purposes, refers to change or reform that will take society to a higher level, especially relating to social, economic, political, and environmental well-being. As we noted in chapter 1, our definition of *social well-being* means all people have access to basic social institutions and relationships that support their ability to thrive; *economic well-being* means all people have opportunities to achieve a wide variety of livelihoods and that wages should pay enough to meet a family's need for shelter, food, health care, and transportation; *political well-being* means that all people should have freedom to associate, speak, vote, and participate in the governments that make policy for them; *environmental well-being* means that present generations must not live beyond the resources available in the biosphere and must restore, to the extent possible, damage to air, water, soil, fisheries, forests, and other species.

Both progressive and negative social movements may grow from reactions to a rapidly changing world, either in a local or global arena. Kriegman (2007) writes that

> psychological responses to a shrinking world include some mixture of fear and hope. When fear dominates, [this may promote] xenophobia, retreating into protected enclaves, and projecting militaristic solutions. [Fear may stimulate] fundamentalist movements that offer reassurance and simple answers for an increasingly perplexing world. When hope is strong, people's highest aspirations motivate them to uphold their moral responsibilities to their fellow humans and the larger community of life. (Kriegman 2007:3)

We identify movements for progressive social change in both developed and developing countries with those whose organizations connect their sense of fairness with current and future generations and whose goals are focused on improved social, economic, political, and environmental outcomes. We contrast these with movements initiated out of fear of rapid global change and frame their response in protectionist intolerance and militaristic oppression. This difference seems simple, but it is never so clear-cut as the "either/or" way stated above. Human beings and their cultural and social institutions are dynamic and multilayered, resulting in varied responses to changing conditions that come in many shades of grey.

Historically, scholars have described missed opportunities in the United States to follow a much more progressive path in the early part of the last century. Led in part by settlement house residents, the Women's International League for Peace and Freedom (WILPF), the Young Women's Christian Association (YWCA), the National Consumers League, and trade union organizations, progressive social policies were promoted in the early twentieth century only to be opposed and contravened by the hysterical fear and scare tactics of conservative government and powerful organizations calling such enlightened social policy "socialist" and "communist" (Reisch and Andrews 2001). These "red scare" tactics would rise again during the McCarthy era in the early 1950s, and with the 1954 Department of the Army pamphlet entitled *How to Spot a Communist* that warned people to be on the lookout for Communist sympathizers who used words such as "unions," "civil rights," "exploitation," "discrimination," and "progressive" (Andrews and Reisch 1997:32–33). If we have learned anything in our democracy, we have learned the many values of discussing ideas in public discourse and the destructive costs of scare tactics, fear mongering, and witch hunts to discredit new and different ideas presented to resolve current problems and confront the status quo (Alderman and Kennedy 1991; Ravitch and Thernstrom 1992).

Challenges to move in the direction of progressive change come from many places. For example, Fisher and Karger (1997) highlight the United States government's recent withdrawal from the more inclusive and human development-focused social policies of the 1930s New Deal and the 1960s Great Society Programs, saying "The state's retreat from progressive social policy is a retreat from social responsibility. . . . The guiding principle behind governmental action must be to advance an inclusive and egalitarian vision of the public good" (177). Social workers themselves, working within the broader norms and institutions of society, are sometimes criticized for not understanding the structural causes of poverty and oppression, not embracing the meaning of "progressive," and not working toward a vision of social justice (Mullaly 2007; Reisch 2008; Reisch and Wenocur 1986; Rubin and Rubin 2007; Specht and Courtney 1994). In this chapter we offer a vision of progressive social policies to help social workers identify with social movements that can bring societies to a higher level of social justice and human rights.

NEW SOCIAL MOVEMENTS

Before the 1960s, major social movements in the United States were linked to issues such as antislavery, voting rights for women and African Americans, utopian communities, peace and reconciliation, and struggles in the labor movement. Labor and workplace movements were based on a broad interpretation of class struggles (Fisher and Karger 1997; Nash 2005; Reisch 2008). More recent social movements are less often linked to the workplace and more likely to be community-based. They tend to be organized around constituencies and cultural identities, rejecting hierarchies in their organizational structure and embracing new visions of democracy, with struggle and resistance based on human rights, and strategies that are based on self-help and empowerment (Fisher and Karger 1997; Oberschall 1993). Nash (2005) describes the focus of new labor movements as the struggle for fair-market practices at the regional as well as global levels. New spaces for social movements are also being created by civil society groups and leapfrogging across borders and oceans stimulating the emergence of international movements with new contours in each new context. Both the civil rights movement and the women's movement in the United States influenced similar movements throughout Asia and Latin America. These movements influenced groups such as the Plaza de Mayo Mothers in Argentina silently demonstrating for information about their "disappeared" family member, or the women's organizations in India going up against Coke and Pepsi for depleting or contaminating the water in the villages surrounding the corporate giants' bottling plants (Asociación Madres de Plaza de Mayo 2008; Shiva 2005). Nash presents one view of the conditions that spawn new social movements and their connections:

> The civil rights movement addressing ethnic and racial discrimination undoubtedly grew out of anti-colonial movements instigated by Gandhi in India and influencing a new generation of nonviolent protest. The reverberations in the American South have found support for long delayed reforms throughout the North, eventually igniting movements to overcome segregation in Africa and other formerly colonized states. Civil society mobilizations against corruption in despotic Asian societies such as Indonesia and the Philippines expanded the range and variety of people's mobilizations. Inequities in the labor scene are now addressed through free-trade associations as well as the revitalized trade union movement. Labor unions seek covenants affirming human rights and democratic negotiations

in regional trade pacts such as NAFTA (the North American Free Trade Agreement), and the European Community, as well as in bilateral agreements such as that between the United States and China. (Nash 2005:9).

Much of the current organization of social movements is motivated by antiglobalization coalitions, a huge network of established organizations operating with a general collective interest in limiting the excesses of corporations and promoting the needs of low-wealth countries and populations (Porta and Diani 2006). Sensing the state's inability to control multinational corporations and mediate the negative excesses of global market processes, organizations supporting global justice have protested directly against international institutions such as the World Trade Organization (WTO), the World Bank, and the General Agreements on Tariffs and Trade (GATT) (Klein 2007; Korten 2001).

Many of these antiglobalization organizations have participated in the World Social Forum, which began in Porto Alegre, Brazil, in 2001 with 16,000 people and three years later was attended by over 100,000. Now the annual World Social Forum has a revolving international meeting in addition to regional meetings in many different countries. Their Web site provides organizing information in twenty-eight languages and declares it is "not a group or an organization but growing from the Zapatista Uprising in Mexico in 1995 and building on the demonstrations against the WTO in Seattle in 1999, it works against neo-liberal globalization, war, patriarchy, racism, colonialism, and environmental disasters" (World Social Forum 2008).

In chapter 7 we described sustainable development as both a development strategy and a movement for progressive change that will have a fundamental effect on the practice and theory of development. The "philosophical foundations" of sustainable development have been identified in a number of earlier social movements:

- Early environmental/human ecology movements of Europe and North America
- Antiwar and antinuclear movements of Europe and North America
- World order movement
- World dynamics modeling movement
- European Green movement
- Alternative economics movement
- Women's movement in North America, Europe, and in Latin America
- Indigenous peoples' movements in Latin America, Asia, and selected areas of the Pacific [and, we would add, in North America]
- Worldwide human rights movement (Estes 1993:6–8)

How these broad community-based social, economic, and environmental justice concerns become tied together into a regional or global movement is a question for social scientists as they watch the rapidity and fluidity with which many different local organizations are able to network and respond to global concerns (Fisher and Karger 1997; Nash 2005; Porta and Diani 2006).

EXAMPLES OF MOVEMENTS FOR PROGRESSIVE CHANGE

The three examples in this chapter help us grasp both the local and global aspects of community-based social movements. The first example is a description of the fair trade movement, which grew out of consumers' interests in avoiding purchases of goods based on child labor, unsafe working conditions, low wages, and environmentally destructive processes. The second is the peace movement, beginning with the efforts of Jane Addams prior to World War I and continuing through to the most recent war in Iraq. In their 2006 *Human Development Report* the UNDP describes the global struggles for water that will increase in this century (UNDP 2006a). The third example comes from the concern in Cochabamba, Bolivia, to privatize water resources and the move by Bolivian citizens to counter that effort.

FAIR TRADE

The difference between fair trade and free trade is becoming clearer to many North American, European, Australian, New Zealand, and Japanese consumers. Free trade allows the "market" to dictate the cost of goods and consequently pays the producer the lowest price possible in order to maximize profit. To cut costs, the ideologically neoliberal-driven globalized market tolerates such negative aspects of production as child slave labor for cocoa bean harvesting and rug making and the contamination of water and earth in low-wage *maquiladora* factories (assembly plants that receive materials, assemble products, and ship them back across the border) in Mexico and scattered throughout Central and South America. Fair trade, on the other hand, is based on a buyer's agreement to

> pay fair wages to the artisans and farmers . . . provide advance payments for working capital; purchase goods directly from the producers, eliminating the chain of middlemen and speculators; and provide technical and financial assistance when necessary. The producers agree to work in an economically, socially, and environmentally sustainable manner; ensure healthy and safe working conditions; support democratic participation of all members, and contribute to the development of the community by increasing jobs and by building schools, health-care centers and other infrastructure projects that a particular community deems a priority. (Grimes 2005:239)

(continued)

It is one answer to people who do not want to buy chocolate or rugs, for example, produced by children enslaved by the producers, or produced by adults who are not paid a living wage.

In the 1940s the Mennonite/Brethren organizations started the principle of fair trade consumer products with their Ten Thousand Villages and SERRV (formerly Sales Exchange Refugee Rehabilitation and Vocation) centers in the United States. Oxfam UK began selling Chinese refugee products in the 1950s and created the Alternative Trade Organization in Europe in 1964 (Grimes 2005). Now there are Fair Trade organizations in Australia, New Zealand, and Japan as well. Some groups focus on coffee, tea, and chocolate, whereas others arrange for the sale of fair trade textiles, crafts, and art. The largest movement is in Europe, which has twelve importing organizations supplying shops in thirteen countries (Grimes 2005). At the same time, students and middle-class consumers have protested against sweatshop-produced goods on their university campuses and in their malls. Some communities have worked to be identified as sweatshop-free and fair trade communities (Co-op America 2008; SweatFree Communities 2008). Although the movement continues to grow, making more and more direct connections between consumers and agricultural/craft producers in the developing world, it has a long way to go to counter the negative effects of a global free trade economy (Grimes 2005). A parallel movement involving the production and local marketing of farm products so that consumers can eat fresh, organic produce and keep local farmers in business echoes the fair trade principles (National Campaign for Sustainable Agriculture 2008; Pollan 2008; Slow Food USA 2008).

PEACE

The peace movement, sometimes identified as the antiwar movement, has ebbed and flowed throughout recent history. Jane Addams, one of the most respected and eloquent leaders in historical peace movements, provides an intellectual connection between social work and peace work. Prior to World War I, Addams began recognizing that people might be longing for what William James had called a "moral substitute for war" (Stiehm 2006:33–35). Her long experience with the immigrant neighbors surrounding Hull-House in Chicago, many of whom had fled the threat and violence of war and oppression in their own countries, informed her position. She concluded that, in addition to protecting people against international threats and crime, governments also had a responsibility to their citizens for protection against exploitation, poverty, and disease. She rejected socialist arguments that divided people into classes:

> She didn't trust abstraction; she listened attentively to people with the widest range of experience—Chicago's juvenile delinquents, international heads of state, and starving peasants. She was wary of those who claimed to have all

(continued)

the necessary answers, whether they were moguls, ministers, socialists, or academics. She opposed any analysis that separated people into antagonistic groups, whether worker and capitalist, or men and women . . . but she believed women had something special to offer the political world. (Stiehm 2006:38)

Addams believed that young men went to war to die for honor and could not be expected to give up their high ideals without having equally high replacement ideals. In 1914 she helped organize and was elected chair of the Women's Peace Party, a cadre of 40,000 U.S. women, calling for "continuous mediation" in the place of war and an eleven-point platform that set out methods to end World War I. These were women who did not yet have the right to vote, and forty-seven of them traveled to Europe to an International Congress of Women at the Hague, joining more than a thousand delegates from twelve countries (Bussey and Tims 1980). The English press ridiculed them and suggested "to speak of peace in time of war is to undermine the troops, to be unpatriotic, even to be treasonous" (Stiehm 2006:34), a refrain we would hear fifty, and again nearly a hundred, years later when people who opposed the Vietnam and Iraq wars were again vilified as unpatriotic.

The Hague meeting in April 1915 planted the seeds for the formation of the Women's International League for Peace and Freedom (WILPF). While in Europe, women from the congress traveled in teams to the warring countries speaking with political leaders as well as soldiers returning from the war. On her return to the United States, Addams reported on the congress to a large gathering at Carnegie Hall in New York. Near the end of her speech she described the stories from wounded soldiers, in their own words, on both sides of the European conflict. Having spoken with wounded soldiers returning from the front on trains, she described how they were willing to sacrifice themselves, but were reluctant to kill, and how they often were given or took stimulants before they could charge into battle. The next day the newspapers reported that Addams had dishonored the soldiers "by suggesting they were cowards and drunks" (Stiehm 2006:35). She was vilified by the U.S press for having provided first-person accounts of the destructive nature of war in the voices of the soldiers themselves, an example of the first-person qualitative research for which she was famous. The Women's International League for Peace and Freedom continued and was joined by African American women who saw the irony of African American men fighting in the war for freedoms they themselves did not have in their own country (Chandler 2005; Rief 2004). Eventually, in 1931, Addams was awarded the Nobel Peace Prize for these innovative and courageous actions. WILPF continues as a national and international organization today, joining other peace movements such as Peace Action (known as SANE/Freeze until 1993), to form coalitions around specific peace-related mobilizations such as the movement against the Iraq War. The February 15, 2003 gathering of people against the preemptive invasion of Iraq covered five continents and organized millions of people, including U.S. veterans, and is considered one of the largest antiwar demonstrations ever organized (Porta and Diani 2006).

WATER

Bolivia is a poor but resource-rich landlocked country in South America that has had a stormy political history with frequent changes in leadership and ever wider gaps between rich and poor. In the mid-1980s the International Monetary Fund (IMF) and the World Bank approved loans to Bolivia on the condition that it would sell off its public enterprises (Albro 2005; Klein 2007; Shultz and Draper 2008). The government embraced this neoliberal plan and in the beginning of 2000 negotiated, without any public discussion, the sale of the water sources and systems in the city of Cochabamba to a private company in which Bechtel Corporation of California held a 50 percent interest. Within days of the sale the water rates for the residents of Cochabamba, a city of 900,000, increased more than 200 percent, and rural people, who dug cooperative wells for their communities, were told the new private company also owned their water (Albro 2005; Chavez 2006). These price increases and expropriation of rural water rights caused a major public revolt and brought together "rural farmers, industrial proletariats, disillusioned recent in-migrants, largely invisible members of a growing informal economy, environmentalists, retirees, left-leaning economists and technocrats, as well as sympathetic foreigners, in provincial towns, peripheral shantytowns, and the urban streets, in an ultimately successful and spectacular street level demonstration of popular consensus" (Albro 2005:251).

Violent confrontations occurred in early April 2000. Local rural peasants who used the water for irrigation felt their ancestral rights were being stolen. Some urban residents who had established their own communal wells felt robbed, and those whose water bills increased to 20–30 percent of their monthly income without warning were incensed (Albro 2005). Two Americans, Jim Shultz of the Democracy Center, and Tom Kruse, a researcher with Centro de Estudios para el Desarrollo Laboral y Agrario (CEDLA), agreed to spread the word internationally about the coalition and the Cochabamba "Water War." Even though many Bolivian citizens had become accustomed to government secrecy and the extraction of their minerals and petroleum products by foreign corporations leaving behind very little in improved human development, taking the water was the last straw. The demonstrators swarmed the city center confronting the police. By mid-April, the leaders of the demonstration signed an agreement with the government which annulled the contract with the Bechtel-owned company and returned control of the water system to a regional directorate (Albro 2005; Cuba 2000). The message went out to the antiglobalization movements around the world that "a popular coalition in Bolivia had successfully kicked a transnational corporation out of the country" (Albro 2005:253). Although water is now less expensive and the Bolivians have regained their patrimony, the problems with sufficient and efficient water systems have not been solved for the long term. The Bolivian hydrologist Carlos Fernandez Jaurequi, who is the UNESCO water consultant, suggests that the process for changing the water system in Cochabamba should have involved local people: "Water legislation has to be based on consulting local people, as other laws are. If local culture, customs and ways of life had been taken into account, all these problems could have been avoided" (Cuba 2000:1). Jim Shultz takes a more historical perspective. While Bolivians showed courage in confronting the confiscation of

(continued)

their water system by foreign corporations, creating a new, technologically improved system is more difficult: "Two decades of disassembling state enterprises and putting economic conservatives and foreigners at the reigns has left little opportunity for others [e.g., local Bolivians] to gain the experience they need to govern" (Shultz and Draper 2008:293).

SCOPE OF CONCERN

The scope of concern for this model is in the support of social movements that are working for social, economic, and environmental justice within society and in the world. Historically, progressive social movements have influenced social work, and social workers have provided leadership to social movements (Reisch and Andrews 2001). The basic process described in the next section shows how social workers can become more responsive to positive global processes (e.g., access to information; opportunities to share perspectives on human resources and human rights; access to new technology and health resources) while working to stop or mitigate negative aspects of globalization: oppressive working conditions, including slave labor linked with market forces gone amok; the plundering of the biosphere through overuse and dumping of waste; and the increases in unfair distribution of basic resources and lopsided trade agreements that contribute to the widening gap between the rich and the poor (Korten 2001; Skinner 2008). We also describe the important roles social workers have in promoting the value of diversity in cultural practices, livelihoods, and economic and social patterns while at the same time working for human rights, especially the rights of women and girls. Social workers, particularly community practice social workers, can contribute to new visions and paradigms for the healthy development of people and the planet by recognizing and supporting basic principles of social justice and human rights.

BASIC PROCESS: SEVEN STRATEGY LEVELS

In the previous community practice models, we described critical guiding steps for engagement and practice with groups and communities to illuminate how the work gets accomplished. In this model, we borrow from the work of Richard Estes (1993), who described seven strategy levels for engaging in "sustainable development practice" (16–17). Instead of focusing solely on sustainable development, we focus on the arenas we believe are representative of "Movements for Progressive Change." Estes's seven strategy levels, starting with the "individual and group empowerment" level and going to the "world-building level," provide a hierarchy of opportunities for social workers' engagement in social, economic, and environmental justice movements.

1. Individual and Group Empowerment. The first level of involvement begins with individuals and their identity groups. Identity groups might be a family, cultural, social, or professional group. First, the individual begins to explore within his or her personal group "the contradictions that exist in the social, political, and economic structures intrinsic to all societies" (Estes 1993:16), as well as the contradictions that exist in human rights and environmental well-being. By sharing ideas within a group, the contradictions, injustices, and oppressive conditions can be clarified as the group engages in dialogue about the meanings of these conditions. Individuals can clarify meaning for themselves and examine how much they are part of the problem or solution. Going a step beyond, they can explore the implications for more vulnerable people in the community or more oppressed groups anywhere in the world.

Another aspect of the individual or group level would be to take action on one or several of these contradictions toward a more positive outcome in social, economic, political, human rights, or environmental conditions. This process of learning about contradictions and taking action toward some correction or improved state is called conscientization, a term identified by Paulo Freire (1972). After the individual or group takes action, the next step in the process of conscientization is always a reflection on what happened—"Did anything change because of my, or our, action? Why did change happen? What was expected and unexpected? What new learning came from taking the action? What is the meaning of what happened for me and for the group?"

Students in the United States who were successful in getting their universities to purchase only "fair trade" logo clothing are an example of this strategy level. Another example is that of the students who saw the significant need of residents displaced by Hurricane Katrina and traveled to Mississippi and Louisiana to lend a hand. Students in India who boycott the purchase of Coke and Pepsi products until the production companies stop contaminating the water in the villages surrounding the bottling plants are yet another example. Individuals and groups who put a stop to workplace conversations and artifacts that denigrate people because of race, class, religion, sex, sexual orientation, age, or physical or developmental ability are also taking a stand against social oppression. Also, opportunities to become involved in stopping slave labor—estimated to number in the hundreds of thousands in Africa, 2 million in Europe, Asia, and the Americas, and 10 million in South Asia—are available through activities with antislavery movements (Skinner 2008). Taking action to promote social or economic justice and recognizing that personal agency can result in progressive and positive change help the identity group experience a sense of empowerment.

2. Conflict Resolution. A second level of engagement involves a three-pronged effort for conflict resolution:

- Assisting groups with grievances to negotiate a mutually satisfying understanding
- Facilitating dialogue so that difference can be expressed and heard
- Mediating power imbalances so that groups that have consistently been excluded have a more level playing field to access resources and opportunities

Conflict is a given in human relationships and cannot be avoided or ignored. Instead, understanding why there are differences and how to embrace and celebrate differences that are not harmful should be part of all social work. In all the work social workers do, equity and fairness should be a guiding principle.

The following example comes from the Democratic Republic of the Congo, where civil disturbance has caused hundreds of thousands of refugees to flee to neighboring countries during the last ten years and people are now being repatriated. Upon returning "home," multiple conflicts arose around their resettlement because their properties had been confiscated, and jealousies and rumors were rampant, creating a very complicated and tense situation. To respond to these conditions, the organization Search for Common Ground developed participatory theater for "conflict transformation." The theater troupe, trained in conflict resolution and dialogue techniques, first seeks out informal conversation with all sectors of a community. In these conversations they learn about the conflicts simmering below the surface that could turn volatile. Everyone is invited to come to watch the theater group's presentation later in the day. The theater group develops several scenarios created from their discussions with people in the community. The play begins in a very public setting, often outside. It is based on the actual conflicts within the community. At some point before the scene ends the audience is asked, "What went wrong with the scenario"? What could have been done in another way? How could the situation have taken a different direction? The community members are also asked to become actors and show others how they would have changed the scenario. Afterward more discussion helps people transform their thinking about the conflict situation (Slachmuijlder 2007). Participants in these communities have begun to find common interests that can help move their people forward, but trust building will take many years.

Conflict resolution skills are needed in a variety of direct, group, organizational, and community practice situations. As indicated in earlier chapters, the increase in multicultural societies in all parts of the world because of forced and voluntary migration of populations carries the potential for xenophobic responses and cross-cultural conflict. These conflicts can occur within families, neighborhoods, organizations, communities, and across borders. Social workers should acquire conflict resolution training and have skill in facilitating dialogue so that they can employ these skills at any level of their practice. Training opportunities are offered by many local mediation centers and are also available, for example, through the Community Tool Box, University of Kansas, Section 6 (2008b), a service of the Work Group for Community Health and Development.

3. **Community Building.** Estes (1993) defined community building as the increased participation and social animation of people so that their communities would seek an equitable response to people's social and material needs" Cheryl Walter (2004) describes community building as "conceptualizing and relating to community as an inclusive, complex, and dynamic system, of which we are a part . . . The goal is to build the capacity of the entire system, and all of its participants, to operate as community" (67). Community building assumes that each of us is connected to a complex multidimensional entity that is the context for creating and re-creating ourselves and the social, economic, and environmental milieu that supports us. Kretzmann and McKnight (1993) remind us that citizens in all communities have gifts or assets to contribute toward raising the community to a higher level.

Each of us is part of a neighborhood community, an identity community, a workplace community, a professional community, and a number of other communities. As a community member, we come together with others in relationships and from those experiences we develop a consciousness about who we are, affirming our values and practicing how we will name and label certain things and what stories we will tell to describe ourselves and our associations (Walter 2004:69). In these relationships and associations we both explore and affirm our perceptions about social justice and human rights. We learn how to give meaning to concerns for social, economic, and environmental well-being. We may not always be aware of how we shape meaning for ourselves and influence meaning for others, but we can be sure it is happening in all of our community groups. We can also be certain that the stories, values, and labels emerging from our community relationships are influenced by the social movements that are taking place in the larger society—our region, our country, and the world.

We hear reports of news events and react from our own perspectives. Drawing from our earlier examples, consider how you might react to learning that a child enslaved on a cocoa plantation had picked the cocoa beans used to make your chocolate bar. Or how you might have reacted to hearing that U.S. soldiers in Vietnam, or perhaps in current wars, could easily acquire narcotics in order to numb the sheer terror of possibly having to fire on a young boy or girl, or even another soldier, before they knew for sure the person would not try to kill them. Or consider how you feel about a Bolivian farmer whose communal water well had just been confiscated by a large multinational corporation. You cannot decide to build a community response to every example of social injustice or economic oppression you hear about, but you can reaffirm your values and deepen your understanding about these oppressions and injustices as you relate with others and as you see opportunities to connect with progressive social movements. In this level, consciously deciding to work in support of human rights, social justice, and environmental restoration contributes to building the community of which you are a part.

4. **Institution Building.** At the institution building level, Estes (1993) refers to "the process of humanizing existing social institutions and . . . establishing new institutions that respond more effectively to new or emerging social needs" (16). One example of humanizing an institution, presented in more detail in chapter 8, describes how an individual was able to initiate change in response to people who were living longer with the HIV/AIDS virus because of improved medications. The newly designed program was made more effective because it incorporated the perspectives of those living with HIV/AIDS. We emphasize that the key to developing effective and humane institutions for responding to social problems is in the involvement of those who are directly affected by the problems.

Awareness of those working to humanize institutions and create new responses to need is increasing through the emergence of organizations that champion such actions and the ability to rapidly spread their stories electronically. ASHOKA and the Skoll Foundation, for example, are two organizations that are championing leadership for humane and effective responses to social problems.

Although social work literature has traditionally called a person who initiates or facilitates the development of a new response to social problems a community organizer or community leader, the name used by ASHOKA and the Skoll Foundation is "social entrepreneur" (ASHOKA 2008; Skoll Foundation 2008). Bill Drayton founded ASHOKA in 1981 to identify, support, and widely communicate the success of social entrepreneurs from across the globe (ASHOKA 2008). Each year ASHOKA fellows, who now number 1,800 from sixty different countries, are selected for work they have initiated in six areas: civic engagement, economic development, environment, health, human rights, and education/learning. ASHOKA describes social entrepreneurs as "individuals with innovative solutions for society's most pressing social problem. . . . Rather than leaving societal needs to the government or business sectors, social entrepreneurs find what is not working and solve the problem by changing the system, spreading the solution, and persuading entire societies to take new leaps" (ASHOKA 2008). ASHOKA's selection competition seeks out the most innovative approaches to social change. The Skoll Foundation, created by the first president of eBay, describes the work of social entrepreneurs as those who create "innovative and systemic approaches for meeting the needs of the marginalized, the disadvantaged and the disenfranchised populations that lack the financial means or political clout to achieve lasting benefit on their own" (Skoll Foundation 2008).

Community practice within social work is different from a social entrepreneur in that the knowledge, skills, and value base for community organization and facilitation are grounded in the social work profession. In addition, community organizers, while they stimulate and facilitate community-based solutions to problems, understand that real change will also engage supportive government, political and private sector systems. ASHOKA and the Skoll Foundation identify individual social entrepreneurs who then have the potential advantage of being linked to significant resources and global communication networks.

ASHOKA also introduces new language for the concept we know as community-based or nongovernmental organizations (CBOs and NGOs) by calling them citizen sector organizations (CSOs). Currently, ASHOKA is urging its citizen sector organizations to build their resource base by "generating a diverse income of financial and nonfinancial resources" with the expectation that the organization can become self-supporting. Muhammad Yunus also promotes the diversification of organizations for social betterment he calls social businesses. Yunus describes a variety of types of social businesses that, through fees or paid services, are able to financially support their mission and goals and can even generate profits that would be reinvested in the business (Yunus 2007, 2008). Although social work community organizers promote the ability of community-based organizations to be financially sound and would support their ability to produce income, the appropriate balance between government support, foundation support, financial independence, and financial profit should be maintained with the best interests of the most vulnerable populations in mind.

Problems can and do arise for nonprofit community-based organizations (CBOs) that depend on government and foundation grants to carry on their work. In their effort to write proposals that will be accepted by foundations and government funding sources, the nonprofit organization's mission and goals are sometimes subverted. Often the funding sources become the drivers of the CBO's mission and goals, thwarting the innovative or planned structural changes previously designed with community partners. In a critique of grantmaker practices, Aaron Dorfman, executive director of the National Committee for Responsive

Philanthropy, suggests that foundations should invest in community organizing and policy advocacy if they really want to affect changes in negative social issues (Dorfman 2007–2008). He describes the following example of how funding for community organization and policy advocacy pays off:

> The Polk Ecumenical Action Council for Empowerment, Inc. (PEACE), in Polk County, Florida, won a campaign in 2004 to create a series of health clinics to serve uninsured residents. The first clinic opened November 1, 2007, and is serving 11,000 people. In the next five years, four additional clinics are planned and are expected to serve more than 45,000 people. These clinics are funded by a one-half cent sales tax increase, and the proceeds are dedicated exclusively to funding indigent health care in the county—$37 million per year until 2020. Citrus growers dominate Polk County politics, and the sales tax increase was passed due almost exclusively to the work of the PEACE organization. In the year it won that campaign, PEACE had a budget of approximately $100,000. With foundation investments of $100,000 in direct health services, only a handful of residents would have been served. By funding community organizing, the impact of those foundation investments was exponentially greater. If you count the return on investment . . . [for] all 15 years the tax will be in place ($555 million), and if you assume it took three years for PEACE to build the capacity to win the [tax increase] campaign ($300,000), the return is $1,850 for each dollar invested. This rudimentary calculation doesn't capture the social capital benefits produced by the organization, the economic benefits to the community of a healthier population, or the multiplier effect of the medical spending. Of course, major wins like these don't happen every year for advocacy organizations or community organizing groups. Change takes time, and foundations that want to see significant results need to be willing to invest for the long haul. (Dorfman 2007–2008:4–5)

Whether we call the people who do this work community organizers or social entrepreneurs, and whether we call the organizations that respond to serious human needs community-based, citizen sector, or social businesses, these activities are part of a broad social movement for social justice and human rights.

5. Nation Building. Estes (1993) envisions this level as work that integrates social, economic, cultural, political, and environmental well-being at the national level. Each person can envision ways that their own nation might work toward improved social, economic, political, and environmental well-being. A place to start is to ask where one's country stands on the Universal Declaration of Human Rights and the six additional United Nations covenants and conventions described by the "Ethics in Social Work, Statement of Principles" (IFSW/IASSW 2008). These documents, and three additional declarations, conventions, and protocols described in chapter 11 that speak to the right to development, the right not to be subjected to torture and degrading punishment, and the right against the trafficking in persons, are documents that can only come alive if we social workers help move them forward for public discussion in our communities and in our countries.

For example, in the United States there is hard work ahead to promote public discussion about why our country has not yet ratified the Convention on the Rights of the Child, the Convention on the Elimination of all Forms of Discrimination against Women (CEDAW), and the UN Declaration on the Right to Development. Having open and public debates about these conventions, which came into force in the world community in 1990, 1981, and 1986, respectively, would be an important step forward. Moving these conventions and declarations toward ratification in the U.S. Senate can be nation-building work on the part of U.S. social workers.

In addition to human rights issues, we community practice social workers can compare our country's standing in the Human Poverty Index (UNDP 2007) described in chapter 7 and examine factors such as opportunities to have a long and healthy life, education, a livelihood that provides a decent standard of living, and the absence of social exclusion, to determine where our national policies need to be improved. Social movements that are working to help low-income citizens develop assets, livelihoods within alternative economic systems, and fair wages can provide opportunities for social workers to engage in nation-building work.

6. Region Building. Estes (1993) recognizes the importance of regionally integrated social, economic, and cultural institutions. Thinking in terms of world regions begins to blur national borders, as is happening with the European Union. The interconnectedness of regional and global institutions has an extensive literature among those writing about both the positive and negative outcomes of globalization. In their *International Policy Statement on Globalization and the Environment*, the International Federation of Social Workers states:

A more integrated world community brings both benefits and problems for all; it affects the balance of economic, political and cultural power between nations, communities and individuals and it can both enhance and limit freedoms and human rights. Social workers, by the nature of their work, tend to meet those who are more likely to have suffered the damaging consequences of some aspects of globalisation. (International Federation of Social Workers 2008)

In all of our regional settings, social workers will generally be more knowledgeable of and sensitive to interactions with their immediate neighboring countries. Citizens of countries in the European Union will be more knowledgeable about the integration of educational, agricultural, industrial, and monetary systems across their region. In each regional area of the world, people are affected by both the cooperative efforts among their governments and those economic, social, environmental, and political tensions that can prevent progressive policy implementation and unravel into full-blown conflicts. In the United States we are closest to the interconnections with our Mexican and Canadian neighbors.

One issue to examine in our regional effort to improve social, economic, and environmental well-being might be to examine U.S. trade agreements with Mexico. Looking at the recent significant Mexican migration into the United States, described in chapter 11, may require a deeper analysis of bilateral and multilateral trade agreements as well as alternative development strategies that might have been employed. In 1994 the governments of the United States, Canada, and Mexico signed the North American Free Trade Agreement (NAFTA). A deep analysis of this agreement is beyond the scope of this book, but some economists question NAFTA's ability to assist a developing country like Mexico move toward a higher Human Development Index, and believe the agreement should have contained more language and provisions for "fair trade" and fewer provisions for pseudo "free trade." Stiglitz and Charlton's (2006) analysis suggests that "inequality and poverty both increased under NAFTA, and by the end of the decade, Mexico was losing to China many of the jobs that had been created since the signing of the agreement" (11). They describe three lessons from observing the U.S./Mexico trade experience since NAFTA:

- Trade liberalization by itself clearly does not ensure growth. . . . Mexico suffered from low levels of innovation . . . poor regulatory effectiveness and high levels of corruption.
- Mexico fared poorly in competition with China [because] China was able to invest heavily in infrastructure and education.
- NAFTA was not really a free trade agreement. NAFTA pitted the heavily subsidized U.S. agribusiness sector against peasant producers and family farms in Mexico [allowing U.S. exports into Mexico] at costs far below those of the local market, driving down prices for local farmers [and using] non-tariff barriers to keep out some of Mexico's products. (Stiglitz and Charlton 2006:11–12)

Instead of some of the NAFTA provisions that clearly protect corporate agribusiness and maquiladora investors (e.g., factories in Mexico that assemble consumer export products), collaborative agreements between Mexico and the United States could have been negotiated to expand and improve rural educational models (such as those currently used in Colombia), promote sustainable agricultural (such as practices that could decrease a farmer's need for petroleum-based fertilizers), and provide legal assistance to help strengthen regulatory institutions and diminish corruption. We should have looked for regional "best practices" to boost the social, economic, and environmental well-being of people in Mexico, Canada, and the United States instead of what was best for multinational corporations. What was needed was a sensible cooperative plan between Mexico and the United States whereby both countries could contribute something to social, economic, and environmental well-being, allowing Mexican citizens to be real partners in the planning. These are not dreamy-eyed notions; they are simply different approaches stimulated by a set of values that put people's well-being ahead of corporate profits and that invest in long-term social, economic, and environmental improvements. There are many alternative economic and human rights social movements from which to draw wisdom and strength for this kind of work (Cavanagh and Mander 2004; Hawken, Lovins, and Lovins 1999; Henderson 1996; Pollan 2008; Prigoff 2000; Shiva 2005).

7. **World Building.** Estes (1993) expects social workers also to have a role in this highest level strategy of world building. The expectation is that we engage in "the process of working toward the establishment of a new system of international social, political, economic, and ecological relationships guided by the quest for world peace, increased social justice, the universal satisfaction of basic human needs, and protection of the planet's fragile ecosystem" (17).

Part of the world moves forward on these progressive, long-term goals, and another part, working from a different set of values, pushes for a strategy in which freedom is equated with freedom of market forces to solve problems, even to solve problems such as global warming on a voluntary basis. Each side has its strong proponents and examples of success. To explore this deep division of perspectives and to reckon with the significant role the United States has for leadership in these goals, we draw from the words of Peter L. Pellett, professor emeritus of nutrition at the University of Massachusetts, Amherst. In 1999 he spoke to the United Nations Standing Committee on Nutrition (SCN), at a symposium discussing the relationship between human rights and issues of hunger and malnutrition. In effect, he was speaking to Estes's call for "universal satisfaction of basic human needs." He focused on the Declaration of the Right to Development as the instrument that the world community could use to promote programs against hunger. Part of his message follows:

> In the 1986 [UN] General Assembly vote on the Declaration of the Right to Development . . . there were a few abstentions and one vote against by the United States. Nevertheless, at the World Conference on Human Rights, the International Conference on Population and Development, the World Summit on Social Development, the Fourth World Conference on Women and the World Food Summit, the right to development was reaffirmed in declarations adopted by consensus.

Probably, therefore, this right exists (UNHCHR 1997, 1998), albeit not in international treaties and in consequence, the UNDP has adopted the concept of such a right in its development activities. The United States [through their representatives to the UN], in line with their negative vote in 1986, regards the socio-economic rights of the Universal Declaration as having no status. They are, in the words of former UN Ambassador Jeane Kirkpatrick, "a letter to Santa Claus"; "Neither nature, experience, nor probability informs these lists of 'entitlements', which are subject to no constraints except those of the mind and appetite of their authors." On the right to development, Washington's ambassador informed the UN Commission on Human Rights that these are not rights: the proposals "seem preposterous" and even "a dangerous incitement." (Kirkpatrick, J. 1981. *Establishing a Viable Human Rights Policy*. Third World Traveler; Chomsky, N. 1999. *Profit over People*. New York: Seven Stories Press).

An important question thus remains: is there any reality to a right to development when such a right has no basis in international law and is not recognized by the United States, whose financial power and global interests are sufficient to inhibit its application? It appears then, that in the view of the United States a right to development is superfluous since the global free market is the ultimate answer to all development issues. Not all would agree. John Gray, of the London School of Economics (1998), summarizes his concerns about globalization:

> A global free market . . . resembles that other twentieth century experiment in Utopian social engineering, Marxian socialism. Each was convinced that human progress must have a single civilization as its goal. Each denied that a modern economy can come in many varieties. Each was ready to exact a large price in suffering from humanity in order to impose its single vision on the world. Each has run aground on vital human needs. (Gray, J. 1998. *False Dawn: The Delusions of Global Capitalism. Granta*, London, 235)

(Pellett 1999)

One has to wonder how prescient both the words of Pellett and Gray were now as we watch the unfolding of the economic crisis of 2008, not ten years after these observations. Would our world have been more secure if the United States had taken a more pro-development, pro-human rights approach in its foreign aid support and leadership? Would we have met more of the basic needs of the world population if we had allowed a variety of economic experiments to flourish rather than cookie-cutter capitalism and communism?

These contrasting ideas about how to understand rights and how to approach the basic needs of humanity, and the additional goals of the quest for world peace, increased social justice and the protection of the biosphere, form the content of discussion currently engaging movements for progressive change. These discussions should also be part of the curriculum of schools of social work. Some social work organizations and collaborative organizations are deeply involved in the efforts to improve social, economic, and environmental well-being. How, for example, should social work students and social work curricula respond to the following urgent call from Save the Children UK?

Save the Children is calling on developing country governments and international donors to:

- invest in free healthcare, clean water and sanitation, support for women's education and action against poverty
- convene a global summit on child and maternal hunger bringing together governments, international institutions, the private sector and civil society to inspire action
- agree to clear targets focused on the impact of their policies on maternal and child health and nutrition. It is impossible to make progress without facts, openness and clarity
- tackle inequality as part of the Millennium Development Goals by including a target of halving the gap in child mortality between the richest and poorest 20%. (Save the Children UK News 2008)

Or how might community practice social workers already working in the field respond to this call from the International Federation of Social Workers on how to engage with the negative effects of globalization:

IFSW's interpretation of how development programs should proceed: . . . social development programs, whether linked to structural adjustment or other emergency economic recovery programs, must have the following elements:

- Education and lifelong learning programs
- Supportive work programs for those whose physical, mental or emotional problems or caring responsibilities prevent them from taking standard jobs,
- Social protection to sustain those unable to raise income through work, with annual targets to reduce poverty
- Respect for the UN Conventions on Human Rights and the Rights of the Child and arrangements to promote the education and welfare of children
- Consultation with local communities and civil society organizations and the active involvement of "excluded" individuals and communities in decisions which affect them. (IFSW, Globalization Statement 2008)

In each of these seven levels or strategies to engage with progressive social movements, we can choose to engage from a personal, group, organizational, community, national, regional, or global perspective. We can contribute social work's collective wisdom toward improved social, economic, and environmental well-being on multiple levels. It will require extra effort to listen and learn from many different voices and the willingness to move beyond our comfort zones to affirm personal and political values.

THEORIES AND CONCEPTS THAT GROUND THE MODEL

Theory streams that inform this model include *collective behavior; social constructionist theory and frame analysis; social identity; social change;* and *new social movement theory.* These theory streams are discussed in greater detail in chapter 4 and overlap with other models, especially chapter 6, organizing functional communities, chapter 10, coalitions, and chapter 11, political and social action. The conceptual understandings derived from these theories that we feel are most useful to community practice social work for engaging with movements for progressive change are as follows:

- Coalitions and collaborations for social justice and human rights.
- Diversity and Unity: engaging in transformative experiences and practices that recognize the value of diversity in cultural, economic, and political institutions while building toward more unified common goals that provide improved social, economic, and environmental well-being for everyone on the planet.

COALITIONS AND COLLABORATIONS FOR SOCIAL JUSTICE AND HUMAN RIGHTS

Although we have discussed coalitions and the process of collaboration in chapter 10, understanding these processes relates to movements for progressive change as well. A social movement is the broader and deeper manifestation of the coming together of a number of coalitions and interest groups for a common purpose. Diverse coalitions networked by a broader concern united on February 15, 2003, to demonstrate against the United States' planned invasion of Iraq; this is considered the largest antiwar demonstration in history as it took place in 800 cities across the world (CNN.com February 16, 2003; Porta and Diani 2006). Although an event does not necessarily constitute a movement, the ability to bring together such a large demonstration grew from existing social justice and human rights groups already working against the negative aspects of globalization and militaristic responses to conflict.

New social movement theory indicates that social movements are more likely to establish linkages with civil society organizations and cross-national networks rather than revolutionary groups and ideological party politics (Nash 2005). Coalitions that network and become movements are more like the fair trade and peace movements described at the beginning of this chapter, where civil society groups connect across borders to affirm their common concerns, even though their origins might be quite diverse. Estes (1993) described the emergence of the Movement for Sustainable Development that grew from the dissatisfaction with fifty years of failed international development strategies, as well as progressive feminist, indigenous peoples, human rights, antinuclear, ecological, and green movements. Concern for global warming, beginning with scientific evidence and broadening to sustainable agriculture, forest ecology, and anticonsumer groups, now ties into the broader networks of alternative and solidarity economics, biomimicry, appropriate technology, and green building. Indeed, Paul Hawken (2007), in his recent book, *Blessed Unrest*, describes the book's purpose as telling "the story without apologies of what is going *right* on this planet, narratives of imagination and conviction, not defeatist accounts about the limits. Wrong is an addictive, repetitive story; Right is where the movement is" (4). Hawken's Web site hosts an interactive Internet catalog, WiserEarth, which provides opportunities to learn about and network with hundreds of thousands of coalitions and civil society groups working toward social justice, human rights, and environmental preservation all across the globe (WiserEarth 2009).

DIVERSITY AND UNITY

The most interesting and perhaps elusive nature of new social movements is how very diverse organizations can come together for a unified purpose when the need arises. The recognition and respect of diversity is a basic social work value incorporated in definitions of social justice in the NASW Code of Ethics (2008) and the IFSW/IASSW "Ethics in Social Work, Statement of Principles" (2008).

Studies in ecology and biology have shown us the value of diversity in ponds, forests, soils, insects—indeed, the necessity of biodiversity to sustain human societies (Pimentel, Westra, and Noss 2000). Humans have struggled with transferring this knowledge of the essential nature of biodiversity to the need for diversity in institutions created by human societies. Human inventions of culture, economic institutions, and political institutions are different in every corner of the globe. Krishna Guadalupe (2003) suggests that "human diversity can generally be defined as human differences, influenced by the interplay of cognitive, physical, social, and/or spiritual variables, to make each person unique and un-duplicated" (22). The patterns of how we develop and confer knowledge, beliefs, and behaviors, the values we assign to materials and social institutions, as well as our patterns of selecting leaders and making rules for social organization are all very different. However, since the classical civilizations beginning in 3500 B.C.E., and continuing into the rise of nations and on to the present, we have tended to see these differences as reasons to conquer and oppress rather than to celebrate and collaborate (Swimme and Berry 1994).

Only in the last half century, for example, have we begun to appreciate the value of difference resulting from feminist and ethnic studies. Emerging from patriarchal and Western frames of knowledge and understanding, we have come to appreciate the wisdom of women's and ethnic and indigenous people's ways of knowing and being (La Duke 2005; McAdoo 1993; Taylor and Kennedy 2003). More importantly, we have come to realize that each individual woman and each individual indigenous person has unique qualities while also having common qualities with their respective identity groups as well as with all human beings. Building on the knowledge and ways of understanding the planet that men and women everywhere contribute would be in keeping with the social work value of the dignity of persons.

In the new social movements, we are seeing diversity in the cross-border coalitions that come together to challenge the meetings of institutions deemed representative of everything negative about globalization—economic, political, social and cultural exclusion, and oppression. Old and young, male and female, workers and students, peasant farmers from the Philippines and farmers from the United States, scientists from India and indigenous peoples from Brazil, they all came together in Seattle in November 1999 to demonstrate against globalization's negative effects on the environment, on small farmers, on workers' wages, the loss of cultural and seed diversity, and the widening gap between rich and poor. These collaborations are transformative experiences as people learn to value the diverse experiences and perspectives of each other while working toward unified life-affirming goals. The coming together of diverse groups may be what Swimme and Berry (1994) describe as the new Ecozoic era—a time when earth and humans are mutually enhanced by their relationships. They justify the use of the word *universe* to emphasize that "the diversity of things exists not in separation but in a comprehensive unity whereby all things are bonded together in inseparable and everlasting unity" (266). It just may be that when connecting to the new social movements the appropriate greeting could be one used by the Vulcans in an episode of *Star Trek*—"Greetings? I am pleased to see we are different. May we together become greater than the sum of both of us" (quoted in Anderson and Carter 2003:v).

SOCIAL WORK/COMMUNITY PRACTICE ROLES

In the first half of the twentieth century, social workers made up part of the leadership of progressive social movements, and in turn these movements influenced the values and approaches of the profession (Reisch and Andrews 2001). We identify three potential roles for community practice social workers as they connect with new social movements that are based in progressive social, economic, and environmental change. These roles, defined in chapter 2 and discussed in relation to previously described models, are:

- Advocate
- Facilitator
- Leader

There are many potential issues, local to global, that may serve as arenas for work in new social movements. For example, the issues of prison populations and the rate of incarceration are of particular concern in the United States and may also apply to other countries. According to a report from the Pew Center on the States, the United States has incarcerated 2.3 million people as of January 1, 2008, more than China's 1.5 million and Russia's 890,000 (Pew Center on the States:2008). What makes the problem in the United States worse is the disproportionate numbers of people of color who are in jail: one in nine Black men ages 20 to 34; one in fifteen Black men ages 18 or older; one in thirty-six Hispanic men, ages 18 or older; and one in 100 Black women ages 35 to 39. These data raise questions about the options available for treatment of prisoners while they are incarcerated, and the many options for community based programs such as drug court programs, ankle monitors, and daily reporting centers for nonviolent offenders. Most importantly, one must question the disproportionate rate of people of color among those incarcerated and how social and economic resources can be redirected to keep young men and women out of prison in the first place. Perhaps the Books Not Bars project spearheaded by Van Jones at the Ella Baker Center for Human Rights in Oakland, California, could be the catalyst that starts a movement all across our country to invest in the social and economic well-being of families whose children might have been destined for these jails (Ella Baker Center 2008). Watch for the opportunity to get involved or to become a leader on this issue.

Several huge global issues—global warming, which is an environmental threat, and nuclear proliferation, which is a political and humanitarian threat—could also be choices for involvement (Peace Action 2008; Redefining Progress 2008a). These issues have ongoing international, national, and local organizations that provide social workers opportunities to work as advocates, facilitators, or leaders in progressive social movements.

We have chosen the issue of poverty to identify and explore these three roles for the movements for progressive change model. The following data provide reasons for the sense of urgency associated with poverty:

- There are more than 1 billion people—one in six people around the world— who live in extreme poverty, which is defined as living on less than $1 a day.
- More than 800 million people go hungry each day.
- Over 100 million primary school-age children cannot go to school.
- Over half of the world's population—3 billion people—lives on less than US$2 per day.
- Every year, 6 million children die from malnutrition before their fifth birthday.
- Over 11 million children die each year from preventable causes such as malaria, diarrhea, and pneumonia. (Catholic Relief Services Food Fast 2008; Global Issues 2009; Micro Finance Enterprises 2009)

There is a social movement working to cut these devastating numbers in half by the year 2015. You could be part of this movement for progressive change. What can you do as an advocate?

The role of *advocate* is that of a person who is informed on the issues, has adopted a position based on information and social justice and human rights values, and engages in purposeful discussion and activities. Engagement in discussions and activities is for the purpose of improving social, economic, and environmental well-being for everyone, but especially for the most vulnerable populations. As an advocate, you can become very well informed about global and national poverty by researching data from Mercy Corps/Net Aid, Oxfam America, RESULTS, UNICEF, from the UN Millennium Development Goals status reports or the UN *Human Development Reports*. There is no shortage of information about these issues or effective strategies to cut these numbers in half by the year 2015. You may be more interested in working on local or regional poverty, or you may be inspired to work on global poverty. Either way, this social movement needs advocates to help others understand the data and the most effective poverty alleviation strategies available. We can all lend a hand to a social movement already in progress.

One very important place the United States needs advocates now is with our own government. The Millennium Development Goals (MDGs) were established in the year 2000 by agreement of nearly all the world's governments. One aspect of these goals was to cut extreme poverty in half by the year 2015. In addition, the goals included indicators to diminish hunger and gender inequalities, prevent and treat HIV/AIDS, TB, and other diseases, provide health care, clean water, and education, and protect the environment (chapter 1, table 1.1). It was estimated that in order to reach the established goals the poor countries themselves would have to make some investments, but the industrial world would have to double their investment in poor countries to $135 billion by 2006 and increase it to $195 billion by 2015. In addition to these aid investments, the developed world should change the trade rules so that the world would be governed by "fair trade" and policies would have to be approved to provide debt relief for the countries with the lowest Human Development Index. These investments needed from countries that have developed economies seem small when compared with the $600 billion the United States alone had invested in the Afghanistan and Iraq wars as of September 2007 (Bilmes 2008; Congressional Budget Office February 2008), or the more than $700 billion being made available to rescue national banking and Wall Street financial institutions. The financial crisis of 2008 requires even greater attention and support for low-wealth countries from the countries with greatest wealth and should not be used to put the Millennium Development Goals on hold.

At the halfway point toward reaching the goals, the United States has made some contribution to provide assistance for HIV/AIDS and some economic growth, but has not stepped up to the plate to help in significant ways.

Among the twenty-two countries in the Organization for Economic Cooperation and Development (OECD), only Norway, Sweden, Luxembourg, Denmark, and the Netherlands are providing development assistance at levels above the target of .7 percent of gross national income (GNI) promised by developed countries in 1970. The United States, providing only .16 percent of its gross national income in 2007, was the least generous of the twenty-two developed countries (Global Issues 2009). Advocates for cutting the numbers of poor in half by 2015 could help our government leaders understand that development assistance is important to preserve international security as well as to respond to humanitarian needs (Oxfam America 2008; Staub-Bernasconi 2007).

Supporting efforts to alleviate poverty at a community and statewide level by disseminating information about effective local poverty reduction strategies is an equally important advocacy activity. Programs to give the poor a hand-up such as child care subsidies, health care, adult education classes, extended unemployment support, Individual Development Accounts (IDAs), and living wages all need advocates in the United States.

A *facilitator* works with an organization that has already been established and helps its leadership and members become more efficient and effective in carrying out their mission and reaching their goals. The facilitator helps organizational members and leaders clarify the issues, understand the strategies for change, and examine the outcomes by asking hard and deep questions about eliminating social injustice, economic exclusion or oppression, and environmental degradation. In the case of global poverty, a facilitator might work with one of the advocacy organizations collaborating to support the reduction in poverty, or they might work with a host country community-based organization (CBO) in one of the countries where these poverty statistics are starkly visible. The effort should be a partnership with developing country organizations working side by side and providing the cultural context. Poor countries and their CBOs have the responsibility to develop plans with goals and objectives for poverty alleviation strategies and good governance practices that would eliminate corruption and waste. Working with a host country CBO or a government agency to help meet these expectations would be an important effort in facilitation. Working as a facilitator in an international setting with a local CBO is possible through many international organizations (e.g., Mercy Corps, Oxfam, World Neighbors, Peace Corps).

A community practice facilitator may prefer to work with poverty alleviation strategies planned by nonprofit or government-funded programs in their own country. A number of organizations in the United States work on asset development (e.g., IDAs), on alternative or solidarity economics programs such as cooperatives, on new green building and green entrepreneurial projects and on rural development projects such as sustainable agriculture. All of these kinds of organizations have the potential to decrease poverty on a local level and can benefit from skilled facilitators.

The role of *leader* is that of guide and director of the organization as defined above. The leader in community practice is cognizant of developing or "growing" new leadership and training a diverse and deep group of leaders who serve in a variety of capacities. As is true of the advocate, a leader must have done the research to know the issues well. With regard to global poverty and the Millennium Development Goals, studies indicate that U.S. citizens believe the U.S. government should be helping with global poverty. Currently, the United States spends less than one half of 1 percent of its federal budget on aid to poor countries. Survey data show that Americans erroneously believe we are spending 24 percent of the federal budget on aid to poor countries and that we should cut it back to 10 percent (OECD 2009; Singer 2009). This discrepancy between reality and public perception could be a useful opening to help people in your personal group, your organization, and your community understand how to move in a more progressive direction in our relationships with the rest of the world's population.

InterAction, the American Council for Voluntary International Action, laments the fact that, although "there are more than 26 US government agencies involved in foreign assistance, there is no overarching strategy or programmatic coordination of goals . . . [resulting] in inefficiencies, particularly in the area of food aid" (InterAction Press Release, October 18, 2007). Leadership in the area of reducing global poverty is both urgent and essential for moral as well as national interest and global security reasons. The oppression of poverty, affecting every aspect of the lives of poor family members in its total destruction of abilities and opportunities, can be alleviated. This is a movement for progressive change for which we social workers should all provide some leadership.

CORE SKILLS AND COMPETENCIES USED IN MOVEMENTS FOR PROGRESSIVE CHANGE

As in earlier chapters, we are listing the primary skills and competencies expected for working in this model, recognizing that many more skills need to be gained in order to do this kind of work effectively. We list the skills and raise the questions for personal assessment. It is up to community practice social workers to explore their own knowledge, skills, and abilities, and to develop a plan for gaining the practice necessary to be efficient, effective, and ethical. The skills we have identified for this model and assessment questions are as follows:

COLLABORATION AND BUILDING NETWORKS

- What experience do I have in helping groups with different structures and memberships come together around a common concern?
- How do social work values and ethics guide my involvement with movements for progressive change?
- Where do natural collaborations exist that would increase the power and effectiveness of people toward specific goals focused on improved social, economic, and environmental well-being?

FACILITATION

- Do I have sufficient cross-cultural knowledge and skills to be able to contribute to organization building in a country other than my own? in a community different from my own?
- Do I have the patience to work outside my own cultural, social, and political comfort zones to help unite groups interested in making changes to diminish social, economic, and environmental injustice.
- How can I help local groups identify indicators of progress within their social, economic, and environmental contexts?

- Am I sufficiently knowledgeable about and open to participatory evaluation methods so that I can help an organization track its progress and accomplishments?

LEADERSHIP

- Do my personal skills lend themselves to some form of leadership in progressive movements for social change?
- Am I committed to "growing" leadership within organizations so that all kinds of people can become part of the empowered movement for social justice, economic opportunity, and environmental restoration and protection?
- Will I be able to receive critical feedback about my leadership so that I can continue to grow in my ability to direct the organizations in which I work?
- Am I sufficiently grounded in social work values and ethics that I will not lose my way in the work toward social justice and human rights?

The answers to these questions only provide opportunities to plan the next level of knowledge and skill development. Michael Reisch (2008) affirms the connection between social work and new social movements in the recent edition of the *Encyclopedia of Social Work*, where he states:

A consistent thread connecting New Social Movements with social work is that both are linked, philosophically and practically, to the expansion of democracy and the promotion of social justice globally. . . . social workers can help expose the consequences of globalization and develop viable alternatives to existing institutional arrangements. This will require greater imagination, flexibility, and adaptability in defining and addressing new and persistent social issues. . . . [as well as clarifying] the meaning of social justice in an increasingly globalized and multicultural environment. (8)

CONCLUSIONS

This chapter focused on social work community practice involvement in movements for progressive change. We have outlined the need for social work advocacy, facilitation, and leadership in some of the major global concerns of our times, especially poverty, human rights, social justice, and efforts for peace. Social workers have a history and knowledge base to be able to contribute to these global concerns, all of which also have local and regional manifestations. The conditions that contribute to poverty and social and economic oppression are embedded in many of our existing institutions, norms, and practices at all levels of political and social organizations. Although these thick layers of opposition may seem overpowering as one explores their nature, they also present the opportunity to work at every level identified by Estes in developing strategies for social change. There is no shortage of opportunities.

The Global Service Institute (2008), established by the Ford Foundation in 2001, focuses on the range of civic service models scattered around the planet. The research and information agendas of the GSI are located at the Center for Social Development at Washington University in St. Louis, which has begun to build on research and policy knowledge to help social workers, development experts, and policy makers become more grounded in how to frame and measure civic service efforts (McBride and Sherraden 2004). We look to this source as a helpful base from which to draw knowledge about movements for progressive change in the future.

We challenge social work education and social workers to engage in these issues. Every hungry child, every dislocated family, every girl child denied the right to attend school, every woman raped in war, every child sold into slavery, every man denied a living wage, every forest decimated, every stream polluted demand our response.

13

THE CHALLENGES FOR COMMUNITY PRACTICE AHEAD

I have almost reached the regrettable conclusion that the Negro's great stumbling block in his stride toward freedom is not the . . . Ku Klux Klanner, but the white moderate, who is more devoted to "order" than to justice; who prefers a negative peace, which is the absence of tension, to a positive peace, which is the presence of justice.

THE REV. DR. MARTIN LUTHER KING JR., "LETTER FROM A BIRMINGHAM JAIL," APRIL 16, 1963

Poverty, social isolation/exclusion, environmental degradation and violent conflict undermine the opportunity to make the most of human rights and are an affront to human dignity. They limit the life chances of those in poverty and inhibit their opportunity for personal fulfillment.

IFSW POLICY STATEMENT ON GLOBALIZATION AND THE ENVIRONMENT, 2008

THE PURPOSES OF THIS BOOK

It is our intent to inspire and prepare you to become a community practice social worker in the twenty-first century in the United States or anywhere in the world these models can be appropriately applied considering the local context and needs. Throughout the book we provided scenarios for you to consider how and when to become involved with community practice. To help clarify the possibilities, we have organized the approaches into eight different models, with the opportunity to compare them along five characteristics. Comparison of discrete characteristics helps you to see the likely outcome for each of the different approaches. In addition, we have provided many descriptions of current real-world examples as well as guidance for building your knowledge and skills for this work. We hope you will become as inspired as we are for the work ahead.

INSPIRATION Some people are inspired by the nature of the problems, notably their inhumanity and their enormity. Others are inspired by the ongoing work of nonprofit, nongovernmental organizations and the courageous and effective work of their leaders and coalitions. We are definitely inspired by both.

It is sometimes overwhelming to face the degree of violence and inhumanity we see daily reported in the newspapers. Yet, some stories cut so deeply into our hearts they are part of the motivation to keep going in this work. Two examples come from the yellowed newspaper clippings one author keeps on her desk. Each story is accompanied with a photograph, and the eyes of the victims pictured drill into the psyche. These stories are from 2006 and seem too poignant to be thrown away.

The first story is from the *New Mexican,* written by Amanda Lee Myers on March 15, 2006. It tells of Juan Cruz-Torralva, an undocumented immigrant, who lived in California with his wife and 2-year-old son. With his situation somewhat stabilized, he returned to Mexico to bring his 12-year-old daughter, Lourdes, to the United States. She had been left behind in the care of her grandparents when Cruz-Torralva first came to California, but now both grandparents are ill and unable to care for her. Although the trip would be arduous and dangerous, he thought she was old enough to make it, and would have a chance for a good education in the United States. The father and daughter crossed back into the United States at the Arizona-Mexican border, and as they made their way across the desert with a group of immigrants a border patrol agent spotted them. In the process of following the group in his truck, the agent accidentally ran over Cruz-Torralva and his daughter. Lourdes was killed, and Cruz-Torralva's back was severely injured. He was arrested and initially charged with child endangerment for causing the death of his daughter by bringing her into the United States clandestinely. Later, the charges were dropped, and plans were made to deport him. At the jail, where he spoke in his indigenous language through an interpreter, a tearful Cruz-Torralva, who did not know where they had taken his daughter's body, said, "My daughter is dead, and my mom and dad are sick. I've been in jail for a week, I don't have any money, and I'm in pain. I just want to leave this place and never come back" (Myers 2006:C6).

A second story appeared in the *New York Times* on October 29, 2006, written by Sharon LaFraniere. She describes the life of Mark Kwadwo, who spends his life working on a fishing boat on Lake Volta in Ghana. Mark is 6 years old, barely able to carry the wooden boat paddle, and works an average of 14 hours a day. He and other boys working with this fishing company were "leased" to the company for about $20 a year by their parents, who were too poor to continue to feed them. The boys sleep in a shanty with a dirt floor. In the picture accompanying the story, Mark is standing in the fishing boat and does indeed look like an "oversized toddler," just as LaFraniere describes him. These two stories give us a small window into the immense pain caused by poverty and oppression that we must address in social work and community practice.

These two stories inspire with their pain. Other stories, such as the one of Jaime Lerner and his leadership of the humane development of Curitiba, Brazil, or the story of the Ethiopian HIV/AIDS workers in chapter 9, or the stories of Majora Carter and Van Jones on the two coasts of the United States working to turn abandoned people and neighborhoods into thriving, environmentally restored communities—these are stories that inspire with courage and wisdom.

In addition to the stories of current courage and leadership that frame how community practice can improve social, economic, and environmental well-being, we also have the stories of people who came before us, our historic leaders who believed there was a better way and spent their lives showing us how. We think of Jane Addams, Sojourner Truth, Mohandas Gandhi, Martin Luther King Jr., Whitney Young, and many others whose names we will never know, but whose shoulders provided the support for many that we do know.

PREPARATION Our eight-model structure is intended to simplify your own work by giving you a framework for comparisons. It will not provide the full extent of the possibilities to do community practice, but it will allow you to make comparisons between eight different models we believe are dominant models in our own country, as well as many countries around the world. No two settings or contexts for community practice will be alike, so the community practice worker must be knowledgeable, ethical, skilled, and wise, in addition to being flexible and humble. Making judgments while supporting and guiding groups in their efforts to improve social, economic, human rights, and environmental conditions in their community, region, country or the world at large, requires all of these attributes.

The rationale for doing this work is drawn from our national and international codes of ethics, as well as from the knowledge we have about oppression, exclusion, poverty, and environmental degradation and from the examples we have for overcoming those same destructive forces through purposeful organizing, planning, sustainable development, collaboration, and action for progressive change. For each model we provided windows to the work through examples, guiding steps to consider, conceptual understandings to deepen your knowledge base, roles normally taken by people doing work in the model, and core skills and competencies to develop in preparation for the work. In addition we shared the theoretical underpinnings that inform the work to be done in each model, and we provided insight into the major forces that will affect community practice work in the next century—increases in multicultural societies, globalization, and human rights, especially rights for women and girls.

In this summary chapter, we discuss general challenges that can place barriers and detours in your work. We also discuss factors we believe will provide "the wind on your back," supportive forces that can help as you engage in this sometimes difficult but very rewarding work.

CHALLENGES FOR ENGAGEMENT IN COMMUNITY PRACTICE IN THIS CENTURY

A number of forces may interfere with the progressive work community practice social workers will do in the years ahead. Some of these are old and enduring problems that we have faced since work in communities began. They are the deeply embedded problems of racism, sexism, multicultural conflict, human rights violations at all levels of society, and poverty. Others are more recently acknowledged problems such as environmental degradation and global warming. Both the old and the new problems are created by human relationships, organizations, institutions, and production. They can only be solved with equally energetic efforts by human creativity. Community practice has developed a knowledge base, a set of methods, research and evaluation reports, ethical standards, and professional organizations to do its part to overcome these formidable challenges.

OLD AND ENDURING PROBLEMS

Racism, sexism, multicultural conflict, human rights violations, and poverty are embedded in our social and economic fabric from north to south and east to west. The worst outcome for these negative social and economic creations is violence, which in all its forms is costly and prevents the human community from making progress. The continuum of violence described by Jane Crosby and Dorothy Van Soest (1997) for the NASW Project on Violence and Development included three types of threats to "personal security and social stability":

- *Structural,* including "avoidable deprivations built into the structure of society and based on the norms and traditions that subjugate one group in favor of another."
- *Institutional,* including "harmful acts by organizations and institutions (e.g., oppression, unequal treatment under law, police brutality, torture) and official forms of violence (e.g., state-sponsored repression, war, and invasion)."
- *Personal,* including "interpersonal acts of violence against persons or property (e.g., rape, murder, muggings), harmful acts against self (e.g., alcohol and drug abuse, suicide), and acts by organized groups or mobs (e.g., hate crimes, looting, rioting)." (Crosby and Van Soest 1997:3).

Violence in any of its forms—whether state sponsored or domestic, whether caused by development principles based on greed, racial, ethnic, and gender violence based on superiority, or the oppressive nature of poverty—diminishes the resources and opportunities for optimum human development (Van Soest 1997).

Poverty is often described as one of the cruelest forms of violence. Current estimates hold that half the world's population lives on less than $2 a day (Oxfam America 2008; Wronka 2007). Every day 25,000 children die from preventable causes, most of them due to poverty (UNICEF 2009).

Those of us living in relative affluence and security have become inured to the idea that more than 6 million children in the world die every year from preventable diseases and hunger (Catholic Relief Services Food Fast 2008; Micro Finance Enterprises 2009), that 72 million school-age children have never seen the inside of a classroom (RESULTS 2008b), and that trillions of dollars are spent on state-sponsored conflict and civil wars as though we have no alternative. From a recent UNDP report, we learned that the richest 500 individuals in the world have a combined income greater than that of the poorest 416 million people (UNDP 2005). The eloquent words of Nelson Mandela make clear the connection that exists between poverty and violence: "Massive poverty and obscene inequality are such terrible scourges of our times—times in which the world boasts breathtaking advances in science, technology, industry and wealth accumulation—that they have to rank alongside slavery and apartheid as social evils" (UNDP 2003:4).

Natural disasters also pose challenges as negative forces working against community development, and many social workers respond to such disasters when they occur. We encourage a strong focus on things we can change—the harm humans do to themselves, to each other, and to the environment and other species that sustain us—as a guide to motivate community practice social workers.

RECENTLY ACKNOWLEDGED PROBLEMS

Workers in the early settlement house movement warned about the effects on human development of cities clogged with immigrants living in overly dense, disease-prone neighborhoods that housed labor for industrial plants. The pollution of air and water caused by those factories and mills in the early twentieth century was also apparent, but we humans then thought those resources were unlimited and that the "externalities" could be managed. In the 1960s, scientists began alerting us again to the further damage posed to ourselves, other species, and the entire biosphere by unbridled use of natural and chemical resources in everything from food to fuel, and the continuing contamination of the environment by the waste we discarded. These warnings created some new efforts on the part of city and regional planners, social workers, and public health workers, but only recently have the ideas of environmental degradation and global warming become acknowledged as serious problems.

James Speth (2003) speaks of the dual progression of the global economy and environmental pollution when he describes the doubling of the world economy during the 1980s and 1990s and the concurrent increase in environmental degradation: "We now recognize that our species is a global force with little, if any, competition, and that the global-scale problems we face today are more menacing than the predominantly domestic issues that spurred the environmental awakening of the 1960s" (Speth 2003:xi). We humans are the greatest threat to our own future if we continue to behave in ways that provide short-term gain while wasting finite resources and fouling our air, water, food, and social organizations. We are equally misguided if we support such waste and destruction among corporate and government organizations. Each of us has a personal and organizational role to play in responding appropriately to the global warming crisis. Social work should be particularly focused on this issue as it is "the poorest countries and most vulnerable citizens [that] will suffer the earliest and most damaging setbacks [from global warming], even though they have contributed least to the problem" (UNDP 2007/2008:1).

It has taken about 200 years, since the beginning of the Industrial Revolution, to put our planet so perilously close to major environmental disaster, and the message we all carried within us was that this "free" market economic development was bringing us prosperity. The threat is now too great and compels us to find new messages and a new story that can turn these conditions around (Berry 1990). A place to begin, as we mentioned earlier, is for all of us to understand our effect on the world's resources and ecosystems by calculating our own "ecological footprint," in whatever language we prefer and from wherever we are living on the planet (Redefining Progress 2008b). This exercise is not intended to depress you but to make you aware of everyone's need to adopt responsible personal, organizational, and global patterns that allow our children's children to have the opportunity to develop to their fullest potential. Beyond increasing your personal awareness, each person should work to change at least one environmentally damaging thing in your life, and if possible in a larger sphere, for example, family, neighborhood, village, or region. There is work to be done on this issue, and whether or not your special interest in community practice encompasses environmental protection and restoration, some part of your personal time should be committed to repairing the environment.

In our view, nothing measures up to the destructive forces of violence, including the violence of poverty, and global warming. These challenges to effectively working in community practice are much more complex than we have described them here. Violence and global warming are insidious in the way they become part of so many aspects of our lives.

ASSETS AND OPPORTUNITIES FOR FACING CHALLENGES

Although these challenges will buffet and interrupt the work we do toward organizing sustainable development, planning, collaboration, and action for progressive change, there are also many positive forces that we can work with to improve social, economic, and environmental conditions. These forces are "the wind on our back," helping to push us along when we grow weary. The most powerful forces available to keep us moving in progressive directions are human decency and shared values, improvements in human development indicators, human rights research and practice, peace work practice and innovations, and hundreds of thousands of partners in this work. Our challenge is to continue to seek both the knowledge that gives us new insight into effective solutions to these problems and the people who are committed to values we have described throughout this book that strengthen human well-being.

HUMAN DECENCY AND SHARED VALUES

We define *social well-being* as all people having access to basic social relationships that support their ability to thrive, including *political well-being*, which is people having freedom to associate, speak, vote, and participate in the governments that make policy for them. *Economic well-being* occurs when all people have opportunities to achieve a wide variety of livelihoods and that wages pay enough to meet a family's shelter, food, health care, and transportation. *Environmental well-being* requires that present generations not live beyond the resources in the biosphere and that they work to repair the damage to air, water, soil, fisheries, forests, and other species.

We know from experience that basic human decency exists in most individuals and is expressed in hundreds of helping relationships in communities everywhere. We also know that the basic social work values and ethics mirror the shared values of people all across the globe who work for social justice, human rights, economic justice, and environmental restoration. One of our tasks as community practice workers is to help link the networks of people working for social, political, economic, and environmental well-being in communities and institutions all around us (Finn and Jacobson 2008b; Reisch 2005a).

Sources to help community practice workers with shared human values might include each country's code of ethics; the International Federation of

Social Workers/International Association of Schools of Social Work's "Ethics in Social Work, Statement of Principles" (2008; adopted 2004); and the UNDP's annual *Human Development Report.* The basic decency to help one another is reflected most clearly in what the United Nations Development Program calls "caring labor" (UNDP 1999). Caring labor is involved in social well-being— having access to basic social relationships that support the human ability to thrive. Humans are social creatures, and as such, they are dependent on relationships for physical and emotional protection and stability. Caring labor involves nurturing families as well as communities.

CARING LABOR FOR FAMILIES Caring labor or caring tasks constitute a wide range of activity related to nurturing children and youth, helping children and youth develop their capabilities, providing social support for the development and maintenance of adults, as well as the special care provided to people who are ill or to dependent elders.

Caring tasks and skills are well understood by social workers, who are often responsible for organizing, training for, and supervising care provided by surrogates when extended families are not available to provide it. Although these tasks are essential for human development, they have often been invisible to society because, in large part, they are the unpaid or underpaid labor of women and are not part of the equation to measure traditional market economies.

Family caring tasks have become a complex global issue. With more and more women entering the workforce outside the home, the increasing demand for care workers in North America and Europe has stimulated a significant migration of women from low-income countries to care for children and aging parents in developed countries. This migration has an insidious effect on families around the globe because the jobs separate migrant care workers from their own children. Although the work offered in another country offers the promise of a better future for the family, the wages are insufficient to support the care giver's family in the new country, and these women have to leave their children behind in the care of relatives. The question posed by the United Nations concerning caring labor is: "How can societies distribute the costs and burdens of this work equitably—between men and women, and between the state and the family or community, including the private sector?" (UNDP 1999:77).

These are questions social workers need to be engaged with as they support and protect the caring labor necessary to nurture families who are "the strength of every nation" (NASW 2007b).

Social workers around the globe organize caring work in local communities such as reaching out to alienated youth and isolated elders, responding to the needs of young families in economic and emotional stress, or providing support and advocacy for people who are excluded or oppressed by societal norms.

Organized caring work, whether provided by the family, the community, or public or private service, is undertaken to promote individual development and prevent violence. Caring work, wherever it can be promoted, supports the community and is also an antidote to violence.

CARING LABOR FOR COMMUNITIES Human relationships in the form of community networks and social exchange are also vital to creating the social support necessary for human development. Throughout this book we have spoken of social capital, the dense networks of relationships that provide opportunities for developing neighborhood associations, religious and spiritual organizations, recreational associations and sports teams, arts and theater groups, as well as educational, political, and economic institutions. The voluntary contributions of people everywhere on the globe to create and maintain these kinds of community institutions are enormous and are rarely counted in the traditional economic formulas to measure progress.

Community organizers and facilitators contribute to building social capital in a wide variety of community efforts. Earlier we described examples of positive community conditions that result when governments and foundations extend their investments to communities to support people who do community organizing, advocacy, and capacity building (Couto and Guthrie 1999; Dorfman 2007–2008). This organizing, advocacy, and capacity building work connects the people who are already committed to strengthening common decency, social justice, and human rights in communities all across the globe.

HUMAN DEVELOPMENT INDICATORS

Social work, public health, city and regional planning, cooperative extension, development experts, and anthropologists have amassed a significant body of knowledge useful for improving the social, economic, and environmental well-being of communities, only a very small fraction of which we have presented in this book. The expansion of communication technology is truly amazing when you consider what we can know and the speed of sharing that knowledge. Information and technology gains help us reach people in very distant places. Health-Net, for example, uses innovative communications technology to deliver current medical information to health care workers in more than thirty developing countries. HealthNet's use of radiotelephone, computer networks, and low-earth-orbit satellites makes it possible to deliver transforming knowledge to even remote locations that lack any telecommunications infrastructure (UNDP 1999). The advantages of the communication revolution are quite clear when you consider that "a 40 page document can be sent from Madagascar to Côte d'Ivoire . . . by five-day courier for $75, by 30-minute fax for $45 or by two-minute email for less than 20 cents—and the email can go to hundreds of people at no extra cost" (UNDP 1999:58). The potential to bring more and more people into the information age requires us to commit to the Millennium Development Goals to make certain that children everywhere have a chance to go to school.

In addition to general theoretical understandings of human behavior, community and organizational development, and models of sustainable development, ways to measure social, economic, and environmental well-being are particularly helpful to community practice workers. We feel it is essential for people working in community practice to become very familiar with the annual *Human Development Report* prepared by the United Nations Development Program, as well as with the Genuine Progress Indicator developed by Redefining Progress (2008a). In 2007 the Organization for Economic Cooperation and Development (OECD) coordinated the signing of the Istanbul Declaration that acknowledges "emerging consensus on the need to undertake the measurement of societal progress in every country going beyond conventional economic measures such as GDP per capita" (OECD 2007:1). A group within the OECD has already made progress toward measuring gender equality through a formula that calculates the effect of the root causes of inequalities. The measure, called the Social Institutions and Gender Index (SIGI), can be explored by viewing an explanatory video at their Web site (OECD SIGI 2009). Although these existing tools have different formulas for measuring human progress, they help us see the deficits in using the gross domestic product (GDP) as the single indicator of how human communities really make progress in areas of social, economic, and environmental well-being.

HUMAN RIGHTS RESEARCH AND PRACTICE

In the preceding chapters, we have commented extensively on the need to understand the development of human rights knowledge and instruments. This knowledge is essential for all social workers, especially community practice workers. Human rights knowledge is important in two ways: to gain an appreciation for the development of a human rights perspective across time and cultures, and to understand the commonly accepted conventions and instruments as a standard of comparison for each community. Human rights will and should dominate discourse in these next several decades as the increase in multicultural communities also increases the potential for tension and conflict between and among culturally different groups. The role of gender in human rights will have a special focus in that discourse as women and girls pursue their own understanding of what it means to be a human being.

We have excellent resources to draw upon from people who are engaged in research and discussions about human rights (Dominelli 2007; Ife 2006, 2007a;

Link 2007; Reichert 2007; Sen 1998; Wetzel 2007), in addition to the major human rights documents identified in earlier chapters which are available at the United Nations Web site. The University of Minnesota Human Rights Library (2008), which is available in eight languages, holds all the major and minor peace documents from throughout the world and connects with similar libraries in Yemen, South Africa, Australia, Russia, and Geneva, Switzerland. In addition, the Center for Human Rights Education (2008) provides materials for deeper understanding and group discussion of human rights, available in ten languages. Global information with a focus on women's rights is available from the Association for Women's Rights in Development (AWID 2009) Web site, formerly identified as the Women's Human Rights Network.

PEACE WORK AND INNOVATIONS IN PEACEMAKING PRACTICE

While headlines daily describe the global toll of international conflicts and the inhumanity of personal conflicts, a number of organizations are working to change the idea that violence is the norm through research, study, and engagement. Among these organizations in the United States are the Carter Center in Atlanta, Georgia (2008), the Carnegie Endowment for International Peace (2008), and the Friends Committee on National Legislation (FCNL) in Washington, D.C. In their proposal, *Peaceful Prevention of Deadly Conflict* (2004), FCNL has developed five principles from which they are working to promote peace at an international level:

- International cooperation and the rule of law
- Preventive diplomacy and peace operations
- Arms control and disarmament
- Human rights and good governance
- Sustainable development and human security (FCNL 2004:8–11)

These principles, based on their experience with alternatives-to-violence work and the work of international commissions led by the United Nations and the Carnegie Commission, are consonant with social work principles. Social work has formulated additional materials in a *Peace Policy Toolkit* that includes the positions on peace promotion taken by historical leaders as well as recent presidents and executive directors of the National Association of Social Workers (NASW 2007b).

Dorothy Van Soest and Arline Prigoff (1997) explored a variety of approaches to promote healing following experiences of violence. These materials help us develop and implement more interventions that work toward violence prevention at every point along the continuum of violence. To focus on prevention, we have the help of many social work colleagues. Betty Garcia and Dorothy Van Soest (2006) provide an excellent guide for identifying and confronting the embedded nature of racism in our institutions and relationships. King Davis and Tricia Bent-Goodley (2004) track U.S. social policy from colonial times to the present, demonstrating just how carefully our own country has used every legal means to control people of color. Katherine van Wormer (2004) adds to the strong literature on understanding how oppression and internalized oppression work against the gains we make toward helping people reach their optimum potential. Understanding these insidious racist processes helps social workers begin our own transformation toward a social justice commitment.

The Coalition to Stop the Use of Child Soldiers is working to encourage regional governments in Central America to take effective action to diminish the quantity of arms available and to engage children in education and livelihood activities (Coalition to Stop the Use of Child Soldiers 2008).

A global approach to promoting peace was proposed by Paul Hawken (1993) in *The Ecology of Commerce*, in which he suggested that a special tax be placed on the manufacture and sale of missiles, guns, bombs, tanks, and other war materials. Hawken argued that the funds from the weapons tax would be sufficient to support UN peacekeeping operations as well as most UN development programs.

HUNDREDS OF THOUSANDS OF PEOPLE WORKING FOR PROGRESSIVE CHANGE

Throughout this book we have introduced you to people and programs working at the grassroots level to improve conditions in their communities, regions, and countries. While not drawing on every country of the world, we have given you a window into what community organizers, social entrepreneurs, and promoters of effective and progressive communities are doing across the globe, and have provided opportunities for idea and technology exchange to be able to identify effective approaches. There are many sources that continue to connect with people like you who wish to make a difference. Paul Hawken's (2007) WiserEarth Web site expands on the ideas in his recent book, *Blessed Unrest*, to connect people working for the well-being of communities throughout the world (WiserEarth 2009). Other sources might be *Affilia*, the journal of women in social work, the ASHOKA Web site, the *Journal of Community Practice* that is connected with the Association of Community Organization and Social Administration (ACOSA), the *Journal of Social Development* associated with the International Consortium for Social Development (ICSD), the *Journal of Progressive Human Services*, and the *Handbook of Community Practice* (2005), edited by Marie Weil.

CONCLUSIONS: OUR BEST WISHES FOR COMMUNITY PRACTICE WORKERS EVERYWHERE

It is our hope that after reading this book you feel more inspired and more prepared to do this work as you move forward in your career in community practice. Having a more detailed understanding and more specific knowledge of the theoretical underpinnings, basic processes, roles, and skills required of a community practitioner, you are better able to engage in the important work ahead. Building your knowledge base will be a continual activity throughout your career. Keep on asking the questions that get you closer to understanding social justice and human rights and that take you on a path to promote social, economic, and environmental well-being. We give you our best wishes as you move forward.

We leave you with an additional quote of inspiration from the Chilean president, Michelle Bachelet. Her father was murdered, and she and her mother were arrested and eventually exiled by the former dictator Augusto Pinochet. Following the return of democracy, she came back to Chile and was elected president in 2006.

Violence entered my life and destroyed what I loved. I was a victim of hate, and so I have dedicated my life to reversing that hatred by turning it into understanding, tolerance and—why not say it outright?—love.

Michelle Bachelet, president of Chile,
greeting the people upon winning the presidency
January 15, 2006

REFERENCES

Abbott, Grace. 1938. *The Child and the State*. Chicago: University of Chicago Press.

About Canada. Multiculturalism. 2008. http://www.mta.ca/about_canada/multi/index.htm.

Act Up. "Civil Disobedience Guide." 2008. http://www.actupny.org/documents/CDdocuments/CDindex.html.

Addams, Jane. 1910/1911/1960. *Twenty Years at Hull-House*. New York: Signet Classic with arrangements of Macmillan Company. (First publication by Phillips Publishing.)

Addams, Jane. 1922/1983. *Peace and Bread in Time of War*. NASW Classics Series, Silver Spring, MD: NASW. (First published by Macmillan Company.)

Agger, Ben. 1998. *Critical Social Theories: An Introduction*. Boulder, CO: Westview.

Albro, Robert. 2005. "'The Water Is Ours, Carajo!': Deep Citizenship in Bolivia's Water War." In *Social Movements: An Anthropological Reader*, ed. J. Nash, pp. 249–71. Malden, MA: Blackwell Publishing.

Alderman, Ellen, and Caroline Kennedy. 1991. *In Our Defense: The Bill of Rights in Action*. New York: Avon Books.

Alinsky, Saul D. 1971. *Rules for Radicals*. New York: Random House.

Allen, Mark. 2006, January 16. "I Wrapped a Giant Condom over Jesse Helms' House." http://blog.wfmu.org/freeform/i_wrapped_a_gia.htlm.

Alter, Catherine F. 2000. "Interorganizational Collaboration in the Task Environment." In *The Handbook of Social Welfare Management*, ed. Rino Patti, pp. 283–302. Thousand Oaks, CA: Sage Publications.

Alter, Catherine. 2008. "Interorganizational Practice Interventions." In *Encyclopedia of Social Work*, ed. Terry Mizrahi and Larry E. Davis, pp. 528–33. Washington, DC: NASW Press; New York: Oxford University Press.

American Friends Service Committee. 2008. "Guide to Civil Disobedience." http://www.afsc.org/ht/display/ContentDetails/i/2947/pid/268.

Anderson, Joseph, and Robin Wiggins Carter. 2003. *Diversity Perspectives for Social Work Practice*. Boston: Pearson Education, Allyn & Bacon.

Andrews, Janice, and Michael Reisch. 1997. "Social Work and Anti-Communism: A Historical Analysis of the McCarthy Era." *Journal of Progressive Human Services* 8(2): 29–49.

Anner, John. 1996. Introduction to *Beyond Identity Politics: Emerging Social Justice Movements in Communities*, ed. J. Anner, pp. 5–13. Boston: South End Press.

Anwar, Duaa. 2004. *The Everything Koran Book*. Avon, MA: Adams Media.

Apastamba Dharma Sutra. 1996. In *The Religion of the Hindus*, ed. Kenneth W. Morgan and D. S. Sama. Delhi: Motilal Banarsidass Publishers.

Arizmendi, Lydia Gonzalez, and Larry Ortiz. 2004. "Neighborhood and Community Organizing in Colonias: A Case Study in the Development and Use of Promotoras." *Journal of Community Practice*, 12(1/2): 23–35.

Arnold, Rick, Bev Burke, Carl James, D'Arcy Martin, and Barb Thomas. 1991. *Educating for a Change.* Toronto, Ontario: Between the Lines.

Asad, Muhammad, trans. 2008. *The Message of the Qur'an.* 2nd ed. Watsonville, CA: The Book Foundation.

ASHOKA. 2008. Definition of social entrepreneur. At http://ashoka.org/fellows/social_entrepreneur.cfm.

ASHOKA. 2009. Innovators for the Public, Ashoka Fellow Karen Tse. http://www.ashoka.org/node/2986.

ASHOKA Conversations Network. 2007. Fazel H. Abed. BRAC. Thinking Big and Scaling Up. http://sic.conversationsnetwork.org/shows/detail3217.html.

Aspen Institute. 1996. *Measuring Community Capacity Building: A Workbook-in-Progress for Rural Communities.* Washington, DC: Aspen Institute Rural Economic Policy Program.

Asociación Madres de Plaza de Mayo. 2008. Retrieved February 22, 2008, from http://www.madres.org/.

Association for Community Organization and Social Administration (ACOSA) Symposium. 1998. Council on Social Work Education, Washington, DC.

Association for Women's Rights in Development (AWID). 2009. http://www.awid.org/.

Atlee, Tom. 2009. "The Co-Intelligence Institute." http://www.co-intelligence.org/P-dialogue.html.

Austin, David M. 2002. *Human Services Management: Organizational Leadership in Social Work Practice.* New York: Columbia University Press.

Austin, Michael, and Neil Betten. 1990. Rural Organizing and the Agricultural Extension Service. In *The Roots of Community Organizing, 1917–1939,* ed. Neil Betten and Michael Austin, pp. 94–105. Philadelphia: Temple University Press.

Baby Milk Action. 2008. Baby Milk Action history. http://www.babymilkaction.org/pages/history.html.

Bailey, Darlyne, and Kelly McNally Koney. 2000. *Strategic Alliances among Health and Human Services Organizations: From Affiliations to Consolidations.* Thousand Oaks, CA: Sage Publications.

Bandura, Albert. 1985. "Reflections on Human Agency." In *Contemporary Psychology in Europe: Theory, Research, and Applications,* ed. J. Georgas, M. Manthouli, E. Besevegis, and A. Kokkevi, pp. 194–210. Seattle, WA: Hogrefe & Huber.

Bandura, Albert. 1986. *Social Foundations of Thought and Action: A Social Cognitive Theory.* Englewood Cliffs, NJ: Prentice-Hall.

Bandura, Albert. 1995. *Self-Efficacy in Changing Societies.* Cambridge, UK: Cambridge University Press.

Bandura, Albert. 1997. *Self-Efficacy: The Exercise of Control.* New York: W. H. Freeman.

Bank, Richard. 2002. *The Everything Judaism Book.* Avon, MA: Adams Media.

Bankhead, Teiahsha, and John L. Erlich. 2005. "Diverse Populations and Community Practice." In *The Handbook of Community Practice,* ed. Marie Weil, pp. 59–83. Thousand Oaks, CA: Sage Publications.

Barker, Jonathan. 1999. *Street Level Democracy: Political Settings at the Margins of Global Power.* West Hartford, CT: Kumarian Press.

Barker, Robert L. 2003. *The Social Work Dictionary.* Washington, DC: NASW Press.

Barney, Gerald O. 1980. *The Global 2000 Report to the President.* 3 vols. Washington, DC: U.S. Government Printing Office.

Barney, Gerald O. 2007. "Finding a Path to the Ecozoic Era." *Ecozoic Reader,* 4(4): 3–6.

Beer, Jennifer E., and Eileen Stief. 1997. *The Mediator's Handbook*. Gabriola Island, BC: New Society Publishers.

Bennis, Warren, Kenneth D. Benne, Robert Chin, and Kenneth E. Corey. 1976. *The Planning of Change*, 3rd ed. New York: Holt, Rinehart and Winston. (Originally published in 1967.)

Beresford, Peter, and Suzy Croft. 1993. *Citizen Involvement: A Practical Guide for Change*. Basingstoke, UK: Macmillan.

Beresford, Peter, and Suzy Croft. 2001. "Service Users, Knowledges and the Social Construction of Social Work." *Journal of Social Work* 1(3): 295–316.

Bernstein, Jared. 2007, October 2. "Alleviating Poverty Forum," Washington, DC, edited transcript. Agenda for a Shared Prosperity. Economic Policy Institute.

Berry, Thomas. 1990. *The Dream of the Earth*. San Francisco, CA: Sierra Club Books.

Berry, Thomas. 2007. *Ecozoic Reader* 5(1):cover.

Berry, Wendell. 1992. *Sex, Economy, Freedom and Community*. New York: Pantheon Books.

Bethel New Life Community Corporation. Retrieved 2008 from http://www.bethelnewlife.org/.

Betten, Neil, and Michael Austin, eds. 1990. *The Roots of Community Organizing, 1917–1939*. Philadelphia: Temple University Press.

Bhagavad Gita. 2000. Translated by Stephen Mitchell. New York: Three Rivers Press.

Bilmes, Linda J. 2008, March/April. "Iraq's 100-Year Mortgage: The Price Tag for Caring for the Americans Who Fight This War Could Exceed What It Costs to Wage It." *Foreign Policy*, 84–85.

Birkenmaier, Julie, and Sabrina Watson Tyuse. 2005. "Affordable Financial Services and Credit for the Poor: The Foundation of Asset Building." *Journal of Community Practice* 13(1): 69–85.

Black Mesa Indigenous Support. 2008. http://www.blackmesais.org/.

Black Mesa Water Coalition. 2008. http://www.blackmesawatercoalition.org/.

Blank, Rebecca M. 1998. *It Takes a Nation: A New Agenda for Fighting Poverty*. Princeton, NJ: Princeton University Press.

Blue Ridge Women in Agriculture (BRWIA). 2007. Home page. http://brwia.org/.

Blue Ridge Women in Agriculture 2nd Annual Conference. 2004, August 27. "Cultivating Dreams, Breaking New Ground, Harvesting Profits." Boone, NC: Watauga County Cooperative Extension.

Boal, Augusto. 2000. *Theatre of the Oppressed*. London: Pluto Press.

Bobo, Kimberley, Jackie Kendall, and Steve Max. 1991. *Organize: Organizing for Social Change*. Cabin John, MD: Seven Locks Press.

Boehm, Werner, ed. 1959. *Social Work Curriculum Study*. New York: Council on Social Work Education.

Borden, Lynne M, and Daniel Perkins. 1999, April. "Assessing Your Collaboration: A Self Evaluation Tool." *Journal of Extension* 37(2). E-version at http://www.joe.org/joe/1999april/tt1.html.

Bornstein, David. 2007. *How to Change the World: Social Entrepreneurs and the Power of New Ideas*. New York: Oxford University Press.

Boston Foundation. 1992. Building the Dudley Street Neighborhood. *Boston Foundation Report*, pp. 1–3.

Bradford, Bonnie, and Margaret A. Gwynne, eds. 1995. *Down to Earth: Community Perspectives on Health, Development and the Environment*. West Hartford, CT: Kumarian Press.

Bradshaw, Catherine P., Steven Soifer, and Lorraine Gutierrez. 1994. "Toward a Hybrid Model for Effective Organizing with Women of Color." *Journal of Community Practice* 1: 25–41.

Brager, George, and Harry Specht. 1973. *Community Organizing*. New York: Columbia University Press.

Brager, George, Harry Specht, and James L. Torczyner. 1987. *Community Organizing*, 2nd ed. New York: Columbia University Press.

Brandwein, Ruth A. 1981. "Toward Androgyny in Community and Organizational Practice." In *Women, Power and Change*, ed. Ann Weick and Sally Vandiver, pp. 158–70. Washington, DC: NASW Press.

Braverman, Lois. 1988. *Women, Feminism, and Family Therapy*. New York: Hawthorne Press.

Brazil, Wayne D. 1988. *Howard W. Odum: The Building Years, 1884–1930*. New York: Garland Publications.

Brechin, Ann, and Moyra Sidell. 2000. "Ways of Knowing." In *Using Evidence in Health and Social Care*, ed. Roger Gomm and Celia Davies. Open University, London: Sage Publications.

Breckenridge, Sophonisba P. 1934. *Social Work and the Courts: Select Documents*. Chicago: University of Chicago Press.

Bricker-Jenkins, Mary, Carrie Young, and Cheri Honkala. 2007. "Using Economic Human Rights in the Movement to End Poverty: The Kensington Welfare Rights Union and the Poor People's Economic Human Rights Campaign." In *Challenges in Human Rights: A Social Work Perspective*, ed. Elizabeth Reichert, pp. 122–37. New York: Columbia University Press.

Brisson, Daniel. 2004. "The Bonds and Bridges to Economic Success: An Application and Test of Social Capital in Lower-Income Urban Neighborhoods." Dissertation, North Carolina Collection, Chapel Hill, NC: University of North Carolina.

Brody, Ralph. 2004. *Effectively Managing Human Service Organizations*. Thousand Oaks, CA: Sage Publications.

Brooks, Fred. 2007. "Living Wage Movement: Potential Implications for the Working Poor." *Families in Society* 88(3): 437–42.

Brown, Michael Jacoby. 2006. *Building Powerful Community Organizations: A Personal Guide to Creating Groups That Can Solve Problems and Change the World*. Arlington, MA: Long Haul Press.

Brueggemann, William G. 2006. *The Practice of Macro Social Work*. 3rd ed. Belmont, CA: Thompson/Brooks/Cole Higher Education.

Buddhist Scriptures. 2004. Ed. Donald Lopez. London: Penguin Classics.

Bullard, Sara. 1994. *Free at Last: A History of the Civil Rights Movement and Those Who Died in the Struggle*. New York: Oxford University Press.

Burford, Gale, and Joe Hudson, eds. 2000. *Family Group Conferences: New Directions in Community-centered Child and Family Practice*. Hawthorne, NY: Aldine de Gruyter.

Bussey, Gertrude, and Margaret Tims. 1980. *Pioneers for Peace: Women's International League for Peace and Freedom, 1915–1965*. Oxford, UK: Alden Press.

Butterfield, Alice Johnson. 2008. "Community Development." In *Encyclopedia of Social Work*, 20th ed., ed. Terry Mizrahi and Larry Davis, vol. 1, pp. 375–81. Washington, DC: NASW Press.

Carlton-LaNey, Iris. 2001. *African American Leadership: An Empowerment Tradition in Social Welfare History*. Washington, DC: NASW Press.

Carlton-LaNey, Iris, Susan Murty, and Lynne Clemmons Morris. 2005. "Rural Community Practice: Organizing, Planning and Development." In *Handbook of Community Practice*, ed. Marie Weil, pp. 402–17. Thousand Oaks, CA: Sage Publications.

Carnegie Endowment for International Peace. 2008. Home page. http://www.carnegieendowment.org/.

Carniol, B. 1990. *Case Critical*. Toronto: Between the Lines.

Carson, Rachel. 1962. *Silent Spring*. Boston: Houghton Mifflin.

Carter Center. 2008. "The Carter Center: Waging Peace, Advancing Human Rights and Alleviating Suffering." http://www.cartercenter.org/homepage.html.

Castelloe, Paul. 1999. "Community Change: An Integrated Model." In Community Change and Community Practice: An Organic Model of Community Practice. Ph.D. diss., Chapel Hill, NC: University of North Carolina at Chapel Hill, School of Social Work.

Castelloe, Paul, and Dorothy N. Gamble. 2005. "Participatory Methods in Community Practice: Popular Education and Participatory Rural Appraisal." In *The Handbook of Community Practice*, ed. Marie Weil, pp. 261–75. Thousand Oaks, CA: Sage Publications.

Castelloe, Paul, and Thomas Watson. 2000. "The Toolbox: Skills for Effective Organizing: Entering the Community." http://www.cpcwnc.org/Toolbox/tbxentercom.html.

Catholic Relief Services Food Fast. 2008. World Hunger and Poverty Data. http://www.food fast.org/resources/eng/poverty-hunger-data.pdf.

Cauthen, Nancy. 2007, October 2. Alleviating Poverty Forum, Washington, DC, edited transcript. Agenda for a Shared Prosperity. Economic Policy Institute.

Cavanagh, John, and Jerry Mander, eds. 2004. *Alternatives to Economic Globalization: A Better World Is Possible*, 2nd ed. San Francisco, CA: Berrett-Koehler.

Centers for Disease Control. 2005, September 9. "Unintentional Deaths from Drug Poisoning by Urbanization Area, New Mexico, 1994–2003." *MMWR Weekly* 54(35): 870–73. http://www.cdc.gov/mmwR/preview/mmwrhtml/mm5435a3.htm.

Center for Participatory Change. 2007. http://www.cpcwnc.org/.

Center for Responsive Politics. 2009. OpenSecrets.org. http://www.opensecrets.org/about/index.asp.

Center for the Study of Violence and Reconciliation (CSVR). 2004. *Justice for All: The Rights to Know*. Braamfontein, South Africa: CSVR.

Center for the Study of Violence and Reconciliation (CSVR). 2008. Home page. http://www.csvr.org.za/.

Center on Budget and Policy Priorities. 2008. Analysis of presidential budget for 2009. http://www.cbpp.org/2-4-08bud2.htm.

Centre for Human Rights Education. 2008. Retrieved April 25, 2008, from http://www.hrea.org/index.php?baseid=10&languageid=1.

Chambers, Robert. 1995. *Ideas for Development*. London: Earthscan Publications.

Chambers, Robert. 1997. *Whose Reality Counts? Putting the First Last*. London: Intermediate Technology Publications.

Chambers, Robert. 2002. *Participatory Workshops: A Sourcebook of 21 Sets of Ideas and Activities*. Sterling, VA: Earthscan Publications.

Chandler, Susan. 2005. "Addie Hunton and the Construction of an African American Female Peace Perspective." *Affilia: Journal of Women and Social Work* 20(3): 270–83.

Chandler, Susan, and Jill Jones. 2003. "Because a Better World Is Possible: Women Casino Workers, Union Activism, and the Creation of a Just Work Place." *Journal of Sociology and Social Welfare* 30(4): 57–78.

Chaskin, Robert J. 1997. "Perspectives on Neighborhood and Community: A Review of the Literature." *Social Service Review*, 71: 522–47.

Chaskin, Robert J. 2001. "Building Community Capacity: A Definitional Framework and Case Studies from a Comprehensive Community Initiative." *Urban Affairs Review* 36(3): 291–323.

Chaskin, Robert J., Prudence Brown, Sudir Venkatesh, and Avis Vidal. 2001. *Building Community Capacity*. Chicago: University of Chicago Press.

Chaskin, Robert J., and Jona M. Rosenfeld, eds. 2008. *Research for Action: Cross-national Perspectives on Connecting Knowledge, Policy and Practice for Children*. New York: Oxford University Press.

Chavez, Franz. 2006, November 8. "Cochabamba's 'Water War': Six Years On." Inter Press Service News Agency (IPS). http://ipsnews.net/news.asp?idnews=35418.

Chen, Jiagang. 2006. "Participatory Budgeting." Unpublished paper. The Sanford Center for Public Policy, Duke University.

Chicanos Por La Causa. 2008. Retrieved June 12, 2008, from http://www.cplc.org/.

Chief Seattle Speech: Washington State Library. 2008. Historical Debate on Chief Seattle's Speech. Nancy Zussy, State Librarian, 1993. http://www.synaptic.bc.ca/ejournal/wslibrry .htm.

Chow, Julian Chun-Chung, and Kelsey Crowe. 2005. "Community-Based Research and Methods in Community Practice." In The Handbook of Community Practice, ed. Marie Weil, pp. 604–19. Thousand Oaks, CA: Sage Publications.

Citizen Health Care Working Group. Retrieved August 15, 2007, from http://www.citizen shealthcare.gov/about/invorgs.php.

City Farmer. 2006. Bi-annual Newsletter of SEEDS. Spring 6(1). Durham, NC: SEEDS.

CIVICUS. 2009. World Alliance for Citizen Participation. http://www.civicus.org/ who-we-are.

Clean Election Institute. 2008. Arizona. http://www.azclean.org/.

Cliteur, Paul. 2007. "Falling Prey to Relativism." Sign and Sight. http://www.signandsight. com/features/1174.html.

CNN.com. 2003, February 16. Cities Jammed in Worldwide Protest of War in Iraq. At http:// www.cnn.com/2003/US/02/15/sprj.irq.protests.main/.

Coalition to Stop the Use of Child Soldiers. 2008. http://www.child-soldiers.org/home.

Cohen, David, Rosa de la Vega, and Gabrielle Watson. 2001. Advocacy for Social Justice: A Global Action and Reflection Guide. Bloomfield, CT: Kumarian Press.

Coleman, James Samuel. 1990. Foundations of Social Theory. Cambridge, MA: Harvard University Press.

Collier, Paul. 2009. Wars, Guns and Votes: Democracy in Dangerous Places. New York: Harper/ HarperCollins.

Common Cause. 2007 Public Financing in States. http://www.commoncause.org/site/pp .asp?c=dkLNK1MQIwG&b=507399.

Community Tool Box. 2008a. Kansas University Work Group. http://ctb.ku.edu/en/.

Community Tool Box. 2008b. Training for Conflict Resolution. University of Kansas at http://ctb1.ku.edu/en/tablecontents/section_1164.htm.

Comprehensive Dialogue among Civilizations. 2007. At http://thinktanks.fpri.org/compre hensive-dialogue-among-civilizations.

Concerned Citizens of Tillery. 2003. "25th Anniversary." Tillery, NC.

Confucius. 1979. The Analects. Trans. D. C. Lau. London: Penguin Books.

Congressional Budget Office (CBO). 2008, February 8. The Cost of Iraq, Afghanistan and Other Global War on Terror Operations since 9/11. At http://www.fas.org/sgp/crs/natsec/ RL33110.pdf.

Constitutional Court of South Africa. 2008. Constitution of the Republic of South Africa— 1996. http://www.info.gov.za/documents/constitution/index.htm.

The Constitution of the United States of America, with the Declaration of Independence; and the Articles of Confederation. 2006. New York: Barnes & Noble.

Convention on the Elimination of All Forms of Discrimination Against Women (CEDAW). 2008. http://www.un.org/womenwatch/daw/cedaw/.

Co-op America. 2008. Retrieved February 22, 2008, from http://www.coopamerica.org/pubs/ realmoney/articles/nosweatshops.cfm.

Cottrell, Leonard S., Jr. 1976. "The Competent Community." In Further Explorations in Social Psychiatry, ed. Berton H. Kaplan, Robert N. Wilson, and Alexander H. Leighton, pp. 195–209. New York: Basic Books.

Coulton, Claudia. 2005. "The Place of Community in Social Work Practice Research: Conceptual and Methodological Developments." *Social Work Research* 29: 73–86.

Council on Social Work Education, Educational Policy and Accreditation Standards, Adopted 2001, Revised October 2004. Retrieved August 10, 2007, from http://www.cswe.org/NR/rdonlyres/111833A0-C4F5-475C-8FEB-EA740FF4D9F1/0/EPAS.pdf.

Couto, Richard A., with Catherine S. Guthrie. 1999. *Making Democracy Work Better: Mediating Structures, Social Capital, and the Democratic Prospect.* Chapel Hill: University of North Carolina Press.

Cox, David, and Manohar Pawar. 2006. *International Social Work: Issues, Strategies, and Programs.* Thousand Oaks, CA: Sage Publications.

Cox, Fred, John L. Erlich, Jack Rothman, and John Tropman. 1970. *Strategies of Community Organization.* Itasca, IL: F. E. Peacock.

Coyle, Grace L. 1947. *Group Experience and Democratic Values.* New York: Women's Press.

Creed, Gerald W. 2006. *The Seductions of Community, Emancipations, Oppressions, Quandaries.* Santa Fe, NM: School of American Research Press.

Cropper, Steve, Mark Ebers, Chris Huxham, and Peter Smith Ring. 2008. *The Oxford Handbook of Inter-organizational Relations.* New York: Oxford University Press.

Crosby, Jane, and Dorothy Van Soest. 1997. *Challenges of Violence Worldwide: An Educational Resource.* Violence and World Development Project. Washington, DC: NASW Press.

Cuba, Jorge. 2000, December. "Free or Foreign: The Water Battle in Bolivia." *UNESCO Courier.* http://www.unesco.org/courier/2000_12/uk/planet2.htm.

Cumming-Bruce, Nick. 2008, June 18. "World's Refugee Count in 2007 Exceeded 11 Million, U.N. Says." *New York Times.* http://www.nytimes.com/2008/06/18/world/18refugees.html?_r=1&oref=slogin.

Dalai Lama. 2001. *Ethics for the New Millennium.* New York: Riverhead Books.

Daley-Harris, Sam. 2007. *State of the Microcredit Summit Campaign Report 2007.* http://www.microcreditsummit.org/pubs/reports/socr/EngSOCR2007.pdf.

Daly, Herman E., and John B. Cobb Jr. 1989. *For the Common Good: Redirecting the Economy toward Community, the Environment, and a Sustainable Future.* Boston: Beacon Press.

Davis, King E., and Tricia B. Bent-Goodley. 2004. *The Color of Social Policy.* Washington, DC: NASW Press.

Day, Phyllis J. 2009. *A New History of Social Welfare.* 6th ed. Boston: Pearson Learning.

Delbecq, Andre L., Andrew H. Van de Ven, and David H. Gustafson. 1975. *Group Techniques for Program Planning: A Guide to Nominal Group and Delphi Processes.* Glenview, IL: Scott, Foresman.

Democracy North Carolina. 2007, January 5. "Voter-Owned, Clean Elections Candidates Win More than 200 State Offices in 2006." http://www.democracy-nc.org/improving/voterowned elections/victories2006.pdf.

Department of Labor. 2008. http://www.dol.gov/esa/minwage/america.htm#NewMexico.

Dessel, Adrienne, Mary E. Rogge, and Sarah B. Garlington. 2006. "Using Intergroup Dialogue to Promote Social Justice and Change." *Social Work* 51: 303–16.

Dewey, John. 1967. *Philosophy, Psychology and Social Practice.* Ed. Joseph Ratner. New York: Capricorn Books.

Dierenfield, Bruce J. 2004. *The Civil Rights Movement.* Boston: Longman Publishing.

Dolgoff, Ralph, Frank M. Loewenberg, and Donna Harrington. 2008. *Ethical Decisions for Social Work Practice.* 8th ed. Belmont, CA: Wadsworth/Brooks-Cole.

Dominelli, Lena. 2002. *Anti-oppressive Social Work Theory and Practice.* London: Palgrave.

Dominelli, Lena. 2007. "Human Rights in Social Work Practice: An Invisible Part of the Social Work Curriculum." In *Challenges in Human Rights: A Social Work Perspective,* ed. Elizabeth Reichert, pp. 16–43. New York: Columbia University Press.

Dorfman, Aaron. 2007–2008. "Bang for the Buck: Why Grantmakers Should Provide More Funding for Policy Advocacy and Community Organizing." *Responsive Philanthropy Quarterly* (Winter): 2–5.

Drake, Robert F. 2001. *The Principles of Social Policy.* New York: Palgrave Macmillan.

Dromi, Paula, and Marie O. Weil. 1984, November. "Social Work Values: Their Role in a Technological Age." Paper presented at the Sixth Annual Symposium for the Advancement of Social Work with Groups, Chicago, Illinois.

Drug Policy Alliance, New Mexico, 2007. Retrieved August 15, 2007, from http://www. drugpolicy.org/about/stateoffices/newmexico/overdose/.

Earth Charter. 2008. http://www.earthcharter.org/.

Ebadi, Shirin. 2003. "In the Name of the God of Creation and Wisdom." Nobel Lecture. http://nobelprize.org/nobel_prizes/peace/laureates/2003/ebadi-lecture-e.html.

Ecklein, Joan, and Armand A. Lauffer. 1972. *Community Organizers and Social Planners.* New York: John Wiley & Sons.

Economic Policy Institute. 2008. http://www.epinet.org.

Edwards, Richard L., David M. Austin, and Mary A. Altpeter. 1998. "Managing Effectively in an Environment of Competing Values." In *Skills for Effective Management of Nonprofit Organizations,* ed. Richard L. Edwards, John A. Yankey, and Mary A. Altpeter, pp. 5–21. Washington, DC: NASW Press.

Eichler, Michael. 2007. *Consensus Organizing: Building Communities of Mutual Self Interest.* Thousand Oaks, CA: Sage Publications.

Einstein, Albert. Retrieved August 13, 2008, from http://www.famousquotesand authors. com/topics/observation_quotes/html.

Ella Baker Center for Human Rights. 2008. Van Jones Project, "Books Not Bars." At http://ellabakercenter.org/page.php?pageid=45.

El Pueblo, Inc. 2008. At http://www.elpueblo.org.

Encyclopedia of Public Health. 2008. "World Health Organization Elements of Healthy Communities—1986." http://www.enotes.com/public-health-encyclopedia/healthy-communities.

Eng, Eugenia, and Edith Parker. 1994. "Measuring Community Competency and the Mississippi Delta: Interface between Program Evaluation and Empowerment." *Health Education Quarterly* 21: 199–220.

Escobar, Arturo. 1995. *Encountering Development: The Making and Unmaking of the Third World.* Princeton, NJ: Princeton University Press.

Estes, Richard J. 1993. "Toward Sustainable Development: From Theory to Praxis." *Social Development Issues* 15(3): 1–29.

Estrella, Marisol, Jutta Blauert, Dinda Campilon, and John Gaventa. 2002. *Learning from Change: Issues and Experiences in Participatory Monitoring and Evaluation.* London: Intermediate Technology Publishers.

Ewalt, Patricia L., Edith M. Freeman, and Dennis L. Poole, eds. 1998. *Community Building: Renewal, Well-Being, and Shared Responsibility.* Washington, DC: NASW Press.

Ezell, Mark. 2001. *Advocacy in the Human Services.* Belmont, CA: Wadsworth/Thompson Learning.

Falk, Richard. 1971. *This Endangered Planet: Prospects and Proposals for Human Survival.* New York: Random House.

Fals-Borda, Orlando, ed. 1998. *People's Participation: Challenges Ahead.* New York: Apex/Intermediate Technology Press.

Fals-Borda, Orlando, and Mohammad Anisur Rahman, eds. 1991. *Action and Knowledge: Breaking the Monopoly with Participatory Action Research.* New York: Intermediate Technology Pubs/Apex Press.

Fauri, David P., Stephen P. Wernet, and Ellen F. Netting, eds. 2008. *Cases in Macro Social Work Practice*. Needham Heights, MA: Allyn & Bacon.

Fellin, Philip A. 2001. *The Community and the Social Worker*, 3rd ed. Itasca, IL: F.E. Peacock.

Fetterman, David M., Shakeh Kaftarian, and Abraham Wandersman, eds. 1996. *Empowerment Evaluation: Knowledge and Tools for Self-Assessment and Accountability*. Thousand Oaks, CA: Sage Publications.

Fetterman, David M., and Abraham Wandersman. 2004. *Empowerment Evaluation Principles in Practice*. Chicago: Guilford Press.

Figuera-McDonough, Josephina. 2001. *Community Analysis and Praxis*. Philadelphia: Brunner-Routledge.

Finn, Janet L. 2005. "La Victoria: Claiming Memory, History, and Justice in a Santiago Población." *Journal of Community Practice* 13(3): 9–31.

Finn, Janet L., and Maxine Jacobson. 2008a. *Just Practice: A Social Justice Approach to Social Work*, 2nd ed. Peosta, IA: Eddie Bowers Publishing.

Finn, Janet L., and Maxine Jacobson. 2008b. "Social Justice." In *Encyclopedia of Social Work*, ed. Terry Mizrahi and Larry E. Davis, vol. 4, pp. 44–52. Washington, DC: NASW Press.

Finn, Janet L., Maxine Jacobson, and Jillian Dean Campana. 2004. "Participatory Research, Popular Education, and Popular Theater: Contributions to Group Work." In *Handbook of Social Work with Groups*, ed. C. D. Garvin, L. M. Gutierrez, and M. J. Galinsky, pp. 326–43. New York: Guilford Press.

Fisher, Robert. 1994. *Let the People Decide: Neighborhood Organizing in America*. Boston: Twayne.

Fisher, Robert. 2005. "History, Context, and Emerging Issues for Community Practice." In *The Handbook of Community Practice*, ed. Marie Weil, pp. 34–58. Thousand Oaks, CA: Sage Publications.

Fisher, Robert, and Howard Jacob Karger. 1997. *Social Work and Community in a Private World: Getting Out in Public*. White Plains, NY: Longman.

Fisher, Roger, William Ury, and Bruce Patton. 1991. *Getting to Yes*. New York: Penguin Books.

Flacks, Richard. 1995. "Think Globally, Act Politically: Some Notes toward New Movement Strategy." In *Cultural Politics and Social Movements*, ed. M. Darnovsky, B. Epstein, and R. Flacks, pp. 251–363. Philadelphia: Temple University Press.

Fook, Jan. 2002. *Social Work: Critical Theory and Practice*. London: Sage Publications.

Foucault, Michel. 1980. *Power/Knowledge: Selected Interviews and Other Writings, 1972–77*. Ed. and trans. Charles Gordon. New York: Pantheon.

Frankl, Viktor E. 2006. *Man's Search for Meaning*. Boston: Beacon Press.

Freedom House. 2008. http://www.freedomhouse.org/template.cfm?page=1.

Freire, Paulo. 1972. *Pedagogy of the Oppressed*. Baltimore, MD: Penguin Books.

Freire, Paulo. 2000. *Pedagogy of the Oppressed*. 30th anniversary ed. New York: Continuum International.

Freire, Paulo. 2005. *Education for Critical Consciousness*, 2nd ed. New York: Continuum International Publishing.

Friedmann, J., and B. Hudson. 1974. "Knowledge and Action: A Guide to Planning Theory." *Journal of the American Institute of Planners* 40: 147–66.

Friedmann, John. 1979. *The Good Society*. Cambridge, MA: MIT Press.

Friedmann, John. 1992. *Empowerment: The Politics of Alternative Development*. New York: Blackwell Publishers.

Friends Committee on National Legislation (FCNL). 2004. *Peaceful Prevention of Deadly Conflict*. Washington, DC: FCNL.

Friends Committee on National Legislation. 2009. "Where Do Our Income Tax Dollars Go?" http://www.fcnl.org/pdfs/taxDay08.pdf.

Gamble, Dorothy N., and Marie Hoff. 2005. "Sustainable Community Development." In *The Handbook of Community Practice*, ed. Marie Weil, pp. 169–88. Thousand Oaks, CA: Sage Publications.

Gamble, Dorothy N., and Marie Weil. 1995. "Citizen Participation." In *Encyclopedia of Social Work*, 19th ed., ed. R. L. Edwards, pp. 483–94. Washington, DC: NASW Press.

Gamble, Dorothy N., and Marie Weil. 2008. "Community: Practice Interventions." In *Encyclopedia of Social Work*, ed. Terry Mizrahi and Larry Davis, pp. 355–68. Washington, DC: NASW Press.

Gamble, Dorothy N., Marie Weil, and Nicole Kiefer with community collaborators. 2005. *Measuring a Movement: Evaluating Outcomes in Community Sustainable Development.* Unpublished workbook for The Conservation Fund's Resourceful Communities Program, Chapel Hill, NC: The Conservation Fund.

Gandhi, Mohandas K. 1956. *The Gospel of Selfless Action, or The Gita According to Ghandi*, ed. Mahadev Desai. Ahmedabad, India: Navajivan Publishing House.

Gandhi, Mohandas K. 1993. *Gandhi: An Autobiography: The Story of My Experiments with Truth*. Boston: Beacon Press.

Gandhi, Mohandas K. 1995. *The Penguin Gandhi Reader*, 2nd ed. Baltimore, MD: Penguin.

Garcia, Betty, and Dorothy Van Soest. 2006. *Social Work Practice for Social Justice: Cultural Competence in Action*. Washington, DC: NASW Press.

Garvin, Charles D., and John E. Tropman. 1992. *Social Work in Contemporary Society*. Englewood Cliffs, NJ: Prentice-Hall.

Gaventa, John. 1981. "Land Ownership in Appalachia, USA: A Citizens' Research Project." In *Research for the People: Research by the People*, ed. F. Dubell, pp. 118–30. Linkoping, Sweden: Linkoping University Department of Education.

Gaventa, John. 1982. *Power and Powerlessness: Quiescence and Rebellion in an Appalachian Valley*. Champaign-Urbana: University of Illinois Press.

Georgetown University Study Abroad Program. 2007. Retrieved August 15, 2007, from http://www3.georgetown.edu/departments/sociology/programs/sjastudyabroad/.

Gibson-Graham, J. K. [Katherine Gibson and Julie Graham]. 1996. *The End of Capitalism (as We Knew It): A Feminist Critique of Political Economy*. Oxford, UK: Blackwell Publishers.

Glendinning, Chellis. 2005. *Chiva: A Village Takes on the Global Heroin Trade*. Gabriola Island, BC: New Society Publishers.

Global Health Council. 2008. http://www.globalhealth.org/.

Global Issues. 2009. United States and Foreign Aid Assistance. http://www.globalissues.org/article/35/us-and-foreign-aid-assistance.

Global Service Institute. 2008. http://gwbweb.wustl.edu/csd/gsi/about/index.htm.

Goldsmith, William W. 2006. Participatory Budgeting in Brazil. Cornell University. http://www.plannersnetwork.org/resources/pdfs/brazil_goldsmith.pdf#search=%22Origins%20.

Goodwin, Jan. 2008, January. "From Mutilation to Salvation." *Marie Claire*, 93–97.

Gore, Al. 2006. *An Inconvenient Truth: The Planetary Emergency of Global Warming and What We Can Do About It*. Emmaus, PA: Rodale Press

Gore, Al. 2007, December 10. Nobel Laureate Lecture. http://nobelprize.org/nobel_prizes/peace/laureates/2007/gore-lecture.html.

Gramsci, Antonio. 1987. *The Modern Prince and Other Stories*. New York: International Publishers.

Green Belt Movement. 2006. *GBM Kenya: Highlights of Thirty Years of Achievements*. http://greenbeltmovement.org/w.php?id=33.

Grimes, Kimberly M. 2005. "Changing the Rules of Trade with Global Partnerships: The Fair Trade Movement." In *Social Movements: An Anthropological Reader,* ed. J. Nash, pp. 237–48. Malden, MA: Blackwell Publishing.

Guadalupe, Krishna. 2003. "Empowerment Perspectives." In *Diversity Perspectives for Social Work Practice,* ed. Joseph Anderson and Robin Wiggins Carter, pp. 21–38. Boston: Allyn & Bacon.

Guadalupe, Krishna L., and Doman Lum. 2004. *Multidimensional Contextual Practice: Diversity and Transcendence.* Belmont, CA: Brooks/Cole.

Gun, C., and H. D. Gun. 1991. *Reclaiming Capital: Democratic Initiatives and Community Development.* Ithaca, NY: Cornell University Press.

Gurin, Arnold. 1970. *Community Organization Curriculum in Graduate Social Work Education: Report and Recommendations.* New York: CSWE.

Gutierrez, Lorraine M. 1992. "Empowering Clients in the 21st Century: The Role of Human Service Organizations." In *Human Service Organizations as Complex Organizations,* ed. Y. Hasenfeld, pp. 320–38. Newbury Park, CA: Sage Publications.

Gutierrez, Lorraine M., and Ann R. Alvarez. 2000. "Educating Students for Multicultural Community Practice." *Journal of Community Practice,* 7: 39–56.

Gutierrez, Lorraine M., and Edith A. Lewis. 1994. "Community Organizing with Women of Color: A Feminist Approach." *Journal of Community Practice,* 1: 23–44.

Gutierrez, Lorraine M., and Edith Lewis. 1999. *Empowering Women of Color.* New York: Columbia University Press.

Gutierrez, Lorraine M., Edith A. Lewis, Biren A. Nagda, Laura Wernick, and Nancy Shore. 2005. "Multicultural Community Practice Strategies and Intergroup Empowerment." In *The Handbook of Community Practice,* ed. Marie O. Weil, pp. 341–59. Thousand Oaks, CA: Sage Publications.

Gutierrez, Lorraine M., Ruth J. Parsons, and Enid Opal Cox, eds. 1998. *Empowerment in Social Work Practice: A Sourcebook.* Pacific Grove, CA: Brooks/Cole.

Hacker, Andrew. 2004, August 29. "How Different Is New York City?" *New York Times.*

Hall, Antony, and James O. Midgley. 2004. *Social Policy for Development.* Thousand Oaks, CA: Sage Publications.

Hall, Bob, ed. 1988. *Environmental Politics: Lessons from the Grassroots.* Durham, NC: Institute for Southern Studies.

Hallman, Howard W. 1984. *Neighborhoods: Their Place in Urban Life.* Beverly Hills, CA: Sage Publications.

Halpern, Robert. 1995. *Rebuilding the Inner City.* New York: Columbia University Press.

Hammersley, M., and P. Atkinson. 1983. *Ethnography: Principles in Practice.* London: Tavistock.

Hands Across Cultures. 2007. Española, New Mexico. http://www.hacc95.org/index.htm.

Hanh, Thich Nhat. 1998. *The Heart of the Buddha's Teaching.* New York: Broadway Books.

Hanh, Thich Nhat. 2000. *Plum Village Chanting and Recitation Book.* Compiled by Thich Nhat Hanh and the Monks and Nuns of Plum Village. Berkeley, CA: Parallax Press.

Hardcastle, David A., and Patricia R. Powers, with Stanley Wenocur. 2004. *Community Practice: Theories and Skills for Social Workers,* 2nd ed. New York: Oxford University Press.

Harper, Ernest B., and Arthur Dunham, eds. 1959. *Community Organization in Action.* New York: Association Press.

Harper-Dorton, Karen V. 2007. *Cross-Cultural Social Work Practice: Purpose and Meaning.* Chicago: Lyceum Books.

Harrington, Michael. 1962. *The Other America.* New York: Macmillan.

Hart, Maureen. 1999. *Guide to Sustainable Community Indicators,* 2nd ed. North Andover, MA: Hart Environmental Data. Retrieved February 8, 2008, from http://www.sustainablemeasures.com/.

Hart, Stuart L. 2007. *Capitalism at the Crossroads: Aligning Business, Earth, and Humanity*, 2nd ed. Philadelphia, PA: Wharton School Publishing.

Hasenfeld, Yzekial, ed. 1992. *Human Services as Complex Organizations*. Thousand Oaks, CA: Sage Publications.

Hashi, Khadija, Leyla Sharafi, and Barbara Ryan. 2007. *A Holistic Approach to the Abandonment of Female Genital Mutilation /Cutting*. New York: United Nations Population Fund (UNFPA).

Hatch, Mary J. 1997. *Organization Theory*. London: Oxford University Press.

Hawken, Paul. 1993. *The Ecology of Commerce*. New York: Collins.

Hawken, Paul. 2007. *Blessed Unrest: How the Largest Movement in the World Came into Being and Why No One Saw It Coming*. New York: Viking.

Hawken, Paul, Amory Lovins, and L. Hunter Lovins. 1999. *Natural Capitalism: Creating the Next Industrial Revolution*. Boston: Little, Brown.

Health Care Now. 2007. http://www.healthcare-now.org/.

Healy, Lynne M. 2001. *International Social work: Professional Action in an Interdependent World*. New York: Oxford University Press.

Heierbacher, Sandy. 2006. "What Are Dialogue and Deliberation?" National Coalition for Dialogue and Deliberation. http://www.thataway.org/?page_id=713.

Henderson, Hazel. 1996. *Building a Win-win World: Life Beyond Global Economic Warfare*. San Francisco, CA: Berrett-Koehler.

Herring, Hal. 2008, January 22. "Oil and Gas Symposium: Montana Cannot Become Another Wyoming." New West Network. http://www.newwest.net/topic/article/oil_gas_symposium_montana_cannot_become_another_wyoming/C38/L38/.

Herrnstein, Richard J., and Charles Murray. 1994. *The Bell Curve*. New York: Free Press.

Hersey, Paul, Kenneth H. Blanchard, and Dewey E. Johnson. 2000. *Management of Oganizational Behavior: Leading Human Resources*, 8th ed. New York: Prentice Hall.

Hick, Steven, and John McNutt, eds. 2002. *Advocacy, Activism and the Internet: Community Organization and Social Policy*. Chicago: Lyceum Books.

Hill Collins, Patricia. 2000. *Black Feminist Thought: Knowledge, Consciousness and the Politics of Empowerment*, 2nd ed. New York: Routledge..

Hillier, Amy E., and Dennis A. Culhane. 2005. "Integrating and Distributing Agency Data." In *The Handbook of Community Practice*, ed. M. Weil, pp. 647–58. Thousand Oaks, CA: Sage Publications.

Hines, Brian. 2004. *Return to the One: Plotinus' Guide to God-Realization. A Modern Exposition of an Ancient Classic: The Enneads*. Bloomington, IN: Unlimited Publishing.

Hinsdale, Mary Ann, Helen M. Lewis, and Maxine S. Waller. 1995. *It Comes from the People: Community Development and Local Theology*. Philadelphia, PA: Temple University Press.

Hirshman, Albert O. 1984. "Against Parsimony: Three Easy Ways of Complicating Some Categories of Economic Discourse." *American Economic Association Papers and Proceedings*, 74(2): 89–96.

Hirsi Ali, Ayaan. 2007. *Infidel*. New York: The Free Press.

Hobbes, Thomas. 1985. *Leviathan*. Reprinted in Penguin Classic Books. London: Penguin Classic Books.

Hoff, Marie D. 1994. "Environmental Foundations of Social Welfare: Theoretical Resources." In *The Global Environmental Crisis: Implications for Social Welfare and Social Work*, ed. M. D. Hoff and J. G. McNutt, pp. 12–35. Aldershot, England: Ashgate Publishing/Avebury Books.

Hoff, Marie D., ed. 1998. *Sustainable Community Development: Studies in Economic, Environmental and Cultural Revitalization*. Boca Raton, FL: Lewis Publishers.

Hoffman, Lily. 1989. The Politics of Knowledge: Activist Movements in Medicine and Planning. Albany, NY: State University of New York Press.

Hogan-Garcia, Mikel. 2003. *The Four Skills of Cultural Diversity Competence: A Process for Understanding and Practice*. Belmont, CA: Wadsworth.

Hogue, Teresa. 1994. "Wellness Multiplied." Oregon Center for Community Leadership. http://www.uwsp.edu/CNR/landcenter/pdffiles/CompPlanBinder/Public%20Partici pation%20in%20Planning/What%20We%20Mean%20by%20Working%20Together.pdf.

Hokenstad, M. C., and James Midgley, eds. 1997. *Issues in International Social Work: Global Challenges for a New Century*. Washington, DC: NASW Press.

Homan, Mark S. 2008. *Promoting Community Change: Making It Happen in the Real World*. 4th ed. Belmont, CA: Thomson, Brooks/Cole.

hooks, bell. 1984. *Feminist Theory from Margin to Center*. Boston: South End Press.

Hope, Anne, Sally Timmel, and Chris Hodzi. 1995. *Training for Transformation: A Handbook for Community Workers*, vols. 1–3, revised. Gweru, Zimbabwe: Mambo Press.

Horton, Myles, Judith Kohl, and Herbert Kohl. 1990. *The Long Haul: An Autobiography*. New York: Anchor Books, Doubleday.

Hoy Recovery Program. 2007. Española, New Mexico. http://www.hoyrecovery.org/.

Hudson, B. M. 1979. "Comparison of Current Planning Theories: Counterparts and Contradictions." *Journal of the American Planning Association* 45(4): 387–98.

Hufstader, Chris. Fall 2007. "This Is the Future: Landmark Victory in Bolivia." *Oxfam Exchange* 7(3): 12–13.

Hull-House Maps and Papers, by Residents of Hull-House, a Social Settlement. A Presentation of Nationalities and Wages in a Congested District of Chicago, Together with Comments and Essays on Problems Growing Out of the Social Conditions. 1895. New York: Cromwell.

Hurst, Charles E. 2006. *Social Inequality: Forms, Causes and Consequences*, 6th ed. Boston: Allyn & Bacon.

Hyde, Cheryl. 1986. "Experiences of Women Activists: Implications for Community Organizing Theory and Practice." *Journal of Sociology and Social Welfare* 13(3): 545–62.

Hyde, Cheryl. 1989. "A Feminist Model for Macro Practice: Promises and Problems." *Administration in Social Work* 13(3/4): 145–81.

Hyde, Cheryl. 1995. "Feminist Social Movement Organizations Survive the New Right." In *Feminist Organizations: Harvest of the New Women's Movement*, ed. M. Ferree and P. Martin, pp. 306–22. Philadelphia: Temple University Press.

Hyde, Cheryl A. 2003. "Multicultural Development in Non-profit Human Services: Views from the Field." *Journal of Community Practice* 11(1): 39–59.

Hyde, Cheryl A. 2004. "Multicultural Development in Human Service Agencies: Challenges and Solutions." *Social Work* 49(1): 7–16.

Hyde, Cheryl A. 2005. "Feminist Community Practice." In *The Handbook of Community Practice*, ed. Marie Weil, pp. 360–71. Thousand Oaks, CA: Sage Publications.

Hyde, Cheryl A., and Karen Hopkins. 2004. "Assessing the Diversity Climates in Human Service Agencies." *Journal of Ethnic and Cultural Diversity in Social Work* 13(2): 25–43.

Ife, Jim. 2006. "Human Rights beyond the 'Three Generations.'" In *Activating Human Rights*, ed. Elizabeth Porter and Baden Offord, pp. 29–45. New York: Peter Lang/Oxford.

Ife, Jim. 2007a. "Cultural Relativism and Community Activism." In *Challenges in Human Rights: A Social Work Perspective*, ed. Elisabeth Reichert, pp. 76–96. New York: Columbia University Press.

Ife, Jim. 2007b, October. "The New International Agendas: What Role for Social Work." Hokenstad International Social Work Lecture. Council on Social Work Education, San Francisco, California.

Ife, Jim. 2008. *Human Rights and Social Work: Toward Rights-Based Practice*. Rev. ed. Cambridge, UK: Cambridge University Press.

Iglehart, Alfreda, and Rosina M. Becerra. 2000. *Social Services and the Ethnic Community.* Longrove, IL: Waveland Press.

InterAction. Press Release. 2007, October 18. "At Halfway Mark, New Report Shows U.S. Falling Short of U.N. Millennium Goals to Combat Global Poverty." At http://www.inter action.org/media/MDGsReport/20071018-MDGReport2.htm.

International Baby Food Action Network (IBFAN). 2008. http://www.ibfan.org/site2005/ Pages/article.php?art_id=23&iui=1.

International Campaign to Ban Landmines (ICBL). 2009. http://www.icbl.org/campaign/history.

International Federation of Social Workers (IFSW). 2008. International Policy Statement on Globalization and the Environment. At http://www.ifsw.org/en/p38000222.html.

International Federation of Social Workers and International Association of Schools of Social Work (IFSW and IASSW). 2008. "Ethics in Social Work, Statement of Principles, adopted 2004." http://www.ifsw.org/en/p38000324.html.

International Herald Tribune. 2008, February 26. "UN Says Half the World's Population Will Live in Urban Areas by End of 2008." Associated Press. http://www.iht.com/bin/print friendly.php?id=10447430.

International Publishers. Internet World Stats. 2008. http://www.internetworldstats.com/stats .htm.

Israel, Barbara A., Eugenia Eng, Amy J. Schulz, and Edith Parker, eds. 2005. *Methods in Community-Based Participatory Research for Health.* San Francisco: Jossey-Bass.

Israel, Barbara A., E. A. Parker, Z. Rowe, A. Salvatore, M. Minkler, J. López, A. Butz, A. Mosley, L. Coates, G. Lambert, P. A. Potito, B. Brenner, M. Rivera, H. Romero, B. Thompson, G. Coronado, and S. Halstead. 2005. "Community-Based Participatory Research: Lessons Learned from the Centers for Children's Environmental Health and Disease Prevention Research." *Environmental Health Perspectives* 113(10): 1463–71.

Itzhaky, Haya., and Alan S. York. 2002. "Showing Results in Community Organization." *Social Work* 47: 125–31.

Jacobs Center for Neighborhood Innovation. 2008. http://www.jacobscenter.org/.

Jacobson, Maxine, and Chris Rugeley. 2007. "Community-based Participatory Research: Group Work for Social Justice and Community Change." *Social Work with Groups* 30(4): 21–39.

Jansson, Bruce S. 2007. *Becoming an Effective Policy Advocate: From Policy Practice to Social Justice,* 5th ed. Belmont, CA: Wadsworth/Thompson Learning.

Jansson, Bruce S., David Dempsey, Jacquelyn McCorskey, and Robert Schneider. 2005. "Four Models of Policy Practice." In *The Handbook of Community Practice,* ed. Marie Weil, pp. 319–38. Thousand Oaks, CA: Sage Publications.

Jewish Study Bible. 2004. Ed. and trans. Adele Berlin and Mark Zvi Brittler. New York: Oxford University Press.

Johnson, Douglas. 2004. "New Tactics in Human Rights: A Resource for Practitioners from the New Tactics Project." Center for Victims of Torture. http://www.newtactics.org/len/ ToolsforAction/TheNewTacticsWorkbook/read or download files.

Johnson, James H., and Walter C. Farrell Jr. 2000. *Strategies for Engaging the Private Sector in Inner City Job Creation and Poverty Alleviation: An Overview of Proposed Initiatives.* Chapel Hill: University of North Carolina at Chapel Hill, Frank Hawkins Kenan Institute of Private Enterprise.

Jones, Malcolm. 2008. "Katrina Diary." *The American Interest* 3: 40–41.

Kafuko, Mary. 2007. http://www.onemen.org/templates/dispatcher.asp?page_id=2313.

Kahn, Alfred J. 1969. *Theory and Practice of Social Planning.* New York: Russell Sage Foundation.

Kahn, Si. 1991. *Organizing: A Guide for Grassroots Leaders,* rev. ed. Washington, DC: NASW Press.

Kahn, Si. 1994. *How People Get Power*, rev. ed. Washington, DC: NASW Press.

Kane, Mary, and William M. K. Trochim. 2007. *Concept Mapping for Planning and Evaluation*. Thousand Oaks, CA: Sage Publications.

Kaner, Sam, with Lenny Lind, Catherine Toldi, Sarah Fisk, and Duane Berger. 1996. *Facilitator's Guide to Participatory Decision Making*. Gabriola Island, BC: New Society Publishers.

Kavanagh, Brian, Lucy Mayo, Steve Carbo, and Mike Slater. 2005, July. "Ten Years Later a Promise Unfulfilled: The National Voter Registration Act in Public Assistance Agencies, 1995–2005." http://projectvote.org/fileadmin/ProjectVote/pdfs/Tens_Years_Later_A_Promise_Unfulfilled.pdf.

Kean, Yeong Joo, and Annelies Allain. 2004a. *State of the Code by Company 2004*. Penang, Malaysia: International Baby Food Action Network (IBFAN). http://www.ibfan.org.english/pdfs/btro4/socompany04.pdf.

Kean, Yeong Joo, and Annelies Allain, eds. 2004b. *Breaking the Rules, Stretching the Rules*. International Code Documentation Centre. Penang, Malaysia: IBFAN http://www.ibfan.org/site2005/abm/paginas/articles/arch_art/302-3.pdf.

Kellogg Foundation. 2004. *Logic Model Development Guide*. Battle Creek, MI: W. K. Kellogg Foundation.

Kemper, Robert V. 2006. "Robert Ezra Park." In *Encyclopedia of Anthropology*, ed. H. James Brix. Thousand Oaks, CA: Sage Publications.

Kensington Welfare Rights Organization. 2008. http://www.kwru.org/kwru/abtkwru.html.

Kettner, Peter M., Robert M. Maroney, and L. L. Martin. 2008. *Designing and Managing Programs*, 3rd ed. Thousand Oaks: CA: Sage Publications.

Khor, Martin, and Lim Li Lin, eds. 2001. *Good Practices and Innovative Experiences in the South*, vol. 1, *Economic, Environmental and Sustainable Livelihood Initiatives*. London: Zed Books and UNDP.

Kindon, Sara. 2008. *Participatory Action Research and Methods: Connecting People, Participation and Place*. London: Routledge.

King, Rev. Martin Luther, Jr. 1963. "Letter from a Birmingham Jail, 1963." http://www.africa.upenn.edu/Articles_Gen/Letter_Birmingham.html.

Klein, Naomi. 2007. *The Shock Doctrine: The Rise of Disaster Capitalism*. New York: Metropolitan Books/Henry Holt.

Kleymeyer, Charles David, ed. 1994. *Cultural Expressions and Grassroots Development: Cases from Latin America and the Caribbean*. Boulder, CO: Lynne Rienner Publishers.

Knight, E. 1997. "A Description of the Effectiveness of Promoting Rural Opportunity in Mississippi (PRO-MISS) Leadership Program over Time." *Masters Abstracts International* 36(03): 660 (UMI No. 1388114).

Korten, David. 2001. *When Corporations Rule the World*, 2nd ed., West Hartford, CT: Kumarian Press.

Korten, David. 2009. *Agenda for a New Economy: From Phantom Wealth to Real Wealth*. San Francisco, CA: Berrett-Koehler Publishers.

Kramer, Robert M., and Harry Specht. 1975. *Readings in Community Organization Practice*, 2nd ed. Englewood Cliffs, NJ: Prentice-Hall.

Kretzmann, John P., and John L. McKnight. 1993. *Building Communities from the Inside Out: A Path toward Finding and Mobilizing a Community's Assets*. Chicago: ACTA Publications.

Kriegman, Orion (Lead Author); Great Transitions Initiative; Cutler J. Cleveland (Topic Editor). 2007. "Global Citizens Movement." In *Encyclopedia of Earth*, ed. Cutler J. Cleveland. Washington, DC: Environmental Information Coalition, National Council for Science and the Environment. First published in the Encyclopedia of Earth, October 31,

2006; last revised November 9, 2007. Retrieved February 19, 2008, from http://www.eoearth.org/article/Global_citizens_movement.

Kriesberg, Daniel A. 1999. *A Sense of Place: Teaching Children about the Environment with Picture Books*. Portsmouth, NH: Teacher Ideas Press.

Krishna, Anirudh. 2002. *Active Social Capital: Tracing the Roots of Democracy and Development*. New York: Columbia University Press.

Krishna, Anirudh, and Roland Bunch. 1997. "Farmer-to-Farmer Experimentation and Extension: Integrated Rural Development for Smallholders in Guatemala." In *Reasons for Hope: Instructive Experiences in Rural Development*, ed. Anirudh Krishna, Norman Uphoff, and Milton J. Esman, pp. 137–52. West Hartford, CT: Kumarian Press.

Krishna, Anirudh, Norman Uphoff, and Milton J. Esman, eds. 1997. *Reasons for Hope: Instructive Experiences in Rural Development*. West Hartford, CT: Kumarian Press.

Kroeger, O., and J. M. Thuesen. 1988. *Type Talk*. New York: Dell.

Kromm, Chris, and Sue Sturgis. 2008, January. *Hurricane Katrina and the Guiding Principles on Internal Displacement: A Global Human Rights Perspective on a National Disaster*. Durham, NC: Institute for Southern Studies. http://www.southernstudies.org/ISSKatrinaHumanRightsJan08.pdf.

Kuhn, Thomas S. 1970. *The Structure of Scientific Revolutions*, 2nd ed., enlarged. Chicago: University of Chicago Press.

Kumar, Krishna, ed. 1998. *Postconflict Elections, Democratization, and International Assistance*. Boulder, CO: Lynne Rienner Publishers.

Kurzman, Paul. 1985. "Program Development and Service Coordination as Components of Community Practice." In *Theory and Practice of Community Social Work*, ed. Samuel H. Taylor and Robert W. Roberts, pp. 95–124. New York: Columbia University Press.

LaDuke, Winona. 2005. *Recovering the Sacred: The Power of Naming and Claiming*. Cambridge, MA: South End Press.

LaFraniere, Sharon. 2006, October 29. "Africa's World of Forced Labor, in a 6-Year-Old's Eyes." *New York Times*, p. A1. Also http://www.nytimes.com/2006/10/29/world/africa/29ghana.html.

Lakoff, George, and Sam Ferguson. 2006. "Crucial Issues Not Addressed in the Immigration Debate: Why Deep Framing Matters." The Rockridge Institute. http://www.rockridgeinstitute.org/research/lakoff/imm-response.

Lao Tsu. 1994. *Tao Te Ching*. Trans. and appendices by D. C. Lau. New York: Alfred A. Knopf.

Lao Tsu. 1997. *Tao Te Ching*. Trans. Gia-Fu Feng and Jane English. New York: Vintage.

Lauffer, Armand. 1978. *Social Planning at the Community Level*. Englewood Cliffs, NJ: Prentice-Hall.

Lawrence, Bruce. 2006. *The Qur'an: A Biography*. New York: Grove Press.

League of Women Voters. 2007, December 6. "League Urges Senators to Co-sponsor Presidential Public Financing Legislation." http://www.lwv.org/AM/Template.cfm?Section=Campaign_Finance_Reform&CONTENTID=10292&TEMPLATE=/CM/ContentDisplay.cfm.

Lee, Bill. 1997. *Pragmatics of Community Organization*, 2nd ed. Toronto, Ontario: Commonact Press.

Lee, Bill, and Mike Balkwill. 1996. *Participatory Planning for Action*. Toronto, Ontario: Commonact Press.

Lee, Judith A. B. 2001. *The Empowerment Approach to Social Work Practice*, 2nd ed. New York: Columbia University Press.

Lee, William Keng Mun, and Hong-kin Kwok. 2006. "Aging and Elder Care in China: The Case of Guangzhou." *Social Development Issues* 28(1): 20–33.

Lewin, Kurt. 1947. "Frontiers in Group Dynamics," *Human Relations*, 1: 5–41.

Lewis, Edith A., and Kris Kissman. 1989. "Factors Linking Ethnic-Sensitive and Feminist Social Work Practice with African-American Women." *Arete* 14(2): 23–31.

Liberty Guide to Human Rights. 2008. "Peaceful Protest." http://www.yourrights.org.uk/your-rights/chapters/the-right-of-peaceful-protest/.

Lindbloom, Charles E. 1959. "The Science of Muddling Through." *Public Administration Review* 19(2): 79–88.

Lindeman, Eduard C. 1949. "Democracy and Social Work." In *Proceedings National Conference of Social Work, 1948*. New York: Columbia University Press.

Link, Rosemary J. 2007. "Children's Rights as a Template for Social Work Practice." In *Challenges in Human Rights: A Social Work Perspective*, ed. Elisabeth Reichert, pp. 215–38. New York: Columbia University Press.

Linnell, Deborah, Zora Radosevich, and Jonathan Spack. 2002. *Executive Directors Guide: The Guide for Successful Nonprofit Management*. Boston: Third Sector New England.

Lippitt, Roland, Jeanne Watson, and Bruce Westley. 1958. *The Dynamics of Planned Change*. New York: Harcourt, Brace & World.

Living Wage Network, Santa Fe, New Mexico. 2008. "History of the Campaign." http://www.santafelivingwage.org/history.html/.

Living Wage Resource Center. 2008. http://www.livingwagecampaign.org/.

Lohmann, Roger A., and John McNutt. 2005. "Practice in the Electronic Community." In *Handbook of Community Practice*, ed. M. Weil, pp. 636–46. Thousand Oaks, CA: Sage Publications.

Long, Dennis D., Carolyn J. Tice, and John D. Morrison. 2006. *Macro Social Work Practice: A Strengths Perspective*. Belmont, CA: Thomson/Brooks/Cole.

Lopach, James J., and Jean A. Luckowski. 2005. *Jeannette Rankin: A Political Woman*. Boulder: University Press of Colorado.

Lorenz, Jan, and Frederico Menino B. de Oliveira. 2005. "Designing Participatory Budgeting: Mathematics of Opinion Dynamics and Aggregation." FES-Brasilienprojeckt, retrieved September 13, 2006, from http://www.informatik.uni-bremen.de/~jlorinz/policypaper_lorenzmenina.

Lum, Doman, ed. 2006. *Culturally Competent Practice: A Framework for Understanding Diverse Groups and Justice Issues*, 3rd ed. Belmont, CA: Brooks/Cole, Cengage Learning.

Lynch, Kevin A. 1960. *The Image of the City*. Cambridge, MA: MIT Press.

Maathai, Wangari. 2004. Nobel Peace Prize Autobiography by Tore Frangsmyr. http://nobelprize.org/nobel.prizes/peace/laureates/2004/maathai-bio.html.

Mandela, Nelson R. 1995. *Long Walk to Freedom*. Boston: Little, Brown.

Mapp, Susan C. 2008. *Human Rights and Social Justice in a Global Perspective: An Introduction to International Social Work*. New York: Oxford University Press.

Markkula Center for Applied Ethics. 2008. http://www.scu.edu/ethics/.

Marley, Marsha, and Mary Rogge. 2008. "Lee and the Amazing Multifaceted Community Needs Assessment." In *Cases in Macro Social Work Practice*, ed. David P. Fauri, Steven P. Wernet, and F. Ellen Netting, pp. 13-30. Needham Heights, MA: Allyn & Bacon.

Martinez-Brawley, Emilia. 1990. *Perspectives on the Small Community: Humanistic Views for Practitioners*. Washington, DC: NASW Press.

Martinez-Brawley, Emilia. 1995. "Community." In *Encyclopedia of Social Work*, 19th ed., ed. Richard L. Edwards, pp. 539–48. Washington, DC: NASW Press.

Matsuoka, Jon K. 1997. *Economic Change and Mental Health of Lana'i: A Longitudinal Analysis*. Report to the National Institute of Mental Health. Honolulu: University of Hawaii, School of Social Work.

Mattessich, Paul W., Marta Murray-Close, and Barbara R. Monsey. 2001. *Collaboration: What Makes It Work*, 2nd ed. Saint Paul, MN: Fieldstone Alliance.

Max-Neef, Manfred, A. 1992. "Development and Human Needs." In *Real Life Economics: Understanding Wealth Creation*, ed. Paul Ekins and Manfred A. Max-Neef, pp. 197–214. London: Routledge.

Mayer, Robert. 1972. *Social Planning and Social Change*. Englewood Cliffs, NJ: Prentice Hall.

McAdoo, Harriette Pipes, ed. 1993. *Family Ethnicity: Strength in Diversity*. Thousand Oaks, CA: Sage.

McBride, Amanda Moore, and Michael Sherraden. December, 2004. "Toward a Global Research Agenda on Civic Service: Editors' Introduction to This Special Issue." *Nonprofit and Voluntary Sector Quarterly* 33(4): 3S–7S.

McCoy, Jennifer L., ed. 1999. *Political Learning and Redemocratization in Latin America: Do Politicians Learn from Political Crises?* Boulder, CO: Lynne Rienner Publishers.

McIntyre, Alice. 2007. *Participatory Action Research*. Thousand Oaks, CA: Sage Publications.

Mckernan, Signe-Mary, and Michael Sherraden. 2008. *Asset Building and Low-Income Families*. Baltimore, MD: Urban Institute Press.

McKibben, Bill. 1995. *Hope, Human and Wild*. New York: Little, Brown. Also, excerpted Summer 1999 in "Cities of Exuberance, Curitiba: Story of a City." http://www.yesmagazine.org/article.asp?ID=1258.

McKibben, Bill. 2007. *Deep Economy: The Wealth of Communities and the Durable Future*. New York: Times Books/Henry Holt and Company.

McLaughlin, L. A., and G. B. Jordan. 1999. "Logic Models: A Tool for Telling Your Program's Performance Story." *Evaluation and Program Planning* 22: 65–72.

Medoff, Peter, and Holly Sklar. 1994. *Streets of Hope: The Fall and Rise of an Urban Neighborhood*. Boston: South End Press.

Melaville, Atelia, and Martin J. Blank, with Gelareh Asayesh. 1993. *Together We Can: A Guide for Crafting a Profamily System of Education and Human Services*. Pittsburgh, PA: Diane Publishing.

Merriam-Webster OnLine Dictionary. 2009. http://www.merriam-webster.com.

Merton, Robert K. 1968. *Social Theory and Social Structure*. New York: Free Press.

Message of the Qur'an. 2nd ed. 2008. Trans. Muhammad Asad. Watsonville, CA: The Book Foundation.

Micro Finance Enterprises. 2009. http://www.mcenterprises.org/userimages/file/global_poverty_the_sorry_facts_compiled_2005.pdf.

Midgley, James. 1995. *Social Development: The Developmental Perspective in Social Welfare*. Thousand Oaks, CA: Sage Publications.

Midgley, James, and Michelle Livermore. 2005. "Development Theory and Community Practice." In *Handbook of Community Practice*, ed. M. Weil, pp. 153–68. Thousand Oaks, CA: Sage Publications.

Midgley, James, and Michael Sherraden. 2000. "The Social Development Perspective in Social Policy." In *The Handbook of Social Policy*, ed. James Midgley, M. B. Tracy, and Michelle Livermore, pp. 435–46. Thousand Oaks, CA: Sage Publications.

Milanovic, Branko. 2006. "Global Income Inequality: A Review." *World Economics* 7(1): 131–57.

Milewski, Jennifer. 2007. *Quantum Leadership: The Power of Community in Motion*. New York: Leadership for a Changing World; Research Center for Leadership in Action, Robert F. Wagner Graduate School of Public Service, New York University.

Miller, Ethan. 2006, September 9. "Other Economies Are Possible! Organizing toward an Economy of Cooperation and Solidarity. http://www.zmag.org/content/showarticle.cfm?ItemID=10926.

Miller, S. J., D. J. Hickson, and D. C. Wilson. 1996. "Decision-Making in Organizations." In *Handbook of Organization Studies*, ed. S. R. Clegg, C. Hardy, and W. R. Nord, pp. 293–312. London: Sage Publications.

Milligan, Sharon. 2008. "Community Building." In *Encyclopedia of Social Work*, 20th ed., ed. Terry Mizrahi and Larry Davis, vol. 1, pp. 371–75. Washington, DC: NASW Press.

Minkler, Meredith, ed. 2004. *Community Organizing and Community Building for Health.* New Brunswick, NJ: Rutgers University Press.

Minkler, Meredith, and Cheri Pies. 2004. "Ethical Issues and Practical Dilemmas in Community Organization and Community Participation." In *Community Organizing and Community Building for Health*, 2nd ed., ed. Meredith Minkler, pp. 116–33. Piscataway, NJ: Rutgers University Press.

Minkler, Meredith, and Nina Wallerstein, eds. 2003. *Community-Based Participatory Research for Health.* San Francisco: Jossey-Bass.

Mizrahi, Terry. 2009. "Community Organizing Principles and Practice Guidelines." In *Social Workers Desk Reference*, ed. Albert R. Roberts and Gilbert J. Greene, pp. 872–81. New York: Oxford University Press.

Mizrahi, Terry, and Beth Rosenthal. 2001. "Complexities of Effective Coalition Building: A Study of Leaders' Strategies, Struggles, and Solutions." *Social Work* 46: 63–78.

Mondros, Jacqueline B., and Lee Staples. 2008. "Community Organization." *In Encyclopedia of Social Work*, 20th ed., ed. Terry Mizrahi and Larry Davis, vol. 1, pp. 387–98. Washington, DC: NASW Press.

Mondros, Jacqueline B., and Scott M. Wilson. 1994. *Organizing for Power and Empowerment.* New York: Columbia University Press.

Moraga, Cherrie, and Gloria Anzaldua. 1984. *This Bridge Called My Back: Written by Radical Women of Color and Home Girls.* New York: Kitchen Table Press.

Morning Star Development. 2008. Retrieved July 12, 2008, from http://msdev.homestead.com/.

Morrison, John. 2005. "Service Coordination: Practical Concerns for Community Practitioners." In *The Handbook of Community Practice*, ed. Marie Weil, pp. 387–401. Thousand Oaks, CA: Sage Publications.

Mortenson, Greg, and David Oliver Relin. 2006. *Three Cups of Tea: One Man's Mission to Promote Peace . . . One School at a Time.* New York: Penguin Books.

Mota, Ana Elizabete. 2005. "Social Needs, Global Solutions: Creative Solutions for Social Development." Dan Sanders Memorial Lecture, Keynote address, 14th International Symposium, International Consortium for Social Development, Recife, Brazil. http://www.iucisd.org/dansanders/lecture4.htm.

Mullaly, Bob. 2007. *New Structural Social Work: Ideology, Theory, Practice*, 3rd ed. Don Mills, Ontario: Oxford University Press.

Mulroy, Elizabeth A. 2001, November. "Transforming Community Based Collaborations: Planning the Pace of Development." Paper presented at the Association for Research on Nonprofit Organizations and Voluntary Action (ARNOVA), Miami, Florida.

Mulroy, Elizabeth A. 2008. "Community Needs Assessment." In *Encyclopedia of Social Work*, 20th ed., ed. Terry Mizrahi and Larry Davis, pp. 385–87. New York: Oxford University Press.

Mulroy, Elizabeth A., and Jon K. Matsuoka. 2008. "The Native Hawaiian Children's Center: Changing Methods from Casework to Community Practice." In *Cases in Macro Social Work Practice*, ed. D. P. Fauri, S. Wernet, and F. E. Netting, pp. 107–20. Boston: Allyn & Bacon.

Mulroy, Elizabeth A., Kristine E. Nelson, and Denise Gour. 2005. "Community-Building and Family-Centered Service Collaboratives." In *The Handbook of Community Practice*, ed. Marie Weil, pp. 460–74. Thousand Oaks, CA: Sage Publications.

Myers, Amanda Lee. 2006, March 15. "Border Crossing Ends in Grief over Girl's Death." *New Mexican* (Santa Fe), p. C6.

Nabhan, Gary, and Gay Chanler. 2008. Navajo-Churro Sheep, Production Area—Navajo Nation Reserve, Arizona and New Mexico. http://slowfoodfoundation.com/eng/predidi/dettaglio.lasso?cod=331.

Nash, June, ed. 2005. *Social Movements: An Anthropological Reader*. Malden, MA: Blackwell Publishers.

National Association of Black Social Workers (NABSW). 2008. "Code of Ethics." http://www.nabsw.org/mserver/CodeofEthics.aspx.

National Association of Planning Councils. 2008. Retrieved April 26, 2008, from http://www.communityplanning.org/.

National Association of Social Workers (NASW). 2007a. *Institutional Racism and the Social Work Profession: A Call to Action*. Washington, DC: NASW Press.

National Association of Social Workers (NASW). 2007b. *Peace Policy Toolkit 2007*. Washington, DC: NASW Press.

National Association of Social Workers (NASW). 2008. "Code of Ethics of the National Association of Social Workers, Approved 1996, Revised 2008." http://www.socialworkers.org/pubs/code/code.asp.

National Campaign for Sustainable Agriculture. 2008. http://www.sustainableagriculture.net/.

National Coalition for Dialogue and Deliberation. 2007. http://thataway.org.

National Immigrant Solidarity Network. 2008. http://www.immigrantsolidarity.org/.

National Priorities Project. 2008. "Bringing the Federal Budget Home." http://www.national-priorities.org/costofwar_home.

Nazer, Mende, and Damien Lewis. 2002. *Slave*. New York: Public Affairs.

Netting, F. Ellen, Peter M. Kettner, and Steven L. McMurtry. 2008. *Social Work Macro Practice*, 4th ed. Boston: Allyn & Bacon, Pearson Education.

Netting, F. Ellen, Mary Katherine O'Connor, and David P. Fauri. 2008. *Comparative Approaches to Program Planning*. Hoboken, NJ: John Wiley & Sons.

New Mexico Department of Health. 1996. *New Mexico Drug Abuse-related Mortality Rates, 1993–1995*. Santa Fe, NM: Public Health Division.

New Mexico Drug Court. 2008. http://corrections.state.nm.us/programs/drugcourt.html.

New Oxford Annotated Bible: An Ecumenical Study Bible. 2007. 3rd ed., New Revised Standard Version, ed. Michael D. Coogan. New York: Oxford.

Nixon, P., G. Burford, and A. Quinn (with J. Edelbaum). 2005. *A Survey of International Practices, Policy and Research on Family Group Conferencing and Related Practices*. Retrieved August 26, 2006, from http://www.americanhumane.org/site/DocServer/FGDM_www_survey.pdf?docID=2841.

Noponen, Helzi. 2001. "The Internal Learning System for Participatory Assessment of Micro-finance." *Small Enterprise Development* 12(4): 45–53.

Noponen, Helzi. 2002. "The Internal Learning System: A Tool for Participant and Program Learning in Micro-finance and Livelihoods Interventions." *Development Bulletin* 57(1): 106–10.

Nyden, Philip, Anne Figert, Mark Shibley, and Darryl Burrows. 1997. *Building Community: Social Science in Action*. Thousand Oaks, CA: Pine Forge Press.

Obama, Barack. 1995/2004. *Dreams of My Father: A Story of Race and Inheritance*. New York: Three Rivers Press.

Oberschall, Anthony. 1993. *Social Movements: Ideologies, Interests, and Identities*. New Brunswick, NJ: Transaction Publishers.

O'Connor, Mary Katherine, and F. Ellen Netting. 2007. "Emergent Program Planning as Competent Practice: The Importance of Considering Context." *Journal of Progressive Human Services* 18(2): 57–75.

Odum, Eugene P. 1997. *Ecology: A Bridge between Science and Society*, 3rd ed. Sunderland, MA: Sinauer Associates.

Odum, Howard T., and Elizabeth C. Odum. 2001. *A Prosperous Way Down: Principles and Policies*. Boulder, CO: University of Colorado Press.

Odum, Howard W. 1936/1969. *Southern Regions of the United States*. New York: Agathon Press.

Ohmer, Mary L., and Wynne S. Korr. 2006. "The Effectiveness of Community Practice Interventions: A Review of the Literature." *Research on Social Work Practice* 16(2): 132–45.

Orenstein, Peggy. 2008, March 23. "Mixed Messenger." *New York Times Magazine*, pp. 9–10.

Organization for Economic Co-operation and Development (OECD). 2007. Istanbul Declaration 2007. http://www.oecd.org/dataoecd/14/46/38883774.pdf.

Organization for Economic Co-operation and Development (OECD). 2009. Social Institutions and Gender Index (SIGI). http://www.oecd.org/document/39/0,3343,en_2649_33935_42274663_1_1_1_1,00.html.

Ottawa Charter for Health Promotion. 2008. http://www.who.int/hpr/NPH/docs/ottawa_charter_hp.pdf.

Oxfam America. 2008. *SmartDevelopment*. http://www.oxfamamerica.org/newsandpublications/publications/briefing_papers/smart-development.

Pádilla, Yolanda C., and Michael Sherraden. 2005. "Communities and Social Policy Issues: Persistent Poverty, Economic Inclusion and Asset Building." In *The Handbook of Community Practice*, ed. Marie Weil, pp. 103–16. Thousand Oaks, CA: Sage Publications.

Park, Robert E. 1952. *Human Communities*. Glencoe, IL: Free Press.

Parris, Thomas M., and Robert W. Kates. 2003. "Characterizing and Measuring Sustainable Development." *Annual Review of Environmental Resources*, 28(13): 1–13.

Parsons, Talcott. 1954. *Essays in Sociological Theory*. New York: Free Press.

Parton, Nigel, and Patrick O'Byrne. 2005. *Constructive Social Work: Towards a New Practice*. New York: Palgrave Macmillan.

Pawlek, Edward J., and Robert D. Vinter. 2004. *Designing and Planning Programs for Nonprofit and Government Organizations*. San Francisco, CA: John Wiley & Sons.

Payne, Malcolm. 2005. *Modern Social Work Theory*, 3rd ed. Houndmills, Basingstoke, Hampshire, UK: Palgrave Macmillan.

Payne, Malcolm, and Gurid Aga Askeland. 2008. *Globalization and International Social Work: Postmodern Change and Challenge*. Hampshire, UK: Ashgate Publishers Ltd.

Peace Action. 2008. At http://www.peace-action.org/.

Peace Majority Report, 2007. http://www.peacemajority.us.index.html.

Peace Talks Radio (6/29/07). Nobel peace laureate Jody Williams. http://www.goodradioshows.org/peaceTalksL50.htm.

Pellett, Peter L. 1999, April 12–13. "A Human Rights Approach to Food and Nutrition Policies and Programs." ACC/SCN Symposium: The Substance and Politics of a Human Rights Approach to Food and Nutrition Policies and Programs," Geneva. At http://www.unsystem.org/SCN/archives/scnnews18/ch06.htm.

Pennell, Joan. 2007. "Safeguarding All Family Members—FGC and Family Violence." *Social Work Now: The Practice Journal of Child, Youth and Family* 37:4–8. Retrieved March 16, 2008, from http://www.cyf.govt.nz/documents/swn37.pdf.

Pennell, Joan, and Gary Anderson, eds. 2005. *Widening the Circle: The Practice and Evaluation of Family Group Conferencing with Children, Youths, and Their Families*. Washington, DC: NASW Press.

Pennell, Joan, Helzi Noponen, and Marie O. Weil. 2005. "Empowerment Research." In *The Handbook of Community Practice*, ed. Marie O. Weil, pp. 620–35. Thousand Oaks, CA: Sage Publications.

Penninx, Rinus, Maria Berger, and Karen Kraal, eds. 2006. *The Dynamics of International Migration and Settlement in Europe: A State of the Art.* Amsterdam: Amsterdam University Press.

People's Decade of Human Rights Education. 2008. *Passport to Dignity.* http://www.pdhre.org/passport.html.

Pete Seeger: The Power of Song. 2007. Documentary directed by Jim Brown.

Peterson, Brooks. 2004. *Cultural Intelligence: A Guide to Working with People from Other Cultures.* London: Intercultural Press.

Pew Center on the States. 2008. Pew Charitable Trusts. *One in 100: Behind Bars in America.* At http://www.pewcenteronthestates.org/uploadfiles/1%20in%20100.pdf.

Pibel, Doug. 2006. "When the People Decide." *Yes!,* No. 37 (Spring), 45.

Pillay, Navanethem, ed. 2007, December. "Gender and Transitional Justice." Special issue, *International Journal of Transitional Justice* 1(3).

Pimentel, David, Laura Westra, and Reed F. Noss, eds. 2000. *Ecological Integrity: Integrating Environment, Conservation and Health.* Washington, DC: Island Press.

Pincus, Allen, and Anne Minahan. 1973. *Social Work Practice: Method and Model.* Itasca, IL: Peacock.

Pirkei Avos: Ethics of the Fathers. 1994. Ed. Meir Zlotowitz and Nosson Scherman. Brooklyn, NY: Artscroll.

Plato. 1968. *The Republic.* Trans. Allan Bloom. New York: Basic Books.

Policy Research Initiative. 2005. "Social Capital in Action: Thematic Policy Studies." Ottawa, Canada: http://policyresearch.gc.ca/doclib/SC_thematic_E.pdf.

Pollan, Michael. 2008, October 12. "Farmer in Chief: What the Next President Can and Should Do to Remake the Way We Grow and Eat Our Food." *New York Times Magazine,* pp. 62–71, 92.

Poor People's Economic Human Rights Campaign. 2008. http://www.economichumanrights.org/index.shtml.

Popova, Deliana. 2006. "Trafficking in Women, Female Migration, and Identity." *Social Development Issues* 28(3): 70–86.

Population Reference Bureau. 2006. "World Population Data Sheet: International Migration Is Reshaping United States, Global Economy." http://www.prb.org/Publications/Datasheets/2006/2006WorldPopulationDataSheet.aspx?p=1.

Porta, Donatella Della, and Mario Diani. 2006. *Social Movements: An Introduction.* Malden, MA: Blackwell Publishing.

Portes, Alejandro. 1998. "Social Capital: Its Origins and Applications in Modern Sociology." *Annual Review of Sociology* 24: 1–24.

Pretty, Jules N., Irene Guijt, John Thompson, and Ian Scoones. 1995. *Participatory Learning and Action: A Trainers Guide.* London: International Institute for Environment and Development, Sustainable Agriculture Programme.

Price, Sara K. 2005. "Experience as Educator: The Journey from Clinician to Practice-Based Researcher." *Reflections: Narratives of Professional Helping* 11(4): 37–47.

Prigoff, Arline. 2000. *Economics for Social Workers: Social Outcomes of Economic Globalization with Strategies for Community Action.* Stamford, CT: Wadsworth, Brooks/Cole, Thomson Learning.

Professional Assistance for Development Action (PRADAN). 2009. http://www.pradan.net/index.php?option=com_content&task=view&id=16&Itemid=2.

Public Agenda. 2008. "Immigration Fact File." http://www.publicagenda.org/issues/factfiles_detail.cfm?issue_type=immigration&list=5.

Putnam, Robert D. 1993. *Making Democracy Work: Civic Traditions in Modern Italy.* Princeton, NJ: Princeton University Press.

Putnam, Robert D. 1995. "Bowling Alone: America's Declining Social Capital." *Journal of Democracy* 6: 65–73.

Putnam, Robert D., and Lewis M. Feldstein, with Don Cohen. 2003. *Better Together: Restoring the American Community*. New York: Simon and Schuster.

Quinn, R. E. 1988. *Beyond Rational Management: Mastering the Paradoxes and Competing Demands of High Performance*. San Francisco, CA: Jossey-Bass.

Quivira Coalition. 2008. Preserving Lifeway Traditions and Heritage Breeds for a Resilient Future. Seventh Annual Conference. http://quiviracoalition.org/Detailed/Annual -Conference/Archives/Seventh-An . . . rence/Preserving-Lifeways-T . . . _900.html.

Rahnema, Majid, and Victoria Bawtree, eds. 1997. *The Post Development Reader*. London: Zed Books.

Ramanathan, Chathapuram S., and Rosemary J. Link. 1999. *All Our Futures: Principles and Resources for Social Work Practice in a Global Era*. Belmont, CA: Wadsworth/Thomson Publishing.

Rangihau, J. 1986. *Pau-te-Ata-tu (Daybreak): Report of the Ministerial Advisory Committee on a Maori Perspective for the Department of Social Welfare*. Wellington, NZ: Department of Social Welfare, N.Z. Government Printing Office.

Rao, Aruna, Rieky Stuart, and David Kelleher. 1999. "Building Gender Capital at BRAC: A Case Study." In *Gender at Work: Organizational Change for Equality*, ed. Aruna Rao, Rieky Stuart, and David Kelleher, pp. 31–76. West Hartford, CT: Kumarian Press.

Ravitch, Diane, and Abigail Thernstrom, eds. 1992. *The Democracy Reader: Classic and Modern Speeches, Essays, Poems, Declarations and Documents on Freedom and Human Rights Worldwide*. New York: HarperCollins.

Rawls, John. 2001. *Justice as Fairness: A Restatement*. Ed. Erin Kelly. New York: Belknap Press.

Ray, Karen. 2002. *The Nimble Collaboration: Fine-Tuning Your Collaboration for Lasting Success*. Saint Paul, MN: Amherst H. Wilder Foundation.

Reagan, Bernice Johnson. 1993. *We Who Believe in Freedom*. Harpswell, ME: Anchor.

Redefining Progress. 2008a. Genuine Progress Indicators. http://www.rprogress.org/sustainability_indicators/genuine_progress_indicator.htm.

Redefining Progress. 2008b. http://www.rprogress.org/. Also see Ecological Footprint Quiz http://www.myfootprint.org/.

Reed, Beth. 2005. "Theorizing in Community Practice." In *Handbook of Community Practice*, ed. Marie Weil, pp. 84–202. Thousand Oaks, CA: Sage Publications.

Reichert, Elizabeth. 2006. *Understanding Human Rights: An Exercise Book*. Thousand Oaks, CA: Sage Publications.

Reichert, Elizabeth, ed. 2007. *Challenges in Human Rights: A Social Work Perspective*. New York: Columbia University Press.

Reisch, Michael. 2005a. "American Exceptionalism and Critical Social Work: A Retrospective and Prospective Analysis." In *Globalization, Global Justice and Social Work*, ed. Iain Ferguson, Michael Lavalette, and Elizabeth Whitmore, pp. 157–72. London: Routledge.

Reisch, Michael. 2005b. "Radical Community Organizing." In *The Handbook of Community Practice*, ed. Marie Weil, pp. 287–304. Thousand Oaks, CA: Sage Publications.

Reisch, Michael. 2008. "Social Movements." *Encyclopedia of Social Work*, 20th ed., ed. Terry Mizrahi and Larry E. Davis, vol. 4, pp. 52–56. Washington, DC: NASW Press.

Reisch, Michael, and Janice Andrews. 2001. *The Road Not Taken: A History of Radical Social Work in the United States*. Philadelphia: Brunner-Routledge.

Reisch, Michael, and Stanley Wenocur. 1986. "The Future of Community Organization in Social Work: Social Activism and the Politics of Profession Building." *Social Service Review* 60(1): 70–91.

Reisch, Michael, Stanley Wenocur, and Wendy Sherman. 1981. "Empowerment, Conscientization and Animation as Core Social Work Skills." *Social Development Issues* 5(2/3): 108–20.

RESULTS. 2008a. "Strategic Goals: Microcredit." http://www.results.org/website/article.asp?id=2097.

RESULTS. 2008b. "U.S. Must Do More on Global Education." http://www.results.org/website/article.asp?id=3381.

Reynolds, David, and Jen Kern. 2003. *Living Wage Campaign: An Activist's Guide to Organizing a Movement for Economic Justice.* Detroit, MI: Wayne State University Labor Studies Center. Also available online at http://www.laborstudies.wayne.edu/research/Living Wage.html.

Richmond, Mary Ellen. 1907. *The Good Neighbor in the Modern City.* Philadelphia: J. B. Lippincott.

Ridings, John W., Dian M. Powell, James E. Johnson, Carrie J. Pullie, Colleen M. Jones, Richard L. Jones, and Katie J. Terrill. 2008. "Using Concept Mapping to Promote Community Building: The African American Initiative at Roseland." *Journal of Community Practice* 16: 39–63.

Rief, Michelle. 2004. "Thinking Locally, Acting Globally: The International Agenda of African American Club Women, 1880–1940." *Journal of African American History* 89(3): 203–22.

Rig Veda: An Anthology. 1982. Trans. Wendy Donigen O'Flaherty. London: Penguin Classics.

Rio Arriba County Comprehensive Plan. Adopted January 24, 2008. http://www.rio-arriba.org/pdf/20/comprehensive_plan.pdf.

Rio Arriba County Data. 2000. http://www.epodunk.com/cgi-bin/popInfo.php?locIndex=17939.

Rivera, Felix, and John Erlich, eds. 1998. *Community Organizing in a Diverse Society,* 3rd ed. Boston: Allyn & Bacon.

Robbins, Susan P., Pranab Chatterjee, and Edward Canda. 2006. *Contemporary Human Behavior Theory: A Critical Perspective for Social Work,* 2nd ed. Boston: Pearson/ Allyn & Bacon.

Robert, Henry M., III, and others. 2004. *Robert's Rules of Order Newly Revised in Brief.* Cambridge, MA: Da Capo Press.

Roberts, Brandon, and Deborah Povich. 2008. *Still Working Hard, Still Falling Short.* Working Poor Families Project. www.workingpoorfamilies.org.

Roberts-DeGennaro, Maria. 1986. "Building Coalitions for Political Advocacy Efforts in the Human Services." *Social Work* 31: 308–11.

Roberts-DeGennaro, Maria. 1997. "Conceptual Framework of Coalitions in an Organizational Context." *Journal of Community Practice* 4(1): 91–107.

Roberts-DeGennaro, Maria, and Terry Mizrahi. 2005. "Coalitions as Social Change Agents." In *Handbook for Community Practice,* ed. Marie Weil, pp. 305–18. Thousand Oaks, CA: Sage Publications.

Robinson, Christine. 1996. "The Who Questions." Unpublished paper. School of Social Work, University of North Carolina.

Rocha, Cynthia J. 2007. *Essentials of Social Work Policy Practice.* Hoboken, NJ: John Wiley and Sons.

Rogge, Mary E. 1995. "Coordinating Theory, Evidence, and Practice: Toxic Waste Exposure in Communities." *Journal of Community Practice* 2: 55–75.

Rogge, Mary E. 1998. "Toxic Risk, Community Resilience, and Social Justice in Chattanooga, Tennessee." In *Sustainable Community Development: Studies in Economic, Environmental, and Cultural Revitalization,* ed. M. D. Hoff, pp. 105–22. Boca Raton, FL: Lewis Publishers.

Rohe, William M., and Lauren B. Gates. 1985. *Planning with Neighborhoods*. Chapel Hill: University of North Carolina Press.

Rosenthal, Beth. 2004. "Appendix 5: How to Build Effective Multicultural Coalitions/ Innclusivity Checklist." In *Community Organizing and Community Building for Health*, ed. Meredith Minkler, pp. 448–49. New Brunswick, NJ: Rutgers University Press.

Ross, Murray G. 1955. *Community Organization: Theory and Principles*. New York: Harper & Row.

Ross, Murray G. 1958. *Case Histories in Community Organization*. New York: Harper & Row.

Ross, Murray G. 1967. *Community Organization: Theory, Principles and Practice*, 2nd ed. New York: Harper & Row.

Rotabi, Karen Smith. 2004. "Theory Bridging between Sociology, Social Work and Ecology: Dynamic Interchanges and Cross-Fertilizations: The Intellectual Legacy of the Odum Family." Dissertation, North Carolina Collection, University of North Carolina, Chapel Hill.

Rothman, Jack. 1968. "Three Models of Community Organization Practice." In *National Conference on Social Welfare, Social Work Practice 1968*. New York: Columbia University Press.

Rothman, Jack. 2001. "Approaches to Community Intervention." In *Strategies of Community Intervention*, ed. Jack Rothman, John L. Erlich, and John E. Tropman, pp. 27–64. Itasca, IL: Peacock Publishers.

Rothman, Jack. 2007. "MultiModes of Intervention at the Macro Level." *Journal of Community Practice* 15(4): 11–37.

Rothman, Jack. 2008. "Multi Modes of Community Intervention" In *Strategies of Community Intervention*, 7th ed., ed. Jack Rothman, John L. Erlich, and John E. Tropman, pp. 141–70. Peosta, IA: Eddie Bowers.

Rothman, Jack, John L. Erlich, and John E. Tropman, eds. 2008. *Strategies of Community Intervention*, 7th. ed. Peosta, IA: Eddie Bowers.

Royse, David, Bruce Thyer, Debra Padgett, and T. K. Logan. 2006. *Program Evaluation: An Introduction*, 4th ed. Pacific Grove, CA: Wadsworth.

Rubin, Herbert J., and Irene S. Rubin. 2005. "The Practice of Community Organizing." In *The Handbook of Community Practice*, ed. Marie O. Weil, pp.189–203. Thousand Oaks, CA: Sage Publications

Rubin, Herbert J., and Irene S. Rubin. 2007. *Community Organizing and Development*, 4th ed. Needham Heights, MA: Allyn & Bacon.

Rubin, Herbert J., and Margaret Sherrard Sherraden. 2005. "Community Economic and Social Development." In *The Handbook of Community Practice*, ed. Marie O. Weil, pp. 475–93. Thousand Oaks, CA: Sage Publications.

Sachs, Jeffrey D. 2005. *The End of Poverty*. New York: Penguin.

Sager, Jon. 2008. "Social Planning." In *Encyclopedia of Social Work*, 20th ed., ed. Terry Mizrahi and Larry Davis, vol. 4, pp. 56–61. New York: Oxford University Press.

Saguaro Seminar. 2006, September. "The Saguaro Seminar: Civic Engagement in America." http://www.ksg.harvard.edu/saguaro/index.htm.

Saleebey, Dennis. 2005. *The Strengths Perspective in Social Work Practice*, 4th ed. San Francisco, CA: Harper.

Sartre, Jean-Paul. 2007. *Existentialism Is a Humanism*. Trans. Carol Macomber. New Haven, CT: Yale University Press.

Save the Children UK News. 2008, February. "The Life-or-Death Lottery: Inequality and Injustice in the Fight to Save Children's Lives." At http://www.savethechildren.org.uk/en/41_4251.htm.

Schattschneider, Elmer E. 1975. *The Semisovereign People: A Realist's View of Democracy*. New York: Harcourt Brace College Publishers.

Schermerhorn, John, Jr., John G. Hunt, and Richard Osborne. 2008. *Organizational Behavior*, 10th ed. Hoboken, NJ: John Wiley & Sons.

Schmid, Hillel, and Hatem Salman. 2005. "Citizens' Perceptions of the Neighborhood Council: The Case of Arab Neighborhoods in East Jerusalem." *Journal of Community Practice* 13(2): 61–75.

Schneider Robert L., and Lori Lester 2001. *Social Work Advocacy: A New Framework for Action*. Belmont, CA: Wadsworth/Thompson Learning.

Schopler, Janice H. 1987. "Interorganizational Groups: Origins, Structure and Outcomes." *Academy of Management Review* 12: 702–13.

Schwartz, Meyer. 1965. "Community Organization." In *Encyclopedia of Social Work*, 15th ed. Washington, DC: NASW Press.

Schwarz, Sidney. 2008. *Judaism and Justice*. Woodstock, VT: Jewish Light Publishing.

Sen, Amartya. 1973. *On Economic Inequality*. New York: W. W. Norton.

Sen, Amartya. 1998, December 8. "The Possibility of Social Choice." Nobel Lecture. http://nobelprize.org/nobel_prizes/economics/laureates/1998/sen-lecture.pdf.

Senge, Peter M., Art Kleiner, Charlotte Roberts, and Rick Ross. 2006. *The Fifth Discipline Fieldbook*. New York: Doubleday Business.

Sherraden, Margaret. 2008. "Community Economic Development." In *Encyclopedia of Social Work*, 20th ed., ed. Terry Mizrahi and Larry Davis, vol. 1, 381–85. New York: Oxford University Press.

Sherraden, Michael. 2001. "Asset-Building Policy and Programs for the Poor." In *Assets for the Poor: The Benefits of Spreading Asset Ownership*, ed. T. Shapiro and E. Wolff, pp. 302–23. New York: Russell Sage Foundation.

Sherraden, Michael. 2008. "Asset Building." In *Encyclopedia of Social Work*, 20th ed., ed. Terry Mizrahi and Larry E. Davis, pp. 180–82. Washington, DC: NASW Press.

Shiva, Vandana. 2005. *Earth Democracy: Justice, Sustainability, and Peace*. Cambridge, MA: South End Press.

Shultz, Jim, and Melissa Crane Draper. 2008. *Dignity and Defiance: Stories from Bolivia's Challenge to Globalization*. Berkeley: University of California Press.

Simmel, Georg. 1964. *The Sociology of Georg Simmel*. Trans. Kurt H. Wolff. New York: Schocken Books.

Simmons, Jeremiah Jason. 2008. "Cultural Sensitivity: Importance and Impact on International Development." Unpublished paper for Certificate in International Development, University of North Carolina, Chapel Hill.

Simon, Barbara Levy. 1994. *The Empowerment Tradition in American Social Work: A History*. New York: Columbia University Press.

Singer, Peter. 2009. *The Life You Can Save: Acting Now to End World Poverty*. New York: Random House.

Skinner, E. Benjamin. 2008. *A Crime So Monstrous: Face-to-Face with Modern-Day Slavery*. New York: Free Press.

Sklar, Kathryn Kish. 1995. *Florence Kelley and the Nation's Work: The Rise of Women's Political Culture, 1830–1900*. New Haven, CT: Yale University Press.

Skoll Foundation. 2008. "What Is a Social Entrepreneur?" At http://www.skollfoundation.org/aboutsocialentrepreneurship/whatis.asp.

Slachmuijlder, Lena. 2007. "Ashoka Changemaker: Participatory Theater for Conflict Transformation. Search for Common Ground in the Democratic Republic of the Congo." Retrieved February 27, 2007, from http://proxied.changemakers.net/journal/peace/display peace.cfm?ID=226.

Slife, Brent D., and Richard N. Williams. 1995. *What's Behind the Research? Discovering Hidden Assumptions in the Behavioral Sciences*. Thousand Oaks, CA: Sage Publications.

Slocum, Rachel, Lori Wichart, Dianne Rocheleau, and Barbara Thomas-Slayter. 1995. *Power, Process and Participation: Tools for Change*. London: Intermediate Technology Publications.

Slow Food USA. 2008. http://www.slowfoodusa.org/index.html.

Smith, Court. 2007. "Wealth and Poverty, History of Minimum Wage." Oregon State University. http://oregonstate.edu/instruction/anth484/wpout.html.

Smith, Huston. 1994. *The Illustrated World's Religions: A Guide to Our Wisdom Traditions*. New York: HarperOne.

Smith, Norma. 2002. *Jeannette Rankin, America's Conscience*. Helena, MT: Montana Historical Society Press.

Soeteman, Kees, and Eric Harkink. 2005. "Collaboration of National and Global Corporations in Environmental Management." In *A Handbook of Globalisation and Environmental Policy: National Government Interventions in a Global Arena*, ed. Frank Wijen, Zees Soeteman, and Jan Pieters, pp. 179–210. Cheltenham, UK: Edward Elgar Publishing.

Solomon, Barbara. 1986. *Black Empowerment: Social Work in Oppressed Communities*. New York: Columbia University Press.

Southern Poverty Law Center (SPLC). 2008. http://www.splcenter.org/.

Southern Rural Development Initiative (SRDI). 2009. http://www.srdi.org/.

Sowers, Karen M., and William S. Rowe. 2006. *Social Work and Social Justice: From Local to Global Perspectives*. Belmont, CA: Brooks/Cole Thompson Learning.

Specht, Harry, and Mark E. Courtney, 1994. *Unfaithful Angels: How Social Work Has Abandoned Its Mission*. New York: The Free Press.

Speth, James Gustave. 2003. "Two Perspectives on Globalization and the Environment." In *Worlds Apart: Globalization and the Environment*, ed. James G. Speth, pp. 1–18. Washington, DC: Island Press.

St. Onge, Patricia. 2009. *Cultural Competency in the Non Profit Sector: Starting the Conversation*. St. Paul, MN: Fieldstone Alliance.

Staples, Lee. 2004. *Roots to Power: A Manual for Grassroots Organizing*, 2nd ed. Westport, CT: Praeger Publishers.

Staub-Bernasconi, Sylvia. 2007. "Economic and Social Rights: The Neglected Human Rights." In *Challenges in Human Rights: A Social Work Perspective*, ed. Elizabeth Reichert, pp. 138–61. New York: Columbia University Press.

Stegner, Wallace E. 1993. *Where the Bluebird Sings to the Lemonade Springs: Living and Writing in the West*. New York: Penguin.

Stein, Maurice R. 1960. *The Eclipse of Community: An Interpretation of American Studies*. New York: Harper Torchbooks, Harper & Row.

Stiehm, Judith Hicks. 2006. *Champions for Peace: Women Winners of the Nobel Peace Prize*. Lanham, MD: Rowman & Littlefield.

Stiglitz, Joseph. 2003. *Globalization and Its Discontents*. New York: W. W. Norton.

Stiglitz, Joseph. 2009. "Progress, What Progress?" http://www.oecdobserver.org/news/fullstory.php/aid/2793/Progress,_what_progress_.html.

Stiglitz, Joseph, and Linda Bilmes. 2008, February 23. "The Three Trillion Dollar War." *The Times OnLine*. http://www.timesonline.co.uk/tol/comment/columnists/guest_contributors/article3419840.ece.

Stiglitz, Joseph, and Andrew Charlton. 2006, March/April. "Fair Trade for All: How Trade Can Promote Development." *World Ark, Heifer International*. Excerpted and adapted from *Fair Trade for All*. New York: Oxford University Press.

Stoecker, Randy. 2005. *Research Methods for Community Change: A Project-Based Approach*. Thousand Oaks, CA: Sage Publications.

Stop the Traffic. 2008. http://www.stopthetraffik.org/default.aspx.

Streeter, Calvin. 2008. "Community: Overview." In *Encyclopedia of Social Work*, 20th ed., ed. Terry Mizrahi and Larry Davis, vol. 1. pp. 347–55. New York: Oxford University Press.

Stretch, John J., William J. Hutchison, Jan Wilson, and Ellen Burkemper. 2003. *Practicing Social Justice*. New York: Haworth Press.

Suarez-Balcazar, Yolanda, and Gary W. Harper, eds. 2003. *Empowerment and Participatory Evaluation of Community Interventions: Multiple Benefits*. New York: Haworth.

Suber, Peter. 1999. "Civil Disobedience." In *Philosophy of Law: An Encyclopedia*, ed. Christopher B. Gray, pp. 110–13. New York: Garland Publishing. Also at http://www.earlham.edu/~peters/writing/civ-dis.htm.

Sue, Derald Wing, and Monica McGoldrick. 2005. *Multicultural Social Work Practice*. Hoboken, NJ: John Wiley & Sons.

Sustainable South Bronx. 2008. http://www.ssbx.org.

SweatFree Communities. 2008. Sweatfree Community Tool Kit. Retrieved February 22, 2008, from http://www.sweatfree.org/resources_campaigntools.

Swimme, Brian, and Thomas Berry. 1994. *The Universe Story: From the Primordial Flaring Forth to the Ecozoic Era*. New York: HarperCollins.

TANAKH Translation. 1999. Philadelphia: Jewish Publication Society.

Tarbuck, Edward J., and Frederick K. Lutgens. 2000. *Earth Science*. Upper Saddle River, NJ: Prentice Hall.

Tarnas, Richard. 1993. *The Passion of the Western Mind*. New York: Ballantine Books.

Taylor, Samuel H. 1985. "Community Social Work and Social Work: The Community Liaison Approach." In *Theory and Practice of Community Social Work*, ed. S. H. Taylor and R. W. Roberts, pp. 179–214. New York: Columbia University Press.

Taylor, Samuel H., and Robert W. Roberts, eds. 1985. *Theory and Practice of Community Social Work*. New York: Columbia University Press.

Taylor, Susan, and Robin Kennedy. 2003. "Feminist Framework." In *Diversity Perspectives in Social Work Practice*, ed. J. Anderson and R. W. Carter, pp. 171–97. Boston: Allyn & Bacon.

Temkin, Kenneth, and William Rohe. 1996. "Neighborhood Change and Urban Policy." *Journal of Planning Education and Research* 15(3):101–12.

Temkin, Kenneth, and William Rohe. 1998. "Social Capital and Neighborhood Stability: An Empirical Investigation." *Housing Policy Debate* 9(1): 61–88.

Thyer, Bruce A. 2001. *The Handbook of Social Work Research Methods*. Thousand Oaks, CA: Sage Publications.

Tocqueville, Alexis de. 1835/2000. *Democracy in America*. Introduction by Sanford Kessler. Trans. Stephen Grant. Indianapolis, IN: Hackett.

Tönnies, Ferdinand. 1957 (1887). *Community and Society*. Trans. and ed. Charles P. Loomis. East Lansing: Michigan State University Press.

Toseland, Roland, and Robert F. Rivas. 2008. *An Introduction to Group Work Practice*, 6th ed. Boston: Allyn & Bacon.

Tropman, John E., John L. Erlich, and Jack Rothman. 2001. *Tactics and Techniques of Community Intervention*, 4th ed. Belmont, CA: Thomson Brooks/Cole Publishing.

Twelvetrees, Alan. 1989. *Organizing for Neighborhood Development*. Brookfield, VT: Avebury.

Twersky, Isadore, ed. 1972. *A Maimonides Reader*. Springfield, NJ: Behrman House.

UN Habitat: UN News Center. 2008.

UN High Commission for Human Rights. 2008. Universal Declaration of Human Rights. http://www.unhchr.ch/udhr/.

UN High Commission for Refugees (UNHCR). 2007. http://www.unhcr.org/basics.html.

UN High Commission for Refugees (UNHCR). 2008, June 20. "World Refugee Day." UN-HCR Briefing Notes. http://www.unhcr.org/news/NEWS/485b8a892.html.

UNICEF. 2006. *Women and Children: Double Dividend. State of the World's Children 2007* Report. http://www.unicef.org/sowc07/.

UNICEF. 2009. United States Fund. http://www.unicefusa.org/.

United Nations. 1987. *Human Rights: Questions and Answers.* New York: UN. http://info.human rights.curtin.edu.au/.

United Nations Department of Economic and Social Affairs. 2007, October. *Indicators of Sustainable Development: Guidelines and Methodologies.* New York: Commission on Sustainable Development, United Nations. http://www.un.org/esa/sustdev/natlinfo/indicators/guidelines.pdf.

United Nations Development Program (UNDP). 1999. *Human Development Report 1999.* New York: Oxford University Press.

United Nations Development Program (UNDP). 2000a. *Annual Report 2000: Building Human and Institutional Capacity for Sustainable Development.* Retrieved April 26, 2008, from http://capacity.undp.org/index.cfm?module=Library&page=Document&DocumentID=4075.

United Nations Development Program (UNDP). 2000b. *Human Development Report 2000.* New York: Oxford University Press.

United Nations Development Program (UNDP). 2001. *Human Development Report 2001.* New York: Oxford University Press.

United Nations Development Program (UNDP). 2002. *Annual Report 2002.* Retrieved April 26, 2008, from http://www.undp.org/annualreports/2002/english/.

United Nations Development Program (UNDP). 2003. *Human Development Report 2003.* New York: Oxford University Press.

United Nations Development Program (UNDP). 2005. *Human Development Report 2005.* New York: Oxford University Press.

United Nations Development Program (UNDP). 2006a. *Human Development Report 2006: Beyond Scarcity: Power, Poverty and the Global Water Crisis.* New York: Oxford University Press

United Nations Development Program (UNDP). 2006b. *Millennium Development Goals.* http://www.undp.org/mdg/basics.shtml.

United Nations Development Program (UNDP). 2007. *Human Development Report 2007–2008.* New York: Oxford University Press. Also http://hdr.undp.org/en/reports/global/hdr2007-2008/.

United Nations Development Program for Women (UNIFEM). 2008. http://www.unifem.sk/index.cfm?module=project&page=country&CountryISO=ba.

United Nations Office on Drugs and Crime (UNODC). 2008. "Status of the Protocol to Prevent, Suppress and Punish Trafficking in Persons." http://www.unodc.org/en/human-trafficking/index.html.

United States Census Bureau. Retrieved April 16, 2008, from www.census.gov/compendia/statab/tables/0850687.pdf.

United Way of America. 1996. *Measuring Program Outcomes: A Practical Approach.* Alexandria, VA: United Way of America.

United Way of America. Program Evaluation. http://www.liveunited.org/Outcomes/Library/pgmomres.cfm.

Universal Declaration of Human Rights (UDHR). 1948. At http://www.unhchr.ch/udhr/index.htm.

University of Minnesota Human Rights Library. 2008. Main Page. http://www1.umn.edu/humanrts/.

Unrau, Yvonne A., Peter A. Gabor, and Richard M. Grinnell Jr. 2007. *Evaluation in Social Work: The Art and Science of Practice*, 4th ed. New York: Oxford University Press.

Uphoff, Norman, Milton J. Esman, and Anirudh Krishna. 1998. *Reasons for Success: Learning from Instructive Experiences in Rural Development*. West Hartford, CT: Kumarian Press.

Van den Berg, Nan, and Lynn B. Cooper, eds. 1986. *Feminist Visions for Social Work*. Silver Spring, MD: NASW Press.

Van Soest, Dorothy. 1997. *The Global Crisis of Violence: Common Problems, Universal Causes, Shared Solutions*. Washington, DC: NASW Press.

Van Soest, Dorothy, and Arline Prigoff. 1997. "Toward Solutions: Approaches to Healing from Violence-Related Trauma." In *The Global Crisis of Violence: Common Problems, Universal Causes, Shared Solutions*, ed. Dorothy Van Soest, pp. 229–328. Washington, DC: NASW Press.

van Wormer, Katherine. 2004. *Confronting Oppression, Restoring Justice: From Policy Analysis to Social Action*. Washington, DC: NASW Press.

VeneKlasen, Lisa, and Valerie Miller. 2002. *A New Weave of Power, People, and Politics: The Action Guide for Advocacy and Citizen Participation*. Oklahoma City: World Neighbors.

Vidal, Avis C. 1992. *Rebuilding Communities: A National Study of Urban Community Development Corporations*. New York: New School of Social Research.

Wackernagel, Mathis, and William E. Rees. 1996. *Our Ecological Footprint: Reducing Human Impact on Earth*. Gabriola Island, B.C., Canada: New Society Publishers.

Walter, Cheryl L. 2004. "Community Building Practice: A Conceptual Framework." In *Community Organizing and Community Building for Health*, 2nd ed., ed. M. Minkler, pp. 66–78. New Brunswick, NJ: Rutgers University Press.

Wandersman, Abraham, Robert M. Goodman, and Frances D. Butterfoss. 2004. "Understanding Coalitions and How They Operate as Organizations." In *Community Organizing and Community Building for Health*, 2nd ed., ed. Meredith Minkler, pp. 292–313. New Brunswick, NJ: Rutgers University Press.

Warren, Roland. 1963. *The Community in America*. Chicago: Rand McNally.

Warren, Roland. 1965. *Studying Your Community*. New York: The Free Press. (Originally published by the Russell Sage Foundation, 1955).

Warren, Roland, ed. 1966. *Perspectives on the American Community: A Book of Readings*. Chicago: Rand McNally.

Wates, Nick. 2000. *The Community Planning Handbook: How People Can Shape Their Cities, Towns, and Villages in Any Part of the World*. London: Earthscan Publications, Ltd.

Weber, Max. 1978. *Selections in Translation*. Ed. W. G. Runciman. Cambridge, UK: Cambridge University Press.

Weber, Max. 1903–1917/1997. *The Methodology of Social Sciences*. Ed. and trans. Edward A. Shils and Henry A. Finch. New York: The Free Press.

Weick, Ann, Charles Rapp, W. Patrick Sullivan, and Walter Kisthardt. 1989. "A Strengths Perspective for Social Work Practice." *Social Work* 34(4): 350–54.

Weick, K. E. 1995. *Sensemaking in Organizations: Foundations for Organizational Science*. Thousand Oaks, CA: Sage Publications.

Weil, Marie. 1986. "Women, Community, and Organizing." In *Feminist Visions for Social Work*, ed. Nan Van Den Bergh and Lynn B. Cooper. Silver Spring, MD: NASW Press.

Weil, Marie. 1993. "Introduction to Diversity and Development in Community Practice." *Journal of Community Practice* 1(1): xxiv–xxxiii.

Weil, Marie. 1996. "Model Development in Community Practice: An Historical Perspective." In *Community Practice Conceptual Models*, ed. M. Weil, pp. 5–67. New York: Haworth Press.

Weil, Marie. 2000. "Services for Families and Children: The Changing Context and New Challenges." In *The Handbook of Social Welfare Management*, ed. Rino Patti, pp. 481–510. Thousand Oaks, CA: Sage Publications.

Weil, Marie. 2005a. Introduction to *Handbook of Community Practice*, ed. Marie Weil, pp. 3–33. Thousand Oaks CA: Sage Publications.

Weil, Marie. 2005b. "Social Planning with Communities." In *The Handbook of Community Practice*, ed. M. Weil, pp. 215–43. Thousand Oaks, CA: Sage Publications.

Weil, Marie, ed. 2005c. *Handbook of Community Practice*. Thousand Oaks, CA: Sage Publications.

Weil, Marie, and Judith Dunlop. 2008. *Family-Centered Services Community Planning Manual*. London, Ontario: Kings University College School of Social Work.

Weil, Marie, and Dorothy N. Gamble. 1995. "Community Practice Models." In *Encyclopedia of Social Work*, 19th ed., ed. Richard L. Edwards and June Gary Hopps, pp. 577–94. Washington, DC: NASW Press.

Weil, Marie, and Dorothy N. Gamble. 2005. "Evolution, Models, and the Changing Context of Community Practice." In *The Handbook of Community Practice*, ed. Marie Weil, pp. 117–50. Thousand Oaks, CA: Sage Publications.

Weil, Marie, and Dorothy N. Gamble. 2008. "Community Practice Models for the Twenty-first Century." In *Social Worker's Desk Reference*, 2nd ed., ed. Albert R. Roberts and Gilbert J. Greene, pp. 882–900. New York: Oxford University Press.

Weil, Marie, Dorothy N. Gamble, and Emily R. MacGuire. 2010. *Community Practice Skills Workbook: Local to Global Perspectives*. New York: Columbia University Press.

Weil, Marie, Dorothy N. Gamble, and Evelyn Williams. 1998. "Women, Communities and Development." In *The Role of Gender in Practice Knowledge: Claiming Half the Human Experience*, ed. Josephina Figueira-McDonough, F. Ellen Netting, and Ann M. Nichols-Casebolt (chapter 9), pp. 241–86. Chicago: Garland Publishing.

Weil, Marie, and Jean Kruzich. 1990. "Introduction to the Special Issue." *Administration in Social Work* 14(2): 1–12.

Weinbach, Robert W. 2003. *The Social Worker as Manager*, 4th ed. Needham Heights, MA: Allyn & Bacon.

Wentzel, Wilfred. 2003. *Poverty Reduction, Land Reform and Integrated Rural Development. Report for the CIRD*. Cape Town, South Africa: Center for Integrated Rural Development.

West, Cornel. 2005, September 11. "Exiles from a City and from a Nation." *London Observer*. http://www.guardian.co.uk/world/2005/sep/11/hurricanekatrina.comment.

Westlake, Jennifer. 2004. "Ebadi on Democracy." Quebec, Canada: *McGill Reporter*. http://www.mcgill.ca/reporter/37/04/ebadi/.

Westley, Frances, Brenda Zimmerman, and Michael Quinn Patton. 2006. *Getting to Maybe: How the World Has Changed*. Toronto: Random House.

Wetzel, Janice W. 2007. "Human Rights and Women: A Work in Progress." In *Challenges in Human Rights: A Social Work Perspective*, ed. Elizabeth Reichert, pp. 62–87. New York: Columbia University Press.

Wilderness Society. 2008. Defending Australia's Wild Country. http://www.wilderness.org .au/campaigns/forests/nsw/protlegal2/.

Wilson, Maureen, and Elizabeth Whitmore. 2000. *Seeds of Fire: Social Development in an Era of Globalism*. New York: Apex Press.

Wilson, William J. 1987. *The Truly Disadvantaged*. Chicago: University of Chicago Press.

Winer, Michael, and Karen Ray. 1994. *Collaboration Handbook: Creating, Sustaining, and Enjoying the Journey*. Saint Paul, MN: Fieldstone Alliance.

WiserEarth. 2009. "A Worldwide Community Directory and Networking Forum That Maps and Connects Non-governmental Organizations and Individuals Addressing the Central

Issues of Our Day: Climate Change, Poverty, the Environment, Peace, Water, Hunger, Social Justice, Conservation, Human Rights and More." At http://wiserearth.org/.

Wolff, Tom. 2003. "The Healthy Communities Movement: A Time for Transformation." *National Civic Review* 92(2): 95–112. Also at http://www.tomwolff.com/healthy-communities -tools-and-resources.html#pubs.

Wolff, Tom. 2008a. "Coalition Building Tips: What Coalitions Are Not." http://www .tomwolff.com/resources/cb_what_not.pdf.

Wolff, Tom. 2008b. "Power-Based vs. Relationship-Based Social Change." http://www.tom wolff.com/resources/organizing-v-building.pdf.

Wolff, Tom. 2008c. "Coalition Building Tips: Principles of Success." http://tomwolff. com/resources/cb_principles.pdf.

Wolff, Tom, and Gillian Kaye, eds. 1995. *From the Ground Up: A Workbook on Coalition Building and Community Development.* Amherst, MA: AHEC Community Partners. Also, 2008. E-version: http://www.tomwolff.com/coalition-empowerment-self-assessment -tool.htm.

Women's Environment and Development Organization (WEDO). 2008. http://www.whrnet .org/

Women's Human Rights Network (WHRnet). 2008. http://www.whrnet.org/. Also see Association for Women's Rights in Development (AWID 2009).

Woolcock, Michael, and Deepa Narayan. 2000. "Social Capital: Implications for Develop-ment Theory, Research, and Policy." *World Bank Research Observer,* 15(2): 225–49.

World Bank. 2006. "Poverty Rates, 1981–2002." http://siteresources.worldbank.org/DATASTA-TISTICS/Resources/table2-7.pdf.

World Commission on Environment and Development (WCED). 1987. *Our Common Fu-ture: From One Earth to One World.* New York: Oxford University Press.

World Conference on Human Rights 1993. *Vienna Declaration and Program of Action, 1993.* http://www.tamilnation.org/humanrights/instruments/vienna.htm.

World Health Organization (WHO). 2000, June 21. "World Health Organization Assesses the World's Health Systems." WHO Press Release/44. http://www.photius.com/rank-ings/who-world-health-ranks.html.

World Health Organization, Regional Office for Europe. 2008. "Vahid's Story." http://www .euro.who.int/mentalhealth/topics/2007113_4?PrinterFriendly=1&.

World Social Forum. 2008. Retrieved February 22, 2008, from http://www.wsf2008.net/.

Wronka, Joseph. 2007. "Global Distributive Justice as a Human Right: Implications for the Creation of a Human Rights Culture." In *Challenges in Human Rights: A Social Work Perspective,* ed. Elisabeth Reichert, pp. 44–75. New York: Columbia University Press.

Xu, Yan. 1995. "Sense of Place and Identity." East St. Louis Action Research Project, Univer-sity of Illinois at Urbana-Champaign. http://www.eslarp.uiuc.edu/la/la437-f95/reports/yards/main.html.

Yankey, John A., and Richard L. Edwards. 2006. *Effectively Managing Nonprofit Organiza-tions.* Washington, DC: NASW Press.

York, Alan S., and Hank Havassy. 1997. "Can Community Activists Be Taught Their Job?" *Journal of Community Practice* 4: 77–92.

Yuen, Francis K. O., and Kenneth L. Terao. 2004. *Practical Grant Writing and Program Evaluation.* San Diego, CA: Wadsworth.

Yunus, Muhammad. 1997. "The Grameen Bank Story: Rural Credit in Bangladesh." In *Reasons for Hope: Instructive Experiences in Rural Development,* ed. Anirudh Krishna, Norman Uphoff, and Milton J. Esman, pp. 9–24. West Hartford, CT: Kumarian Press.

Yunus, Muhammad. 2004, September. *Grameen Bank at a Glance.* Dhaka, Bangladesh: Grameen Bank.

Yunus, Muhammad. 2007. *Creating a World without Poverty: Social Business and the Future of Capitalism*. New York: Public Affairs.

Yunus, Muhammad. 2008. "Social Business Entrepreneurs Are the Solution." http://www.grameen-info.org/bank/socialbusinessentrepreneurs.htm.

Zachery, E. J. 1998. "An Exploration of Grassroots Leadership Development: A Case Study of a Training Program's Effort to Integrate Theory and Method." Dissertation Abstracts International 59(01):327A (UMI No. 9820259/6).

Zander, Alvin. 1990. *Effective Social Action by Community Groups*. San Francisco, CA: Jossey-Bass.

INDEX

CPSIA information can be obtained
at www.ICGtesting.com
Printed in the USA
JSHW020033251120
9817JS00006B/195